Watson W. Dewees

A Brief History of Westtown Boarding School

Watson W. Dewees

A Brief History of Westtown Boarding School

ISBN/EAN: 9783337338961

Printed in Europe, USA, Canada, Australia, Japan

Cover: Foto ©ninafisch / pixelio.de

More available books at **www.hansebooks.com**

A BRIEF HISTORY

OF

WESTTOWN BOARDING SCHOOL

WITH A

GENERAL CATALOGUE

OF

OFFICERS, STUDENTS, ETC.

COMPILED CHIEFLY FROM MINUTES OF THE COMMITTEE IN CHARGE, AND
THE RECORDS PRESERVED AT THE INSTITUTION.

Third Edition.

PHILADELPHIA:
PRINTED BY SHERMAN & CO.
1884.

Entered according to Act of Congress, in the year 1872, by
WATSON W. DEWEES,
In the Office of the Librarian of Congress at Washington.

COPYRIGHT,
WATSON W. DEWEES.
1884.

CONTENTS.

INTRODUCTION: PAGE
    EDUCATION AMONG EARLY FRIENDS 9

HISTORY:
    CHAPTER I.—1790 TO 1810 17
    CHAPTER II.—1810 TO 1865 34
    CHAPTER III.—1865 TO 1884 46
    CHAPTER IV.—WESTTOWN 55

OFFICERS:
    SUPERINTENDENTS AND MATRONS 79
    GOVERNORS AND GOVERNESSES 80
    TEACHERS 83
    FARMERS 92
    BOOK-KEEPERS 92

COMMITTEES 95

STUDENTS:
    MALES 105
    FEMALES 223

SUMMARY 375

TABLE OF AVERAGES 376

ALPHABETICAL INDEX TO NAMES IN FOREGOING
    LISTS 377

PREFACE.

THE almost universal possession of at least a good common-school education by members of the Society of Friends, is generally conceded. Among the establishments in America which have contributed to this, *Westtown Boarding School* occupies a prominent position. Most of the families of Friends within the limits of Philadelphia Yearly Meeting, and many in surrounding parts, have each contributed one or more to swell the number of students; in many cases *all* the members have in succession passed some portion of time at the institution. And such is its age, that those who now assemble within its walls are the grandchildren of those first enrolled as students. Patronized thus extensively, it has also served another important purpose. It has been a point of common interest to all classes, and the acquaintances there formed by those just on the threshold of active life, have bound together in closer union the members from distant sections of the country. To those with whom the name of Westtown has thus become very familiar, who retain pleasant recollections of the time spent there, and who wish to possess, in a form convenient for reference, most of the accessible information relating to the School, it is hoped the present compilation will prove acceptable.

The short history, prepared by the aid of some members of the committee in charge of the institution, will be found to chronicle the important events, in connection with the origin and progress of the concern, and the means by which the school attained its present condition. In the preparation of other matter included in the volume, the records in possession of the book-keeper and librarian were resorted to. With what degree of correctness these were kept in past times, will be best known should these pages meet the eyes of those who alone are competent to verify the entries,—the many whose names are herein enrolled. Care has been taken to follow the records in all essential particulars.

The use of register numbers is peculiar to Westtown, but the system is so well understood by its patrons, that it was believed no other order of arrangement would serve so well in a work of this kind. It corresponds generally with the chronological order, and most persons will turn readily to their own entries. It is to be regretted that a more uniform policy was not pursued at all times in the assignment of numbers. In the earlier years of the school, students returning after an absence, in some cases received new numbers. From this cause, the *highest register number issued* does not indicate truly the number of *different persons* entered. These re-admissions, when known to the compiler, were omitted in the second instance, and a summary on page 289 shows the result.

To obviate all difficulty in finding particular names, as well as to group together those of one family name, a complete alphabetical index has been added. In cases where students have in after years been connected with the school as officers or otherwise, the same has been indicated by reference in the index.

Only those who have attempted a labor of this kind can realize the difficulty experienced in regard to the spelling of many names. In the space of seventy years, some families change the spelling slightly, or a branch but distantly related may adopt a different spelling as a distinction, or names pronounced exactly alike, but spelled differently, may lead to confusion in many ways. Hence, it will not be surprising if persons bearing the name of Baily (Bailey),

Ballinger (Ballenger), Evans (Evens), Lea (Lee), Philips (Phillips), Swain (Swayne), Eayre (Eyre), or any one of a score of other like doubtful names, will notice a spelling unlike that generally used by them.

The frontispiece, although most of the large trees in the vicinity have been omitted, in order to show the buildings, will yet, it is hoped, convey a tolerably correct impression of the place, and show to those who have not visited it since 1869–70 the location of the boys' school-building.

The compiler wishes to express his obligation to many Friends for encouragement and assistance in the prosecution of the labor. Especially is he indebted to the present Superintendent and Matron, Aaron and Susanna F. Sharpless, whose extensive acquaintance with those connected with the school for many years past, rendered their advice and assistance peculiarly valuable.

The result of many days' pleasant employment is herewith submitted, hoping that *The History and General Catalogue of Westtown School* may suggest to many the thought of how much they owe to the institution in its past, and at the same time tend to perpetuate that degree of interest which will insure its usefulness in the future.

WATSON W. DEWEES,
Westtown Boarding School, Westtown P. O.,
Chester County, Pa.

Eighth Month 15th, 1872.

NOTE TO THIRD EDITION.

The stereotype plates of this work being now the property of the Committee in charge of Westtown School, this edition is issued under their supervision. The Historical sketch has been extended, and the Catalogue made complete to the summer of 1884 by the addition of about one thousand names of officers and students not in former editions.

INTRODUCTION.

EDUCATION AMONG EARLY FRIENDS.

THE ministry of George Fox began in the year 1647. Only a short time elapsed before those who came to have a common bond of interest in the adoption of the doctrines he taught, turned their attention to the care and instruction of the youth. A history of the educational movement in the Society of Friends would, therefore, cover nearly the same period as the history of the Society itself. To what extent private schools were established and patronized at that early day, we know not. In the journal of George Fox, under date of 1667, occurs the following (page 409):

"I advised the setting up of a school there (at Waltham) for teaching boys; also a woman's school to be opened at Shackelwell for instructing girls and young maidens in whatsoever things were civil and useful in the creation."

This advice seems to have been at once acted upon. In four years from that time there were reported to be fifteen boarding schools in operation. These, of course, were small, and became wholly insufficient, as the number to be taught increased.

London Yearly Meeting strove to impress upon both

subordinate meetings and individuals the importance of providing for the education of the children of Friends in schools under the care of members of the Society. From 1700 to 1740 there were earnest appeals, issued by that body annually, in reference to their literary as well as religious instruction. The following is the advice of the Yearly Meeting in 1706:

"And forasmuch as, next to our own souls, our children and offspring are the most immediate objects of our care and concern, it is tenderly recommended to all that are or may be parents or guardians of children, that they be diligently exercised in this care and concern for the education of those committed to their charge; that, in their tender years, they may be brought to a sense of God, — his wisdom, power, omnipresence, so as to beget an awe and fear of Him in their hearts (which is the beginning of wisdom); and, as they grow up in capacity, to acquaint them with and bring them up in the frequent reading of the Scriptures of Truth, and also to instruct them in the great love of God, through Jesus Christ and the work of salvation by Him, and of sanctification through His blessed Spirit; and also to keep them out of the vain and foolish ways of the world, and in plainness of language, habit, and behaviour, that, being thus instructed in the way of the Lord when they are young, they may not forget it when they are old."

Some of the difficulties of a later day are shadowed forth in the following extract:

"The want of proper persons among Friends — qualified for schoolmasters — has been the occasion of great damage to the Society in many places.

"We desire Friends would, in their monthly meetings, assist young men of low circumstances, whose genius and conduct may be suitable for that office, with the means requisite to obtain the proper qualifications;

and, when so qualified, afford them the necessary encouragement for their support." (*Minutes London Yearly Meeting*, 1715.)

A particular description of the various efforts made in compliance with the oft expressed concern of London Yearly Meeting will not be here attempted. They finally resulted in the establishment of a national boarding school at Ackworth in 1779. This institution, through the liberality and constant care of Friends, was made an instrument of great good to the youth of the Society. It continues in operation at the present time. The number of scholars admitted since its commencement in 1779, to 1871, was 8,753.

Should any one query what kind of an education early Friends desired for their children, abundant material for an answer could be found in the recorded minutes of that period. While they, in common with all other classes, were satisfied with a course of study very much shorter than that now considered essential, it cannot be denied that the prevailing standard was a liberal one. When we view the subject in connection with the state of schools among other classes, their plan of education seems surprisingly broad and practical. An emphatically religious education was desired — an education, which, while it made the mind the receptacle of such human wisdom as would conduce to the greatest usefulness upon earth, encouraged that obedience to the manifestations of Divine grace which would restrain and bring under right control the natural propensities of the child. That which puffeth up was to find no place, while that which teaches the accountability that must attach to all human action, and the due subordination of all desires and feelings to the one great end of man's existence on earth, was to be the corner-stone of the system. The spirit which animated many, is shown in the advice to parents to "be good examples in all things, as become men and women professing godliness, that good footsteps may be left by us to future generations, which may be helpful to the preservation of those who succeed us in the right way of the Lord." (*Lon. Y. M. Epistle*, 1712.)

In 1682, a considerable number of Friends arrived in America, and founded the colony of which Philadelphia was the centre. The first mention of schools was at a meeting of a council in Philadelphia, held 18th of Tenth month, 1683, at which time, it is easy to imagine, the settlers were not all comfortably housed. The following is the minute:

"The Governor (William Penn) and council, having taken into their serious consideration the necessity there is for the instruction and sober education of youth in the town of Philadelphia, sent for Enoch Flower, an inhabitant of said town, who, for twenty years past, hath been exercised in that care and employment in England, to whom having communicated their minds, he embraced it upon the following terms:

"To learn to read English, . . . 4s. by the quarter.
 "   "   "   "   and write . . . 6s.   "   "
 "   "   "   "   "   and cast
  accounts . . . . 8s.   "   "

"For boarding a scholar, that is to say, diet, washing, lodging, and schooling, £10 for one whole year."

Six years later, the "Friends' Public School," in Philadelphia, was opened. This was regularly incorporated by Deputy-Governor Markham in 1697; and afterward confirmed by fresh patent from William Penn himself, the final one bearing date Eleventh month

29th, 1711. The objects of the corporation are thus stated:

"*Whereas*, The prosperity and welfare of any people depend in great measure upon the good education of youth and their early introduction into the principles of true religion and virtue, and qualifying them to serve their country and themselves, by breeding them in reading, writing, and learning of languages, and useful arts and science, suitable to their age, sex, and degree, which cannot be effected in any manner so well as by erecting public schools for the purposes aforesaid," &c.

George Keith, formerly of Aberdeen, in Scotland, was employed as teacher. He was followed, at the end of a year, by his usher, Thomas Makin, who is described as having been a "good Latinist." Several schools have been maintained, and are still in operation, under the provisions of the original charter.

The following, from Smith's "History of Delaware County, Pa.," is of interest in this connection:

"Friends now (1692) began to give their attention to the subject of schools. At a monthly meeting, held at Darby the 7th of the Seventh month, it was agreed 'that Benjamin Clift is to teach scoole, Beging° ye 12th of ye 7th m°·; and to continue one whole yeare, except 2 weekes.' The annual salary of this worthy teacher, as appears by an agreement for employing him another year, was but £12. He probably boarded with his employers." (Page 183.)

Thus early did the subject claim the attention of Friends in America; nor were the efforts confined to a few localities. Schools were established in various places, and their improvement made a subject of special and frequent care, both by individuals and meetings

Difficulty was experienced in procuring suitable teachers, and, we may readily suppose, the schools, when established, were not always such as satisfied concerned parents. Philadelphia Yearly Meeting Minutes, in 1746, say:

"We desire you, in your several Monthly Meetings, to encourage and assist each other in the settlement and support of schools for the instruction of your children, at least to read and write, and some further useful learning to such whose circumstances will permit it; and that you observe as much as possible, to employ such masters and mistresses as are concerned, not only to instruct your children in their learning, but are likewise careful, in the wisdom of God, and a spirit of meekness, gradually to bring them to the knowledge of their duty to God and one with another; and, we doubt not, such endeavors will be blessed with success."

The same body, a few years after, still further advised, that

"The most likely means to induce 'religious prudent persons' to undertake the business of teaching, would be to provide a certain and stated income, for such persons, by the establishment of funds for the purpose. In 1777 the 'consideration of the sorrowful complaint of deficiency in the religious care and education of the youth, brought up from Philadelphia Quarterly Meeting, was entered upon;' and the minute, then made, states, that 'a lively concern impressed our minds for the advancement of righteousness and the real benefit of the rising generation, both with respect to their pious education in Friends' families and also their school education.'"

The subject rested with weight upon the minds of many, and the exercise of the meeting, at that time, resulted in the appointment of a committee of fourteen Friends, "to take the matter relating to the youth and their religious education and schooling particularly under their care, and give such advice and assistance therein, and respecting other deficiencies, as they in the wisdom of Truth may see expedient."

This committee deemed it right to issue an epistle upon the subject, and from their report the following is taken:

"It is the opinion of the committee that Friends having united with others in employing such persons for masters, who have not submitted to the operation of Truth, hath had a tendency to strengthen a disposition in our youth, to avoid the cross and unite with the spirit of the world, whereby many hurtful and corrupt things have gained ground amongst us."

After alluding to the concern manifested upon the same subject for many years previous, and the fact, that, "notwithstanding these pressing recommendations, little has been effectually done therein,"—after proposing that it should be again urged upon the attention of subordinate meetings,—they conclude:

"We, also, think it necessary that this weighty concern should, in future, become the continued care of the Quarterly Meetings by an annual query, that so the matter may rest on a solid foundation, and every possible encouragement and assistance may be afforded to Friends in the settlement of schools, procuring masters, &c., through the whole extent of the Yearly Meeting."

It was also recommended:

"*First*, That a lot of ground be provided in each monthly or preparative meeting, sufficient for a garden, orchard, grass for a cow, &c., and a suitable house erected thereon. *Second*, That funds be raised by contribution, bequests, &c., in each meeting; the interest of which to be applied either in aid of the tutor's salary, or lessening the expense of Friends in straitened circumstances, in the education of their children. *Third,* That a committee be appointed in each monthly or preparative meeting, to have the care of schools, and the funds for their support, and that no tutor be employed but with their consent."

Some years after (1783), upon receipt of reports from the Quarterly Meetings, the Minutes say:

"Though in divers places some care has been taken, school-houses built, and schools instituted under care of Monthly Meetings, importing a degree of promising progress; yet respecting other parts, it is acknowledged that little improvement has been made, not much having been done toward establishing permanent funds for the regular and liberal support of schools, under well qualified, discreet, and religious instructors." *

* It should be borne in mind that the period to which these Minutes refer was one of great unsettlement, owing to the Revolutionary contest, and the political agitations growing out of it.

THE HISTORY

OF

WESTTOWN BOARDING SCHOOL.

CHAPTER I.

1790—1810.

ABOUT the year 1790, the propriety of establishing a boarding school began to arrest attention. A tract put forth by Owen Biddle in this year,—rehearsing some facts in the experience of Friends in England, and discussing, at some length, the adaptation of a large boarding school to the needs of the youth of the Society in this country,—probably contributed to ripen the concern in the minds of many Friends. In the Fourth month, 1791, the subject was introduced into Philadelphia Monthly Meeting, whence it was carried to the Quarterly Meeting. That body, in the succeeding year, introduced the subject into the Yearly Meeting. Effort on the part of individuals had already resulted in the formation of a fund of several thousand pounds in aid of the enterprise when it should be undertaken.

A subject of the magnitude of that now brought before the Yearly Meeting, of course, required much consideration before action could be taken. It was successively referred to the meetings held in 1793 and 1794. In the latter meeting a large committee was appointed to take the whole subject into consideration,—consult with such Friends as had for a length of time had the matter weightily on their minds,—and report their united judgment when ready. At a subsequent sitting they made a report, from which the following is extracted:

"On taking the subject into deliberate consideration, we are united in the sentiment that an institution of the kind proposed, if managed with religious care and circumspection, may tend to the prosperity of Truth by promoting the real good of the rising generation; we do, therefore, recommend the said proposal from the Quarterly Meeting of Philadelphia, to the patronage of the Yearly Meeting, and propose that a committee thereof be appointed to consider and digest a plan and rules for the government and management of the house, school, and other parts of the economy," &c.

They proposed that the said committee should be the agents for carrying out the concern, and should report regularly their progress. The Meeting agreeing to this, a standing committee of forty-seven Friends was appointed, as recommended. The women's Yearly Meeting appointed seven of their number to join with men Friends in the service as occasion might require.

The men Friends thus appointed held their first meeting for deliberation on the evening of the 3d of Tenth month, 1794, in the old Fourth Street Meeting-House.* Thomas Morris was chosen clerk, and Thomas

---

* This building has lately been removed, and its site is now occupied by an extension of the Forrest Building in Fourth Street below Chestnut Street.

Fisher, treasurer. A sub-committee was appointed to solicit further subscriptions. The selection of a site for the proposed institution was one of the first subjects to be decided. Some of the members, whose attention had already been turned to this, proposed a tract of land on the Neshamony Creek, some miles below Bristol, in Bucks County, containing about four hundred and fifty acres, known as Langhorne Park. This land was indeed purchased by a few Friends in the expectation that it would be selected for the purpose. A delegation was sent to view this spot, as well as any others, thought more likely to answer the end designed. After visiting various places, they expressed themselves in favor of selecting the farm of James Gibbons in Westtown township, Chester County, as the one in all respects best adapted to the purpose. This land, about six hundred acres in extent, was accordingly purchased. The amount paid James Gibbons was £6,083 6s. 8d. = $16,222.22. A small sum was expended to obtain the entire water-power of Chester Creek. This was accomplished by buying the adjoining farm on the west side, and selling with a reservation of the entire water privilege. At the time of purchase only a small portion of the farm had been cleared; not only that which is timbered at the present day, but much of that which has since been brought under cultivation, was then covered by a dense growth of forest-trees, of a size and age now represented by a few trees in the "South woods." Near the present site of the farm-house stood the dwelling known in those days as the "Mansion house." This was repaired and soon after occupied. Edward Churchman was the first tenant. Preparations were at once made for erecting a sawmill. This was completed by the end of the year 1795, and afforded the means of preparing the lumber to be used in the future buildings. This mill and dam in the creek were near the northern line of the farm, and the curious may yet see the remains of the latter, and the race which wound around the western base of Walnut Hill, to the spot where the mill was situated.

Meanwhile the selection of a site for the main building occupied the attention of the committee. By agreement, several members met at the farm on the 17th of the Eighth month, 1795. Their report says, they " viewed the eminence north of the Mansion house remarkable for the fine prospect it affords." Judging this to be the right place, the exact front was staked out. It was the original design to make the main front parallel " to the new road from Marlborough Street road to the Goshen township road." But a south-eastern front was afterward decided upon. In the following spring a barn was built near the farm-house; and arrangements were made for the burning of bricks for the school-building, — a plentiful supply of clay for which, as well as of good building-stone, exists on the farm.

The *plan* of the building was a subject requiring careful consideration; and it was only after much labor had been expended that one was agreed upon. The generally prevailing opinion was, that accommodations should be provided for one hundred and fifty students and the requisite number of teachers, &c. For this a building, one hundred feet long and fifty-six wide, three stories in height, was thought to be sufficient. Special care was taken that an extension could be readily made, if circumstances should render it desirable in after-years. The sub-committee intrusted with the oversight of the work of building were David Evans, Jonathan Evans,

Thomas Morris, Philip Price, Jr., Daniel Thomas, Samuel Canby, James Marshall, John Talbot, Eli Yarnall, and Abram Sharpless. The work progressed steadily from the time of its beginning in 1796 to the period of its completion in 1799. If it should occur to any that the time thus occupied was long, it must be remembered that builders had not, then, all the modern facilities at their command, and material was not to be had in a complete state of preparation at short notice. Those of the committee, who resided in or near Philadelphia, had a carriage, or horse-back ride, of twenty miles, in order to get to the scene of their labors. The expenditure of time on their part must therefore have been considerable.

The building thus slowly constructed has proved to be of a very substantial character, and although the floors in some places, and other parts of the wood-work, have, in the many years that have since elapsed, required renewal, yet the walls still bear witness to the care which was exercised in the selection of the materials and the thoroughness of the work.

During the erection of the building, roads were laid out, a garden was enclosed, furniture obtained for the school-rooms, and other preparations made for the accommodation of its future inmates.

The total expense of the improvements thus made, including a new barn at the farm-house, general repairs, fencing, &c., increased the total cost of the premises by the year 1802 to $46,020.19. An inspection of the books of the Institution shows that the total amount expended up to the year 1870, in the further enlargements of the main building, the erection of additional structures, alterations, repairs, and permanent improvements generally, to the buildings and upon the farm, forms an aggregate of $228,335.36.

In the Yearly Meeting which convened near the close of 9th mo., 1796, report was made of the transactions up to that period, in the progress of the building, the condition of the farm, and the exhausted state of the funds. Some "constitutional rules," also, were presented at the same time, describing several of the main features in the organization of the proposed establishment. The first of these defined the nature and powers of the standing committee to have the permanent care of the school. Others made provision for a superintendent under the direction of the acting committee, for meetings for worship in the house on First and Fifth days, for the support of discipline by the officers, aided, when needful, by the acting committee, &c. Some of these "rules" were as follows:

"That spelling, reading, writing, arithmetic, and book-keeping, shall be taught in the different schools, and such other useful branches of learning as the circumstances of the pupils may require, and the state of the Institution shall permit."

"That the board and lodging of the children shall be plain and frugal, without distinction, except in cases of sickness."

"That boys and girls be accommodated in separate apartments under care of separate tutors."

"That no tutors, assistants, or domestics, be retained in the Institution, whose deportment is not sober and exemplary."

"That no children shall be taken in under the age of *eight* years, or entered for less than *one* year."

"That if children are sent with clothing not sufficiently plain as to color, or which shall require washing, it shall be returned; but if the *make* only be exceptionable, it shall be altered and the expense charged."

The meeting also took measures to replenish the funds, and strengthen the hands of the committee. As the house progressed toward completion, other details began to receive attention. Efforts were made to engage teachers, though with only partial success at first, and especial difficulty was found in procuring men Friends who were qualified for the service. A report in 1799 says:

"Encouragement hath, however, been derived from the free and disinterested offer of our Friends, Richard and Catharine Hartshorne, to devote their time and attention to the oversight of the general order and management of the house and its appendages."

These Friends, who were the first superintendents, entered on their duties in the early part of the year 1799. Women Friends interested themselves to good purpose in procuring beds, bedding, and many other articles requisite in housekeeping. The books, opened for the purpose, contained in 4th mo., 1799, the names of seventy-three boys and sixty girls, applicants for admission; but, from the difficulty of starting at once into successful operation with a full house, it was concluded to begin with a much smaller number, and to admit at first only twenty of each sex. This number was to be increased by ten of each sex monthly, if it was found to be advisable. The price of board and tuition was fixed at £24 per annum = $64; it being decided to put it at this low price, in order that the charge should not be an obstacle "in depriving any proper objects of the benefit intended."

The school was opened on the 6th of 5th mo., 1799, with John Forsythe, Elizabeth Bellerby, and Phebe Cox as teachers. Some members of the committee were also present, as appears by the following extract from the Minutes:

"Our Friends, Samuel Smith and John Cox, being willing to devote a portion of their time for this purpose, their dedication to the service is very acceptable to the committee, and they are encouraged to attend as soon after the school shall be opened as is convenient to them. Rebecca Archer, having agreed to attend, and it being hoped that Rebecca Jones and Ann Lloyd may also find it their duty to give up to unite with the two men Friends above mentioned."

It would be interesting to know more of those eventful days, the 6th and 7th of the month, when most of the forty pupils were arriving and finding places in the new institution. Busy days they doubtless were, as it is scarcely possible but that even the most careful foresight had failed to secure every needed arrangement, and many times the officers found themselves poorly provided with facilities for their work. A glance at the list of students will show who the first admissions were. One of them, William Evans, late of Philadelphia, makes the following mention of his early experiences at the school. (See *Journal of William Evans*, p. 8.)

"In the Fifth month, 1799, the boarding school at Westtown, instituted by our Yearly Meeting, was open for the reception of scholars, and I was one of the first twenty admitted there, my brother Joseph also remaining a few months. It was quite a novel scene, and required time before a proper system of order and government was established. Everything seemed in a crude state; the yards not laid out and regulated, shavings and chips from the hewed timber and the shingles, the woods grown up very thick with bushes, so that it was difficult to get through them, all contributed to give the whole a rude appearance. All this made work and amusement for the boys, who employed themselves under the supervision of the teachers in burning up the great beds of shavings, cutting openings for walks through the woods, and making arbors with seats to recreate themselves in during the warm weather."

According to the arrangement made, additional pupils were afterwards admitted, until the number was considerably above the estimated capacity of the house, being as many as one hundred of each sex at the beginning of winter. At this time there were about one hundred applications on file, and it was ordered that no more names should be registered. To meet the requirements of the growing family, other teachers were added during the summer. Ann Thomas came in the 7th mo., Elihu Pickering in the 8th mo., Ann Bacon in the 10th mo., and Enoch Lewis in the 11th mo. of 1799. The progress up to this time must have been very gratifying to those who had labored in the cause. If they foresaw in the future of the establishment a long career of usefulness, it surely was not more than they reasonably had ground to hope.

After a period of seventy-two years, it is difficult to obtain an insight into the daily life of the inmates of the house. At first the galleries were used as collecting-rooms, and the children stood during the periods in which they were there assembled. Rooms on the first floor were afterwards used for this purpose, which were furnished with benches without backs, on which the pupils sat closely side by side, without desks. Dining-rooms were in the basement, as also the laundry. The tables were doubtless furnished in a simple manner. There are those who still remember the large drinking-cups which used to be passed up and down the long bare tables to accommodate all who were thirsty, one or two sufficing for all. There were no wash-rooms, but the pumps in the yard furnished water, to which the children carried their basins and took turns before the spout, and where morning ablutions in winter were probably quickly performed. One pump was in the space where the boys' bath-house now stands; another in the same relative situation at the opposite end of the house. No pupils entered this school for a less time than one year, and two months' notice was required before a child was removed. When a vacancy occurred, the next applicant on the list was admitted to fill it. There were no vacations. Children when entered were expected to remain until they had completed their studies. Being thus debarred from the opportunity of going home, the services of the tailor and shoemaker were often needed, who resided in the house, and kept their accounts with each scholar.*

Teachers, if they had any vacation, were released one at a time. The salaries during the first year were as follows: Male teachers, £100 = $266, and if married, a house to live in beside; female teachers, £30 = $80.

---

* As illustrating this, observe the following; being the sundries charged to one of the first twenty boys:

J—— J——, Dr. to Sundries.

Tailor's Account for Son.

7th mo. 28th, 1799,	Mending Coat,	1s. 2d.	
8th mo. 6th, "	" Trowsers,	9d.	
8th mo. 20th, "	Making Coattee,	10s. 6d.	
11th mo. 30th, "	Mending Coat and Breeches,	2s. 6d.	
12th mo. 20th, "	Mending Coat,	9d.	—15s. 8d.

Merchandise.

| 8th mo. 14th, " | 5¼ yds. Fustian, | 14s. | |
| | 1 yd. Linen, 2s. 6d., Silk Twist, mould, 1s. 7½d. = | 4s. 1½d. | —18s. 1½ d. |

As indicated in the "Constitutional Rules," the education proposed was practical in its nature. Much attention was given to spelling, reading, and writing. If visitors came into the school, a reading class was called out for their entertainment. In the First-day afternoon reading of religious books before the whole school, the older pupils assisted by turns. With the girls especially it was a favorite custom to meet and transact business after the manner of their elders in society affairs; quaint and often beautifully expressed were the "certificates" prepared for those about leaving the school. The letters written home were produced first as essays and, after being corrected by the teachers, were copied with strictest regard to neatness. When complete, they were placed in the rack in the parlor to await the coming of visitors who could forward them to their respective neighborhoods.

Very early in the progress of the institution there were on each side of the house two principal rooms, promotion to which was determined largely by mathematical attainments, and from which classes were drawn for exercise in other things. There were two long sessions per day, and during the winter season an evening school, and in the summer an hour of recitation before breakfast.

The care of the pupils between schools devolved upon the teachers in rotation. This duty was arduous; and the difficulties were probably increased by the changes of caretakers which this system implied. It was inevitable that, however conscientious all might be, the children realized the change from one to another; and, since upon the teacher in "care" devolved many of those minor duties so essential to the welfare of a large company of young persons, we are not surprised that many of the trying experiences of the teachers in early times were connected with this portion of their duties, nor that in after years it was found expedient to secure uniformity in the exercise of this care by the employment of persons specially for the service.

The female department had some features peculiar to itself. There appears to have been at first a monitorial system, not unlike that yet found in some schools for deaf mutes and the blind. Each older pupil had under her immediate care one of the little girls. The responsibility of the older for the younger pupil extended to such details as the neatness of the toilet and politeness and deportment at all times; and any punishment merited by the child was endured by the caretaker. A compensating feature was the privilege of changing in case any child was not readily controlled.

The name monitor was not used in this sense, however; but that distinguishing title was applied to some older girls who performed more important duties in aid of the teachers, having charge of rooms at times and reporting the names of those who were disorderly. This was regarded as a very responsible office, and those who held it were allowed to sit up in the evenings until a later hour, or sometimes to eat at the family table as a reward.

All of the girls over fourteen years of age wore caps, and a degree of skill in making and caring for these was regarded as essential to the future housewife. Indeed, the education offered the girls was even more "practical" than that provided for the boys, for we find a "sewing-room" to have been an established feature of the school. This was under the care of a responsible person, and the instruction was regular and systematic. Attention was given to plain sewing, to mending in all its branches, and to such forms of fancy work as seemed to possess an element of usefulness and led to familiarity with the use of the needle. Knitting was taught; and in darning, "a patch eight by twelve inches" was reckoned a sufficient test of the skill of the operator. At one time we find that all the younger girls spent two weeks at a time in the sewing-room, going out at intervals during the day for lessons in spelling and reading. Four weeks were then spent in the "arithmetical room," followed again by two weeks at sewing. How important this department was considered we may judge from the proportion of time devoted to it, and the many items charged to the pupils upon the books of the institution, such as thread, ribbon, vandyke, zephyr, galloon, etc. Boys were sometimes employed in the gardens and in some minor operations about the premises, but there does not appear to have been any attempt at systematic instruction in manual labor.

Human nature is much the same in all ages. The officers of the institution in these earlier years were patient, conscientious workers, who, no doubt, endeavored to impress upon their pupils the propriety of doing right for its own sake. But offences came and punishments were necessary. For the boys, the use of the rod was well-nigh universal, Westtown being in this respect not unlike other schools of the period. Those who transgressed by going "out of bounds" were punished also by deprivation of their customary privileges. There was a rule, often changed and apparently not satisfactory in its operation, which excluded boys from the school after they attained a certain age, generally fourteen or fifteen years.

Milder punishments sufficed for the girls. A "disgrace-table" in the dining-room, a "dunce-stool" near the teacher's desk, and the regular practice of requiring so much "poetry" for each trifling offence, were the instruments of punishment. The production of rhyme—poetry it was called—seems to have been almost as common as whipping among the boys. These effusions of course perished with the using, but there must have been strong temptation to dwell upon the personal peculiarities of their careful teachers, and to versify in sport concerning the offences for which the punishment was exacted.

A hard-worked and hard-working body of people were the caretakers of the institution, and obliged to submit to much real hardship in the discharge of their duties. From the busy superintendent, everybody's friend and universal helper in time of trouble, charged with the care of all duties which did not plainly belong to others, even to extracting the teeth of the children on occasion, to the equally busy teacher armed, it may be, with a penknife and a bundle of quills for making pens, or leading the procession of children toward the chamber, preceded by half a dozen older pupils bearing tallow dips, all found themselves busied with many cares, and often obliged to work with but very imperfect appliances and poor accommodations. As late as 1807, probably later, there was not a carpet about the establishment, almost no maps, and all the furniture was of the simplest kind. The food supplied was simple and generally nutritious. Pie and milk, which was the regular supper three times per week, was much enjoyed, and Westtown pie is still remembered with pleasure by pupils of former times. The pies were served on large pewter plates some sixteen or eighteen inches in diameter, and the milk drunk from "porringers" of the same material. This pewter ware was gradually replaced by more modern kinds, and finally became almost a curiosity. The porringers were made at the school and remolded as they became worn.

Persons visiting the school were, as now, accommodated at the farm-house. The committee were desirous that this latter "should not be viewed as a *tavern*, where arbitrary conduct in calling for meals, commanding the servants, etc., is often observed, but that, as much as possible, a Christian and meek deportment be maintained; that the table be provided with victuals, plain cooked, and served in a decent way, merely for needful accommodation, avoiding all profusion and unnecessary expense."

Richard and Catharine Hartshorne, believing they felt released from further care at the school, retired about the close of the year 1799. Some members of the committee assisted in the oversight of the family until 4th mo., 1800, when Joshua and Ann Sharpless assumed the charge as superintendents. The experience of a year now began to make manifest the further wants of the establishment. Women Friends, having observed the inconveniences to which the sick were exposed in the apartments allotted for their use, proposed, and were encouraged to raise a sum of money principally among themselves, and erect an infirmary, in which such cases might be treated, at a suitable distance from the main building. With funds principally procured by private contributions, a building was erected on the south side of the lane, in the summer of 1803. Rooms in the basement were appropriated to the tailor and shoemaker of the institution, leaving the upper portions of the main building to be devoted to the family proper. This infirmary was never used to any considerable extent as originally designed. The expense and difficulty of supporting two separate nurseries at a distance from the remainder of the family were sufficient to prevent the house from being thus used. It has, however, been occupied as a residence for married teachers, by whom members of the committee were temporarily accommodated when in attendance at the school.

About this period, another improvement was projected and carried out. Difficulty having been experienced in getting the wheat converted into flour for so large a family, twelve Friends formed a company in 11th mo., 1800, and put up a grist-mill, with the requisite dam and race for securing power from the water of Chester Creek, taking the usual toll from all grain ground. The mill eventually passed into the ownership of the school, some shares being donated and some purchased, and has been in successful operation since. In 1815, a pump was attached to the wheel to force water up for the supply of the school.

While the institution was thus acquiring valuable additions, it was not exempt from sore trials. In the spring of 1801, as also in the autumn of 1803, sickness* prevailed to such an extent that parents were allowed to remove the children for a short time. The number in attendance was so far reduced that for the year ending 4th mo., 1803, only one hundred and thirty pupils were reported. It was a period of some discouragement to the friends of the institution, in alluding to which, the committee say:

"As many engagements, however clearly directed in their origin, and in early progress attended with confirming evidence of their rectitude, are subject to the introduction of discouraging prospects and consequently close exercises, so in the prosecution of this religious concern, the minds of the committee have not been without a share of trials of this kind."

* Scarlet fever.

A few months later:

"The minds of Friends were turned to the general state of the school, so far as relates to *morals, manners,* and religious education of the youth; and it being apprehended there is ground to fear that the improvement of the rising generation, so much desired, and for which this institution, as one means, was originally designed to promote, is not advancing in such a degree as to afford a satisfactory prospect to many concerned minds, it is hoped the importance of this deeply interesting subject may claim the weighty consideration of Friends generally; and that we of the committee, to whom the concern of the Yearly Meeting has been more particularly intrusted, may solidly ponder and carefully examine how far our duty has been performed, that should a greater portion of our time, and more earnest exertion of endeavors be pointed out to individuals, it is desired that a faithful dedication of talents in a cause of such importance may be rendered, under a hope that so benevolent a work will be rewarded with the comfortable enjoyment of true peace."

One source of discouragement, during the years 1802–3–4, was the weak force of men teachers, and the difficulty of obtaining others. Assistant teachers, then called "apprentices," were now first proposed, as a means of lightening the labors of the principal teachers, and also as likely to lead more persons to qualify themselves for the profession of teaching. It was also hoped "that any members of the standing committee having a concern to give up a portion of their time to be spent at the school for the furtherance of good order and decorum amongst the children there, be encouraged to offer themselves to the acting committee for this end." Thomas Scattergood at one time remained in the school for some months, aiding in the labor of instruction, as well as by his advice and religious exercise.

The following extracts from the minutes and reports of the committee further show the religious concern which was maintained:

9th mo., 1805: "In the evening a season of solemn religious waiting with the scholars, teachers, and various care-takers was experienced, in which the minds of some of the committee were qualified by Divine Goodness to communicate pertinent counsel, calculated to encourage the superintendent and teachers in the performance of their arduous duties, and the children to submit themselves to wholesome discipline."

3d mo., 1807: "We can inform the meeting that an improvement in salutary order and discipline has been pleasingly observable, and an encouraging hope revives, that as the exercise which led into this undertaking for the advancement of the youth in piety and virtue is singly kept to, the propitious eye of Divine regard will support under the various difficulties and trials with which this and other works of righteousness are frequently assailed."

CHAPTER II.

1810—1865.

IN external appearance the Westtown of 1810 differed largely from that of a later day. The building still retained the steep roof which figures in all early drawings and representations. On the east the woods came close to the house, furnishing natural shade. In front and on the west some trees had been planted, but were yet small.

There was a yard of limited extent in front, and beyond

a garden for vegetables and sometimes flowers. Farther over the brow of the hill the road wound around toward the east end of the house, passing near the barn, which stood nearly on the spot afterward occupied by the greenhouse. Below the road there was at first continuous woods, but early in the century an opening was made, thus securing a fine view and permitting the circulation of air.

A small yard, extending a few rods from the western end of the house, was set apart for the exclusive use of the girls. Beyond this was the regular vegetable garden of the institution, occupying the space afterward called the "girls' bounds." The pupils always had some use of this ground, however, for they might enter at a gate opposite the west door, and a walk quite around the garden, with two transverse walks, gave opportunity for exercise. "Three times around once across" was said to make a mile. Both this garden and the one in front were carefully fenced.

The boys had little open playground, but the dense woods presented unlimited scope for amusement of certain kinds. In this they built their huts, and at seasons stored their supply of nuts. The open space north of the lane was an apple orchard. The trees which now occupy each side of the lane were not planted until twenty years later.

It is not essential to this sketch to record all the changes which occurred in the building itself. Partitions were erected or removed, and rooms devoted to different purposes, with the varying demands of the school. The erection of buildings partially or wholly detached from the principal structure liberated various portions, which were appropriated to the better accommodation of the inmates. A slight mention only of some of the more important additions will be attempted. In the year 1809 a slight fire in one of the rooms warned the inmates of the danger which threatened them, and led to the employment of a watchman to patrol the house, and to the procuring of a supply of fire-buckets.

The boys' play-shed was erected the same year. About the year 1811, the want of additional room, especially for the boys, began to be felt. A subscription was set on foot, with the design of raising a sum sufficient to extend the main building East and West a distance of thirty feet. The East, or boys' wing, was ready for use in 1813. The basement was used at first for storing wood, afterward as a wash-room. The first floor was divided into two school-rooms; and the second floor eventually became the room for the meetings for worship of the family. The erection of the western wing was delayed some years for want of funds. The small tenement opposite the end of the lane came into the possession of the school in 1811. It being feared that this property would be used for purposes injurious to the interests of the students, the stone building now there, and a few acres of land attached, were purchased by the committee, and it has since been the residence of some of the married teachers, or others connected with the school.

During a period of several subsequent years, little change was made in the surroundings of the institution. Internally, however, it was gradually undergoing transformations to adapt it more fully to the end designed. Efforts were made to secure the more complete classification of the scholars, as well as to procure better text-books for their use. The range of studies was gradually enlarged in conformity with the general improvements in education. The desire of some scholars to pursue the study of the Latin and Greek languages, led to the employment of a regular classical teacher in 1830.

The following extract from a report of the committee in 1824, gives a pleasing view of the results obtained up to this period in one very important direction:

"Among the many advantages which it was contemplated would accrue from an institution of this description, several of both sexes have so profited by the course of studies and the mode of instruction thus derived as to be qualified for teachers of schools in many parts of the country; and so far as can at present be ascertained, the number who have thus devoted a part of their time and talents is at least sixty-nine young men and one hundred and eighty-one young women, the ability and example of many of whom, we trust, have diffused such views of the economy and management of schools, as have tended to raise in due estimation this important and highly useful occupation."

Up to this period, the number of children admitted had been 3,482, viz., 1,337 boys, and 2,145 girls.

The troubles of 1827-8, growing out of a defection in principle among members of the Society of Friends, were felt at Westtown, as elsewhere, very severely. A spirit of insubordination showed itself among the boys, which was a source of great anxiety and care to the officers and committee, as also to many parents. Careful and persevering labor on the part of those immediately concerned, was eventually followed by a more satisfactory state of things among the students. It was found necessary to remove a few from the school, and with a view to promote order among those remaining, some members of the committee spent a portion of their time at the institution.

The following extract from a report of the committee shows the feelings experienced at this depressing and critical period by deeply exercised Friends, who were then charged with the oversight of the institution. After stating some particulars connected with the recent disorder, they remark:

"Discouraging as this representation may appear, we have a hope that by patient, persevering labor, under the guidance of Divine Wisdom, who has, we believe, in great condescension regarded this seminary as an effort towards the promotion of righteousness and truth in the earth, a much better and more comfortable state may be effected, and many of the children, as heretofore, have, with grateful hearts, to acknowledge the benefits and solid advantages derived to them by being placed under the concern and guardianship of the Yearly Meeting."

After the separation of 1827, it was found that Westtown School was even more indispensable than before to the Society. Friends in many sections of the country were left few in number, and so scattered in location that it was difficult to support the requisite neighborhood schools of a select character.

The difficulties of such Friends claimed the serious attention of the Yearly Meeting in 1830, and many looked to Westtown as being the best means for remedying the evils likely to result from the crippled condition of the schools. It was finally decided to reduce the charge from $80 to $60 per year, in order that pecuniary considerations should not deter any from deriving such advantages as the school afforded. Such a low charge, it was foreseen, would be attended with a deficiency in the funds of the school, and it was recommended that such deficit should be made up by the meeting at large.*

---

* As expected, a deficiency in the funds resulted from the reduction in the amount charged. During the period from 1830 to 1836, it was calculated that each student only paid about four-fifths of the actual expense incurred on his account. The amount undercharged

For some years following, the school was in a very crowded condition. This made some addition to the building necessary. The long-delayed west wing was erected and brought into use in 1833. The increased labors of the instructors, from the additional number of students, and from the more comprehensive course of instruction required, led to the employment, in 1831, of persons whose special business it was to have charge over the pupils in the intervals of school. Davis Reece was the first governor and Hannah Wood the first governess. Their appointment was an experiment, which, proving satisfactory, has been continued.

In 1832–3, the cholera raged in and around Philadelphia with violence. A report of the committee to the Yearly Meeting in 1833, makes the following mention of it:

"In alluding to the occurrences of the past year, the committee feel it to be cause of gratitude to the Preserver of men that the institution has escaped the epidemic which has so extensively prevailed throughout our country. Although much may be attributed to the healthfulness of the situation, and the salutary regulations exercised over the scholars, yet we cannot but acknowledge the exemption as an evidence of the preserving care of that beneficent Providence to whom we owe all our blessings. Several cases of the cholera having occurred in the vicinity of the school, and the rapid course of the disease rendering prompt medical advice necessary, the committee deemed it expedient to employ a physician to reside for a time on the farm, and also to engage experienced nurses to attend at the institution

during this time was over eighteen thousand dollars; this, with the expense of erecting the west wing, and other permanent improvements, at a cost of about eight thousand dollars, made it necessary for the Yearly Meeting to raise a considerable amount to cancel the remaining indebtedness.

should their services be required. The expense of these arrangements, we believe, was more than compensated by their influence in allaying the anxiety of parents and calming the agitation and fears which had been excited in the minds of some of the scholars."

In 1836, the committee brought before the Yearly Meeting a proposal for dividing the year into terms, with two short vacations. An experience of thirty-seven years had shown that the system of having no stated intervals of rest was attended with serious disadvantages. It was also found that the requirements of the modern mode of instruction could not be so perfectly secured as now desired without a more complete classification than was possible when students were allowed to begin or discontinue their attendance at irregular intervals. The needful relaxation to the teachers, and a better opportunity for making repairs to the property, thus afforded, were also among the reasons for recommending such a change. The proposition was adopted in the following year, and stated terms, with vacations of three weeks, which were afterwards increased to four weeks each, in the spring and autumn, were established — that in the spring including the time of the Yearly Meeting. This change proved a very satisfactory one, and it is probable that in a majority of cases as much has been accomplished in the two terms of forty-four weeks by the scholars as formerly in the fifty-two.

About this time the two collecting-rooms assumed their present form and appearance, by the removal of partitions and the addition of new desks.

The old tin-plate stove, which once graced the centre of the girls' collecting room, had given place to stoves of more improved pattern. Blackboards of small size began to appear in the school-rooms about 1836, and in many details both the building, as regards the use of the various apartments, and the school, in its system of education, began to assume more nearly the character presented in recent times.

The appointment of a governor in 1831 was followed in 1834 by the addition of a teacher on the boys' side for the instruction of classes in Latin and Greek. The rule which terminated the residence of boys at the school on their attaining a certain age had been rescinded, and the number of studies which might be pursued was rapidly increased. Higher mathematics became very popular, and this tendency in the school was probably promoted by the presence at different times of some teachers eminently qualified by character and attainments for inspiring an interest in this department. Mention of the names of Enoch Lewis, Joseph G. Harlan, and others scarcely less known, will readily suggest a partial explanation for what seemed in after years a distinctive feature of Westtown.

On the girls' side of the house the sewing-room became a less important department. Either from natural inclination, or as an incidental result of instruction in this art, needlework was for many years the principal amusement, it might seem, of many students. Samplers, pin-cushions, mottoes, even globes to illustrate the geography of the world, were favorite articles of production, and these were wrought with so much care as to make them heirlooms in many of the families then represented at the school. But as school studies increased in variety the sewing-room lost some of its attraction. First the instruction was limited to small girls, then became voluntary, and finally, about the year 1845, was discontinued. The one relic of the sewing-room, which continued for yet another generation, was a "drawer" in one of the school-rooms, stocked as before with little articles likely to be required by the girls in their fancy work. This, too, passed away in quite recent times, and the governess instead made occasional visits to West Chester, charged with numerous small errands.

Few summer visitors at Westtown in the period under review failed to see the boys' gardens. Just east of the boys' woods, and flanking the old orchard, a strip of ground two or three rods in width was fenced off and divided into small lots. These the boys cultivated, and great was the rivalry as to which company could show the prettiest flowers and neatest arrangement of walks, seats, and arbors. Persons yet living testify that much taste was manifested in the care and cultivation of these miniature gardens, and no small amount of enjoyment received therefrom. Why they were afterward neglected is not explained. As late as 1870 the outline of beds and walks was plainly visible in the sod where the gardens had been, and some hardy flowers, surviving the changed treatment, have become naturalized in the neighboring woods. As the orchard decayed the boys acquired a footing there for games of ball, and finally, in 1865, the game of base-ball having previously been introduced, their playground was extended to its present size. The last of the apple trees was removed in 1868. The traditions of the boys' gardens still cling to the spot, and there are those who lament the decay of the old custom.

A play-shed for the girls, about thirty by ninety feet in size, erected in 1840, gave opportunity for exercise under cover, and was a useful addition to their rather meager accommodations. In 1846–7 a new roof was put on the main building, and at the same time the side walls were raised about four feet, thus giving the whole a more modern appearance than formerly. The change materially added to the comfort of the boys in their sleeping-apartment, and made it possible to secure better ventilation. At this time also the problem of providing apartments for the occasional invalids attained a satisfactory solution. A benevolent Friend * having offered to defray most of the expense, two nurseries were erected, each twenty by thirty-two feet, two stories high. At first they were connected with the galleries by narrow passage-ways, but afterward they were extended so as to reach the galleries, thus still further increasing their size. Few of the additions to the original structures have been more useful than these buildings. They were found to be well adapted to the end designed. The rooms vacated in the central building were appropriated in other ways.

The bath-house for the girls was completed about the beginning of 1850. The next year witnessed the removal of the laundry from the basement to the building specially designed for it. Both these improvements contributed to the health and comfort of the family. The buildings at the farm were undergoing extensive modifications at the same time. The farm-house itself was pronounced inadequate to the wants of the place, and was much out of repair. The barn was in like condition. The Yearly Meeting in 1849 authorized the collection of funds for the erection of new buildings to replace them, and $10,000 was soon obtained. Including the wood-house, the introduction of water, and various other improvements in and around the house (made chiefly in 1851), the cost of the farm-house was $8,474.98, and it was occupied in the early part of 1851. The

* The late Samuel Bettle, Sr.

remainder of the funds, with some additions, was used in erecting the proposed barn in the summer of 1853, the cost of which was $3,953. Both these buildings are large and well arranged, and have added much to the comfort of those concerned, as well as promoted the economy of the farm management.

The danger and inconvenience resulting from the use of lamps in the school building were removed, in 1854, by the erection of apparatus for the manufacture of gas, the expenses of which, as of several previous improvements, were defrayed by private individuals. The present wheel-house on the race bank, some distance above the grist-mill, was erected about this time, and the forcing-pump, which had previously been at the grist-mill, was removed to it, and a new forcing-main, consisting of fourteen hundred feet of three-inch cast-iron pipe, was laid from the wheel-house to the school. The girls' piazza was built in 1855. The boys' bath-house was completed in the same year, and both this and the girls' furnished with apparatus for heating the water. No one will question the sanitary value of these arrangements. In the years 1855-6-7, upwards of $11,000 were expended in painting and repairing the school building throughout, repairing and putting new roofs on the houses in the lane, and in making various repairs and additions to the buildings at the school, the farm-house, and the mill, among which may be particularly mentioned the new barn and carriage-house at the school. This latter was a great improvement over the old school barn, which stood nearly on the site of the present greenhouse. Of the $11,000 thus expended, $9,800 were contributed by two interested members of the committee.

In the autumn of 1858 the West Chester and Philadelphia Railroad was completed, and Street Road Station, distant one and a half miles, became the point of arrival and departure for those connected with the institution. Travel to and from the place was thus rendered much easier. At the opening, and for more than fifty years thereafter, all travel was on horseback or in carriages. While the school was without vacations, and the pupils were coming and going nearly all the time, it was seldom that many needed conveyances at any one time. Effort was made to keep up a regular stage line from Philadelphia, but it was attended with much trouble from insufficient patronage. But when the session system was introduced, and the children met in Philadelphia, and came out in stage loads, the twenty mile ride became quite an important event in the career of the Westtown scholar. The trip back to the city was a renewal of the excitement and bustle. After the branch road was built from the Pennsylvania Central to West Chester, some of the travel took that course. In 1852 the stage route was changed to meet passengers in West Chester, and so remained until the final change above mentioned diverted all travel to the new road.

The period during which the Civil War raged in this country, was not characterized by any serious depression in the operations of the school. Indeed, as an asylum for many young persons, where they were measurably free from the great excitement prevailing elsewhere, its usefulness seemed even greater.

Several pupils from those portions of the Southern States devastated by the contending armies, spent the time quietly and profitably at the school, until they could safely return home.

CHAPTER III.

1865—1884.

IT may be desirable to describe more fully the workings of the school as exhibited in the decade from 1860 to 1870, before any accommodations were provided outside the main building. Except such modifications as resulted from the employment of additional teachers little change had taken place since 1830. There were now six men and five women teachers, and a governor and governess. On each side of the house there was a primary department, including, usually, about one-fifth of all the pupils, but with no definite standard requisite for promotion. These rooms were entirely separate from the others in their routine work. The remaining portion of the school was divided into equal parts, under the care of the first and second mathematical teachers respectively. From the rooms presided over by these teachers, the pupils went out in classes for instruction in reading and writing, and the boys for Latin and Greek. No regular provision was yet made for instructing the girls in the classics. The evening school in winter and the morning hour in summer, now the first hour after breakfast, was devoted, usually, to grammar, each teacher having a class. At another time in the day the whole school was divided into spelling classes and sent to the different rooms.

In mathematics, no attempt was made to instruct by classes. Each pupil did much or little, as suited him, and, reporting from day to day at the teacher's desk, was usually examined at the board to test his proficiency, then allowed to proceed. Those who were fond of mathematics made rapid progress, while others advanced very slowly. So unequal was the development that no regular classification was attempted. New scholars entering the school were not examined closely, but allowed to choose their own studies to a great extent, unless they undertook something manifestly beyond their powers.

Just previous to the visitation by the General Committee in the Sixth and Twelfth months, there was a week of review and a day of oral examination on the work accomplished in the first portion of the term. A longer review and a three days' examination marked the end of the term.

Upon the pages of the catalogue appeared the courses of study, classical and scientific, but they were rather formidable, and it was not the custom of the school to take up these branches in the prescribed order and finish them. Many remained in the school almost or quite long enough to finish, but having passed no examinations on the earlier parts of the work they were deterred from seeking a diploma before leaving. Thus, the courses of study were not much used. The few who did graduate (seven boys and seventeen girls previous to 1870) can scarcely be said to have much influenced the school at large in favor of a systematic course of study.

Dining-rooms were three in number, the superintendent's and those teachers not immediately engaged in the care of the pupils, occupying what was known as the "family dining-room." The experiment made many years before, of having the boys and girls in the same room, but at different tables, had been thought unsatisfactory. The furniture of these rooms was the same which had been in use for half a century, except the pewter porringers and plates had pretty much disappeared, and the long tables were covered with cloths. At the head of each table a short bench was placed, on which a teacher sat. At the teacher's side were two scholars, chosen by turn from the table, whose business it was to replenish the dishes from the kitchen and act in general as waiters. About thirty persons were seated at each table. The provision, except bread, was kept at the head of the table, and plates were helped, under the immediate supervision of the teacher, by some older pupils designated for the purpose. Meals were eaten in silence, or nearly so, except the subdued calls upon the waiters. When all were done, and, after a moment of silence, had passed out, the waiters themselves ate their meal, being under the care, for the time, of an assistant teacher.

Speaking for the boys' school more particularly, these ten years seemed to cover a transition period, in which some old customs were dying out and new ideas obtaining a foothold. Many things contributed to bring about these changes. The introduction of base-ball, and the presence of teachers regularly on the playground, had a good effect in promoting harmony of feeling between officers and students. The construction of ponds for swimming and skating, and other facilities for healthy out-door exercise, materially increased the comfort and happiness of the boys, and promoted a better feeling toward the disciplinary department of the institution. This was shown especially by the voluntary association of the boys for securing good order in the chambers without the immediate presence and surveillance of any officer. These "chamber organizations" form a pleasant feature in the history of the school. Although in after years the movement lost the enthusiasm which first gave it an impulse, and the organizations were finally discontinued, yet they served a useful purpose, since they tended to establish the principle of self-government, and the power of organization to enforce the moral sentiment of the best members of the community. The essential principle has reappeared in many ways, and power for self-government may be said to distinguish Westtown boys.

Certain forms of disorder, such as going beyond the prescribed bounds in a spirit of bravado and for the sake of adventure, now became more unusual; and he who continued these practices, instead of being lionized by his fellows as most worthy of imitation, began to feel, instead, that he had offended a certain moral sentiment of the school. This feeling disinclined him to boast of his exploits, and was a most effective agency in causing him to discontinue such practices. As the officers were less engaged in the detection and punishment of disorder, they were able to devote themselves more unreservedly to the intellectual wants of their pupils. These results were not all produced at once; but comparing periods of time somewhat remote from each other a marked difference may be observed, the change being in the direction of a healthier moral tone and feeling of individual responsibility.

The construction of the ponds above alluded to, added another illustration of the willingness of Friends to provide the means for necessary improvements when their desirability became manifest. This was a subject which enlisted the efforts of the students themselves, and chiefly through them contributions to the amount of nearly one thousand dollars were secured for this purpose. The boys also assisted by their own labors, and experienced a satisfaction in seeing their efforts crowned with success.

From 1865 to 1870 an unusually large number of

pupils were occupying the various departments. This brought under notice more forcibly the want, which had been previously felt, of additional class-rooms for both sexes. The plan most in favor for remedying the difficulty, was to erect a building to accommodate the boys, and thus vacate portions of the main building for the use of the girls. Other plans were proposed, and some time elapsed before any was fully matured. No one was more interested in the movement than the then superintendent, Dubré Knight. But he at least was not permitted to assist in carrying out any of the plans. He died suddenly, on the morning of the 3d of Second month, 1868. In the course of a long life, almost wholly devoted to the cause of education, he had made many friends, and his death left a painful vacancy, not only at Westtown, but elsewhere. Joseph and Hannah Snowdon, who had before for several years acted as superintendents, temporarily filled the vacancies thus suddenly occasioned, during the remainder of the session.

The Yearly Meeting in 4th mo., 1868, authorized subscriptions for the purpose of erecting additional accommodations for the boys. A fire occurring just before, had made some rebuilding also necessary,— the boys' bath-house and play-shed having been destroyed. The contributions received amounted to $23,226. Work was at once commenced, a plan having finally been agreed upon. The school building was first used at the opening of the Winter term of 1869–70. It is situated east of and adjoining the boys' play-shed, a covered connection with the main building being thus secured; is sixty-eight by fifty-four feet in extent, with two stories devoted to school purposes, and has a basement and an attic. A large room in the basement, immediately adjoining the play-shed, affords additional space for exercise within doors during stormy weather. On the first and second floors are a study room and six recitation rooms. These are much more comfortable than the crowded accommodations previously afforded. The rooms vacated by the boys in the main building were now appropriated mainly to the use of the girls, and thus both schools were greatly benefited. Some of the space gained is allotted also to the teachers of both departments, who had previously no private rooms.

Again in 1869 the Yearly Meeting encouraged subscriptions in aid of Westtown. This time an excellent dairy barn was the result, finished in the autumn of that year at a cost of nearly six thousand dollars. The greatly improved supply of butter and milk has demonstrated the wisdom of that movement.

In the report of the Committee to the Yearly Meeting of 1873 occurs the following paragraph:

It is with feelings of sadness that we have to record the death of the Governess, Sarah W. Moore, which occurred on the 10th of Third month, after an illness of about two weeks. We feel that in her removal we have lost a valuable and faithful officer, whose exemplary Christian deportment exerted an important influence over the pupils under her charge, and was a strength to her younger coadjutors in the discharge of their duties.

It is a source of consolation to know that in the winding up of her useful life she was favored with a peaceful mind, and an evidence that while she had nothing of her own to trust to, she could rely on the mercy of that Redeemer whom she had sought faithfully to follow.

Again in 1876 they record the death of Martha Heacock, teacher of the boys' primary department. She had served very acceptably in this station for several years, and her removal was felt to be a real loss to the institution.

In 1873 the Committee called attention to the small number of persons, especially men, who, possessing the requisite qualifications, were willing to engage in teaching, and the frequent changes among those who did for a time seek employment in the school-room. Under the impression that inadequate compensation had much to do with this, they proposed the raising of a fund, the income of which might be applicable only to increasing the salaries of teachers. Two years later they reported that contributions to the amount of $61,000 had been paid in, and the income arising therefrom would enable them to materially increase the salaries. The fund has since received some additions.

Several changes have been made of recent times in the workings of the schools. These began in 1876, with the abolition of evening school in winter and the substitution of a quiet study hour. About the same time considerable attention was given to the course of study, resulting in modifications which brought it into more general use by the pupils. Next a plan was matured by the teachers for classifying and grading the schools, so that all the members of a class would pursue the same studies at the same time. This was adopted, and was followed soon after by a system of written examinations, upon which promotions are based. This was arranged to occur during the last few days of each term, and the oral examination was shortened to one day's work to gain time for this. The union of the two introductory departments under the care of one teacher belongs also to this period.

These various changes, so recent that it seems not necessary to describe them, have greatly increased the regularity and efficiency of the instruction. The class feeling and the prospect of a written examination have proved a healthy stimulus. The alteration in the course of study has induced a considerable number of students to remain and finish it. One hundred and thirty-four thus far (to 1884) have received the diploma of the institution. It is the aim, however, to render the instruction useful to all who attend, whether for a longer or shorter period, and, while recognizing the value to the school of the prolonged residence of such as remain to graduate, not to consider their interests alone. The true alumni of Westtown are not those incidentally designated by length of residence and intellectual acquirements only, but those who, having received any portion of their education within its walls, profit thereby and continue to cherish a kindly feeling toward the principles of the institution, as well as the institution itself.

The Westtown report in 1880 contained this cautionary paragraph:

In accordance with our previous practice the Committee has continued to give to those pupils who have completed the prescribed course of study at the institution, the encouragement and assistance which may be derived from its Certificate. But the desire has-been felt to guard them from that which may tend to make them think more highly of themselves than they ought to think, or lead them to forget that they are then but entering upon the more serious responsibilities of life; and that the final reward of well doing is not promised to those who have obtained a name among men, but to the humble learners and doers of the Divine will.

In the summer of 1882 a Normal Class was organized

in connection with the girls' school. It continues in successful operation, and is aiding to raise the standard of teaching in the Yearly Meeting. The growing tendency to seek for such instructors as have professional skill and knowledge, as well as general intelligence, indicates a more extended field of usefulness for this department of the school work.

Not only is the theory taught by the study of the best educational authorities, but actual practice is given, under the immediate supervision of an experienced teacher. Young teachers frequently take advantage of the summer vacations elsewhere to spend some weeks or months in this department.

Such indications lead to the belief that this experiment, the first attempt at normal instruction within the limits of Phila. Yearly Meeting, though small in its beginning, will be increasingly useful in improving the methods of instruction in all the schools under the care of that body.

Within the last ten years, more association by pupils of opposite sexes has been allowed; the joint literary society which has existed since 1874, the union of the Latin classes and occasionally of those on other subjects, and the arrangement made in 1881, by which the pupils eat in the same dining-room with the rest of the family, boys and girls sitting at the same tables, all point to a willingness to profit by the results of experience. These changes have been made with caution, and not till the Committee were well satisfied of their utility.

CHAPTER IV.

WESTTOWN.

IT is impossible to record within the limits of a few pages all the steps in the growth of Westtown. As we look back over the past, we are forcibly reminded of the humble, teachable spirit in which the enterprise was undertaken, and can but regard its success as due to the watchful care of those engaged in the work, who, as they have kept close to that guidance which animated them in the beginning, have been enabled to move aright in enlarging the undertaking. It may be proper to add a brief outline of the school as it now exists.

The discipline of the school is largely paternal. Pupils are taught to govern their actions by considerations of right and propriety. Rules are found necessary, but effort is made that these commend themselves to the minds of all as the necessary restrictions of a well-ordered community. The opening paragraph of the "Rules and Advices" is as follows:

In all their conduct the pupils are enjoined to do right for its own sake, and because it is the Divine Will. This requires some sacrifice of self-interest and self-will; but it must ever be remembered that unrestrained liberty of action is incompatible with either civil laws or the requirements of Christian morality.

The summer session usually opens on the first Third day in the Fifth month, and continues nearly twenty-two weeks. After a vacation of one month the school again opens for the winter term, about the first of Eleventh month. One day at the opening of each term is devoted to the reception of students and the examination of those who enter for the first time.

The course of study covers a period of three years, and is equal to that of the best high schools. Greek is wholly elective, while Latin may be omitted by those who desire only the scientific course. The intermediate department comprises five grades for the boys and four for the girls. The recitations of the two sexes are separate, except in the Latin and some of the more advanced classes in scientific and English studies. The introductory department includes those least advanced of both sexes, and is chiefly under the care of one teacher.

The five weeks preceding the close of each term are devoted to review and examination. The latter is mainly by written work, and upon the result depends the future standing of each pupil. The close of the term is always attended by some of the Committee in charge of the school, and one day is devoted to the oral examination of several of the classes. Graduating exercises, if there are any, occur on Fifth day at noon, and mark the final close.

Pupils spend five and one-half hours per day in school; and when not engaged in reciting, they remain in their respective study rooms, occupied in the preparation of other lessons. There are also facilities for study between the regular school hours, either in collections presided over by a teacher, or under restrictions imposed by the students themselves.

Lectures upon scientific and other subjects are delivered regularly during the winter, and frequently at other times. For the purposes of illustration, both in lectures and recitations, there is an abundant supply of apparatus. This collection received its first large addition in 1852, when some of the men teachers raised a sum of money by subscription and visited Boston to make purchases. Some of the pieces which then came to the school are yet in frequent use. Latterly, valuable additions have been made in all departments to keep pace with the improved methods of the times.

The mineralogical collection belonging to the school is an excellent one. Many specimens were collected by the officers of the school in former years, which have been increased by valuable donations from Dr. George Martin of West Chester, the late Jane Watson of Ohio, and the heirs of Isaac Jones, late of Camden, N. J. These together now form an extensive and varied collection. The space at present applicable is utterly inadequate to the display of these specimens, and many of them must remain packed in boxes until such time as the institution possesses facilities for their proper classification and arrangement.

The "Westtown Literary Society," organized in 1836, by the men teachers and older pupils, was for many years a source of great interest and usefulness. Bound volumes of "The Cabinet," the monthly paper published by the Society, attest the excellence of much of the work done by the members. A collection of specimens in Natural History, chiefly collected and prepared by the first governor, Davis Reece, was given into the care of this organization in 1865. Among the girls literary societies existed under various names until 1869, when "The Lyonian" was organized, and promised to be permanent. Its paper, "The Casket," vied with "The Cabinet" in the excellence of its contributions. Finally, in 1874, by permission of the Committee, these two societies were merged in "The Literary Union," to which all the possessions of both were transferred, and it is now one of the established features of the institution. Members are chosen by election from the older and more advanced pupils of both sides of the house; meetings are held weekly, and they are often occasion of much interest. Other societies exist among the younger students, but membership is restricted to their respective departments.

A well-selected library of three thousand seven hundred volumes is open to the pupils at frequent intervals, and encyclopedias and other reference books are kept at points so near their living rooms as to invite their frequent use by the students. The library began in 1806, at which time it was under the care of one of the older boys. It received material enlargement, and was first catalogued in 1856. It now receives additions annually, and is under care of one of the teachers, who gives personal attention to advising the students and directing them to suitable works upon particular subjects.

In the intervals between school hours the students are principally under the care of the governor and governess. Though children are not sent to Westtown in search of recreation, yet the various amusements resorted to are of no slight importance. The absolute necessity of some provision of the kind in any system of education is fully recognized. But little attention has been paid to gymnastic or calisthenic exercises, but this is largely compensated for by the free access to the fine walks and extensive playgrounds which they enjoy. In summer the boys have their frequent games of ball, and the girls other lighter games. Not least among the attractions of the place for the young are the facilities for long rambles near Chester Creek and around Walnut Hill. The belt of woodland nearer the school buildings has always been a favorite resort, the occasional cart tracks having been appropriated as footpaths. In this was the "Labyrinth" of olden time. During the summer of 1878 numerous paths were opened up, to which appropriate names were given. These are kept in order by the students, and are much used. It is the policy of the institution to preserve this piece of timber as a natural park, in which, by a few minutes' walk, one reaches almost the quiet and seclusion of a dense woodland.

The large farm, traversed by the winding creek and mill-race, and still occupied in parts by a fine growth of timber, contains many sequestered and beautiful resorts, well known to all Westonians, and connected, perhaps, with not a few of the cherished recollections of their childhood. Every year makes more apparent the wisdom of the founders of Westtown in securing abundance of land while it was yet comparatively cheap. Few institutions possess such ample facilities for varied pastimes within their own borders. So valuable is this feature esteemed, that less land has been cleared and brought under cultivation than if money profit had been the sole consideration. Of the 600 acres in the entire tract, about 125 acres, including one considerable belt of woodland, are under the care of the superintendent. This includes the playgrounds, lawns, gardens, orchards, etc. Several acres are attached to the mill, and of the portion under the care of the farmer, 75 acres are woodland, or occupied by the public road, which traverses the tract for at least two miles, and less than 400 acres under cultivation. On this portion a fine dairy of sixty cows is kept, and the abundant supply of pure milk and butter is not least among the blessings enjoyed by pupils at Westtown.

The skating pond covers about four acres, and in season

affords exhilarating exercise for both boys and girls. The swimming pond for the boys is of equal interest in the summer. Foot-ball in winter and base-ball and lawn tennis in summer are the most popular games with the boys, and the last mentioned is also a favorite with the girls. These exercises contribute largely to the general good health enjoyed by inmates of the establishment.

Meetings for worship are held in the house on First and Fifth days. Through the Scripture recitations, religious readings, and the personal association of the officers with the students, as well as the labors of the members of the Committee, efforts are made to instil into them proper motives of action, and the principles of a sound moral character, and give a practical acquaintance with the doctrines and testimonies of the Society of Friends. Whatever may be the degree of success in these respects, although there may be among those who leave the school some who show little evidence of religious improvement by a sojourn there, cases are in no wise infrequent, now as formerly, of those who attribute seasons of true growth in the best life to the instructions received and the influences thrown around them while at Westtown.

In every department of the institution there continues to be a special and personal oversight by members of the Yearly Meeting's Committee. Originally that body appointed an acting committee of ten members, who had the entire supervision of all the departments. More recently, a system of rotation in the appointment of visiting committees has been adopted, by which all members are expected to attend at least once in the course of the year. There are also important sub-committees, specially intrusted with certain duties. Principal among these are the "Instruction," "Farm," "Admission's," and

"Household" Committees, each of which reports to the General Committee.

The immediate surroundings of the house are those which come only with age. The fine trees which grace the lawns have become almost a part of the institution. Around them cling the pleasant memories of successive generations of students and teachers, and universal regret is expressed that any future enlargement of the building may result in the destruction of some of these. Another fifty years must elapse before a second "Maple Grove" could replace that of the present.

The main building, though good for some years of service, having sheltered the large family for more than fourscore years, and endured many alterations in that time, begins to show the effects of age. During recent years the minds of many have been turned to consider the advisability of replacing it with a new structure, in which approved accommodations and facilities might be afforded. It is no charge against the wisdom and foresight of Friends in 1800 that the building, which was thought an admirable structure then, is found inadequate to the changed requirements of almost a century later.

The aim has been steadily kept in view to place the price of board and tuition as low as possible, in order to be within the reach of all classes. The present price is $160 per year, about one-half that charged by other schools of equal grade. The average annual expense per pupil for the ten years preceding 1884 was about $214. The deficiency is made up from the income of invested funds, profits of the farm, donations, and bequests. From the two latter sources a considerable fund has arisen, the income of which is applied to assist in educating the children of parents whose means are limited. The fund is in this way productive of much good to many in various parts of Philadelphia Yearly Meeting, but it is not the property of the school itself. The income derived from it is not applicable to the support of the institution, except as it is received in payment for the education of children entitled to its benefit.

But it has not been to the liberal donations of money alone, or even to these principally, that the success of the school has been owing. Primarily the praise is due to Him from whom cometh every good and perfect gift, and who, while He opened the hearts of some to contribute of their worldly substance to this cause, made others willing to incur the labor, anxiety, and religious exercise inseparable from the right management of such a concern. The continuance of this success will much depend on the maintenance in the hearts of Friends of that earnest desire for the preservation and true welfare of the children, which encouraged many in time past to labor faithfully for their good. If a succession of honest and devoted laborers can be preserved on the committee and in the officers entrusted with the care of this school, there is good reason to hope that Westtown shall continue to be in the future what it has been in the past, a place where the principles of purity and peace are upheld and instilled; that it shall be a home from whence may go forth sons and daughters whose upright walk in the world will say emphatically unto others, "Come and have fellowship with us, for truly our fellowship is with the Father and with his Son Jesus Christ."

LIST OF

SUPERINTENDENTS, MATRONS, GOVERNORS, GOVERNESSES, TEACHERS, FARMERS, AND BOOK-KEEPERS, WHO HAVE SERVED IN WESTTOWN SCHOOL.

SUPERINTENDENTS AND MATRONS.

RICHARD and CATHARINE HARTSHORNE were appointed previous to the opening of the school, Fifth month 6th, 1799, and left on the 16th of Twelfth month of that year. Some members of the Committee resided at the Institution for a few months, before other persons were appointed.

JOSHUA and ANN SHARPLESS were appointed Fourth month 1st, 1800, and continued until Tenth month 17th, 1811.

JOSEPH and HANNAH WHITALL were appointed Tenth month 15th, 1811, and remained until Tenth month 13th, 1818.

PHILIP and RACHEL PRICE commenced Tenth month 13th, 1818, and retired Fifth month 3d, 1830.

PENNOCK and SARAH PASSMORE commenced Fifth month 1st, 1830, and served until Third month 29th, 1836.

NATHAN SHARPLESS and MARTHA JEFFERIS began Third month 28th, 1836, and served until Tenth month 27th, 1843.

PENNOCK and SARAH PASSMORE served a second term, beginning Tenth month 27th, 1843, and ending Fourth month 7th, 1848.

JOSEPH and HANNAH E. SNOWDON commenced Fourth month 8th, 1848, and served until Tenth month 20th, 1858.

DAVID and RACHEL H. ROBERTS commenced Tenth month 16th, 1858, and retired Fourth month 16th, 1861.

Dubré and Jane W. Knight began Fourth month 15th, 1861. Dubré Knight deceased Second month 3d, 1868. Jane Knight remained until Fourth month following.

Charles J. and Martha D. Allen began Fourth month 30th, 1868, and remained until Fifth month 2d, 1869.

Aaron and Susanna F. Sharpless commenced Fifth month, 1869, and remained until Fourth month, 1874.

Benjamin W. and Rebecca G. Passmore began Fourth month, 1874, and remained until Fourth month, 1881.

Jonathan G. and Susanna R. Williams began Fourth month, 1881.

GOVERNORS.

Davis Reece, from Twelfth month 16th, 1831, to Tenth month 1st, 1859.

David J. Scott, from Eleventh month 1st, 1860, to Tenth month 1st, 1869.

Watson W. Dewees, from Eleventh month, 1869, to Tenth month, 1874.

Thompson Frame, Eleventh month, 1874.

GOVERNESSES.

Hannah S. Wood, from Twelfth month 16th, 1831, to Sixth month 13th, 1834.

Lydia A. Buffington, from Sixth month 13th, 1834, to Twelfth month 11th, 1835.

GOVERNESSES.

Rebecca McCollin, from Twelfth month 11th, 1835, to Fourth month 7th, 1843.

Deborah B. Smith, from Fourth month 7th, 1843, to Fourth month 1st, 1846.

Elizabeth Walter, from Fourth month 10th, 1846, to Tenth month 10th, 1851.

Abigail Williams, from Tenth month 10th, 1851, to Fourth month 11th, 1857.

Hannah Forsythe, from Fifth month 1st, 1857, to Second month 10th, 1862.

Hannah A. Warner, from Second month 10th, 1862, to Fourth month 10th, 1863.

Elizabeth W. Hoopes, from Fifth month 1st, 1863, to Fourth month 1st, 1865.

Martha Sankey, from Fifth month 1st, 1865, to Fourth month 1st, 1867.

Sarah W. Moore,* from Fifth month, 1867, to Third month 10th, 1873.

Ruth Anna Brown, from Third month 10th, 1873, to Tenth month, 1873.

Mary H. Woolman, from Eleventh month, 1873, to Fourth month, 1875.

Sylvania Cooper, from Fifth month, 1875, to Tenth month, 1876.

Sarah A. Collins, from Eleventh month, 1876, to Fourth month, 1877.

Sylvania Cooper (2d Term), Fifth month, 1877.

* Deceased at the school. See page 51.

A LIST OF TEACHERS

From the Opening of the School to the Present Time,

Arranged in the Order of their Appointment, and showing also the Times of Entering and Retiring from the Service.

	APPOINTED.	RETIRED.
Elizabeth Bellerby,	4th mo. 30, 1799;	6th mo. 7, 1800.
Phebe Cox,	5th mo. 6, "	3d mo. 1, 1801.
John Forsythe,	5th mo. 6, "	4th mo. 6, 1801.
Ann Thomas,	7th mo. 21, "	7th mo. 21, 1802.
Elihu Pickering,	8th mo. 7, "	4th mo. 8, 1802.
Ann Bacon,	10th mo. 15, "	10th mo. 1, 1801.
Alexander Wilson,	.... "	.... 1799.
Rebecca Budd,	11th mo. 1, "	2d mo. 20, 1803.
Enoch Lewis,	11th mo. 10, "	3d mo. 1, 1808.
Emmor Kimber,	2d mo. 10, 1800;	" 31, 1800.
Samuel Comfort,	4th mo. 1, "	11th mo. 17, "
John Comly,	" 11, "	2d mo. 7, 1802.
Ann Gilbert,	" 27, "	" 10, 1804.
Abigail Hoskins,	6th mo. 1, "	8th mo. 21, 1800.
Martha Barker,	7th mo. 1, "	" 26, 1808.
John Baldwin,	11th mo. 17, "	1st mo. 16, 1809.
Martha West,	" 1, 1801;	5th mo. 14, 1805.
Charity Cope,	6th mo. 19, 1802;	" 10, 1803.
Joseph Black,	10th mo. 15, "	2d mo. 2, 1806.
Martha Sharpless,	3d mo. 1, 1803;	11th mo. 21, 1809.
Mary Allinson,	3d mo. 1, 1804;	9th mo. 12, 1804.
Sarah Jacobs,	5th mo. 17, "	1st mo. 7, 1813.
Hannah Albertson,	9th mo. 7, "	9th mo. 5, 1807.
Sarah Woodward,	3d mo. 1, 1805;	8th mo. 2, 1806.
William Adams,	4th mo. 28, 1806;	9th mo. 10, "
Ann Woodward,	8th mo. 20, "	7th mo. 19, 1808.
Eli Hilles,	9th mo. 1, "	3d mo. 23, 1811.
Hannah Foulke,	10th mo. 19, 1807;	5th mo. 21, 1815.
Samuel Hilles,	3d mo. 1, 1808;	8th mo. 3, 1811.
Sarah Martin,	7th mo. 1, "	9th mo. 19, 1814.

	APPOINTED.	RETIRED.
John Bullock,	12th mo. 1, 1808;	12th mo. 7, 1813.
Sally Page,	5th mo. 2, 1809;	2d mo. 28, 1814.
Septimus Roberts,	" 4, "	9th mo. 26, 1812.
Elizabeth Barker,	6th mo. 8, "	6th mo. 11, 1811.
Blakey Sharpless,	4th mo. 9, 1810;	9th mo. 12, 1814.
Robert Parry,	" 1, 1811;	8th mo. 4, 1816.
Sarah Farquhar,	6th mo. 15, "	1st mo. 16, "
John Gummere,	10th mo. 5, 1812;	3d mo. 19, 1814.
John Mason,	12th mo. 6, 1813;	6th mo. 11, "
Rachel Parry,	1st mo. 21, 1814;	4th mo. 8, 1816.
Mary Blackledge,	3d mo. 21, "	2d mo. 8, 1815.
Ann Stockton,	4th mo. 25, "	" 1, 1817.
Amos Bullock,	6th mo. 1, "	6th mo. 15, 1816.
David Whitall,	" 13, "	2d mo. 1, 1815.
Jacob Haines,	2d mo. 1, 1815;	11th mo. 6, 1823.
Hannah W. Butcher,	4th mo. 4, "	2d mo. 7, 1817.
Sibilla Embree,	5th mo. 22, "	12th mo. 30, 1822.
Samuel R. Gummere,	6th mo. 22, "	8th mo. 6, 1816.
Sarah West,	1st mo. 13, 1816;	2d mo. 7, 1822.
Margaretta T. Jacobs,	4th mo. 29, "	8th mo. 7, 1817.
Joseph Cooper,	6th mo. 25, "	5th mo. 18, "
William Neal,	" " "	11th mo. 25, 1820.
Seth Smith,	8th mo. 12, "	10th mo. 23, 1821.
Pennock Passmore,	12th mo. 7, "	3d mo. 29, 1836.
Mary Passmore,	2d mo. 7, 1817;	5th mo. 14, 1826.
Elizabeth Pyle,	" 8, "	1st mo. 3, 1820.
Abigail Passmore,	8th mo. 6, "	" 28, 1825.
Elizabeth S. Walton,	1st mo. 8, 1820;	4th mo. 12, 1830.
Benjamin Hallowell,	" 12, 1821;	9th mo. 8, 1824.
Sarah Conard,	9th mo. 6, "	" 24, 1830.
Alice Comfort,	2d mo. 7, 1822;	" 5, 1822.
Mary Hallowell,	" 8, 1823;	1st mo. 9, 1826.
Charles Farquhar,	11th mo. 10, "	12th mo. 29, 1824.
Oliver Paxson,	9th mo. 21, 1824;	6th mo. 18, 1826.
Jacob Heald,	12th mo. 29, "	2d mo. 24, 1826.
Hannah S. Wood,	1st mo. 24, 1825;	12th mo. 16, 1831.
Elizabeth H. Knight,	9th mo. 7, "	10th mo. 6, 1828.
Davis Reece,	2d mo. 27, 1826;	12th mo. 16, 1831.
Lydia Ann Buffington,	5th mo. 1, "	6th mo. 13, 1834.

TEACHERS. 85

	APPOINTED.	RETIRED.
Samuel W. Black,	10th mo. 9, 1826;	3d mo. 16, 1830.
George W. Taylor,	3d mo. 28, 1830;	6th mo. 30, 1831.
Bartram Kaighn,	7th mo. 20, "	7th mo. 9, 1834.
Mary Passmore (2d Term),	9th mo. 15, "	10th mo. 1, 1832.
Catharine V. West,	" 20, "	12th mo. 4, 1830.
Howard Yarnall,	10th mo. 6, "	10th mo. 4, 1844.
Deborah Cope,	" 25, "	8th mo. 15, 1832.
Hannah Gillingham,	12th mo. 21, "	9th mo. 7, "
Harvey Thomas,	6th mo. 30, 1831;	5th mo. 1, 1835.
Zillah Embree,	9th mo. 13, "	8th mo. 31, 1833.
Hannah Allen,	10th mo. 3, "	2d mo. 17, 1834.
Enoch Lewis (2d Term),	12th mo. 19, "	9th mo. 27, "
Samuel M. Day,	7th mo. 5, 1832;	11th mo. 28, "
Elizabeth Cowgill,	" 25, "	9th mo. 5, "
Rebecca S. Leeds,	10th mo. 8, "	5th mo. 19, 1837.
Amy Eastlack,	9th mo. 2, 1833;	4th mo. 7, 1838.
Martha Gibbons,	4th mo. 29, 1834;	10th mo. 30, 1834.
Moses B. Lockwood,	7th mo. 10, "	9th mo. 9, 1835.
Rebecca McCollin,	8th mo. 2, "	12th mo. 11, 1835.
William Forsythe,	9th mo. 29, "	10th mo. 29, 1836.
Mary L. Smith,	10th mo. 30, "	" 3, 1835.
Edward Richie,	11th mo. 29, "	" 23, "
Sarah Baily,	12th mo. 15, "	" 1, 1869.
James Emlen,	5th mo. 4, 1835;	12th mo. 27, 1848.
David S. Burson,	10th mo. 7, "	9th mo. 2, 1836.
Mary Dent,*	" 19, "	1st mo. 23, "
Samuel Leeds,	" 24, "	7th mo. 26, "
Sarah Ann Dillin,	12th mo. 24, "	9th mo. 20, 1839.
Susanna Lightfoot,	3d mo. 28, 1836;	4th mo. 10, 1841.
James C. Jackson,	8th mo. 8, "	11th mo. 7, 1838.
Ann Jefferis,	" 17, "	10th mo. 10, 1840.
Joseph Walton,	9th mo. 30, ."	1st mo. 9, 1846.
John G. Jackson,	10th mo. 29, "	4th mo. 7, 1838.
Sidney Stevenson,	5th mo. 19, 1837;	10th mo. 10, 1840.
Levis Newlin, ·	4th mo. 30, 1838;	5th mo. 21, 1841.
Enoch Lewis (3d Term),	" " "	10th mo. 16, 1838.
Elizabeth Baily,	5th mo. 2, "	" 8, 1841.
Rebecca Kite,	6th mo. 18, "	" " 1838.

* Deceased at the School.

	APPOINTED.	RETIRED.
Hugh D. Vail,	6th mo. 18, 1838;	4th mo. 10, 1847.
Yardley Warner,	12th mo. 31, "	" " 1841.
Mary Emlen,	11th mo. 2, 1839;	10th mo. 8, "
Rebecca Kite (2d Term),	7th mo. 8, "	" " 1839.
Abigail Williams,	11th mo. 2, 1840;	4th mo. 5, 1844.
Lydia Philips.	" " "	" 10, 1841.
Martha C. Barton,	5th mo. 3, 1841;	" 1, 1867.
Rebecca Biddle,	" " "	10th mo. 8, 1842.
John Newlin,	" " "	" 9, 1847.
Rebecca Kite (3d Term),	10th mo. 28, "	7th mo. 8, 1845.
Henry Rodman,	" " "	4th mo. 9, 1842.
Jesse Edgerton,	4th mo. 28, 1842;	10th mo. 8, "
Elizabeth Walter,	10th mo. 28, "	4th mo. 10, 1846.
Rebecca Conard,	" " "	" 5, 1843.
Jas. C. Jackson (2d Term),	11th mo. 9, "	" " 1843.
Joseph G. Harlan,	4th mo. 28, 1843;	10th mo. 1, 1853.
Priscilla Walter,	" 26, 1844;	" 7, 1849.
Margaret Lightfoot,	10th mo. 30, 1845;	" 1, 1859.
Martha D. House,	5th mo. 1, 1846;	" 1, 1853.
Benjamin Hoopes,	10th mo. 29, "	4th mo. 9, 1852.
James Smedley,	" " "	2d mo. 28, 1851.
George Baily,	" " "	10th mo. 7, 1848.
James M. Price,	" 28, 1848;	" 1, 1853.
Charles Potts,	11th mo. 13, "	" 10, 1851.
Richard J. Allen,	4th mo. 26, 1849;	" 9, 1857.
Rebecca E. Haines,	1st mo. 15, 1850;	" 8, 1852.
Lewis Palmer,	6th mo. 2, 1851;	" 1, 1854.
Edward Potts,	11th mo. 3, "	4th mo. 1, 1859.
Isaac Hall,	5th mo. 3, 1852;	10th mo. 1, 1857.
Hannah Forsythe,	11th mo. 1, 1852;	5th mo. 1, "

TEACHERS.

From the printed catalogues of late years information is obtained as to the branches taught by each.

	APPOINTED.	RETIRED.
William B. Morgan, Classics,	10th mo., 1853;	10th mo., 1855.
Samuel Alsop, Sen., Mathematics,	" "	4th mo., 1860.
Sarah Henly, Primary Department,	" "	10th mo., 1854.
Asenath Hill, Second Department,	11th mo., 1854;	4th mo., 1859.
Thomas Waring, Writing,	" "	" 1857.
Joseph Passmore, Classics,	" 1855;	" 1856.
Ephraim Smith, History, Geography, etc.,	5th mo., 1856;	" 1858.
Jane W. Edwards, Primary Department,	" 1857;	" 1861.
Benjamin Hoopes (2d Term), Arithmetical Department,	11th mo., "	" 1860.
Jesse S. Cheyney, Classics,	11th mo., 1857;	8th mo., 1866.
David J. Scott, Writing,	5th mo., 1858;	10th mo., 1860.
Samuel Alsop, Jr., Reading,	" 1859;	4th mo., "
Martha Sankey, Second Dep.,	" "	" 1865.
Ephraim Smith (2d Term), Arithmetical Department,	12th mo., 1859;	" "
Elizabeth Rhoads, Reading,	" "	1st mo., 1861.
Benjamin Hoopes, Mathematics,	5th mo., 1860;	4th mo., 1863
Ziba D. Walter, Primary Department,	11th mo., "	12th mo., 1861.
Nathan H. Edgerton, Reading,	" "	6th mo., 1863.
Elizabeth Chambers, Reading,	5th mo., 1861;	10th mo., 1865.
Esther Kite, Primary Department,	" "	4th mo., 1862.
Yardley Warner (2d Term), Primary Department,	1st mo., 1862;	" 1863.
Rebecca Smedley, Primary Department,	5th mo., "	" "

88 GENERAL CATALOGUE.

	APPOINTED.	RETIRED.
Thomas A. Bell, Primary Department,	5th mo., 1863;	4th mo., 1865.
Mary L. Michener, Primary Department,	" "	10th mo., 1866.
Samuel Alsop, Jr. (2d Term), Mathematics,	" "	7th mo., 1868.
Charles Potts (2d Term), Reading,	6th mo., "	....
William Kite, Writing,	11th mo., "	10th mo., 1867.
Thomas A. Bell, Arithmetical Department,	5th mo., 1865;	11th mo., 1867.
William G. Embree, Primary Department,	" "	4th mo., "
Mary Anna Forsythe, Second Department,	" "	10th mo., 1865.
Mary Maule, Second Department,	11th mo., "	4th mo., 1867.
Sarah W. Moore, Primary Department,	" "	" "
Watson W. Dewees, Assistant Governor,	5th mo., 1866;	10th mo., 1869.
Thomas C. Hoge, Primary Department,	11th mo., "	2d mo., 1870.
Mary L. Michener, Reading,	" "	5th mo., 1868.
C. Canby Balderston, Arithmetical Department,	" "	10th mo., 1869.
Sarah B. Boswell, Primary Department,	5th mo., 1867;	" 1868.
Cidney E. Williams, Second Department,	" "	1st mo., "
Martha Sankey, Writing,	" "	5th mo., "
Henry N. Hoxie, Classics,	" "	10th mo., 1871.
Zebedee Haines, Writing,	11th mo., "	8th mo., 1869.
Rachel A. Cooper, Primary Department,	5th mo., 1868;	4th mo., "
Martha Sankey, Second Department,	" "	10th mo., "
Dorothy Hobson, Writing,	11th mo., "	" "
Martha Heacock, Reading,	" "	" 1870.

TEACHERS.

	APPOINTED.	RETIRED.
Isaac Sharpless, Mathematics,	11th mo., 1868;	10th mo., 1872.
Sylvania Cooper, Third Department,	5th mo., 1869;	10th mo., 1869.
Sylvania Cooper, Second Department,	11th mo., "	4th mo., 1875.
Elizabeth Evans, Third Department,	" "	4th mo., 1870.
Cidney E. Williams (2d Term), Writing,	" "	7th mo., 1871.
Martha Sankey, First Department,	" "	4th mo., 1876.
John W. Cloud, Jr., Geography, etc.,	" "	5th mo., 1871.
C. Canby Balderston, Writing and Ass't Governor,	" "	4th mo., 1872.
David J. Scott, Arithmetical Department,	" "	" 1871.
Elizabeth Rhoads, Reading,	5th mo., 1870;	10th mo., 1870.
Mary Anna Brown, Third Department,	" "	" 1871.
Anne Warner, Reading,	10th mo., "	4th mo., 1872.
Martha Heacock, Primary Department, (Boys',)	" "	2d mo., 1876.*
John W. Cloud, Jr., Arithmetical Department,	5th mo., 1871;	4th mo., 1872.
Lydia Embree, Third Department,	10th mo., "	" "
Anna J. Cooper, Writing,	" "	" "
Henry Evaul, Classics,	" "	5th mo., "
Isaac N. Vail, Writing and Assistant Governor,	4th mo., 1872;	10th mo., "
C. Canby Balderston, Arithmetical Department,	" "	" "
Sarah R. Harmer, Reading,	" "	4th mo., 1875.
Ann Sharpless, Writing,	" "	10th mo., 1881.
Ruth Anna Brown, Third Department,	" "	5th mo., 1873.
William B. Kaighn, Classics,	5th mo., "	10th mo., 1873.

* Deceased at the school, 21st of Second mo., 1876.

	APPOINTED.	RETIRED.
C. Canby Balderston, Mathematics,	11th mo., 1872;	10th mo., 1873.
Isaac N. Vail, Arithmetical Department,	" "	" "
Edwin Thorp, Writing,	" "	....
Benjamin Vail, Care of Study Room, &c.,	" "	5th mo., 1873.
Julia T. Walter, Girls' Introductory Department.	5th mo., 1873;	10th mo., 1874.
Isaac N. Vail, Care of Study Room, &c.,	11th mo., "	4th mo., 1875.
John E. Forsythe, Classical Department,	" "	" 1876.
Isaac Sharpless, Mathematics,	" "	10th mo., 1875.
C. Canby Balderston, Natural and Physical Science,	" "	....
Phebe Nicholson, Arithmetic and Natural Philosophy,	5th mo., 1874;	10th mo., 1874.
Mary Anna Forsythe, Girls' Introductory Department,	11th mo., "	" 1875.
Watson W. Dewees, History and Care of Study Room,	5th mo., 1875;	....
Sarah W. Passmore, Arithmetic and Nat. Philosophy,	" "	10th mo., 1875.
Anne Balderston, Grammar and Elocution,	" "	4th mo., 1883.
Thomas K. Brown, Mathematics,	11th mo., "	....
Anna Livezey, Girls' Introductory Department,	" "	10th mo., 1876.
Sarah W. Passmore, Mathematics,	" "	4th mo., "
Sarah F. Jones, Writing and History,	" "	10th mo., "
Mary Anna Forsythe, Instructor in the Study Room,	" "	" 1877.
William Trimble, Classical Department,	5th mo., 1876;	" 1876.

TEACHERS. 91

	APPOINTED.	RETIRED.
Joseph Rhoads, Jr., Introductory Department,	5th mo., 1876;	10th mo., 1877.
Phebe Nicholson, Mathematics,	" "	4th mo., 1879.
Eliza A. Cheyney, Arithmetic and Natural Philosophy,	" "	" 1880.
John E. Forsythe, Classical Department,	11th mo., "	10th mo., 1877.
Sarah F. Jones, Girls' Introductory Department,	" "	4th mo., 1881.
Albert H. Votaw, Classical Department,	" 1877;	....
Albert B. Cope, Introductory Department,	" "	4th mo., 1878.
Sarah W. Passmore, Instructor in Study Room,	" "	" 1879.
Wilmer P. Leeds, Introductory Department,	5th mo., 1878;	" "
Sarah W. Passmore, Mathematics,	" 1879;	10th mo., "
Mary Anna Forsythe, Instructor in Study Room,	" "	....
Phebe Nicholson, Mathematics,	11th mo., "	....
Mary Anna Balderston, Arithmetic and Natural History,	5th mo., 1880;	4th mo., 1881.
Agnes V. McGrew, Arithmetic and Natural History,	" 1881;	8th mo., "
Anna Walton, Introductory Department,	" "	10th mo., 1883.
Mary Anna Balderston, Arithmetic and Natural History.	10th mo., "	5th mo., 1882.
Margaret M. McCollin, Writing and History,	" "	10th mo., "
Ann Sharpless, Normal Department,	5th mo , 1882;	....
Agnes V. McGrew, Arithmetic and Natural History,	" "	4th mo., 1883.
Rebecca J. Allen, Arithmetic and Natural History,	" 1883;	8th mo., "

	APPOINTED.	RETIRED.
Lucinda Lake, Grammar and Elocution,	5th mo., 1883;	....
Miriam Elfreth, Introductory Department,	11th mo., "	....
Anna Walton, Arithmetic and Natural History,	" "	....

FARMERS.

	APPOINTED.	RETIRED.
Edward Churchman,	3d mo., 1795;	3d mo., 1796.
Robert Green,	" 1796;	" 1800.
David Branson,	" 1800;	" 1804.
Andrew Steel,	" 1804;	1st mo., 1813.
William Reed,	1st mo., 1813;	12th mo., 1831.
Joseph Bailey,	12th mo., 1831;	1st mo., 1838.
Hughes Bell,	1st mo., 1838;	4th mo., 1847.
Isaac Hayes,	4th mo., 1847;	" 1853.
John Bennington,	" 1853;	" 1860.
Phineas Ash,	" 1860;	" 1864.
Elisha Roberts,	" 1864;	" 1868.
Caleb Hoopes,	" 1868;	" 1875.
James Davis,	" 1875;	....

BOOK-KEEPERS.

	APPOINTED.	RETIRED.
Jesse Meredith,	10th mo., 1801;	8th mo., 1806.
Jesse Williams,	8th mo., 1806;	6th mo., 1808.
Thomas Kimber,	6th mo., 1808;	" 1810.
Blakey Sharpless,	" 1810;	" 1811.
John Gummere,	" 1811;	10th mo., 1812.
Isaac Jackson,	10th mo., 1812;	7th mo., 1815.
Jacob Elfreth,	7th mo., 1815;	10th mo., 1816.
Pennock Passmore,	12th mo., 1816;	3d mo., 1817.
Thos. Williamson,	3d mo., 1817;	6th mo., 1827.

BOOK-KEEPERS.

	APPOINTED.	RETIRED.
Pennock Passmore,	6th mo., 1827;	5th mo., 1830.
Cyrus Mendenhall,	12th mo., 1830;	" 1858.
Dubré Knight,	5th mo., 1858;	" 1861.
Samuel Alsop, Jr.,	" 1861;	" 1863.
Benjamin Hoopes,	" 1863;	" 1865.
Joshua P. Edge,	6th mo., 1865;	12th mo., 1866.
Lewis Forsythe,	12th mo., 1866;	4th mo., 1879.
Jonathan Eldridge,	4th mo., 1879;	" 1883.
J. Henry Bartlett,	" 1883;	....

F

A LIST OF FRIENDS

WHO HAVE SERVED ON THE COMMITTEE IN CHARGE OF WESTTOWN BOARDING SCHOOL, WITH DATE OF FIRST APPOINTMENT.

NOTE.—Some in the following list were continued by reappointment for many years. Only the new names are given.

Tenth Month 3d, 1794.

Henry Drinker,	Samuel P. Griffiths,	George Churchman,
Owen Biddle,	William Jackson,	Joseph Sansom,
John Drinker,	Humphrey Marshall,	John Cox,
Thomas Fisher,	John Jones,	John Wistar,
Jesse Foulke,	Joshua E. Pusey,	Benjamin Swett,
John Shoemaker,	Samuel Howell,	John Reeve,
David Cumming,	Thomas Stewardson,	John Collins,
Joseph Potts,	John Field,	Joseph Shotwell,
Robert Kirkbride,	Thomas Morris,	Britton White,
William Blakey,	Warner Mifflin,	William Hartshorne,
John Stapler,	John Needles,	Henry Clifton,
Sam'l Smith (Bucks),	Robert Moore,	John Morton,
Samuel Canby,	Benjamin Clark,	Nicholas Waln,
John Pierce,	Peter Ellis,	Sam'l Smith (Phila.),
Roger Dicks,	John Hoskins,	Jonathan Evans, Jr.
Josiah Bunting,	Caleb Carmalt,	
Rebecca Jones,*	Mary Hough,	Catharine Howell,

* "Men Friends have handed us for communication here, their proceedings and progress as far as they stept, in regard to the establishment of a Boarding School, and as they apprehend a committee of women Friends might be useful, Rebecca Jones (and others as above) are nominated on this occasion."—*Minutes Women's Meeting, Tenth Mo. 4th, 1794.*

Mary Pleasants,   Sarah Waln,   Deborah Field.
Margaret Hart,

Tenth Month 2d, 1795.

Philip Price, Jr.,   James Emlen,   James Marshall,
William Savery,   Daniel Thomas,   Eli Yarnall.
John Talbot,   David Evans,

Sarah Newlin,*   Phebe Pemberton,   Rachel Hunt,
Ann Pierce,   Ann Lloyd,   Rebecca Archer,
Catharine Wistar,   Margaret Marshall,   Hannah West.

Ninth Month 30th, 1796.

Abraham Sharpless.

Fourth Month 19th, 1799.

Sarah Savery,   Rachel Malin,   Sarah Cresson.

Fourth Month, 1800.

Oliver Wilson,   William Webb,   George Massey,
William Garrigues,   William Mode,   Richard Strode,
Peter Barker,   John Cox, Jr.,   Isaac Bonsall,
Alexander Wilson,   William Newbold,   Abraham Pennell,
John Shoemaker, Jr., Richard Hartshorne, Jacob Lindley,
John Brown,   Ellis Yarnall,   James Cooper,
Caspar Wistar,   Thomas Norton,   Daniel Cowgill,
Cyrus Newlin,   Benjamin Wright,   Abra'm Warrington,
Jehu Roberts,   Geo. Williams,   Josiah Reeve,
Cheyney Jefferis,   Jonathan Pickering, James Cooper
Nathan Sharpless,   John Hunt (Darby),   (Jersey),

* "The report of the committee on a Boarding School, sent us by men Friends, was read, by which it appears some progress is made therein, and a desire expressed for an additional number of women Friends to that committee, believing their services will be useful. This meeting uniting therewith, nominates the following Friends, to be added to the committee appointed last year" (see above).—*Minutes Women's Meeting, Tenth Month 3d,* 1795.

COMMITTEES.

Hannah Evans,	Anna Mifflin,	Jane Downing,
Amy Coates,	Mary Newbold, Jr.,	Hannah Pusey, Jr.,
Anna Stewardson,	Hannah Hopkins,	Sarah Cowgill,
Rachel Richards,	Rachel Crukshank,	Ann Cox,
Catharine Morris,	Mary Morton,	Sarah Maule,
Hannah Yarnall,	Elizabeth Dorsey,	Margary Mickle,
Mary Mott,	Ann Warder,	Phebe Miller,
Margaret Canby,	Mary Taylor,	Agnes Elston,
Rachel Cope,	Sarah Wilson,	Cath'rine Hartshorne,
Elizabeth Pennock,	Hannah Kirkbride,	Elizabeth Howell.

Fourth Month, 1801.

Elizabeth Roberts.

Fourth Month, 1802.

Ruth Ely,	Rachel Price,	Mary Swett,
Mary Smith,	Mary Newlin,	Sarah Hartshorne.

Fourth Month, 1803.

Catharine Sharpless,	Mary Allinson,	Jane Shoemaker,
Rebecca Churchman,	Ann Mifflin, Jr.,	Mary Wheeler.

Fourth Month, 1804.

Stephen Comfort,	Jacob Wooley,	Isaac W. Morris,
Edmund Smith,	Samuel Bettle,	Geo. Williams (Phila.)
Amos Harvey,	John Forsythe,	Joseph Malin,
Ephraim Wilson,	Holiday Jackson,	John Philips,
Joseph Turner,	John Tatum, Jr.,	Jeffrey Smedley,
Thomas Berry,	John Morton, Jr.,	Samuel Harlan,
George Dillwyn,	John Johnson,	Joseph Sharp,
Benjamin Cooper,	Joseph Howell,	Hugh Ely.
Joseph Whitall,		

Mary Swain, Lydia Philips.

Fourth Month, 1805.

Thomas Scattergood.

Susanna Haydock,   Letitia Murphy,   Elizabeth Balderston,
Ruth Richardson,   Sarah Shotwell,   Jane Downing,
Sally N. Dickinson, Hannah Fisher, Sr.,   Mary Moore,
Hannah Pusey,   Hannah Lewis, Jr.,   Sarah Haines,
Susanna Emlen,   Alice Comfort,   Hannah Whitall,
Sarah Hopkins, Jr., Hannah Yarnall,   Patience Corlies.

Fourth Month, 1808.

Oliver Paxson,   John Roberts,   Edward Garrigues,
Simon Gillam,   John Jacobs,   John Parker,
William Poole,   John Turner,   Samuel Emlen,
Jesse Kersey,   Emmor Kimber,   Nathan Sharpless
John Letchworth,   Phineas Lord,   (Downingtown).
John Kinsey,   Charles Shoemaker,

Hannah Elliott.

Fourth Month, 1811.

Nathan Harper,   Charles Townsend,   John H. Bunting,
Caleb Swayne,   William Roberts,   Nathan H. Sharpless.
Jonathan Hunn,   Joseph Kaighn,

Beulah Sansom,   Sarah Cooper,   Margaret Resin,
Anne Biddle,   Rebecca Wilson,   Hannah Gibbons,
Ann Scattergood,   Mary Wistar,   Alice Lewis,
Sarah Tatnall,   Mary Bonsall,   Elizabeth Coleman,
Sarah Lindley,   Ann Paul,   Charlotte Wistar.
Patience Hunn,

Fourth Month, 1814.

Jesse Jones,   John Paul,   Benjamin Cope,
Clayton Cowgill,   Josiah Roberts,   Philip Garrett,
William Allinson,   Charles Allen,   John Cook
Joseph Bassett,   William Evans,   (High Street),
Isaac Sharpless   Enoch Lewis,   Benjamin Sharpless
    (Birmingham),   Joshua G. Rowland,   (Birmingham),
Nathan Sharpless   Thomas Lawrie,   Samuel Swayne,
    (Middletown),   Joseph Walcott,   Robert L. Pitfield.
Daniel Elliott,   Moses Palmer,

COMMITTEES. 99

Martha Jefferis,	Ann Grigg,	Sarah Saunders,
Rest Swayne,	Abigail Barker,	Mary Corlies,
Mary Fisher,	Ann West,	Mary Cope,
Elizabeth Reeve,	Rachel Sharpless,	Anne Richardson,
Esther Smith,	Hannah J. Alston,	Mary Williams,
Hannah Hartshorne,	Susanna Newbold,	Jane M. Rogers,
Jane Johnson,	Elizabeth F. Paul,	Hannah Evans, Jr.

Fourth Month, 1817.

Richard Barnard,	Nathan Sharpless	Henry Warrington, Jr.
John Cooke.	(Concord),	

Margaret Morton,	Sarah Poole,	Deborah Howell,
Rachel Yarnall,	Deborah Coates,	Elizabeth Waln,
Elizabeth Cresson,	Mary H. Morris,	Hannah Tatum.

Fourth Month, 1820.

Sarah Latimer,	Jane Bettle,	Rest Cope,
Rebecca B. Comly,	Martha Reeve,	Sidney Temple,
Sarah Buckley,	Elizabeth Robeson,	Elizabeth Kirk.

Fourth Month, 1822.

William F. Miller,	Joseph M. Paul,	William Cooper.
David Hoopes,	Benjamin Ferris,	

Rachel C. Bartram,	Lydia L. Miller,	Anne Potts,
Rebecca Allen,	Sarah Cresson,	Margaret Smith,
Martha Hilles,	Elizabeth Pitfield,	Rachel H. Roberts,
Mary W. Davis,	Philena Marshall,	

Fourth Month, 1828.

Joseph Evans,	Henry Cope,	Josiah Tatum,
James Forsythe,	James Emlen,	Joshua B. Sharpless,
George G. Ashbridge,	John James,	Bartholomew Wistar.
David Roberts,	John W. Tatum,	
Hannah Paul,	Phebe Sharpless,	Margaret H. Hilles,

Sarah B. Cope,   Anne Tatum,   Grace Evans.
Elizabeth C. Mason, Mary Clarke,

Fourth Month, 1831.

Edward Tatnall,   Charles Yarnall,   Thomas Kimber,
George Malin,   Clayton Wistar,   Thomas Evans.
William Rhoads,

Margaret Parker,   Jane Jackson,   Ann Buckley,
Eliz. Richardson, Miriam Lippincott, Lydia Hughes, Jr.
Hannah Rhoads,   Jane Clark,

Fourth Month, 1834.

John Forsythe, Jr., John M. Kaighn,   Joseph Snowdon.
Thomas Bacon,

Jane Moon,   Margaret Malin,   Sarah Folwell,
Eliz. K. Passmore, Lydia Cole,   Sidney Coates,
Mercy Shotwell,   Beulah Hopkins,   Elizabeth Smith,
Rebecca Warder,   Phebe Hoopes,   Hannah Richardson,
Anne Spencer,   Hannah Warrington, Elizabeth Pierson.
Jane Malin,

Fourth Month, 1837.

Thomas Kite,   Jesse Spencer,   Isaac Pusey,
Samuel Hilles,   John Kirkbride,   Charles Downing.

Phebe Middleton,   Elizabeth Evans,   Amelia Smith,
Eliz. R. Shotwell, Hannah Williams,   Martha Wistar.

Fourth Month, 1840.

John E. Sheppard,   Pennock Passmore, Nathaniel N. Stokes.

Beulah H. Nicholson, Eliz. D. Valentine, Sarah Scull.
Amy Y. Tatum,   H. Regina Shober,

COMMITTEES.

Fourth Month, 1843.

John Benington, Solomon Lukens, Samuel B. Morris.
Robert Thomas,

Sarah Trimble, Margaret M. Smith.

Fourth Month, 1846.

Aaron Sharpless, Joel Evans.

Fourth Month, 1848.

Joseph Scattergood.

Fourth Month, 1849.

Alfred Cope, Samuel Bettle, Jr.,
Charles Williams, Samuel Nicholson.

Edith Edge, Margaret Churchman, Margaret Sheppard.
Abigail Williams, Rebecca Biddle,

Fourth Month, 1852.

Moses Comfort, Joshua B. Pusey.

Lydia Starr, Sarah Allen, Jane Gibbons,
Beulah M. Hacker, Abigail Wood, Susanna L. Wood.
Caroline M. Smith, Hannah P. Davis, Rebecca B. Cope.

Fourth Month, 1858.

Joseph Passmore, Thomas Savery,
Horatio C. Wood, Abraham Gibbons,
Clarkson Sheppard,

Lydia S. Wills, Sarah C. Paul, Mary Evens (Cropwell),
Mary Maris, Mary Passmore, Deborah Rhoads.

Fourth Month, 1861.

Jeremiah Hacker, John M. Sharpless,
Jacob Edge Charles J. Allen

Catharine Evans, Eliz. C. Scattergood, Rebecca S. Allen.
Elizabeth Allen, Abigail W. Hall,

Fourth Month, 1864.

Samuel Allinson, Samuel Morris,
Thomas Conard, William Balderston.

Hannah F. Wood, Anna V. Edge, Mercy Comfort,
Abigail Hutchinson, Margaret Maule, Hannah E. Snowdon,
Beulah S. Morris, Lydia W. Sheppard, Rebecca S. Conard,
Hannah A. Warner, Susanna F. Sharpless, Elizabeth R. Evans.
Margaret G. Sheppard,

Fourth Month, 1867.

Jacob Roberts, Richard B. Baily, Jonathan E. Rhoads,
Yardley Warner, William Biddle, Charles Evans,
Geo. J. Scattergood, John Bishop, Edward Richie.
Charles Rhoads,

Elizabeth Rhoads, Phebe W. Roberts, Susan E. Comfort,
Susan E. Lippincott, Martha D. Allen, Sarah M. Tatum.
Sarah A. Richie,

Fourth Month, 1869.

Edward Sharpless.

Fourth Month, 1870.

Philip P. Dunn, Benjamin W. Passmore,
Joseph Walton, Isaac Hall.

Elizabeth C. Dunn, Lydia L. Walton, Rachel Scattergood.

Fourth Month, 1873.

William Evans, Oliver Paxson, Thomas P. Cope,
Isaac Morgan, Jonathan G. Williams, Wm. P. Townsend.
John S. Comfort, Samuel Emlen,

Hannah Evans, Han'h W. Richardson, Ann Eliz. Comfort,
Mary Wistar, Sarah Forsythe, Anna W. Hooton.
Dinah H. Lippincott, Martha N. Warrington,

COMMITTEES.

Fourth Month, 1876.

William L. Bailey, Thomas M. Harvey, John E. Carter,
George M. Comfort, Caleb Hoopes.
Susanna R. Williams, Anna Mary Townsend, Jane M. Cope.

Fourth Month, 1879.

Zebedee Haines, Joshua L. Harmer, Charles S. Carter,
James Smedley, Truman Forsythe.
Ruth S. Abbott, Sarah E. Smith,
Anna E. Howell, Catharine C. Balderston.

Fourth Month, 1882.

John W. Biddle, Joseph Scattergood, George Abbott.
Ephraim Smith, John Trimble,
Sarah Pike, Rebecca G. Rhoads, Elizabeth D. Meredith,
Rebecca G. Passmore, Rebecca C. Sheppard, Esther Roberts.

The Committee at present under appointment (1884) are as follows:

Joseph Passmore, Philip P. Dunn, John E. Carter,
Clarkson Sheppard, Joseph Walton, Caleb Hoopes,
Jacob Edge, Benj. W. Passmore, Zebedee Haines,
Charles J. Allen, Isaac Hall, Joshua L. Harmer,
Samuel Morris, William Evans, Truman Forsythe,
John Bishop, John S. Comfort, Charles S. Carter,
Charles Rhoads, Samuel Emlen, John W. Biddle,
Jonathan E. Rhoads, Thomas P. Cope, Ephraim Smith,
George J. Scattergood, Wm. P. Townsend, Joseph Scattergood,
Edward Richie, William L. Bailey, John Trimble,
William Biddle, George M. Comfort, George Abbott.
Edward Sharpless,

Sarah A. Richie, Susan E. Comfort, Jane M. Cope,
Deborah Rhoads, Lydia L. Walton, Ruth S. Abbott,
Elizabeth Allen, Elizabeth C. Dunn, Anna E. Howell,
Anna V. Edge, Rachel S. Maris, Sarah E. Smith,
Beulah M. Rhoads, Hannah Evans, Sarah Pike,
Hannah F. Wood, Han'h W. Richardson. Rebecca G. Passmore,
Susanna F. Sharpless, Martha N. Warrington, Rebecca G. Rhoads,
Elizabeth R. Evans, Ann Eliz. Comfort, Rebecca C. Sheppard,
Elizabeth Rhoads, Anna W. Hooton, Elizabeth D. Meredith,
Martha D. Allen, Anna M. Townsend, Esther Roberts.

A LIST OF STUDENTS
AT
WESTTOWN SCHOOL
FROM 1799 TO 1872.

MALES.

FIRST THOUSAND.

NAME.	RESIDENCE.	DATE OF ENTRY.	
1. Samuel R. Fisher,	Philadelphia, Pa.,	5th mo.,	1799.
2. George Aston,	"	"	"
3. Lloyd Mifflin,	"	"	"
4. David Wilson,	Cantwell's Bridge, Del.,	6th mo.,	"
5. Thomas Stapler,	Makefield, Pa.,	"	"
6. Israel Thompson,	Waterford, Va.,	5th mo.,	"
7. Mark Whitall,	Woodbury, N. J.,	6th mo.,	"
8. Solomon Jones,	Frankford, Pa.,	5th mo.,	"
9. Rees Cadwallader,	Brownsville, Pa.,	7th mo.,	"
10. Asher Cumming,	Horsham, Pa.,	5th mo.,	"
11. Jonathan Dawes,	Philadelphia, Pa.,	"	"
12. Samuel F. Dawes,	"	"	"
13. Edward Dawes,	"	"	"
14. James Lloyd,	Darby, Pa.,	"	"
15. William W. Moore,	Easton, Md.,	6th mo.,	"
16. George Bartram,	Philadelphia, Pa.,	5th mo.,	"
17. Thomas Say,	"	"	"
18. William C. Ellis,	Muncy, Pa.,	"	"
19. John C. Allinson,	Burlington, N. J.,	"	"
20. William Evans,	Philadelphia, Pa.,	"	"
21. Joseph Evans,	"	"	"
22. Samuel Hildeburn,	"	"	"
23. Reuben Haines,	"	"	"
24. Jacob Elfreth,	Haddonfield, N. J.,	6th mo.,	"
25. David Bacon,	Philadelphia, Pa.,	"	"
26. Andrew Robeson,	Germantown, Pa.,	"	"
27. Abel Green,	Westtown, Pa.,	"	"

GENERAL CATALOGUE.

FIRST THOUSAND.

NAME.	RESIDENCE.	DATE OF ENTRY.
28. Joseph Sharpless,	E. Bradford, Pa.,	6th mo., 1799
29. Thomas Lea,	Wilmington, Del.,	7th mo., "
30. William Way,	"	6th mo., "
31. Samuel Hanson,	"	" "
32. Philip Price,	Philadelphia, Pa.,	" "
33. William F. Corbit,	Appoquinimink, Del.,	8th mo., "
34. Thomas Shipley,	Philadelphia, Pa.,	7th mo., "
35. Charles Longstreth,	"	" "
36. Jacob Robinson,	Wilmington, Del.,	" "
37. J. W. Mayberry,	Philadelphia, Pa.,	" "
38. Edward Randolph,	"	" "
39. William Randolph,	"	" "
40. James Wright,	Columbia, Pa.,	8th mo., "
41. Lewis Eddy,	Philadelphia, Pa.,	11th mo., "
42. John Hirons,	Appoquinimink, Del.,	7th mo., "
43. John L. Williams,	Abington, Pa.,	8th mo., "
44. Samuel Rowland,	"	7th mo., "
45. John Hutchinson,	Philadelphia, Pa.,	8th mo., "
46. Thomas Butcher,	Mt. Holly, N. J.,	" "
47. George West,	"	" "
48. Thomas Bonsall,	Philadelphia, Pa.,	" "
49. William Haydock,	"	" "
50. Isaac Cleaver,	"	" "
51. Bartholomew Mather,	Abington, Pa.,	10th mo., "
52. Joseph Mickle,	Cooper's Ferry, N. J.,	1st mo., 1800.
53. David B. Cumming,	Horsham, Pa.,	2d mo., "
54. Robert Sharpless,	Aston, Pa.,	10th mo., 1799.
55. John Warder,	Philadelphia, Pa.,	9th mo., "
56. Samuel Williams,	Trenton, N. J.,	10th mo., "
57. William Wynn,	Philadelphia, Pa.,	11th mo., "
58. Joshua Gilbert,	Fallsington, Pa.,	" "
59. Samuel Knight,	Haddonfield, N. J.,	10th mo., "
60. Caleb Carr,	Mt. Holly, N. J.,	9th mo., "
61. William M. Gibbons,	Philadelphia, Pa.,	12th mo., "
62. Joseph Wood,	"	11th mo., "
63. James Wood,	"	" "
64. Norris Hibberd,	Upper Darby, Pa.,	10th mo., "
65. Samuel Blackwood,	Woodbury, N. J.,	11th mo., "
66. Walker Yarnall,	Middletown, Pa.,	10th mo., "
67. Richard Smith,	Burlington, N. J.,	" "
68. William Price,	E. Bradford, Pa.,	9th mo., "
69. Jacob Smith,	Philadelphia, Pa.,	3d mo., 1800.
70. Clayton Decou,	Mt. Holly, N. J.,	11th mo., 1799.
71. Josiah Clement,	Haddonfield, N. J.,	" "
72. William Earl,	Springfield, N. J.,	12th mo., "
73. John N. Reeve,	Evesham, N. J.,	11th mo., "
74. John N. Offley,	Philadelphia, Pa.,	" "

STUDENTS.

FIRST THOUSAND.

NAME.	RESIDENCE.	DATE OF ENTRY.
75. William L. Stevenson,	Salem, N. J.,	12th mo., 1799.
76. James Thornton,	Byberry, Pa.,	11th mo., "
77. Thomas Hanson,	Wilmington, Del.,	8th mo., "
78. Thomas H. Oldden,	Philadelphia, Pa.,	11th mo., "
79. James Glover,	Haddonfield, N. J.,	" "
80. Joshua Emlen,	Middletown, Pa.,	1st mo., 1800.
81. Samuel Emlen,	"	" "
82. Gibbons Hunt,	Darby, Pa.,	12th mo., 1799.
83. John Hutton,	Philadelphia, Pa.,	" "
84. Benjamin H. Yarnall,	"	4th mo., 1800.
85. Joshua Henzey,	"	1st mo., "
86. James Forsythe,	E. Bradford, Pa.,	12th mo., 1799.
87. Benjamin Say,	Philadelphia, Pa.,	4th mo., 1800.
88. John Cope,	E. Bradford, Pa.,	2d mo., "
89. Joseph Green,	Westtown, Pa.,	12th mo., 1799.
90. David Hoopes,	West Chester, Pa.,	2d mo., 1800.
91. Charles Smith,	Philadelphia, Pa.,	3d mo., "
92. Arthur Collins,	Evesham, N. J.,	" "
93. James Skull,	Salem Co., N. J.,	" "
94. Gideon Skull,	"	" "
95. Stephen Stapler,	Stanton, Del.,	" "
96. John J. Shoemaker,	Philadelphia, Pa.,	" "
97. Richard Randolph,	"	" "
98. Aaron Bellangee,	Egg Harbor, N. J.,	2d mo., "
99. David Willis,	Philadelphia, Pa.,	4th mo., "
100. William Morris,	"	3d mo., "
101. Isaac Cooper,	"	4th mo., "
102. Mordecai Yarnall,	E. Bradford, Pa.,	" "
103. William Painter,	Concord, Pa.,	" "
104. William Walker,	Wilmington, Del.,	5th mo., "
105. James Walker,	"	" "
106. Henry Warrington,	Westfield, N. J.,	" "
107. Joseph Jones,	Germantown, Pa.,	6th mo., "
108. William Morris,	Philadelphia, Pa.,	7th mo., "
109. Edward Pole,	"	6th mo., "
110. Joseph W. Pole,	"	" "
111. Thomas Luff,	Motherkill, Del.,	" "
112. Samuel E. Mifflin,	Philadelphia, Pa.,	8th mo., "
113. Caleb Carter,	E. Bradford, Pa.,	" "
114. Ziba Ferris,	Wilmington, Del.,	" "
115. Charles Smith,	Philadelphia, Pa.,	9th mo., "
116. Samuel Canby, Jr.,	Wilmington, Del.,	8th mo., "
117. Josiah Gaskill,	Springfield, N. J.,	9th mo., "
118. Joseph Rhoads,	" Pa.,	10th mo., "
119. Mahlon Gillingham,	Frankford, Pa.,	12th mo., "
120. James Moon,	Fallsington, Pa.,	11th mo., "
121. John Wiley,	Maiden Creek, Pa.,	" "

GENERAL CATALOGUE.

FIRST THOUSAND.

NAME.	RESIDENCE.	DATE OF ENTRY.
122. David Ellis,	Springfield, N. J.,	12th mo., 1800.
123. Charles Garrett,	Upper Darby, Pa.,	" "
124. William Levis,	Kennet, Pa.,	11th mo., "
125. Thomas Jacobs,	Providence, Pa.,	2d mo., 1801
126. Benjamin Mather,	Abington, Pa.,	12th mo., 1800.
127. Merrit Canby,	Wilmington, Del.,	1st mo., 1801.
128. Isaac Seal,	"	" "
129. Cyrus Mendenhall,	Middletown, Pa.,	" "
130. James Miller,	Salem, N. J.,	2d mo., "
131. Edward G. Corlies,	Shrewsbury, N. J.,	" "
132. William Garrigues,	Philadelphia, Pa.,	" "
133. Milton Painter,	Concord, Pa.,	1st mo., 1802.
134. Thomas Trotter,	Philadelphia, Pa.,	2d mo., 1801.
135. Vincent King,	Little Britain, Pa.,	1st mo., "
136. Charles Warder,	Philadelphia, Pa.,	" "
137. Jeremiah Emlen,	"	2d mo., "
138. Josiah Coates,	"	5th mo., "
139. Richard Paxson,	Middletown, Pa.,	2d mo., "
140. Henry Landis,	"	" "
141. Samuel Comly,	Byberry, Pa.,	1st mo., "
142. John Thomas,	Philadelphia, Pa.,	2d mo., "
143. Jacob Lindley,	New Garden, Pa.,	3d mo., "
144. James Harper,	Frankford, Pa.,	" "
145. Thomas Richardson,	Middletown, Pa.,	4th mo., "
146. George Lea,	Wilmington, Del.,	" "
147. William Mitchell,	Bristol, Pa.,	" "
148. Thomas Willis,	Philadelphia, Pa.,	" "
149. Nathan Trotter,	"	" "
150. Thomas Lea,	Wilmington, Del.,	6th mo., "
151. Samuel Lawrence,	....	5th mo., "
152. Jonathan W. Mifflin,	Little Creek, Del.,	6th mo., "
153. Samuel Howell,	Camden, Del.,	" "
154. Evan Morrison,	Philadelphia, Pa.,	5th mo., "
155. William Folwell,	"	" "
156. David Pierce,	W. Bradford, Pa.,	7th mo., "
158. Samuel S. Smith,	Philadelphia, Pa.,	8th mo., "
159. Benjamin Lightfoot,	Uwchlan, Pa.,	5th mo., "
160. Thomas Morgan.	Georgetown, D. C.,	6th mo., "
161. Allen Moore,	Mt. Holly, N. J.,	6th mo., "
162. Henry Drinker,	Philadelphia, Pa.,	" "
164. John Stapler,	Stanton, Del.,	8th mo., "
165. Isaac Garrigues,	Philadelphia, Pa.,	9th mo., "
166. Mordecai L. Gordon,	"	10th mo., "
167. Benjamin Kester,	Muncy, Pa.,	12th mo., 1801.
168. Owen Churchman,	Concord, Pa.,	10th mo., "
169. Benjamin Moore,	Harford, Pa.,	" "
170. Thomas Bacon,	Philadelphia, Pa.,	" "

STUDENTS.

FIRST THOUSAND.

NAME.	RESIDENCE.	DATE OF ENTRY.
171. Joseph Tomkins,	Philadelphia, Pa.,	4th mo., 1802.
172. Edward Simmons,	"	7th mo., 1801.
173. William Philips,	Kennet, Pa.,	10th mo., "
174. James Baily,	W. Marlborough, Pa.,	12th mo., "
175. Joshua Baily,	"	1st mo., 1802.
177. Nathan Pennell,	Chichester, Pa.,	12th mo., 1801.
178. John Jones,	Plymouth, Pa.,	11th mo., "
179. Nicholas Hopkins,	Philadelphia, Pa.,	10th mo., "
180. Samuel Marshall,	Concord, Pa.,	11th mo., "
181. Ellis Yarnall,	"	" " .
182. Isaac Levis,	Middletown, Pa.,	1st mo., 1802.
183. Edward Johnson,	Abington, Pa.,	10th mo., 1801.
184. Isaac Wilkinson,	Wilmington, Del.,	11th mo., "
185. Joseph Dixon,	Philadelphia, Pa.,	" "
186. Ethan Comly,	Byberry, Pa.,	" "
187. Samuel Longstreth,	Philadelphia, Pa.,	
188. Evan Clement,	Haddonfield, N. J.,	12th mo., "
189. William George,	Lower Merion, Pa.,	1st mo., 1802.
190. Amos George,	"	" "
191. Jonathan Jarrett,	Horsham, Pa.,	12th mo., 1801.
192. Thomas Ross,	New Garden, Pa.,	3d mo., 1802.
193. James Emlen,	Middletown, Pa.,	4th mo., "
194. John Shreeve,	Alexandria, Va.,	1st mo., "
195. Jonathan Mitchell,	Fallsington, Pa.,	" "
196. Joseph Harlan,	Little Britain, Pa.,	" "
197. Reece Thomas,	Radnor, Pa.,	2d mo., "
198. Sinnick Sinnickson,	Salem, N. J.,	11th mo., "
199. Joshua Hoopes,	Thornbury, Pa.,	4th mo., "
200. Charles Roberts,	Gwynedd, Pa.,	9th mo., "
201. Joseph Mendenhall,	Wilmington, Del.,	5th mo., "
202. Lemuel Mifflin,	Philadelphia, Pa.,	" "
203. Cyrus Pierce,	Sadsbury, Pa.,	6th mo., "
204. Thomas Rowland,	Abington, Pa.,	5th mo., "
205. Evan Lewis,	Radnor, Pa.,	" "
206. William Lightfoot,	Uwchlan, Pa.,	8th mo., "
207. Lea Pusey,	London Grove, Pa.,	7th mo., "
208. Caleb Pusey,	"	1st mo., 1803.
209. Isaac Williams,	Plymouth, Pa.,	7th mo., 1802.
210. Richard Brooke,	Sandy Spring, Md.,	3d mo., 1803.
211. Meredith Pennell,	Aston, Pa.,	1st mo., "
212. John T. Brooke,	Sandy Spring, Md.,	3d mo., "
213. Joshua Richards,	New Garden, Pa.,	11th mo., 1802.
214. Isaac Jacobs,	Uwchlan, Pa.,	11th mo., 1802.
215. Thomas Rutter,	Pottsgrove, Pa.,	" "
216. John Townsend,	E. Bradford, Pa.,	6th mo., 1803.
217. Isaiah Ingham,	Solebury, Pa.,	1st mo., "
219. Francis Fairlamb,	Chester, Pa.,	" "

GENERAL CATALOGUE.

FIRST THOUSAND.

NAME.	RESIDENCE.	DATE OF ENTRY.
220. Samuel Wood,	Philadelphia, Pa.,	3d mo., 1803.
221. David Saunders,	White Clay Creek, Pa.,	" "
222. Isaac Tyson,	Baltimore, Md.,	4th mo., "
223. William Johnson,	Germantown, Pa.,	5th mo., "
224. Thomas Reece,	Baltimore, Md.,	4th mo., "
225. James Lippincott,	....	8th mo., "
226. James Martin,	Rahway, N. J.,	5th mo., "
227. William Jacobs,	"	" "
228. Burnett Burdsall,	"	" "
229. Isaac Wilson,	Philadelphia, Pa.,	" "
231. Thomas Wood,	"	" "
232. Septimus Roberts,	Gwynedd, Pa.,	6th mo., "
233. Isaac Sharpless,	Middletown, Pa.,	5th mo., "
234. Abiah Baily,	E. Marlborough, Pa.,	" "
235. Matthew Fitzwater,	Baltimore, Md.,	" "
236. Daniel Janney,	Alexandria, Va.,	11th mo., "
237. Joseph Paul,	Byberry, Pa.,	5th mo., "
238. George Burr,	Burlington, N. J.,	6th mo., "
239. Jacob Fitzwater,	Baltimore, Md.,	" "
240. Jesse Evans,	Gwynedd, Pa.,	5th mo., "
241. Carleton Passmore,	Kennet, Pa.,	5th mo., "
242. Elijah Weaver,	Haddonfield, N. J.,	6th mo., "
243. Joseph W. Corlies,	Shrewsbury, N. J.,	" "
244. Samuel Carr,	Mt. Holly, N. J.,	12th mo., "
245. William Taylor,	Little York, Pa.,	6th mo., "
246. Mordecai Morgan,	Georgetown, D. C.,	" "
247. Ziba Pyle,	Londonderry, Pa.,	" "
248. Jacob Ridgway,	Springfield, N. J.,	7th mo., "
250. Thomas Evans,	Gwynedd, Pa.,	10th mo., "
251. John H. Hill,	Middletown, Pa.,	8th mo., "
252. Daniel J. Rhoads,	Upper Darby, Pa.,	" "
253. Benjamin Pusey,	London Grove, Pa.,	" "
254. Thomas E. Deacon,	Burlington, N. J.,	9th mo., "
255. Joseph Buzby,	"	" "
256. Josiah Albertson,	Plymouth, Pa.,	" "
258. Charles Hampton,	Solebury, Pa.,	10th mo., "
259. Eusebius Townsend,	E. Bradford, Pa.,	11th mo., "
260. Samuel E. Spencer,	Horsham, Pa.,	" "
262. Isaac Pierce,	Sadsbury, Pa.,	10th mo., "
263. Aaron Philips,	New Hope, Pa.,	" "
264. Nathan Tyson,	Baltimore, Md.,	" "
265. John Ellicott,	Alexandria, Va.,	11th mo., "
266. Samuel Kirk,	Little York, Pa.,	12th mo., "
267. Mahlon Kirk,	Harford, Md.,	" "
268. Jonathan Dutton,	Chichester, Pa.,	" "
269. Joseph Lownes,	Springfield, Pa.,	" "
270. John O. Rhoads,	"	" "

STUDENTS. 111

FIRST THOUSAND.

NAME.	RESIDENCE.	DATE OF ENTRY.
271. Charles Paist,	Providence, Pa.,	11th mo., 1803.
272. James Brinton,	Lampeter, Pa.,	" "
273. John Gest,	Sadsbury, Pa.,	" "
274. Abraham Gibbons,	Lampeter, Pa.,	12th mo., "
275. Thomas Lee,	Exeter, Pa.,	" "
276. Blakey Sharpless,	Downingtown, Pa.,	11th mo., "
278. James Starr,	Philadelphia, Pa.,	" "
279. Samuel Bacon,	"	" "
280. Britton Corlies,	Shrewsbury, N. J.,	" "
281. Nathan Shotwell,	Plainfield, N. J.,	12th mo., "
282. Samuel Shoemaker,	Horsham, Pa.,	1st mo., 1804
283. Caleb Taylor,	Little York, Pa.,	4th mo., "
286. Marshall Smith,	Wrightstown, Pa.,	8th mo., "
287. Caleb Kirk,	Centre, Del.,	1st mo., "
288. Ebenezer Reynolds,	Pennsbury, Pa.,	3d mo., "
290. Abel Townsend,	Beaver, Pa.,	" "
291. Samuel Hoopes,	Downingtown, Pa.,	" "
293. Israel Janney,	Goose Creek, Va.,	6th mo., "
294. Jesse Gover,	Waterford, Va.,	" "
295. John P. Kirkbride,	Philadelphia, Pa.,	12th mo., 1803.
296. John Malin,	E. Whiteland, Pa.,	2d mo., 1804.
297. Thomas Kimber,	Philadelphia, Pa.,	" "
298. Samuel Carey,	Baltimore, Md.,	4th mo., "
299. James Carey,	"	" "
300. John Bullock,	Springfield, N. J.,	" "
301. George Eddy,	Philadelphia, Pa.,	" "
302. Seth Lippincott,	Westfield, N. J.,	5th mo., "
303. Edmund Pryor,	New York city, N. Y.,	" "
304. Jesse Bond,	Evesham, N. J.,	" "
305. Timothy Rogers,	Upper Canada,	" "
306. David Hutchinson,	Newtown, Pa.,	6th mo., "
307. Samuel Bunting,	Philadelphia, Pa.,	" "
308. Jacob Bunting,	"	" "
309. Thomas S. Roberts,	"	" "
310. Charles Starr,	"	" "
311. Azor Gregory,		7th mo., "
312. John Gummere,	Burlington, N. J.,	8th mo., "
313. Edward Leedom,	Newtown, Pa.,	" "
316. Watson Jenks,	Philadelphia, Pa.,	11th mo., "
317. Robert Wright,	Trenton, N. J.,	10th mo., "
320. Samuel Walker,	Wilmington, Del.,	7th mo., "
321. Hartshorne Moore,	Rahway, N. J.,	6th mo., "
322. George T. Trimble,	Newburg, N. Y.,	7th mo., "
323. Yeamans Paul,	Germantown, Pa.,	" "
324. George Lownes,	Springfield, Pa.,	9th mo., "
325. James Greaves,	Philadelphia, Pa.,	" "
326. John Hewes,	Chichester, Pa.,	10th mo., "

FIRST THOUSAND.

NAME.	RESIDENCE.	DATE OF ENTRY.
327. Maris Taylor,	Springfield, Pa.,	9th mo., 1804.
328. Samuel Stokes,	Richland, Pa.,	11th mo., "
329. Henry Dickinson,	Sadsbury, Pa.,	4th mo., 1805.
330. William P. Palmer,	Concord, Pa.,	12th mo., 1804.
331. Samuel Lee,	Exeter, Pa.,	" "
332. Peter Yarnall,	E. Bradford, Pa.,	" "
333. James Smith,	Sadsbury, Pa.,	11th mo., "
335. William Trimble,	Baltimore, Md.,	12th mo., "
336. Eli Yarnall,	Middletown, Pa.,	11th mo., "
337. Jeremiah Reynolds,	Nottingham, Md.,	1st mo., 1805.
338. John F. Randolph,	Philadelphia, Pa.,	12th mo., 1804.
340. Joseph Wilson,	White Marsh, Pa.,	1st mo., 1805.
341. Thos. T. Hutchinson,	Newtown, Pa.,	12th mo., 1804.
342. Joseph R. Smith,	....	" "
343. Josiah M. Reeve,	Evesham, N. J.,	" "
344. John Lukens,	Horsham, Pa.,	" "
345. Townsend Speakman,	Richland, Pa.,	6th mo., 1805.
346. Isaac Lawrence,	Springfield, Pa.,	12th mo., 1804.
347. Thomas Longstreth,	Abington, Pa.,	1st mo., 1805.
348. Mahlon Taylor,	Newtown, Pa.,	" "
349. Jonathan Paxson,	"	" "
350. Samuel H. Carver,	Buckingham, Pa.,	2d mo., "
351. Thomas Allen,	Middletown, Pa.,	4th mo., "
352. Bartholomew Wistar,	Salem, N. J.,	3d mo., "
353. Clayton Wistar,	"	" "
354. Robert Smith,	Burlington, N. J.,	4th mo., "
355. Robert Garrigues,	Philadelphia, Pa.,	" "
356. William Douglas,	Fallsington, Pa.,	" "
357. Joseph Elkinton,	Philadelphia, Pa.,	7th mo., "
358. William Bettle,	"	5th mo., "
359. Crowell Webster,	Plainfield, N. J.,	6th mo., "
360. Thomas Clark,	Woodbury, N. J.,	7th mo., "
361. Isaac Moore,	Haverford, Pa.,	4th mo., "
362. Henry Howard,	——— Ohio,	5th mo., "
363. Edward Webster,	Rahway, N. J.,	6th mo., "
364. John Willits,	Maiden Creek, Pa.,	" "
365. William Wilkinson,	London Grove, Pa.,	7th mo., "
366. Elias Marsh,	Rahway, N. J.,	6th mo., "
367. James Ellicott,	Baltimore, Md.,	7th mo., "
368. Mahlon Chandlee,	E. Nottingham, Pa.,	9th mo., "
369. Thomas Trump,	Horsham, Pa.,	8th mo., "
370. Moses Coates,	W. Caln, Pa.,	9th mo., "
371. Joseph Y. Tomkins,	Baltimore, Md.,	6th mo., "
372. Francis Cope,	Philadelphia, Pa.,	" "
373. Henry Cope,	"	" "
374. Isaac Gillam,	Middletown, Pa.,	7th mo., "
375. Andrew C. Wright,	Trenton, N. J.,	" "

STUDENTS. 113

FIRST THOUSAND.

NAME.	RESIDENCE.	DATE OF ENTRY.
376. Caleb Maule,	Richmond, Pa.,	7th mo., 1805.
377. Evan T. Ellicott,	Baltimore, Md.,	" "
378. Joel Laing,	Plainfield, N. J.,	8th mo., "
379. Clarkson Vail,	"	" "
380. Thomas Tyson,		" "
381. Jacob Albertson,	Plymouth, Pa.,	9th mo., "
382. John Nesbit,	Philadelphia, Pa.,	" "
383. Nathaniel Pettit,	Buckingham, Pa.,	10th mo., "
384. Stogdell Stokes,	Richland, Pa.,	11th mo., "
385. Sam'l Satterthwaite,	Crosswicks, N. J.,	" "
386. Thomas Cumming,	Horsham, Pa.,	10th mo., "
387. Benjamin Albertson,	Plymouth, Pa.,	11th mo., "
388. Paul Scull,	Pilesgrove, N. J.,	" "
390. Joshua Sharpless,	Middletown, Pa.,	9th mo., "
391. Stephen Hambleton,	West Grove, Pa.,	" "
392. William Ellicott,	Baltimore, Md.,	" "
393. Isaac Powell,	Chester, Pa.,	10th mo., "
394. Henry Sharpless,	"	" "
395. William Pusey,	London Grove, Pa.,	" "
396. Randall Malin,	E. Whiteland, Pa.,	11th mo., "
397. Josiah Tatum,	Woodbury, N. J.,	10th mo., "
398. James Townsend,	....	" "
399. Lewis Sharpless,	West Chester, Pa.,	11th mo., "
400. Daniel Milnor,	Little Britain, Pa.,	10th mo., "
401. James Smith,	Salem, N. J.,	11th mo., "
402. Elisha Bassett,	"	" "
403. Joshua B. Sharpless,	Downingtown, Pa.,	12th mo., "
404. David Pancoast,	Pilesgrove, N. J.,	11th mo., "
405. William Jackson,	London Grove, Pa.,	" "
406. Wm. W. Downing,	Downingtown, Pa.,	12th mo., "
407. Samuel Peach,	Baltimore, Md.,	11th mo., "
408. James Jefferis,	E. Bradford, Pa.,	12th mo., "
409. Morris Hall,	Salem, N. J.,	" "
410. Joseph Turner,	Chestertown, Md.,	" "
411. Joseph Newbold,	Springfield, N. J.,	" "
412. Benjamin C. Cooper,	Evesham, N. J.,	11th mo., "
413. John R. Trimble,	Newburg, N. Y.,	" "
414. Robert Pitman,	Burlington, N. J.,	" "
415. Thomas D. Shotwell,	Rahway, N. J.,	" "
416. Nathaniel Parsons,	Providence, Pa.,	12th mo., "
417. George G. Williams,	Trenton, N. J.,	" "
418. William Adams,	Greenwich, N. J.,	" "
419. Nathaniel Newlin,	Darby, Pa.,	" "
420. John Hunt,	"	2d mo., 1806.
421. Joseph W. Thomas,	Radnor, Pa.,	1st mo., "
422. Thomas J. Carlisle,	Philadelphia, Pa.,	" "
423. Jesse Williams,	—— N. C.,	3d mo., "

9*

GENERAL CATALOGUE.

FIRST THOUSAND.

NAME.	RESIDENCE.	DATE OF ENTRY.	
424. James Bringhurst,	Philadelphia, Pa.,	3d mo.,	1806.
425. David W. Ridgway,	Springfield, N. J.,	4th mo.,	"
426. John Thomas,	Philadelphia, Pa.,	"	"
427. Joseph Thomas,	"	"	"
428. Daniel Thomas,	Germantown, Pa.,	"	"
429. Daniel Pound,	Plainfield, N. J.,	"	"
431. Jacob Pusey,	London Grove, Pa.,	10th mo.,	"
432. Isaac Dillon,	Gunpowder, Md.,	3d mo.,	"
433. John Tyson,	Baltimore, Md.,	12th mo.,	1805.
434. Eli Hilles,	Brownsville, Pa.,	"	"
436. Isaac Wilkinson,	Head of Chester, Md.,	"	"
437. Ellis Comfort,	Middletown, Pa.,	1st mo.,	1807.
438. John Bartlett,	Easton, Md.,	"	1806
439. Thomas P. Stabler,	Sandy Spring, Md.,	2d mo.,	"
440. John S. Newlin,	Chichester, Pa.,	10th mo.,	"
441. Benjamin Davids,	Rahway, N. J.,	3d mo.,	"
442. Joseph Husband,	Deer Creek, Md.,	4th mo.,	"
443. Edward H. Bonsall,	Philadelphia, Pa.,	5th mo.,	"
444. Thomas Hilyard,	Rancocas, N. J.,	4th mo.,	"
445. Caleb Stabler,	Sandy Spring, Md.,	6th mo.,	"
446. John B. Ellison,	Philadelphia, Pa.,	"	"
447. Lownes Taylor,	West Chester, Pa.,	5th mo.,	"
448. James Winston,	Richmond, Va.,	"	"
449. Charles Denny,	New Garden, Pa.,	11th mo.,	"
450. Isaac Hewes,	Darby, Pa.,	"	"
451. Joseph Fell,	Makefield, Pa.,	5th mo.,	"
452. William Ridgway,	Springfield, N. J.,	6th mo.,	"
453. John Sinton,	Wilkesbarre, Pa.,	4th mo.,	"
454. Ridgway Thomas,	Mt. Holly, N. J.,	5th mo.,	"
455. Franklin Comly,	Byberry, Pa.,	6th mo.,	"
456. Edward Mott,	New York city, N. Y.,	"	"
457. Alexander Neave,	Philadelphia, Pa.,	7th mo.,	"
458. Joseph Cooper,	Newtown, N. J.,	"	"
459. Joseph Mather,	Cheltenham, Pa.,	10th mo.,	"
460. Thomas Irwin,	Washington, D. C.,	5th mo.,	"
462. Peter Wilson,	Alexandria, Va.,	"	"
463. Jehu House,	Kennet, Pa.,	6th mo.,	"
464. Evan Thomas,	E. Marlborough, Pa.,	8th mo.,	"
465. Jacob Dingee,	"	9th mo.,	"
466. Samuel D. Thomas,	W. Whiteland, Pa.,	"	"
467. Edward Stabler,	Sandy Spring, Md.,	11th mo.,	"
468. John Stabler,	"	"	"
469. William Stabler,	Alexandria, Va.,	"	"
470. Moses Philips,	Solebury, N. J.,	"	"
471. Andrew C. Ridgway,	Springfield, N. J.,	9th mo.,	"
474. Phineas Marsh,	Rahway, N. J.,	11th mo.,	"
475. Joseph Smith,	Burlington, N. J.,	"	"

STUDENTS.

FIRST THOUSAND

NAME.	RESIDENCE.	DATE OF ENTRY.
476. Charles Stroud,	Stroudsburg, Pa.,	12th mo., 1806.
477. George M. Stroud,	"	" "
479. Samuel R. Turner,	Head of Chester, Md.,	7th mo., 1807.
480. David Nock,	Little Creek, Del.,	" "
481. Obadiah Dingee,	E. Marlborough, Pa.,	8th mo., 1807.
482. Hill Pennell,	Darby, Pa.,	11th mo., 1806.
483. John R. Latimer,	Wilmington, Del.,	1st mo., 1807.
484. Peter R. Walker,	Burlington, N. J.,	7th mo., "
485. Jesse B. Eyre,	Chester, Pa.,	6th mo., "
486. Benjamin Price,	E. Bradford, Pa.,	8th mo., "
487. Isaac Sharpless,	Downingtown, Pa.,	" "
488. Isaac Starr,	Wilmington, Del.,	12th mo., "
489. Gouverneur Emerson,	Little Creek, Del.,	3d mo., 1808.
490. John Dutton,	Chichester, Pa.,	9th mo., "
491. William Ray,	....	6th mo., 1807.
492. Thomas C. Burling,	New York, N. Y.,	" "
493. Asa Moore,	Sandy Spring, Md.,	" "
494. Warwick Miller,	Alexandria, Va.,	7th mo., "
495. Jacob T. Bunting,	Philadelphia, Pa.,	8th mo., "
496. Samuel Cox,	"	" "
497. Edward Walters,	....	9th mo., "
498. John Smith,	Burlington, N. J.,	10th mo., "
499. Samuel Webb,	Philadelphia, Pa.,	8th mo., "
500. Robert W. Jordan,	——, N. C.,	4th mo., "
501. George Williams,	Abington, Pa.,	5th mo., "
502. John Stapler,	Makefield, Pa.,	" "
503. John Little,	Washington, D. C.,	4th mo., "
504. Charles Little,	"	" "
505. William Haydock,	New York, N. Y.,	" "
506. Joseph Johnson,	"	5th mo., "
507. Joseph James,	Philadelphia, Pa.,	6th mo., 1808.
508. Cyrus Smith,	"	" 1807.
509. Joseph Rowland,	"	" "
510. James Nicholson,	Salem, N. J.,	11th mo., "
511. Samuel Matthews,	Gunpowder, Md.,	" "
512. Thomas Hoopes,	Kennet, Pa., .	2d mo., 1808.
513. Passmore Hoopes,	"	" "
514. John W. Stubbs,	Middletown, Pa.,	6th mo., "
515. Joseph Taylor,	West Chester, Pa.,	4th mo., "
516. Isaac Vickers,	E. Caln, Pa.,	5th mo., "
518. Joshua Walker,	Wilmington, Del,	6th mo., "
519. William Baldwin,	Downingtown, Pa.,	7th mo., "
520. Rowland Dutton,	Chichester, Pa.,	9th mo., "
521. Jacob Taylor,	Inley's Town, N. J.,	12th mo., 1807.
522. Thomas M. Coffin,	Nantucket, Mass.,	9th mo., "
523. John Roberts,	Downingtown, Pa.,	10th mo., "
524. Joseph Schofield,	Middletown, Pa.,	11th mo., "

FIRST THOUSAND.

NAME.	RESIDENCE.	DATE OF ENTRY.
525. Oliver Parry,	New Hope, Pa.,	10th mo., 1807.
526. John K. Garrett,	Upper Darby, Pa.,	" "
527. Charles Ely,	Buckingham, Pa.,	" "
528. Benjamin Garrigues,	Kingsessing, Pa.,	11th mo., "
529. Joseph R. Hulme,	Middletown, Pa.,	" "
530. Caleb Earl,	Springfield, N. J.,	" "
531. Thomas Earl,	"	" "
532. George Britt,	Philadelphia, Pa.,	" "
533. William W. King,	Burlington, N. J.,	" "
534. Stephen Pancoast,	Springfield, N. J.,	12th mo., "
535. Charles Folwell,	Philadelphia, Pa.,	11th mo., "
537. Joseph Bonsall,	"	" "
538. Moses Barnard,	Nantucket, Mass.,	12th mo., "
539. Joseph Ely,	Buckingham, Pa.,	" "
540. Charles Stapler,	Makefield, Pa.,	" "
541. John Paxson,	Solebury, Pa.,	" "
542. Gilbert T. Pell,	———, N. Y.,	1st mo., 1808.
543. George Roberts,	Plymouth, Pa.,	3d mo., "
544. John Rose,	Abington, Pa.,	" "
545. Thomas Penrose,	Philadelphia, Pa.,	" "
546. Jonathan G. Macy,	Nantucket, Mass.,	" "
547. William S. Bartram,	Philadelphia, Pa.,	8th mo., "
548. Joshua C. Oliver,	Lynn, Mass.,	5th mo., "
549. Anthony Thomas,	Germantown, Pa.,	" "
550. Israel Jones,	Wilmington, Del.,	6th mo., "
551. Thomas R. Hazard,	Bristol, Pa.,	7th mo., "
552. Isaac P. Hazard,	"	" "
553. William Stroud,	Stroudsburg, Pa.,	10th mo., "
554. Thomas Mifflin,	Columbia, Pa.,	8th mo., "
555. Charles Eddy,	Philadelphia, Pa.,	" "
556. James Hutton,	"	9th mo., "
558. Elisha Shoemaker,	Horsham, Pa.,	10th mo., "
559. Abiah Brown,	Philadelphia, Pa.,	11th mo., "
560. Benjamin Yarnall,	E. Bradford, Pa.,	10th mo., "
561. Jacob Hewes,	Chichester, Pa.,	11th mo., "
563. Joseph Kersey,	Downingtown, Pa.,	1st mo., 1809.
564. Samuel Sinclair,	New Garden, Pa.,	3d mo., "
565. William Baker,	W. Bradford, Pa.,	5th mo., "
566. Thos. S. Pleasants,	James River, Va.,	4th mo., "
567. Oliver Ladd,	"	" "
568. George Fox,	———, N. Y.,	" "
569. Nicholas Taylor,	Little York, Pa.,	" "
570. Robert V. Massey,	W. Whiteland, Pa.,	12th mo., 1808
571. John M. Foulke,	Gwynedd, Pa.,	11th mo., "
573. David R. Evans,	Philadelphia, Pa.,	" "
574. Robert Evans,	"	" "
575. Isaac Pugh,	"	12th mo., "

STUDENTS.

FIRST THOUSAND.

NAME.	RESIDENCE.	DATE OF ENTRY.	
576. Alban Smith,	Philadelphia, Pa.,	1st mo.,	1809.
577. Samuel Rogers,	....	"	"
578. George Downing,	Wilmington, Del.,	3d mo.,	"
579. Joseph Starr,	Philadelphia, Pa.,	4th mo.,	"
580. James B. Smith,	"	"	"
581. Samuel E. Clement,	Haddonfield, N. J.,	"	"
582. N. H. Gillingham,	Frankford, Pa.,	"	"
583. John L. Kite,	Philadelphia, Pa.,	"	"
584. Isaac L. Shoemaker,	"	5th mo.,	"
585. John Brown,	Middletown, Pa.,	4th mo.,	"
586. Joseph B. Shinn,	Julia Town, N. J.,	9th mo.,	"
587. Joshua Mitchell,	Fallsington, Pa.,	5th mo.,	"
588. Emley Oldden,	Princeton, N. J.,	"	"
589. William Cope,	Philadelphia, Pa.,	6th mo.,	"
590. Anthony P. Morris,	"	5th mo.,	"
591. Samuel E. Coe,	Burlington, N. J.,	"	"
592. William Dawson,	Philadelphia, Pa.,	"	"
593. Elijah Laws,	"	6th mo.,	"
594. James Walker,	"	7th mo.,	"
595. Joseph Hutchinson,	"	5th mo.,	"
696. Thos. W. Hathaway,	"	"	"
597. Caleb Hathaway,	"	"	"
598. George W. Burr,	Mt. Holly, N. J.,	"	"
599. Isaac Stowe,	Philadelphia, Pa.,	"	"
600. Davis Hoopes,	E. Caln, Pa.,	"	"
601. Benjamin Maule,	Radnor, Pa.,	"	"
602. Isaac P. Cox,	Mt. Holly, N. J.,	"	"
603. George Carey,	Baltimore, Md.,		
604. Robert Pearsall,	New York, N. Y.,	9th mo.,	"
605. William Vail,	Plainfield, N. J.,	10th mo.,	"
606. Joseph Shipley,	Wilmington, Del.,	"	"
607. Joseph Pleasants,	James River, Va.,	"	"
609. Joseph Sharpless,	Concord, Pa.,	11th mo.,	"
610. B. H. Hollinshead,	Chester, N. J.,	8th mo.,	"
611. Jonathan Bell,	Plymouth, Pa.,	6th mo.,	"
613. John Livezey, Jr.,	Germantown, Pa.,	8th mo.,	"
614. Samuel Biddle,	Philadelphia, Pa.,	6th mo.,	"
615. George Abbott,	Trenton, N. J.,	"	"
616. Joseph O. Clarke,	Princeton, N. J.,	"	"
617. John Biddle,	Philadelphia, Pa.,	"	"
618. Andrew Underhill,	"	"	"
619. John T. Vail,	Plainfield, N. J.,	"	"
620. Thomas Wistar,	Philadelphia, Pa.,	7th mo.,	"
621. Edward Edwards,	Abington, Pa.,	8th mo.,	"
622. William Lawrie,	Trenton, N. J.,	9th mo.,	"
623. William Black,	Springfield, N. J.	"	"
624. Edward Newbold,	Ridley, Pa.,	"	"

FIRST THOUSAND.

NAME.	RESIDENCE.	DATE OF ENTRY.
625. William L. Newbold,	Ridley, Pa.,	9th mo., 1809.
626. Thomas Ridgeway,	Springfield, N. J.,	10th mo., "
627. Edward Garrigues,	Philadelphia, Pa.,	9th mo., "
628. Robert Kirby,	Springfield, N. J.,	10th mo., "
629. Barzillai Smith,	Burlington, N. J.,	11th mo., "
630. Samuel Starr,	Philadelphia, Pa.,	6th mo., 1810.
631. John James,	"	11th mo., 1809.
632. Clayton Newbold,	Springfield, N. J.,	" "
633. William F. Hussey,	Nantucket, Mass.,	" "
634. Andrew Swain,	"	" "
635. Elias Ely,	New Hope, Pa.,	1st mo., 1810.
636. John Elliott,	Baltimore, Md.,	4th mo., "
637. Caspar Garrigues,	Philadelphia, Pa.,	3d mo., "
638. James R. Garrigues,	"	" "
639. Wm. H. Gillingham,	Frankford, Pa.,	5th mo., "
640. Gilpin Bennett,	Pennsbury, Pa.,	12th mo., 1809.
642. James Carter,	E. Bradford, Pa.,	5th mo., 1810.
643. Ferree Brinton,	Lampeter, Pa.,	" 1811.
644. Robert Vail,	Plainfield, N. J.,	6th mo., 1810.
645. Samuel Poole,	Wilmington, Del.,	5th mo., "
646. Samuel Davis,	Birmingham, Pa.,	4th mo., "
647. Charles Wright,	Columbia, Pa.,	5th mo., "
648. Robert Wright,	"	" "
649. Cyrus Jones,	Wilmington, Del.,	4th mo., "
650. John Kaighn,	Kaighnston, N. J.,	8th mo., "
651. John Haydock,	———, N. Y.,	5th mo., "
652. Thomas Bedford,	Philadelphia, Pa.,	" "
653. Richard Cook,	"	" "
654. Charles Mears,	"	" "
655. Thos. S. Trueman,	"	6th mo., "
656. Sam'l R. Simmons,	"	5th mo., "
657. William Richards,	"	11th mo., "
658. William Jones,	"	6th mo., "
660. Benjamin Pennock,	London Grove, Pa.,	5th mo., 1811.
661. James B. Price,	Philadelphia, Pa.,	8th mo., 1810.
662. Henry Newbold,	Chester, Pa.,	10th mo., "
663. Samuel Darlington,	Aston, Pa.,	9th mo., "
664. Joseph Freeman,	Rahway, N. J.,	7th mo., "
665. William Davis,	Willistown, Pa.,	12th mo., "
667. Caleb Swayne,	London Grove, Pa.,	5th mo., 1811.
669. Joseph Preston,	W. Nottingham, Md.,	12th mo., 1810.
670. George Walker,	Charleston, Pa.,	10th mo., "
671. Francis J. Folger,	Nantucket, Mass.,	12th mo., "
672. Joseph Baily,	Abington, Pa.,	4th mo., 1811.
673. James Folwell,	Philadelphia, Pa.,	9th mo., 1810.
674. Jason L. Fennimore,	Julia Town, N. J.,	" "
675. Benjamin Corlies,	Shrewsbury, N. J.,	8th mo., "

STUDENTS. 119

FIRST THOUSAND.

NAME.	RESIDENCE.	DATE OF ENTRY.	
676. James Eddy,	Philadelphia, Pa.,	8th mo.,	1810.
677. Isaac Bartram,	"	"	"
678. John J. Smith,	Burlington, N. J.,	10th mo.,	"
679. Morris Smith,	"	"	"
680. Raper Smith,	"	9th mo.,	"
681. Stephen Phipps,	Philadelphia, Pa.,	10th mo.,	1810.
682. Isaac Kimber,	"	9th mo.,	"
683. William Gray,	Kingsessing, Pa.,	10th mo.,	"
684. Joseph Gibbons,	Philadelphia, Pa.,	9th mo.,	"
685. Richards Johnson,	"	10th mo.,	"
686. Wm. R. Maxfield,	"	4th mo.,	1811.
687. William Coe,	Burlington, N. J.,	10th mo.,	1810.
688. Samuel Mason,	Philadelphia, Pa.,	1st mo.,	1811.
689. Stacy Lippincott,	Haddonfield, N. J.,	2d mo.,	"
690. Samuel Cooper,	Pleasant View, N. J.,	3d mo.,	"
691. Hugh Smith,	Philadelphia, Pa.,	10th mo.,	1810.
692. Charles Oakford,	Darby, Pa.,	"	"
693. Henry Carver,	Buckingham, Pa.,	11th mo.,	"
694. Isaac W. Pennock,	Fallowfield, Pa.,	2d mo.,	1811.
695. James S. Newbold,	Frankford, Pa.,	4th mo.,	"
696. Benjamin L. Walton,	"	10th mo.,	1810.
697. Levi Foulke,	Gwynedd, Pa.,	4th mo.,	1811.
699. Robert Haydock,	Philadelphia, Pa.,	2d mo.,	"
700. Benjamin Haydock,	"	"	"
701. Isaiah Large,	Buckingham, Pa.,	1st mo.,	"
702. Thomas Cook,	Philadelphia, Pa.,	5th mo.,	"
703. Joseph Evans,	"	"	"
704. Jacob Stroud,	Stroudsburg, Pa.,	"	"
705. James Stroud,	"	"	"
706. Nathan T. Knight,	Byberry, Pa.,	2d mo.,	"
707. Warder Cresson,	Philadelphia, Pa.,	5th mo.,	"
708. William Kimber,	"	4th mo.,	"
709. Charles Remington,	"	6th mo.,	"
710. Joseph Knight,	Byberry, Pa.,	5th mo.,	"
711. Samuel C. Cooper,	Cropwell, N. J.,	9th mo.,	"
712. Arthur D. Shreeve,	Philadelphia, Pa.,	5th mo.,	"
713. Caleb Shreeve,	"	"	"
714. Oliver Martin,	Rahway, N. J.,	6th mo.,	"
715. John G. Merrifield,	Philadelphia, Pa.,	7th mo.,	"
716. Jonathan Jones,	Abington, Pa.,	8th mo.,	"
717. James Squibb,	Wilmington, Del.,	7th mo.,	"
718. Jacob Jeans,	Philadelphia, Pa.,	6th mo.,	"
719. Job W. Reeve,	Evesham, N. J.,	7th mo.,	"
720. Isaac Miller,	Providence, Pa.,	4th mo.,	"
721. Warner Cowgill,	Little Creek, Del.,	10th mo.,	"
723. Benjamin Whitall,	Woodbury, N. J.,	"	"
724. Joshua Whitall,	"	"	"

GENERAL CATALOGUE.

FIRST THOUSAND.

NAME.	RESIDENCE.	DATE OF ENTRY.
725. Ebenezer Whitall,	Woodbury, N. J.,	10th mo., 1811
726. John G. Lewis,	Robeson, Pa.,	12th mo., "
727. Charles Pusey,	Sadsbury, Pa.,	6th mo., 1812.
730. Thomas Longstreth,	Philadelphia, Pa.,	7th mo., 1811.
731. Edwin P. Atlee,	"	10th mo., "
732. Thomas Livezey,	Germantown, Pa.,	9th mo., "
734. Caleb Johnson,	Philadelphia, Pa.,	3d mo., 1812.
735. Morris Longstreth,	"	12th mo., 1811.
736. James Walton,	Fallowfield, Pa.,	10th mo., "
738. William Rhoads,	Springfield, Pa.,	8th mo., "
739. Chalkley Jarrett,	Horsham, Pa.,	9th mo., "
740. Timothy Zane,	Philadelphia, Pa.,	8th mo., "
741. Joseph Large,	Solebury, Pa.,	11th mo., "
742. Jotham Townsend,	Plainfield, N. J.,	" "
743. Samuel T. Jones,	Philadelphia, Pa.,	10th mo., "
744. John Blackwood,	Woodbury, N. J.,	11th mo., "
745. Daniel T. Tyson,	Philadelphia, Pa.,	12th mo., "
746. John L. Newby,	Perquimons Co., N. C.,	10th mo., "
747. Robert B. Newby,	"	" "
748. Joseph Chapman,	Philadelphia, Pa.,	11th mo., "
749. Charles Ward,	Woodbury, N. J.,	" "
750. Samuel Evans,	Gwynedd, Pa.,	" "
751. Samuel Kimber,	Philadelphia, Pa.,	3d mo., 1812.
752. Erwin J. Leedom,	"	4th mo., "
753. Howard Abbott,	"	" "
754. Charles S. Cope,	"	5th mo., "
755. Wm. A. Robinson,	"	12th mo., 1811.
756. Edward Robinson,	"	" "
758. Mordecai L. Dawson,	"	2d mo., 1812.
759. Nathan T. Zane,	"	" "
760. Edward Yarnall,	"	3d mo., "
761. Edward Chandlee,	E. Nottingham, Md.,	4th mo., "
762. Benjamin Kite,	Philadelphia, Pa.,	5th mo., "
764. Thomas Laws,	"	4th mo., "
765. George W. Laws,	"	" "
766. Caspar Wistar,	"	" "
768. William Wilson,	"	6th mo., "
769. Thomas Newlin,	Chichester, Pa.,	" "
770. Daniel Troth,	....	5th mo., "
771. Jacob H. Squibb,	Wilmington, Del.,	6th mo., "
772. Eli K. Price,	E. Bradford, Pa.,	5th mo., "
774. Thomas Watson,	Buckingham, Pa.,	" "
775. Elijah Lewis,	Robeson, Pa.,	12th mo., "
776. Evan Lewis,	"	11th mo., "
777. Thomas Corbit,	Odessa, Del.,	7th mo., "
778. Joseph Bonsall,	....	6th mo., "
779. Thomas S. Newlin,	Wilmington, Del.,	7th mo., "

STUDENTS. 121

FIRST THOUSAND.

NAME.	RESIDENCE.	DATE OF ENTRY.
780. James Bennett,	Philadelphia, Pa.,	5th mo., 1812.
781. Samuel G. Morton,	"	4th mo., "
782. Charles Bonsall,	"	" "
783. Thomas Williams,	Abington, Pa.,	5th mo., "
784. Ad'm B. Williamson,	Newtown, Pa.,	" "
785. Charles Hooton,	Philadelphia, Pa.,	" "
786. Thomas Gillingham,	Frankford, Pa.,	10th mo., "
787. Ezra Jones,	Buckingham, Pa.,	" "
788. Robert Miller,	Alexandria, Va.,	8th mo., "
789. Matlack Church,	Moorestown, N. J.,	" "
790. Jacob Hayes,	W. Bradford, Pa.,	2d mo., 1816.
791. James Davis,	Birmingham, Pa.,	4th mo., 1813.
792. Benjamin Parrott,	....	" "
793. John Tatum,	Woodbury, N. J.,	5th mo., "
794. David Ogden,	Swedesborough, N. J.,	" "
795. Samuel S. Jackson,	Reading, Pa.,	11th mo., "
796. James Bellach,*	Chichester, Pa.,	8th mo., "
797. Daniel S. Cowgill,	Smyrna, Del.,	5th mo., "
798. Charles Cowgill,	"	8th mo., 1812.
799. Charles Farquhar,	Little York, Pa.,	7th mo., 1813.
800. Edwin Bonsall,	Philadelphia, Pa.,	11th mo., 1812.
801. William Earl,	....	10th mo., "
802. Henry L. Bonsall,	Philadelphia, Pa.,	" "
803. John Chapman,	....	1st mo., 1813.
804. John Stokes,	Darby, Pa.,	5th mo., "
805. Rowland G. Hazard,	Bristol, Pa.,	4th mo., "
806. Joseph Wills,	Rancocas, N. J.,	5th mo., "
807. George Pleasants,	Philadelphia, Pa.,	4th mo., "
808. Robert Pleasants,	"	" "
809. Henry G. Hoskins,	Radnor, Pa.,	2d mo., "
810. Job Ridgway,	....	3d mo., "
811. David Jordan,	Suffolk, Va.,	11th mo., "
812. William Laws,	Philadelphia, Pa.,	4th mo., "
813. Wm. W. Longstreth,	"	5th mo., "
814. Richard B. Gilpin,	Wilmington, Del.,	" "
815. Thomas Scattergood,	Philadelphia, Pa.,	" "
816. Joseph Smith,	"	" "
817. Joshua T. Seal,	Wilmington, Del.,	4th mo., "
818. Timothy A. Conrad,	Philadelphia, Pa.,	" "
819. William Abbott,	"	5th mo., "
820. Marmaduke Cope,	"	7th mo., "
822. John Evans,	"	5th mo., "
823. George F. Garretson,	....	" "
824. Robert Morton,	Philadelphia, Pa.,	" "
825. George Branner,	....	

* Deceased at the school 7th mo., 1814.

10

FIRST THOUSAND.

NAME.	RESIDENCE.	DATE OF ENTRY.
826. John Starr,	Philadelphia, Pa.,	5th mo., 1813.
827. Daniel Laws,	"	" "
828. Edward Bettle,	"	" "
829. Griffith Hinchman,	Woodbury, N. J.,	7th mo., "
830. John Newbold,	Chester, Pa.,	" "
831. David Chambers,	London Grove, Pa.,	8th mo., "
832. George P. Harlan,	Kennet, Pa.,	11th mo., "
833. Isaac Trimble,	E. Bradford, Pa.,	10th mo., "
834. James Bonsall,	———, Ohio,	" "
835. Isaac Price,	E. Bradford, Pa.,	" "
836. James Cowgill,	Duck Creek, Del.,	9th mo., "
837. Benj. Blackwood,	Woodbury, N. J.,	12th mo., "
838. Jacob Dutton,	Chichester, Pa.,	11th mo., "
839. Samuel Bassett,	Salem, N. J.,	10th mo., "
843. William W. Burr,	Mt. Holly, N. J.,	" 1813.
844. Elisha Nicholson,	....	" "
845. Ben. H. Lippincott,	Mt. Holly, N. J.,	11th mo., "
846. Reynell Coates,	Philadelphia, Pa.,	10th mo., "
847. James Gillingham,	Frankford, Pa.,	" "
848. S. H. Gillingham,	Philadelphia, Pa.,	" "
850. Hughes Bell,	Plymouth, Pa.,	11th mo., "
851. Thomas M. Lewis,	Willistown, Pa.,	12th mo., "
852. Joseph Davis,	"	" "
853. William Sinclair,	Baltimore, Md.,	4th mo., 1814.
854. John Powell,	"	12th mo., 1813.
855. Benjamin Powell,	"	" "
856. Wm. Penn Thomas,	Radnor, Pa.,	4th mo., 1814.
857. Andrew Griscom,	Salem, N. J.,	" "
858. Isaac Meredith,	Kennet Square, Pa.,	" "
859. Abraham Bell,	W. Nottingham, Md.,	5th mo., "
860. Abraham Resin,	Camden, Del.,	6th mo., "
861. Elisha Townsend,	Philadelphia, Pa.,	12th mo., 1813.
862. James G. McCurach,*	Salem, N. J.,	11th mo., "
863. John Carter,	Philadelphia, Pa.,	12th mo., "
864. Henry Carter,	"	" "
865. Charles Randolph,	"	5th mo., 1814.
866. George A. Downing,	Downingtown, Pa.,	1st mo., "
867. Robert Coe,	Philadelphia, Pa.,	" "
868. Isaac P. Morris,	"	3d mo., "
869. Samuel S. Grubb,	Wilmington, Del.,	5th mo., "
870. Edward Grubb,	"	" "
871. Harman Husband,	Deer Creek, Md.,	" "
872. George Bullock,	Springfield, N. J.,	11th mo., "
873. Ezekiel Jenkins,	Camden, Del.,	6th mo., "
874. Benjamin Taylor,	Kennet, Pa.,	10th mo., "
875. David Fell,	Makefield, Pa.,	11th mo., "
876. Isaac Massey,	Deer Creek, Md.,	10th mo., "

* Deceased at the school, 4th of Second month, 1814.

STUDENTS.

FIRST THOUSAND.

NAME.	RESIDENCE.	DATE OF ENTRY.
878. William B. Price,	Gunpowder, Md.,	11th mo., 1814.
879. John Husband,	Deer Creek, Md.,	" "
880. William Hazard,	Bristol, Pa.,	5th mo., "
881. John M. Laws,	Philadelphia, Pa.,	3d mo., "
882. Henry Abbott,	"	5th mo., "
883. Ezra Evans,	Evesham, N. J.,	" "
884. William Wilson,	Baltimore, Md.,	4th mo., "
885. Howell Longstreth,	Philadelphia, Pa.,	" "
886. Samuel Rowland,	Camden, Del.,	5th mo., "
887. Mifflin Rowland,	"	" "
888. Richard Thomas,	West Whiteland, Pa.,	" "
889. Charles Reynolds,	....	" "
890. Thomas R. Lindley,	New Garden, Pa.,	8th mo., "
891. William Lindley,	"	" "
892. James C. Biddle,	Philadelphia, Pa.,	6th mo., "
893. George B. Allen,	"	7th mo., "
894. Evan T. Tyson,	Baltimore, Md.,	9th mo., "
895. Wallace Lippincott,	Haddonfield, N. J.,	10th mo., "
896. Giles Oldden,	Stonybrook, N. J.,	11th mo., "
897. William G. Chandler,	Philadelphia, Pa.,	9th mo., "
898. William Hallowell,	"	1st mo., 1815.
899. Edward Garrett,	Darby, Pa.,	11th mo., 1814.
900. George V. Massey,	W. Whiteland, Pa.,	" "
901. Samuel Reckerfuse,	Frankford, Pa.,	12th mo., "
902. Clayton Reeve,	Evesham, N. J.,	3d mo., 1816.
903. Jacob Jackson,	Darby, Pa.,	1st mo., 1815.
904. Mordecai Lawrence,	....	3d mo., "
907. Jacob Ridgway,	Springfield, Pa.,	4th mo., "
908. Thomas Chandler,	Philadelphia, Pa.,	" "
909. Thomas Downing,	Uwchlan, Pa.,	5th mo., "
910. Joseph Harvey,	Kennet, Pa.,	" "
911. Edward Hicks,	Goshen, Pa.,	" "
912. Robinson Stabler,	Alexandria, Va.,	" "
913. Joseph Dixon,	Wilmington, Del.,	4th mo., "
914. Nathaniel N. Stokes,	Darby, Pa.,	6th mo., "
915. John S. Miller,	Alexandria, Va.,	5th mo., "
916. David Reed,	Westtown, Pa.,	7th mo., "
918. Jonathan Tyson,	Baltimore, Md.,	" "
919. William Tyson,	"	" "
920. John Lancaster,	Rancocas, N. J.,	5th mo., "
921. Joseph Baldwin,	Downingtown, Pa.,	6th mo., "
922. Thomas Ballenger,	Philadelphia, Pa.,	5th mo., "
923. Samuel Hutchinson,	"	" "
924. Charles D. Howard,	"	6th mo., "
925. James A. Hewes,	——, Va.,	5th mo., "
926. Wilson Balderston,	Baltimore, Md.,	" "
927. Isaiah Balderston,	"	" "

GENERAL CATALOGUE.

FIRST THOUSAND.

NAME.	RESIDENCE.	DATE OF ENTRY.
928. Thomas Abbott,	Philadelphia, Pa.,	5th mo., 1815.
929. Amos Lower,	"	6th mo., "
930. John H. Stewardson,	"	" "
931. John E. Lamb,	Wilmington, Del.,	" "
932. John C. McCoy,	Baltimore, Md.,	8th mo., "
933. William McCoy,	"	" "
934. Philip Price,	E. Bradford, Pa.,	7th mo., "
935. William Barnard,	E. Marlborough, Pa.,	8th mo., "
936. Jesse Cook,	Baltimore, Md.,	" "
937. Andrew Ellicott,	Ellicott's Mills, Md.,	— " "
938. Joshua Lord,	Woodbury, N. J.,	10th mo., "
939. Thomas Squibb,	Wilmington, Del.,	" "
941. Robert Stackhouse,	Philadelphia, Pa.,	6th mo., "
942. Wm. W. Wood,	Woodbury, N. J.,	7th mo., "
945. Job Darnell,	Evesham, N. J.,	9th mo., "
946. Watson Newbold,	Springfield, N. J.,	8th mo., "
947. George R. Justice,	Philadelphia, Pa.,	1st mo., 1816.
948. Clement H. Kay,	Woodbury, N. J.,	9th mo., 1815.
949. Edward R. Justice,	Philadelphia, Pa.,	1st mo., 1816.
950. Daniel Carter,	Delaware Co., Pa.,	11th mo., 1815.
951. William Biddle,	Philadelphia, Pa.,	" "
952. Jacob Maule,	Radnor, Pa.,	" "
953. Charles W. Wilson,	Philadelphia, Pa.,	12th mo., "
954. Pancoast Levis,	Springfield, Pa.,	" "
955. William Folger,	Nantucket, Mass.,	2d mo., 1816.
956. Edm'd T. Williams,	Shrewsbury, N. J.,	6th mo., "
957. Esek H. Williams,	"	" "
958. William W. Owen,	Philadelphia, Pa.,	3d mo., "
959. Milton Smith,	"	" "
962. Mar. Balderston,	Baltimore, Md.,	10th mo., 1815.
963. Eli West,	"	11th mo., "
964. Nathan Haines,	Nottingham, Md.,	12th mo., "
965. James Paist,	Providence, Pa.,	" "
966. Haines Reynolds,	Nottingham, Md.,	" "
967. Cheyney Jefferis,	E. Bradford, Pa.,	1st mo., 1816
968. Matthias Brown,	———, Pa.,	" "
969. Pierce Hoopes,	West Chester, Pa.,	" "
970. George Roberts,	Downingtown, Pa.,	4th mo., "
971. Henry D. Ellis,	Muncy, Pa.,	" "
972. Charles Denny,	New Garden, Pa.,	6th mo., "
973. John B. Ward,	Woodbury, N. J.,	" "
974. Elisha L. Clark,	Stonybrook, N. J.,	5th mo., "
975. John Reeve,	Woodbury, N. J.,	" "
976. Daniel Bonsall,	Salem, Ohio,	8th mo., "
977. Joseph Hazard,	Bristol, Pa.,	6th mo., "
978. Isaac Dixon,	Wilmington, Del.,	7th mo., "
979. William Poits,	Easton, Md.,	8th mo., "

STUDENTS.

FIRST THOUSAND.

NAME.	RESIDENCE.	DATE OF ENTRY.
980. Elisha Cook,	Philadelphia, Pa.,	5th mo., 1816.
982. Caleb Pleasants,	"	4th mo., "
983. Charles Iredell,	"	5th mo., "
984. Wm. A. Widdefield,	"	4th mo., "
985. H. W. Ridgway,	"	" "
986. Richard Waln,	Springfield, N. J.,	" "
987. Isaac Richards,	Upper Merion, Pa.,	6th mo., "
988. John Folwell,	Philadelphia, Pa.,	" "
989. William H. Stabler,	Alexandria, Va.,	" "
990. Charles Walmsley,	Byberry, Pa.,	" "
991. Michael Forsythe,	....	" "
992. James Hulme,	Mt. Holly, N. J.,	7th mo., "
993. Ambrose Webb,	Philadelphia, Pa.,	" "
994. H. Hollingshead,	"	" "
995. Jonathan Byrnes,	Wilmington, Del.,	11th mo., "
996. Wm. Scattergood,	Philadelphia, Pa.,	10th mo., "
997. Y. Gillingham,	Schuylkill Falls, Pa.,	9th mo., "
998. Joseph Reeves,	Philadelphia, Pa.,	" "
999. Wm. Griscom,	——, N. Y.,	10th mo., "
1000. Charles Atherton,	Middletown, Pa.,	9th mo., "

SECOND THOUSAND.

NAME.	RESIDENCE.	DATE OF ENTRY.
1. Eusebius Barnard,	E. Marlborough, Pa.,	11th mo., 1816.
2. Joseph Thomas,	"	" "
3. Joseph Tomlinson,	Woodbury, N. J.,	10th mo., "
7. Richard Townsend,	Plainfield, N. J.,	1st mo., 1817.
8. Enos Massey,	Concord, Pa.,	4th mo., "
9. Jacob Richards,	Upper Merion, Pa.,	12th mo., 1816.
10. Samuel Richards,	Providence, Pa.,	" "
11. Samuel D. Howell,	Philadelphia, Pa.,	10th mo., "
12. Richard Smith,	"	" "
13. William Buzby,	Egg Harbor, N. J.,	12th mo., "
14. William Evans,	Philadelphia, Pa.,	10th mo., "
15. Septimus Smith,	Bucks Co., Pa.,	11th mo., "
16. Tylee W. Burr,	Mt. Holly, N. J.,	" "
17. Charles W. Burr,	"	" "
18. James Bolton,	Philadelphia, Pa.,	" "
19. Joseph Tatum,	Woodbury, N. J.,	" "
20. James Remington,	Philadelphia, Pa.,	" "
21. Henry Smith,	Burlington, N. J.,	12th mo., "
22. Wm. Satterthwaite,	Crosswicks, N. J.,	6th mo., 1817.
23. Edwin Hallowell,	Philadelphia, Pa.,	4th mo., "
24. Edward Townsend,	"	3d mo., "
25. William Lukens,	Abington, Pa.,	4th mo., "
26. Charles B. Allen,	Philadelphia, Pa.,	" "

10* H

GENERAL CATALOGUE.

SECOND THOUSAND.

NAME.	RESIDENCE.	DATE OF ENTRY.
27. Daniel Wills,	Rancocas, N. J.,	5th mo., 1817
28. John Wills,	"	" "
29. John Cook,	Philadelphia, Pa.,	4th mo., "
30. James Lord,	Woodbury, N. J.,	3d mo., "
31. Enoch Walker,	Charlestown, Pa.,	12th mo., "
32. John C. Deacon,	Burlington, N. J.,	11th mo., "
33. Emmor Hunt,	Brownsville, Pa.,	10th mo., "
34. Mifflin Cadwallader,	"	" "
35. Stephen Speakman,	Concord, Pa.,	12th mo., "
37. Enoch P. Hoopes,	Kennet, Pa.,	5th mo., "
38. William Pennock,	W. Marlborough, Pa.,	6th mo., "
39. Shotwell Powell,	Plainfield, N. J.,	8th mo., 1819.
40. William Chapman,	Bucks Co., Pa.,	4th mo., 1817.
41. Benjamin Cooper,	Pleasant View, N. J.,	5th mo., "
42. Daniel Vail,	Rahway, N. J.,	4th mo., "
43. Charles Kaighn,	Kaighnton, N. J.,	5th mo., "
44. Jesse North,	Philadelphia, Pa.,	2d mo., 1825.
45. William H. Jones,	"	5th mo., 1817.
46. Benjamin C. Tucker,	"	6th mo., "
47. George W. Foster,	Mt. Holly, N. J.,	" "
48. Joseph Line,	Rahway, N. J.,	5th mo., "
49. Benjamin Leedom,	Philadelphia, Pa.,	6th mo., "
50. Henry Drinker,	"	" "
51. Nelson Laws,	"	" "
52. Jeremiah Fincher,	Robeson, Pa.,	12th mo., "
53. Edward Wilson,	Philadelphia, Pa.,	7th mo., "
54. Thomas Bacon,	Salem, N. J.,	11th mo., "
55. Jacob W. Paul,	Germantown, Pa.,	10th mo., "
56. James Cresson,	Philadelphia, Pa.,	" "
57. Marshall Slocum,	Germantown, Pa.,	" "
58. Peter R. Moore,	Philadelphia, Pa.,	11th mo., "
59. Joseph Smith,	Rahway, N. J.,	" "
60. Paul C. Budd,	Philadelphia, Pa.,	" "
61. Thomas Phipps,	Frankford, Pa.,	8th mo., 1818.
62. Charles Phipps,	"	" "
63. Henry Corlies,	Shrewsbury, N. J.,	11th mo., 1817.
64. Josiah Middleton,	Philadelphia, Pa.,	12th mo., "
65. Thomas J. Fell,	"	" "
66. William E. Baily,	Abington, Pa.,	3d mo., 1818
67. James Wilson,	Burlington, N. J.,	2d mo., "
68. Josiah Chapman,	Northumb'l'd Co., Pa.,	4th mo., "
69. Samuel Reeve,	Philadelphia, Pa.,	3d mo., "
70. John White,	"	" "
71. Lukens Grant,	Abington, Pa.,	4th mo., "
72. Barclay Brown,	Burlington, N. J.,	5th mo., "
73. Samuel Bonsall,	Frankford, Pa.,	6th mo., "
74. William S. Johnson,	Philadelphia, Pa.,	" "

STUDENTS.

SECOND THOUSAND.

NAME.	RESIDENCE.	DATE OF ENTRY.
75. Joseph P. Morris,	Philadelphia, Pa.,	7th mo., 1818
76. George Meeteer,	Makefield, Pa.,	10th mo., "
77. Jerem'h Manchester,	Utica, N. Y.,	9th mo., "
78. Oliver Hough,	Makefield, Pa.,	10th mo., "
79. Parker Owen,	Philadelphia, Pa.,	3d mo., 1819.
80. Owen Rhoads,	Springfield, Pa.,	7th mo., 1818.
81. Joel Swayne,	London Grove, Pa.,	8th mo., "
82. James Lawrie,	Woodstown, N. J.,	11th mo., "
84. Gideon G. Palmer,	Concord, Pa.,	" "
85. Lewis Palmer,	"	12th mo., "
86. George Matthews,	Gunpowder, Md.,	1st mo., 1819.
87. Edward Matthews,	"	12th mo., 1818.
88. Abel C. Vail,	Plainfield, N. J.,	2d mo., 1819.
89. Nathan Walton,	Fallowfield, Pa.,	3d mo., "
90. Eli Skelton,	Doe Run, Pa.,	" "
91. Daniel R. Bennett,	Philadelphia, Pa.,	11th mo., 1818.
94. Richard T. Downing,	Wilmington, Del.,	" "
95. John C. Allen,	Philadelphia, Pa.,	12th mo., "
96. Jacob R. Middleton,	"	1st mo., 1819.
97. Charles J. Walton,	"	" "
98. Samuel Allinson,	"	2d mo., "
99. Samuel Townsend,	"	4th mo., "
100. William A. Smith,	"	5th mo., "
101. David Hunt,	Fallowfield, Pa.,	4th mo., "
102. Joseph Matthews,	Gunpowder, Md.,	6th mo., "
103. Gibbons Marsh,	Concord, Pa.,	" "
104. William Starr,	Baltimore, Md.,	" "
105. Abraham Pennell,	Middletown, Pa.,	8th mo., "
107. David Price,	Gunpowder, Md.,	10th mo., "
109. John R. Carpenter,	Salem, N. J.,	" "
110. Norris Temple,	Pennsbury, Pa.,	" "
111. Joseph Carpenter,	Muncy, Pa.,	1st mo., "
112. Isaac Shoemaker,	Abington, Pa.,	4th mo., "
113. Joshua S. Hulme,	Hulmeville, Pa.,	2d mo., "
114. Thomas C. Hulme,	"	" "
115. John H. Mifflin,	Columbia, Pa.,	" "
116. Franklin Smith,	Philadelphia, Pa.,	4th mo., "
117. Josiah R. Reeve,	Evesham, N. J.,	5th mo., "
118. Isaac W. Potts,	Plymouth, Pa.,	4th mo., "
119. Edward T. Smith,	Philadelphia, Pa.,	5th mo., "
120. John K. Townsend,	"	3d mo., "
121. Edward Paxson,	"	5th mo., "
122. James Kite,	"	4th mo., "
123. Samuel Morton,	"	5th mo., "
125. Barton Cook,	"	4th mo., "
126. Joseph C. Clement,	"	" "
127. William Evans,	"	5th mo., "

SECOND THOUSAND.

NAME.	RESIDENCE.	DATE OF ENTRY.	
128. David Scattergood,	Philadelphia, Pa.,	5th mo.,	1819.
129. David D. Potts,	Valley Forge, Pa.,	"	"
130. Levi Bell,	Plymouth, Pa.,	"	"
131. Charles W. Bacon,	Philadelphia, Pa.,	"	"
132. Joseph Price,	"	"	"
133. John Hulme,	Mt. Holly, N. J.,	10th mo.,	"
134. William Bell,	Plymouth, Pa.,	8th mo.,	"
138. Joseph Lippincott,	Philadelphia, Pa.,	6th mo.,	"
139. Samuel Y. Atlee,	"	7th mo.,	"
140. Thomas T. Lea,	"	6th mo.,	"
141. John Brown,	Brownsville, N. Y.,	"	"
142. Darling Lippincott,	Haddonfield, N. J.,	11th mo.,	"
143. Dillwyn Parrish,	Philadelphia, Pa.,	9th mo.,	"
144. Rathmell Wilson,	"	11th mo.,	"
146. James Cresson,	"	10th mo.,	"
147. Owen Biddle,	"	11th mo.,	"
150. Thomas Jackson,	Darby, Pa.,	"	"
151. Levis Pennock,	W. Marlborough, Pa.,	10th mo.,	1820.
152. Thomas Bartram,	Darby, Pa.,	12th mo.,	1819.
153. Townsend Scott,	Baltimore, Md.,	"	"
154. Caspar W. Sharpless,	Aston, Pa.,	"	"
155. James Canby, Jr.,	Wilmington, Del.,	5th mo.,	1820.
156. Samuel R. Canby,	"	"	"
157. William F. Leggett,	———, N. Y.,	"	"
158. James Pennell,	Middletown, Pa.,	9th mo.,	1821.
159. William Hibberd,	E. Whiteland, Pa.,	11th mo.,	1820.
160. Levi Morris,	Lower Merion, Pa.,	"	1819.
161. Powell Morris,	Philadelphia, Pa.,	11th mo.,	"
162. Richard S. Shreeve,	Mt. Holly, N. J.,	1st mo.,	1820.
163. Alexander Shreeve,	"	"	"
164. David Tatum,	Wilmington, Del.,	5th mo.,	"
165. William Mcgear,	"	1st mo.,	"
166. Robert Alsop,	Philadelphia, Pa.,	4th mo.,	"
167. Charles Owen,	"	3d mo.,	"
168. Thomas Remington,	"	"	"
170. Charles Davis,	"	5th mo.,	"
171. Samuel Bolton,	"	"	"
172. Ed. C. Gillingham,	"	4th mo.,	"
173. Edward Brown,	"	5th mo.,	"
174. Benjamin Johnson,	"	3d mo.,	"
175. Thomas Garrett,	"	5th mo.,	"
177. Joseph D. Stratton,	"	4th mo.,	"
178. William L. Jenkins,	———, N. Y.,	5th mo.,	"
179. Aaron Llewellyn,	Salem Co., N. J.,	6th mo.,	"
180. Percival Seaman,	———, N. Y.,	5th mo.,	"
181. Willet Seaman,	"	"	"
182. John M. Bacon,	Philadelphia, Pa.,	"	"

STUDENTS.

SECOND THOUSAND.

NAME.	RESIDENCE.	DATE OF ENTRY.
183. Callender Price,	Philadelphia, Pa.,	5th mo., 1820.
186. Edward Biddle,	"	" "
187. Samuel Evans,		" "
188. Edward Folwell,	"	8th mo., "
191. Abraham Sharpless,	Aston, Pa.,	10th mo., "
192. Joseph G. Clark,	Doe Run, Pa.,	12th mo., "
193. Jacob Heald,	Hockessing, Del.,	" "
194. William B. Smith,	Baltimore, Md.,	6th mo., 1821.
195. Ellis Webb,	Kennet, Pa.,	5th mo., "
196. Charles Pearsall,	———, N. Y.,	7th mo., "
197. Robert Pearsall,	"	" "
198. John Palmer,	Little Creek, Del.,	" "
199. Samuel Jacobs,	E. Bradford, Pa.,	9th mo., "
201. George B. Deacon,	Burlington, N. J.,	11th mo., 1820.
202. Samuel M. Day,	Haddonfield, N. J.,	" "
203. Charles Curtis,	....	" "
204. Daniel Smith,	Philadelphia, Pa.,	" "
205. George D. Smith,	Burlington, N. J.,	" "
206. Joseph Warrington,	Westfield, N. J.,	12th mo., "
207. William R. Kaighn,	Kaighnton, N. J.,	" "
208. Joshua Husband,	Deer Creek, Md.,	2d mo., 1821.
209. Thomas Shipley,	———, N. Y.,	1st mo., "
210. Rowen Smith,	Philadelphia, Pa.,	12th mo., 1820.
211. Samuel Rhoads,	Upper Darby, Pa.,	1st mo., 1821.
212. Joshua Rhoads,	Philadelphia, Pa.,	" "
213. Mickle Clement,	Haddonfield, N. J.,	" "
214. Charles B. Evans,	"	4th mo., "
215. Richard Humphreys,	Philadelphia, Pa.,	5th mo., "
216. Daniel S. Earl,	New Mills, N. J.,	" "
217. Stanton Dorsey,	Philadelphia, Pa.,	" "
218. William Dorsey,	"	" "
219. Clayton Richardson,	Middletown, Pa.,	" "
220. Caspar Morris,	Lower Merion, Pa.,	" "
221. Thomas Evans,	Evesham, N. J.,	" "
222. James H. West,	Trenton, N. J.,	6th mo., "
223. William Evans,	Evesham, N. J.,	5th mo., "
224. Joseph W. Stokes,	"	" "
225. Alexander Cooper,	Camden, N. J.,	" "
227. Samuel Johnson,	Philadelphia, Pa.,	6th mo., "
228. Wm. W. Clement,	Haddonfield, N. J.,	7th mo., "
229. Daniel White,	Philadelphia, Pa.,	6th mo., "
230. Morris L. Hallowell,	"	7th mo., "
231. Caleb Hallowell,	"	" "
232. Israel Morris,	Lower Merion, Pa.,	" "
233. James S. Crim,	Burlington, N. J.,	8th mo., "
234. William Pitfield,	Philadelphia, Pa.,	10th mo., "
235. John F. Laing,	Plainfield, N. J.,	" "

SECOND THOUSAND.

NAME.	RESIDENCE.	DATE OF ENTRY.
236. Samuel C. Taylor,	Philadelphia, Pa.,	12th mo., 1821.
237. Charles T. Deacon,	Burlington, N. J.,	11th mo., "
238. Ellis Middleton,	Philadelphia, Pa.,	" "
239. Robert Thomas,	Germantown, Pa.,	" "
240. Sam'l F. Balderston,	Baltimore, Md.,	10th mo., "
241. George Thomas,	W. Whiteland, Pa.,	" "
242. Joseph Jobson,	Middletown, Pa.,	11th mo., "
243. Jacob Smedley,	"	10th mo., "
244. Isaac Eldridge,	Charlestown, Pa.,	11th mo., "
245. William Bassett,	Salem, N. J.,	" "
246. William W. Palmer,	Concord, Pa.,	12th mo., "
247. Rossiter Scott,	Baltimore, Md.,	1st mo., 1822.
248. Aquila B. Massey,	Deer Creek, Md.,	12th mo., 1821.
249. Thomas B. Hartley,	Haddonfield, N. J.,	2d mo., 1822.
250. Ezra Price,	Gunpowder, Md.,	1st mo., "
251. Asa Lippincott,	Westfield, N. J.,	12th mo., 1821.
253. Isaac J. Smith,	Philadelphia, Pa.,	" "
254. James W. Smith,	"	" "
256. Richard H. Bowne,	——, N. Y.,	4th mo., 1822.
257. Richard M. Acton,	Salem, N. J.,	1st mo., "
258. George W. Corlies,	——, N. Y.,	4th mo., "
259. Stephen Paschall,	Darby, Pa.,	2d mo., "
260. Benjamin Wilson,	Burlington, N. J.,	4th mo., "
261. James Mott,	Baltimore, Md.,	2d mo., "
262. David Thompson,	Salem, N. J.,	4th mo., "
263. Ezekiel Hunn,	Camden, Del.,	" "
264. Charles Trump,	Bristol, Pa.,	5th mo., "
265. Halliday Jenkins,	Camden, N. J.,	" "
266. James M. Corse,	Smyrna, Del.,	6th mo., "
267. Henry Smith,	Baltimore, Md.,	" "
268. Richard Mott,	"	7th mo., "
269. Levis Miller,	Springfield, Pa.,	" "
270. Richard M. Reeve,	Evesham, N. J.,	8th mo., 1824.
271. Charleton Ferris,	——, N. Y.,	4th mo., 1822.
272. James M. Woodnutt,	Salem, N. J.,	" "
273. William L. Shipley,	——, N. Y.,	3d mo., "
274. Edward Shotwell,	Rahway, N. J.,	6th mo., "
275. Oliver Cope,	Philadelphia, Pa.,	4th mo., "
276. Sam. H. Hartshorne,	Shrewsbury, N. J.,	6th mo., "
277. Edward A. Warner,	Darby, Pa.,	3d mo., 1825.
278. Lindley Vail,	Plainfield, N. J.,	5th mo., 1822.
279. Jonathan Pim,	Woodstown, N. J.,	" "
280. Joseph Scattergood,	Philadelphia, Pa.,	" "
281. Samuel A. Pancoast,	Springfield, N. J.,	6th mo., "
282. Emlen Cresson,	Philadelphia, Pa.,	" "
284. Clement Remington,	"	" "
285. George M. Alsop,	——"	" "

STUDENTS.

SECOND THOUSAND.

NAME.	RESIDENCE.	DATE OF ENTRY.
286. Alfred Greaves,	Valley Forge, Pa.,	1st mo., 1823.
287. Isaac Massey,	W. Whiteland, Pa.,	11th mo., 1822.
289. Anthony Williams,	Abington, Pa.,	9th mo., "
290. Samuel Richards,	Philadelphia, Pa.,	10th mo., "
291. William Cowgill,	Duck Creek, Del.,	7th mo., "
292. Samuel Parry,	Abington, Pa.,	11th mo., "
293. George M. Coale,	W. Nottingham, Md.,	9th mo., "
294. William Sharpless,	West Chester, Pa.,	" "
296. Isaac Darlington,	E. Bradford, Pa.,	10th mo., "
297. John Roberts,	Pipe Creek, Md.,	" "
298. Thomas Booth,	Londonderry, Pa.,	12th mo., "
299. Aaron Sharpless,	E. Bradford, Pa.,	1st mo., 1823.
301. Chas. M. Valentine,	Philadelphia, Pa.,	10th mo., 1822.
302. Joseph F. Warner,	Bristol, Pa.,	12th mo., "
303. Moses Livezey,	Springfield, N. J.,	11th mo., "
306. Nathan Wilkinson,	Wilmington, Del.,	" "
307. Jonathan D. Smith,	Springfield, Pa.,	1st mo., 1823.
308. James Mifflin,	Philadelphia, Pa.,	3d mo., "
309. Joseph Mifflin,	"	" "
310. Henry Book,	Germantown, Pa.,	4th mo., "
311. Jacob Jefferis,	W. Caln, Pa.,	2d mo., "
312. Thomas Baldwin,	Springfield, Pa.,	5th mo., "
313. John Trimble,	Baltimore, Md.,	4th mo., "
314. James E. Atkinson,	Easton, Md.,	" "
315. Joseph E. Poits,	"	" "
316. William Denny,	Smyrna, Del.,	5th mo., "
317. James S. Sterling,	Trenton, N. J.,	6th mo., "
318. Eli W. Lamborn,	Wilmington, Del.,	8th mo., "
319. Samuel Painter,	E. Bradford, Pa.,	" "
320. J. Morton Poole,	Wilmington, Del.,	10th mo., "
321. Jonah Hallowell,	Philadelphia, Pa.,	4th mo., "
322. Antrim Church,	Moorestown, N. J.,	6th mo., "
323. Joseph E. Temple,	Pennsbury, Pa.,	5th mo., "
324. Thomas J. Mcgear,	Wilmington, Del.,	" "
325. John Hallowell,	Abington, Pa.,	" "
326. Samuel Trotter,	Philadelphia, Pa.,	" "
328. Edward Remington,	"	" "
329. William Remington,		" "
331. Samuel Middleton,	Mt. Holly, N. J.,	6th mo., "
332. Samuel Vail,	Plainfield, N. J.,	8th mo., "
333. Richard Lloyd,	Philadelphia, Pa.,	9th mo., "
334. Watson J. Welding,	Frankford, Pa.,	11th mo., "
335. Edmund Lippincott,	Shrewsbury, N. J.,	12th mo., "
336. Benjamin Bonner,	Byberry, Pa.,	11th mo., "
337. Thomas Comfort,	"	" "
338. Jonathan C. Jones,	Germantown, Pa.,	" "
339. Hugh O. Smith,	Philadelphia, Pa.,	

9*

SECOND THOUSAND.

NAME.	RESIDENCE.	DATE OF ENTRY.
340. Josiah Phillips,	Kennet Square, Pa.,	10th mo., 1823.
341. Jasper Cope,	Philadelphia, Pa.,	8th mo., 1824.
342. James Oldden,	Stony Brook, N. J.,	12th mo., 1823.
343. John Mechem,	E. Bradford, Pa.,	" "
344. Jesse Jones,	Tredyffrin, Pa.,	3d mo., 1824.
345. Samuel Dixon,	Wilmington, Del.,	7th mo., "
346. William Garrett,	Upper Darby, Pa.,	5th mo., "
347. Richard Jacobs,	E. Bradford, Pa.,	12th mo., "
348. David Trimble,	Baltimore, Md.,	4th mo., "
349. Joseph Trimble,	"	" "
350. Robert R. Moore,	Easton, Md.,	6th mo., "
351. Samuel Bell,	Plymouth, Pa.,	11th mo., 1823.
352. John Jackson,	Darby, Pa.,	12th mo., "
353. Peter Thomas,	Abington, Pa.,	" "
354. John Wilson,	Camden, Del.,	" "
355. Edward L. Wood,	Woodbury, N. J.,	" "
356. Matthew Roberts,	Lower Merion, Pa.,	1st mo., 1824.
357. Thomas Blakey,	Middletown, Pa.,	12th mo., 1823.
358. Hewlings Bryant,	Philadelphia, Pa.,	" "
359. Isaac R. Davis,	"	" "
360. James C. Hallock,	Egg Harbor, N. J.,	2d mo., 1824.
361. Edward Roberts,	Philadelphia, Pa.,	4th mo., "
362. William Page,	"	5th mo., "
364. Thomas Shreeve,	Trenton, N. J.,	" "
365. John T. Child,	Philadelphia, Pa.,	4th mo., "
366. John W. Oldden,	Stony Brook, N. J.,	5th mo., "
367. Edward H. Trotter,	Philadelphia, Pa.,	7th mo., "
368. John Lippincott,	Mauch Chunk, Pa.,	8th mo., "
369. Wm. Warrington,	Westfield, N. J.,	" "
370. John G. Hewes,	Concord, Pa.,	" "
371. Richard B. Bailey,	W. Bradford, Pa.,	9th mo., "
372. Lloyd Oakford,	Darby, Pa.,	10th mo., "
373. George Sharpless,	E. Bradford, Pa.,	9th mo., "
374. Joseph Grubb,	Wilmington, Del.,	10th mo., "
375. Lewis Evans,	Lampeter, Pa.,	11th mo., "
376. Brinton Dilworth,	E. Whiteland, Pa.,	" "
377. William A. Gibbons,	E. Bradford, Pa.,	" "
378. Edward Hibberd,	E. Whiteland, Pa.,	" "
379. Joseph Bartlett,	Brownsville, Pa.,	
380. Abner G. Kirk,	Lampeter, Pa.,	12th mo., "
381. J. H. McIlvain,	W. Philadelphia, Pa.,	11th mo., "
382. Edmund Deacon,	Burlington, N. J.,	" "
383. Joseph M. Shipley,	———, N. Y.,	9th mo., "
384. John H. McIlvain,	W. Philadelphia, Pa.,	11th mo., "
385. Franklin Miller,	Salem, N. J.,	10th mo., "
386. Clarkson Sheppard,	Greenwich, N. J.,	11th mo., "
387. Samuel Scattergood,	Philadelphia, Pa.,	" "

STUDENTS.

SECOND THOUSAND.

NAME.	RESIDENCE.	DATE OF ENTRY.
388. Stacy B. Shreeve,	Mt. Holly, N. J.,	11th mo., 1824.
389. William L. Oakford,	Philadelphia, Pa.,	10th mo., "
390. Chas. D. Stackhouse,	"	" "
391. Benjamin Acton,	Salem, N. J.,	" "
392. George Waters,	Philadelphia, Pa.,	" "
394. James Bell,	Plymouth, Pa.,	" "
395. Abraham Shotwell,	Plainfield, N. J.,	12th mo., "
396. Nathaniel Cowgill,	Chester, Pa.,	11th mo., "
397. Joshua Stokes,	Evesham, N. J.,	12th mo., "
398. David Evans,	"	" "
399. Josiah B. Evans,	Haddonfield, N. J.,	" "
400. Rich'd Satterthwaite,	Crosswicks, N. J.,	
401. Benjamin Hunt,	Darby, Pa.,	5th mo., 1825.
402. Thomas Conard,	New London, Pa.,	" "
403. John M. Sharpless,	Chester, Pa.,	10th mo., "
404. Andrew Harman,	Middletown, Pa.,	5th mo., "
405. John A. Harman,	"	" "
406. Thomas S. Parker,	Philadelphia, Pa.,	7th mo., "
407. Charles Parker,	"	" "
408. Joseph Parker,	"	" "
409. Joseph C. Burdsall,	Trenton, N. J.,	4th mo., 1826.
410. Harvey Phillips,	Hockessing, Del.,	9th mo., 1825.
411. Nath. Hendrickson,	Crosswicks, N. J.,	6th mo., "
412. Alfred Smith,	Philadelphia, Pa.,	4th mo., "
413. Seneca Ely,	Buckingham, Pa.,	5th mo., "
414. Isaac Parry,	Philadelphia, Pa.,	" "
415. Jacob Stratton,	"	" "
416. David Webster,	Plainfield, N. J.,	6th mo., "
417. Allen Hallock,	Egg Harbor, N. J.,	1st mo., 1827.
418. John Kirkwood,	Columbia, Pa.,	5th mo., 1825.
419. John Kester,	Frankford, Pa.,	6th mo., "
420. Edward Richie,	Philadelphia, Pa.,	5th mo., "
421. Samuel Richie,	"	" "
422. John L. Passmore,	Darby, Pa.,	10th mo., "
423. Marshall J. Hunt,	"	" "
424. Nathan Jones,	E. Bradford, Pa.,	9th mo. "
425. Thos. S. Dawson,	Easton, Md.,	11th mo., "
426. Charles Comly,	Byberry, Pa.,	10th mo., "
427. Thomas D. Lindley,	New Garden, Pa.,	12th mo., "
428. Samuel N. Pusey,	Hockessing, Del.,	" "
429. Ezekiel Palen,	Cairo, N. Y.,	4th mo., 1826.
430. Arthur Palen,	"	" "
431. Elihu Roberts,	Philadelphia, Pa.,	7th mo., 1825.
432. George Lippincott,	Westfield, N. J.,	9th mo., "
433. Charles Shoemaker,	Abington, Pa.,	7th mo., "
434. Israel Knight,	Philadelphia, Pa.,	8th mo., "
435. Henry Ely,	Buckingham, Pa.,	9th mo., "

GENERAL CATALOGUE.

SECOND THOUSAND.

NAME.	RESIDENCE.	DATE OF ENTRY.
436. Wm. T. McCollin,	Philadelphia, Pa.,	9th mo., 1825.
437. Joseph Canby,	Hulmeville, Pa.,	11th mo., "
438. Jacob Carter,	Philadelphia, Pa.,	10th mo., "
439. Joshua M. Allen,	"	" "
440. Benj. W. Paxson,	Trenton, N. J.,	11th mo., "
441. Eden Shotwell,	Rahway, N. J.,	" "
442. Joseph Jobson,	Philadelphia, Pa.,	" "
443. Edward B. Mears,	Mauch Chunk, Pa.,	" "
444. George Maulsby,	Plymouth, Pa.,	" "
445. John Dixon,	Philadelphia, Pa.,	1st mo., 1826.
446. James Rhoads,	Blockley, Pa.,	12th mo., 1825.
447. Benjamin Stratton,	Philadelphia, Pa.,	" "
448. Stephen Proctor,	Baltimore, Md.,	" "
449. Isaac Martin,	Philadelphia, Pa.,	10th mo., 1826.
450. Philip Sharpless,	West Chester, Pa.,	12th mo., 1825.
451. Emmor Reeve,	Evesham, N. J.,	11th mo., "
452. Samuel L. Steer,	Waterford, Va.,	1st mo., 1826.
453. Lea Gause,	E. Bradford, Pa.,	12th mo., 1825.
454. Samuel Coale,	W. Nottingham, Md.,	" "
455. Samuel Painter,	Concord, Pa.,	11th mo., 1826.
456. Robert Register,	Smyrna, Del.,	7th mo., "
457. Edward Painter,	Concord, Pa.,	11th mo., "
458. Joseph Clement,	Woodbury, N. J.,	" "
459. Garrett Thatcher,	Concord, Pa.,	12th mo., "
460. Stephen Trimble,	"	" "
461. Edward Johnson,	Philadelphia, Pa.,	3d mo., "
462. Reuben Williams,	Abington, Pa.,	4th mo., "
463. Joseph Middleton,	Philadelphia, Pa.,	" "
464. John Middleton,	"	" "
465. Josiah Bacon,	Greenwich, N. J.,	" "
466. Isaac J. Cox,	Easton, Md.,	3d mo., 1827.
467. Samuel Oldden,	Stony Brook, N. J.,	4th mo., 1826.
468. Jonathan Leedom,	Philadelphia, Pa.,	" "
469. James Vail,	Plainfield, N. J.,	" "
470. Sandwith Drinker,	Philadelphia, Pa.,	5th mo., "
471. John Lamborn,	New Garden, Pa.,	11th mo., "
472. Samuel Denny,	Smyrna, Del.,	8th mo., "
473. Daniel C. Denny,	"	" "
474. Thomas Russell,	New Market, N. J.,	10th mo., "
475. Jacob V. Shotwell,	Rahway, N. J.,	11th mo., "
476. William Hampton,	"	" "
477. John W. Haines,	Westfield, N. J.,	" "
478. John Longstreth,	Westtown, Pa.,	10th mo., "
479. Jacob R. Shotwell,	Rahway, N. J.,	11th mo., "
480. Day Wood,	Little Britain, Pa.,	12th mo., "
481. Levi Tyson,	Abington, Pa.,	5th mo., "
482. Ed. R. Simmons,	Philadelphia, Pa.,	6th mo., "

STUDENTS.

SECOND THOUSAND.

NAME.	RESIDENCE.	DATE OF ENTRY.
483. Charles Corlies,	Shrewsbury, N. J.	9th mo., 1826.
484. M. S. Kirkbride,	Fallsington, Pa.,	11th mo., "
485. Joseph W. Pharo,	Tuckerton, N. J.,	10th mo., "
486. Archelaus R. Pharo,	"	" "
487. Edward Remington,	Philadelphia, Pa.,	" "
488. William Remington,	"	" "
489. Edward M. Davis,	Germantown, Pa.,	" "
490. Aaron Cox,	Philadelphia, Pa.,	" "
492. John R. Barker,	Bristol, Pa.,	2d mo., 1827.
493. Charles W. Bacon,	Philadelphia, Pa.,	4th mo., "
494. Edward Woodnutt,	Salem, N. J.,	9th mo., "
495. Lewis P. Lee,	Valley Forge, Pa.,	5th mo., "
496. Duncan S. Oliphant,	Tuckerton, N. J.,	8th mo., "
497. Edwin A. Weaver,	Philadelphia, Pa.,	10th mo., "
498. Robert Pharo,	Barnegat, N. J.,	9th mo., "
499. John L. Smith,	Philadelphia, Pa.,	11th mo., "
500. Richard Price,	Gunpowder, Md.,	4th mo., "
501. Washington Irish,	Brownsville, Pa.,	" "
502. Franklin Irish,	"	" "
503. Samuel Mickle,	Sadsbury, Pa.,	5th mo., "
504. Thomas Dent,	Westtown, Pa.,	10th mo., 1828.
505. Joseph Snowden,	Indian Spring, Va.,	4th mo., 1827.
506. Jesse Parker,	Rahway, N. J.,	6th mo., "
507. William Sheward,	W. Marlborough, Pa.,	4th mo., "
508. J. H. Mendenhall,	Chichester, Pa.,	6th mo., "
509. Josiah Haines,	Pipe Creek, Md.,	11th mo., "
510. Edward Sharpless,	E. Bradford, Pa.,	10th mo., "
511. William Forsythe,	"	" "
512. Humphrey Yearsley,	Concord, Pa.,	" "
513. James C. Comfort,	Byberry, Pa.,	11th mo., "
514. Eli Y. Reece,	Providence, Pa.,	" "
515. Nathan Haines,	Pipe Creek, Md.,	" "
516. John P. Jones,	Pennsbury, Pa.,	12th mo., "
517. John Haines,	Pipe Creek, Md.,	11th mo., "
518. Henry P. Sharpless,	West Chester, Pa.,	" "
519. Joel Cook,	Deer Creek, Md.,	" "
520. Nathan Cook,	"	" "
521. Charles Seal,	E. Marlborough, Pa.,	12th mo., "
522. Josiah Evans,	Willistown, Pa.,	" "
523. Isaac G. Sheward,	W. Marlborough, Pa.,	" "
524. Milton Painter,	Concord, Pa.,	1st mo., 1828.
525. Benj. D. Garrigues,	Philadelphia, Pa.,	3d mo., "
526. James Phillips,	Hockessing, Del.,	1st mo., "
527. Nathan Conard,	Egg Harbor, N. J.,	2d mo., "
528. John R. Corse,	Wilmington, Del.,	3d mo., "
529. Thomas Knight,	Frankford, Pa.,	5th mo., "
530. Caleb W. Pusey,	E. Marlborough, Pa.,	" "

SECOND THOUSAND.

NAME.	RESIDENCE.	DATE OF ENTRY.	
531. Thos. J. Husband,	Deer Creek, Md.,	12th mo.,	1827.
532. George W. Taylor,	Philadelphia, Pa.,	"	"
533. Charles W. Taylor,	"	"	"
534. Charles Janney,	"	10th mo.,	1830.
535. Hugh H. Bowne,	Rahway, N. J.,	1st mo.,	1828.
536. William Bowne,	"	"	"
537. Charles Walton,	Philadelphia, Pa.,	4th mo.,	"
538. Abel North,	"	3d mo.,	"
539. James Coleman,	Trenton, N. J.,	5th mo.,	"
540. George Wilson,	Cantwell's Bridge, Del.,	7th mo.,	"
541. Robert Garrett,	Willistown, Pa.,	9th mo.,	"
542. John Forsythe,	E. Bradford, Pa.,	10th mo.,	"
543. Davis Garrett,	Upper Darby, Pa.,	"	"
544. Hugh M. Lownes,	Springfield, Pa.,	"	"
545. George R. Baker,	W. Bradford, Pa.,	"	"
546. Francis W. Evans,	Hamilton, Pa.,	"	"
547. Edwin James,	E. Bradford, Pa.,	"	"
548. Howard Yarnall,	Edgmont, Pa.,	11th mo.,	"
549. Moses Palmer,	Concord, Pa.,	"	"
550. William Davidson,	Frankford, Pa.,	5th mo.,	"
551. George Kinsey,	"	"	"
552. Morgan Hinchman,	Philadelphia, Pa.,	9th mo.,	"
553. Barclay Hinchman,	"	"	"
554. Samuel Stokes,	Evesham, N. J.,	"	"
555. John Hicks,	E. Goshen, Pa.,	11th mo.,	"
556. William Bancroft,	Providence, Pa.,	12th mo.,	"
557. Harvey Bancroft,	"	11th mo.,	"
558. Lee W. Buffington,	Middletown, Pa.,	12th mo.,	"
559. Lewis G. Mason,	Wilmington, Del.,	1st mo.,	1829.
560. Caleb S. Cope,	E. Bradford, Pa.,	4th mo.,	"
561. Isaac R. Walker,	Tredyffrin, Pa.,	5th mo.,	"
562. Pearson Kinsey,	Hockessing, Del.,	6th mo.,	"
563. John Mendenhall,	Marcus Hook, Pa.,	9th mo.,	"
564. Daniel O. Tatum,	Woodbury, N. J.,	10th mo.,	"
565. Joseph Jones,	Camden, N. J.,	"	1828.
566. Arthur Howell,	Middletown, Pa.,	12th mo.,	"
567. Charles L. Willits,	Haddonfield, N. J.,	3d mo.,	1829.
568. William W. Corlies,	Shrewsbury, N. J.,	"	"
569. Benjamin Allen,	"	4th mo.,	"
570. Joseph Corlies,	Philadelphia, Pa.,	3d mo.,	"
571. Jabez Jenkins,	Westfield, N. J.,	5th mo.,	"
572. Charles Painter,	Concord, Pa.,	9th mo.,	"
573. John Thomas,	Goshen, Pa.,	10th mo.,	"
574. William Wetherill,	Springfield, Pa.,	9th mo.,	"
575. Charles Smith,	Sadsbury, Pa.,	12th mo.,	"
576. Amos Darlington,	E. Bradford, Pa.,	10th mo.,	"
577. John Tudor,	Adams Co., Pa.,	11th mo.,	"

STUDENTS.

SECOND THOUSAND.

	NAME.	RESIDENCE.	DATE OF ENTRY.
578	David G. Pratt,	Newtown, Pa.,	1st mo., 1830.
579	William Kemp,	King's Creek, Md.,	4th mo., "
580.	Abram Brown,	Middletown, Pa.,	" "
581.	Walter Knight,	Frankford, Pa.,	" "
582.	Joseph Cox,	Baltimore, Md.,	5th mo., 1829.
583.	James M. Thomas,	Philadelphia, Pa.,	" "
584.	William B. Cooper,	Pleasant View, N. J.,	" "
585.	William P. Newlin,	Darby, Pa.,	6th mo., "
586.	Edward E. Palmer,	Philadelphia, Pa.,	5th mo., "
587.	David Welding,	Stroudsburg, Pa.,	" "
588.	Dillwyn Smith,	Burlington, N. J.,	" "
589.	Joseph K. Williams,	Philadelphia, Pa.,	" "
590.	James Wilson,	Salem, N. J.,	6th mo., "
591.	Joseph Lea,	Philadelphia, Pa.,	" "
592.	B. Wyatt Wistar,	"	" "
593.	Charles Welding,	Frankford, Pa.,	10th mo., "
594.	Lindley Haines,	Evesham, N. J.,	" "
595.	Richard W. Davis,	Philadelphia, Pa.,	9th mo., "
596.	Mahlon Moon,	Middletown, Pa.,	10th mo., "
597.	Wm. A. Pancoast,	Springfield, N. J.,	9th mo., "
598.	Edward Snowdon,	Philadelphia, Pa.,	" "
599.	Ambrose Smith,	"	10th mo., "
600.	John Cassin,	Providence, Pa.,	" "
601.	John Wistar,	Salem, N. J.,	11th mo., "
602.	Wm. W. Humphreys,	Philadelphia, Pa.,	10th mo., "
603.	James Saunders,	Woodbury, N. J.,	11th mo., "
604.	Wm. Morris Davis,	Upper Merion, Pa.,	" "
605.	Charles M. Cooper,	Camden, N. J.,	" "
606.	Francis L. Altemus,	Philadelphia, Pa.,	12th mo., "
607.	Jonathan Richards,	Darby, Pa.,	" "
608.	Henry W. Lippincott,	Shrewsbury, N. J.,	4th mo., 1830.
609.	Joseph Walton,	Philadelphia, Pa.,	3d mo., "
610.	Milton Conard,	New London, Pa.,	8th mo., "
611.	Clarkson West,	Little Falls, Md.,	11th mo., "
612.	Mahlon Vail,	Plainfield, N. J.,	8th mo., "
613.	John W. Vail,	" "	" "
614.	Albert L. Vail,	" "	" "
615.	William Thorn,	Rahway, N. J.,	7th mo., "
616.	Joseph Pennock,	W. Marlborough, Pa.,	11th mo., "
617.	Jasper Hoopes,	West Chester, Pa.,	8th mo., "
618.	James C. Jackson,	Hockessing, Del.,	10th mo., "
619.	John H. Marsh,	Concord, Pa.,	11th mo., "
620.	Jacob Painter,	Middletown, Pa.,	9th mo., "
621.	George Ashbridge,	Downingtown, Pa.,	5th mo., "
622.	Ellwood Welding,	Frankford, Pa.,	" "
623.	Israel Maule,	Philadelphia, Pa.,	" "
624.	William Parker,	"	" "

11*

SECOND THOUSAND.

NAME.	RESIDENCE.	DATE OF ENTRY.
625. Elias Parker,	Philadelphia, Pa.,	5th mo., 1830.
626. Wm. L. Humphreys,	"	" "
627. Chalkley N. Thorn,	"	" "
628. Joshua P. Wilkins,	Evesham, N. J.,	" "
629. Charles L. Sharpless,	Philadelphia, Pa.,	" "
630. Nathan Hilles,	Frankford, Pa.,	" "
631. Joseph E. Maule,	Philadelphia, Pa.,	" "
632. Elisha P. Maule,	"	" "
633. David S. Burson,	Richland, Pa.,	7th mo., "
634. William W. Parker,	Philadelphia, Pa.,	6th mo., "
635. Edward A. Parker,	"	" "
636. Evan Thomas,	"	5th mo., "
637. Nixon White,	Perquimons Co., N. C.,	" "
638. John B. Cresson,	Philadelphia, Pa.,	" "
639. Joseph L. Maule,	"	6th mo., "
640. Thomas Corlies,	"	5th mo., "
641. Edward Middleton,	"	7th mo., "
642. Nathan Middleton,	"	" "
643. Samuel L. Garrett,	Darby, Pa.,	10th mo., 1832.
644. Samuel B. Woolman,	Burlington, N. J.,	6th mo., 1830.
645. Charles Greaves,	———, Pa.,	7th mo., "
646. Thomas Kite,	Philadelphia, Pa.,	" "
647. Joseph Carter,	Darby, Pa.,	" "
648. Samuel Bunting,	Crosswicks, N. J.,	9th mo.; "
649. Clayton Stratton,	Philadelphia, Pa.,	7th mo., "
650. Samuel Haines,	"	9th mo., "
651. Joseph H. Atkinson,	Crosswicks, N. J.,	" "
652. Charles Jones,	Cheltenham, Pa.,	10th mo., "
653. Isaac B. Brown,	Fallsington, Pa.,	9th mo., "
654. Isaac C. Price,	Philadelphia, Pa.	8th mo., "
655. Jeremiah Comfort,	Plymouth, Pa.,	10th mo., "
656. Samuel N. Smith,	Chester, Pa.,	" "
657. Nathaniel Randolph,	Philadelphia, Pa.,	" "
658. Wm. H. Balderston,	Baltimore, Md.,	" "
659. Jonathan Fell,	Philadelphia, Pa.,	" "
660. Biddle Reeves,	Crosswicks, N. J.,	8th mo., "
661. William B. Smith,	Sadsbury, Pa.,	" "
662. John Lightfoot,	Uwchlan, Pa.,	9th mo., "
663. John M. Maris,	Chester, Pa.,	10th mo., "
664. William Sharpless,	"	" "
665. Samuel Dutton,	Aston, Pa.,	9th mo., "
666. William Lownes,	Springfield, Pa.,	10th mo., "
667. Jesse Evans,	Lampeter, Pa.,	11th mo., "
668. Abner G. Hawley,	Concord, Pa.,	10th mo., "
669. Abraham P. Morgan,	Chichester, Pa.,	9th mo., "
670. Robert Wetherill,	Springfield, Pa.,	6th mo., 1831.
671. Spencer Bonsall,	Germantown, Pa.,	10th mo., 1830.

STUDENTS.

SECOND THOUSAND.

NAME.	RESIDENCE.	DATE OF ENTRY.
672. William Whitall,	Woodbury, N. J.,	10th mo., 1830.
673. Louis Paxson,	Frankford, Pa.,	" "
674. Rowland Johnson,	Germantown, Pa.,	11th mo., "
675. James V. Emlen,	Philadelphia, Pa.,	10th mo., "
676. Yardley Warner,	Fallsington, Pa.,	9th mo., "
677. Jesse Comfort,	Middletown, Pa.,	11th mo., "
678. Joseph Gardiner,	Evesham, N. J.,	" "
679. Stephen Coffin,	Guilford Co., N. C.,	9th mo., "
680. Joseph Pennell,	Concord, Pa.,	10th mo., "
681. William Pennell,	Concord, Pa.,	10th mo., "
682. John D. Pierce,	Providence, Pa.,	3d mo., 1831.
683. Thomas Pratt,	Middletown, Pa.,	9th mo., 1830.
684. Owen Rhoads,	Springfield, Pa.,	3d mo., 1831.
685. Benjamin Lord,	Woodbury, N. J.,	10th mo., 1830.
686. Robert G. Hopkins,	Spring Mills, Md.,	4th mo., 1831.
687. Isaac Craft,	Crosswicks, N. J.,	9th mo., "
688. Joseph May,	W. Marlborough, Pa.,	4th mo., "
689. Willis W. Wright,	Spring Mills, Md.,	" "
690. William E. Haines,	Muncy, Pa.,	11th mo., "
691. Charles Foulke,	Gwynedd, Pa.,	3d mo., "
692. Jehu L. Kite,	Susquehanna Co., Pa.,	10th mo., "
693. Thos. H. Newbold,	Frankford, Pa.,	5th mo., "
694. Joseph H. Deacon,	Mt. Holly, N. J.,	4th mo., "
695. Rich'd M. Kirkbride,	Philadelphia, Pa.,	" "
696. John W. Paxson,	Horsham, Pa.,	3d mo., "
697. George Williams,	Shrewsbury, N. J.,	5th mo., "
698. Jesse W. Taylor,	Philadelphia, Pa.,	4th mo., "
699. Samuel Leeds,	G. Egg Harbor, N. J.,	3d mo., "
700. William Bowne,	Rahway, N. J.,	4th mo., "
701. John Bowne,	"	" "
702. Benjamin Marsh,	"	" "
703. Samuel Hulme,	Bristol, Pa.,	5th mo., "
704. M. W. Allen,	"	" "
705. Oliver Livezey,	Medford, N. J.,	" "
706. Peter L. Levick,	Philadelphia, Pa.,	3d mo., "
707. George B. Abbott,	Trenton, N. J.,	5th mo., "
708. Joseph Baily,	Staunton, Del.,	7th mo., "
709. Isaac M. Donaldson,	Philadelphia, Pa.,	5th mo., "
710. John Cresson,	"	4th mo., "
711. Caleb S. Hunt,	"	9th mo., "
712. Benajah Antrim,	"	" "
713. Wm. M. Downing,	Bristol, Pa.,	10th mo., "
714. Sam. A. Downing,	"	" "
715. Samuel Hilles,	Frankford, Pa.,	8th mo., "
716. Josiah Jones,	Cheltenham, Pa.,	11th mo., "
717. John A. Barrington,	Susquehanna Co., Pa.,	10th mo., "
718. Jonathan H. Lowler,	Camden, N. J.,	11th mo., "

SECOND THOUSAND.

NAME.	RESIDENCE.	DATE OF ENTRY.
719. Howard White,	Philadelphia, Pa.,	10th mo., 1832
720. Barclay White,	"	" "
721. William Edge,	Downingtown, Pa.,	6th mo., 1831.
722. John R. Howell,	Edgmont, Pa.,	7th mo., "
723. William Reed,	Westtown, Pa.,	5th mo., "
724. Darwin Painter,	Concord, Pa.,	6th mo., "
725. Richard Thatcher,	"	7th mo., "
726. Samuel Abbott,	Salem, N. J.,	11th mo., "
727. George Abbott,	"	5th mo., "
728. Edward Waters,	Baltimore, Md.,	4th mo., "
729. Joseph Pusey,	Sadsbury, Pa.,	9th mo., "
730. George Brown,	Middletown, Pa.,	11th mo., "
731. Beaumont Maris,	New Hope, Pa.,	6th mo., "
732. William Maris,	"	" "
733. George Randolph,	Philadelphia, Pa.,	" "
734. I. H. Satterthwaite,	Crosswicks, N. J.,	9th mo., "
735. John Healy,	Fallsington, Pa.,	10th mo., "
736. James Boustead,	Philadelphia, Pa.,	6th mo., "
737. Solomon Conrad,	"	3d mo., 1832.
738. Benjamin Parry,	"	4th mo., "
739. Thomas Brown,	Middletown, Pa.,	11th mo., 1831.
740. Edward Comfort,	Byberry, Pa.,	" "
741. Preston Woodnutt,	Salem, N. J.,	9th mo., "
742. George Guell,	Wilmington, Del.,	" "
743. Samuel Williams,	Fallsington, Pa.,	11th mo., "
744. Britton Corlies,	Philadelphia, Pa.,	3d mo., 1832.
745. Charles Reeve,	Greenwich, N. J.,	12th mo., 1831.
746. David Trump,	Newport, Pa.,	3d mo., 1832.
747. James M. Saunders,	Woodbury, N. J.,	" "
748. Samuel S. Willits,	Haddonfield, N. J.,	4th mo., "
749. Alfred Thomas,	Bensalem, Pa.,	3d mo., "
750. Amos Middleton,	Crosswicks, N. J.,	11th mo., 1831.
751. John Hunn,	Camden, Del.,	5th mo., "
752. Isaac Wetherill,	Providence, Pa.,	10th mo., "
753. William Alexander,	Middletown, Pa.,	11th mo., "
754. Josiah Tatum,	Woodbury, N. J.,	9th mo., "
755. Richard Gibbons,	Lampeter, Pa.,	4th mo., 1832.
756. William Daniel,	"	8th mo., "
757. Thomas Marshall,	Concord, Pa.,	10th mo., "
758. Ephraim Barnard,	London Grove, Pa.,	3d mo., "
759. Cyrus Hoopes,	"	9th mo., "
760. Benj. Sharpless,	London Britain, Pa.,	12th mo., 1831.
761. Lewis P. Wilkinson,	London Grove, Pa.,	5th mo., 1832.
762. Abel Breaor,	Wilmington, Del.,	4th mo., "
763. Isaac Yearsley,	Coatesville, Pa.,	" "
764. Richard Taylor,	West Chester, Pa.,	11th mo., "
765. Seth Warrington,	Westfield, N. J.,	10th mo., "

STUDENTS.

SECOND THOUSAND.

NAME.	RESIDENCE.	DATE OF ENTRY.
766. George Fitzwater,	Abington, Pa.,	6th mo., 1832.
767. Wilson Barnard,	New Garden, Pa.,	10th mo., "
768. Samuel B. Evans,	Evesham, N. J.,	" "
769. Davis Lewis,	Springfield, Pa.,	5th mo., "
770. Enoch Lewis,	Philadelphia, Pa.,	6th mo., "
771. Benj. S. Bellangee,	"	5th mo., "
772. Samuel Schooley,	Trenton, N. J.,	9th mo., "
773. Michael Trump,	Newport, Pa.,	" "
774. Robert K. Wright,	Philadelphia, Pa.,	4th mo., "
775. James M. Hall,	Salem, N. J.,	" 1833.
776. Samuel Comfort,	Middletown, Pa.,	10th mo., "
777. Benj. Atkinson,	Mansfield, N. J.,	5th mo., 1832.
778. J. Satterthwaite,	Fallsington, Pa.,	" "
779. Joseph Merrefield,	Philadelphia, Pa.,	" "
780. George Martin,	"	" "
781. Henry Martin,		" "
782. Levi P. Rhoads,	Pottsville, Pa.,	4th mo., "
783. Samuel J. Levick,	Philadelphia, Pa.,	5th mo., "
784. Isaac Morgan,	"	9th mo., "
785. James S. Lippincott,	"	5th mo., "
786. Samuel W. Bacon,	"	" "
787. Stacy Cook,	Frankford, Pa.,	10th mo., "
788. Edmund H. Bonsall,	Germantown, Pa.,	11th mo., "
789. Richard Randolph,	Philadelphia, Pa.,	7th mo., "
790. John W. Chambers,	New Garden, Pa.,	11th mo., "
791. Charles L. Baily,	Westtown, Pa.,	" "
792. James Forsythe,	West Goshen, Pa.,	" "
793. Edward Hoopes,	"	9th mo., "
794. Amos H. Yarnall,	Edgmont, Pa.,	11th mo., "
795. Wm. P. Thatcher,	Concord, Pa.,	10th mo., "
796. Elisha Roberts,	Moorestown, N. J.,	11th mo., "
797. John G. Jackson,	Hockessing, Del.,	5th mo., "
798. Cyrus G. Kinsey,	Wilmington, Del.,	" "
799. Thomas Trimble,	W. Whiteland, Pa.,	9th mo., 1833.
800. William Ogden,	Springfield, Pa.,	2d mo., "
801. Caleb Jones,	Valley Forge, Pa.,	9th mo., 1832.
802. Joseph Thompson,	Salem, N. J.,	10th mo., "
803. Daniel R. Harper,	Bristol, Pa.,	9th mo., "
804. Joseph Townsend,	Baltimore, Md.,	4th mo., 1834.
805. William Kinsey,	Frankford, Pa.,	11th mo., 1832.
806. Oliver A. Taylor,	Taylorsville, Pa.,	10th mo., "
807. H. Satterthwaite,	Crosswicks, N. J.,	11th mo., "
808. Samuel L. Baily,	Philadelphia, Pa.,	6th mo., 1833.
809. Richard S. Folwell,	"	10th mo., 1832.
810. Joseph E. Dixon,	"	" "
811. Richard Thatcher,	Kennet Square, Pa.,	
812. Edward Bell,	Philadelphia, Pa.,	4th mo., 1833.

I

142　　　GENERAL CATALOGUE.

SECOND THOUSAND.

NAME.	RESIDENCE.	DATE OF ENTRY.
813. Samuel C. Willits,	Philadelphia, Pa.,	3d mo., 1833.
814. John Bishop,	Mansfield, N. J.,	11th mo., 1832.
815. Thomas Edge,	Downingtown, Pa.,	9th mo., "
816. Joel Willis,	Mount Pleasant, Ohio,	3d mo., 1835.
817. David Paxson,	Horsham, Pa.,	" 1833.
818. Joseph S. Cohn,	Bordentown, N. J.,	10th mo., "
819. Isaac Scull,	Woodstown, N. J.,	4th mo., "
820. Joshua Hunt,	Downingtown, Pa.,	3d mo., "
821. Hugh D. Vail,	Plainfield, N. J.,	5th mo., "
822. Phineas Lownes,	Springfield, Pa.,	11th mo., 1832.
823. William Webster,	Rahway, N. J.,	5th mo., "
824. John L. Pennell,	Concord, Pa.,	2d mo., 1833.
825. S. S. G. Eachus,	Edgmont, Pa.,	3d mo., "
826. Samuel Register,	Smyrna, Del.,	5th mo., "
827. Joseph W. Thorn,	West Fallowfield, Pa.,	10th mo., "
828. Osborn Hamilton,	Oxford, Pa.,	9th mo., "
829. Joseph Wetherill,	Springfield, N. J.,	11th mo., "
830. Vincent Mason,	Newlin, Pa.,	5th mo., "
831. Charles E. Smith,	Philadelphia, Pa.,	3d mo., "
832. Alexander Shaw,	"	4th mo., "
833. Thomas N. Black,	Bordentown, N. J.,	5th mo., "
834. Nath. B. Hillman,	Haddonfield, N. J.,	4th mo., "
835. Oborn Levis,	Upper Darby, Pa.,	3d mo., "
836. William Levis,	"	" "
837. Joseph A. Miller,	Greenwich, N. J.,	4th mo., "
838. George K. Johnson,	Philadelphia, Pa.,	5th mo., "
839. Chalkley Bell,	White Marsh, Pa.,	10th mo., 1834.
840. Benjamin Davidson,	Frankford, Pa.,	11th mo., 1832.
841. John Burson,	Stroudsburg, Pa.,	4th mo., 1833.
842. Thomas Wilson,	Little Creek, Del.,	" "
843. Lea Pusey,	Sadsbury, Pa.,	3d mo., 1834.
844. Henry Walter,	Hockessing, Del.,	3d mo., 1832.
845. Samuel Ogden,	Springfield, Pa.,	4th mo., 1833.
846. Isaac D. Phillips,	Hockessing, Del.,	5th mo., "
847. Stephen A. Webb,	Pennsbury, Pa.,	" ".
848. William Marsh,	Concord, Pa.,	" "
849. John Painter,	Birmingham, Pa.,	3d mo., 1834.
850. Henry C. Townsend,	West Chester, Pa.,	4th mo., "
851. Edward Maule,	Philadelphia, Pa.,	4th mo., 1833.
852. George C. Townsend,	"	5th mo., "
853. Jacob V. Thomas,	Bellefonte, Pa.,	" "
854. Josiah T. Cook,	Isle of Wight Co., Va.,	4th mo., 1835.
855. Jacob D. Valentine,	Bellefonte, Pa.,	5th mo., 1833.
856. Allen Hinchman,	Philadelphia, Pa.,	10th mo., "
857. Joseph S. Redman,	Haddonfield, N. J.,	5th mo., "
858. Oliver Paxson,	Solebury, Pa.,	10th mo., 1834.
859. Jonathan E. Parke,	Downingtown, Pa.,	6th mo., "

STUDENTS.

SECOND THOUSAND.

NAME.	RESIDENCE.	DATE OF ENTRY.
860. Jesse Hewes,	Upper Chichester, Pa.,	5th mo., 1833.
861. James Lord,	Woodbury, N. J.,	1st mo., "
862. George W. Trimble,	Concord, Pa.,	10th mo., "
863. Nathan Pennell,	Upper Chichester, Pa.,	5th mo., "
864. Samuel Marshall,	Concord, Pa.,	9th mo., "
865. Mordecai Lewis,	Springfield, Pa.,	5th mo., "
866. John Ogden,	"	10th mo., "
867. Joseph Hooton,	Moorestown, N. J.,	2d mo., "
868. William L. Green,	Providence, Pa.,	6th mo., "
869. Amos W. House,	Pennsbury, Pa.,	11th mo., "
870. Charles Sharpless,	London Britain, Pa.,	9th mo., "
871. William Boustead,	Philadelphia, Pa.,	5th mo., 1834.
872. Charles Middleton,	"	6th mo., 1833.
873. Richard Walmsley,	Byberry, Pa.,	4th mo., 1834.
874. Samuel Roberts,	Cropwell, N. J.,	4th mo., 1833.
875. Abm. P. Rudolph,	Springfield, Pa.,	3d mo., 1834.
876. Henry L. Shotwell,	Philadelphia, Pa.,	5th mo., "
877. Thomas Ballenger,	"	5th mo., 1833.
878. Albanus Smith,	"	6th mo., 1834.
879. William Thomas,	Bensalem, Pa.,	6th mo., 1833.
880. Isaac Evans,	Lampeter, Pa.,	11th mo., "
881. Charles Canby,	Philadelphia, Pa.,	2d mo., 1834.
882. John Canby,	"	" "
883. George Pratt,	New London, Pa.,	" "
884. Truman Forsythe,	Goshen, Pa.,	" "
885. Edwin A. Tyson,	Philadelphia, Pa.,	4th mo., 1833.
886. Charles Moon,	Fallsington, Pa.,	" "
887. Levis Newlin,	Middletown, Pa.,	10th mo., "
888. John Newlin,	"	10th mo., 1834.
889. Joshua Newbold,	Byberry, Pa.,	6th mo., "
890. Joshua Jefferis,	Birmingham, Pa.,	3d mo., "
891. Joseph O. Ely,	Buckingham, Pa.,	6th mo., 1833.
892. William H. Trotter,	Philadelphia, Pa.,	" "
893. William H. Corse,	Wilmington, Del.,	7th mo., "
894. William Canby,	Wilmington, Del.,	4th mo., 1834.
895. William Tatnall,	"	" "
896. James Willits,	Philadelphia, Pa.,	2d mo., "
897. Henry Haines,	Evesham, N. J.,	3d mo., "
898. Joseph Mather,	Plymouth, Pa.,	10th mo., 1833.
899. Elias A. White,	———, N. C.,	4th mo., 1834.
900. Thomas W. Gardiner,	Evesham, N. J.,	3d mo., "
901. Joshua Haines,	Chester, N. J.,	11th mo., 1833.
902. Samuel R. Williams,	Philadelphia, Pa.,	4th mo., 1834.
903. Edward H. Taylor,	Taylorsville, Pa.,	11th mo., 1833.
904. Henry Taylor,	"	" "
905. George White,	Philadelphia, Pa.,	3d mo., 1834.
906. Peter S. Levick,	"	" "

GENERAL CATALOGUE.

SECOND THOUSAND.

NAME.	RESIDENCE.	DATE OF ENTRY.
907. James B. Dolby,	Philadelphia, Pa.,	3d mo., 1834.
908. Mahlon Kirkbride,	Fallsington, Pa.,	10th mo., 1833.
909. William A. Page,	Tuckerton, N. J.,	7th mo., 1835.
910. William H. Miller,	Philadelphia, Pa.,	5th mo., "
911. Chalkley Stokes,	Evesham, N. J.,	5th mo., 1834.
912. Charles Stokes,	"	" "
913. Samuel J. Wills,	Rancocas, N. J.,	11th mo., 1833.
914. Chalkley Wills,	"	" "
915. Paul H. Troth,	Waterford, N. J.,	10th mo., "
916. David Comfort,	White Marsh, Pa.,	10th mo., 1834.
917. Francis White,	———, N. C.,	5th mo., "
918. William Lloyd,	Philadelphia, Pa.,	5th mo., 1835.
919. James Ladd,	Smithfield, Ohio,	8th mo., 1833.
920. Harvey Sharpless,	Goshen, Pa.,	9th mo., 1834.
921. Mahlon Chambers,	New Garden, Pa.,	7th mo., "
922. Amos Evans,	Evesham, N. J.,	5th mo., 1833.
923. William Hughes,	London Grove, Pa.,	3d mo., 1834.
924. Caleb Parry,	Concord, Pa.,	9th mo., "
925. Amos Whitson,	Sadsbury, Pa.,	10th mo., "
926. Charles Paxson,	Philadelphia, Pa.,	3d mo., 1835.
927. Alb't L. Letchworth,	"	6th mo., 1834.
928. Thomas Evans,	Evesham, N. J.,	5th mo., 1833.
929. Joseph Chambers,	New Garden, Pa.,	9th mo., 1835.
930. Hibberd Puscy,	West Fallowfield, Pa.,	5th mo., 1834.
931. Caspar W. Acton,	Salem, N. J.,	11th mo., "
932. Jonathan T. Jones,	Lower Merion, Pa.,	3d mo., "
933. Caleb Taylor,	Philadelphia, Pa.,	" "
934. Clement W. Smith,	Salem, N. J.,	" "
935. John Bushman,	Fallsington, Pa.,	11th mo., "
936. J. C. Cowperthwaite,	"	8th mo., "
937. William Whitall,	Woodbury, N. J.,	4th mo., "
938. Edward H. Garrigues,	Philadelphia, Pa.,	3d mo., "
939. Wm. H. Garrigues,	"	" "
940. Benjamin W. Morris,	Muncy, Pa.,	10th mo., 1833.
941. Thomas Lamborn,	New Garden, Pa.,	5th mo., 1834.
942. William G. Phillips,	Hockessing, Del.,	2d mo., "
943. Dell P. Peters,	Concord, Pa.,	6th mo., "
944. Jefferis Wilson,	Philadelphia, Pa.,	" "
945. Robert H. Thomas,	Abington, Pa.,	2d mo., 1835.
946. John P. Lewis,	Pottsville, Pa.,	3d mo., 1836.
947. Edward Tatum,	Woodbury, N. J.,	9th mo., 1834.
948. Edwin Roberts,	Moorestown, N. J.,	11th mo., "
949. Thomas Baily,	East Bradford, Pa.,	10th mo., "
950. Samuel P. Baily,	"	" "
951. John Street,	Salem, Ohio,	9th mo., "
952. William C. Ivins,	Shrewsbury, N. J.,	5th mo., "
953. Caleb Emlen,	Philadelphia, Pa.,	3d mo., "

* Deceased at the school.

STUDENTS. 145

SECOND THOUSAND.

NAME.	RESIDENCE.	DATE OF ENTRY.
954. Dillwyn Woodward,	Crosswicks, N. J.,	5th mo., 1834.
955. Asa Hancock,	Burlington, N. J.,	3d mo., 1835.
956. Jesse Lippincott,	Haddonfield, N. J.,	5th mo., 1834.
957. Thomas Ball,	Richland, Pa.,	10th mo., "
958. Thomas L. Baily,	Philadelphia, Pa.,	6th mo., "
959. Abm. S. Ashbridge,	Downingtown, Pa.,	" "
960. Samuel Styer,	White Plain, Pa.,	11th mo., "
961. Henry Whitall.	Woodbury, N. J.,	4th mo., 1835.
962. Charles Bell,	White Marsh, Pa.,	2d mo., "
963. Samuel W. Taylor,	Camden, N. J.,	11th mo., 1834.
964. Benjamin H. Pitfield,	Philadelphia, Pa.,	9th mo., "
965. Joseph H. Branson,	"	6th mo., "
966. Henry Warrington,	Westfield, N. J.,	11th mo., "
968. Edgar Thorn,	Rahway, N. J.,	7th mo., "
969. Ridgway Moore,	Newtown, N. J.,	12th mo., "
970. Zebedee Nicholson,	Haddonfield, N. J.,	6th mo., "
971. James H. Ogden,	Springfield, N. J.,	2d mo., "
972. Stephen Atkinson,	Wrightstown, Pa.,	3d mo., 1835.
973. Thomas F. Barnett,	Philadelphia, Pa.,	7th mo., 1834.
974. Albin Pierce,	Pennsbury, Pa.,	11th mo., "
975. Joshua Fulton,	Sadsbury, Pa.,	8th mo., "
976. David C. Woodward,	Marshallton, Pa.,	" "
977. Thomas Gibbons,	Lampeter, Pa.,	11th mo., "
978. William Kinsey,	Wilmington, Del.,	6th mo., 1835.
979. Samuel S. Lewis,	Springfield, Pa.,	5th mo., "
980. Larkin Pennell,	Chichester, Pa.,	12th mo., 1834.
981. Morris R. Stroud,	Philadelphia, Pa.,	6th mo., "
982. Dell Pennell,	Darby, Pa.,	" "
983. William D. Stroud,	Philadelphia, Pa.,	1st mo., 1835.
984. Richard Wistar,	Salem, N. J.,	9th mo., 1834.
985. J. H. Satterthwaite,	Fallsington, Pa.,	" "
986. Joseph E. Haines,	Medford, N. J.,	5th mo., 1835.
987. Mifflin Morris,	Philadelphia, Pa.,	2d mo., "
988. Wm. F. Lippincott,	Salem, N. J.,	5th mo., "
989. Charles B. Williams,	Philadelphia, Pa.,	6th mo., 1834.
990. Joseph E. Allen,	———, N. Y.,	" "
991. James B. Mode,	East Fallowfield, Pa.,	8th mo., "
992. William B. Coale,	Deer Creek, Md.,	" "
993. James Worthington,	"	5th mo., 1835.
994. William Powell,	Easton, Md.,	9th mo., 1834.
995. Samuel Dugdale,	Trenton, N. J.,	4th mo., 1835.
996. Charles H. Parker,	Pennsbury, Pa.,	11th mo., 1834.
997. John James,	East Bradford, Pa.,	10th mo., "
998. William Pusey,	New Garden, Pa.,	" "
999. Nathan S. Yarnall,	Edgmont, Pa.,	5th mo., 1835.
1000. Benjamin Betts,	Unionville, Pa.,	4th mo., "

12

GENERAL CATALOGUE.

THIRD THOUSAND.

NAME.	RESIDENCE.	DATE OF ENTRY.
1. Nathan Garrett,	Upper Darby, Pa.,	5th mo., 1835.
2. Samuel S. Boone,	Georgetown, Pa.,	4th mo., "
3. Joseph B. Taylor,	Springfield, Pa.,	11th mo., "
4. Joseph Stapler,	Newtown, Pa.,	5th mo., "
5. Joshua Cresson,	Philadelphia, Pa.,	1st mo., 1836.
6. Benjamin J. Edwards,	"	2d mo., 1835.
7. Orrin Pharo,	Barnegat, N. J.,	5th mo., "
8. George Collins,	"	" "
9. Samuel B. Walton,	Byberry, Pa.,	" "
10. Charles Janney,	Philadelphia, Pa.,	4th mo., "
11. Francis Janney,	"	" "
12. Thomas Dilworth,	Lumberville, Pa.,	6th mo., "
13. Abra'm G. McIlvain,	Philadelphia, Pa.,	12th mo., "
14. Amos Taylor,	Recklesstown, N. J.,	6th mo., "
16. Jeremiah Bonsall,	Philadelphia, Pa.,	12th mo., "
17. James L. Webb,	"	5th mo., "
18. Joseph Jones,	Abington, Pa.,	12th mo., "
19. John Spencer,	Gwynedd, Pa.,	10th mo., "
20. Joseph A. Malin,	Whiteland, Pa.,	5th mo., "
21. Robert P. Thomas,	Philadelphia, Pa.,	3d mo., "
22. Alfred Walton,	West Chester, Pa.,	4th mo., "
23. Parvin Smith,	Sadsbury, Pa.,	9th mo., "
24. Lewis Gause,	Concord, Pa.,	3d mo., "
25. Samuel Kimberly,	Salem, Ohio,	6th mo., "
26. Hiram Roberts,	Montgomery Co., Pa.,	9th mo., "
27. John Edge,	Downingtown, Pa.,	5th mo., "
28. John E. Klein,	Madison Co., Va.,	4th mo., 1844.
29. William Burgess,	Fallsington, Pa.,	11th mo., 1835.
30. Joseph Rhoads,	Springfield, Pa.,	5th mo., "
31. Thomas B. Dallam,	Deer Creek, Md.,	" "
32. William Dallam,	"	" "
33. Levick Palmer,	Smyrna, Del.,	6th mo., "
34. Daniel Palmer,	"	" "
35. George Williamson,	Newtown, Pa.,	" "
36. James M. Price,	Wilmington, Del.,	" "
37. Henry Handy,	Baltimore, Md.,	" "
38. William Pyle,	Hockessing, Del.,	7th mo., "
39. Nathan J. Sharpless,	Downingtown, Pa.,	10th mo., "
40. William W. Smedley,	Middletown, Pa.,	" "
41. Hugh Pound,	Plainfield, N. J.,	5th mo., 1836.
42. Samuel Pound,	"	" "
43. William Wetherill,	Stroudsburg, Pa.,	" 1835.
44. Aaron N. Haines,	Medford, N. J.,	4th mo., 1836.
45. Isaac Pedrich,	Pedrictown, N. J.,	7th mo., 1835.
46. Richard W. Tyson,	Baltimore, Md.,	6th mo., "
47. Joseph R. Fisher,	Woodbury, N. J.,	9th mo., "
48. John W. Wilson,	Baltimore, Md.,	6th mo., "

STUDENTS. 147

THIRD THOUSAND.

NAME.	RESIDENCE.	DATE OF ENTRY.
49. Ellwood Kay,	Swedesborough, N. J.,	10th mo., 1835
50. Gideon Cotant,	Stroudsburg, Pa.,	12th mo., "
51. Thomas Owen,	Woodbury, N. J.,	8th mo., "
52. Milton Smith,	Unionville, Pa.,	9th mo., "
53. Emmor Hickman,	Goshen, Pa.,	" "
54. Samuel W. Maris,	Chester, Pa.,	11th mo., "
55. William Maris,	"	" "
56. James Pusey,	Sadsbury, Pa.,	9th mo., "
57. James Cooper,	"	" "
58. Benjamin Taylor,	West Goshen, Pa.,	10th mo., "
59. John Deprefontaine,	Chichester, Pa.,	4th mo., "
60. Robert Morris,	———, Ind.,	11th mo., "
61. Ebenezer L. Bruff,	Philadelphia, Pa.,	6th mo., "
62. Joseph Elfreth,	"	10th mo., "
63. Joseph P. Risley,		
65. Joshua Woolston,	Fallsington, Pa.,	10th mo., "
66. Benj. H. Woolman,	Burlington, N. J.,	" "
67. William Fisher,	Woodbury, N. J.,	9th mo., "
68. Nathan Roberts,	Newportville, Pa.,	4th mo., 1836.
69. Elisha Clark,	Princeton, N. J.,	" "
70. Wm. Worthington,	Deer Creek, Md.,	12th mo., 1835.
71. Pennell Larkin,	Chichester, Pa.,	4th mo., 1836.
72. Nathan R. Vail,	Plainfield, N. J.,	" "
73. Richard B. McCay,	———, Md.,	" "
74. Samuel J. Peters,	Aston, Pa.,	6th mo., "
75. James Smith,	Unionville, Pa.,	10th mo., "
76. Joseph Wilson,	Hockessing, Del.,	4th mo., "
77. Francis Lightfoot,	Goshen, Pa.,	10th mo., 1837.
78. Jonas Edge,	Downingtown, Pa.,	5th mo., 1836.
79. Benj. Thatcher,	Thornbury, Pa.,	4th mo., "
80. Caleb Baldwin,	Downingtown, Pa.,	7th mo., "
81. William F. Lukens,	Plymouth, Pa.,	5th mo., "
82. Edward Thomas,	———, Pa.,	4th mo., "
83. Jonathan Thomas,	"	" "
84. Micajah Gardiner,	Evesham, N. J.,	" "
85. Henry Corlies,	Shrewsbury, N. J.,	" "
86. Thomas S. Pike,	Burlington, N. J.,	
87. Thomas K. Taylor,	Mt. Holly, N. J.,	10th mo., "
88. George S. Elliott,	Philadelphia, Pa.,	3d mo., 1837.
89. Jeremiah Healy,	Morrisville, Pa.,	5th mo., 1836.
90. Josiah Warrington,	Moorestown, N. J.,	9th mo., "
91. Joseph J. Edwards,	Philadelphia, Pa.,	3d mo., "
92. Edward T. Parker,	"	8th mo., "
93. William Thompson,	Tullytown, Pa.,	10th mo., "
94. Samuel Woolston,	Fallsington, Pa.,	" "
95. Edward M. Smith,	Philadelphia, Pa.,	2d mo., 1837.
96. Charles B. Ely,	Buckingham, Pa.,	3d mo., "

GENERAL CATALOGUE.

THIRD THOUSAND.

NAME.	RESIDENCE.	DATE OF ENTRY.
97. William P. Ely,	Buckingham, Pa.,	3d mo., 1837.
98. Warner M. Raisin,	Philadelphia, Pa.,	11th mo., 1836.
99. Wm. L. Mendenhall,	Muncy, Pa.,	4th mo., 1837.
100. John W. Buzby,	Moorestown, N. J.,	5th mo., 1836.
101. Ezra Hunt,	Mt. Holly, N. J.,	" "
102. James A. Willits,	Philadelphia, Pa.,	" "
103. Charles Leeds,	Egg Harbor, N. J.,	3d mo., 1837.
104. Charles Wetherill,	Stroudsburg, Pa.,	5th mo., 1836.
105. Robert C. White,	Shrewsbury, N. J.,	4th mo., "
106. William Pennell,	Darby, Pa.,	10th mo., "
107. Jesse J. Baily,	Bradford, Pa.,	" "
108. Joshua B. Lee,	Exeter, Pa.,	12th mo., "
109. Emmor Haines,	Lockport, Pa.,	8th mo., "
110. William B. Cole,	Sadsbury, Pa.,	4th mo., 1837.
111. M. H. Gillingham,	Philadelphia, Pa.,	6th mo., 1836.
112. C. W. Thompson,	Salem, N. J.,	9th mo., "
113. John E. Deacon,	Mt. Holly, N. J.,	8th mo., "
114. David H. Livezey,	Medford, N. J.,	6th mo., "
115. Charles Potts,	Philadelphia, Pa.,	7th mo., "
116. Gideon D. Scull,	Sculltown, N. J.,	8th mo., "
117. John Brown,	Fallsington, Pa.,	10th mo., "
118. Joseph K. Bacon,	Philadelphia, Pa.,	6th mo., "
119. Charles S. Ogden,	Woodstown, N. J.,	8th mo., "
120. William G. Palmer,	Sandy Spring, Md.,	11th mo., "
121. Moses G. Palmer,	"	11th mo., "
122. Richard J. Hillman,	Haddonfield, N. J.,	10th mo., "
123. Barzillai Leeds,	Egg Harbor, N. J.,	" "
124. Ellis Hancock,	Burlington, N. J.,	12th mo., "
125. Wardell Ivins,	Plainfield, N. J.,	10th mo., "
126. David L. Vail,	"	9th mo., "
127. Preston Wickersham,	New Garden, Pa.,	10th mo., "
128. Benjamin Hoopes,	"	" "
129. Charles V. Peters,	Aston, Pa.,	1st mo., 1837.
130. William Webster,	Middletown, Pa.,	10th mo., 1836.
131. George Spencer,	Gwynedd, Pa.,	" "
132. John P. Hutchinson,	Philadelphia, Pa.,	" "
133. C. C. W. Taylor,	"	" "
134. John W. Taylor,	"	" "
135. Henry Willits,	Tuckerton, N. J.,	" "
136. Nathan B. Willits,	Haddonfield, N. J.,	4th mo., 1837.
137. Charles Lippincott,	Mauch Chunk, Pa.,	12th mo., 1836.
138. Samuel Smith,	Philadelphia, Pa.,	5th mo., 1837.
139. Ed. A. Crenshaw,	Richmond, Va.,	4th mo., "
140. Thomas Seal,	Unionville, Pa.,	10th mo., 1836.
141. Howard Pugh,	"	" "
142. Josiah Hibberd,	Whiteland, Pa.,	4th mo., 1837.
143. John F. Brinton,	Lancaster Co., Pa.,	5th mo., "

STUDENTS.

THIRD THOUSAND.

NAME.	RESIDENCE.	DATE OF ENTRY.
144. Thomas C. Carey,	Baltimore, Md.,	10th mo., 1836.
145. Frederic Richards,	Wilmington, Del.,	" "
146. James H. Crew,	Richmond, Va.,	11th mo., "
147. Thomas M. Crew,	"	" "
148. Silas D. Pound,	Plainfield, N. J.,	" "
149. John E. Baldwin,	Downingtown, Pa.,	" "
150. Thornton Smith,	Sadsbury, Pa.,	" "
151. Joshua Howell,	Edgmont, Pa.,	5th mo., 1837.
152. John B. Parrott,	Still Pond, Md.,	4th mo., "
153. Charles Cooper,	Sadsbury, Pa.,	3d mo., "
154. Oliver Scott,	Montgomery Co., Md.,	12th mo., 1843.
155. Townsend Hoopes,	Downingtown, Pa.,	4th mo., 1837.
156. Henry Hoopes,	"	" "
157. N. D. Comstock,*	Lockport, N. Y.,	5th mo., "
158. Isaac T. Comstock,	"	" "
159. Benjamin Warner,	Muncy, Pa..	4th mo., "
160. John Ridgway,	Tuckerton, N. J.,	6th mo., "
161. Joseph S. Elkinton,	Philadelphia, Pa.,	4th mo., 1839.
162. J. Clemson Sharpless,	Downingtown, Pa.,	5th mo., 1844.
163. Isaac C. Quinby,	Brandywine, Pa.,	3d mo., 1837.
164. Watson F. Quinby,	"	" "
165. Spencer Middleton,	Moorestown, N. J.,	4th mo., "
166. George F. Perry,	———, N. Y.,	4th mo., 1844.
167. William H. Bines,	Germantown, Pa.,	4th mo., 1837.
168. Samuel M. Bines,	"	" "
169. William J. Canby,	Philadelphia, Pa.,	" "
170. Caleb Canby,	"	" "
171. Ezra Leeds,	"	" "
172. Thomas Lamborn,	New Garden, Pa.,	" "
173. John B. Wickersham,	Philadelphia, Pa.,	" "
174. Joseph Brown,	"	10th mo., "
175. Charles Taylor,	Mt. Holly, N. J.,	" "
176. Joseph Brinton,	Lancaster Co., Pa.,	4th mo., "
178. Ellwood Comfort,	Fallsington, Pa.,	10th mo., "
179. Thomas Wistar,	Philadelphia, Pa.,	" "
180. Benj. W. M. Ellis,	Muncy, Pa.,	5th mo., "
181. Benjamin Philips,	Sadsbury, Pa.,	10th mo., "
182. Charles J. Allen,	Philadelphia, Pa.,	6th mo., "
183. John Tatum,	Woodbury, N. J.,	10th mo., "
184. Abraham M. Vail,	Plainfield, N. J.,	4th mo., 1844.
185. Ellis Smedley,	Middletown, Pa.,	10th mo., 1837.
186. Isaac Yarnall,	Edgmont, Pa.,	" "
187. Nicholas Newlin,	Middletown, Pa.,	" "
188. Joseph Passmore,	Goshen, Pa.,	" "
189. William Trimble,	Whiteland, Pa.,	" "

* Deceased at the school, Third mo. 1st, 1839.

GENERAL CATALOGUE.

THIRD THOUSAND.

NAME.	RESIDENCE.	DATE OF ENTRY.
190. George Spencer,	Gwynedd, Pa.,	10th mo., 1837.
191. James C. Valentine,	Philadelphia, Pa.,	5th mo., "
192. Jacob Valentine,	"	" "
193. Nathaniel B. Brown,	"	6th mo., "
194. John W. Parker,	Long Branch, N. J.,	10th mo., "
195. Benjamin C. Parker,	"	" "
196. Reuben Ellis,	Plymouth, Pa.,	" "
197. John J. Wilson,	"	" "
198. Oliver Wilson,	"	" "
199. Edwin Scott,	Baltimore, Md.,	5th mo., 1844.
200. Charles Wills,	Rancocas, N. J.,	10th mo., 1837.
201. Daniel B. Price,	Fallsington, Pa.,	10th mo., "
202. Nathaniel Lippincott,	Chester, N. J.,	4th mo., 1838.
203. Thomas Kimber,	Philadelphia, Pa.,	7th mo., 1837.
204. Samuel R. Shipley,		4th mo., 1838.
205. Charles Mather,	White Marsh, Pa.,	10th mo., 1837.
206. Emmor K. Massey,	Philadelphia, Pa.,	" "
207. John N. Reeve,	Medford, N. J.,	10th mo., 1838.
208. Cyrus Linton,	Newtown, Pa.,	10th mo., 1844.
209. Aaron J. Michener,	"	" "
210. John G. Pusey,	Sadsbury, Pa.,	10th mo., 1837.
211. Henry Sharpless,	Chester, Pa.,	" "
212. David Eldridge,	Goshen, Pa.,	" "
213. David B. Griscom,	Nottingham, Pa.,	" "
214. Ezra Kinsey,	Wilmington, Del.,	" "
215. William J. Parker,	Philadelphia, Pa.,	" "
216. Richard Bruff,	"	" "
217. Samuel Mitchell,	Wilmington, Del.,	" "
218. Clarkson Ogden,	Buttertown, N. J.,	" "
219. Benj. W. Passmore,	Goshen, Pa.,	11th mo., "
220. Samuel Trimble,	Concord, Pa.,	10th mo., "
221. Isaac Morgan,	Aston, Pa.,	" "
222. Thomas H. Hall,	Uwchlan, Pa.,	" "
223. Wm. S. Thompson,	New Garden, Pa.,	" "
224. Charles Mather,	Plymouth, Pa.,	" "
225. J. C. Satterthwaite,	Tecumseh, Mich.,	" "
226. David Nields,	Makefield, Pa.,	4th mo., 1838.
227. Charles Lewis,	New Garden, Pa.,	" "
228. Edmund Hunt,	Moorestown, N. J.,	" "
229. Henry Parker,	Philadelphia, Pa.,	5th mo., "
230. Isaac Pyle,	Hockessing, Del.,	4th mo., "
231. James R. Squibb,	Philadelphia, Pa.,	" "
232. Benjamin Lippincott,	Mauch Chunk, Pa.,	4th mo., 1839.
233. Charles Eldridge,	Sculltown, N. J.,	4th mo., 1838.
234. John F. Edmondson,	Philadelphia, Pa.,	6th mo., "
235. Joshua L. Baily,	"	4th mo., "
236. Isaac M. Lowry,		

STUDENTS.

THIRD THOUSAND.

NAME.	RESIDENCE.	DATE OF ENTRY.
237. Samuel C. Clement,	Wilmington, Del.,	4th mo., 1838.
238. Henry Maule,	Philadelphia, Pa.,	" "
239. Jeremiah Willits,	"	" "
240. George D. Kimber,	New York city, N.Y.,	" "
241. James L. Clemson,	Sadsbury, Pa.,	" "
242. Richard H. Wilson,	Salem, N. J.,	" "
243. Samuel Ogden,	Springfield, N. J.,	" "
244. Jacob Hewes,	Chichester, Pa.,	" "
245. Samuel Knight,	Philadelphia, Pa.,	10th mo., 1845.
246. George Coates,	Coatesville, Pa.,	4th mo., 1838.
247. George Baily,	"	6th mo., "
248. Lewis Forsythe,	Birmingham, Pa.,	4th mo., "
249. Emmor Brinton,	"	" "
250. George Martin,	Chichester, Pa.,	" "
251. Nathan S. Martin,	"	" "
252. William Evans,	Springfield, Pa.,	" "
253. Joseph M. Kaighn,	Kaighn's Point, N. J.,	" "
254. Joseph Stevenson,	Plainfield, N. J.,	" "
255. James W. Stevenson,	"	" "
256. Nathan S. Brinton,	Lampeter, Pa.,	10th mo., "
257. Parvin Masters,	Muncy, Pa.,	4th mo., "
258. William M. Walton,	——, N. Y.,	" "
259. Benjamin Davis,	Radnor, Pa.,	" "
260. James W. Kay,	Buttertown, N. J.,	" "
261. William P. Wilson,	Plainfield, N. J.,	5th mo., "
262. Eayre Oliphant,	New Lisbon, N. J.,	10th mo., "
263. Albert Pharo,	Tuckerton, N. J.,	4th mo., "
264. Benjamin Sleeper,	Philadelphia, Pa.,	" "
265. Mordecai L. Maule,	Radnor, Pa.,	" "
266. Thomas M. Yardley,	Yardleyville, Pa.,	" "
267. Thomas E. Lukens,	Philadelphia, Pa.,	10th mo., "
268. Reuben Lukens,	"	" "
269. Evan Levis,	"	4th mo., "
270. James J. Levick,	"	" "
271. Joseph Williams,	Sadsbury, Pa.,	10th mo., "
272. David Chambers,	White Clay Creek, Del.,	4th mo., "
273. Edward Baily,	Coatesville, Pa.,	" "
274. David Buzby,	Wilmington, Del.,	" "
275. Thomas M. Harvey,	Penn, Pa.,	
276. Oliver Knight,	Philadelphia, Pa.,	10th mo., "
277. John B. Hillman,	Haddonfield, N. J.,	4th mo., 1844.
278. Joseph Reeve,	....	" 1839.
279. Thomas J. Bell,	Whitemarsh, Pa.,	10th mo., 1838.
280. Henry Mendenhall,	Edgmont, Pa.,	" "
281. J. P. Hutchinson,	——, N. Y.,	4th mo., "
282. J. F. Hutchinson,	"	" "
283. Ellwood Johnson,	Germantown, Pa.,	" "

GENERAL CATALOGUE.

THIRD THOUSAND.

NAME.	RESIDENCE.	DATE OF ENTRY.
284. Charles Parry,	Moorestown, N. J.,	10th mo., 1838.
285. Job Haines,	———, N. J.,	4th mo., "
286. H. D. Thompson,	Philadelphia, Pa.,	" "
287. Samuel Levis,	"	10th mo., "
288. Edward Reeve,	Medford, N. J.,	" "
289. John M. Bacon,	Greenwich, N. J.,	4th mo., 1839.
290. George Rhoads,	Springfield, Pa.,	10th mo., 1838.
291. Job M. Lewis,	Philadelphia, Pa.,	4th mo., 1839.
292. Francis W. Lee,	Exeter, Pa.,	10th mo., "
293. Samuel Walton,	Philadelphia, Pa.,	5th mo., 1840.
294. Gilpin F. Walton,	New Garden, Pa.,	10th mo., 1844.
295. Sam'l M. Sheppard,	Greenwich, N. J.,	4th mo., 1839
296. James Phipps,	Whitemarsh, Pa.,	10th mo., "
297. Elton B. Gifford,	Tuckerton, N. J.,	5th mo., 1840.
298. Isaac J. Wistar,	Philadelphia, Pa.,	4th mo., 1839.
299. Marshall Taylor,	Makefield, Pa.,	" "
300. Solomon Jones,	Byberry, Pa.,	11th mo., 1838.
301. William H. Webb,	Kennet, Pa.,	10th mo., "
302. Joseph R. Marsh,	Concord, Pa.,	" "
303. Jesse E. Maris,	Chester, Pa.,	" "
304. Ellis Pusey,	Unionville, Pa.,	" "
305. John Walker,	Mill Creek, Del.,	" "
306. James Davis,	East Caln, Pa.,	" "
307. Joel Thompson,	New Garden, Pa.,	4th mo., 1839.
308. Jacob Howell,	Edgmont, Pa.,	10th mo., 1838.
309. Albert Hall,	Ilestonville, Pa.,	" "
310. George E. Hall,	"	" "
311. Joseph Poole,	Uwchlan, Pa.,	" "
312. Gerard C. Kersey,	West Chester, Pa.,	" "
313. Pennock Pusey,	Wilmington, Del.,	" "
314. James Thompson,	New Garden, Pa.,	" "
315. Richard Sloan,	Mt. Holly, N. J.,	4th mo., 1839.
316. Hibberd Yarnall,	Edgmont, Pa.,	10th mo., 1844.
317. Josiah F. Jones,	Plymouth, Pa.,	6th mo., 1839.
318. James S. Jones,	"	" "
319. Wm. L. Marshall,	Kennet, Pa.,	10th mo., "
320. Samuel Stevenson,	Plainfield, N. J.,	4th mo., "
321. Charles Coates,	Coatesville, Pa.,	4th mo., "
322. Elisha H. Hunt,	Moorestown, N. J.,	" "
323. Charles Cooper,	Sadsbury, Pa.,	" "
324. Edward C. Phillips,	Christiana, Del.,	10th mo., "
325. Wm. P. Eldridge,	Goshen, Pa.,	" "
326. Jonathan Cleaver,	King of Prussia, Pa.,	4th mo., "
327. Charles P. Hewes,	Concord, Pa.,	10th mo., "
328. Wm. Marshall,	"	4th mo., "
329. William Rhoads,	Springfield, Pa.,	10th mo., "
330. Thomas Yearsley,	Coatesville, Pa.,	4th mo., "

STUDENTS.

THIRD THOUSAND.

NAME.	RESIDENCE.	DATE O ENTRY.
331. L. M. Elkinton,	Philadelphia, Pa.,	4th mo., 1839.
332. William L. Baily,	"	" "
333. William J. Smedley,	"	" "
334. George Haines,	Medford, N. J.,	" "
335. Benjamin Harper,	Philadelphia, Pa.,	" "
336. Edwin M. Haines,	Medford, N. J.,	" "
337. Nathan Shotwell,	Philadelphia, Pa.,	" "
338. George W. Sheppard,	Greenwich, N. J.,	" "
339. Isaac Jones,	Camden, N. J.,	" "
340. Lindley M. Perkins,	Philadelphia, Pa.,	" "
341. Charles F. Redman,	Haddonfield, N. J.,	" "
342. Daniel Fletcher,	Philadelphia, Pa.,	" "
343. Sam'l P. Nicholson,	"	" "
344. Jesse W. Heacock,	Germantown, Pa.,	" "
345. Ezra Stokes,	Marlton, N. J.,	10th mo., "
346. Edwin Stokes,	"	" "
347. Thomas Warrington,	Moorestown, N. J.,	" "
348.		
349. Jesse Smith,	Philadelphia, Pa.,	4th mo., 1839.
350. John Richardson,	Wilmington, Del.,	" "
351. Jos. P. Richardson,	"	" "
352. David Evans,	Willistown, Pa.,	" "
353. Charles Handy,	Baltimore, Md.,	" "
354. William Handy,	"	" "
355. Elisha Griffin,	Poughkeepsie, N. Y.,	10th mo., "
356. Joseph L. Ballance,	Kirk's Mills, Pa.,	" "
357. Jesse Haines,	Muncy, Pa.,	" "
358. Thomas Pierson,	Concord, Pa.,	" "
359. J. M. Albertson,	Plymouth, Pa.,	" "
360. Joseph Sharpless,	East Caln, Pa.,	" "
361. Oliver Sharpless,	"	" "
362. Enos Thomas,	Goshen, Pa.,	" "
363. Thomas Rudolph,	Springfield, Pa.,	" "
364. Eber Heston,	Parkesburg, Pa.,	" "
365. Samuel S. Downing,	Downingtown, Pa.,	" "
366. Samuel Benington,	Concord, Pa.,	" "
367. George B. Lownes,	Springfield, Pa.,	" "
368. Pennock Hucy,	Kennet, Pa.,	" "
369. William Stephens,	Tredyffrin, Pa.,	" "
370. George Jones,	Cheltenham, Pa.,	" "
371. Powell Stackhouse,	Philadelphia, Pa.,	" "
372. J. Gardiner Taylor,	Cinnaminson, N. J.,	" "
373. Chas. H. Pancoast,	Philadelphia, Pa.,	5th mo., "
374. Bolton Lloyd,	"	10th mo., "
375. Robert Underhill,	New York, N. Y.,	" "
376. Robert W. Titus,	———, L. I.,	" "
377. Daniel Titus,	"	" "

THIRD THOUSAND.

NAME.	RESIDENCE.	DATE OF ENTRY.
378. Robert D. Congdon,	Poughkeepsie, N. Y.,	10th mo., 1839.
379. Ellwood Thomas,	Philadelphia, Pa.,	" "
380. Benjamin F. Taylor,	Taylorsville, Pa.,	5th mo., 1840.
381. Lambert Ivins,	Shrewsbury, N. J.,	10th mo., 1839.
382. Elton Thomas,	Philadelphia, Pa.,	" "
383. Henry J. Williams,*	"	5th mo., 1840.
384. Joseph Stokes,	Moorestown, N. J.,	" "
385. Abraham Trimble,	Whiteland, Pa.,	" "
386. John Sloan,	Mt. Holly, N. J.,	" "
387. Charles Sloan,	"	" "
388. Joseph Willits,	Philadelphia, Pa.,	" "
389. George Canby,	"	" "
390. Ezra Bell,	Westtown, Pa.,	10th mo., 1839.
391. Mark Healy,	Fallsington, Pa.,	" "
392. John Roberts,	West Chester, Pa.,	5th mo., 1840.
393. Samuel Hewes,	Chichester, Pa.,	10th mo., 1839.
394. Wm. P. Sharpless,	Concord, Pa.,	5th mo., 1840.
395. Eli Thompson,	New Garden, Pa.,	" "
396. Jacob Chandler,	New London, Pa.,	11th mo., "
397. Joseph H. Peters,	Concord, Pa.,	5th mo., "
398. William Denny,	Wilmington, Del.,	" "
399. Elies Dawson,	Easton, Md.,	" "
400. Joshua Eyre,	Chichester, Pa.,	" "
401. Samuel Troth,	Camden, N. J.,	" "
402. William Tudor,	Adams Co., Pa.,	" "
403. Isaac Tudor,	"	" "
404. Samuel E. Lloyd,	Wilmington, Del.,	6th mo., "
405. Joseph B. Cooper,	Sadsbury, Pa.,	5th mo., "
406. Benj. W. Swayne,	London Grove, Pa.,	" "
407. Wm. Marshall Swayne,	"	" "
408. Edward H. Hall,	Hestonville, Pa.,	" "
409. William Kirk,	Goshen, Pa.,	" "
410. William H. Walter,	Kennet, Pa.,	" "
411. Sam. B. Middleton,	Crosswicks, N. J.,	" "
412. John J. Murray,	New York, N. Y.,	" "
413. Henry Tatnall,	Brandywine, Pa.,	" "
414. Nicholas Taylor,	Chester Co., Pa.,	11th mo., 1840.
415. Philip P. Townsend,	West Chester, Pa.,	5th mo., "
416. Israel Pusey,	Columbia, Pa.,	" "
417. Isaac Pusey,	"	" "
418. George Wilson,	West Grove, Pa.,	" "
419. Lewis Pusey,	New Garden, Pa.,	" "
420. William R. Peters,	Aston, Pa.,	" "
421. Erasmus W. Haines,	Christiana, Pa.,	" "
422. Benjamin H. Haines,	"	" "
423. John P. Rhoads,	Philadelphia, Pa.,	" "
424. Edward H. Magill,	New Hope, Pa.,	" "

*Deceased at the school, Twelfth mo., 1842.

STUDENTS. 155

THIRD THOUSAND.

NAME.	RESIDENCE.	DATE OF ENTRY.
425. Caspar P. Lukens,	Philadelphia, Pa.,	5th mo., 1840.
426. Samuel Biddle,	"	" "
427. James E. Underhill,	New York, N. Y.,	" "
428. Edm'd A. Crenshaw,	Richmond, Va.,	" "
429. Edward R. Maule,	Philadelphia, Pa.,	" "
430. Edward Potts,	"	" "
431. Wm. C. Sheppard,	Greenwich, N. J.,	" "
432. David Heston,	Fallsington, Pa.,	" "
433. John Hoopes,	East Caln, Pa.,	10th mo., 1844.
434. Joseph S. Lewis,	Smyrna, Del.,	5th mo., 1840.
435. Richard Wood,	Philadelphia, Pa.,	" "
436. William Chambers,	"	11th mo., "
437. Charles Darnell,	Evesham, N. J.,	5th mo., 1841.
438. Oliver Norris,	Franklinville, Md.,	10th mo., 1844.
439. Albanus Styer,	White Plain, Pa.,	" "
440. James Yarnall,	Edgmont, Pa.,	" "
441. William L. Baily,	Coatesville, Pa.,	11th mo., 1841.
442. Joseph P. Smedley,	Edgmont, Pa.,	" 1840.
443. Lewis Passmore,	Strickersville, Pa.,	" "
444. Cloud Pyle,	Chester Co., Pa.,	" "
445. Samuel Hughes,	Chatham, Pa.,	" 1841.
446. Amos Forsythe,	Chesterfield, N. J.,	5th mo., "
447. William D. Griffin,	Poughkeepsie, N. Y.,	11th mo., 1840.
448. Jacob Griffin,	"	" "
449. Lewis Palmer,	Upper Providence, Pa.,	10th mo., 1844.
450. Charles Cotant,	Stroudsburg, Pa.,	11th mo., 1840.
451. Job Scott,	Worcester, Pa.,	" "
452. Thomas Middleton,	Philadelphia, Pa.,	" "
453. Henry W. Puckett,	Newport, Ind.,	" "
454. Septimus Roberts,	———, Pa.,	" "
455. David Haines,	Medford, N. J.,	" "
456. George D. Leaver,	Burlington, N. J.,	" "
457. James Butler,	Uwchlan, Pa.,	5th mo., 1841.
458. James H. Wilson,	Easton, Md.,	" "
459. Caleb Hewes,	Middletown, Pa.,	" "
460. Joel B. Pusey,	London Grove, Pa.,	4th mo., 1844.
461. Wm. H. Nicholson,	Haddonfield, N. J.,	11th mo., 1840.
462. Abm. L. Pennock,	Upper Darby, Pa.,	5th mo., 1841.
463. John Humphreys,	Philadelphia, Pa.,	11th mo., "
464. John C. Snowdon,	"	5th mo., "
465. Benj. H. Lightfoot,	Dublin, Pa.,	" "
466. Richard Stephens,	King of Prussia, Pa.,	10th mo., 1844.
467. Amos Eastburn,	Attleboro, Pa.,	5th mo., 1841.
468. Nathan Folwell,	Springfield, N. J.,	" "
469. Edmund T. Wooley,	Shrewsbury, N. J.,	" "
470. Wm. T. Hopkins,	Easton, Md.,	" "
471. Amos S. Collins,	———, N. Y.,	" "

GENERAL CATALOGUE.

THIRD THOUSAND.

NAME.	RESIDENCE.	DATE OF ENTRY.
472. Owen Evans,	Springfield Pa.,	5th mo., 1841
473. Joseph G. Harlan,	W. Marlborough, Pa.,	" "
474. John P. Cheyney,	Doe Run, Pa.,	" "
475. John M. Lindley,	Downingtown, Pa.,	4th mo., 1842.
476. Nathan H. Johnson,	Germantown, Pa.,	5th mo., 1841.
477. William Eldridge,	Evesham, N. J.,	" "
478. John Ballenger,.	Woodbury, N. J.,	" "
479. George Massey,	Philadelphia, Pa.,	" "
480. Jesse Edgerton,	Barnesville, Ohio,	" "
481. Joseph Fell,	Springfield, Pa.,	" "
482. Jones Yerkes,	West Chester, Pa.,	4th mo., 1842.
483. Charles Wood,	——, N. Y.,	5th mo., 1841.
484. George Wood,	"	" "
485. R. H. Benington,	Garretsville, N. Y.,	11th mo., "
486. Joseph Good,	Jennerville, Pa.,	" "
487. Isaac Y. Smedley,	Edgmont, Pa.,	" "
488. Abram P. Smedley,	"	" "
489. Ellwood Garrett,	Birmingham, Pa.,	" "
490. John H. Stokes,	Moorestown, N. J.,	" "
491. Jacob M. Troth,	Camden, N. J.,	5th mo., "
492. Franklin Lloyd,	Philadelphia, Pa.,	" "
493. John Roberts,	Bristol, Pa.,	10th mo., 1844.
494. Amos Forsythe,	Chesterfield, N. J.,	5th mo., 1841.
495. Joseph Swayne,	York Co., Pa.,	10th mo., 1844.
496. John H. Ballenger,	Medford, N. J.,	11th mo., 1841.
497. J. T. Ballenger,	"	" "
498. Ezra Magarge,	Germantown, Pa.,	5th mo., "
499. Thomas Woolman,	Philadelphia, Pa.,	11th mo., "
500. George D. Heston,	Newtown, Pa.,	5th mo., "
501. Isaac S. Cassin,	Providence, Pa.,	11th mo., "
502. William B. Dixon,	Philadelphia, Pa.,	5th mo., "
503. William R. Grubb,	"	" "
504. William H. Black,	Jacksonville, N. J.,	11th mo., "
505. Levi Pownall,	Penningtonville, Pa.,	10th mo., 1844.
506. Joseph B. Cooper,	Newtown, N. J.,	11th mo., 1841.
507. Richard Wetherill,	Manayunk, Pa.,	4th mo., 1842.
508. Charles Lee,	Stonersville, Pa.,	11th mo., 1841.
509. John L. Trasel,	Blockley, Pa.,	" "
510. Edward G. Trasel,	"	" "
511. William M. Canby,	Wilmington, Del.,	" "
512. Ziba Ferris,	"	" "
513. William Betts,	"	" "
514. Nathan B. Smith,	Philadelphia, Pa.,	" "
515. John W. Hazard,	Dutchess Co., N. Y.,	" "
516. Francis Wistar,	Germantown, Pa.,	4th mo., 1842.
517. John Q. Adams,	Warren Co., N. J.,	10th mo., 1844.
518. Richard Pound,	Plainfield, N. J.,	" "

STUDENTS. 157

THIRD THOUSAND.

NAME.	RESIDENCE.	DATE OF ENTRY.
519. Robert S. Moore,	Baltimore, Md.,	4th mo., 1842.
520. Randall Malin,	Whiteland, Pa.,	11th mo., 1841.
521. John Rhoads,	Springfield, Pa.,	" "
522. Cheyney James,	Birmingham, Pa.,	" "
523. Alfred Williamson,	Newtown, Pa.,	" "
524. Isaac Good,	London Grove, Pa.,	" "
525. John Barton,	Haddonfield, N. J.,	" "
526. Isaac Mickle,	Camden, N. J.,	" "
527. William Janney,	Loudon Co., Va.,	4th mo., 1844.
528. Benj. H. Lightfoot,	Goshen, Pa.,	11th mo., 1841.
529. Thomas Pancoast,	Springfield, Pa.,	4th mo., 1842.
530. Thomas Bartram,	Marple, Pa.,	11th mo., 1841.
531. Jonathan Scott,	Worcester, Pa.,	" "
532. Joseph H. Cotant,	Stroudsburg, Pa.,	4th mo., 1842.
533. Barton Hoopes,	West Chester, Pa.,	" "
534. Charles Hayes,	Philadelphia, Pa.,	" "
535. Robert B. Bell,	Whitemarsh, Pa.,	" "
536. Henry W. Taylor,	Cinnaminson, N. J.,	" "
537. Albert Hendrickson,	Crosswicks, N. J.,	" "
538. Robert B. Rowand,	....	" "
539. Josiah J. Watson,	New Hope, Pa.,	" "
540. Sam'l M. Albertson,	Plymouth, Pa.,	5th mo., "
541. Thomas W. Harlan,	W. Marlborough, Pa.,	" "
542. William Smedley,	Edgmont, Pa.,	10th mo., "
543. Joseph Mendenhall,	"	" "
544. Joseph Hughes,	Chatham, Pa.,	" "
545. Aaron Davis,	Downingtown, Pa.,	" "
546. Joseph G. Taylor,	West Chester, Pa.,	" "
547. Richard Matthews,	Baltimore, Md.,	5th mo., 1845.
548. William W. Parker,	Parkersville, Pa.,	10th mo., 1842.
549. Joseph Lownes,	Springfield, Pa.,	" "
550. Francis Good,	Jennerville, Pa.,	" "
551. Richard J. Williams,	Philadelphia, Pa.,	4th mo., "
552. Josiah Wistar,	Salem, N. J.,	" "
553. Jos. W. Lippincott,	Moorestown, N. J.,	" "
554. Sam. L. Albertson,	Plymouth, Pa.,	5th mo., 1845.
555. George E. Elkinton,	Philadelphia, Pa.,	4th mo., 1842.
556. Edward R. Parry,	"	" "
557. Jacob W. Magill,	New Hope, Pa.,	" "
558. Jon. H. Woolman,	Rancocas, N. J.,	" "
559. Charles Hunt,	Philadelphia, Pa.,	" "
560. John B. Mickle,	Camden, N. J.,	" "
561. Francis Wistar,	Philadelphia, Pa.,	" "
562. Richard J. Allen,	Springfield, Pa.,	" "
563. John Gill,	Haddonfield, N. J.,	" "
564. John C. Remington,	Philadelphia, Pa.,	" "
565. Emlen Satterthwaite,	Crosswicks, N. J.,	10th mo., "

13   K

THIRD THOUSAND.

NAME.	RESIDENCE.	DATE OF ENTRY.
566. Samuel L. Burrough,	Haddonfield, N. J.,	4th mo., 1842.
567. John D. Haines,	Evesham, N. J.,	" "
568. George H. Sellers,	Seller's Mill, Pa.,	" "
569. Edward Taylor,	West Chester, Pa.,	10th mo., 1844.
570. Bolton L. Taylor,	"	" "
571. William Wilson,	Muncy, Pa.,	4th mo., 1842.
572. Thomas Yardley,	Yardleyville, Pa.,	" "
573. Evert J. Wendell,	Philadelphia, Pa.,	" "
574. Cyrus Cadwallader,	Fallsington, Pa.,	10th mo., "
575. Joseph H. Middleton,	Crosswicks, N. J.,	" "
576. William Pierson,	Concord, Pa.,	5th mo., 1845.
577. Charles Folwell,	Columbus, N. J.,	10th mo., 1842.
578. Israel Woodward,	Crosswicks, N. J.,	" "
579. Joseph K. Lippincott,	Haddonfield, N. J.,	" "
580. James E. Rhoads,	Springfield, Pa.,	" "
581. Charles E. Rhoads,	"	" "
582. Lewis W. Leeds,	Moorestown, N. J.,	" "
583. James B. Bellangee,	Yardville, N. J.,	" "
584. Rich'd L. Nicholson,	Philadelphia, Pa.,	" "
585. Edmund G. Webster,	"	" "
586. Samuel Sellers,	"	" "
587. George Sellers,	"	" "
588. Jacob Valentine,	"	" "
589. Richard Wood,	"	4th mo., 1843.
590. Thomas Evans,	Springfield, Pa.,	5th mo., 1845.
591. James Smedley,	Middletown, Pa.,	10th mo., 1842.
592. Thos. R. Matthews,	Baltimore, Md.,	4th mo., 1843.
593. Ashton Richardson,	Wilmington, Del.,	5th mo., 1845.
594. Asa Elkinton,	Philadelphia, Pa.,	4th mo., 1843.
595. William P. Dawson,	Easton, Md.,	" "
596. Everett G. Passmore,	Edgmont, Pa.,	5th mo., 1845.
597. Otto Smedley,	Lumberville, Pa.,	4th mo., 1843.
598. Benj. D. Smedley,	"	" "
599. Charles H. Fox,	Philadelphia, Pa.,	5th mo., 1845.
600. Stacy Buzby,	Bordentown, N. J.,	4th mo., 1843.
601. William Walmsley,	Frankford, Pa.,	". ".
602. Franklin Bell,	Philadelphia, Pa.,	" "
603. Edwin Harvey,	Concord, Pa.,	10th mo., "
604. Enos Larkin,	"	" "
605. Daniel W. Chandler,	Kennet, Pa.,	" "
606. Levi Wickersham,	Sadsbury, Pa.,	" "
607. William B. Trump,	Philadelphia, Pa.,	" "
608. Jonathan Eldridge,	Goshen, Pa.,	" "
609. Benjamin Hayes,	Newlin, Pa.,	" "
610. Paschall Cope.	East Bradford, Pa.,	" "
611. Reuben Barnard,	W. Marlborough, Pa.,	" "
612. Joseph S. Walter,	Kennet, Pa.,	" "

STUDENTS.

THIRD THOUSAND.

NAME.	RESIDENCE.	DATE OF ENTRY.
613. Barclay Smith,	Doe Run, Pa.,	10th mo., 1843.
614. Morris Levis,	Springfield, Pa.,	" "
615. Thomas H. Webb,	Birmingham, Pa.,	" "
616. Joseph D. Huey,	Kennet, Pa.,	
617. Charles E. Gause,	Hamorton, Pa.,	5th mo., 1845.
619. Joseph S. Townsend,	Plainfield, N. J.,	" "
620. William Lawrie,	Parkesburg, Pa.,	10th mo., "
621. William Edwards,	Muncy, Pa.,	4th mo., 1843.
622. Bethuel Haines,	Evesham, N. J.,	10th mo., 1842.
623. Edwin M. Bunting,	Crosswicks, N. J.,	4th mo., 1843.
624. Henry W. Stokes,	Philadelphia, Pa.,	" "
625. Francis Stokes,	"	" "
626. Isaac S. Eastburn,	Attleboro, Pa.,	" "
627. Samuel Paxson,	Trenton, N. J.,	" "
628. William H. Wistar,	Philadelphia, Pa.,	" "
629. Edward Cumming,	"	" "
630. Charles Cumming,	"	" "
631. Alfred Jones,	"	" "
632. Edward Sharpless,	"	" "
633. Joseph Fox,	"	" "
634. Edward Maris,	Chester, Pa.,	10th mo., 1845.
635. Richard Paxson,	Buckingham, Pa.,	4th mo., 1843.
636. Benjamin D. Perkins,	Philadelphia, Pa.,	" "
637. James Neville,	———, N. Y.,	" "
638. Joseph W. Neville,	———, N. Y.,	" "
639. Benjamin G. Neville,	———, N. Y.,	" "
640. William E. House,	Marlborough, Pa.,	5th mo., 1842.
641. George B. Wood,	Philadelphia, Pa.,	4th mo., 1843.
642. Daniel W. Walmsley,	Frankford, Pa.,	" "
643. William T. Norris,	Harford Co., Md.,	6th mo., "
644. James Kite,	Philadelphia, Pa.,	7th mo., "
645. William B. Haines,	Burlington Co., N. J.,	10th mo., "
646. Joseph H. Borton,	Rancocas, N. J.,	" "
647. Howard Tucker,	Cincinnati, Ohio,	" "
648. Thomas J. Levick,	Philadelphia, Pa.,	" "
649. Samuel W. Smedley,	Middletown, Pa.,	" "
650. Jacob W. Shipley,	Peekskill, N. Y.,	" "
651. Joseph F. Shotwell,	"	" "
652. August F. Shotwell,	"	12th mo., "
653. Wallace Vail,	Plainfield, N. J.,	10th mo., "
654. Edward N. Bishop,*	Mt. Holly, N. J.,	" "
655. Ellis Branson,	Bristol, Pa.,	4th mo., 1844.
656. George T. Coates,	Doe Run, Pa.,	10th mo., 1845.
657. Samuel Coates,	"	" "
658. John J. Parker,	Parkersville, Pa.,	" "

* Deceased at school, 17th of Twelfth mo., 1843.

GENERAL CATALOGUE.

THIRD THOUSAND.

NAME.	RESIDENCE.	DATE OF ENTRY.
659. Samuel J. Parker,	Parkersville, Pa.,	10th mo., 1845.
660. Richard Chambers,	White Clay Creek, Del.,	" "
661. Alban Webb,	Pennsbury, Pa.,	" "
662. Samuel L. Smedley,	Edgmont, Pa.,	" "
663. William Gibbons,	West Chester, Pa.,	" "
664. Abiah Passmore,	London Britain, Pa.,	" "
665. Joseph L. Baily,	Coatesville, Pa.,	" "
666. George Levis,	Mt. Holly, N. J.,	4th mo., 1844.
667. Sanderson R. Martin,	Philadelphia, Pa.,	" "
668. James Reed,	Brandywine, Pa.,	10th mo., 1845.
669. Jonathan E. Rhoads,	Springfield, Pa.,	4th mo., 1844.
670. John W. Rulon,	Philadelphia, Pa.,	" "
671. John H. Jackson,	Darby, Pa.,	" "
672. Ephraim J. Jackson,	"	" "
673. John Woolman,	Philadelphia, Pa.,	" "
674. James Webb,	Pennsbury, Pa.,	5th mo., "
675. Jacob L. Crew,	Richmond, Va.,	4th mo., "
676. Asa Branson,	Flushing, Ohio,	" "
677. John Needles,	Baltimore, Md.,	" "
678. Jehu Roberts,	Chester Valley, Pa.,	5th mo., "
679. Joseph Warrington,	Philadelphia, Pa.,	4th mo., "
680. Calvin C. Moore,	Sadsbury, Pa.,	5th mo., 1846.
681. John Pierson,	Concord, Pa.,	5th mo., "
682. Elisha Fogg,	Philadelphia, Pa.,	" "
683. George W. Ivins,	Shrewsbury, N. J.,	10th mo., "
684. Nathaniel N. Stokes,	Moorestown, N. J.,	" "
685. Jesse James,	East Bradford, Pa.,	5th mo., "
686. Charles Moore,	Strickersville, Pa.,	10th mo., "
687. Joshua G. Allen,	Springfield, Pa.,	" "
688. William Cope,	East Bradford, Pa.,	" "
689. Aaron Ball,	Quakertown, Pa.,	" "
690. Samuel Cooper,	Sadsbury, Pa.,	" "
691. Frederick Underhill,	New York, N. Y.,	" "
692. George A. Roberts,	Chester Valley, Pa.,	" "
693. Wm. F. Kirkwood,	Sadsbury, Pa.,	" "
694. Henry E. Lownes,	Pineville, Pa,	" "
695. Isaac C. Fallas,	Cincinnati, Ohio,	" "
696. George Wetherill,	Chester, Pa.,	" "
697. Charles G. Ogden,	Springfield, Pa.,	" "
698. Henry Benington,	Concord, Pa.,	" "
699. Granville Bassett,	———, Del.,	10th mo., 1847.
700. Charles M. Harlan,	Doe Run, Pa.,	10th mo., 1846.
701. J. Borton Hayes,	"	" "
702. Isaac I. Hayes,	"	" "
703. J. Hanover Baldwin,	Downingtown, Pa.,	" "
704. Gerard Hopkins,	Frederick Co., Va.,	" "
705. David B. Trimble,	Baltimore, Md.,	11th mo., "

STUDENTS.

THIRD THOUSAND.

NAME.	RESIDENCE.	DATE OF ENTRY.
706. Jacob Dingee,	West Bradford, Pa.,	5th mo., 1847.
707. George P. Hughes,	London Grove, Pa.,	" "
708. James D. Simmons,	Bart, Pa.,	1st mo., 1848.
709. Daria W. Hunt,	Guilford Co., N. C.,	5th mo., 1847.
710. John Pleasants,	———, N. Y.,	" "
711. Alfred Satterthwaite,	Crosswicks, N. J.,	4th mo., 1844.
712. Coleman Nicholson,	Philadelphia, Pa.,	5th mo., "
713. James A. Remington,	"	" "
714. Reuben H. Underhill,	Poughkeepsie, N. Y.,	4th mo., "
715. Joseph Taylor,	Cinnaminson, N. J.,	10th mo., "
716. William R. Dutton,	Burlington, N. J.,	" "
717. Moses Cadwallader,	Fallsington, Pa.,	" "
718. Allen P. Tilton,	Barnegat, N. J.,	5th mo., 1845.
719. Robert Pennell,	Darby, Pa.,	10th mo., 1844.
720. George C. Hancock,	Burlington, N. J.,	" "
721. Reuben Battin,	Elkland, Pa.,	" "
722. Armat W. Lee,	Maiden Creek, Pa.,	" "
723. James Wilson,	Philadelphia, Pa.,	" "
724. George D. Hilyard,	New York, N. Y.,	" "
725. William H. Gill,	Haddonfield, N. J.,	" "
726. Rowland J. Dutton,	Burlington, N. J.,	" "
727. Caspar Wistar,	Salem, N. J.,	" "
728. Albert Comfort,	Morrisville, Pa.,	" "
729. Oliver Norris,	Franklinville, Md.,	" "
730. Thomas Serrill,	Darby, Pa.,	" "
731. Philip P. Dunn,	Trenton, N. J.,	" "
732. Charles C. Sellers,	Philadelphia, Pa.,	" "
733. Marshall B. Smith,	"	" "
734. Albert H. Smith,	"	" "
735. Charles Sharpless,	Providence, Pa.,	" "
736. Alfred Willits,	Philadelphia, Pa.,	" "
737. Edward Darnell,	Evesham, N. J.,	" "
738. George Wood,	New York, N. Y.,	" "
739. William E. Coale,	Baltimore, Md.,	" "
740. Thomas E. Coale,	"	" "
741. Isaac Tyson,		" "
742. William C. Matlack,	....	11th mo., "
743. John S. Palmer,	Upper Providence, Pa.,	10th mo., "
744. H. R. Woodward,	Moorestown, N. J.,	5th mo., 1845.
745. Joseph W. Eastburn,	Middletown, Pa.,	" "
746. William P. Cook,	Deer Creek, Md.,	10th mo., 1847.
747. George S. Booth,	Philadelphia, Pa.,	5th mo., 1845.
748. William Thomas,	Burlington, N. J.,	" "
749. Richard Parry,	Philadelphia, Pa.,	" "
750. Wm. C. Shoemaker,	Cheltenham, Pa.,	" "
751. George Valentine,	Bellefonte, Pa.,	- " "
752. Wm. T. Valentine,	"	" "

13*

GENERAL CATALOGUE.

THIRD THOUSAND.

NAME.	RESIDENCE.	DATE OF ENTRY.
753. Howard Edwards,	Philadelphia, Pa.,	5th mo., 1845.
754. Samuel L. Albertson,	Plymouth, Pa.,	" "
755. Franklin Levis,	Mt. Holly, N. J.,	" "
756. Thomas Parry,	Plattekill, N. Y.,	" "
757. William W. Janney,	Philadelphia, Pa.,	" "
758.		
759. Edward Sellers,	Upper Darby, Pa.,	" "
760. James H. Moon,	Fallsington, Pa.,	" "
761. Thos. E. Lippincott,	Mauch Chunk, Pa.,	10th mo., "
762. John C. Tatum,	Woodbury, N. J.,	" "
763. Daniel Wills,	Rancocas, N. J.,	" "
764. Isaac Nicholson,	Haddonfield, N. J.,	" "
765. Samuel Eves,	Medford, N. J.,	" "
766. John Watson,	New Hope, Pa.,	" "
767. Jacob M. Watson,	"	" "
768. Joseph S. Dell,	Townsbury, N. J.,	" "
769. Edward A. Warner,	Kingsessing, Pa.,	" "
770. Charles L. Warner,	Muncy, Pa.,	" "
771. John W. Janney,	Philadelphia, Pa.,	" "
772. John Scott,	Norristown, Pa.,	" "
773. Geo. J. Scattergood,	Philadelphia, Pa.,	5th mo., 1846.
774. David J. Scott,	W. Bradford, Pa.,	10th mo., 1847.
775. Ellwood W. Scott,	"	" "
776. Percival Collins,	Philadelphia, Pa.,	5th mo., 1846.
777. Stephen G. Collins,	"	" "
778. Stephen W. Savery,	"	" "
779. Thomas H. Savery,	"	" "
780. Charles Ware,	Kensington, Pa.,	" "
781. John C. Corbit,	Cantwell's Bridge, Del.,	" "
782. Caspar Wistar,	Philadelphia, Pa.,	" "
783. William F. Spencer,	Horsham, Pa.,	" "
784. William Albertson,	Plymouth, Pa.,	" "
785. Samuel A. Janney,	Baltimore, Md.,	" "
786. Johns H. Janney,	"	" "
787. Lewis N. Hopkins,	Frederic Co., Va.,	" "
788. Henry H. Smith,	Philadelphia, Pa.,	" "
789. William R. Wills,	Rancocas, N. J.,	" "
790. George B. Borton,	"	" "
791. John K. Bartlett,	Talbot Co., Md.,	" "
792. Stacy B. Haines,	Marlton, N. J.,	" "
793. Charles P. Pleasants,	Philadelphia, Pa.,	" "
794. Samuel T. Proctor,	Baltimore, Md.,	" "
795. Ellwood Hunt,	Philadelphia, Pa.,	" "
796. Samuel Cooper,	Camden, N. J.,	10th mo., "
797. Benjamin Cooper,	"	" "
798. Joseph Potts,	Springfield, Pa.,	" "
799. Thomas Warner,	Muncy, Pa.,	" "

STUDENTS.

THIRD THOUSAND.

NAME.	RESIDENCE.	DATE OF ENTRY.
800. John M. Roberts,	Moorestown, N. J.,	10th mo., 1846.
801. Henry W. Roberts,	Moorestown, N. J.,	" "
802. James H. Bonsall,	Philadelphia, Pa.,	" "
803. Thomas Hoopes,	Newtown, Pa.,	" "
804. Ed. B. Underhill,	Poughkeepsie, N. Y.,	" "
805. Charles Decou,	Trenton, N. J.,	" "
806. Wistar Stokes,	Philadelphia, Pa.,	" "
807. James Ecroyd,	Muncy, Pa.,	" "
808. Edward Y. Cope,	Bradford, Pa.,	" "
809. George Wetherill,	Chester, Pa.,	" "
810. Jabez H. Jenkins,	Camden, Del.,	" "
811. Elliston P. Morris,	Germantown, Pa.,	" "
812. Joseph R. Stroud,	Rancocas, N. J.,	" "
813. Joseph R. Murray,	New York, N. Y.,	" "
814. William R. Murray,	"	" "
815. Charles Elkinton,	Philadelphia, Pa.,	12th mo., "
816. David Scull,	"	5th mo., 1847.
817. John Dickinson,	"	" "
818. Horatio W. Pharo,	"	" "
819. George B. Pharo,	"	" "
820. J. G. Richardson,	"	" "
821. Francis Richardson,	"	" "
822. Henry Lawrence,	Petersburg, Va.,	" "
823. Thornton Brown,	Philadelphia, Pa.,	" "
824. Howell Brown,	"	" "
825. William R. Bishop,	Burlington, N. J.,	" "
826. Charles Albertson,	Philadelphia, Pa.,	" "
827. Clayton Cooper,	Camden, N. J.,	" "
828. William R. Newbold,	Philadelphia, Pa.,	" "
829. Mark S. Reeve,	Medford, N. J.,	" "
830. Pemberton Janney,	Philadelphia, Pa.,	" "
831. William Evans,	"	" "
832. Bailey Llewellyn,	Pennsville, Ohio,	" "
833. William Savery,	Philadelphia, Pa.,	" "
834. Samuel L. Fox,	Haddonfield, N. J.,	" "
835. Stacy Jones,	Germantown, Pa.,	" "
836. Mor. M. Dawson,	Philadelphia, Pa.,	" "
837. Edward Darnell,	Burlington, N. J.,	" "
838. John W. Cadbury,	Philadelphia, Pa.,	" "
839. Thomas Burdsall,	———, N. Y.,	" "
840. Robert Walker,	"	7th mo., "
841. Sam'l R. Valentine,	Philadelphia, Pa.,	10th mo., 1847.
842. Jon. J. Comfort,	Tecumseh, Mich.,	" "
843. Joseph Albertson,	Plymouth, Pa.,	" "
844. Benjamin B. Taylor,	Mt. Holly, N. J.,	" "
845. William R. Deacon,	Burlington, N. J.,	" "
846. James Deacon,	"	" "

GENERAL CATALOGUE.

THIRD THOUSAND.

NAME.	RESIDENCE.	DATE OF ENTRY.
847. Nicholas W. Hoag,	Dutchess Co., N. Y.,	10th mo., 1847
848. Rob't K. Tomlinson,	Brownsburg, Pa.,	" "
849. John Cumming,	Philadelphia, Pa.,	" "
850. Issachar Eldridge,	Goshen, Pa.,	" "
851. Thomas C. Eldridge,	"	" "
852. John T. Evans,	Springfield, Pa.,	" "
853. Joshua Hoopes,	West Chester, Pa.,	" "
854. Isaiah Kirk,	Goshen, Pa.,	" "
855. Thomas Smedley,	Middletown, Pa.,	" "
856. George L. Smedley,	"	" "
857. Edward Harry,	Uwchlan, Pa.,	" "
858. Benj. H. Tomlinson,	Middletown, Pa.,	" "
859. Charles T. Bonsall,	Trenton, N. J.,	" "
860. Joseph G. Rowland,	Newtown, Pa.,	" "
861. Charles W. Thomas,	Waynesville, Ohio,	" "
862. Robert Dixon,	Talbot Co., Md.,	4th mo., 1848.
863. Samuel Roberts,	Downingtown, Pa.,	" "
864. Morris Walmsley,	Kensington, Pa.,	" "
865. Reading K. Hancock,	Burlington, N. J.,	" "
866. Barzillai B. Stokes,	Medford, N. J.,	" "
867. Isaac B. Webb,	Birmingham, Pa.,	" "
868. Merrick Ballance,	Lancaster Co., Pa.,	10th mo., "
869. James Bell,	Camden Co., N. J.,	" "
870. Thomas D. Hoopes,	East Caln, Pa.,	" "
871. James T. Hughes,	West Chester, Pa.,	" "
872. Thomas H. Poole,	New Castle Co., Del.,	" "
873. Thomas Pim,	Downingtown, Pa.,	" "
874. Benjamin Sharpless,	Birmingham, Pa.,	" "
875. Edward G. Smedley,	Middletown, Pa.,	" "
876. Cidney Lytle,	Winchester, Va.,	" "
877. Stephen Reynolds,	Cecil Co., Md.,	" "
878. Jacob Reynolds,	"	" "
879. Mich'l N. Woolman,	Philadelphia, Pa.,	" "
880. Edward Temple,	Pennsbury, Pa.,	" "
881. Benjamin Williams,	Frankford, Pa.,	" "
882. Alfred C. Merritt,	Salem, N. J.,	" "
883. Thomas C. Batty,	Collins, N. Y.,	" "
884. David Reynolds,	Rising Sun, Md.,	" "
885. Isaac H. Thompson,	London Grove, Pa.,	" "
886. William Hoopes,	Baltimore, Md.,	4th mo., 1849.
887. Robert M. Sharpless,	Chester, Pa.,	" "
888. Jonas Janney,	Loudon Co., Va.,	" "
890. Jeremiah Jones,	Whitemarsh, Pa.,	" "
891. Benjamin Lamborn,	London Grove, Pa.,	" "
892. Edward Hayes,	Doe Run, Pa.,	" "
893. John M. Harlan,	"	" "
894. Henry S. Garrett,	Willistown, Pa.,	" "

STUDENTS.

THIRD THOUSAND.

NAME.	RESIDENCE.	DATE OF ENTRY.
895. Theodore Reynolds,	Cecil Co., Md.,	4th mo., 1849.
896. Daniel T. Burdsall,	New York, N. Y.,	" "
897. Samuel Hopkins,	Frederic Co., Va.,	" "
898. Joseph Larkin,	Concord, Pa.,	" "
899. Thomas Sharpless,	Chester, Pa.,	" "
900. James Dixon,	Talbot Co., Md.,	" "
901. Job Bacon,	Greenwich, N. J.,	" 1847.
902. Cyrus Eastburn,	Newtown, Pa.,	" "
903. Joseph B. Evans,	Camden, N. J.,	" "
904. John D. Griffin,	New York, N. Y.,	" "
905. Henry Albertson,	Philadelphia, Pa.,	" "
906. Paul S. Reeves,	Woodbury, N. J.,	" "
909. Richard Hughes,	....	" "
910. Nathaniel Barton,	Marlton, N. J.,	" "
911. Morris Hacker,	Philadelphia, Pa.,	" "
912. Thomas S. Bonsall,	Trenton, N. J.,	" "
913. Ellwood Bonsall,	"	" "
914. Benj. K. Wetherill,	Chester, Pa.,	" "
915. Isaac Hall,	Mt. Pleasant, Ohio,	10th mo., "
916. William H. Macy,	Nantucket, Mass.,	4th mo., "
917. Joseph T. Moore,	Sandy Spring, Md.,	" 1848.
918. George Adams,	Philadelphia, Pa.,	" "
919. Joseph W. Stokes,	"	" "
920. John B. Garrett,	"	" "
921. Philip C. Garrett,	"	" "
922. Henry R. Tilton,	Barnegat, N. J.,	" "
923. Thomas Ridgway,	Egg Harbor, N. J.,	" "
924. Thomas J. Edge,	Wilmington, Del.,	" "
925. William B. Kimber,	Philadelphia, Pa.,	" "
926. Samuel S. Kimber,	"	" "
927. Nathaniel B. Stokes,	"	" "
928. Albert H. Hillman,	Camden, N. J.,	" "
929. Charles Scott,	Norristown, Pa.,	" "
930. John C. Griffith,	Frederic Co., Va.,	" "
931. Samuel Jones,	Philadelphia, Pa.,	" "
932. James T. Shinn,	"	" "
933. Josiah Bacon,	Greenwich, N. J.,	10th mo., "
934. Joseph E. Ballenger,	Gloucester, N. J.,	" "
935. George E. Yardley,	Bucks Co., Pa., .	" "
936. Lewis J. Albertson,	Plymouth, Pa.,	" "
937. Spencer Thompson,	New Garden, Pa.,	" "
938. Joseph Whitall,	Philadelphia, Pa.,	" "
939. Theo. T. Gillingham,	Alexandria, Va.,	" "
940. Henry Parker,	Parkersville, Pa.,	" "
941. Clement Ogden,	Springfield, N. J.,	" "
942. John Deacon,	Birmingham, N. J.,	" "
944. Isaac Chrisman,	Stonersville, Pa.,	4th mo., 1849.

* Deceased at the school.

THIRD THOUSAND.

NAME.	RESIDENCE.	DATE OF ENTRY.
945. Joseph Austin,	Nantucket, Mass.,	4th mo., 1849.
946. Oliver D. Martin,	Philadelphia, Pa.,	" "
947. William Miller,	Bellefonte, Pa.,	" "
948. Isaac Thomas,	"	" "
949. Ebenezer Roberts,	Moorestown, N. J.,	" "
950. Edwin L. Dickinson,	Philadelphia, Pa.,	" "
951. Robert G. Allen,	Bristol, Pa.,	" "
952. George R. Parry,	Philadelphia, Pa.,	" "
953. Samuel Kitchen,	Lumberville, N. J.,	" "
954. John Evans,	Marlton, N. J.,	" "
955. George Haines,	Medford, N. J.,	" "
956. Wm. W. Underhill,	Burlington, N. J.,	" "
957. William K. Knight,	Philadelphia, Pa.,	" "
958. William P. Jones,	"	" "
959. J. Henry Cowgill,	Camden, N. J.,	" "
960. Jacob Smedley,	Middletown, Pa.,	" "
961. Jesse Garrett,	Birmingham, Pa.,	10th mo., "
962. Edward G. Dennis,	Wilmington, Del.,	" "
963. John S. Kirk,	Goshen, Pa.,	" "
964. Charles Cowgill,	Camden, Del.,	" "
965. Caleb M. Cooper,	Lancaster Co., Pa.,	" "
966. William Wilkins,	Easton, N. J.,	" "
967. Wm. H. Davidson,	Bradford, Pa.,	" "
968. Aaron Ward,	Camden, N. J.,	" "
969. Isaac P. Jackson,	Rising Sun, Md.,	" "
970. Samuel Worth,	Bradford, Pa.,	" "
971. Francis Worth,	"	" "
972. Ziba Lamborn,	Chatham, Pa.,	" "
973. Samuel P. Webb,	Pennsbury, Pa.,	" "
974. Morton Morris,	West Chester, Pa.,	" "
975. Wm. Hendrickson,	Crosswicks, N. J.,	" "
976. Sam. S. Thompson,	London Grove, Pa.,	" "
977. Daniel B. Cotant,	Stroudsburg, Pa.,	" "
978. Thomas Gifford,*	Ledyard, N. Y.,	4th mo., 1850.
979. Charles Gifford,	"	" "
980. Richard Walker,	New York, N. Y.,	" "
981. William Fothergill,	Strickersville, Pa.,	" "
982. William C. Alderson,	Cincinnati, Ohio,	" "
983. William Poole,	New Castle Co., Del..	" "
984. Benj. F. Thomas,	Waynesville, Ohio,	" "
985. Edwin Roberts,	Haddonfield, N. J.,	" "
986. Thomas Waring,	Rising Sun, Md.,	" "
987. Edward S. Preston,	"	" "
988. Charles Downing,	Downingtown, Pa.,	" "
990. Samuel H. Jenkins,	Camden, Del.,	" "

* Deceased at the school, 24th of Third month, 1851.

STUDENTS.

THIRD THOUSAND.

NAME.	RESIDENCE.	DATE OF ENTRY.
991. Thomas Bowers,	....	4th mo., 1850.
992. Thomas Smedley,	Sugartown, Pa.,	" "
993. Thomas Sharpless,	Birmingham, Pa.,	" "
994. Webster Edget,	New Baltimore, N. Y.,	" "
996. Charles Temple,	Pennsbury, Pa.,	" "
997. Enoch W. Heston,	Sadsbury, Pa.,	" "
998. Alfred Hughes,	West Chester, Pa.,	" "
999. Samuel Leeds,	Westfield, N. J.,	" "
1000. Dan. Satterthwaite,	Tecumseh, Mich.,	" "

FOURTH THOUSAND.

NAME.	RESIDENCE.	DATE OF ENTRY.
1. H. D. Thompson,	Wilmington, Del.,	6th mo., 1851.
2. B. E. Hendrickson,	Crosswicks, N. J.,	10th mo., 1849.
3. Aaron R. Comfort,	Tecumseh, Mich.,	" "
4. William Stevenson,	Marlton, N. J.,	" "
5. George R. Wood,	Philadelphia, Pa.,	" "
6. Barton T. Thorn,	Crosswicks, N. J.,	" "
7. T. T. Sharpless,	Chester, Del.,	" "
8. Joseph Wills,	Rancocas, N. J.,	" "
9. Gideon S. Bolton,	Philadelphia, Pa.,	" "
10. Joseph Brinton,	Lampeter, Pa.,	" "
11. Allen Ward,	Camden, N. J.,	" "
12. Edward B. Alsop,	Philadelphia, Pa.,	" "
13. John Wetherill,	Chester, Pa.,	" "
14. Mark Hughes,	West Grove, Pa.,	5th mo., 1859.
15. Nathaniel Robinson,	Highland, N. Y.,	4th mo., 1850.
16. John Whitacre,*	Muncy, Pa.,	10th mo., "
17. Thomas S. Bolton,	Philadelphia, Pa.,	4th mo., "
18. William Potts,	Springfield, Pa.,	" "
19. Edward H. Smith,†	Philadelphia, Pa.,	" "
20. Harvey Linton,	West Grove, Pa.,	5th mo., 1859.
21. George K. Taylor,	Philadelphia, Pa.,	4th mo., 1850.
22. Edward R. Wood,	"	- " "
23. William Winner,	Williamsport, Pa.,	" "
24. William Gould,	....	5th mo., "
25. Nathan C. Hunt,	Philadelphia, Pa.,	4th mo., "
26. Reece Alsop,	"	" "
27. Robert F. Raley,	Hanover, Ohio,	" "
28. Robert P. Lovett,	Fallsington, Pa.,	10th mo., "
29. Edward Balderston,	"	" "
30. Cyrus C. Comfort,	"	" "
31. George M. Comfort,	"	" "
32. Alfred S. Conard,	West Grove, Pa.,	" "
33. Uriah Borton,	Rancocas, N. J.,	" "

* Deceased at the school, 6th of Fourth month, 1852.
† Deceased at the school, 23d of Third month, 1851.

FOURTH THOUSAND.

NAME.	RESIDENCE.	DATE OF ENTRY.
34. Samuel S. Haines,	Marlton, N. J.,	10th mo., 1850.
35. Silas Warner,	Rancocas, N. J.,	" "
36. Dallas Reeve,	Allowaystown, N. J.,	" "
37. John T. Pound,	Plainfield, N. J.,	" "
38. Samuel S. Cope,	Wt. Marlborough, Pa.,	" "
39. Rich'd M. Chambers,	Strickerville, Pa.,	5th mo., 1859.
40. Thos. H. Bedell,	New Baltimore, N.Y.,	10th mo., 1850.
41. Joshua Kimber,	Flushing, N. Y.,	" "
42. George C. Stokes,	Philadelphia, Pa.,	" "
43. Edwin Hendrickson,	Crosswicks, N. J.,	" "
44. Caspar W. Haines,	Medford, N. J.,	" "
45. Edgar Cope,	Susquehanna Co., Pa.,	" "
46. Sam. E. Dickinson,	Philadelphia, Pa.,	6th mo., 1851.
47. Edward Pyle,	New Garden, Pa.,	" "
48. William H. Whitall,	Philadelphia, Pa.,	" "
49. Edward B. Stevenson,	Bloomsburg, N. J.,	" "
50. Joseph E. Barton,	Fellowship, N. J.,	10th mo., 1850.
51. William K. Williams,	Frankford, Pa.,	" "
52. George E. Pim,	Downingtown, Pa.,	" "
53. William Eldridge,	Concord, Pa.,	" "
54. Robert Hayes,	Westtown, Pa.,	" "
55. Thomas H. Passmore,	Edgmont, Pa.,	6th mo., 1851.
56. Edward Congdon,	Oswego, N. Y.,	11th mo., "
57. Benjamin Hallowell,	Alexandria, Va.,	6th mo., "
58. Ephraim Haines,	Pipe Creek, Md.,	" "
59. John H. Jenkins,	Camden, Del.,	" "
60. Lawrence H. Hopkins,	Baltimore, Md.,	" "
61. Henry C. Matthews,	"	5th mo., 1859.
62. Kirkwood Moore,	West Grove, Pa.,	6th mo., 1851.
63. Joshua Moore,	Bart, Pa.,	" "
64. William J. Roberts,	Haddonfield, N. J.,	" "
65. Edward Maule,	Colerain, Ohio,	" "
66. Silas A. Underhill,	Brooklyn, N. Y.,	5th mo., 1852.
67. Henry Fothergill,	Parkersville, Pa.,	11th mo., 1851.
68. Joseph J. Pound,	Plainfield, N. J.,	5th mo., 1852.
69. Coleman Packer,	Woodbury, N. J.,	11th mo., 1851.
70. Clarkson Moore,	West Grove, Pa.,	" "
71. William Lamborn,	New Garden, Pa.,	" "
72. Charles G. Carpenter,	Clarkesville, Ohio,	" "
73. Yardley Brown,	Pughtown, Pa.,	" "
74. George S. Dewell,	Stanton, N. Y.,	" "
75. Stephen Wood,	Brooklyn, N. Y.,	" "
76. James Wood,	Bedford, N. Y.,	" "
77. James Mekeel,	Hector, N. Y.,	" "
78. Ebenezer Worth,	Bradford, Pa.,	" "
79. Mordecai Larkin,	Guthrieville, Pa.,	" "
80. Amos J. Michener,	Rising Sun, Md.,	" "

STUDENTS.

FOURTH THOUSAND.

NAME.	RESIDENCE.	DATE OF ENTRY.
81. Isaac Haviland,	South Dover, N. Y.,	11th mo., 1851.
82. Henry Palmer,	Providence, Pa.,	" "
83. Samuel Cope,	West Chester, Pa.,	" "
84. Benj. H. Miller,	Alexandria, Va.,	" "
85. Joseph Thompson,	W. Bradford, Pa.,	" "
86. William Smedley,	Middletown, Pa.,	" "
87. Wilson Hall,	Harrisville, Ohio,	" "
88. William R. Ash,	West Caln, Pa.,	" "
89. Isaac Yearsley,	"	" "
90. David R. Hoopes,	Newtown, Pa.,	" "
91. Henry Gibbons,*	Salem, N. J.,	5th mo., 1853.
92. Jesse S. Cheyney,	Thornbury, Pa.,	11th mo., 1851.
93. William Hunt,	Gloucester, Pa.,	5th mo., 1852.
94. Thomas Dell,	Philadelphia, Pa.,	" "
95. Irena Bassett,	Wilmington, Del.,	" "
96. Samuel J. Evans,	Evesham, N. J.,	11th mo., "
97. William B. Gifford,	Ledyard, N. Y.,	5th mo., "
98. Enoch Harlan,	Doe Run, Pa.,	" 1853.
99. George B. Painter,	Concord, Pa.,	" 1852.
100. Stephen Underhill,	Croton Point, N. Y.,	" "
101. J. B. Middleton,	Crosswicks, N. J.,	6th mo., 1851.
102. John Blakey,	Attleboro', Pa.,	" "
103. John W. Hilyard,	Rancocas, N. J.,	" "
104. Elliott Winn,	Philadelphia, Pa.,	" "
105. James B. Temple,	"	" "
106. William K. Carlisle,	"	" "
107. John W. Evans,	"	" "
108. Francis C. Williams,	"	" "
109. Joseph Scattergood,	"	" "
110. Thomas Scattergood,	"	" "
111. Horace Lloyd,	"	" "
112. Charles I. Shipley,	Cincinnati, Ohio,	" "
113. James S. Newbold,	Philadelphia, Pa.,	" "
114. Thomas Wistar,	"	" "
115. William W. Wistar,	"	" "
116. Charles Smith,	"	" "
117. John M. Sheppard,	Greenwich, N. J.,	" "
118. Eayre P. Bartlett,	Newark, N. J.,	" "
119. Gideon L. Richie,	Philadelphia, Pa.,	" "
120. Richard W. Chase,	"	11th mo., "
121. David Brown,	Lahaska, Pa.,	" "
122. Allen Lippincott,	Fallsington, Pa.,	" "
123. Joseph Lloyd,	Wilmington, Del.,	" "
124. Isaac B. Lloyd,	"	" "
125. William Vivian,	Burlington, N. J.,	" "

* Deceased at the school, 25th of Fifth month, 1855.

GENERAL CATALOGUE.

FOURTH THOUSAND.

NAME.	RESIDENCE.	DATE OF ENTRY.
126. Charles Evans,	Springfield, Pa.,	11th mo., 1851.
127. George W. Tatum,	Woodbury, N. J.,	" "
128. James Taylor,	Mt. Holly, N. J.,	" "
129. Joseph Wistar,	Salem, N. J.,	" "
130. John R. Carpenter,	"	" "
131. Thos. L. Chambers,	New Garden, Pa.,	5th mo., 1854.
132. Josiah A. Roberts,	Goshen, Pa.,	11th mo., 1851.
133. James Ogborn,	Germantown, Pa.,	" "
134. John E. Balderston,	Philadelphia, Pa.,	" "
135. Samuel Alsop, Jr.,	Wilmington, Del.,	" "
136. Rowland H. Hazard,	Wash'n Hollow, N. Y.,	" "
137. Alfred Morris,	Wellsborough, Pa.,	5th mo., 1852.
138. Samuel L. Allen,	Philadelphia, Pa.,	" "
139. Canby B. Shoemaker,	Milestown, Pa.,	" "
140. Horatio C. Wood,	Philadelphia, Pa.,	" "
141. Edward S. Lowry,	"	" "
142. Charles Lowry,	"	" "
143. Clement E. Lloyd,	"	" "
144. Joseph Evans,	Marlton, N. J.,	" "
145. Jacob Parker,	Rahway, N. J.,	" "
146. George Wood,	Philadelphia, Pa.,	" "
147. Jos. S. Middleton,	Crosswicks, N. J.,	" "
148. Levi Cowperthwaite,	Philadelphia, Pa.,	" "
149. John Richie,	"	" "
150. Isaac H. Richards,	Winchester, Va.,	" "
151. Wilson Thompson,	Avondale, Pa.,	11th mo., "
152. William Green,	Edgmont, Pa.,	5th mo., 1854.
153. William C. Corbit,	Cantwell's Bridge, Del.,	11th mo., 1852.
154. Howard Thomas,	Cincinnati, Ohio,	10th mo., 1853.
155. Bennett L. Smedley,	Edgmont, Pa.,	11th mo., 1852.
156. Daniel Lippincott,	Moorestown, N. J.,	" "
157. George R. Haines,	Millville, N. J.,	" "
158. William P. Buzby,	Columbia, N. J.,	" "
159. Thomas Good,	West Grove, Pa.,	" "
160. Ed. W. Woolman,	Blockley, Pa.,	" "
161. Lewis Sharpless,	Chester, Pa.,	" "
162. Jesse H. Garrett,	Willistown, Pa.,	" "
163. Ed. B. Stevenson,	Bloomsburg, N. J.,	" "
164. Dan. W. Stevenson,	"	" "
165. Samuel L. Moore,	Coopersville, Pa.,	" "
166. Reece Larkin,	Concord, Pa.,	" "
167. Joseph R. Downing,	Downingtown, Pa.,	" "
168. Arthur Miller,	Wheatland, Va.,	" "
169. Richard Carpenter,	Port Chester, N. Y.,	" "
170. John W. Storer,	———, N. Y.,	" "
171. Robert B. Underhill,	Clinton, N. Y.,	5th mo., 1853.
172. Alfred A. Underhill,	"	" "

STUDENTS. 171

FOURTH THOUSAND.

NAME.	RESIDENCE.	DATE OF ENTRY.
173. Robert Wood,	Brooklyn, N. Y.,	5th mo., 1853.
174. Henry Underhill,	Katonah, N. Y.,	" "
175. Philip H. Haviland,	New Milford, Conn.,	" "
176. Joseph H. Miller,	Vermont, Ill.,	" "
177. John Lee,	Stonersville, Pa.,	" "
178. George B. Allen,	Springfield, Pa.,	" "
179. Dillwyn Parker,	West Chester, Pa.,	" "
180. George Herendeen,	Farmington, N. Y.,	10th mo., "
181. Joseph P. Forsythe,	West Chester, Pa.,	" "
182. James H. Jones,	Frankford, Pa.,	" "
183. Isaac E. Windle,	Westtown, Pa.,	" "
184. Joseph Roberts,	Paoli, Pa.,	" "
185. Isaac Pusey,	London Grove, Pa.,	" "
186. James Maule,	Colerain, Ohio,	" "
187. Ambrose J. Boone,	Pickering, Canada,	" "
188. Joshua Waring,	Pictou, Canada,	" "
189. Edward Waring,	"	" "
190. Wilson Thompson,	Avondale, Pa.,	" "
191. Robert Garrett,	Edgmont, Pa.,	" "
192. Isaac Y. Ash,	Sadsbury, Pa.,	" "
193. George Lovett,	Fallsington, Pa.,	" "
194. Samuel Evans,	Marple, Pa.,	" "
195. Alphonso Kirk,	West Chester, Pa.,	" "
196. Llewellyn Miller,	Wheatland, Va.,	" "
197. James Hoge,	Hamilton, Va.,	" "
198. Joseph P. Eldridge,	East Goshen, Pa.,	" "
199. Wm. H. Underhill,	Indianapolis, Ind.,	11th mo., 1854.
200. Isaac H. Griffith,	Winchester, Va.,	5th mo., "
201. George G. Bartlett,	Tuckerton, N. J.,	11th mo., 1852.
202. Samuel Pancoast,	Springfield, Pa.,	" "
203. George Matlack,	Moorestown, N. J.,	" "
204. Robert B. Engle,	Rancocas, N. J.,	" "
205. William T. Borton,	Mt. Laurel, N. J.,	" "
206. Benjamin Warner,	Muncy, Pa.,	" "
207. Benjamin Dickinson,	Reading, Pa.,	" "
208. Charles Ballenger,	Mt. Laurel, N. J.,	" "
209. Amos E. Kaighn,	Chew's Landing, N. Y.,	" "
210. Edwin Wright,	Columbus, N. J.,	" "
211. Willet Lukens,	Horsham, Pa.,	" "
212. Elmer Levis,	Newtown, Pa.,	" "
213. Isaiah Balderston,	Philadelphia, Pa.,	" "
214. John Maule,	Port Royal, Pa.,	" "
215. Charles Woolman,	Frankford, Pa.,	" "
216. Sam'l Worthington,	Philadelphia, Pa.,	" "
217. Charles Parker,	Rahway, N. J.,	" "
218. William C. Johnson,	Parkesburg, Pa.,	" "
219. Charles M. Palmer,	Sandy Spring, Md.,	1st mo., 1853.

FOURTH THOUSAND.

NAME.	RESIDENCE.	DATE OF ENTRY.
220. Joseph H. Palmer,	Sandy Spring, Md.,	1st mo., 1853.
221. Samuel Allen,	Salem, N. J.,	5th mo., "
222. Francis J. Bell,	Experiment Mills, Pa.,	" "
223. Edwin A. Bell,	"	" "
224. David Branson,	Philadelphia, Pa.,	" "
225. Sam'l C. Woolman,	Rancocas, N. J.,	" "
226. Joseph E. Bacon,	Philadelphia, Pa.,	" "
227. Jonah M. Bacon,	"	" "
228. Joseph W. Jones,	"	" "
229. Samuel Whitall,	"	" "
230. James A. Coffin,	"	" "
231. Oliver G. Coffin,	"	" "
232. Edward Savery,	"	" "
233. Richard Haines,	Medford, N. J.,	" "
234. Clayton Haines,	"	" "
235. Edward Sheppard,	Philadelphia, Pa.,	" "
236. Samuel R. Evans,	Evesham, N. J.,	" "
237. Edward D. Cope,	Germantown, Pa.,	" "
238. Edward A. Thomas,	Cayuga Co., N. Y.,	" "
239. Robert Mitchell,	Philadelphia, Pa.,	" "
240. Amos A. Ridgway,	Tuckerton, N. J.,	10th mo., "
( ) Leonard Snowdon,	Westtown, Pa.,	" "
241. Thomas R. Bartlett,	Tuckerton, N. J.,	" "
242. George S. Garrett,	Upper Darby, Pa.,	" "
243. John Trimble,	Chester, Pa.,	" "
244. Isaac Maule,	Radnor, Pa.,	" "
245. Elijah Bowerman,	Scottsville, N. Y.,	" "
246. Wager H. Wood,	Rahway, N. J.,	" "
247. John H. Wood,	"	" "
248. Alfred Wood,	"	" "
249. Samuel W. Stokes,	Woodbury, N. J.,	" "
250. Richard W. Hutton,	Chester, Pa.,	" "
251. Morris Bacon,	Greenwich, N. J.,	" "
252. William B. Chase,	Burlington, N. J.,	" "
253. Charles Bettle,	Philadelphia, Pa.,	" "
254. Earl Shinn, Jr.,	"	" "
255. Charles Pancoast,	Marple, Pa.,	" "
256. Clayton N. Wills,	Rancocas, N. J.,	" "
257. Wm. J. Hedley,	Medina, N. Y.,	" "
258. Henry Cope,	London Grove, Pa.,	" "
259. Francis Decou,	Columbus, N. J.,	" "
260. Philip G. Biddle,	Philadelphia, Pa.,	" "
261. John L. Deacon,	Burlington, N. J.,	" "
262. Edward B. Kaighn,	Philadelphia, Pa.,	5th mo., 1854.
264. Thomas P. Conard,	West Grove, Pa.,	" "
265. Jos. A. Wickersham,	"	" "
266. William T. Reed,	Darlington, Md.,	" "

STUDENTS.

FOURTH THOUSAND.

NAME.	RESIDENCE.	DATE OF ENTRY.
267. Albert Underhill,	Brooklyn, N. Y.,	5th mo., 1854.
268. Walter C. Moore,	Rochester, N. Y.,	" "
269. Edward D. Cowgill,	Camden, Del.,	" "
270. Charles P. Janney,	Hillsboro', Va.,	" "
271. Enos E. Thatcher,	West Chester, Pa.,	11th mo., 1859.
272. Francis Thompson,	New Garden, Pa.,	" 1854.
273. George Wright,	Springfield, N. J.,	" "
274. Jos. P. Eldridge,	Goshen, Pa.,	" "
275. Daniel Garwood,	Evesham, N. J.,	" "
276. George Temple,	Parkersville, Pa.,	" "
277. Joseph Thompson,	West Bradford, Pa.,	" "
278. Joel A. Seal,	Avondale, Pa.,	" "
279. A. H. Griffith,	Winchester, Va.,	" "
280. Jos. John Duell,	Norwichville, C. W.,	" "
( ) John Benington,	Westtown, Pa.,	" "
281. Carpenter Walter,	West Chester, Pa.,	" "
282. Nathan Bundy,	Barnesville, Ohio,	" "
283. Chalkley Dawson,	"	" "
284. Jacob Maule,	Colerain, Ohio,	" "
285. Jacob V. Edge,	Downingtown, Pa.,	" "
286.		
287. Nathan Sharpless,	Chester, Pa.,	11th mo., 1854.
288. John M. Sheppard,	Greenwich, N. J.,	" "
289. Thomas P. Miller,	Wheatland, Va.,	5th mo., 1855.
290. Ralston R. Hoopes,	East Bradford, Pa.,	11th mo., 1854.
291. Paschall Morris,	West Chester, Pa.,	" "
292. Isaac Larkin,	Concord, Pa.,	" "
293. David Garrett,	Birmingham, Pa.,	" "
294. Joshua G. Embree,	Marshallton, Pa.,	" "
295. William Cope,	Bradford, Pa.,	" "
296. Gilbert Cope,	West Chester, Pa.,	" "
297. Isaac Lippincott,	Salem, N. J.,	" "
298. William B. Moore,	Nine Points, Pa.,	11th mo., 1860.
299. Francis Masters,	Greenwood, Pa.,	5th mo., 1855.
300. William E. Dingee,	Uwchlan, Pa.,	" "
301. Samuel Maule,	Port Royal, Pa.,	11th mo., "
302. Ellis Pennington,	Jennerville, Pa.,	5th mo., "
303. Charles Smedley,	Fulton House, Pa.,	" "
304. William E. Bell,	Richmond, Ind.,	" "
305. Edward S. Yarnall,	Howellville, Pa.,	11th mo., 1860.
306. Daniel W. Corbit,	Cantwell's Bridge, Del.,	5th mo., 1855.
307. Thomas M. Coulson,	Green, Pa.,	" "
308. Joseph Branson,	Flushing, Ohio,	" "
309. Nath. E. Janney,	Hillsboro', Va.,	" "
310. Edward D. Moore,	Rochester, N. Y.,	" "
311. John G. Henley,	Caraway, N. C.,	" "
312. Ephraim Smith,	Barnesville, Ohio,	" "

GENERAL CATALOGUE.

FOURTH THOUSAND.

NAME.	RESIDENCE.	DATE OF ENTRY.	
313. Edward Downing,	Downingtown, Pa.,	5th mo.,	1855.
314. J. D. Schureman,	New Rochelle, N. Y.,	"	"
315. Jesse Mekeel,	Searsburg, N. Y.,	"	"
316. George W. Cloud,	Woodbury, N. J.,	"	"
317. Morris Pennington,	Jennerville, Pa.,	"	"
318. Charles R. Cloud,	Woodbury, N. J.,	11th mo.,	1859.
319. Bernard T. Janney,	Purcellsville, Va.,	"	"
320. William R. Knight,	Philadelphia, Pa.,	"	"
321. Thomas R. Preston,	Rock Springs, Md.,	"	"
322. Amos R. Bartlett,	West Creek, N. J.,	"	1857.
323. Job Ridgway,	Tuckerton, N. J.,	"	1855.
324. Charles C. Bedell,	Clinton Corners, N. Y.,	5th mo.,	1856.
325. Robert M. Brinton,	Lampeter, Pa.,	11th mo.,	1855.
326. John S. Harris,	Westminster, N. C.,	"	"
327. Benjamin Cope,	West Chester, Pa.,	"	"
328. Joseph E. Cope,	"	"	1859.
329. William Seal,	Avondale, Pa.,	"	1855.
330. Jonathan Smedley,	Wakefield, Pa.,	5th mo.,	1856.
331. Edwin C. Forsythe,	West Chester, Pa.,	11th mo.,	1855.
332. Moses Worth,	Marshallton, Pa.,	"	"
333. Paschall Worth,	"	"	"
334. Abraham Jones,	Fallsington, Pa.,	"	"
335. John Moore,	Nine Points, Pa.,	"	"
336. Benjamin S. House,	Parkersville, Pa.,	"	"
337. William G. Embree,	Marshallton, Pa.,	"	"
338. Cyrus Pennington,	Jennerville, Pa.,	"	"
339. Edward Tatnall,	Wilmington, Del.,	"	"
340. Benjamin Dickinson,	Guiger's Mills, Pa.,	"	"
341. Joseph Jones,	Frankford, Pa.,	"	"
342. Albert Pardoe,	Eldredville, Pa.,	5th mo.,	1858.
343. William B. Jackson,	Wilmington, Del.,	"	1857.
344. Thomas Jackson,	"	"	"
345. Hugh Townsend,	Plainfield, N. J.,	"	1856.
346. John Llewellyn,	Pennsville, Ohio,	1st mo.,	"
347. William H. Cook,	Rowlandsville, Md.,	5th mo.,	"
348. James Eldridge,	Concord, Pa.,	"	"
349. Charles B. Sheppard,	West Chester, Pa.,	"	"
350. John T. Cook,	Darlington, Md.,	"	1854.
351. John B. Wood,	Philadelphia, Pa.,	"	"
352. Dillwyn Wistar,	"	"	"
353. William G. Ash,	"	"	"
354. Richardson S. Reeve,	Medford, N. J.,	"	"
355. Josiah Reeve,	"	"	"
356. Robert Levick,	Philadelphia, Pa.,	"	"
357. James Gubbings,	Germantown, Pa.,	"	"
358. Caleb G. Evans,	Brooklyn, N. Y.,	"	"
359. Jon. H. Hilyard,	....	11th mo.,	"

STUDENTS.

FOURTH THOUSAND.

NAME.	RESIDENCE.	DATE OF ENTRY.
360. Sam'l M. McCollin,	Philadelphia, Pa.,	11th mo., 1854.
361. Henry Albertson,	Plymouth, Pa.,	5th mo., "
362. James E. Bell,	West Chester, Pa.,	" "
363. Walter Bell,	"	" "
364. Charles Richardson,	Philadelphia, Pa.,	" "
365. Joseph J. Wilson,	Germantown, Pa.,	" "
366. Joseph Healy,	Philadelphia, Pa.,	" "
367. Daniel Cope,	West Chester, Pa.,	11th mo., "
368. William C. Stokes,	Woodbury, N. J.,	" "
369. Howard Darnell,	Mt. Laurel, N. J.,	" "
370. Thomas Wildman,	Morrisville, Pa.,	" "
371. Ellwood Evans,	Camden, N. J.,	" "
372. J. Gardiner Haines,	Medford, N. J.,	" 1859.
373. Thomas A. Bell,	Experiment Mills, Pa.,	" 1854.
374. Howard Deacon,	Burlington, N. J.,	" "
375. Willits Parker,	Tuckerton, N. J.,	" "
376. Mark M. Reeve,	Allowaystown, N. J.,	" "
377. Richard H. Reeve,	"	" "
378. James Allinson,	Yardville, N. J.,	" "
379. Richard Ecroyd,	Muncy, Pa.,	5th mo., 1855.
380. James S. Conrad,	Darby, Pa.,	" "
381. Henry Sheppard,	Philadelphia, Pa.,	" "
382. Nathan Whinery,	Salem, Ohio,	11th mo., 1859.
383. Peter Ellis Decou,	Trenton, N. J.,	5th mo., 1855.
384. Walter R. Stevenson,	Allamuchy, N. J.,	" "
385. Philip G. Sheppard,	Greenwich, N. J.,	" "
386. Edward C. Jones,	Philadelphia, Pa.,	" "
387. Randolph Wood,	"	" "
388. Thomas C. Stokes,	"	" "
389. Samuel Trimble,	Chester, Pa.,	" "
390. Benjamin Albertson,	Philadelphia, Pa.,	" "
391. Alfred Bolton,	"	" "
392. John Brown,	Lahaska, Pa.,	11th mo., "
393. Lewis Woolman,	Philadelphia, Pa.,	" "
394. John H. Taylor,	Mt. Holly, N. J.,	" "
395. George P. Stokes,	Woodbury, N. J.,	" "
396. Charles A. Clement,	Leeds' Point, N. J.,	" "
397. Josh. C. Ballenger,	Mt. Laurel, N. J.,	" "
398. Charles P. Taylor,	West Grove, Pa.,	" "
399. R. Satterthwaite,	Crosswicks, N. J.,	" "
400. John Kaighn,	Haddonfield, N. J.,	" "
401. James Saunders,	Woodbury, N. J.,	" "
402. Adrian Moore,	Nine Points, Pa.,	" 1859.
403. Ed. L. Fenimore,	Philadelphia, Pa.,	5th mo., 1856.
404. Joseph H. Gibbons,	Winneshiek Co., Iowa,	" "
405. Albert Pancoast,	Philadelphia, Pa.,	" "
406. Morris E. Masters,	Muncy, Pa.,	" "

FOURTH THOUSAND.

NAME.	RESIDENCE.	DATE OF ENTRY.	
407. Robert T. Martin,	Philadelphia, Pa.,	5th mo.,	1856.
408. James R. Kite,	"	"	"
409. Robert Burton,	Fallsington, Pa.,	"	"
410. William H. Phillips,	Wilmington, Del.,	"	"
411. Wm. O. Bartlett,	Bethlehem, Pa.,	"	"
412. Jon. C. Baldwin,	Downingtown, Pa.,	"	"
413. Richard E. Griffith,	Winchester, Va.,	"	"
414. Lewis N. Hoge,	Hamilton, Va.,	"	"
415. Charles C. Bedell,	Clinton Corners, N. Y.,	"	"
416. Asahel Cooper,	Christiana, Pa.,	"	"
417. Sam'l K. Chambers,	Strickersville, Pa.,	11th mo.,	1859.
418. Barclay Cope,	Kimbleville, Pa.,	"	1856.
419. Caleb Bundy,	Barnesville, Ohio,	"	"
420. Melmoth H. Way,	Centreville, Del.,	"	"
421. Pemberton Moore,	Gap, Pa.,	"	"
422. William E. Windle,	Milltown, Pa.,	"	"
423. James L. Forsythe,	West Chester, Pa.,	"	"
424. Samuel Miller,	Wheatland, Va.,	"	"
425. Levi Moore,	Gap, Pa.,	"	"
426. John Ballance,	Kirk's Mills, Pa.,	"	"
427. Jas. M. Ballance,	Oak Hill, Pa.,	"	"
428. Thos. H. Jolliffe,	Stephenson's Sta., Va.,	"	"
429. Thomas Kinsey,	New Garden, Pa.,	"	"
430. David Cope,	London Grove, Pa.,	"	"
431. Samuel H. Edge,	Wilmington, Del.,	"	"
432. Edwin E. Embree,	Marshallton, Pa.,	"	"
433. John M. James,	West Chester, Pa.,	"	"
434. Charles W. Ash,	Sadsburyville, Pa.,	"	1859.
435. Charles S. Wilson,	Loveville, Del.,	4th mo.,	1857.
436. Elias P. Lownes,	Taylorsville, Pa.,	11th mo.,	"
437. Franklin M. Grubb,	Philadelphia, Pa.,	4th mo.,	"
438. George W. Harlan,	Doe Run, Pa.,	"	"
439. James W. Tatnall,	Wilmington, Del.,	"	"
440. Levi Haines,	Pleasant Grove, Pa.,	5th mo.,	"
441. Charles C. Way,	Kennet Square, Pa.,	"	"
442. James Garrett,	West Chester, Pa.,	11th mo.,	1859.
444. Albin Garrett,	"	"	1857.
445. Nathan Cope,	"	"	"
446. William H. Jolliffe,	Baltimore, Md.,	"	"
447. Jesse P. Thatcher,	Warren Tavern, Pa.,	"	"
448. David L. Griffith,	White Hall, Va.,	"	"
449. Nelson W. Scott,	Marshallton, Pa.,	"	"
451. Joel Evans,	Marple, Pa.,	"	"
452. Levi Hoopes,	Willistown Inn, Pa.,	"	"
453. Chris. H. Alexander,	Philadelphia, Pa.,	5th mo.,	1858.
454. Phineas P. James,	West Chester, Pa.,	11th mo.,	1857.
455. Henry C. Carlile,	W. Philadelphia, Pa.,	"	"

STUDENTS.

FOURTH THOUSAND.

NAME.	RESIDENCE.	DATE OF ENTRY.
456. Henry E. Gould,	Newport, R. I.,	11th mo., 1857.
457. John T. Jones,	Fawn Grove, Pa.,	" "
458. Lewis B. George,	White Hall, Va.,	" "
459. Ed. W. Pierson,	Avondale, Pa.,	" "
460. Ziba D. Walter,	Centreville, Del.,	" "
461. James T. Wood,	Philadelphia, Pa.,	5th mo., 1856.
462. George J. French,	Milestown, Pa.,	" "
463. Daniel Decou,	Georgetown, N. J.,	" "
464. Joseph G. Seal,	Avondale, Pa.,	" "
465. William Scattergood,	Philadelphia, Pa.,	" "
466. Charles Gruwell,	Damascoville, Ohio,	" "
467. George W. Bacon,	Greenwich, N. J.,	" "
468. Richard Maris,	Lionville, Pa.,	" "
469. Asabel W. Cooper,	Christiana, Pa.,	" "
470. Charles Horney,	Philadelphia, Pa.,	" "
471. Joseph E. Carlile,	W. Philadelphia, Pa.,	" "
472. William W. Stapler,	Wilmington, Del.,	" "
473. Penrose Maule,	Port Royal, Pa.,	" "
474. Ellwood Cooper,	Christiana, Pa.,	" "
475. Marcellus Balderston,	Philadelphia, Pa.,	" "
476. Samuel H. Cloud,	Woodbury, N. J.,	" "
477. Timothy A. Pharo,*	Tuckerton, N. J.,	11th mo., "
478. Norris J. Scott,	West Haverford, Pa.,	5th mo., "
479. J. W. Worthington,	Philadelphia, Pa.,	" "
480. William P. Jones,	Conshohocken, Pa.,	11th mo., "
481. Robert Taylor,	Columbus, N. J.,	" "
482. William Balderston,	Fallsington, Pa.,	" "
483. George B. Taylor,	Philadelphia, Pa.,	" "
484. Elias Wildman,	Morrisville, Pa.,	" "
485. Atkinson H. Rich,	Three Tons, Pa.,	" "
486. D. C. Satterthwaite,	Crosswicks, N. J.,	" "
487. Jonathan L. Cresson,	Philadelphia, Pa.,	" "
488. John E. Darnell,	Mt. Laurel, N. J.,	" "
489. Robert B. Ivins,	Shrewsbury, N. J.,	" "
490. William W. Dilks,	Germantown, Pa.,	" "
491. Ellis P. Lee,	Stonersville, Pa.,	" "
492. Jos. B. Scattergood,	Philadelphia, Pa.,	" "
493. Thomas J. Windle,	Guthrieville, Pa.,	" 1859.
494. David Tomlinson,	Ivy Mills, Pa.,	" 1856.
496. William W. Hazard,	Poplar Ridge, N. Y.,	" 1859.
497. Benj. W. Gauntt,	Jobstown, N. J.,	" 1856.
498. Charles M. Tatnall,	Wilmington, Del.,	5th mo. 1857.
499. William E. Allen,	Philadelphia, Pa.,	" "
500. William H. Jenks,	"	" "
501. Nath. B. Crenshaw,	Richmond, Va.,	" "

* Deceased at the school, Second mo. 16th, 1857.

GENERAL CATALOGUE.

FOURTH THOUSAND.

NAME.	RESIDENCE.	DATE OF ENTRY.	
502. Charles R. Deacon,	Burlington, N. J.,	5th mo.,	1857
503. Isaac Stokes,	Woodbury, N. J.,	"	"
504. Samuel A. Willits,	Haddonfield, N. J.,	"	"
505. William Hutton,	Chester, Pa.,	"	"
506. Benjamin C. Reeve,	Allowaystown, N. J.,	"	"
507. John Blackwood,	Haddonfield, N. J.,	"	"
508. Phillips Chambers,	Fairville, Pa.,	"	"
509. Walter A. Ricks,	Ruther Glenn, Va.,	"	"
510. Ed. L. Murray,	Flushing, N. Y.,	"	"
511. John C. Maule,	Philadelphia, Pa.,	"	"
512. Joseph G. Evans,	Haddonfield, N. J.,	"	"
513. William W. Biddle,	West Chester, Pa.,	11th mo.,	"
514. Charles S. Dutton,	Philadelphia, Pa.,	"	"
515. Caspar T. Sharpless,	Moorestown, N. J.,	"	"
516. Eli Sharpless,	"	"	"
517. Isaac P. Garrett,	Upper Darby, Pa.,	"	"
518. Samuel B. Darnell,	Marlton, N. J.,	"	"
519. George G. King,	Burlington, N. J.,	"	"
520. William G. King,	"	"	"
( ) Joseph Tomlinson,	Westtown, Pa.,	"	1858.
521. Benjamin A. Vail,	Rahway, N. J.,	"	1857.
522. Franklin Eastburn,	Attleboro', Pa.,	"	"
523. Robert G. Lear,	Warren Tavern, Pa.,	"	1859.
524. Rich. W. Randolph,	Philadelphia, Pa.,	"	1857.
525. William Taylor,	"	"	"
526. Ed. Mendenhall,	Parkersville, Pa.,	"	"
527. Nehemiah Whitacre,	Muncy, Pa.,	"	"
528. Samuel J. Scott,	Sandy Spring, Md.,	"	1859.
529. T. Scattergood, Jr.,	Philadelphia, Pa.,	"	1857.
530. George W. Ivins,	Shrewsbury, N. J.,	5th mo.,	1858.
531. Chas. E. Woodward,	Marshallton, Pa.,	11th mo.,	"
534. William Harry,	Lionville, Pa.,	"	"
535. R. H. Johnson,	Parkesburg, Pa.,	7th mo.,	"
536. David S. Haviland,	Harrison, N. Y.,	11th mo.,	"
537. Walter Haviland,	"	"	"
539. Caleb P. Cooper,	Parkesburg, Pa.,	"	1859.
540. Thos. F. Matthews,	Cockeysville, Md.,	"	1858.
541. Ed. H. Matthews,	"	"	"
542. H. B. Gilkeson,	Mount Sidney, Va.,	5th mo.,	1860.
543. Joseph K. Cally,	Camden, Del.,	"	"
544. Isaac N. Vail,	Lloydsville, Ohio,	"	"
545. Albert W. Preston,	Conowingo, Md.,	11th mo.,	1862.
546. Alfred Haines,	Trout Run, Pa.,	5th mo.,	1860.
547. Jas. Wilson Masters,	Millville, Pa.,	11th mo.,	"
548. Henry C. Scull,	Woodstown, N. J.,	"	"
549. John Eldridge,	Johnstown, Pa.,	"	"
550. William Jolliffe,	Stephenson's Sta., Va.,	"	"

STUDENTS. 179

FOURTH THOUSAND.

NAME.	RESIDENCE.	DATE OF ENTRY.
551. Charles T. Abbott,	Salem, N. J.,	11th mo., 1860.
552. Isaac P. Hazard,	Poplar Ridge, N. Y.,	" "
553. Isaac C. Hoge,	Hamilton, Va.,	" "
554. Stephen W. Post,	N. Hempstead, L. I.,	" 1862.
555. Abiah Cope,	Marshallton, Pa.,	" 1860.
556. Benjamin F. Cloud,	Woodbury, N. J.,	" "
557. George Cooper,	Ercildoun, Pa.,	" "
558. Isaac L. Troth,	Columbus, N. J.,	" "
559. Alfred Whitacre,	Muncy, Pa.,	" "
560. Joseph Heacock,	Greenwood, Pa.,	" "
( ) Ellwood Tomlinson,	Westtown, Pa.,	" 1861.
561. Edmund Wood,	Rahway, N. J.,	" 1860.
562. Samuel W. Moore,	Christiana, Pa.,	" "
563. Wilmer W. Marshall,	Newport, Del.,	5th mo., 1861.
564. Wm. H. Tomlinson,	Willistown Inn, Pa.,	11th mo., 1860.
565. James E. Bangs,	Philadelphia, Pa.,	5th mo., 1861.
566. George Balderston,	Port Deposit, Md.,	11th mo., 1860.
567. Wm. P. Husband,	Dublin, Md.,	5th mo., 1861.
568. Mifflin Bell,	Bloomington, Ill.,	" "
569. Ed. C. Hopkins,	Darlington, Md.,	" "
570. Samuel Johnson,	Lima, Pa.,	" "
571. Samuel C. Hatton,	Sugartown, Pa.,	11th mo., "
572. Skipwith H. Coale,	Baltimore, Md.,	6th mo., "
573. Samuel G. Painter,	Fallston, Md.,	11th mo., "
574. J. Howard Palmer,	Centreville, Del.,	" "
575. Amor Nichols,	"	" "
576. Alban Harvey,	"	" "
577. George Thomas, Jr.,	W. Whiteland, Pa.,	" "
578. Chas. T. Thomas,	"	" "
579. William L. Jefferis,	Chandlerville, Pa.,	" "
580. Nathan Sharpless,	"	" "
581. Joseph Conrow,	Flushing, Ohio,	" "
582. Frank N. Hopkins,	Baltimore, Md.,	" "
583. Morris S. Cope,	Marshallton, Pa.,	" "
584. Joshua H. Shaw,	Darlington, Md.,	" "
585. Alfred B. Taylor,	Doe Run, Pa.,	" "
586. William B. Bell,	Experiment Mills, Pa.,	" "
587. Edward B. Temple,	Doe Run, Pa.,	" "
588. John F. Davis,	Barnesville, Ohio,	" "
589. Thomas W. Bundy,	"	" "
590. William E. Bundy,	Pugh, Ohio,	" "
591. John F. Kinsey,	Quakertown, Pa.,	5th mo., 1862
592. Ellwood Ball,	"	" "
593. Alexis Thomas Cope,	Philadelphia, Pa.,	" "
594. Henry C. Valentine,	Bellefonte, Pa.,	" "
595. John B. Valentine,	"	" "
596. George W. Taylor,	West Grove, Pa.,	" "

GENERAL CATALOGUE.

FOURTH THOUSAND.

NAME.	RESIDENCE.	DATE OF ENTRY.
597. Walter O. Shreeve,	Long-a-coming, N. J.,	5th mo., 1862
598. William T. Forsythe,	West Chester, Pa.,	11th mo., "
599. Isaac Sharpless,	Birmingham, Pa.,	" "
600. C. Canby Balderston,	W. Nottingham, Md.,	" "
601. James W. Morris,	Mansfield, Pa.,	5th mo., 1858.
602. Joseph S. Haines,	Philadelphia, Pa.,	" "
603. Henry W. Sharpless,	"	" "
604. Howard A. Hunt,	"	" "
605. Samuel F. Rudolph,	Marcus Hook, Pa.,	" "
606. Wm. P. G. Shotwell,	Plainfield, N. J.,	" "
607. John Haines,	Oxford Valley, Pa.,	" "
608. Thomas Walmsley,	Burlington, N. J.,	" "
609. Samuel R. Matlack,	Philadelphia, Pa.,	" "
610. Josiah N. Woolman,	W. Philadelphia, Pa.,	" "
611. Ira J. Parker,	Millville, Pa.,	" "
612. Joshua Brown,	Fallsington, Pa.,	11th mo., "
613. David J. Brown,	"	" "
614. Henry Lippincott,	"	" "
615. Enos Thomas,	Philadelphia, Pa.,	" "
616. Aaron E. Borton,	Mt. Laurel, N. J.,	" "
617. N. Newlin Smith,	Darlington, Md.,	" "
618. S. Preston Carpenter,	Salem, N. J.,	" "
619. John K. Hulme,	Bristol, Pa.,	" "
620. Joseph H. Haines,	Medford, N. J.,	" "
621. Jos. H. Balderston,	Port Deposit, Md.,	" "
622. Nathan H. Edgerton,	Barnesville, Ohio,	5th mo., 1860.
623. Levi S. Thomas,	New Brighton, Pa.,	11th mo., 1862.
624. Thomas B. Jones,	Fallsington, Pa.,	" 1858.
625. Wm. Mendenhall,	Parkersville, Pa.,	" "
626. William Roberts,	Medford, N. J.,	" "
627. Lemuel Brackin,	Colerain, Ohio,	" 1862.
628. Milton Starbuck,	Barnesville, Ohio,	" "
629. John C. Hall,	East Fairfield, Ohio,	" "
630. Job McCarty,	Eldredville, Pa.,	" 1858.
631. Alfred K. Smith,	Philadelphia, Pa.,	" "
632. Isaac Jones,	Fallsington, Pa.,	" "
633. Lewis Pennington,	West Grove, Pa.,	" 1862.
634. Charles Burton, Jr.,	Fallsington, Pa.,	" 1858.
635. John M. Palmer,	Sandy Springs, Md.,	" "
636. Lee H. Buffington,	Philadelphia, Pa.,	5th mo., 1859.
637. Jos. K. Lippincott,	Woodstown, N. J.,	" "
638. Wm. H. Welding,	Brooklyn, N. Y.,	" "
639. Walter Wood,	Philadelphia, Pa.,	" "
640. Cleayton Wistar,	Salem, N. J.,	" "
641. Thomas Dutton,	Philadelphia, Pa.,	" "
642. Joseph H. Wills,	Mt. Holly, N. J.,	" "
643. Lindley Haines, Jr.,	Philadelphia, Pa.,	" "

STUDENTS.

FOURTH THOUSAND.

NAME.	RESIDENCE.	DATE OF ENTRY.
644. Francis Morris,	Philadelphia, Pa.,	11th mo., 1859
645. Joseph A. Haines,	Medford, N. J.,	" "
646. James W. Haines,	"	" "
647. Israel R. Scott,	Concordville, Pa.,	" "
648. Thomas Hall,	Spencer's Station, Ohio,	" "
649. Edward Bonsall,	Philadelphia, Pa.,	" "
650. Reuben Eldridge,	Goshenville, Pa.,	" "
651. Joseph Mathis,	Mt. Laurel, N. J.,	" "
652. William J. Evans,	Marlton, N. J.,	" "
653. S. Smith Griffith,	Eagle P. O., Pa.,	" "
654. William Sharpless,	Chester, Pa.,	" "
655. Wm. S. Woolman,	Fallsington, Pa.,	" "
656. William H. Taylor,	West Chester, Pa.,	" "
657. Samuel C. Collins,	Trenton, N. J.,	" "
658. Jonathan Jones, Jr.,	Branchtown, Pa.,	" "
659. Henry Cope, Jr.,	Philadelphia, Pa.,	" "
660. Arthur W. Palmer,	Sandy Springs, Md.,	" "
661. Wm. H. Warrington,	Cinnaminson, N. J.,	" "
662. Hudson B. Taylor,	Rancocas, N. J.,	" "
663. William B. Conrad,	Philadelphia, Pa.,	" "
664. Joseph Pennell,	Lima, Pa.,	" "
665. C. Henry Leeds,	Cinnaminson, N. J.,	5th mo., 1860.
666. Thomas S. Bishop,	Columbus, N. J.,	" "
667. Edward W. Twining,	Yardleyville, Pa.,	" "
668. James Hilyard, Jr.,	Rancocas, N. J.,	" "
669. Samuel P. Bartlett,	Tuckerton, N. J.,	" "
670. Stephen Wood,	New York, N. Y.,	" "
671. Chas. L. Sharpless,	Philadelphia, Pa.,	" "
672. Edward B. Richie,	"	" "
673. Charles Bell,	Experiment Mills, Pa.,	11th mo., 1862.
674. John C. Deacon, Jr.,	Burlington, N. J.,	5th mo., 1860.
675. Wm. H. Randolph,	Philadelphia, Pa.,	" "
676. John B. Jones,	Fallsington, Pa.,	11th mo., "
677. Henry B. Abbott,	Salem, N. J.,	" "
678. Welding Ring,	Cornwall, N. Y.,	" "
679. John B. Buckman,	Newtown, Pa.,	" "
680. J. M. Mendenhall,	Westminster, N. C.,	" "
681. Edmund W. Scott,	Sandy Spring, Md.,	12th mo., 1862.
682. William Matlack,	Moorestown, N. J.,	11th mo., 1860.
683. Enos P. Eldridge,	Goshenville, Pa.,	" "
684. George Trimble,	Chester, Pa.,	" "
685. Benj. H. Middleton,	Crosswicks, N. J.,	" "
686. Joshua S. Wills,	Rancocas, N. J.,	" "
687. Josiah Hall,	Harrisville, Ohio,	" "
688. Howard H. Wills,	Rancocas, N. J.,	" "
689. William C. Haines,	Medford, Pa.,	" "
690. Charles J Taylor,	Philadelphia, Pa.,	" "

FOURTH THOUSAND.

NAME.	RESIDENCE.	DATE OF ENTRY.
691. John Hopkins,	Port Deposit, Md.,	11th mo., 1860
692. Zebedee Haines,	Medford, N. J.,	" "
693. William E. Tatum,	Woodbury, N. J.,	" "
695. William Livezey,	Centre Bridge, Pa.,	" "
696. Richard J. Brown,	Fallsington, Pa.,	" "
697. Edmund D. Wills,	Princeton, N. J.,	5th mo., 1861.
698. Joseph Frame,	Lloydsville, Ohio,	" "
699. Isaac S. Lowry,	Philadelphia, Pa.,	" "
700. John S. Lowry,	"	" "
701. Davis P. Walter,	Parkersville, Pa.,	" "
702. Henry Bacon,	Philadelphia, Pa.,	" "
703. N. H. Middleton,	Crosswicks, N. J.,	" "
704. Samuel R. Matlack,	Moorestown, N. J.,	11th mo., "
705. David E. Darnell,	Mt. Laurel, N. J.,	" "
706. John I. Bishop,	Columbus, N. J.,	" "
707. Robert P. Brown,	Fallsington, Pa.,	" "
708. B. C. Satterthwaite,	Oxford Valley, Pa.,	" "
709. Charles Collins,	Morrisville, Pa.,	" "
710. John P. Balderston,	Port Deposit, Md.,	" "
711. Giles S. Woolman,	Fallsington, Pa.,	" "
713. W. Henry Taylor,	Columbus, N. J.,	" "
714. Christopher H. Jones,	Fallsington, Pa.,	" "
715. John Wistar,	Salem, N. J.,	" "
716. George C. Kinsey,	Quakertown, Pa.,	5th mo., 1863
717. Henry P. Whitacre,	Muncy, Pa.,	11th mo., 1861.
718. Nathan C. Gauntt,	Jobstown, N. J.,	" "
719. Joshua Sharpless,	McClellansville, Del.,	" "
720. Lloyd Baily,	Germantown, Pa.,	" "
721. Joseph G. Fogg,	Philadelphia, Pa.,	" "
722. Paul S. Lippincott,	Woodstown, N. J.,	" "
723. Wm. H. Blackwood,	Haddonfield, N. J.,	" "
724. Evert P. Maule,	Philadelphia, Pa.,	5th mo., 1862
725. David Scattergood,	"	" "
726. John W. Bartlett,	Tuckerton, N. J.,	" "
727. Jonathan Bell, Jr.,	Plymouth, Pa.,	" "
728. Ezra Comfort,	Conshohocken, Pa.,	" "
729. Ellis Middleton,	Crosswicks, N. J.,	" "
730. Edward H. Coffin,	Newburg, N. Y.,	" "
731. Wistar Newbold,	Philadelphia, Pa.,	" "
732. Joshua D. Evans,	Elizabethtown, N. J.,	" "
733. James P. Cooper,	Ercildoun, Pa.,	11th mo., "
734. •William S. Jenness,	Burlington, N. J.,	" "
735. John M. Griffith,	White Hall, Va.,	12th mo., "
736. Joseph K. Evens,	Marlton, N. J.,	11th mo., "
737. Ezra E. Darnell,	Mt. Laurel, N. J.,	" "
738. John P. Canby,	Hulmeville, Pa.,	" "
739. Joseph S. Moore,	Nine Points, Pa.,	" "

STUDENTS. 183

FOURTH THOUSAND.

NAME.	RESIDENCE.	DATE OF ENTRY.
740. Joseph Lownes,	New Hope, Pa.,	11th mo., 1862.
741. William H. House,	Goshenville, Pa.,	5th mo., 1863.
742. J. Howard Masters,	Benton, Pa.,	11th mo., 1862.
743. Edwin Whitacre,	Muncy, Pa.,	" "
744. Franklin Bassett,	Stanton, Del.,	5th mo., 1863.
745. Henry T. Gardiner,	Mt. Laurel, N. J.,	11th mo., 1862.
746. Thomas M. Warren,	Burlington, N. J.,	" "
747. Joseph G. Painter,	Fallston, Md.,	5th mo., 1863
748. Marshall J. Walter,	Parkersville, Pa.,	11th mo., 1862
749. Henry H. Elkinton,	Philadelphia, Pa.,	5th mo., 1863
750. James C. Roberts,	West Chester, Pa.,	" "
751. Edward M. Wistar,	Germantown, Pa.,	" "
752. T. Ellicott Lindley,	Avondale, Pa.,	" "
753. Isaac Remington,	Philadelphia, Pa.,	" "
754. Samuel S. Williams,	"	" "
755. Duncan O. Bartlett,	Bethlehem, Pa.,	" "
756. William Trimble,	Chester, Pa.,	" "
757. Chas. F. Welding,	Brooklyn, N. Y.,	" "
758. Thomas K. Carey,	Baltimore, Md.,	" "
759. William B. Harlan,	West Chester, Pa.,	" "
760. R. Albert Wills,	Mt. Holly, N. J.,	" "
761. S. H. Edwards,	Huntington, Ind.,	" "
762. Alfred P. Edge,	London Grove, Pa.,	" "
763. William K. Smith,	Smyrna, Ohio,	" "
764. George Abbott, Jr.,	Salem, N. J.,	" "
765. James M. Rote,	Millville, Pa.,	" "
766. J. Franklin Hilyard,	New York, N. Y.,	" "
767. Richard Wistar, Jr.,	Salem, N. J.,	" "
768. James W. Janney,	Hillsboro', Va.,	" "
769. Abram H. Smith,	Philadelphia, Pa.,	" "
770. Edward B. Taylor,	Cinnaminson, N. J.,	11th mo., "
771. Wm. C. Holloway,	Flushing, Ohio,	5th mo., "
772. Stuart Wood,	Philadelphia, Pa.,	" "
773. John B. Comfort,	Moorestown, N. J.,	11th mo., "
774. William D. Maule,	Port Royal, Pa.,	" "
775. John W. Stokes,	Long Branch, N. J.,	" "
776. Newbold R. Haines,	Philadelphia, Pa.,	" "
777. Lewis E. Bonsall,	"	" "
778. Thomas K. Brown,	"	" "
779. Samuel C. Eastburn,	Attleboro', Pa.,	" "
780. Edward H. Cloud,	Woodbury, N. J.,	" "
781. Hamilton Haines,	Medford, N. J.,	" "
782. Henry H. Wilkins,	Rancocas, N. J.,	" "
783. James Cope,	West Chester, Pa.,	" "
784. William Carpenter,	Salem, N. J.,	" "
785. Joseph C. Sharpless,	McClellansville, Del.,	" "
786. Walter B. Smith,	Philadelphia, Pa.,	5th mo., "

GENERAL CATALOGUE.

FOURTH THOUSAND.

NAME.	RESIDENCE.	DATE OF ENTRY.
787. Ellis H. Masters,	Millville, Pa.,	11th mo., 1863
788. J. Parvin Masters,	"	" "
789. Francis Haviland,	Harrison, N. Y.,	" "
790. H. W. Worthington,	Leavenworth, Ks.,	5th mo., 1865
791. Alfred England,	Landsdale, Pa.,	11th mo., 1863
792. Lewis C. Kinsey,	Centreville, Del.,	" "
793. Morgan Troth,	Bordentown, N. J.,	" "
794. William P. Evans,	London Grove, Pa.,	" "
795. Samuel Speakman,	Coatesville, Pa.,	" "
796. Edward Garrigues,	Woodbury, N. J.,	5th mo., 1864.
797. M. C. Kimber,	Philadelphia, Pa.,	" "
798. George M. Lamb,	Philopolis, Md.,	11th mo., 1863.
799. George S. Hutton,	Chester, Pa.,	5th mo., 1864.
800. J. Howell Leeds,	Philadelphia, Pa.,	" "
801. Samuel A. Bacon,	Greenwich, N. J.,	11th mo., 1863.
802. Henry S. Williams,	Philadelphia, Pa.,	5th mo., 1864.
803. John Wm. Cook,	Glenville, Md.,	11th mo., "
804. Thomas M. Janney,	Purcellsville, Va.,	" 1863.
805. John G. Haines,	Medford, N. J.,	" 1864.
806. William McCluen,	Marple, Pa.,	5th mo., "
807. Thomas Phillips, Jr.,	Waterford, Va.,	11th mo., 1863.
808. Joseph Kester,	Millville, Pa.,	5th mo., 1864.
809. C. Carroll Cook,	Philadelphia, Pa.,	" "
810. J. Barclay Hilyard,	Rancocas, N. J.,	11th mo., 1863.
811. William Bangs,	Germantown, Pa.,	5th mo., 1864.
812. George A. Hunt,	Philadelphia, Pa.,	" "
813. Edward Matthews,	Philopolis, Md.,	11th mo., 1863.
814. Henry K. Peckham,	Smyrna, N. Y.,	5th mo., 1866.
815. William M. Parker,	Millville, Pa.,	11th mo., 1864.
816. Benjamin Price,	Philopolis, Md.,	" 1863.
817. Howard Rich,	Danboro', Pa.,	" 1864.
818. Isaac H. Lear,	Warren Tavern, Pa.,	" "
819. Jacob L. Price,	Philopolis, Md.,	" 1863.
820. John W. Borton,	Rancocas, N. J.,	5th mo., 1866.
821. William Jones,	Moorestown, N. J.,	11th mo., 1864.
822. Alfred S. Wills,	Rancocas, N. J.,	" 1863.
823. E. C. Shoemaker,	Upper Dublin, Pa.,	" 1864.
824. T. S. Shoemaker,	"	" "
825. Wilmer Cheyney,	Street Road, Pa.,	" 1863.
826. John N. Haines,	Medford, N. J.,	" 1864.
827. George Williams,	Rancocas, N. J.,	" "
828. William J. Street,	Salem, Ohio,	" 1863.
829. Charles G. Clark,	Indianapolis, Ind.,	" 1864.
830. Biddle Reeves,	Woodbury, N. J.,	" "
831. Sam. H. Lippincott,	Cinnaminson, N. J.,	" 1863.
832. William H. Moon,	Morrisville, Pa.,	" 1864.
833. Charles N. Thorp,	Salem, N. J.,	" "

STUDENTS.

FOURTH THOUSAND.

NAME.	RESIDENCE.	DATE OF ENTRY.
834. Edward Webster,	Glen Riddle, Pa.,	11th mo., 1863.
835. Joshua Barton,	Marlton, N. J.,	" 1864.
836. Albert Gardiner,	"	" "
837. Charles W. Lewis,	Jerusalem Md.,	" 1863.
838. Joseph J. Jolliffe,	Martinsburg, Va.,	" 1864.
839. Samuel E. Bell,	Bloomington, Ill.,	5th mo., 1865.
840. Lindley M. Hoge,	Flushing, Ohio,	11th mo., 1863.
841. Thomas M. Webster,	Lima, Pa.,	5th mo., 1864.
842. Charles T. Malone,	Philadelphia, Pa.,	" "
843. Benjamin P. Hoopes,	Avondale, Pa.,	11th mo., 1863.
844. William C. Malone,	Philadelphia, Pa.,	5th mo., 1865.
845. Edward P. Allinson,	Burlington, N. J.,	" "
846. Davis Yearsley,	Coatesville, Pa.,	11th mo., 1863.
847. John G. Willits,	Haddonfield, N. J.,	5th mo., 1865.
848. Wm. Henry Haines,	Philadelphia, Pa.,	" "
849. Webster Gibson,	Circleville, Va.,	11th mo., 1863.
850. Henry Taylor,	Philadelphia, Pa.,	5th mo., 1865.
851. George L. Jennings,	Sandy Spring, Md.,	11th mo., 1864.
852. John S. Pennell,	Lima, Pa.,	" 1863.
853. John J. Chambers,	Strickerville, Pa.,	" 1864.
854. Geo. Fitzwater, Jr.,	Philopolis, Md.,	" "
855. William Kite, Jr.,	Birmingham, Pa.,	" 1863.
856. Joseph Fawcett,	Sandy Spring, Md.,	" 1864.
857. Walter Stabler,	Baltimore, Md.,	" "
858. Robert H. Miller,	Sandy Spring, Md.,	5th mo., "
859. Charles M. Stabler,	Baltimore, Md.,	11th mo., "
860. William Wright,	Chester Hill, Ohio,	5th mo., 1865.
861. Alfred Haviland,	Harrison, N. Y.,	" 1864.
862. Joseph Evans,	Onarga, Ill.,	11th mo., "
863. Joseph Webster,	Ercildoun, Pa.,	" "
864. H. M. Cromwell,	New York, N. Y.,	5th mo., "
865. Joseph Evans,	Lima, Pa.,	11th mo., "
866. Joshua M. Shelley,	Phœnix, Md.,	" "
867. Watson W. Dewees,	Pennsville, Ohio,	5th mo., 1865.
868. Lindley B. Steer,	Colerain, Ohio,	11th mo., 1864.
869. Isaac Nicholson,	Haddonfield, N. J.,	" "
870. Jonas P. Cook,	Port Deposit, Md.,	5th mo., "
871. Lewis P. Ash,	Wagontown, Pa.,	11th mo., "
872. Walter Reese,	Baltimore, Md.,	" "
873. Johnson P. Strawn,	Quakertown, Pa.,	5th mo., "
874. Robert V. Miller,	Baltimore, Md.,	11th mo., "
875. William G. Price,	Philopolis, Md.,	" "
876. Francis Woodward,	New York, N. Y.,	5th mo., "
877. William J. Pusey,	London Grove, Pa.,	11th mo., "
878. Eli M. Hibberd,	New Windsor, Md.,	" "
879. Webster Street,	Salem, Ohio,	5th mo., "
880. William H. Wilkins,	Rancocas, N. J.,	11th mo., "

15*

GENERAL CATALOGUE.

FOURTH THOUSAND.

NAME.	RESIDENCE.	DATE OF ENTRY.
881. Joshua Husband, Jr.,	Dublin, Md.,	5th mo., 1864
882. Joseph Johnson,	Glen Riddle, Pa.,	" "
883. John W. Kinsey,	Quakertown, Pa.,	" "
884. Henry Marshall,	Hamorton, Pa.,	" "
885. J. Leander Haines,	Pleasant Grove, Pa.,	" "
886. Ezra H. Brown,	Mt. Laurel, N. J.,	11th mo., "
887. Alfred Troth,	Bordentown, N. J.,	" "
888. Joshua Matthews,	Philopolis, Md.,	" "
889. William J. Corse,	Baltimore, Md.,	" "
890. Frank Corse,	"	" "
891. George Wood,	Trenton, N. J.,	" "
892. Wm. G. Hoyle,	Lloydsville, Ohio,	5th mo., 1865.
893. Alfred Sharpless,	Strickersville, Pa.,	11th mo., 1864.
894. W. Walter Hoopes,	Westtown, Pa.,	" "
895. Frederic D. Gove,	Hamilton, Min.,	" "
896. Samuel G. Redmond,	New York, N. Y.,	" "
897. David B. Hedley,	Medina, N. Y.,	" "
898. William L. Atwater,	Somerset, N. Y.,	" "
899. John Janney,	Hillsboro', Va.,	" "
900. Robert M. Janney,	"	" "
901. David W. Garrigues,	Woodbury, N. J.,	5th mo., 1865.
902. Marshall Fell, Jr.,	West Chester, Pa.,	" "
903. Richard Thomas,	Bellefonte, Pa.,	" "
904. James H. Crenshaw,	Richmond, Va.,	" "
905. Charles Cranstone,	Yorktown, Va.,	" "
906. Alfred H. Cranstone,	"	" "
907. Albert L. Hilles,	Frankford, Pa.,	" "
908. William P. Hilles,	"	" "
909. Edward Lippincott,	Rising Sun, Pa.,	" "
910. Francis L. Price,	Media, Pa.,	" 1866.
911. I. Powell Leeds,	Cinnaminson, N. J.,	11th mo., 1865.
912. Thomas B. Decou,	Trenton, N. J.,	" "
913. Howard Middleton,	Crosswicks, N. J.,	" "
914. Charles B. Heston,	Bristol, Pa.,	" "
915. Edward A. Kashner,	Columbus, N. J.,	" "
916. J. Miller Scarlett,	Birdsboro', Pa.,	" "
917. Nathaniel Jones,	Moorestown, N. J.,	" "
918. Richard T. Cadbury,	Philadelphia, Pa.,	5th mo., 1866.
919. Mark B. Taylor,	"	" 1865.
920. Robert R. Hulme,	Bristol, Pa.,	" 1866.
921. J. Paul Kirkbride,	Burlington, N. J.,	" "
922. Geo. B. Kirkbride,	"	" "
923. H. A. Pennock,	Upper Darby, Pa.,	" "
924. Chas. D. Stackhouse,	Howellville, Pa.,	" "
925. J. Larkin Smedley,	Chelsea, Pa.,	" 1867.
927. Charles J. Walton,	Philadelphia, Pa.,	" 1866
928. Benjamin Thorp, Jr.,	Salem, N. J.,	" "

STUDENTS. 187

FOURTH THOUSAND.

NAME.	RESIDENCE.	DATE OF ENTRY.
929. Joseph G. Woolman,	W. Philadelphia, Pa.,	5th mo., 1866.
930. William Mathis,	Jobstown, N. J.,	11th mo., "
931. Alex. Underhill,	Brooklyn, N. Y.,	5th mo., "
932. Charles Penrose,	Pennsville, Ohio,	" "
933. Dillon Gibbons,	Barnesville, Ohio,	" "
934. Frank Adams,	Indianapolis, Ind.,	" "
935. Robert H. Adams,	"	" "
936. Joseph H. Branson,	Flushing, Ohio,	" "
937. Eph. W. Holloway,	"	" "
938. Edward A. Powell,	Trappe, Md.,	" "
939. Samuel C. Thomas,	New Brighton, Pa.,	" "
940. Henry Trimble,	Chester, Pa.,	" 1867.
941. Joseph Hall,	Salem, Ohio,	" 1866.
942. Wm. D. Hartshorne,	Brighton, Md.,	" "
943. Joseph Williams,	Flushing, Ohio,	" 1867.
944. William H. Smedley,	Frankford, Pa.,	11th mo., 1866.
945. James C. Borton,	Rancocas, N. J.,	" "
946. Nehemiah Wright,	Chester Hill, Ohio,	5th mo., "
947. Adna H. Sutton,	Clintondale, N. Y.,	" "
948. Daniel Cromwell,	New York, N. Y.,	" "
949. Josiah P. Engle,	Mt. Laurel, N. J.,	11th mo., "
950. Barclay Thomas,	Concordville, Pa.,	" "
951. Joseph Eldridge,	Muscatine, Iowa,	" 1864.
952. Thomas C. Hoge,	Flushing, Ohio,	" "
953. Wilson Pennington,	West Grove, Pa.,	" "
954. Sam. J. Wetherald,	West Haverford, Pa.,	" "
955. Sam. H. Scattergood,	Sereno, Pa.,	5th mo., 1865.
956. Hastings England,	Quakertown, Pa.,	11th mo., "
957. Charles S. Taylor,	Cincinnati, Ohio,	5th mo., "
958. Frank W. Hillyard,	Rancocas, N. J.,	" "
959. Alfred Jessop,	York, Pa.,	" "
960. Joseph E. Mickle,	Oakdale, Pa.,	" "
961. John L. Balderston,	W. Nottingham, Md.,	" "
962. Philip Dunn,	Trenton, N. J.,	" "
963. David L. Matthews,	Cockeysville, Md.,	" "
964. John D. Branson,	Chester Hill, Ohio,	" "
965. John E. Forsythe,	Oak Hill, Pa.,	" "
966. Frederic H. Deacon,	Burlington, N. J.,	" "
967. George E. Deacon,	"	" "
968. Dan. L. Pennington,	West Grove, Pa.,	11th mo., "
969. Edward Haviland,	Harrison, N. Y.,	5th mo., "
970. Samuel R. Pusey,	Thorndale, Pa.,	11th mo., "
971. John W. Moore,	Nine Points, Pa.,	" "
972. Nathan G. Green,	West Chester, Pa.,	" "
973. W. Henry Kashner,	Columbus, N. J.,	" "
974. Wm. C. Nicholson,	Mt. Ephraim, N. J.,	" "
975. Richard P. Pim,	Thorndale, Pa.,	

GENERAL CATALOGUE.

FOURTH THOUSAND.

NAME.	RESIDENCE.	DATE OF ENTRY.
976. Howard Comfort,	Germantown, Pa.,	11th mo., 1865.
977. William Comfort,	"	" "
978. E. Satterthwaite,	Crosswicks, N. J.,	" "
979. Lewis P. Sharpless,	Strickersville, Pa.,	" "
980. Vincent Edge,	Downingtown, Pa.,	" "
981. Charles T. Wills,	Princeton, N. J.,	" "
982. Charles Wright, Jr.,	Columbus, N. J.,	" "
983. Hilles Lippincott,	Rising Sun, Pa.,	" "
984. Samuel Abbott,	Salem, N. J.,	" "
985. Nathan S. Roberts,	Mt. Laurel, N. J.,	" "
986. Geo. R. Chambers,	Strickersville, Pa.,	" "
987. M. C. Satterthwaite,	Attleboro', Pa.,	" "
988. John S. Garrigues,	West Haverford, Pa.,	" "
989. Mulford Haines,	Medford, N. J.,	" "
990. John Gardiner,	Mt. Laurel, N. J.,	" "
991. Walter T. Moore,	Salem, Ohio,	" "
992. Barclay Decou,	Trenton, N. J.,	" "
993. C. N. Balderston,	Port Deposit, Md.,	5th mo., 1867.
994. John W. Cloud,	Woodbury, N. J.,	11th mo., 1866.
995. Samuel S. Leeds,	Barnegat, N. J.,	5th mo., "
996. Charles Lee,	Stouersville, Pa.,	" "
997. Samuel B. Kester,	Millville, Pa.,	11th mo., "
998. R. Harlan Whitacre,	Muncy, Pa.,	5th mo., "
999. Barclay Lear,	Warren Tavern, Pa.,	" "
1000. Elisha Cook,	Glenville, Md.,	" "

FIFTH THOUSAND.

NAME.	RESIDENCE.	DATE OF ENTRY.
1. B. Gilpin Smith,	Darlington, Md.,	11th mo., 1866.
2. William T. Cooper,	Woodbury, N. J.,	" "
3. Joshua Taylor,	Columbus, N. J.,	" "
4. Charles E. Zelley,	Moorestown, N. J.,	5th mo., 1867.
5. Thos. B. Taylor,	West Chester, Pa.,	" "
6. Joseph Heacock,	Greenwood, Pa.,	11th mo., "
7. Ev. P. Roberts,	Moorestown, N. J.,	5th mo., "
8. Josiah T. Henrie,	Greenwood, Pa.,	" "
9. Henry M. Jones,	Germantown, Pa.,	" "
10. Wistar P. Brown,	West Chester, Pa.,	" "
11. Josiah T. Baily,	Yardville, N. J.,	" "
12. John C. Stokes,	Philadelphia, Pa.,	" "
13. J. How'd Yarnall,	Lima, Pa.,	" "
14. S. Mason Bines,	Germantown, Pa.,	" "
15. William T. Bines,	"	" "
16. J. K. Worthington,	Darlington, Md.,	" "
17. Ezra E. Prickitt,	Vincenttown, N. J.,	11th mo., "
18. Thomas B. Gould,	Moorestown, N. J.,	5th mo., "

STUDENTS.

FIFTH THOUSAND.

NAME.	RESIDENCE.	DATE OF ENTRY.
19. Edward B. Hilles,	Frankford, Pa.,	5th mo., 1867.
20. Edward Allen, Jr.,	Moorestown, N. J.,	" "
21. Charles Willits,	Haddonfield, N. J.,	" "
22. Howard Hamblin,	Philadelphia, Pa.,	" 1868
23. Alfred R. Bartlett,	Tuckerton, N. J.,	" 1867.
24. Rowland D. Allen,	Philadelphia, Pa.,	" "
25. William B. Crew,	Chester Hill, Ohio,	" "
26. Caspar W. Haines,	Cheltenham, Pa.,	" "
27. Biddle Bishop,	Columbus, N. J.,	11th mo., "
28. I. Henry Roberts,	Lumberton, N. J.,	" "
29. Ellis Haines,	Medford, N. J.,	" "
30. William K. Thorp,	West Chester, Pa.,	" "
31. John Griffith,	Winchester, Va.,	5th mo., 1868.
32. M. H. Jenks,	Philadelphia, Pa.,	" "
33. Chas. W. Warrington,	Greenwich, N. J.,	" "
34. Archie P. Willits,	Philadelphia, Pa.,	" "
35. Joseph B. Willits,	"	" "
36. Walter Price,	Media, Pa.,	" 1867.
37. Edward Brinton,	Chadd's Ford, Pa.,	" 1870.
38. Benjamin C. Comfort,	Conshohocken, Pa.,	5th mo., 1868.
39. John M. Kaighn,	Camden, N. J.,	" "
40. Samuel C. Moon,	Morrisville, Pa.,	" "
( ) Edwin A. Hoopes,	Westtown, Pa.,	
41. William W. Minster,	Goshenville, Pa.,	11th mo., 1866.
42. Harvey Sharpless,	Cinnaminson, N. J.,	" "
43. Charles Hoopes,	New Garden, Pa.,	" "
44. William W. Leeds,	Cinnaminson, N. J.,	" "
45. Charles H. Roberts,	Mt. Holly, N. J.,	" "
46. George E. Embree,	West Chester, Pa.,	" "
47. Chas. E. Huntington,	Philadelphia, Pa.,	" "
48. Milton Rote,	Millville, Pa.,	" "
49. Chas. E. Mendenhall,	Muncy, Pa.,	5th mo., 1869.
50. John H. Thomas,	Avondale, Pa.,	11th mo., 1866.
51. James Gardiner,	Mt. Laurel, N. J.,	" "
52. Charles W. Comfort,	Conshohocken, Pa.,	" "
53. Lawrence Tatum,	——, Ind.,	7th mo., "
54. Benjamin Edge,	Downingtown, Pa.,	11th mo., "
55. Jonathan Hatton,	Goshenville, Pa.,	" "
56. James Chambers,	New Garden, Pa.,	" "
57. John P. Sharpless,	McClellandsville, Del.,	" "
58. Edward Philips,	Avondale, Pa.,	" "
59. Ashton R. Tatnall,	Wilmington, Del.,	" "
60. William S. Bacon,	Greenwich, N. J.,	" "
61. Edwin Thorp,	Howellville, Pa.,	" "
62. James B. Cope,	Germantown, Pa.,	" "
63. Ashton R. Tatum,	Wilmington, Del.,	5th mo., 1867.
64. Milnor D. Smith,	West Chester, Pa.,	" "

M

FIFTH THOUSAND.

NAME.	RESIDENCE.	DATE OF ENTRY.
65. Chas. Balderston,	W. Nottingham, Md.,	5th mo., 1867
66. James L. Hedley,*	Medina, N. Y.,	" "
67. Alfred Hedley,	"	" "
68. Joseph E. Bonsall,	Salem, Ohio,	" "
69. Harmon L. Hutton,	Philadelphia, Pa.,	" "
70. Edward Cromwell,	New York, N. Y.,	" "
71. William C. Palmer,	Stanfordville, N. Y.,	" "
72. Abiah I. Palmer,	"	" "
73. Levis P. Newlin,	West Chester, Pa.,	" 1869.
74. William T. Zook,	Downingtown, Pa.,	11th mo., 1867.
75. C. H. Warrington,	West Chester, Pa.,	" "
76. H. Lea Forsythe,	"	" "
77. Charles H. Brown,	Mt. Laurel, N. J.,	" "
78. William H. Zelley,	Moorestown, N. J.,	" "
79. James F. Sharpless,	Birmingham, Pa.,	" "
80. Reece L. Thomas,	Chelsea, Pa.,	" "
( ) William H. Roberts,	Westtown, Pa.,	5th mo., "
( ) Davis H. Forsythe,	"	" "
81. Richard R. Tatnall,	Wilmington, Del.,	" 1869.
82. Maurice Comfort,	Moorestown, N. J.,	11th mo., 1867.
83. Harvey S. Comfort,	Conshohocken, Pa.,	" "
84. Wm. Henry Kite,	Cincinnati, Ohio,	" "
85. Thomas Tatnall,	Wilmington, Del.,	" "
86. Wm. E. Albertson,	Norristown, Pa.,	5th mo., 1868.
87. Henry A. Bell,	Experiment Mills, Pa.,	" "
88. J. John H. Taber,	Mt. Pleasant, Ohio,	" "
89. Wm. Edgar Henley,	Richmond, Ind.,	" "
90. Daniel W. Hopkins,	Havre-de-Grace, Md.,	" "
91. Edwin Cook,	Salem, Ohio,	" "
92. T. S. Cadwallader,	Philadelphia, Pa.,	" "
93. Jas. Albin Thorp,	Howellville, Pa.,	" "
94. William E. Curtis,	Cincinnati, Ohio,	" "
95. Frederic B. Johnson,	West Chester, Pa.,	" "
96. Louis P. Good,	West Grove, Pa.,	" 1869
97. Ed. Cadwallader,	Philadelphia, Pa.,	11th mo., 1868
98. Maris H. Eldridge,	Goshenville, Pa.,	" "
99. Alfred Embree,	Marshallton, Pa.,	" "
100. Amos L. Albertson,	Norristown, Pa.,	" "
101. Henry Tatnall,	Wilmington, Del.,	5th mo., "
102. Edward H. Jones,	Camden, N. J.,	" "
103. J. Barclay Hoge,	Flushing, Ohio,	" "
104. Arthur H. Bell,	Bloomington, Ill.,	" "
105. George H. Thompson,	Muscatine, Iowa,	" "
106. Isaac Buzby,	Rancocas, N. J.,	" "
107. T. Franklin Pharo,	Tuckerton, N. J.,	11th mo., "
108. Albert E. Pharo,	"	" "

* Deceased at the school, 7th of Seventh month, 1869.

STUDENTS.

FIFTH THOUSAND.

NAME.	RESIDENCE.	DATE OF ENTRY.
109. Mahlon Kirkbride,	Morrisville, Pa.,	" "
110. Ezra Parker,	Philadelphia, Pa.,	" "
111. W. L. Hendrickson,	Long Branch, N. J.,	" "
112. Henry W. Williams,	Rancocas, N. J.,	" "
113. Caspar Pennock,	Upper Darby, Pa.,	" "
114. Edmund Willits,	Philadelphia, Pa.,	5th mo., 1869
115. Joseph Rhoads,	Wilmington, Del.,	" "
116. Joseph L. Nicholson,	Camden, N. J.,	" "
117. H. M. Nicholson,	"	" "
118. Henry E. Betts,	Moorestown, N. J.,	11th mo., "
119. J. W. Nicholson,	Haddonfield, N. J.,	5th mo., "
120. Benj. A. Lippincott,	"	" "
121. Charles E. Pennock,	Upper Darby, Pa.,	" "
122. William J. Wood,	Poughkeepsie, N. Y.,	" "
123. George R. Dilks,	New Paris, Ohio,	" "
124. Benj. H. Lowry,	Philadelphia, Pa.,	" "
125. Chas. Lippincott,	"	" "
126. H. W. Satterthwaite,	Fallsington, Pa.,	11th mo., 1868.
127. Thomas Eastburn,	Attleboro', Pa.,	" "
128. Burrwood Moore,	Atlantic City, N. J.,	" "
129. Isaac Evans,	Glen Mills, Pa.,	" "
130. Alvin Cole.	Ridge Farm, Ill.,	" "
131. Townsend W. Hoopes,	Frankford, Pa.,	" "
132. Augustus C. Buzby,	Rancocas, N. J.,	" "
133. George J. Wills,	Princeton, N. J.,	" "
134. George B. Johnson,	West Chester, Pa.,	" "
135. William Webster,	Glen Riddle, Pa.,	" "
136. William Beans, Jr.,	Edgewood, Pa.,	" "
137. Andrew J. Wilson,	Guthrieville, Pa.,	" "
138. James Edgerton, Jr.,	Barnesville, Ohio,	" "
139. Edmund Post,	Old Westbury, L. I.,	" "
140. David Roberts, Jr.,	Moorestown, N. J.,	" "
141. Joseph H. Roberts,	"	" "
142. M. C. Pennington,	West Grove, Pa.,	" "
143. Harvey E. Heacock,	Greenwood, Pa.,	" "
144. Franklin Cope,	West Chester, Pa.,	" 1869.
145. John W. Mendenhall,	Muncy, Pa.,	" 1868.
146. Howard Thomas,*	Avondale, Pa.,	" "
147. Isaac M. Webster,	Lima, Pa.,	" "
148. Nathan B. Leeds,	Barnegat, N. J.,	" "
149. Josiah Collins,	"	" "
150. J. Harper Cloud,	Woodbury, N. J.,	" "
151. Samuel B. Deacon,	Princeton, N. J.,	" "
152. Joseph E. Pennock,	Upper Darby, Pa.	" "
153. E. Eldridge Pennock,	"	" "
154. J. Warner Parker,	West Chester, Pa.,	5th mo., 1869

* Deceased at the school, 5th of Seventh month, 1872.

FIFTH THOUSAND.

NAME.	RESIDENCE.	DATE OF ENTRY.
155. J. Trimble Zook,	Downingtown, Pa.,	11th mo., 1869
156. William T. Sharpless,	Westtown, Pa.,	" "
157. Asahel W. Moore,	Nine Points, Pa.,	" "
158. Morris Hoopes,	Avondale, Pa.,	" "
159. Walter S. Reeve,	Medford, N. J.,	" "
160. Franklin Roberts,	Philadelphia, Pa.,	" "
161. Howard Brinton,	Chadd's Ford, Pa.,	" "
162. Edward Forsythe,	"	" "
163. Franklin M. Potts,	Westtown, Pa.,	" "
164. William Mickle,	Marple, Pa.,	" "
165. Samuel Ash,	Wagontown, Pa.,	" "
166. Luke W. Morris,	Olney, Pa.,	" "
167. Jas. M. Bradshaw,	Somerton, Va.,	" "
168. C. William Arnold,	Stanfordville, N. Y.,	" "
169. Gilbert McGrew,	Smithfield, Ohio,	" "
170. Robert P. Thomas,	New Brighton, Pa.,	" "
171. Dempsey Baily,	Barnesville, Ohio,	" "
172. Eulysses A. McGrew,	Flushing, Ohio,	" "
173. Henry Evens,	Marlton, N. J.,	" "
174. Josiah W. Doudna,	Barnesville, Ohio,	" "
175. S. Clarence Pharo,	Tuckerton, N. J.,	" "
176. Edward B. Williams,	Philadelphia, Pa.,	5th mo., "
177. Richard Kaighn,	Haddonfield, N. J.,	" "
178. Walter P. Stokes,	Philadelphia, Pa.,	" "
179. Franklin W. Smith,	"	" "
180. George S. Wetherill,	"	" "
181. Joseph J. Evens,	Marlton, N. J.,	11th mo., "
182. Joseph H. Darnell,	Mt. Holly, N. J.,	" "
183. Abram L. Pennock,	Upper Darby, Pa.,	" "
184. Henry Tatum,	Woodbury, N. J.,	" "
185. James C. Comfort,	Germantown, Pa.,	" "
186. Jacob Twining,	Richboro', Pa.,	" "
187. John Barclay Jones,	Germantown, Pa.,	" "
188. Howard E. Roberts,	Moorestown, N. J.,	" "
189. Thornton E. Brown,	Brooklyn, N. Y.,	5th mo., 1870.
190. William Bishop,	Columbus, N. J.,	" "
191. Stephen B. Isaac,	Lahaska, Pa.,	" "
192. Frederic McCarty,	Eldredville, Pa.,	" "
193. Alfred Lowry,	Philadelphia, Pa.,	" "
194. William C. Lowry,	"	" "
195. C. Allen Hamblin,		11th mo., 1871
196. Abram S. Eldridge,	Johnstown, Pa.,	5th mo., 1870
197. J. Murray Bacon,	Greenwich, N. J.,	11th mo., "
198. Henry J. Cloud,	Woodbury, N. J.,	" "
199. John Gill, Jr.,	Haddonfield, N. J.,	" "
200. Frank Cadwallader,	Philadelphia, Pa.,	" "
201. Israel H Townsend,	Oak Hill, Pa.,	" 1869.

STUDENTS.

FIFTH THOUSAND.

NAME.	RESIDENCE.	DATE OF ENTRY.
202. T. T. Pennington,	West Grove, Pa.,	11th mo., 1869.
203. Charles Carpenter,	Milton, N. Y.,	" "
204. Lewis H. Walter,	Parkersville, Pa.,	" "
205. Edwin Cooper,	Avondale, Pa.,	" "
206. Lewis Taylor,	Columbus, N. J.,	" 1870.
207. Charles A. Ring,	Buffalo, N. Y.,	" 1869.
208. Walter Jones,	Germantown, Pa.,	5th mo., 1870.
209. J. Morton Brown,	"	11th mo., "
210. T. F. Warrington,	West Chester, Pa.,	5th mo., "
211. Richard P. Tatum,	Philadelphia, Pa.,	" "
212. Edward P. Tatum,	"	" "
213. George Cook,	Glenville, Md.,	" "
214. Jonathan Eldridge,	Goshenville, Pa.,	" "
215. Jesse E. Bundy,	Barnesville, Ohio,	" "
216. Everett Cromwell,	New York, N. Y.,	" "
217. Francis McCarty,	Eldredville, Pa.,	" "
218. William G. Kimber,	Brooklyn, N. Y.,	" "
219. Isaac Forsythe,	Oak Hill, Pa.,	" "
220. Henry D. Downing,	W. Whiteland, Pa.,	" "
221. Pennell Larkin,	Chelsea, Pa.,	11th mo., "
222. Henry Warrington,	Moorestown, N. J.,	" "
223. Joseph Trimble,	Chester, Pa.,	" "
224. George S. Yarnall,	Howellville, Pa.,	" "
225. Wilson Townsend,	Rahway, N. J.,	" "
226. Josiah T. Allinson,	Yardville, N. J.,	" "
227. T. Elwood Parker,	Parkersville, Pa.,	" "
228. J. Walter Parker,	"	" "
229. John B. Moon,	Fallsington, Pa.,	" "
230. Samuel W. Street,	Salem, Ohio,	" "
231. George S. Thorp,	Howellville, Pa.,	" "
232. Richard S. Phillips,	Waterford, Va.,	" "
233. Henry E. Haines,	Muncy, Pa.,	" "
234. Frederic C. Buffum,	Hopkinton, R. I.,	" "
235. William Balderston,	Colora, Md.,	" "
236. Malin Lear,	Warren Tavern, Pa.,	" "
237. John W. Tatum,	Wilmington, Del.,	" "
238. Charles Bell,	Bloomington, Ill.,	" "
239. T. Clarkson Bundy,	Pugh, Ohio,	" "
240. S. Morris Jones,	Germantown, Pa.,	" "
241. Charles Forsythe,	Westtown B. S., Pa.,	" "
242. J. Morris Cooper,	Toughkenamon, Pa.,	" 1871.
243. B. Rush Leeds,	Cinnaminson, N. J.,	" 1870.
244. J. Howard Zelley,	Hartford, N. J.,	" "
245. Warner Cooper,	Woodbury, N. J.,	" "
246. Clemuel R. Henrie,	Greenwood, Pa.,	5th mo., 1871
247. Joseph N. Shreeve,	Berlin, N. J.,	" "
248. Johns Hopkins,	Baltimore, Md.,	" "

16

FIFTH THOUSAND.

NAME.	RESIDENCE.	DATE OF ENTRY.
249. J. Edwin Humes,	Chesterville, Pa.,	5th mo., 1872
250. Edward S. Hulme,	Bristol, Pa.,	11th mo., 1870.
251. Benj. S. Ashead,	Marlton, N. J.,	" "
252. Ezra C. Engle,	Masonville, N. J.,	" "
253. J. Horace Cook,	Philadelphia, Pa.,	5th mo., 1871.
254. J. Benington Elfreth,	Millville, N. J.,	" "
255. Wm. B. Kirkbride,	Morrisville, Pa.,	" "
256. N. Newlin Stokes,	Philadelphia, Pa.,	" "
257. J. Howard Borton,	Rancocas, N. J.,	" "
258. William C. Allen,	Philadelphia, Pa.,	" "
259. Edward A. Thorp,	"	" "
260. Mark P. Chambers,	"	" "
261. Henry D. Lane,	"	" "
262. Charles C. Heacock,	Greenwood, Pa.,	" "
263. Jos. H. Satterthwaite,	Oxford Valley, Pa.,	" "
264. Charles H. Philips,	Philadelphia, Pa.,	11th mo., "
265. William M. Philips,	"	" "
266. William M. Steer,	West Branch, Iowa,	" "
267. John H. Bell,	Mt. Ephraim, N. J.,	" "
268. Edwin R. Bell,	"	" "
269. Geo. W. P. Coates,	Baltimore, Md.,	" "
270. L. Roberts Coates,	"	" "
271. Alban W. Walter,	Norway, Pa.,	" "
272. John H. Lippincott,	Haddonfield, N. J.,	" "
273. John E. Sheppard,	Greenwich, N. J.,	" "
274. Robert R. French,	Medford, N. J.,	5th mo., 1872
275. John Henry Tilton,	Manahawkin, N. J.,	" "
276. Albert Cope,	Redstone, Pa.,	" 1871.
277. Franklin Davis,	Westminster, N. C.,	" "
278. Howard Cooper,	Avondale, Pa.,	11th mo., "
279. Edward B. Smith,	Philadelphia, Pa.,	5th mo., "
280. William H. Pennell,	Linwood, Pa.,	11th mo., "
281. Charles Cheyney,	Doe Run, Pa.,	" "
282. Edward S. Edge,	Darlington, Md.,	" "
283. Thomas G. Rhoads,*	Wilmington, Del.,	" "
284. Joseph C. Harvey,	Brandywine Summit, Pa.,	" "
285. James G. Haines,	Medford, N. J.,	" "
286. Samuel W. Tatnall,	Wilmington, Del.,	" "
287. Arthur H. Buffum,	Hopkinton, R. I.,	" "
288. Geo. J. Jolliffe,	Stephenson's Sta., Va.,	" "
289. William L. Child,	Wilmington, Del.,	" "
290. Charles Chambers,	Strickersville, Pa.,	" "
291. Edward T. Eldridge,	Johnstown, Pa.,	" "
292. Henry E. Jones,	Camden, N. J.,	" "
293. Charles D. Vernon,	Springville, Iowa,	" "
294. Jefferson Bundy,	Barnesville, Ohio,	" "

* Deceased at the school, 31st of Third mo., 1872.

STUDENTS. 195

FIFTH THOUSAND.

NAME.	RESIDENCE.	ATE OF ENTRY.
295. Daniel H. Hallock,	Willow Brook, N. Y.,	11th mo., 1871.
296. J. Harris Reed,	Waterville, Pa.,	" "
297. Crosby M. Brown,	Germantown, Pa.,	" "
298. George W. McGuire,	Flushing, Ohio,	" "
299. John E. Cox,	Goldsboro', N. C.,	" "
300. Henry Forsythe,	Westtown B. S., Pa.,	" "
301. Charles Tatum,	Philadelphia, Pa.,	5th mo., 1872.
302. Enos S. Jones,	Germantown, Pa.,	" "
303. Joseph D. Snowdon,	Philadelphia, Pa.,	" "
304. T. Walter Embree,	West Chester, Pa.,	" "
305. Samuel Forsythe,	Chadd's Ford, Pa.,	11th mo., "
306. Richard M. Cooper,	Haddonfield, N. J.,	5th mo., "
307. Ed. M. Chambers,	Philadelphia, Pa.,	" "
308. Alfred W. Baily,	Marlton, N. J.,	" "
309. Morris Linton,	West Grove, Pa.,	" "
310. John B. Heston,	Bristol, Pa.,	11th mo., "
311. William W. Allinson,	Pemberton, N. J.,	" "
312. John B. Newkirk,	Greenwich, N. J.,	" "
313. Charles Williams, Jr.,	Fellowship, N. J.,	" "
314. William Lewis Brown,	Haddington, Phila.,	5th mo., 1873.
315. William H. Thorp,	Frankford, Pa.,	11th mo., 1872.
316. John P. Thorp,	Lionville, Pa.,	" "
317. Edward Randolph,	Philadelphia, Pa.,	5th mo., 1873.
318. Archie Pharo,	Tuckerton, N. J.,	" "
319. Jos. K. Lippincott, Jr.,	Haddonfield, N. J.,	" "
320. N. Howland Brown,	Philadelphia, Pa.,	" "
321. Henry H. Brown,	" "	" "
322. Stacy L. Heacock,	Greenwood, Pa.,	" "
323. William C. Chase,	Haverford College, Pa.,	" "
324. J. Albertson Jones,	Germantown, Pa.,	" 1874.
325. Edwin S. James,	West Chester, Pa.,	11th mo., "
326. Charles E. Ganse, Jr.,	Plainfield, N. J.,	5th mo., 1872.
327. George C. Webster,	Concordville, Pa.,	" "
328. Jasper C. McGrew,	Pennsville, Ohio,	" "
329. Robert H. Walter,	Norway, Pa.,	" "
330. Henry Ecroyd,	Muncy, Pa.,	" "
331. Louis Lamborn,	West Chester, Pa.,	" "
332. Joshua C. Smith,	Darlington, Md.,	" "
333. Nathan Kite,	Philadelphia, Pa.,	6th mo., "
334. Paschall Moore,	Nine Points, Pa.,	11th mo., "
335. Caleb Moore,	" "	" "
336. Josiah W. Prickitt,	Medford, N. J.,	" "
337. J. Passmore Cheyney,	Colora, Md.,	" "
338. Mordecai S. Parvin,	Leesport, Pa.,	" "
339. Charles Thomas,	Avondale, Pa.,	" "
340. Josiah Cloud, Jr.,	Woodbury, N. J.,	" "
341. John B. Webb,	Chadd's Ford, Pa.,	" "

GENERAL CATALOGUE.

FIFTH THOUSAND.

NAME	RESIDENCE.	DATE OF ENTRY.
342. William Post,	Old Westbury, L. I.,	11th mo., 1872.
343. James Moon,	Morrisville, Pa.,	" "
344. Pennell L. Webster,	Glen Riddle, Pa.,	" "
345. Francis Yarnall,	Howellville, Pa.,	" "
346. Silas W. Cox,	Goldsboro, N. C.,	" "
347. Joseph N. Willits,	Haddonfield, N. J.,	5th mo., 1873.
348. David W. Masters,	Wolf Run, Pa.,	" "
349. Joshua Thomas,	Avondale, Pa.,	" "
350. George W. Henrie,	Greenwood, Pa.,	" "
351. Walter L. Moore,	Avondale, Pa.,	" "
352. Joseph S. Simmons,	Bart P. O., Pa.,	" "
353. Henry Battin,	Canton, Pa.,	" "
354. Edward L. South,	Plainfield, N. J.,	" "
355. William B. Hayes,	Thorndale, Pa.,	" "
356. Brinton P. Cooper,	Christiana, Pa.,	" "
357. Arthur E. Roberts,	Masonville, N. J.,	" "
358. B. F. Wickersham, Jr.,	West Chester, Pa.,	" "
359. William J. A. Hamblin,	Camden, N. J.,	" "
360. William F. Smith,	Pennsville, Ohio,	" "
361. James T. Curtis,	Cincinnati, Ohio,	" "
362. Joseph E. Meyers,	Wolf Run, Pa.,	11th mo., "
363. Walter Brinton,	Chadd's Ford, Pa.,	" "
364. John M. Moore,	Camden, N. J.,	" "
365. Robert P. Nicholson,	Haddonfield, N. J.,	" "
366. John Worth, Jr.,	Marshallton, Pa.,	" "
367. Howard M. Heulings,	Trenton, N. J.,	" "
368. Townsend Sharpless,	Philadelphia, Pa.,	" "
369. J. Henry Bartlett,	Tuckerton, N. J.,	" "
370. Wilmer P. Leeds,	" "	" "
371. Thomas W. Thorp,	Howellville, Pa.,	" "
372. Harrison W. Haines,	Kirkwood, N. J.,	" "
373. Jonathan Cope,	Kimbleville, Pa.,	" "
374. Henry M. Thomas,	Baltimore, Md.,	" "
375. Bond V. Thomas,	" "	" "
376. William E. Jenks,	Philadelphia, Pa.,	5th mo., 1874.
377. Richard L. Jenks,	" "	" "
378. Robert H. Russell,	" "	" "
379. Frank L. Borton,	Rancocas, N. J.,	" "
380. David A. Bines,	Germantown, Pa.,	" "
381. David D. Engle,	Masonville, N. J.,	" "
382. Howard H. Bell,	Mt. Ephraim, N. J.,	" "
383. William L. Collins,	Frankford, Pa.,	" "
384. Stokes Collins,	Barnegat, N. J.,	" "
385. Horace Stokes,	Cinnaminson, N. J.,	" "
386. Edward M. Jones,	Germantown, Pa.,	" "
387. Pennock Cooper,	West Grove, Pa.,	11th mo., "
388. Lewis W. Taylor,	Woodstown, N. J.,	" "

STUDENTS.

FIFTH THOUSAND.

NAME.	RESIDENCE.	DATE OF ENTRY.
389. Stephen Atwater,	Somerset, N. Y.,	11th mo., 1874.
390. Joseph Stokes,	Moorestown, N. J.,	5th mo., 1875.
391. Alexander R. Jenks,	Philadelphia, Pa.,	" "
392. Henry Hall,	Harrisville, Ohio,	" "
393. Walter S. Swayne,	New London, Pa.,	" "
394. Charles Lamborn,	Scipioville, N. Y.,	" "
395. William T. Elkinton,	Philadelphia, Pa.,	" "
396. Ephraim T. Gill,	Haddonfield, N. J.,	" "
397. Milton W. Larkin,	Linwood, Pa.,	11th mo , 1876.
398. Samuel Hulme, Jr.,	Bristol, Pa.,	" 1875.
399. T. Kirkbride Hulme,	" "	" "
400.* Allen H. Roberts,	Moorestown, N. J.,	" "
401. Everett Moon,	Fallsington, Pa.,	" 1873.
402. I. Roberts Comfort,	Wm. Penn P. O., Pa.,	" "
403. J. Alban Kite,	Chester Hill, Ohio,	" "
404. Edward B. Hoge,	Flushing, Ohio,	" "
405. Edwin F. Holloway,	" "	" "
406. Rowland Evans,	Glen Mills, Pa.,	" "
407. William Evans,	" "	" "
408. Hibbard D. Moore,	Avondale, Pa.,	" "
409. John G. Shreve,	Haddonfield, N. J.,	" "
410. Eldaah Wilcox,	Shunk P. O., Pa.,	" "
411. Jesse Williams,	Philadelphia, Pa.,	5th mo., 1874.
412. Franklin T. Hoopes,	Downingtown, Pa.,	" "
413. George A. Rhoads,	Wilmington, Del.,	" "
414. Richard S. Dewees,	Pennsville, Ohio,	" "
415. Elwood Balderston,	Colora, Md.,	" "
416. Edward Warrington,	Moorestown, N. J.,	" "
417. Joseph K. England,	Norristown, Pa.,	" "
418. William W. Heacock,	Benton, Pa ,	" "
419. Charles P. Chambers,	Toughkenamon, Pa.,	" "
420. Samuel L. Whitson,	New Garden, Pa.,	11th mo., "
421. Samuel Worth, Jr.,	Marshallton, Pa.,	" "
422. Richard W. Maris,	Darlington, Md.,	" "
423. T. Chalkley Palmer,	Media, Pa.,	" "
424. William G. Steer,	Barnesville, Ohio,	" "
425. Aaron M. Headley,	Rising Sun, Md.,	" "
426. John W. Mott,	Viola, Iowa,	" "
427. Thomas E. Mott,	" "	" "
428. H. E. Satterthwaite,	Crosswicks, N. J.,	" "
429. Henry Zook,	Downingtown, Pa.,	" "
430. Sam'l L. Smedley, Jr.,	Howellville, Pa.,	" "
431. Eli Heacock,	Greenwood, Pa.,	" "
432. Thomas J. Evens,	Marlton, N. J.,	" "
433. Joshua R. Evens,		" 1875.
434. James Walton,	Barnesville, Ohio,	" 1874.
435. Ephraim G. Shreve,	Haddonfield, N. J.,	" "

16*

FIFTH THOUSAND.

NAME.	RESIDENCE.	DATE OF ENTRY.
436. Horace L. Kille,	Camden, N. J.,	11th mo., 1874.
437. Charles Allinson,	Pemberton, N. J.,	" "
438. Joseph J. Coppock,	Winona, Ohio,	" "
439. Charles Stratton,	" "	" "
440. Joseph C. Stratton,	" "	" "
441. Lindley Fogg,	Damascoville, Ohio,	" "
442. William L. Price,	Philadelphia, Pa.,	5th mo., 1875.
443. Samuel R. Thorp,	Wilmington, Del.,	" "
444. Elmer D. Prickitt,	Masonville, N. J.,	" "
445. Ezra Lamborn,	Avondale, Pa.,	" "
446. Jervis B. Deacon,	Princeton, N. J.,	" "
( ) Joshua H. Davis,	Westtown Farm, Pa.,	" "
447. Joseph C. Chambers,	Toughkenamon, Pa.,	11th mo., "
448. Morris H. Taylor,	Woodstown, N. J.,	5th mo., "
449. William A. Frame,	Barnesville, Ohio,	" "
450. Charles W. L. Wilson,	Waterford, Va.,	" "
451. Oliver H. Headly,	Rising Sun, Md.,	" "
452. Lindley M. Winston,	Richmond, Va.,	" "
453. Alfred R. White,	Franklin Depot, Va.,	" "
454. Cyrus Cooper,	Toughkenamon, Pa.,	11th mo., "
455. E. H. Satterthwaite,	Fairville, Pa.,	" "
456. Joseph S. Leeds,	Moorestown, N. J.,	" "
457. Walton B. Leeds,	" "	" "
458. William B. Harvey,	West Grove, Pa.,	" "
459. Caleb S. Miller,	Spencerville, Md.,	" "
460. Warwick P. Miller, Jr.,	" "	— " "
461. John Scott,	Butler P. O., Md.,	" "
462. Lloyd Balderston, Jr.,	Colora, Md.,	" "
463. Richard L. Bentley,	Sandy Spring, Md.,	" "
464. Elisha Gamble,	East Carmel, Ohio,	" "
465. Joseph H. Ashead,	Salem, Ohio,	" "
466. Ira S. Frame,	Barnesville, Ohio,	" "
467. Isaac Brown,	Mt. Laurel, N. J.,	" "
468. Edwin H. Cooper,	Toughkenamon, Pa.,	" "
469. Ralph Lee Brinton,	Chadd's Ford, Pa.,	" "
470. Henry A. Lippincott,	Salem, N. J.,	" "
471. William S. Prickitt,	Vincenttown, N. J.,	" "
472. Isaac Lippincott,	Moorestown, N. J.,	" "
473. Samuel C. Webster,	Concordville, Pa.,	" "
474. Wilson T. Sidwell,	Colerain, Ohio,	" "
475. John A. Hopkins,	Thompson P. O., Del.,	" "
476. William T. Cooper,	Rutherford Park, N. J.,	" "
477. John Wetherill,	West Branch, Iowa,	" "
478. Thomas M. Reed,	West Chester, Pa.,	5th mo., 1876.
479. Joseph E. Steer,	Philadelphia, Pa.,	" "
480. Samuel Lamborn,	Thompson P. O., Del.,	" "
481. John N. Reeve,	Medford, N. J.,	" "

STUDENTS.

FIFTH THOUSAND.

NAME.	RESIDENCE.	DATE OF ENTRY.
482. Thomas H. Thompson,	Darlington, Md.,	5th mo., 1876.
483. Wakeman H. Scott,	Darlington, Md.,	" "
484. Lindley F. Johnson,	West Chester, Pa.,	" "
485. Benjamin H. Taylor,	Fallsington, Pa.,	11th mo., "
486. Isaac S. Evens,	Marlton, N. J.,	" "
487. William C. Passmore,	Strickersville, Pa.,	" "
488. Elmer E. Eldridge,	Johnstown, Pa.,	" "
489. Horace L. F. Aaronson,	Columbus, N. J.,	" "
490. George Satterthwait.	Langhorne, Pa.,	" "
491. William S. Comfort,	Tecumseh, Mich.,	" "
492. Townsend Sexton,	Crosswicks, N. J.,	" "
493. William S. Yarnall,	Glen Mills, Pa.,	" "
494. Frank W. Prickitt,	Vincenttown, N. J.,	" "
495. Joseph T. Whitson,	Chatham, Pa.,	" "
496. Walter Smedley,	Lima P. O., Pa.,	" "
497. William T. Reed,	Philadelphia, Pa.,	" "
498. Alfred W. Leeds,	Moorestown, N. J.,	" "
499. George R. Meloney,	Avondale, Pa.,	" "
500. Walter South,	Plainfield, N. J.,	5th mo., 1877.
501. Charles E. Winner,	Wolf Run, Pa.,	11th mo., 1875.
502. Samuel N. Shreve,	Mt. Laurel, N. J.,	" "
503. Samuel N. Rhoads,	Haddonfield, N. J.,	" "
504. Alfred E. Maris,	Philadelphia, Pa.,	5th mo., 1876.
505. Robert W. Maris,	" "	" "
506. John W. Patterson,	" "	" "
507. Oliver P. Tatum,	" "	" "
508. William P. Morgan,	Parkersville, Pa.,	" "
509. Robert B. Bradshaw,	Franklin Depot, Va.,	" "
510. Joseph T. Lippincott,	Philadelphia, Pa.,	" "
511. William Tatnall, Jr.,	Wilmington, Del.,	" "
512. Joseph F. Smedley,	Philadelphia, Pa.,	" "
513. Thomas M. Dawson,	Baltimore, Md.,	" "
514. Samuel F. Pennell,	Linwood, Pa.,	11th mo., "
515. George L. Pennock,	Philadelphia, Pa.,	" "
516. Henry W. Comfort,	Fallsington, Pa.,	" "
517. Joseph H. Matlack,	Moorestown, N. J.,	" "
518. Thomas T. Buzby,	Rancocas, N. J.,	" "
519. Charles Canby,	Philadelphia, Pa.,	" "
( ) Caleb W. Davis,	Westtown Farm, Pa.,	" "
( ) J. Wetherill Hutton,	Westtown Mills, Pa.,	" "
520. Henry G. Balderston,	Philadelphia, Pa.,	5th mo., 1877.
521. Edgar Clement,	Camden, N. J.,	" "
522. Edward Hacker,	Germantown, Pa.,	" "
523. Edward Lownes,	Oakdale, Pa.,	" "
524. Hill Pennell,	Philadelphia, Pa.,	" "
525. Thomas J. De Cou,	Columbus, N. J.,	11th mo., "
526. O. Martin Wilcox,	Shunk P. O., Pa.,	" 1876.

FIFTH THOUSAND.

NAME.	RESIDENCE.	DATE OF ENTRY.
527. M. Ellis Wilcox,	Shunk P. O., Pa.,	11th mo., 1876.
528. Clayton H. Evans,	Medford, N. J.,	" "
529. John B. Evans,	" "	" "
530. Horatio W. Bacon,	Greenwich, N. J.,	" "
531. John Bacon,	" "	" "
532. George Bailey,	Thorndale, Pa.,	" "
533. Charles C. Haines.	Moorestown, N. J.,	" "
534. I. Roberts Newkirk,	Greenwich, N. J.,	" 1878.
535. Richard G. Webster,	Glen Riddle, Pa.,	" 1876.
536. Samuel Alan Wilson,	Newportville, Pa.,	" "
537. Gnion Miller,	Sandy Spring. Md.,	" "
538. Irving M. Scott,	Darlington, Md.,	" "
539. Dubre K. Masters,	Muncy, Pa.,	5th mo., 1877.
540. James Smith,	Parkesburg, Pa.,	11th mo., 1876.
541. Benjamin S. Thorp,	Frankford, Pa.,	" "
542. George T. Whitcley.	Philadelphia, Pa.,	5th mo., 1877.
543. Edwin Evans,	Thompson P. O., Del.,	" "
544. C. Canby Hopkins,	" "	" "
545. Edward B. Fox,	Philadelphia, Pa.,	" "
546. Joseph J. Fox,	" "	" "
547. Walter P. Ash,	Wagontown, Pa.,	" "
548. Stephen C. Hinshaw,	Emporia, Kansas,	" "
549. William S. Whitacre,	Pottstown, Pa.,	" "
550. Adolph Brackman,	Shunk P. O., Pa.,	" "
551. Wilmer Cope,	Kimbleville, Pa.,	11th mo., 1878.
552. Howard F. Jones,	Philadelphia, Pa.,	5th mo., 1877.
553. Edward B. Jones,	" "	" "
554. C. Sharpless Mercer,	Kennett Square, Pa.,	" "
555. Alfred H. Moon,	Fallsington, Pa.,	" "
556. John W. Warner,	Wolf Run, Pa.,	11th mo., "
557. Henry W. Whitacre,	Pottstown, Pa.,	" "
558. Walter M. Jones,	Camden, N. J.,	" "
559. Benjamin H. Cope,	Kimbleville, Pa.,	" "
560. David E. Cooper,	Marlton, N. J.,	" "
561. Edward G. Rhoads,	Wilmington, Del.,	" "
562. Jeptha E. Outland,	Woodland, N. C.,	" "
563. C. William Roberts,	Bristol, Pa.,	" "
564. Joseph Thorp,	Howellville, Pa.,	" "
565. J. Howard Mendenhall,	" "	" "
566. William B. Smith,	Parkesburg, Pa.,	" "
567. Chalkley C. Holloway,	Flushing, Ohio,	". "
568. Wm. F. Wickersham,	Kennett Square, Pa,,	" "
569. Newlin Mendenhall,	" " "	" "
570. Charles J. Mercer,	" " "	" "
571. William P. Phipps, Jr.,	Lionville, Pa.,	" "
572. Edward E. Scott,	Butler P. O., Md.,	" "
573. Jonathan C. Hare,	Suffolk, Va.,	" "

STUDENTS.

FIFTH THOUSAND.

NAME.	RESIDENCE.	DATE OF ENTRY.
574. Edward B. Reeve,	Medford, N. J.,	5th mo., 1878.
575. George H. Mendenhall,	Wolf Run, Pa.,	" "
576. C. Wistar Thompson,	Salem, N. J.,	11th mo., "
577. Samuel W. Paxson,	Aquetong, Pa.,	11th mo., 1877.
578. William C. Warren,	Columbus, N. J.,	" "
579. George Sharpless, Jr.,	Chester, Pa.,	" "
580. Morton Cromwell,	Philadelphia, Pa.,	" "
581. William G. Masters,	Pittsburg, Pa.,	" "
582. Albert G. Newbold,	Moorestown, N. J.,	5th mo., 1878.
583. Joseph Bailey, Jr.,	Pine Iron Works, Pa.,	" "
584. Charles S. Bonsall,	Philadelphia, Pa.,	" "
585. Alfred C. Elkinton,	" "	11th mo., "
586. S. Howard Haines,	Medford, N. J.,	" "
587. Thomas H. Newbold,	Media, Pa.,	" 1879.
588. Morris Longstreth,	Philadelphia, Pa.,	" "
589. Clarkson J. Cox,	Kemp's Mills, N. C.,	" "
590. Howard T. Painter,	Darby P. O., Pa.,	5th mo., 1880.
591. Ed. R. Strawbridge,	Germantown, Pa.,	" "
592. Walter E. De Cou,	Trenton, N. J.,	" "
593. George De Cou,	" "	" "
594. Robert F. Engle,	Mt. Holly, N. J.,	" "
595. Daniel S. Kashner,	Columbus, N. J.,	" "
596. Willard Child,	Henderson, N. Y.	" "
597. John Oxley Littler,	Kemp's Mills, N. C.	" "
598. Thomas W. Russell,*	Philadelphia, Pa.,	6th mo., "
599. Clayton L. Evens,	Marlton, N. J.,	11th mo., "
600. Charles H. Moon,	Woodbourne, Pa.,	" "
601. Richard W. Bailey,	Pottstown, Pa.,	5th mo., 1878.
602. Lambert J. Jones,	Hughesville, Md.,	" "
603. Henry B. Leeds,	Moorestown, N. J.,	" "
604. William M. Walter,	Norway P. O., Pa.,	" "
605. Henry A. Thorp,	Wilmington, Del.,	" "
606. Robert T. Mickle,	Millville, N. J.,	" "
607. Horace C. Moore,	West Creek, N. J.,	" "
608. Samuel S. H. Stokes,	Berlin, N. J.,	" "
609. Shelly Larkin,	Linwood, Pa.,	" "
610. William J. Fisher,	Dymond City, N. C.,	5th mo., 1879.
611. Henry W. Fisher,	" " "	" "
612. Walter A. Scott,	Concordville, Pa.,	5th mo., 1878.
613. John D. Michener,	Colora, Md.,	11th mo., "
614. J. Walter Smith,	Lincoln, Va.,	" "
615. George S. Bacon,	Greenwich, N. J.,	" "
616. S. Harrison Gardiner,	Kirkwood, N. J.,	" "
617. Oliver Wilson Paxson,	New Hope, Pa.,	" "
618. William Gardiner,	Mount Holly, N. J.,	" "

* Drowned at the school, Sixth mo. 19, 1880.

FIFTH THOUSAND.

NAME.	RESIDENCE.	DATE OF ENTRY.
619. Albert Haines,	Moorestown, N. J.,	11th mo., 1878.
620. Howard R. Swayne,	Philadelphia, Pa.,	" "
621. Edward M. Bunting,	Brick M't'g House, Md.,	" "
622. Walter F. Bunting,	" " "	" "
623. James M. Patton,	Millville, Pa.,	" "
624. Francis J. Patton,	" "	" "
625. Joseph W. Pharo,	Tuckerton. N. J.,	" "
626. Wilmer L. McFadgen,	Jennerville, Pa.,	" "
627. Amos Ashead, Jr.,	Hartford, N. J.,	" "
628. William T. Hare,	Suffolk, Va.,	" "
629. Thomas E. Coale,	Baltimore, Md.,	" "
( ) George Forsythe,	Westtown P. O., Pa.,	" "
630. Walter J. Buzby,	Masonville, N. J.,	5th mo., 1879.
631. Thomas Lee Haines,	Rancocas, N. J.,	" "
632. Newlin Haines,	" "	" "
633. William H. Savery,	Wilmington, Del.,	" "
634. Joseph D. Hoopes,	Downingtown, Pa.,	" "
635. O. Walter Borton,	Atlantic City, N. J.,	" "
636. William A. Cooper,	Chatham, Pa.,	" "
637. William B. Cooper,	West Grove, Pa.,	" "
638. J. Howard Mickle,	Millville, N. J.,	" "
639. Edward Sharpless,	Strickersville, Pa.,	" "
640. Charles W. Leeds,	Moorestown, N. J.,	" "
641. Alfred B. Jones,	Camden, N. J.,	" "
642. William Abbott,	Salem, N. J,	" "
643. William Biddle, Jr.,	Philadelphia, Pa.,	" "
644. Roland Smedley,	Bryn Mawr, Pa,	" "
645. Warren C. Goodwin,	Greenwich, N. J.,	11th mo., "
646. Clayton E. Underhill,	Washington, D. C.,	" "
647. Norris G. Temple,	Chadd's Ford, Pa.,	" "
648. J. Howard Cook,	Glenville, Md.,	" "
649. Alfred Smedley,	Howellville, Pa.,	" "
650. Alf. H. Satterthwaite,	Crosswicks, N. J.,	" "
651. Amos A. Zelley,	Moorestown, N. J.,	" "
652. Eber N. Gause,	Emporia, Kansas,	" "
653. John E. Hinshaw,	" "	" "
654. Isaac L. Roberts,	Moorestown, N. J.,	" "
655. Wm. R. Newbold, Jr.,	Media, Pa.,	5th mo., 1880.
656. John B. Rhoads,	Wilmington, Del.,	" "
657. Jonathan T. Phipps,	Lionville, Pa.,	" "
658. Wilbern Hartz,	Reading, Pa.,	" "
659. J. Anderson Johnson,	Nicholson's Mills, N.C.,	" "
660. Maurice D. Engle,	Columbus, N. J.,	5th mo., 1883.
661. Howell S. England,	Wilmington, Del.,	5th mo., 1880.
662. Wilmer J. Moore,	West Grove, Pa.,	" "
663. Richard H. Lytle,	Germantown, Pa.,	" "
664. Charles A. Bartlett,	Tuckerton, N. J.,	" "

STUDENTS.

FIFTH THOUSAND.

NAME.	RESIDENCE.	DATE OF ENTRY.	
665. Howard J. Thorp,	Wilmington, Del.,	11th mo.,	1880.
666. Harvey E. Pharo,	Tuckerton, N. J.,	"	"
667. Francis D. Half,	Barnesville, Ohio,	"	"
668. Thomas L. Passmore,	Strickersville, Pa.,	"	"
669. David F. Bentley,	Horsham, Pa.,	"	"
670. Robert M. Thorp,	Frankford, Phila.,	"	"
671. Edmund Alsop,	Colorado Springs, Col.,	"	"
672. Albert E. Yarnall,	Media, Pa.,	"	"
673. William S. Palmer,	Wallingford, Pa.,	"	"
674. William B. Moon,	Fallsington, Pa.,	"	"
675. George W. Balderston,	Morrisville, Pa.,	"	"
676. Henry E. Warner,	Wolf Run, Pa.,	"	"
677. Joel P. Good,	London Grove, Pa.,	"	"
678. William J. Carslake,	Columbus, N. J.,	"	"
679. A. Lincoln Sholl,	Burlington, N. J.,	"	"
680. George G. Williams,	Fellowship, N. J.,	5th mo.,	1881.
681. Henry F. Ogborn,	Philadelphia, Pa.,	"	1883.
682. J. Snowdon Rhoads,	Marple P. O., Pa.,	"	1881.
683. T. Wistar Stanley,	Americus, Kansas,	"	"
684. David S. Haines,	Medford, N. J.,	11th mo.,	"
685. William B. Cooper,	Marlton, N. J.,	"	"
686. William R. Tatum,	Glenelg P. O., Md.,	"	"
687. Joseph E. De Cou,	Columbus, N. J.,	"	"
688. Solomon E. Barker,	Kemp's Mills, N. C.,	"	"
689. Peter Ellis Ivins,	Trenton, N. J.,	"	"
690. Alfred C. Haines,	Rancocas, N. J.,	5th mo.,	1882.
691. Clarkson S. French,	Salem, Ohio,	"	"
692. William J. Blackburn,	East Carmel, Ohio,	"	"
693. William E. Mott,	Burlington, N. J.,	"	"
694. Edward T. Middleton,	Crosswicks, N. J.,	"	"
695. Charles E. Ecroyd,	Muncy, Pa.,	"	"
696. Townsend S. Jolliffe,	Stephenson's Depot, Va.,	"	"
697. Aaron Engle Haines,	Mount Laurel, N. J.,	"	"
698. J. Clifford Haines,	Vincenttown, N. J.,	11th mo.,	"
699. George D. Zook,	Downingtown, Pa.,	"	"
700. James P. Wetherill,	Chester, Pa.,	"	"
701. Walter P. Mendenhall,	Howellville, Pa.,	"	1880.
702. Lee D. Hartz,	Reading, Pa.,	"	"
703. Andrew J. Battin,	Canton P. O., Pa.,	"	"
704. Edward Satterthwaite,	Fairville P. O., Pa.,	"	"
705. Roland T. Satterthwaite.	" " "	"	"
706. William S. Garrett,	Willistown, Pa.,	"	"
707. William E. Priest,	Wolf Run, Pa.,	"	"
708. Elwood Longstreth,	Philadelphia, Pa.,	5th mo.,	1881.
709. D. Howard Williams,	West Branch, Iowa,	"	"
710. Harry E. Moore,	West Grove, Pa.,	"	"
711. Henry W. Leeds,	Cinnaminson, N. J.,	"	1883.

GENERAL CATALOGUE.

FIFTH THOUSAND.

NAME.	RESIDENCE.	DATE OF ENTRY.
712. J. Edwin James,	West Chester, Pa.,	5th mo., 1881.
713. Harry E. Cooper,	Chatham, Pa.,	" "
714. John S. Hartz,	Reading, Pa.,	" "
715. Howard Cox,	Toughkenamon, Pa.,	" "
716. S. Bolton Leeds,	Spread Eagle, Pa.,	" "
717. Allen B. Clement,	Camden, N. J.,	" "
718. Benjamin W. Cooper,	Westtown P. O., Pa.,	" "
719. Daniel Griffin,	Clinton Corners, N. Y.,	" "
720. Charles Livezey,	Barnesville, Ohio,	" "
721. Morris Ashead,	Hartford, N. J.,	" 1883.
722. Herbert M. Bacon,	Greenwich, N. J.,	" 1881.
723. Henry Lloyd Sholl,	Burlington, N. J.,	" "
724. Delbert L. Brown,	Shunk P. O., Pa.	" "
725. Charles C. Birdsall.	East Coldenham, N.Y.,	11th mo., "
726. Richard J Matthews,	Baltimore, Md.,	" "
727. Frederick H. Cope,	Lincoln Univer., Pa.,	" "
728. Jesse M. Otis,	Sherwood, N. Y.,	" "
729. Franklin H. Goodwin,	Greenwich, N. J.,	" "
730. Lewis W. Thorp,	Frankford, Pa.,	" "
731. Horace W. Smedley,	Media, Pa.,	" "
732. William L. Meloney,	Avondale, Pa.,	" "
733. Wm. Alfred Smedley.	Media, Pa.,	" "
734. Edward A. Moore,	West Grove, Pa.,	" "
735. Cyrus W. McFadgen,	West Chester. Pa.,	" "
736. J. Herbert Deacon,	Columbus, N. J.,	" "
737. Herman H. Leeds,	Spread Eagle, Pa.,	" "
738. Benjamin F. Whitson.	Avondale, Pa.,	" "
739. John W. Palmer,	Media, Pa.,	" "
740. Dillwyn Stratton,	Winona, Ohio,	" "
( ) Henry W. Forsythe,	Westtown P. O., Pa.,	" "
741. Edward W. Comfort,	Tecumseh, Mich.,	" "
742. Charles E. Coates,	Baltimore, Md.,	5th mo., 1882.
743. Jesse Coates,	" "	" "
744. William H. Thompson,	Darlington, Md.,	" "
745. Daniel Thompson,	Thompson P. O., Del.,	" "
746. James L. Peele,	Rich Square, N. C.,	" "
747. Francis J. Seal,	Londonderry, Pa.,	" "
748. Robert E. Fox,	Philadelphia, Pa.,	" "
749. Caleb D. Cope,	Kimbleville, Pa.,	11th mo., "
750. William Evans,	Thompson P. O., Del.,	5th mo., "
751. Hilt H. Harris,	Colorado Springs, Col.,	" "
752. John J. Scarlett,	Reading, Pa.,	11th mo., "
753. Lewis N. Scofield,	Sandy Spring, Md.,	" "
754. Russell Stabler,	Brighton, Pa.,	" "
755. Joseph T. Hilles,	Wilmington, Del.,	" "
756. Theodore E. Elder,	Angora, Pa.,	" "
757. Merritt W. Pharo,	Tuckerton, N. J.,	" "

STUDENTS.

FEMALES.

FIRST THOUSAND.

NAME.	RESIDENCE.	DATE OF ENTRY.
1 Hannah Hunt,	Darby, Pa.,	5th mo., 1799
2. Martha Price,	East Bradford, Pa.,	" "
3. Rebecca Cumming,	Horsham, Pa.,	" "
4. Mary Ellis,	Muncy, Pa.,	" "
5. Rachel Ellis,	"	" "
6. Sarah Phipps,	Philadelphia, Pa.,	" "
7. Sarah Spencer,	Germantown, Pa.,	" "
8. Jane Green,	Edgmont, Pa.,	" "
9. Sarah Sharpless,	Burlington, N. J.,	" "
10. Ruth James,	Philadelphia, Pa.,	" "
11. Hannah Jones,	"	" "
12. Martha Newlin,	Darby, Pa.,	" "
13. Edith Newbold,	Springfield, N. J.,	8th mo., "
14. Margaret Lea,	Wilmington, Del.,	12th mo., "
15. Rebecca Budd,	Philadelphia, Pa.,	5th mo., "
16. Rebecca Budd,	Mt. Holly, N. J.,	" "
17. Ann Aston,	Philadelphia, Pa.,	" "
18. Lydia Fisher,	"	" "
19. Elizabeth Williams,	Abington, Pa.,	" "
20. Catharine Rowland,	"	" "
21. Hannah Albertson,	Plymouth, Pa.,	" "
22. Ann Gilpin,	Birmingham, Pa.,	" "
23. Deborah Mifflin,	Philadelphia, Pa.,	" "
24. Hannah Forsythe,	East Bradford, Pa.,	" "
25. Rebecca Butcher,	Mt. Holly, N. J.,	6th mo., "
26. Elizabeth Letchworth,	Philadelphia, Pa.,	" "
27. Sarah Butcher,	Mt. Holly, N. J.,	" "
28. Elizabeth Butcher,	"	" "
29. Rachel Richards,	Philadelphia, Pa.,	" "
30. Lydia Richards,	"	" "
31. Mary H. Oldden,	"	" "
32. Mary Bartram,	"	" "
33. Sarah Ridgway,	Burlington, N. J.,	" "

GENERAL CATALOGUE.

FIRST THOUSAND.

NAME.	RESIDENCE.	DATE OF ENTRY.	
34. Catherine Smith,	Burlington, N. J.,	7th mo.,	1799.
35. Martha West,	Mt. Holly, N. J.,	6th mo.,	"
36. Elizabeth Humphreys,	Darby, Pa.,	7th mo.,	"
37. Margaret Wilson,	Philadelphia, Pa.,	"	"
38. Lydia Williams,	"	"	"
39. Mary Hill,	"	"	"
40. Esther Fisher,	"	"	"
41. Mary Wistar,	Salem, N. J.,	1st mo.,	1800.
42. Rebecca B. Oldden,	Philadelphia, Pa.,	8th mo.,	1799.
43. Rachel V. Sharpless,	Chester Creek, Pa.,	7th mo.,	"
44. Zillah Maule,	Radnor, Pa.,	"	"
45. Sarah Reeves,	Woodbury, N. J.,	"	"
46. Tabitha Rowland,	Camden, Del.,	1st mo.,	1800.
47. Mary Webster,	Abington, Pa.,	8th mo.,	1799.
48. Ann Newbold,	Trenton, N. J.,	"	"
49. Mary Budd,	Philadelphia, Pa.,	"	"
50. Ann Emlen,	"	"	"
51. Mary Emlen,	"	"	"
52. Sarah Elston,	Rahway, N. J.,	"	"
53. Amelia Evans,	Philadelphia, Pa.,	"	"
54. Martha Mendenhall,	Middletown, Pa.,	9th mo.,	"
55. Sidney Hill,	"	"	"
56. Lydia Poultney,	Philadelphia, Pa.,	2d mo.,	1800.
57. Rebecca Jones,	Montgomery Co., Pa.,	3d mo.,	"
58. Elizabeth Rowland,	Camden, Del.,	1st mo.,	"
59. Sarah Craig,	Salem, N. J.,	10th mo.,	1799.
60. Priscilla Kirk,	Byberry, Pa.,	9th mo.,	"
61. Martha Reeve,	Evesham, N. J.,	11th mo.,	"
62. Phebe Emlen,	Philadelphia, Pa.,	10th mo.,	"
63. Sarah Yarnall,	Middletown, Pa.,	"	"
64. Mary Jones,	Wilmington, Del.,	"	"
65. Catharine Ridgway,	Burlington, N. J.,	"	"
66. Ann Vanlaw,	Moorestown, N. J.,	"	"
67. Mary Stevenson,	Salem, N. J.,	12th mo.,	"
68. Rebecca Yarnall,	Byberry, Pa.,	10th mo.,	"
69. Ann Longstreth,	Philadelphia, Pa.,	11th mo.,	"
70. Margaret Garrett,	Upper Darby, Pa.,	9th mo.,	"
71. Ann Rowland,	Abington, Pa.,	7th mo.,	1800.
72. Janet Rowland,	Camden, Del.,	2d mo.,	"
73. Hannah C. Rockhill,	Burlington, N. J.,	1st mo.,	"
74. Keziah Mickle,	Cooper's Ferry, N. J.,	11th mo.,	1799.
75. Sarah Hartshorne,	Alexandria, Va.,	12th mo.,	"
76. Charity Cope,	East Bradford, Pa.,	11th mo.,	"
77. Sarah Tomlinson,	Haddonfield, N. J.,	"	"
78. Deborah Smith,	Philadelphia, Pa.	"	"
79. Rebecca Hopkins,	"	"	"
80. Abigail B. Smith,	"	"	"

STUDENTS.

FIRST THOUSAND.

NAME.	RESIDENCE.	DATE OF ENTRY.
81. Rachel Warrington,	Westfield, N. J.,	12th mo., 1799.
82. Mary French,	"	" "
83. Sarah Buckbee,	Philadelphia, Pa.,	2d mo., 1800.
84. Abigail Scull,	Salem Co., N. J.,	" "
85. Elizabeth Thomas,	West Whiteland, Pa.,	" "
86. Ellen Atkinson,	Frankford, Pa.,	12th mo., 1799.
87. Elizabeth Hunt,	Downingtown, Pa.,	2d mo., 1800.
88. Sarah Yarnall,	Philadelphia, Pa.,	5th mo., "
89. Ann J. Haydock,	"	4th mo., "
90. Mary Willis,	"	" "
91. Harriet Logan,	"	" "
92. Sarah Janney,	Alexandria, Va.,	3d mo., "
93. Jane McPherson,	Baltimore, Md.,	" "
94. Eliz. McPherson,	"	" "
95. Margaret Williams,	Trenton, N. J.,	" "
96. Esther Hewlings,	Philadelphia, Pa.,	" "
97. Ann Paxson,	Trenton, N. J.,	4th mo., "
98. Rachel Pole,	Philadelphia, Pa.,	3d mo., "
99. Martha Roberts,	Allowaystown, N. J.,	" "
100. Mary Pennock,	Philadelphia, Pa.,	4th mo., "
101. Letitia Miller,	Salem, N. J.,	6th mo., "
102. Hannah Price,	East Bradford, Pa.,	4th mo., "
103. Mary Haworth,	Philadelphia, Pa.,	5th mo., "
104. Jane Longstreth,	Crosswicks, N. J.,	" "
105. Anna Oldden,	Princeton, N. J.,	" "
106. Sarah Canby,	Wilmington, Del.,	" "
107. Sarah Miller,	Salem, N. J.,	6th mo., "
108. Jane Malin,	West Whiteland, Pa.,	" "
109. Mary Evans,	Philadelphia, Pa.,	7th mo., "
110. Mary Wiley,	Maiden Creek, Pa.,	6th mo., "
111. Elizabeth Miller,	Salem, N. J.,	8th mo., "
112. Elizabeth Barnard,	E. Marlborough, Pa.,	7th mo., "
113. Sarah Ann Robeson,	Abington, Pa.,	8th mo., "
114. Sarah Williams,	"	7th mo., "
115. Hannah Williams,	"	" "
116. Elizabeth Cresson,	Philadelphia, Pa.,	" "
117. Elizabeth Wright,	Exeter, Pa.,	9th mo., "
118. Priscilla Mickle,	Cooper's Ferry, N. J.,	8th mo., "
119. Ann Gaskill,	Springfield, N. J.,	10th mo., "
120. Mary Garrigues,	Philadelphia, Pa.,	7th mo., "
121. Margaret Smith,	Burlington, N. J.,	8th mo., 1800.
122. Sarah Cresson,	Philadelphia, Pa.,	10th mo., "
123. Ann Bacon,	Salem, N. J.,	9th mo., "
124. Mercy Maule,	Salem Co., N. J.,	11th mo., "
125. Margery Smith,	Philadelphia, Pa.,	1st mo., 1801.
126. Rebecca Smith,	"	" "
127. Esther Knight,	Byberry, Pa.,	2d mo., "

FIRST THOUSAND.

NAME.	RESIDENCE.	DATE OF ENTRY.
128. E. Cowperthwaite,	Moorestown, N. J.,	1st mo., 1801
129. Elizabeth Dawes,	Philadelphia, Pa.,	10th mo., 1800.
130. Edith Pusey,	London Grove, Pa.,	" "
131. Elizabeth Folwell,	Philadelphia, Pa.,	" "
132. Mary Lea,	Wilmington, Del.,	" "
133. Sidney Pennell,	Upper Darby, Pa.,	11th mo., "
134. Elizabeth Brinton,	Lampeter, Pa.,	" "
135. Massey Gibbons,	"	" "
136. Ann Brian,	Wilmington, Del.,	" "
137. Sarah Fletcher,	Abington, Pa.,	" "
138. Susanna Lightfoot,	Uwchlan, Pa.,	" "
139. Lydia Coates,	Philadelphia, Pa.,	4th mo., 1801.
140. Elizabeth Downing,	"	" "
141. Phebe Downing,	Downingtown, Pa.,	12th mo., 1800.
142. Sarah Thomas,	West Whiteland, Pa.,	" "
143. Thomazine Thomas,		" "
145. Rebecca Hopkins,	Philadelphia, Pa.,	" "
146. Mary Garrigues,	"	" "
147. Esther Stapler,	Fallsington, Pa.,	1st mo., 1801.
148. Sarah Woolston,	"	" "
149. Phebe Miller,	Salem, N. J.,	12th mo., 1800.
150. Sarah West,	Mt. Holly, N. J.,	" "
151. Mary Gill,	Haddonfield, N. J.,	2d mo., 1801.
152. Elizabeth Reeve,	Greenwich, N. J.,	" "
153. Abigail Pancoast,	Philadelphia, Pa.,	4th mo., "
154. Sarah Richardson,	"	" "
155. Eliz. Richardson,	"	" "
156. Lydia Cooper,	Newtown, N. J.,	" "
157. R. Scattergood,	Philadelphia, Pa.,	" "
158. Elizabeth Cooper,	Newtown, N. J.,	" "
159. Mary Richards,	Wilmington, Del.,	" "
160. Helena Abbott,	Philadelphia, Pa.,	" "
161. Sarah Abbott,	"	" "
162. Esther Warner,	Wilmington, Del.,	" "
163. Hannah Nichols,	"	" "
164. Mary Denny,	Smyrna, Del.,	" "
165. Phebe Pusey,	London Grove, Pa.,	5th mo., "
166. Sarah Newlin,	Concord, Pa.,	6th mo., "
167. Sarah Salter,	Shrewsbury, N. J.,	5th mo., "
168. Ann Wheeler,	Philadelphia, Pa.,	6th mo., "
169. Sarah Burr,	Mt. Holly, N. J.,	" "
170. Mary Edge,	Downingtown, Pa.,	" "
171. Rebecca White,	Woodstown, N. J.,	8th mo., "
172. Mary Reeves,	Woodbury, N. J.,	" "
173. Susanna Luff,	Camden, Del.,	" "
174. Elizabeth Pleasants,	———, Va.,	7th mo., "
175. Mary Pleasants,	"	" "

STUDENTS.

FIRST THOUSAND.

NAME.	RESIDENCE.	DATE OF ENTRY.
176. Hannah Tunis,	Philadelphia, Pa.,	8th mo., 1801
177. Hannah Ash,	Darby, Pa.,	9th mo., "
178. Hannah Brinton,	Lampeter, Pa.,	10th mo., "
179. Eliz. Cowperthwaite,	Moorestown, N. J.,	11th mo., "
180. Anna Shipley,	Wilmington, Del.,	9th mo., "
181. Deborah Phillips,	New Garden, Pa.,	10th mo., "
182. Mary Haworth,	Philadelphia, Pa.,	11th mo., "
183. Rebecca Hopkins,	"	10th mo., "
184. Elizabeth Robinson,	———, N. Y.,	" "
185. Abigail Robinson,	"	" "
186. Ann Robinson,	"	" "
187. Rebecca Hewes,	Swedesboro, N. J.,	" "
188. Zillah Maule,	Radnor, Pa.,	" "
189. Rebecca Potts,	Abington, Pa.,	11th mo., "
190. Deborah Potts,		" "
191. Elizabeth Woodnutt,	Salem, N. J.,	10th mo., "
192. Rebecca Marshall,	Concord, Pa.,	11th mo., "
193. Sarah Austin,	Salem, N. J.,	" "
194. Sarah Bartram,	Philadelphia, Pa.,	" "
195. Hannah Chandlee,	Sandy Spring, Md.,	" "
196. Sarah Thomas,	Radnor, Pa.,	2d mo., 1802
197. Ann Jones,	Montgomery Co., Pa.,	" "
198. Ann Stroud,	Philadelphia, Pa.,	3d mo., "
199. Mary Ingham,	Buckingham, Pa.,	2d mo., "
200. Naomi Hunt,	Darby, Pa.,	3d mo., "
201. Rebecca Smith,	Burlington, N. J.,	" "
202. Sarah Taylor,	Pennsbury, Pa.,	" "
203. Jane Lewis,	Radnor, Pa.,	6th mo., "
204. Susanna Cox,	Burlington, N. J.,	" "
205. Abigail Wollaston,	....	4th mo., "
206. Rachel Cumming,	Horsham, Pa.,	3d mo., "
207. Rachel Schofield,	....	5th mo., "
208. Susanna Howell,	Philadelphia, Pa.,	" "
209. Hannah Howell,	"	" "
210. Anna Thomas,	W. Whiteland, Pa.,	" "
211. Priscilla Fletcher,	Abington, Pa.,	" "
212. Mary Downing,	Philadelphia, Pa.,	" "
213. Ann Carlisle,*	Buckingham, Pa.,	6th mo., "
214. Susanna Fairlamb,	Marple, Pa.,	" "
215. Rachel Wilson,	London Grove, Pa.,	" "
216. Rest Swayne,	E. Marlborough, Pa.,	" "
217. Deborah Emlen,	Philadelphia, Pa.,	7th mo., "
218. Edith Sharpless,	East Bradford, Pa.,	" "
219. Rachel Yarnall,	Wilmington, Del.,	5th mo., "
220. Esther Hoopes,	New Garden, Pa.,	11th mo., "

* Deceased at the school, Tenth mo. 30th, 1802.

GENERAL CATALOGUE.

FIRST THOUSAND.

NAME.	RESIDENCE.	DATE OF ENTRY.
221. Rebecca Marsh,	Baltimore, Md.,	6th mo., 1802.
222. Rhoda Matthews,	Gunpowder, Md.,	" "
223. Lydia Baily,	E. Marlborough, Pa.,	" "
224. Phebe Trimble,	Concord, Pa.,	7th mo., "
225. Phebe Millhouse,	Uwchlan, Pa.,	8th mo., "
226. Eleanor Brown,	Waterford, Va.,	6th mo., "
227. Sarah Thompson,	"	" "
228. Pleasant Thompson,	"	" "
229. Elizabeth Moore,	"	" "
230. Phebe Embree,	West Bradford, Pa.,	" "
231. Lydia Nichols,	Wilmington, Del.,	7th mo., "
232. Jemima Corbitt,	Appoquinimink, Del.,	" "
233. Lucy Wright,	Burlington, N. J.,	8th mo., "
234. Beulah Lippincott,	"	" "
235. Jane Havard,	Radnor, Pa.,	9th mo., "
236. Ann Paul,	Abington, Pa.,	10th mo., "
237. Beulah Lippincott,	Mt. Holly, N. J.,	" "
238. Phebe Way,	Lampeter, Pa.,	" "
239. Mary Lippincott,	Mt. Holly, N. J.,	" "
240. Sarah Jacobs,	Uwchlan, Pa.,	" "
241. Mary Cooper,	Woodbury, N. J.,	" "
242. Eliz. Cowperthwaite,	Moorestown, N. J.,	12th mo., "
243. Susanna Jones,	Baltimore, Md.,	10th mo., "
244. Hannah Jones,	"	" "
245. Lydia Gibbons,	Lampeter, Pa.,	12th mo., "
246. Mary Brinton,	"	" "
247. Ann Deacon,	Burlington, N. J.,	11th mo., "
248. Elizabeth Buzby,	"	" "
249. Hannah Thompson,	Philadelphia, Pa.,	" "
250. Ann Cooper,	"	" "
251. Sarah Moore,	Harford, Pa.,	12th mo., "
252. Elizabeth Atkinson,	Frankford, Pa.,	" "
255. Ann Hunn,	Camden, Del.,	11th mo., "
256. H. Cowperthwaite,	Moorestown, N. J.,	12th mo., "
257. Mary Hussey,	Baltimore, Md.,	11th mo., "
258. Mary Howell,	London Grove, Pa.,	12th mo., "
259. Esther Smith,	Salem, N. J.,	1st mo., 1803
260. Mary Pennell,	Aston, Pa.,	" "
261. Martha Reeve,	Evesham, N. J.,	2d mo., "
262. Ann Levis,	Springfield, Pa.,	4th mo., "
263. Elizabeth Shourds,	Egg Harbor, N. J.,	5th mo., "
264. Ann Riley,	Baltimore, Md.,	4th mo., "
265. Sarah Thomas,	Sandy Spring, Md.,	3d mo., "
266. Hannah Irwin,	Alexandria, Va.,	" "
267. Elizabeth Rowland,	Camden, Del.,	4th mo., "
268. Ruth Emerson,	"	" "
269. Judith Willits,	Egg Harbor, N. J.,	5th mo., "

STUDENTS.

FIRST THOUSAND.

NAME.	RESIDENCE.	DATE OF ENTRY.	
270. Sarah Shaw,	Chester, Pa.,	5th mo.,	1803.
271. Lydia Bullock,	Springfield, N. J.,	"	"
272. Ann Haines,	Philadelphia, Pa.,	4th mo.,	"
273. Tabitha Rowland,	Camden, Del.,	"	"
274. Mary Carr,	Mt. Holly, N. J.,	5th mo.,	"
275. Rachel White,	Buckingham, Pa.,	4th mo.,	"
276. Sarah Martin,	Rahway, N. J.,	5th mo.,	"
277. Mary Lynn,	Philadelphia, Pa.,	"	"
278. Rachel Owen,	Little York, Pa.,	"	"
279. Mary Cookson,	Pipe Creek, Md.,	"	"
280. Hannah Janney,	Alexandria, Va.,	- 11th mo.,	"
281. Ann Woodward,	Crosswicks, N. J.,	5th mo.,	"
282. Sarah Woodward,	"	"	"
283. Sarah Hopkins,	Philadelphia, Pa.,	6th mo.,	"
284. Mary Britt,	"	"	"
285. Ann Pim,	East Bradford, Pa.,	10th mo.,	"
286. Elizabeth Butcher,	Mt. Holly, N. J.,	11th mo.,	"
287. Hannah Hutton,	Philadelphia, Pa.,	8th mo.,	"
288. Mary Butcher,	Mt. Holly, N. J.,	11th mo.,	"
289. Sarah Evans,	Philadelphia, Pa.,	9th mo.,	"
290. Janet Shaw,	Chester, Pa.,	"	"
291. Sarah Smith,	Sadsbury, Pa.,	10th mo.,	"
292. Rebecca Truman,	"	"	"
293. Sarah Ware,	Salem, N. J.,	8th mo.,	"
294. Mary Welsh,	Little York, Pa.,	9th mo.,	"
295. Phebe Emlen,	Thornbury, Pa.,	10th mo.,	"
296. Sarah Pierce,	"	"	"
297. Mercy Hampton,	New Hope, Pa.,	"	"
298. Elizabeth Phillips,	"	"	"
299. Elizabeth Wright,	Little York, Pa.,	"	"
300. Elizabeth Warder,	Philadelphia, Pa.,	"	"
301. Hannah Ellicott,	Alexandria, Va.,	11th mo.,	"
302. Mary Kirk,	Harford, Md.,	12th mo.,	"
303. Ann Pusey,	East Bradford, Pa.,	"	"
304. Hannah Albertson,	Plymouth, Pa.,	"	"
305. Mary Hampton,	New Hope, Pa.,	"	"
306. Martha Ogden,	Springfield, Pa.,	11th mo.,	"
307. Mary Wiley,	Maiden Creek, Pa.,	12th mo.,	"
308. Mary Way,	West Caln, Pa.,	"	"
309. Mary Darlington,	West Chester, Pa.,	"	"
310. Alice Ann Wilson,	New Garden, Pa.,	10th mo.,	"
311. Jane Pratt,	Edgmont, Pa.,	12th mo.,	"
312. Esther M. Thomas,	Philadelphia, Pa.,	1st mo.,	1804.
313. Lucy Abbott,	Springfield, N. J.,	"	"
314. Susanna Bullock,	"	"	"
315. Hannah Maule,	Radnor, Pa.,	"	"
316. Mary Branson,	Westtown, Pa.,	"	"

GENERAL CATALOGUE.

FIRST THOUSAND.

NAME.	RESIDENCE.	DATE OF ENTRY.
317. Jane Hoopes,	Downingtown, Pa.,	1st mo., 1804
318. Lydia Jackson,	London Grove, Pa.,	" "
319. Deborah Phillips,	Kennet, Pa.,	" "
320. Hannah Price,	East Bradford, Pa.,	" "
321. Elizabeth Rhoads,	Springfield, Pa.,	3d mo., "
322. Elizabeth Rhoads,	"	" "
323. Sarah Taylor,	East Bradford, Pa.,	4th mo., "
324. Hannah Pim,	East Caln, Pa.,	5th mo., "
325. Mary Townsend,	Beaver, Pa.,	3d mo., "
326. Sarah Merritt,	Troy, N. Y.,	1st mo., "
329. Frances Kirkbride,	Frankford, Pa.,	" "
330. Mary Buzby,	Rancocas, N. J.,	3d mo., "
331. Martha Gray,	Darby, Pa.,	4th mo., "
332. Rebecca Potts,	Abington, Pa.,	6th mo., "
333. Mary Merritt,	Troy, N. Y.,	" "
334. Elizabeth Moore,	Lancaster Co., Pa.,	4th mo., "
335. Elizabeth Passmore,	Pleasant Garden, Pa.,	" "
336. Alice Levis,	West Chester, Pa.,	" "
337. Hannah England,	East Marlborough, Pa.,	" "
338. Hannah Updegraff,	Little York, Pa.,	5th mo., "
339. Phebe Harvey,	Pennsbury, Pa.,	" "
340. Elizabeth Wright,	Burlington, N. J.,	7th mo., "
341. Lydia Trimble,	West Bradford, Pa.,	5th mo., "
342. Phebe Trimble,	"	" "
343. Margaret M. Smith,	Burlington, N. J.,	6th mo., "
344. Rachel Smith,	"	" "
345. Hannah Paul,	Horsham, Pa.,	" "
346. Ann Richardson,	Wilmington, Del.,	8th mo., "
347. Mary Comfort,	Fallsington, Pa.,	6th mo., "
348. Elizabeth Heston,	Solesbury, Pa.,	8th mo., "
349. Ann Newlin,	Darby, Pa.,	" "
350. Jane Hewes,	Chichester, Pa.,	10th mo., "
351. Hannah Sheppard,	Pipe Creek, Md.,	5th mo., "
352. Ann Hughes,	New Market, Md.,	" "
353. Massey Pusey,	Bush Creek, Md.,	" "
354. Asenath Roman,	West Bradford, Pa.,	6th mo., "
355. Maria Fell,	Springfield, Pa.,	" "
356. Sarah Edwards,	Thornbury, Pa.,	" "
357. Rebecca Matlack,	Radnor, Pa.,	10th mo., "
358. Elizabeth Tyson,	Baltimore, Md.,	8th mo., "
359. Hannah Howell,	London Grove, Pa.,	9th mo., "
360. Elizabeth Stevenson,	Burlington Co., N. J.,	10th mo., "
361. Hannah Spencer,	Horsham, Pa.,	" "
362. Sarah Vickers,	Philadelphia, Pa.,	8th mo., "
363. Elizabeth Williams,	Plymouth, Pa.,	10th mo., "
364. Hannah Croxson,	....	8th mo., "
365. Hannah Rhoads,	Darby, Pa.,	9th mo., "

STUDENTS. 231

FIRST THOUSAND.

NAME.	RESIDENCE.	DATE OF ENTRY.
366. Sarah Woodward,	Crosswicks, N. J.,	10th mo., 1804.
367. Susanna Spencer,	Horsham, Pa.,	" "
368. Esther Smith,	....	11th mo., "
369. Ann Wheeler,	Philadelphia, Pa.,	10th mo., "
370. Mary Smith,	London Grove, Pa.,	11th mo., "
371. Rebecca Wilson,	"	" "
372. Hannah Pennock,		" "
373. Sarah Pennock,	W. Marlborough, Pa.,	" "
374. Rachel Pennell,	Chichester, Pa.,	10th mo., "
375. Mary Jones,	....	" "
376. Rachel Lee,	Exeter, Pa.,	12th mo., "
377. Mary Jarrett,	Horsham, Pa.,	11th mo., "
378. Hannah Foulke,	Gwynedd, Pa.,	" "
379. Grace Stalker,	East Caln, Pa.,	1st mo., 1805.
380. Susanna Stokes,	Rancocas, N. J.,	11th mo., 1804.
382. Hannah Ellis,	Mansfield, N. J.,	" "
383. Ann Shoemaker,	Plymouth, Pa.,	" "
384. Hannah Jones,	Merion, Pa.,	" "
385. Hannah Jarrett,	Horsham, Pa.,	1st mo., 1805.
386. Martha Buzby,	Burlington, N. J.,	10th mo., 1804.
387. Sarah Ann Robeson,	Germantown, Pa.,	" "
388. Mary Burrough,	Westfield, N. J.,	12th mo., "
389. Susanna Lightfoot,	Maiden Creek, Pa.,	" "
390. Ann Reeve,	Evesham, N. J.,	" "
391. Rachel Rogers,	"	" "
392. Hannah Davis,	Woodstown, N. J.,	3d mo., 1805.
393. Lydia Lippincott,	Westfield, N. J.,	2d mo., "
394. Mary Pearson,	Philadelphia, Pa.,	12th mo., 1804.
395. Deborah Potts,	Abington, Pa.,	1st mo., 1805.
396. Tacy Wood,	Woodbury, N. J.,	12th mo., 1804.
397. Susanna Lightfoot,	Uwchlan, Pa.,	5th mo., 1805.
398. Elizabeth Holmes,	Pilesgrove, Pa.,	3d mo., "
399. Rachel Ward,	Woodbury, N. J.,	4th mo., "
400. Margaret Morris,	Philadelphia, Pa.,	11th mo., 1804.
401. Hannah Clemson,	Pequea Valley, Pa.,	1st mo., 1805.
402. Deborah Williams,	Sadsbury, Pa.,	12th mo., 1804.
403. Sarah Townsend,	Pughtown, Pa.,	11th mo., "
404. Ruth Cook,	London Grove, Pa.,	12th mo., "
405. Elizabeth Williams,	Sadsbury, Pa ,	" "
406. Lydia Brinton,	Lampeter, Pa.,	" "
407. Margaret Pound,	Rahway, N. J.,	" "
408. Sibilla Price,	East Bradford, Pa.,	1st mo., 1805.
409. Ann Wright,	Exeter, Pa.,	12th mo., 1804.
410. Jane Millhouse,	Uwchlan, Pa.,	2d mo., 1805.
412. Martha Newbold,	Burlington, N. J.,	4th mo., "
413. Sarah Miller,	Salem, N. J.,	3d mo., "
414. Elizabeth Smith,	Woodstown, N. J.	" "

18

GENERAL CATALOGUE.

FIRST THOUSAND.

NAME.	RESIDENCE.	DATE OF ENTRY.	
415. Jane Jones,	Wilmington, Del.,	4th mo.,	1805.
416. Esther Canby,	"	"	"
417. Rebecca Thomas,	....	"	"
418. Martha Pettitt,	Philadelphia, Pa.,	"	"
419. Mary Boone,	"	"	1806.
420. Beulah Smith,	Salem, N. J.,	"	1805.
421. Anna Bonsall,	Philadelphia, Pa.,	2d mo.,	"
422. Esther Speakman,	Concord, Pa.,	"	"
423. Pamela Lewis,	Little York, Pa.,	"	"
424. Margaret Hughes,	Exeter, Pa.,	"	"
425. Susanna Phipps,	....	"	"
426. Hannah Baldwin,	West Bradford, Pa.,	4th mo.,	"
427. Ann Truman,	Sadsbury, Pa.,	5th mo.,	"
428. Willianna Smith,	Downingtown, Pa.,	6th mo.,	"
429. Priscilla Smith,	"	"	"
430. Hannah Hurford,	London Grove, Pa.,	5th mo.,	"
431. Hannah Hooton,	Philadelphia, Pa.,	"	"
432. Hannah C. Ellet,	Woodstown, N. J.,	4th mo.,	"
433. Elizabeth Goodwin,	Salem, N. J.,	"	"
435. Elizabeth Williams,	Shrewsbury, N. J.,	5th mo.,	"
436. Elizabeth Burr,	Mt. Holly, N. J.,	"	"
437. Elizabeth Ellicott,	Sandy Spring, Md.,	4th mo.,	"
438. Mary Mifflin,	Camden, Del.,	5th mo.,	"
439. Susanna Webster,	Abington, Pa.,	"	"
440. Lydia Stratton,	Upper Evesham, N. J.,	6th mo.,	"
441. Sarah Bolton,	Philadelphia, Pa.,	5th mo.,	"
442. Mary Heston,	Solesbury, Pa.,	"	"
443. Anna Ellis,	Muncy, Pa.,	4th mo.,	"
444. Hannah Pryor,	——, L. I.,	8th mo.,	"
445. Rebecca Scattergood,	Philadelphia, Pa.,	7th mo.,	"
446. Catharine Webster,	Plainfield, N. J.,	6th mo.,	"
447. Phebe Webster,	"	"	"
448. Esther Speakman,	....	"	"
449. Eliza Jenks,	Philadelphia, Pa.,	"	"
451. Sarah Pennock,	"	5th mo.,	"
452. Rebecca Way,	West Caln, Pa.,	"	"
453. Sidney Painter,	Brandywine, Pa.,	6th mo.,	"
454. Catharine Marsh,	Rahway, N. J.,	"	"
455. Hannah J. Alston,	Camden, Del.,	5th mo.,	"
456. Casandra Moore,	Pleasant Garden, Pa.,	6th mo.,	"
457. Lydia Mann,	Doe Run, Pa.,	9th mo.,	"
458. Hannah Pierce,	Thornbury, Pa.,	6th mo.,	"
459. Rachel Matthews,	Easton, Md.,	7th mo.,	"
460. Amy Cox,	Willistown, Pa.,	10th mo.,	"
461. Sarah Vanhorn,	Little York, Pa.,	9th mo.,	"
462. Mary L. Cox,	Philadelphia, Pa.,	7th mo.,	"
463. Rachel Ellicott,	Baltimore, Md.	"	"

STUDENTS. 233

FIRST THOUSAND.

NAME.	RESIDENCE.	DATE OF ENTRY.
464. Ann C. Whitall,	Woodbury, N. J.,	10th mo., 1805.
465. Hephzibah Roberts,	Moorestown, N. J.,	9th mo., "
466. Elizabeth Bunting,	Philadelphia, Pa.,	8th mo., "
467. Annabella Laing,	Rahway, N. J.,	" "
468. Bethiah Vail,		" "
469. Ann Spencer,	Horsham, Pa.,	10th mo., "
470. Lydia Davis,	Radnor, Pa.,	11th mo., "
471. Beulah Gaskill,	Springfield, N. J.,	10th mo., "
472. Rachel Gaskill,	"	" "
473. Ann Matlack,	Moorestown, N. J.,	9th mo., "
474. Keturah Deacon,	Burlington, N. J.,	10th mo., "
475. Kezia Eayre,	Eayrstown, N. J.,	" "
476. Mary Evans,	Philadelphia, Pa.,	11th mo., "
477. Letitia Smith,	Bucks Co., Pa.,	10th mo., "
478. Tacy Fletcher,	Abington, Pa.,	11th mo., "
479. Deborah Cumming,	Horsham, Pa.,	10th mo., "
480. Rebecca Elkinton,	Philadelphia, Pa.,	11th mo., "
481. Sarah Coates,	West Caln, Pa.,	9th mo., "
482. Lydia Williams,	Goshen, Pa.,	10th mo., "
483. Sarah Ross,	New Garden, Pa.,	12th mo., "
484. Lydia Sharpless,	Middletown, Pa.,	9th mo., "
485. Lydia Burr,	Mt. Holly, N. J.,	10th mo., "
486. Rebecca Burr,	"	" "
487. Hannah Roman,	West Bradford, Pa.,	11th mo., "
488. Jane Pierce,	Sadsbury, Pa.,	" "
489. Maria Reese,	Baltimore, Md.,	" "
491. Rebecca Rhoads,	Springfield, Pa.,	12th mo., "
492. Susanna Rhoads,	"	" "
493. Rebecca Pancoast,	"	" "
494. Anna Pancoast,	"	" "
495. Ruth Lea,	Exeter, Pa.,	" "
496. Sarah W. Coale,	Deer Creek, Md.,	2d mo., 1806.
497. Rebecca Nichols,*	....	" "
498. Martha Jackson,	Hockessing, Del.,	3d mo., "
499. Eliza T. Sipple,	Wilmington, Del.,	4th mo., "
500. Elizabeth T. Starr,	"	" "
501. Martha Betts,	"	12th mo., 1805.
502. Rachel Jeans,	Abington, Pa.,	" "
504. Elizabeth Earl,	Springfield, N. J.,	11th mo., "
505. Lydia White,	Shrewsbury, N. J.,	" "
506. Elizabeth White,	"	" "
507. Rebecca White,	"	" "
508. Ann G. Williams,	Philadelphia, Pa.,	12th mo., "
509. Rachel Hollinshead,	Moorestown, N. J.,	" "
510. Mary Jarrett,	Horsham, Pa.,	1st mo., 1806

* Deceased at the school, Eleventh month 15th, 1806.

GENERAL CATALOGUE.

FIRST THOUSAND.

NAME.	RESIDENCE.	DATE OF ENTRY.
511. Tacy Jarrett,	Horsham, Pa.,	1st mo., 1806.
512. Rebecca Pryor,	Philadelphia, Pa.,	12th mo., 1805
513. Emilia Thomas,	Radnor, Pa.,	1st mo., 1806.
514. Hannah B. Jackson,	Philadelphia, Pa.,	3d mo., "
515. Lydia Lowrie,	Woodstown, N. J.,	11th mo., "
516. Ann Gibson,	Philadelphia, Pa.,	4th mo., "
517. Mary Hibberd,	Darby, Pa.,	" "
518. Rebecca Trotter,	Philadelphia, Pa.,	" "
519. Sarah A. Bringhurst,	"	3d mo., "
520. Phebe Quinby,	Little Britain, Pa.,	" "
521. Sarah Foulke,	Philadelphia, Pa.,	4th mo., "
522. Mary Lippincott,	Mt. Holly, N. J.,	3d mo., "
523. Rachel Townsend,	Pughtown, Pa.,	2d mo., "
524. Mary Husband,	Deer Creek, Md.,	4th mo., "
525. Rachel Cox,	"	" "
526. Lavina Hilyard,	....	" "
527. Junia Hilyard,	....	" "
528. Beulah Sharpless,	Chester, Pa.,	" "
529. Edith Matthews,	Gunpowder, Md.,	3d mo., "
530. Mary Price,	"	" "
531. Hannah Jones,	Baltimore, Md.,	" "
532. Rachel Biles,	New Garden, Pa.,	" "
533. Lucy Harris,	Richmond, Va.,	5th mo., "
534. Deborah Harris,	"	" "
535. Isabella Ladd,	"	" "
536. Hannah Bruff,	Easton, Md.,	" "
537. Lydia Bruff,	"	" "
538. Elizabeth Yarnall,	"	" "
539. Sarah Cox,	Deer Creek, Md.,	11th mo., "
540. Hannah Phillips,	Hockessing, Del.,	5th mo., "
541. Elizabeth Ellis,	Harford, Md.,	4th mo., "
542. Martha Davis,	Pilesgrove, Pa.,	" "
543. Hannah Marsh,	Baltimore, Md.,	3d mo., "
544. Edith Bullock,	Springfield, N. J.,	5th mo., "
547. Catharine Walker,	Egg Harbor, N. J.,	6th mo., "
548. Mary Waterman,	Philadelphia, Pa.,	5th mo., "
549. Martha King,	Cerestown, N. Y.,	6th mo., "
550. Deborah Couch,	Richmond, Va.,	" "
551. Eliz. Hutchinson,	Philadelphia, Pa.,	" "
552. Ann Bruce,		5th mo., "
553. Margery Bunting,	Attleboro', Pa.,	" "
554. Charlotte Longstreth,	Philadelphia, Pa.,	6th mo., "
555. Mary Clark,	Woodbury, N. J.,	5th mo., "
556. Sarah Borton,	Moorestown, N. J.,	6th mo., "
557. E. Cowperthwaite,	"	7th mo., "
558. Mary Thomas,	Springfield, N. J.,	8th mo., "
559. Mary Hibberd,	Darby, Pa.,	10th mo., "

STUDENTS.

FIRST THOUSAND.

NAME.	RESIDENCE.	DATE OF ENTRY.
560. Sarah Ladd,	Richmond, Va.,	5th mo., 1806
561. Ann Forsythe,	Springfield, N. J.,	" "
562. Abigail Ingram,	West Bradford, Pa.,	6th mo., "
563. Ruth Truman,	Sadsbury, Pa.,	" "
564. Sarah Hauxhurst,	New York, N. Y.,	" "
565. Isabella Pennock,	Philadelphia, Pa.,	7th mo., "
566. Zillah Coates,	West Caln, Pa.,	8th mo., "
567. Rebecca W. Pennock,	Buck Run, Pa.,	9th mo., "
568. Elizabeth Dingee,	Newlin, Pa.,	" "
569. Hannah Woodward,	West Bradford, Pa.,	" "
570. Mary Pennock,	London Grove, Pa.,	" "
571. Eliza Newlin,	Chichester, Pa.,	10th mo., "
572. Rebecca Albertson,	Plymouth, Pa.,	8th mo., "
573. Hannah Chandlee,	Nottingham, Pa.,	10th mo., "
575. Margaret Powell,	Chester, Pa.,	" "
576. Elizabeth Caulk,	Cecil Co., Md.,	9th mo., "
577. Susanna Hoopes,	West Chester, Pa.,	" "
578. Margaret Lee,	Exeter, Pa.,	11th mo., "
579. Mary Clemson,	Pequea Valley, Pa.,	" "
580. Rebecca Couch,	Richmond, Va.,	5th mo., 1807.
581. Rachel Hunt,	Darby, Pa.,	9th mo., 1806.
582. Anna Maria Hoskins,	Radnor, Pa.,	11th mo., "
583. Ann Paul,	Abington, Pa.,	" "
584. Jane Evans,	....	" "
585. Jane Iden,	Richland, Pa.,	" "
586. Ann Hauxhurst,	New York, N. Y.,	" "
587. Deborah Engle,	Evesham, N. J.,	" "
588. Sarah Mott,	New York, N. Y.,	" "
589. Hannah Knowles,	Makefield, Pa.,	" "
590. Rachel Mason,	Sandy Spring, Md.,	" "
591. Rebecca Taylor,	———, Ohio,	" "
592. Esther Scott,	Gunpowder, Md.,	" "
593. Elizabeth West,	Baltimore, Md.,	4th mo., 1807.
594. Elizabeth Bruce,	Philadelphia, Pa.,	" "
595. Sarah Clemson,	Pequea Valley, Pa.,	" "
596. Hannah Jefferis,	East Bradford, Pa.,	5th mo., "
597. Lydia West,	Smyrna, Del.,	" "
598. Margaret Price,	East Bradford, Pa.,	" "
599. Hannah Richardson,	....	3d mo., "
600. Ann E. Gregg,	Bristol, Pa.,	11th mo., 1806
601. Grace Rogers,	Evesham, N. J.,	" "
602. Edith Newbold,	Springfield, N. J.,	12th mo., "
604. Hannah Wills,	Rancocas, N. J.,	11th mo., "
605. Elizabeth Hopkins,	Haddonfield, N. J.,	12th mo., "
606. Rachel French,	Moorestown, N. J.,	" "
607. Leah Earl,	Springfield, N. J.,	" "
608. Achsah Willis,	Philadelphia, Pa.,	3d mo., 1807.

18*

O

GENERAL CATALOGUE.

FIRST THOUSAND.

NAME.	RESIDENCE.	DATE OF ENTRY
609. Mary Smith,	Philadelphia, Pa.,	4th mo., 1807
610. Hannah Matlack,	Radnor, Pa.,	10th mo., "
611. Matilda Matthews,	Gunpowder, Md.,	" "
612. Rachel Offley,	Philadelphia, Pa.,	5th mo., "
613. Hannah Evans,	"	" "
614. Phebe Williams,	Abington, Pa.,	" "
615. Mary S. Wood,	Greenwich, N. J.,	6th mo., "
616. Margaret Morris,	Burlington, N. J.,	4th mo., "
617. Rachel Smith,	"	" "
618. Ann Craig,	Darby, Pa.,	5th mo., "
619. Susan H. Cox,	Philadelphia, Pa.,	3d mo., "
620. Hannah Coleman,	Burlington, N. J.,	4th mo., "
621. Hannah Churchman,	Philadelphia, Pa.,	5th mo., "
622. Hannah Haydock,	New York, N. Y.,	6th mo., "
623. Mary Davis,	Radnor, Pa.,	10th mo., "
624. Sarah Taylor,	Horsham, Pa.,	5th mo., "
625. Achsah Stapler,	"	" "
626. Susanna Parker,	Pennsbury, Pa.,	" "
627. Rebecca Woollen,	Horsham, Pa.,	" "
628. Hannah Woollen,	"	" "
629. Bethiah Vail,	Rahway, N. J.,	4th mo., "
630. Christiana Vail,	"	" "
631. Lydia A. Jones,	Wilmington, Del.,	5th mo., "
633. Elizabeth Painter,	East Bradford, Pa.,	" "
635. Grace Trimble,	Uwchlan, Pa.,	7th mo., "
636. Margaret Smith,	London Grove, Pa.,	9th mo., "
637. Eliza Edmondson,	E. Marlborough, Pa.,	8th mo., "
638. Edith Bennett,	Pennsbury, Pa.,	10th mo., "
639. Lydia Austin,	Buckingham, Pa.,	" "
640. Martha Harlan,	West Bradford, Pa.,	11th mo., "
641. Esther Pancoast,	Darby, Pa.,	5th mo., "
642. Abigail Nixon,	Charleston, Pa.,	6th mo., "
643. Esther Wilkins,	Evesham, N. J.,	" "
644. Mary Moore,	Sandy Spring, Md.,	" "
645. Anna Briggs,	"	" "
646. Mary Briggs,	"	" "
647. Catharine Oldden,	Stony Brook, N. J.,	7th mo., "
648. Elizabeth Ash,	Darby, Pa.,	9th mo., "
649. Esther S. Bunting,	Philadelphia, Pa.,	8th mo., "
650. Martha Morris,	"	" "
651. Rachel Johnson,	Germantown, Pa.,	10th mo., "
652. Margaret Smith,	Burlington, N. J.,	" "
653. Eliz. Shoemaker,	Philadelphia, Pa.,	" "
654. Anna Shoemaker,	"	" "
655. Deborah E. Kay,	Woodbury, N. J.,	11th mo., "
656. Eliza B. Wilson,	Buckingham, Pa.,	10th mo., "
657. Elizabeth D. Barker,	Philadelphia, Pa.,	" "

STUDENTS.

FIRST THOUSAND.

NAME.	RESIDENCE.	DATE OF ENTRY.
658. Elizabeth Rowland,	Camden, Del.,	10th mo., 1807
659. Jane Burgess,	Radnor, Pa.,	" "
660. Susanna Pennock,	London Grove, Pa.,	9th mo., "
661. Hannah Wollaston,	E. Marlborough, Pa.,	" "
662. Ann Bernard,	"	" "
663. Elizabeth Pyle,	"	" "
664. Eliz. Cadwallader,	Buckingham, Pa.,	11th mo., "
665. Rebecca Hough,	"	" "
666. Hannah Cope,	East Bradford, Pa.,	10th mo., "
667. Susanna Alston,	Little Creek, Del.,	" "
668. Mary Entriken,	East Bradford, Pa.,	11th mo., "
669. Deborah Brick,	Salem, N. J.,	" "
670. Esther Nicholson,	"	" "
671. Lydia Harlan,	West Bradford, Pa.,	" "
672. Martha Dillon,	Baltimore, Md.,	" "
673. Rebecca Bonsall,	West Whiteland, Pa.,	12th mo., "
674. Charlotte Shourds,	Egg Harbor, N. J.,	" "
675. Hannah Miller,	Brownsville, Pa.,	1st mo., 1808.
676. Mary Paist,	Providence, Pa.,	" "
677. Elizabeth Taylor,	Kennet, Pa.,	2d mo., "
679. Elizabeth Fisher,	East Caln, Pa.,	3d mo., "
680. Sarah Jones,	Radnor, Pa.,	10th mo., "
681. Hannah Zell,	"	" 1807.
682. Mary Trotter,	Philadelphia, Pa.,	" "
683. Rachel Hunt,	Moorestown, N. J.,	11th mo., "
684. Hannah Roberts,	"	" "
685. Rebecca Roberts,	"	" "
686. Ann M. Price,	Darby, Pa.,	" "
687. Elizabeth Conrow,	Moorestown, N. J.,	" "
688. Sarah Stokes,	Philadelphia, Pa.,	" "
689. Mary Matlack,	Moorestown, N. J.,	" "
690. Ann Roberts,	"	" "
691. Sarah H. Richards,	Philadelphia, Pa.,	" "
692. Tacy Wood,	Woodbury, N. J.,	" "
693. Mary Earl,	Springfield, N. J.,	" "
694. Rebecca Nicholson,	Haddonfield, N. J.,	" "
695. Ann Jarrett,	Horsham, Pa.,	" "
696. Beulah Roberts,	Moorestown, N. J.,	" "
697. Mary Rowland,	Abington, Pa.,	" "
698. Rebecca Story,	Wrightstown, Pa.,	4th mo., 1808.
699. Hannah Baily,	Abington, Pa.,	11th mo., 1807.
700. Esther Warrington,	Moorestown, N. J.,	12th mo., "
702. Jane Evans,	Philadelphia, Pa.,	" "
703. Esther Bowman,	Cold Spring, Del.,	1st mo., 1808
704. Hannah Smith,	Philadelphia, Pa.,	2d mo., "
705. Lydia Gibbs,	Salem, N. J.,	" "
706. Beulah Nixon,	Charleston, Pa.,	" "

GENERAL CATALOGUE.

FIRST THOUSAND.

NAME.	RESIDENCE.	DATE OF ENTRY.
707. Hannah Hibberd,	Darby, Pa.,	5th mo., 1808
708. Rachel Wilson,	Woodbury, N. J.,	4th mo., "
709. Sarah Fussell,	Gunpowder, Md.,	3d mo., "
710. Alice Lukens,	Horsham, Pa.,	" "
711. Anna Watson,	Buckingham, Pa.,	" "
713. Mercy Stackhouse,	Horsham, Pa.,	4th mo., "
714. Grace Stackhouse,	"	" "
715. Sarah Lukens,	"	" "
716. Rachel Reeve,	Greenwich, N. J.,	" "
717. Elizabeth Hall,	"	" "
718. Mary Offley,	Philadelphia, Pa.,	5th mo., "
719. Esther Shallcross,	Darby, Pa.,	4th mo., "
720. Margaret Barnard,	W. Marlborough, Pa.	" "
721. Lydia Baker,	"	" "
722. Mary Lamborn,	Kennet, Pa.,	5th mo., "
723. Sarah John,	East Bradford, Pa.,	" "
724. Malinda Jefferis,	West Chester, Pa.,	6th mo., "
725. Lydia Cawley,	Pilesgrove, Pa.,	4th mo., "
726. Mary Taylor,	Kennet, Pa.,	5th mo., "
727. Elizabeth Poole,	Wilmington, Del.,	7th mo., 1809.
729. Rhoda Darlington,	Aston, Pa.,	5th mo., 1808.
730. Mary Sharpless,	Wilmington, Del.,	11th mo., "
731. Rachel Richards,	"	6th mo., "
732. Julia A. Kirkbride,	Philadelphia, Pa.,	5th mo., "
733. Mary Kirkbride,	"	" "
734. Elizabeth Carver,	....	" "
735. Letitia Briggs,	Sandy Spring, Md.,	" "
736. Martha Gray,	Middletown, Pa.,	" "
737. Sarah Iden,	Richland, Pa.,	" "
738. Rachel Shoemaker,	Abington, Pa.,	4th mo., "
739. Sarah Ware,	Darby, Pa.,	5th mo., "
740. Harriet Kirkbride,	Philadelphia, Pa.,	" "
742. Sarah Widdefield,	"	" "
743. Ann Oakford,	Darby, Pa.,	" "
744. Elizabeth Iden,	Richland, Pa.,	" "
745. Abigail Richards,	Philadelphia, Pa.,	" "
746. Priscilla Jones,	Wilmington, Del.,	6th mo., "
747. Sarah Thorn,	Philadelphia, Pa.,	" "
748. Asenath Livezey,	Abington, Pa.,	" "
749. Elizabeth Hazard,	Bristol, Pa..	7th mo., "
750. Elizabeth Dunkin,	Uwchlan, Pa.,	3d mo., "
751. Rebecca Sharpless,	Middletown, Pa.,	5th mo., "
752. Hannah Pennell,	"	6th mo., "
753. Lydia Harvey,	Pennsbury, Pa.,	8th mo., "
754. Hannah Harvey,	"	" "
755. Elizabeth Eastburn,	Wrightstown, Pa.	7th mo., "
756. Leah Jeans,	Abington, Pa.,	4th mo., 1809

STUDENTS.

FIRST THOUSAND.

NAME.	RESIDENCE.	DATE OF ENTRY.
757. Sidney Yarnall,	Middletown, Pa.,	8th mo., 1808.
759. Sarah Harlan,	Kennet, Pa.,	" "
760. Rachel Mendenhall,	Wilmington, Del.,	7th mo., "
761. Mary W. Smith,	....	" "
762. Eliz. B. Harrison,	Philadelphia, Pa.,	" "
763. Hannah Nicholson,	Haddonfield, N. J.,	11th mo., "
764. Rebecca Black,	Mansfield, N. J.,	" "
765. Rebecca Sheppard,	Philadelphia, Pa.,	10th mo., "
766. Martha Newbold,	"	11th mo., "
767. Sarah Dennis,	Greenwich, N. J.,	6th mo., 1809.
768. Beulah Clark,	Woodbury, N. J.,	11th mo., 1808.
769. Lydia Lippincott,	....	" "
770. Eliza Moore,	Willistown, Pa.,	" "
771. Elizabeth Clendenon,	Kennet, Pa.,	10th mo., "
772. Olive Baily,	E. Marlborough, Pa.,	9th mo., "
773. Sarah Pennock,	Philadelphia, Pa.,	10th mo., "
774. Anne Mendenhall,	Middletown, Pa.,	12th mo., "
775. Hannah Patton,	....	11th mo., "
776. Mary Lewis,	....	" "
777. Lydia Carter,	East Bradford, Pa.,	12th mo., "
778. Phebe Passmore,	Pleasant Garden, Pa.,	1st mo., 1809.
779. Ruth Passmore,	"	" "
780. Ruth Hall,	"	" "
781. Hannah C. Pancoast,	Mullica Hill, N. J.,	11th mo., 1808.
782. Rachel Burrough,	Westfield, N. J.,	" "
783. Kezia Burrough,	"	" "
784. Tabitha R. Smith,	Burlington, N. J.,	" "
785. Sidney Pennell,	Darby, Pa.,	" "
786. Mary Pennell,	"	" "
787. Ann Ivins,	Pottsgrove, Pa.,	" "
788. Sidney Foulke,	Richland, Pa.,	" "
789. Sabina Crownover,	Baltimore, Md.,	" "
791. Hannah Andrews,	Darby, Pa.,	" "
792. Anne Sharpless,	Middletown, Pa.,	12th mo., "
793. Mary Shoemaker,	Abington, Pa.,	1st mo., 1809.
794. Jemima Stroud,	Stroudsburg, Pa.,	" "
795. Elizabeth Burr,	Mt. Holly, N. J.,	12th mo., 1808.
796. Elizabeth Dugdale,	Philadelphia, Pa.,	4th mo., 1809.
797. Beulah Paschall,	Darby, Pa.,	3d mo., "
798. Sarah Bacon,	Philadelphia, Pa.,	4th mo., "
799. Sarah Starr,	"	" "
801. Eliza Matthews,	Gunpowder, Md.,	11th mo., 1808
802. Mary Milnor,	Little Britain, Pa.,	12th mo., "
803. Sarah L. Barnes,	Horsham, Pa.,	1st mo., 1809
804. Rachel Yarnall,	Middletown, Pa.,	3d mo., "
805. Mary Moore,	New Garden, Pa.,	" "
806. Mary Barnard,	W. Marlborough, Pa.,	4th mo., "

FIRST THOUSAND.

NAME.	RESIDENCE.	DATE OF ENTRY.
807. Mary P. Barnard,	W. Marlborough, Pa.,	4th mo., 1809
808. Dinah Barnard,	Newlin, Pa.,	" "
809. Mary Ann Pusey,	London Grove, Pa.,	" "
810. Mary Baily,	W. Marlborough, Pa.,	" "
811. Ann Smith,	Philadelphia, Pa.,	" "
812. Margaret Sheppard,	"	" "
813. Mary R. Latimer,	Wilmington, Del.,	" "
814. Sidney A. Gilpin,	"	" "
815. Harriet Jones,	Philadelphia, Pa.,	" "
816. Hannah A. Wood,	Haddonfield, N. J.,	" "
817. Harriet Fairlamb,	West Chester, Pa.,	" "
818. Elizabeth Oldden,	Philadelphia, Pa.,	5th mo., "
819. Mary Shoemaker,	"	" "
820. Elizabeth Shreeve,	"	" "
821. Mary Jones,	Birmingham, Pa.,	" "
822. Hannah Pyle,	E. Marlborough, Pa.,	" "
823. Ann Jenkins,	Camden, Del.,	" "
824. Elizabeth Fisher,	East Caln, Pa.,	" "
825. Rebecca Fisher,	"	" "
826. Mabel Barney,	Kennet, Pa.,	6th mo., "
827. Sally Ann Palmer,	Concord, Pa.,	5th mo., "
828. Hannah Swayne,	"	" "
830. Mary Kirk,	Gunpowder, Md.,	7th mo., "
831. Ann Eliza Gregg,	Bristol, Pa.,	4th mo., "
832. Deborah Gregg,	"	" "
833. Jane Sisom,	"	" "
834. Rebecca Brown,	Fallsington, Pa.,	" "
835. Maria A. Jones,	Merion, Pa.,	5th mo., "
836. Esther Coe,	Burlington, N. J.,	" "
837. Sarah Scull,	Woodstown, N. J.,	4th mo., "
838. Sarah Sinclair,	Baltimore, Md.,	" "
839. Rebecca Sinclair,	"	" "
840. Alice Jarrett,	Horsham, Pa.,	" "
841. Grace Townsend,	Byberry, Pa.,	5th mo., "
842. Susanna Townsend,	"	" "
843. Agnes Craft,	Abington, Pa.,	" "
844. Mary Borton,	Evesham, N. J.,	. " "
845. Ann Jordan,	Richmond, Va.,	6th mo., "
846. Elizabeth Craft,	Abington, Pa.,	5th mo., "
847. Marsha Lawrence,	Richmond, Va.,	6th mo., "
848. Hannah Prior,	——, L. I.,	" "
849. Rebecca Teas,	Philadelphia, Pa.,	5th mo., "
850. Miriam Burr,	Mt. Holly, N. J.,	" "
851. Eliza Bullock,	Springfield, N. J.,	6th mo., "
852. Jane Haines,	Evesham, N. J.,	9th mo., "
853. Mary Coffin,	Philadelphia, Pa.,	5th mo., "
854. Sarah H. Parkins,	....	8th mo., "

STUDENTS. 241

FIRST THOUSAND.

NAME.	RESIDENCE.	DATE OF ENTRY.
855. Maria Parkins,	....	8th mo., 1809
856. Sarah Hillman,	Philadelphia, Pa.,	6th mo., "
857. Elizabeth Coffin,	"	5th mo., "
858. Mary B. Hauxhurst,	———, N. Y.,	6th mo., "
859. Martha Parry,	Abington, Pa.,	" "
861. Elizabeth Walton,	New Garden, Pa.,	10th mo., "
862. Sarah Needles,	Little Creek, Del.,	8th mo., "
863. Elizabeth Baily,	E. Marlborough, Pa.,	10th mo., "
864. Phebe Pennock,	"	11th mo., "
865. Mercy Roberts,	....	" "
866. Ann Clendenon,	Kennet, Pa.,	" "
867. Rachel Darnell,	Evesham, N. J.,	" "
868. Sarah Brinton,	Lampeter, Pa.,	" "
869. Hannah Dillon,	Westtown, Pa.,	" "
870. Sabina Townsend,	Brownsville, Pa.,	10th mo., "
871. Martha Thomas,	Byberry, Pa.,	6th mo., "
873. Anna Biddle,	Philadelphia, Pa.,	" "
874. Sarah B. Thompson,	"	" "
875. Eliz. Stewardson,	"	" "
876. Mary Britt,	"	8th mo., "
877. Esther McPherson,	Baltimore, Md.,	7th mo., "
878. Mary McPherson,	"	" "
879. Elizabeth Marsh,	"	" "
880. Ann Buckley,	Bristol, Pa.,	6th mo., "
881. Hannah Haydock,	New York, N. Y.,	6th mo., "
882. Susanna Lawrie,	Trenton, N. J.,	11th mo., "
883. Martha McKand,	....	10th mo., "
884. Frances Potts,	Philadelphia, Pa.,	8th mo., "
885. Rebecca Edwards,	"	10th mo., "
886. Hannah Longstreth,	"	11th mo., "
887. Elizabeth Waln,	Arneystown, N. J.,	" "
888. Eliz. Blackwood,	Woodbury, N. J.,	" "
889. H. W. Hopkins,	Haddonfield, N. J.,	" "
890. Rebecca Shinn,	Philadelphia, Pa.,	10th mo., "
891. Amy R. Phipps,	"	" "
892. Mary Hough,	Makefield, Pa.,	11th mo., "
893. Mary Longshore,	....	" "
894. Charlotte Wistar,	Salem, N. J.,	12th mo., "
895. Phebe Rhoads,	Springfield, Pa.,	" "
896. Rachel Parry,	Buckingham, Pa.,	" "
898. Anna M. Hoskins,	Radnor, Pa.,	" "
899. Martha G. Bonsall,	Philadelphia, Pa.,	" "
900. Thomazin Trimble,	Newburg, N. Y.,	10th mo., "
901. Hannah Clendenon,	Kennet, Pa.,	12th mo., "
902. Mary Jenkins,	Camden, Del.,	" "
903. Rachel B. Wilson,	Deer Creek, Md.,	" "
904. Rebecca Dutton,	Chichester, Pa.,	1st mo., 1810

GENERAL CATALOGUE.

FIRST THOUSAND.

NAME.	RESIDENCE.	DATE OF ENTRY.
905. Lydia Needles,	Thirdhaven, Md.,	4th mo., 1810
906. Hannah Hoopes,	Thornbury, Pa.,	8th mo., "
907. Mary Poole,	Wilmington, Del.,	2d mo., "
908. Jane Mason,	Newlin, Pa.,	" "
909. Elizabeth Gilpin,	Sandy Spring, Md.,	" "
910. Ellen Atkinson,	Mt. Holly, N. J.,	12th mo., 1809.
911. Priscilla Fenthan,	Philadelphia, Pa.,	" "
912. Hannah Fletcher,	Abington, Pa.,	10th mo., 1810
913. Margaret Wistar,	Philadelphia, Pa.,	1st mo., "
914. Mary Earl,	Springfield, N. J.,	" "
915. Esther Drinker,	Philadelphia, Pa.,	4th mo., "
916. Rebecca Knowles,	Makefield, Pa.,	2d mo., "
917. Jane Gaskill,	Springfield, Pa.,	3d mo., "
918. Susan Yarnall,	Thirdhaven, Md.,	4th mo., "
919. Ann Wilson,	Burlington, N. J.,	" "
920. Rachel Evans,	....	" "
921. Mary Townsend,	East Bradford, Pa.,	" "
922. Ann Sharpless,	"	" "
923. Sarah Ann Cloud,	Concord, Pa.,	5th mo., "
924. Ann Sinclair,	Kennet, Pa.,	" "
925. Sidney Pierce,	"	4th mo., "
926. Mary Passmore,	Edgmont, Pa.,	11th mo., "
929. Philena Pusey,	London Grove, Pa.,	5th mo., "
930. Mary Wilson,	Burlington, N. J.,	4th mo., "
931. Elizabeth Jenkins,	Little Creek, Del.,	" "
932. Amy Yarnall,	Philadelphia, Pa.,	" "
933. Atlantic Matlack,	Moorestown, N. J.,	5th mo., "
934. Margaret Rawlings,	....	4th mo., "
935. Jane Rawlings,	....	" "
936. Frances Pleasants,	Philadelphia, Pa.,	5th mo., "
937. Mary Pleasants,	"	" "
938. Mary Bullock,	Springfield, N. J.,	" "
939. Elizabeth Lea,	Wilmington, Del.,	11th mo., "
940. Eleanor King,	Burlington, N. J.,	4th mo., "
941. Susanna Mears,	Philadelphia, Pa.,	5th mo., "
942. Deborah Hopkins,	"	" "
943. Rebecca Abbott,	Salem, N. J.,	" "
944. Mary Bacon,	Philadelphia, Pa.,	" "
945. Susanna Palmer,	....	" "
946. Eliza Shoemaker,	Philadelphia, Pa.,	6th mo., 1811.
947. Elizabeth Ely,	New Hope, Pa.,	7th mo., 1810.
948. Deborah Thompson,	Darby, Pa.,	6th mo., "
949. Elizabeth Oakford,	"	" "
950. Elizabeth Parvin,	Maiden Creek, Pa.,	5th mo., "
952. Sidney Thatcher,	Aston, Pa.,	7th mo., "
953. Ann Trimble,	E. Nottingham, Md.,	6th mo., "
954. Grace Trump,	W. Nottingham, Md.,	10th mo., "

STUDENTS. 243

FIRST THOUSAND.

NAME.	RESIDENCE.	DATE OF ENTRY.
955. Anna Moore,	W. Nottingham, Md.,	10th mo., 1810
956. Mary Miller,	Greenwich. N. J.,	" "
957. Elizabeth Jarrett,	Horsham, Pa.,	7th mo., "
958. Sarah Turner,	Camden, Del.,	9th mo., "
959. Elizabeth Chance,	Greensburg, Md.,	4th mo., 1811.
960. Rachel Littler,	Wilmington, Del.,	6th mo., 1810.
961. Anne Dawson,	Philadelphia, Pa.,	1st mo., 1811.
962. Elizabeth Lloyd,	"	6th mo., 1810.
963. Sarah Shinn,	Springfield, N. J.,	1st mo., 1811.
964. Mary Vansant,	New Hope, Pa.,	7th mo., 1810.
965. Mary S. Newlin,	Wilmington, Del.,	6th mo., "
966. Frances Canby,	"	" "
967. Sarah M. Garrigues,	Philadelphia, Pa.,	9th mo., "
968. Eliza Jenkinson,	....	8th mo., "
969. Sarah Hopper,	Philadelphia, Pa.,	" "
970. Esther Morton,	"	" "
971. Hannah Yarnall,	Byberry, Pa.,	10th mo., "
972. Rachel French,	Moorestown, N. J.,	8th mo., "
973. Sarah Walker,	Charleston, Pa.,	10th mo., "
974. Priscilla Walker,	"	" "
975. Eliza Hinchman,	Woodbury, N. J.,	9th mo., "
976. Elizabeth Drinker,	Philadelphia, Pa.,	1st mo., 1811.
977. Sidney Bonsall,	"	10th mo., 1810.
978. Marg. Churchman,	"	9th mo., "
979. Catharine Moore,	Rahway, N. J.,	10th mo., "
980. Hannah Ellis,	———, Pa.,	9th mo., "
981. Mary Folwell,	Philadelphia, Pa.,	" "
982. Eleanor Love,	"	" "
983. Hannah Story,	Attleboro', Pa.,	11th mo., "
984. Abigail Ellis,	———, N. J.,	12th mo., "
985. Phebe Miller,	Providence, Pa.,	11th mo., "
986. Martha Lownes,	Springfield, Pa.,	7th mo., 1811.
987. Sarah Hall,	Salem, N. J.,	2d mo., "
988. Susan Hallowell,	Philadelphia, Pa.,	4th mo., "
989. Priscilla Thomas,	Radnor, Pa.,	10th mo., 1810.
990. Anne Sharpless,	Downingtown, Pa.,	" "
992. Betty Dickinson,	Concord, Pa.,	11th mo., "
993. H. Mendenhall,	Wilmington, Del.,	5th mo., "
994. Abigail Blackwood,	Woodbury, N. J.,	12th mo., "
995. Hannah Whitall,	"	" "
996. Eliza Webster,	Wilmington, Del.,	9th mo., "
997. Armily Chance,	Thirdhaven, Md.,	12th mo., "
998. Betty Robinson,	Wilmington, Del.,	" "
999. Sarah Matson,	Concord, Pa.,	1st mo., 1811
1000. Elizabeth Reeve,	Evesham, N. J.,	" "

19

GENERAL CATALOGUE.

SECOND THOUSAND.

NAME.	RESIDENCE.	DATE OF ENTRY.
2. Amy Wills,	Evesham, N. J.,	12th mo., 1810.
3. Mary Lippincott,	Haddonfield, N. J.,	2d mo., 1811.
4. Gulielma Dunkin,	Nantmeal, Pa.,	11th mo., 1810.
5. Susanna M. Watson,	Solebury, Pa.,	4th mo., 1811.
6. Ann Baily,	Abington, Pa.,	" "
7. Sarah Ann Littler,	Wilmington, Del.,	11th mo., 1810.
8. Deborah K. Hall,	Salem, N. J.,	2d mo., 1811.
9. Mary Nisbett,	Philadelphia, Pa.,	11th mo., 1810.
10. Ellen Roberts,	Merion, Pa.,	" "
11. Dorothea Hoskins,	Radnor, Pa.,	6th mo., 1811.
12. Eliza Palmer,	Concord, Pa.,	4th mo., "
13. Susanna Moore,	W. Nottingham, Md.,	1st mo., "
14. Rachel Johnson,	New Garden, Pa.,	11th mo., "
15. Lydia Jefferis,	West Caln, Pa.,	2d mo., "
16. Elizabeth Wilson,	Plymouth, Pa.,	5th mo., "
17. Anna Bonsall,	East Whiteland, Pa.,	6th mo., "
18. Hannah Abbott,	Salem, N. J.,	" "
19. Mary Ann Newbold,	Chester, Pa.,	3d mo., "
20. Susanna Paxson,	Sadsbury, Pa.,	11th mo., "
21. Susan Lea,	Wilmington, Del.,	3d mo., "
22. Elizabeth Barker,	Philadelphia, Pa.,	11th mo., 1810.
23. Lydia Harvey,	Pennsbury, Pa.,	10th mo., 1811.
24. Letitia Jones,	Philadelphia, Pa.,	4th mo., "
25. Sarah West,	Trenton, N. J.,	8th mo., "
26. Hannah Scott,	Burlington, N. J.,	12th mo., 1810.
27. Hannah P. Byrnes,	Philadelphia, Pa.,	4th mo., 1811
28. Hannah Rowland,	Abington, Pa.,	" "
29. Sally Ann Webb,	Philadelphia, Pa.,	3d mo., "
30. Susan H. Garrigues,	"	4th mo., "
31. Elizabeth Troth,	Evesham, N. J.,	" "
32. Mary Troth,	"	" "
33. Martha Jarrett,	Horsham, Pa.,	9th mo., "
34. Sarah Chapman,	Philadelphia, Pa.,	4th mo., "
35. Abigail Hutchinson,	"	5th mo., "
36. Sarah Brantingham,	"	4th mo., "
37. Hannah Tyson,	"	5th mo., "
38. Ann Tyson,	....	" "
39. Hannah T. Richards,	Philadelphia, Pa.,	8th mo., "
40. S. A. Bringhurst,	"	9th mo., "
41. Hannah Garrigues,	Merion, Pa.,	4th mo., "
42. Sidney Matlack,	Radnor, Pa.,	5th mo., "
43. Eliza Matlack,	"	" "
44. Lydia Clement,	Philadelphia, Pa.,	10th mo., "
45. Elizabeth Clement,	"	" "
46. Hannah Newbold,	Trenton, N. J.,	11th mo., "
47. Mary Satterthwaite,	Mansfield, Pa.,	6th mo., "
48. Catharine Leeds,	Philadelphia, Pa.,	10th mo., "

STUDENTS.

SECOND THOUSAND.

NAME.	RESIDENCE.	DATE OF ENTRY.
49. Charlotte Dilworth,	Birmingham, Pa.,	7th mo., 1811.
50. Ann T. Newbold,	Springfield, N. J.,	10th mo., "
51. Sarah Lawrence,	———, N. Y.,	8th mo., "
52. Ann Griffin,	....	9th mo., "
53. Hannah G. Davis,	Philadelphia, Pa.,	4th mo., 1812.
54. Hannah Pierce,	Kennet, Pa.,	8th mo., 1811.
55. Mary Pennell,	Darby, Pa.,	11th mo., "
56. Hannah G. Tyler,	Salem, N. J.,	4th mo., 1812.
57. Abigail Carnahan,	....	10th mo., 1811.
58. Ann Walker,	....	8th mo., "
59. Ann Webster,	Lampeter, Pa.,	10th mo., 1812.
60. Maria Brinton,	"	5th mo., 1811.
61. Rachel Wilson,	....	4th mo., "
62. Lydia Moore,	New Garden, Pa.,	5th mo., "
63. Mary Farson,	Duck Creek, Del.,	8th mo., "
64. Margaret Jacobs,	East Bradford, Pa.,	9th mo., "
65. Hannah Kersey,	Downingtown, Pa.,	11th mo., "
66. Mary Cope,	East Bradford, Pa.,	9th mo., "
67. Margaret Smith,	Sadsbury, Pa.,	11th mo., "
68. Lydia Trimble,	Concord, Pa.,	9th mo., "
69. Edith Sharpless,	"	" "
70. Achsah Clark,	Woodbury, N. J.,	8th mo., "
71. Eliza Clark,	"	" "
72. Elizabeth Kirkbride,	Philadelphia, Pa.,	11th mo., "
73. Martha Lukens,	Upper Dublin, Pa.,	9th mo., "
74. Lydia Jones,	Philadelphia, Pa.,	10th mo., "
75. Rebecca Y. Spencer,	Horsham, Pa.,	" "
76. Susan Jarrett,	"	" "
77. Asenath Hodgin,	———, Ohio,	" "
78. Sidney Steel,	Upper Darby, Pa.,	11th mo., "
79. Susanna Lloyd,	Horsham, Pa.,	" "
81. Susanna Iden,	Richland, Pa.,	9th mo., 1812.
82. Tacy Davis,	Radnor, Pa.,	12th mo., 1811.
83. Ruth Parry,	Abington, Pa.,	4th mo., 1812.
84. Mary Magill,	Solesbury, Pa.,	" "
85. Caroline R. Cope,	Philadelphia, Pa.,	11th mo., 1811.
86. Rachel Jess,	"	" "
87. Rebecca Gaskill,	Springfield, N. J.,	2d mo., 1812.
89. Sarah Richardson,	Middletown, Pa.,	5th mo., "
91. Rebecca Edmondson,	Easton, Md.,	2d mo., "
92. Jane Moore,	W. Nottingham, Pa.,	" "
93. Sarah Phipps,	Plymouth, Pa.,	11th mo., 1811.
94. Mary E. Norris,	Norristown, Pa.,	1st mo., 1812
95. Deborah L. Norris,	"	" "
96. Mary Knowles,	Makefield, Pa.,	" "
97. Elizabeth Haines,	Evesham, N. J.,	12th mo., "
98. Rebecca Hall,	Salem, N. J.,	6th mo., "

GENERAL CATALOGUE.

SECOND THOUSAND.

NAME.	RESIDENCE.	DATE OF ENTRY.	
99. Rachel Pierce,	Kennet, Pa.,	4th mo.,	1812.
100. Lydia Longstreth,	Philadelphia, Pa.,	5th mo.,	"
101. Susanna Longstreth,	"	"	"
102. Rebecca Cooper,	Pleasant View, Pa.,	"	"
103. Eleanor King,	Burlington, N. J.,	"	"
104. Abigail King,	"	"	"
105. Mary Watson,	Buckingham, Pa.,	"	"
106. Sarah Watson,	"	"	"
107. Ann Thompson,	Salem Co., N. J.,	"	"
108. Priscilla Jones,	Germantown, Pa.,	"	"
109. Anna Jones,	"	"	"
110. Margaret Smith,	Philadelphia, Pa.,	"	"
111. Sarah Ann Smith,	"	"	"
112. Elizabeth Downing,	Uwchlan, Pa.,	6th mo.,	"
113. Mary Skyrin,	Philadelphia, Pa.,	"	"
114. Sarah Drinker,	"	"	"
115. Susanna Twining,	Wrightstown, Pa.,	"	"
116. Mary Canby,	Wilmington, Del.,	"	"
117. Mary Gibbons,	Lampeter, Pa.,	"	"
118. Hannah Abbott,	Bordentown, N. J.,	10th mo.,	"
119. Edith Bullock,	Springfield, N. J.,	"	"
120. Rebecca Lukens,	Fallowfield, Pa.,	5th mo.,	"
122. Rebecca Brick,	Salem, N. J.,	6th mo.,	"
123. Sarah Blackwood,	Haddonfield, N. J.,	8th mo.,	"
124. Sarah Taylor,	Pennsbury, Pa.,	7th mo.,	"
125. Hannah Andrews,	Evesham, N. J.,	9th mo.,	"
126. Isabella Peters,	Concord, Pa.,	10th mo.,	"
127. Elizabeth Denny,	New Garden, Pa.,	8th mo.,	"
128. Rachel Painter,	East Bradford, Pa.,	10th mo.,	"
129. Eliza Adams,	Wilmington, Del.,	"	"
130. Mary Ann Cope,	Philadelphia, Pa.,	5th mo.,	"
131. Ann Shoemaker,	"	6th mo.,	"
132. Lydia McCarty,	Muncy, Pa.,	8th mo.,	"
133. Hannah Williamson,	Newtown, Pa.,	9th mo.,	"
134. Lucy Ann Lawrie,	Crosswicks, N. J.,	12th mo.,	1813.
135. Amelia G. Merrefield,	Philadelphia, Pa.,	8th mo.,	1812.
136. Christiana Pratt,	Edgmont, Pa.,	9th mo.,	"
137. Hannah J. Lewis,	New Garden, Pa.,	10th mo.,	"
138. Sarah Pugh,	Philadelphia, Pa.,	"	"
139. Hannah Brown,	New Garden, Pa.,	"	"
140. Phebe Sinton,	Wilkesbarre, Pa.,	8th mo.,	"
141. Jane Kenny,	Uwchlan, Pa.,	10th mo.,	"
142. Beulah Passmore,	Edgmont, Pa.,	9th mo.,	"
143. Mary Davis,	Birmingham, Pa.,	10th mo.,	"
144. Elizabeth Harlan,	Kennet, Pa.,	12th mo.,	"
145. Martha Dilworth,	Birmingham, Pa.,	11th mo.,	"
146. Charlotte Lukens,	Chester Valley, Pa.,	12th mo.,	1814

STUDENTS.

SECOND THOUSAND.

NAME.	RESIDENCE.	DATE OF ENTRY.
147. Rebecca Embree,	West Bradford, Pa.,	11th mo., 1812.
149. Sarah Price,	East Bradford, Pa.,	" "
150. Mercy Sharpless,	Downingtown, Pa.,	12th mo., "
151. Mary Prosser,	Burlington, N. J.,	" "
152. Rebecca Earl,	Springfield, N. J.,	10th mo., "
153. Rachel J. Gummere,	Burlington, N. J.,	11th mo., "
154. Elizabeth Newbold,	Chester, Pa.,	12th mo., "
155. Ann Stockton,	Springfield, N. J.,	10th mo., "
156. Amelia Decou,	Burlington, N. J.,	4th mo., 1813.
157. Mary Stokes,	Woodbury, N. J.,	11th mo., 1812.
158. Susanna Wilson,	Plymouth, Pa.,	12th mo., "
159. Eliza Knight,	Byberry, Pa.,	" "
160. Mary Richardson,	Philadelphia, Pa.,	4th mo., 1813.
161. Minerva Webb,	Kennet, Pa.,	11th mo., 1812.
162. Hannah Darlington,	Pennsbury, Pa.,	12th mo., "
163. Rachel Dickinson,	Sadsbury, Pa.,	" "
164. Hannah Poole,	Wilmington, Del.,	2d mo., 1813.
165. Hannah Baker,	West Bradford, Pa.,	5th mo., "
166. Mary Brookes,	Wilmington, Del.,	11th mo., 1817.
167. Albina Powell,	Baltimore, Md.,	5th mo., 1813.
168. Margaret Marshall,	West Bradford, Pa.,	" "
169. Sarah Scott,	Baltimore, Md.,	" "
170. Rachel Kinsey,	"	" "
171. Rachel Wills,	Rancocas, N. J.,	" "
172. Sarah Lancaster,	Philadelphia, Pa.,	" "
173. Maria Shaw,	Abington, Pa.,	4th mo., "
174. Ann Hibberd,	Darby, Pa.,	5th mo., "
175. Abigail Pierce,	Philadelphia, Pa.,	4th mo., "
176. Eliza Sinclair,	Baltimore, Md.,	" "
177. Ann Sinclair,	"	" "
178. Mary Hinchman,	Woodbury, N. J.,	11th mo., "
179. Mary Proctor,	Baltimore, Md.,	4th mo., "
180. Caroline Warder,	Philadelphia, Pa.,	" "
181. Ann W. Sanderson,	....	" "
182. Ann Jones,	Baltimore, Md.,	" "
183. Eliza Eastburn,	Solesbury, Pa.,	11th mo., 1812
184. Lydia A. Middleton,	Philadelphia, Pa.,	5th mo., 1813
185. Amy Robinson,	"	" "
186. Abigail Gilpin,	Wilmington, Del.,	" "
187. Hannah H. Johnson,	Germantown, Pa.,	" "
188. Rebecca Walker,	Burlington, N. J.,	" "
189. Sarah Walker,	"	" "
190. Sarah Smith,	Philadelphia, Pa.,	" "
191. Rachel Brown,	....	" "
192. Ann Roberts,	West Whiteland, Pa.,	" "
193. Ann Laws,	Philadelphia, Pa.,	" "
194. Martha Woodnutt,	Salem, N. J.,	6th mo., "

SECOND THOUSAND.

NAME.	RESIDENCE.	DATE OF ENTRY.
195. Hannah Hoopes,	Westtown, Pa.,	6th mo., 1813
196. Mary Williams,	Abington, Pa.,	7th mo., "
197. Sarah Williams,	"	" "
198. Eliza McIlvain,	Chester, Pa.,	8th mo., "
199. Mary W. Smith,	Philadelphia, Pa.,	7th mo., "
200. Susanna Ellis,	....	8th mo., "
201. Edith Harlan,	Kennet, Pa.,	6th mo., "
202. Ann Hall,	....	8th mo., "
203. Ann Wilson,	Philadelphia, Pa.,	" "
204. Sidney Moore,	New Garden, Pa.,	11th mo., "
205. Lydia Moore,	"	" "
206. Sarah Griscom,	Salem, N. J.,	4th mo., 1814.
207. Abigail Passmore,	Edgmont, Pa.,	10th mo., "
208. Elma Cadwallader,	Brownsville, Pa.,	" 1813.
209. Abigail Flanner,	Mt. Pleasant, Ohio,	11th mo., "
210. Lydia Johnson,	Richland, Pa.,	7th mo., "
211. Hannah Johnson,	"	" "
212. Sarah Howell,	Philadelphia, Pa.,	8th mo., "
213. Marg. A. Howell,	"	" "
214. Maria McMillan,	Warrington, Pa.,	11th mo., "
215. Susanna J. Thomas,	Germantown, Pa.,	10th mo., "
216. Edith Schofield,	Newtown, Pa.,	11th mo., "
217. Mary Oakford,	Darby, Pa.,	10th mo., "
218. Anna Foulke,	Gwynedd, Pa.,	" "
219. Martha Livezey,	Plymouth, Pa.,	" "
220. Hannah Tyson,	Abington, Pa.,	11th mo., "
222. Martha Gibbons,	Philadelphia, Pa.,	10th mo., "
223. Mary B. Smith,	Buckingham, Pa.,	4th mo., 1814.
224. Lydia Fell,	"	" "
225. Lucy A. Pancoast,	Springfield, N. J.,	11th mo., 1813.
226. Louisa A. Thomas,	Radnor, Pa.,	" "
227. Ann Clement,	Darby, Pa.,	" "
228. Mary Ellis,	Plymouth, Pa.,	10th mo., "
229. Ann Fell,	Solesbury, Pa.,	5th mo., 1814.
230. Orpha Ogden,	Darby, Pa.,	11th mo., 1813.
231. Rebecca Deacon,	Burlington, N. J.,	10th mo., "
232. Kezia Deacon,	"	" "
233. Eliza Woolman,	Rancocas, N. J.,	11th mo., "
234. Lettice Barnard,	Newlin, Pa.,	10th mo., "
235. Amy Thomas,	"	" "
236. Sibilla Embree,	West Bradford, Pa.,	" "
237. Mabel Hutton,	New Garden, Pa.,	11th mo., "
238. Elizabeth Kirk,	Uwchlan, Pa.,	" "
239. Mary Kersey,	Downingtown, Pa.,	" "
240. Ann Garrett,	Upper Darby, Pa.,	" "
241. Elizabeth Prosser,	Burlington, N. J.,	11th mo., "
242. Elizabeth Price,	Westtown, Pa.,	2d mo., 1814.

STUDENTS.

SECOND THOUSAND.

NAME.	RESIDENCE.	DATE OF ENTRY.
243. Rebecca Hibberd,	Goshen, Pa.,	5th mo., 1814.
245. Deborah Haines,	Evesham, N. J.,	2d mo., "
246. Mary Dickinson,	Sadsbury, Pa.,	" "
247. Ruthanna Davis,	....	4th mo., "
248. Lydia Seal,	Wilmington, Del.,	5th mo., "
250. Prudence Hall,	Salem, N. J.,	4th mo., "
251. Annabella King,	Cattaraugus, N. Y.,	3d mo., "
252. Anna Parry,	Philadelphia, Pa.,	4th mo., "
253. Mary Hill,	"	" "
254. Grace Smith,	Burlington, N. J.,	2d mo., "
255. Elizabeth Rogers,	Evesham, N. J.,	" "
257. Ann Maule,	Radnor, Pa.,	4th mo., "
258. Sarah Ann Burr,	Mt. Holly, N. J.,	5th mo., "
259. Anna Lippincott,	Moorestown, N. J.,	4th mo., "
260. Elizabeth Willis,	Philadelphia, Pa.,	" "
261. Ann Thomas,	"	5th mo., "
262. Hannah Townsend,	"	" "
263. Martha Parry,	"	" 1815.
264. Eliza Zelley,	Mt. Holly, N. J.,	9th mo., 1814.
265. Mary Randolph,	Philadelphia, Pa.,	5th mo., "
266. Rachel Randolph,	"	" "
267. Minerva Rogers,	"	4th mo., "
268. Mary Ambler,	Gwynedd, Pa.,	" "
269. Susanna Smith,	Philadelphia, Pa.,	6th mo., "
270. Louisa Webster,	Wilmington, Del.,	5th mo., "
271. Hannah Evans,	....	" "
272. Phebe Pierce,	Philadelphia, Pa.,	
274. Orpha Pratt,	Edgmont, Pa.,	9th mo., 1815.
275. Lydia Leedom,	Philadelphia, Pa.,	6th mo., 1814.
276. Catharine Morris,	"	9th mo., "
277. Hannah Wilson,	Easton, Md.,	8th mo., "
278. Abigail Robinson,	Philadelphia, Pa.,	6th mo., "
279. Hannah Righter,	Plymouth, Pa.,	" "
280. Susanna Carmalt,	Philadelphia, Pa.,	" "
282. Sarah A. Kirkbride,	"	" "
284. Sarah Wilson,	Buckingham, Pa.,	" 1815.
285. Phebe Foulke,	Richland, Pa.,	" "
286. Anna Kimber,	Philadelphia, Pa.,	4th mo., "
287. Ann Stevens,	Trenton, N. J.,	1st mo., 1821.
288. Sarah Baily,	Abington, Pa.,	5th mo., 1815.
289. Mary Lodge,	Darby, Pa.,	10th mo., "
290. Sarah Hall,	Salem, N. J.,	4th mo., "
292. Hannah Harmer,	Columbia, Pa.,	" "
293. Rebecca Cooper,	"	" "
294. Anna Biddle,	Philadelphia, Pa.,	6th mo., "
295. Amy Hoopes,	Willistown, Pa.,	11th mo., "
296. Sarah W. Nock,	....	6th mo., "

SECOND THOUSAND.

NAME.	RESIDENCE.	DATE OF ENTRY.
297. Mary Emerson,	Little Creek, Del.,	6th mo., 1815.
298. Sarah Emerson,	"	" "
299. Thomazin Downing,	Downingtown, Pa.,	" "
300. Mary Leedom,	Philadelphia, Pa.,	10th mo., "
301. Lydia Fairlamb,	West Chester, Pa.,	" "
302. Sarah Zelley,	Mt. Holly, N. J.,	9th mo., "
303. Lydia Starr,	Philadelphia, Pa.,	4th mo., 1815.
304. Eleanor S. Abbott,	"	11th mo., 1814.
305. Sarah Eastburn,	Solesbury, Pa.,	" "
306. Mary Eastburn,	"	" "
307. Mary M. Garrigues,	Merion, Pa.,	10th mo., "
308. Margaret Cox,	Willistown, Pa.,	11th mo., "
309. Sarah A. Pennell,	Chester, Pa.,	10th mo., "
310. Mary D. Rogers,	Evesham, N. J.,	1st mo., 1815.
311. Edith Smedley,	Willistown, Pa.,	11th mo., 1814.
312. Mary Smith,	Philadelphia, Pa.,	3d mo., 1816.
313. Sarah Pierce,	Burlington, N. J.,	10th mo., 1814.
314. Mary Ann Wilson,	——, N. J.,	" "
315. Mary Lancaster,	Philadelphia, Pa.,	1st mo., 1815.
316. Ellen Govett,	"	6th mo., "
317. Elizabeth Waters,	"	10th mo., "
318. Elizabeth Butcher,	Mt. Holly, N. J.,	4th mo., "
319. Ann Jess,	Philadelphia, Pa.,	12th mo., 1814.
320. Mary Hooton,	"	" "
321. Hannah Jones,	Germantown, Pa.,	" "
322. Letitia Reeve,	Evesham, N. J.,	" 1820.
323. Rachel Clark,	....	4th mo., 1815.
324. Margaret Bullock,	Springfield, N. J.,	3d mo., "
326. Leah W. Moore,	Haverford, Pa.,	6th mo., "
327. Sarah Ridgway,	....	4th mo., "
328. Priscilla Morris,	Philadelphia, Pa.,	" "
329. Rebecca Wood,	Haddonfield, N. J.,	" "
330. Ann Pusey,	London Grove, Pa.,	10th mo., 1814.
331. Mary Ann Ayres,	Chichester, Pa.,	11th mo., "
332. Ruth Wright,	Exeter, Pa.,	10th mo., "
333. Ann Somers,	Penn's Neck, N. J.,	11th mo., "
335. Elizabeth Smith,	Sadsbury, Pa.,	" "
336. Ann Carter,	W. Nottingham, Pa.,	" "
337. Hannah Harvey,	Concord, Pa.,	12th mo., "
338. Elizabeth Craft,	Mt. Holly, N. J.,	" "
339. Rebecca Taylor,	West Chester, Pa.,	11th mo., "
340. Elizabeth Rowland,	Abington, Pa.,	5th mo., 1815
341. Harriet Lukens,	"	" "
342. Mary Hallowell,	Philadelphia, Pa.,	4th mo., "
343. Rebecca Carter,	"	" "
344. Mary Garrett,	Willistown, Pa.,	10th mo., "
345. Martha Earl,	Springfield, N. J.,	6th mo., "

STUDENTS.

SECOND THOUSAND.

NAME.	RESIDENCE.	DATE OF ENTRY.
346. Christiana Moore,	....	4th mo., 1815.
348. Rebecca Wilson,	New Garden, Pa.,	5th mo., "
349. Mary A. Yarnall,	Darby, Pa.,	4th mo., "
350. Rebecca Haines,	Evesham, N. J.,	" "
351. Ann Husband,	Deer Creek, Md.,	11th mo., 1814.
352. Sarah G. Pennell,	Concord, Pa.,	1st mo., 1815.
353. Rachel Baker,	West Bradford, Pa.,	4th mo., "
354. Amy C. Hoopes,	West Chester, Pa.,	" "
355. Hannah Shipley,	Wilmington, Del.,	" "
356. Rachel Spencer,	Horsham, Pa.,	" "
357. Lydia Spencer,	"	" "
358. Hannah P. Eldridge,	Woodbury, N. J.,	" "
359. Deborah M. Eldridge,	"	" "
360. Maria Jones,	Brownsville, Pa.,	12th mo., "
361. Mary Earl,	Springfield, N. J.,	5th mo., "
362. Ann Atkinson,	Philadelphia, Pa.,	4th mo., "
363. Hannah Hibberd,	Darby, Pa.,	11th mo., "
365. Hannah Gibbons,	Philadelphia, Pa.,	10th mo., "
366. Sarah R. Smith,	Burlington, N. J.,	5th mo., "
367. Anna Maria Paxson,	Philadelphia., Pa.,	4th mo., "
368. Elizabeth Conard,	"	10th mo., "
369. Maria Pennell,	Brownsville, Pa.,	6th mo., "
370. Grace Barnard,	Newlin, Pa.,	12th mo., "
371. Anna Maria Wood,	Woodbury, N. J.,	7th mo., "
372. Rachel Livezey,	Plymouth, Pa.,	10th mo., "
373. Hannah Maulsby,	"	" "
374. Beulah Glover,	Haddonfield, N. J.,	8th mo., "
375. Mary Dingee,	E. Marlborough, Pa.,	4th mo., "
376. Lydia Neal,	Concord, Pa.,	9th mo., "
377. Rachel Richards,	W. Nottingham, Pa.,	11th mo., "
378. Jane H. Brown,	"	1st mo., 1816.
379. Sidney Phillips,	Hockessing, Del.,	" 1817.
380. Rebecca Price,	Gunpowder, Md.,	" 1822.
381. Mary Ridgway,	Philadelphia, Pa.,	9th mo., 1815.
382. Harriet Lancaster,	Rancocas, N. J.,	10th mo., "
383. Elizabeth Woolman,	"	" "
384. Ann Wills,	"	" "
385. Phebe Vail,	Plainfield, N. J.,	8th mo., "
386. Ann Woolman,	Rancocas, N. J.,	10th mo., "
387. Deborah Oakford,	Darby, Pa.,	11th mo., "
388. Jane Walton,	....	8th mo., "
389. Sarah Ann Pryor,	Philadelphia, Pa.,	12th mo., "
390. Lydia Wilson,	London Grove, Pa.,	" "
391. Esther Downing,	Downingtown, Pa.,	11th mo., "
392. Martha Edmondson,	Easton, Md.,	2d mo., 1816.
393. Mary Bassett,	Wilmington, Del.,	11th mo., 1815.
394. Abigail Jackson,	Reading, Pa.,	12th mo., "

P

GENERAL CATALOGUE.

SECOND THOUSAND.

NAME.	RESIDENCE.	DATE OF ENTRY.	
395. Jane Thomas,	Newlin, Pa.,	12th mo.,	1815.
396. Sarah Gawthrop,	New Garden, Pa.,	"	"
397. Hannah Taylor,	Pennsbury, Pa.,	2d mo.,	1816.
398. Rachel W. Cope,	Brownsville, Pa.,	"	"
399. Hannah Webb,	Kennet, Pa.,	3d mo.,	"
400. Margaret Penrose,	Philadelphia, Pa.,	12th mo.,	1815.
401. Sarah C. Rively,	Darby, Pa.,	11th mo.,	"
402. Susanna Levick,	Little Creek, Del.,	12th mo.,	"
403. Martha N. Austin,	Buckingham, Pa.,	11th mo.,	"
404. Hannah Deacon,	Burlington, N. J.,	10th mo.,	"
405. Ann Corbit,	Philadelphia, Pa.,	11th mo.,	"
406. Martha A. Evans,	"	5th mo.,	1816.
407. Marg. Mendenhall,	Concord, Pa.,	10th mo.,	1815.
408. Mary Richards,	Springfield, N. J.,	"	"
409. Mary Shreeve,	Mt. Holly, N. J.,	12th mo.,	"
410. Rebecca Earl,	"	"	"
411. Lydia Lippincott,	Woodstown, N. J.,	5th mo.,	1816.
412. Hannah Nixon,	Pikeland, Pa.,	"	"
413. Ann Webb,	Muncy, Pa.,	"	"
414. Edith H. Clark,	Woodbury, N. J.,	"	"
415. Jane Pancoast,	Mullica Hill, N. J.,	"	"
416. Anna P. Levis,	Springfield, Pa.,	11th mo.,	"
417. Elizabeth Townsend,	Plainfield, N. J.,	4th mo.,	"
418. Anna Smith,	....	"	"
419. Sarah Roberts,	Goshen, Pa.,	"	"
420. Ann Brick,	Salem, N. J.,	6th mo.,	"
421. Charlotte Wistar,	"	4th mo.,	"
422. Hannah Howell,	Philadelphia, Pa.,	"	"
423. Mary Howell,	"	"	"
424. Mary Whitacre,	Muncy, Pa.,	8th mo.,	"
425. Elizabeth Townsend,	Byberry, Pa.,	5th mo.,	"
426. Elizabeth Thomas,	"	"	"
427. Susan Kimber,	Radnor, Pa.,	4th mo.,	"
428. Elizabeth Haines,	Philadelphia, Pa.,	5th mo.,	"
429. Mary Stokes,	Darby, Pa.,	6th mo.,	"
431. Ruth Johnson,	New Garden, Pa.,	3d mo.,	"
432. Deborah Simmons,	Middletown, Pa.,	4th mo.,	"
433. Rebecca Preston,	W. Nottingham, Md.,	"	"
434. Elizabeth Righter,	Plymouth, Pa.,	3d mo.,	"
435. Phebe Ellis,	Springfield, N. J.,	4th mo.,	"
436. Philena Lamb,	Wilmington, Del.,	"	"
437. Mary Haines,	W. Nottingham, Md.,	"	"
438. Mary Robinson,	Wilmington, Del.,	"	"
439. Sarah Temple,	Pennsbury, Pa.,	"	"
440. Eliza Comfort,	Fallsington, Pa.,	5th mo.,	"
441. Maria Spencer,	Bensalem, Pa.,	"	"
442. Elizabeth Chapman,	Byberry, Pa.,	"	"

STUDENTS.

SECOND THOUSAND.

NAME.	RESIDENCE.	DATE OF ENTRY.
443. Lydia Burrough,	Evesham, N. J.,	5th mo., 1816.
444. Alice Williams,	Abington, Pa.,	10th mo., "
445. Rachel Twining,	Wrightstown, Pa.,	5th mo., "
446. Martha Walton,	Byberry, Pa.,	" "
447. Letitia Lancaster,	Philadelphia, Pa.,	" "
448. Catharine Wood,	"	4th mo., "
449. Elizabeth Paul,	"	8th mo., "
450. Mary Tatum,	Woodbury, N. J.,	5th mo., "
451. Rachel Sharpless,	Downingtown, Pa.,	" "
452. Martha Hobson,	New Garden, Pa.,	" "
453. Mary Ann Green,	Smyrna, Del.,	6th mo., "
454. Ann Blackwood,	Camden, N. J.,	8th mo., "
456. Orpha Thomas,	Willistown, Pa.,	9th mo., "
457. Deborah Passmore,	Edgmont, Pa.,	" "
458. Elizabeth Sharpless,	Concord, Pa.,	" "
459. Charity Thatcher,	"	" "
460. Rachel Garrett,	Willistown, Pa.,	" "
461. Hannah Thomas,	Hatborough, Pa.,	5th mo., 1821.
462. Hannah Hughes,	Philadelphia, Pa.,	11th mo., 1816.
463. Mercy A. Chapman,	———, Pa.,	10th mo., "
464. Mary R. Chapman,	"	" "
465. Mary Saunders,	Woodbury, N. J.,	5th mo., "
466. Hannah Pancoast,	Mullica Hill, N. J.,	7th mo., "
467. Catharine Wistar,	Salem, N. J.,	11th mo., "
468. Abigail Lundy,	Rancocas, N. J.,	5th mo., 1817.
469. Esther Schofield,	Buckingham, Pa.,	10th mo., 1816.
470. Mary Tucker,	Philadelphia, Pa.,	7th mo., "
471. Lucy Bishop,	Springfield, N. J.,	8th mo., "
472. Letitia Wright,	Salem, N. J.,	9th mo., "
473. Phebe Furness,	Colerain, Pa.,	10th mo., "
474. Esther Musgrave,	Philadelphia, Pa.,	7th mo., "
475. Mercy Ellis,	Muncy, Pa.,	9th mo., "
476. Margaret Miller,	Salem, N. J.,	" "
477. Mary Miller,	"	" "
478. Elizabeth Pancoast,	Woodstown, N. J.,	6th mo., "
479. Charlotte Earl,	New Mills, N. J.,	8th mo., "
480. Hannah Forsythe,	Springfield, N. J.,	9th mo., "
481. Sarah A. Lippincott,	Haddonfield, N. J.,	10th mo., "
482. Charlotte Harrison,	Philadelphia, Pa.,	5th mo., 1821.
483. Esther L. Thomas,	Darby, Pa.,	10th mo., 1816.
484. Jane L. Thomas,	Newtown, Pa.,	" "
485. Sarah Jones,	Buckingham, Pa.,	" "
486. Sarah S. Roberts,	Greenwich, N. J.,	" "
487. Susan Hulme,	Hulmeville, Pa.,	9th mo., "
488. Rebecca Hulme,	"	" "
489. Mary Watson,	Fallsington, Pa.,	10th mo., "
490. Rachel Quinby,	Stanton, Del.,	12th mo., "

GENERAL CATALOGUE.

SECOND THOUSAND.

NAME.	RESIDENCE.	DATE OF ENTRY.
491. Mary Hoskins,	Radnor, Pa.,	12th mo., 1816.
492. Ann L. Wilson,	Rahway, N. J.,	2d mo., 1817.
493. Hannah Shoemaker,	Philadelphia, Pa.,	" "
494. Elizabeth Winn,	"	5th mo., 1821.
495. Martha Eastburn,	Solesbury, Pa.,	" 1817.
496. Mary J. Brown,	Rahway, N. J.,	4th mo., "
497. Catharine Evans,	"	" "
498. Susanna Battin,	Muncy, Pa.,	" "
499. Mary Griscom,	Burlington, N. J.,	12th mo., 1816.
501. Sarah Denny,	New Garden, Pa.,	" "
502. Hannah J. Pennock,	London Grove, Pa.,	1st mo., 1817.
503. Charlotte Cleaver,	Radnor, Pa.,	" "
504. Ann Farson,	Duck Creek, Del.,	8th mo., 1818.
505. Rebecca Yarnall,	Easton, Pa.,	6th mo., 1817.
506. Ann Wilson,	London Grove, Pa.,	1st mo., "
507. Anne Embree,	West Bradford, Pa.,	" "
508. Rebecca Dingee,	E. Marlborough, Pa.,	11th mo., "
509. Hannah Massey,	Thornbury, Pa.,	1st mo., "
510. Sarah Elkinton,	Philadelphia, Pa.,	5th mo., "
511. Mary P. Gibbons,	"	" 1821.
512. Ann Hibberd,	E. Whiteland, Pa.,	3d mo., 1817.
513. Abigail Musgrave,	Philadelphia, Pa.,	" "
514. Mary Ann Haines,	....	5th mo., "
515. Mary Ann Walton,	Muncy, Pa.,	" "
516. Mary Ann Hutton,	Philadelphia, Pa.,	6th mo., "
517. Prudence Cooper,	Pleasant View, Pa.,	5th mo., "
518. Anna Thompson,	Abington, Pa.,	" "
519. Mary Lloyd,	Horsham, Pa.,	" "
520. Sarah Walton,	"	" "
521. Rachel B. Pennock,	London Grove, Pa.,	1st mo., "
522. Hannah B. Gibbons,	East Bradford, Pa.,	3d mo., "
523. Mary Hawley,	Uwchlan, Pa.,	5th mo., "
524. Martha Tucker,	Muncy, Pa.,	4th mo., "
525. Eleanor Kemp,	King's Creek, Md.,	9th mo., "
526. Ann Clark,	Woodbury, N. J.,	6th mo., "
527. Hannah Rhoads,	Springfield, Pa.,	" "
528. Ann Chandler,	London Grove, Pa.,	11th mo., "
529. Phebe M. Walker,	Charlestown, Pa.,	12th mo., "
530. Mary T. Dilworth,	Aston, Pa.,	" 1816.
531. Elizabeth G. Clark,	Doe Run, Pa.,	6th mo., 1817.
532. Elizabeth Bartram,	Darby, Pa.,	5th mo., "
533. Betsy Watson,	Buckingham, Pa.,	7th mo., "
534. Lydia Satterthwaite,	Crosswicks, N. J.,	6th mo., "
535. Esther B. Atlee,	Philadelphia, Pa.,	" "
536. Elizabeth Wright,	Tredyffrin, Pa.,	" "
537. Sarah Hannum,	East Caln, Pa.,	4th mo., "
538. Lydia Ingham,	Abington, Pa.,	5th mo., 1821.

STUDENTS. 255

SECOND THOUSAND.

NAME.	RESIDENCE.	DATE OF ENTRY.
539. Lydia Jackson,	W. Nottingham, Pa.,	12th mo., 1817.
540. Eliz. Richardson,	Middletown, Pa.,	8th mo., "
541. Susan Richardson,	"	" "
542. Tacy Lukens,	Abington, Pa.,	9th mo., "
543. Anna Paxson,	Middletown, Pa.,	7th mo., "
544. Sarah Ann Tyson,	Philadelphia, Pa.,	8th mo., "
545. Sarah Conrow,	Shrewsbury, N. J.,	7th mo., "
546. Ann Burson,	Wrightstown, Pa.,	9th mo., "
547. Margaret Maris,	New Hope, Pa.,	12th mo., "
548. Sarah Maris,	"	" "
549. Mary Ann Field,	Crosswicks, N. J.,	9th mo., "
550. Martha Janney,	Newtown, Pa.,	" "
551. Jane Fell,	Richland, Pa.,	" "
552. Elizabeth Lancaster,	Philadelphia, Pa.,	12th mo., "
553. Elizabeth Burr,	"	11th mo., "
554. Hannah Stewart,	Woodstown, N. J.,	9th mo., "
555. Mary Stewart,	"	" "
556. Sarah W. Vail,	Plainfield, N. J.,	12th mo., "
557. Ann Rogers,	Evesham, N. J.,	9th mo., "
558. Martha Davis,	"	" "
559. Phebe Williams,	Shrewsbury, N. J.,	7th mo., "
560. Martha Woolston,	Fallsington, Pa.,	5th mo., 1821.
561. Ruth Bonsall,	West Whiteland, Pa.,	9th mo., 1817.
562. Ann Baker,	West Bradford, Pa.,	11th mo., "
563. Mary W. Reeves,	Philadelphia, Pa.,	9th mo., "
564. Mary A. Sharpless,	Catawissa, Pa.,	10th mo., "
565. Hannah Taylor,	Kennet, Pa.,	" "
566. Harriet Stokely,	Camden, Del.,	9th mo., 1818.
568. Mary Deacon,	Burlington, N. J.,	" "
569. Deborah Smith,	Sadsbury, Pa.,	11th mo., "
570. Margaret Woodward,	Centre, Del.,	12th mo., 1817.
571. Mary Evens,	Cropwell, N. J.,	5th mo., 1821.
572. Sarah Garrett,	Philadelphia, Pa.,	9th mo., 1817.
573. Rebecca W. Cresson,	"	" "
574. Sarah Simmons,	Chester, Md.,	11th mo., "
575. Elizabeth C. Cope,	Philadelphia, Pa.,	6th mo., 1821.
576. Eliza F. Cocks,	New York, N. Y.,	5th mo., "
577. Anna Longstreth,	Horsham, Pa.,	10th mo., 1817.
578. Agnes E. Marsh,	Plainfield, N. J.,	12th mo., "
579. Susanna Stokes,	Rancocas, N. J.,	11th mo., "
580. Sarah Way,	Plainfield, N. J.,	12th mo., "
581. Hannah Lippincott,	Mt. Holly, N. J.,	4th mo., 1818.
582. Priscilla A. Hooton,	Philadelphia, Pa.,	10th mo., 1817.
583. Martha Thomas,	"	11th mo., "
584. Lydia A. Thomas,	West Whiteland, Pa.,	" "
585. Jane Parry,	New Hope, Pa.,	" "
586. Margaret Parry,	"	" "

20

GENERAL CATALOGUE.

SECOND THOUSAND.

NAME.	RESIDENCE.	DATE OF ENTRY.
587. Evelina Denny,	Little Creek, Del.,	6th mo., 1821.
588. Mary Budd,	Philadelphia, Pa.,	12th mo., 1817.
589. Cath. W. Baldwin,	Concord, Pa.,	11th mo., 1821.
590. Priscilla Eves,	Muncy, Pa.,	" 1817.
591. Beulah Hubbs,	Woodstown, N. J.,	5th mo., 1818.
592. Elizabeth Widdefield,	Philadelphia, Pa.,	11th mo., "
593. Elizabeth Lippincott,	Mt. Holly, N. J.,	1st mo., "
594. Mary Baily,	Abington, Pa.,	3d mo., "
595. Violetta Lukens,	Philadelphia, Pa.,	4th mo., "
596. M. Cowperthwaite,	Moorestown, N. J.,	5th mo., "
597. Jane W. Thomas,	Radnor, Pa.,	" "
598. Mary King,	Burlington, N. J.,	9th mo., 1821.
599. Beulah Garrigues,	Merion, Pa.,	4th mo., 1818.
600. Mercy Phillips,	Solesbury, Pa.,	12th mo., 1817.
601. Priscilla Hopkins,	Deer Creek, Md.,	11th mo., "
602. Betsy Greenfield,	New Garden, Pa.,	3d mo., 1818.
603. Hannah B. Stalker,	East Caln, Pa.,	4th mo., "
604. Eliza W. Hunt,	Darby, Pa.,	7th mo., "
605. Eliza Barnard,	W. Marlborough, Pa.,	4th mo., "
606. Phebe A. Speakman,	Concord, Pa.,	6th mo., "
607. Lydia Trimble,	Aston, Pa.,	4th mo., 1819.
608. Lydia Massey,	Springfield, Pa.,	10th mo., 1818.
609. Margaret Hoopes,	West Chester, Pa.,	" "
610. Mary H. Jackson,	Darby, Pa.,	" "
611. Ann Reeves,	Philadelphia, Pa.,	3d mo., "
612. Ann Fletcher,	Abington, Pa.,	4th mo., "
613. Sarah A. Hallowell,	"	" "
614. Susanna M. Payne,	———, N. Y.,	5th mo., "
615. Edith D. Stockton,	Mt. Holly, N. J.,	" "
616. Rebecca Church,	Moorestown, N. J.,	7th mo., "
617. Sarah Church,	"	" "
618. Emeline Cope,	Philadelphia, Pa.,	6th mo., "
619. Susan H. Newbold,	Byberry, Pa.,	11th mo., "
620. Rebecca Newbold,	"	" "
621. Hannah Hall,	Salem, N. J.,	9th mo., "
622. Deborah Frampton,	Hillsborough, Va.,	" "
623. Mary Edmondson,	Camden, Del.,	5th mo., "
624. Abigail Lawrie,	Woodstown, N. J.,	6th mo., "
625. Rebecca Howey,	"	" "
626. Mary Carver,	Plumsted, Pa.,	5th mo., "
627. Ann P. Penrose,	Philadelphia, Pa.,	" "
628. Abigail Penrose,	"	" "
629. Deborah Garrigues,	"	6th mo., "
631. Hannah S. Bolton,	"	" "
633. Mary Ann Roberts,	Merion, Pa.,	10th mo., "
634. Emily Welding,	Frankford, Pa.,	9th mo., "
635. Bathsheba Barton,	Philadelphia, Pa.	" "

STUDENTS.

SECOND THOUSAND.

NAME.	RESIDENCE.	DATE OF ENTRY.
636. Letitia Ely,	Buckingham, Pa.,	10th mo., 1818.
637. Elizabeth Lawrence,	Springfield, Pa.,	" "
638. Mary Paxson,	Trenton, N. J.,	3d mo., "
639. Anna Knowles,	Makefield, Pa.,	11th mo., "
640. Rachel Phillips,	Solesbury, Pa.,	" "
641. Sarah Ogden,	West Chester, Pa.,	10th mo., "
642. Mary Johnson,	New Garden, Pa.,	" "
643. Sarah Miller,	Springfield, Pa.,	" "
644. Rachel Passmore,	Edgmont, Pa.,	12th mo., "
645. Margaret Crawford,	Brownsville, Pa.,	10th mo., "
646. Hannah Crawford,	"	" "
647. Sidney Lownes,	Springfield, Pa.,	1st mo., 1819.
648. Mary S. Jackson,	Reading, Pa.,	4th mo., "
649. Phebe Ann Lewis,	Providence, Pa.,	12th mo., 1818.
651. Hannah A. Oakford,	Darby, Pa.,	10th mo., "
652. Rebecca Hibberd,	Upper Darby, Pa.,	11th mo., "
653. Elizabeth Corbit,	Philadelphia, Pa.,	12th mo., "
654. Lydia Lundy,	Fishing Creek, Pa.,	1st mo., 1819.
655. Hannah Foulke,	Quakertown, Pa.,	11th mo., 1818.
656. Elizabeth Watson,	Buckingham, Pa.,	2d mo., 1819.
657. Judith Smith,	Egg Harbor, N. J.,	1st mo., "
658. Tacy Townsend,	Byberry, Pa.,	4th mo., "
659. Grace Wilson,	"	" "
660. Zillah Embree,	West Bradford, Pa.,	12th mo., 1818.
661. Esther Haines,	E. Nottingham, Pa.,	6th mo., 1819.
662. Rachel Phipps,	Uwchlan, Pa.,	5th mo., "
663. Susanna Swayne,	E. Marlborough, Pa.,	12th mo., 1818.
664. Hannah Griffith,	Columbia, Pa.,	6th mo., 1819.
665. Mary Pennock,	London Grove, Pa.,	10th mo., 1820.
666. Anna Maria Ladd,	Smithfield, Ohio,	6th mo., 1819.
667. Mary Steer,	Waterford, Va.,	4th mo., "
668. Edith Price,	Gunpowder, Md.,	2d mo., "
669. Elizabeth Matthews,	"	" "
670. Sarah Williamson,	Newtown, Pa.,	" "
671. Sarah Ann Lupton,	Waterford, Va.,	4th mo., "
672. Sidney Jacobs,	East Bradford, Pa.,	5th mo., "
673. A. P. Cornthwaite,	Baltimore, Md.,	2d mo., "
674. Rachel Scott,	Gunpowder, Md.,	5th mo., "
675. Eliza H. Smith,	Harford, Md.,	6th mo., "
677. Margaret Wilson,	Baltimore, Md.,	4th mo., "
678. Elizabeth Wilson,	"	" "
679. Eliz. G. Sinclair,	"	" "
680. Sarah E. Thompson,	Waterford, Va.,	5th mo., "
681. Elizabeth Gregg,	Middletown, Pa.,	6th mo., "
682. Mary Wilkinson,	Wilmington, Del.,	2d mo., "
683. Edith B. Stockton,	Springfield, N. J.,	3d mo., "
684. Martha Watson,	Fishing Creek, Pa.,	1st mo., "

SECOND THOUSAND.

NAME.	RESIDENCE.	DATE OF ENTRY.	
685. Eliza Ann Valentine,	Philadelphia, Pa.,	4th mo.,	1819.
686. Elizabeth Knight,	Byberry, Pa.,	"	"
687. Mary Reeve,	Evesham, N. J.,	5th mo.,	"
688. Mira E. Temple,	Philadelphia, Pa.,	4th mo.,	"
689. Mary Ann Jones,	Mt. Holly, N. J.,	8th mo.,	1821.
690. Alice Maulsby,	Plymouth, Pa.,	4th mo.,	1819.
691. Elizabeth Walton,	Frankford, Pa.,	5th mo.,	"
692. Emma Cope,	Philadelphia, Pa.,	"	"
693. Ann Thomas,	Hatborough, Pa.,	4th mo.,	"
694. Ann Wall,	Trenton, N. J.,	"	1821.
695. Mary Bane,	Wilmington, Del.,	"	1819.
697. Mary Phipps,	Frankford, Pa.,	"	"
698. Mary Hallowell,	Abington, Pa.,	"	"
699. Sarah Conrad,	Philadelphia, Pa.,	"	"
700. Susanna Hall,	Springfield, Pa.,	"	"
701. Rebecca Truman,	Sadsbury, Pa.,	"	"
703. Ann West,	Greensborough, Pa.,	6th mo.,	"
704. Mary Pidgeon,	Waterford, Va.,	"	"
705. Hannah Thompson,	New Garden, Pa.,	1st mo.,	1820.
706. Rachel Vail,	Rahway, N. J.,	10th mo.,	1819.
707. Sarah Poole,	Wilmington, Del.,	12th mo.,	"
708. Elizabeth Taylor,	New Garden, Pa.,	1st mo.,	1820.
709. Esther Passmore,	W. Marlborough, Pa.,	11th mo.,	1819.
710. Hannah Pennell,	Middletown, Pa.,	8th mo.,	"
711. Elizabeth Vezey,	Philadelphia, Pa.,	5th mo.,	"
712. Esther Lewis,	Robeson, Pa.,	8th mo.,	"
713. Phebe Carpenter,	Westtown, Pa.,	1st mo.,	1820.
714. Sarah Andrews,	Darby, Pa.,	5th mo.,	1819.
715. Tacy Matlack,	Merion, Pa.,	"	"
716. Ann Pusey,	Darby, Pa.,	"	"
717. Emma Zell,	Germantown, Pa.,	8th mo.,	"
718. Mary C. Jones,	Philadelphia, Pa.,	6th mo.,	"
719. Eleanor Cope,	"	"	"
720. Deborah Shaw,	"	"	"
721. Rachel Hill,	"	"	"
722. Hannah W. Hill,	"	"	"
723. Elizabeth M. Hill,	"	"	"
724. Anna Pierce,	"	7th mo.,	1821.
725. Rebecca Adamson,	Charlestown, Pa.,	8th mo.,	1819.
726. Jane B. Temple,	Edgmont, Pa.,	9th mo.,	"
727. Rachel Watson,	Fallsington, Pa.,	5th mo.,	1820.
728. Martha H. Tyson,	E. Nottingham, Pa.,	11th mo.,	1819.
729. Mary Ann Wright,	Radnor, Pa.,	9th mo.,	"
730. Mary Brown,	Brownsville, N. Y.,	6th mo.,	"
731. Sarah Brown,	"	"	"
732. Hannah Brown,	"	"	"
733. Harriet Shotwell,	Plainfield, N. J.,	9th mo.,	"

STUDENTS. 259

SECOND THOUSAND.

NAME.	RESIDENCE.	DATE OF ENTRY.
734. Jane Temple,	Pennsbury, Pa.,	9th mo., 1819.
735. Rebecca Pierce,	Philadelphia, Pa.,	7th mo., "
736. Mary Ann Miller,	Plainfield, N. J.,	11th mo., "
737. Rebecca Engle,	Haddonfield, N. J.,	9th mo., "
738. Hannah A. Reeve,	Evesham, N. J.,	10th mo., "
739. Sarah W. Reeve,	"	" "
740. Jane Yarnall,	Edgmont, Pa.,	8th mo., "
741. Elizabeth Woodward,	London Grove, Pa.,	11th mo., "
742. Sarah Thatcher,	Concord, Pa.,	9th mo., "
743. Elizabeth Garrett,	Goshen, Pa.,	8th mo., "
744. Hetty Ann Newlin,	Concord, Pa.,	3d mo., 1820.
745. Deborah Davis,	Birmingham, Pa.,	5th mo., "
746. Rachel Denn,	Salem, N. J.,	10th mo., 1819.
747. Sarah Hulme,	Mt. Holly, N. J.,	5th mo., 1820.
748. Ann Crawford,	Brownsville, Pa.,	10th mo., "
749. Mary Painter,	Concord, Pa.,	3d mo., "
751. Rachel Carpenter,	Salem, N. J.,	9th mo., 1819.
752. Jane Matlack,	Moorestown, N. J.,	" "
753. Eliz. M. Thompson,	Salem, N. J.,	10th mo., "
754. Rachel Nicholson,	"	" "
755. Mary Bacon,		" "
756. Deborah A. Mifflin,	Philadelphia, Pa.,	4th mo., 1820.
757. Mary Woolston,	Fallsington, Pa.,	" "
758. Emily Cleaver,	Radnor, Pa.,	1st mo., "
759. Maria Tatum,	Wilmington, Del.,	5th mo., "
760. Mary Edge,	East Caln, Pa.,	" "
761. Massey Pratt,	Springfield, Pa.,	" "
762. Priscilla Pratt,	"	" "
763. Mary Garrett,	Upper Darby, Pa.,	" "
764. Margaret Garrett,	"	" "
765. Mary R. Howland,	New York, N. Y.,	8th mo., "
766. Sophia Haines,	W. Nottingham, Md.,	4th mo., "
767. Mary Ann Starr,	New Garden, Pa.,	" "
768. Rebecca Roberts,	Darby, Pa.,	" "
769. Hannah Dilworth,	Edgmont, Pa.,	" "
770. Rebecca Alsop,	Philadelphia, Pa.,	" "
771. Deborah D. Roberts,	"	2d mo., "
772. Ann Cooper,	"	" "
773. Mary C. Davis,	Evesham, N. J.,	5th mo., "
774. Susanna Conard,	Philadelphia, Pa.,	2d mo., "
775. Elizabeth Pennell,	Concord, Pa.,	4th mo., "
776. Susanna Warrington,	Moorestown, N. J.,	6th mo., "
777. Elizabeth Laws,	Philadelphia, Pa.,	5th mo., "
778. Ann Pleasants,	"	" "
779. Jane Stockton,	Fallsington, Pa.,	4th mo., "
780. Isabel Hustler,	Philadelphia, Pa.,	" "
781. Mary Hustler,	"	" "

20*

SECOND THOUSAND.

NAME.	RESIDENCE.	DATE OF ENTRY.	
782. Sophronia Osborne,	Philadelphia, Pa.,	5th mo.,	1820.
783. Rebecca Shaw,	Jenkintown, Pa.,	"	"
784. Mary Tyler,	Salem, N. J.,	4th mo.,	"
785. Susanna Smith,	Philadelphia, Pa.,	5th mo.,	"
786. Mary Cook,	"	"	"
787. Martha Reeve,	"	4th mo.,	"
788. Eleanor Widdefield,	"	3d mo.,	"
789. Tacy Thomas,	Hatborough, Pa.	5th mo.,	"
790. Rachel Hawley,	Bradford, Pa.,	"	"
791. Ruth Reed,	Westtown, Pa.,	"	"
792. Camilla Jacobs,	East Bradford, Pa.,	"	"
793. Rachel Conard,	New London, Pa.,	"	1821.
794. Ann G. Coates,	Coatesville, Pa.,	8th mo.,	1820.
795. Hannah Wood,	East Bradford, Pa.,	"	"
796. Lydia Hoopes,	Sadsbury, Pa.,	9th mo.,	"
797. Sarah Walton,	New Garden, Pa.,	10th mo.,	"
798. Anne Massey,	Deer Creek, Md.,	"	"
799. Martha Embree,	West Bradford, Pa.,	"	"
800. Ann Richards,	New Garden, Pa.,	11th mo.,	"
801. Lydia Atherton,	Philadelphia, Pa.,	5th mo.,	"
802. Albina N. Roberts,	Middletown, Pa.,	4th mo.,	"
803. Mary Shaw,	Buckingham, Pa.,	5th mo.,	"
804. Prudence Webster,	Rahway, N. J.,	"	"
805. Mary Book,	Germantown, Pa.,	4th mo.,	"
806. Elizabeth Engle,	Mt. Holly, N. J.,	10th mo.,	1823.
807. Jane Heston,	Gwynedd, Pa.,	6th mo.,	1820.
808. Marianna Seaman,	——, N. Y.,	5th mo.,	"
809. Sarah Downing,	Uwchlan, Pa.,	"	"
810. Esther Troth,	Mt. Holly, N. J.,	"	"
811. Mary Gardiner,	Evesham, N. J.,	"	"
812. Lydia Evans,	"	"	"
813. Ann Evans,	"	"	"
814. Mary C. Davis,	Woodstown, N. J.,	"	"
815. Elizabeth P. Seal,	Wilmington, Del.,	"	"
817. Sarah Marshall,	Philadelphia, Pa.,	"	"
818. Ruth Reeve,	"	"	"
819. Hannah Thompson,	Abington, Pa.,	6th mo.,	"
820. Rebecca Allinson,	Philadelphia, Pa.,	5th mo.,	"
821. Martha Howey,	Woodstown, N. J.,	"	"
822. Hannah Lloyd,	Horsham, Pa.,	"	"
823. Hannah Maule,	Philadelphia, Pa.,	"	"
826. Hannah Ely,	Buckingham, Pa.,	6th mo.,	"
827. Lucy Ann Troth,	Mt. Holly, N. J.,	10th mo.,	1823.
828. Ann Lawrie,	Woodstown, N. J.,	7th mo.,	1820.
829. Ann Folwell,	Philadelphia, Pa.,	8th mo.,	"
830. Susan Emerson,	Little Creek, Del.,	11th mo.,	"
831. Mary Green,	Frankford, Pa.,	10th mo.,	"

STUDENTS.

SECOND THOUSAND.

NAME.	RESIDENCE.	DATE OF ENTRY.
832. Sarah H. Taylor,	Attleborough, Pa.,	10th mo., 1820.
833. Rachel McIlvain,	W. Philadelphia, Pa.,	" "
834. Ann Hunt,	Darby, Pa.,	" "
835. Mary Waters,	Philadelphia, Pa.,	11th mo., "
836. Susanna Morris,	"	" "
837. Hannah S. Temple,	Edgmont, Pa.,	" "
838. Abigail B. Roberts,	Mt. Holly, N. J.,	12th mo., "
840. Beulah T. Parker,	Philadelphia, Pa.,	9th mo., "
841. Elizabeth Trimble,	Baltimore, Md.,	10th mo., "
842. Philena Pennock,	London Grove, Pa.,	" "
843. Anne Barnard,	W. Marlborough, Pa.,	
844. Ann Spackman,	Wilmington, Del.,	3d mo., 1821.
845. Sarah Wilson,	Hockessing, Del.,	12th mo., 1820.
846. Susan Clark,	Doe Run, Pa.,	" "
847. Lydia Yeatman,	Hockessing, Del.,	" "
848. Phebe Walker,	"	" "
849. Sarah Phillips,	"	" "
850. Mary Woodward,	Westtown, Pa.,	1st mo., 1821.
851. Sarah Coale,	W. Nottingham, Md.,	3d mo., 1820.
852. H. Worthington,	Deer Creek, Md.,	4th mo., 1821.
853. Eliza Ann Smith,	Baltimore, Md.,	6th mo., "
854. Rachel Atkinson,	Easton, Md.,	4th mo., "
855. Abigail Pyle,	East Marlborough, Pa.,	5th mo., "
856. Hannah Sharpless,	West Chester, Pa.,	" "
857. Ann Matlack,	Radnor, Pa.,	" "
858. Margaret Coale,	W. Nottingham, Md.,	8th mo., "
859. Mary Ann Roberts,	Mt. Holly, N. J.,	5th mo., "
860. Priscilla W. Pennell,	Edgmont, Pa.,	12th mo., 1820.
861. T. R. Pennell,	"	" "
862. Mary T. Dilworth,	"	" "
863. Mary Dixon,	Hockessing, Del.,	" "
864. Mary Harlan,	West Bradford, Pa.,	7th mo., 1821.
865. Anna Seaman,	———, N. Y.,	6th mo., "
866. Patience Howell,	Camden, Del.,	" "
867. Patience Hunn,	"	" "
868. Mary Cowgill,	Duck Creek, Del.,	8th mo., "
869. Susan Roberts,	Mt. Holly, N. J.,	9th mo., "
870. Juliana Randolph,	Philadelphia, Pa.,	4th mo., "
871. Elizabeth Welding,	Frankford, Pa.,	5th mo., "
872. Elizabeth Whitelock,	"	" "
874. Ann B. Powell,	Mt. Holly, N. J.,	4th mo., "
875. Sarah B. Earl,	New Mills, N. J.,	5th mo., "
876. Martha Pancoast,	Mullica Hill, N. J.,	" "
877. Sarah A. Pancoast,	"	" "
878. Emily Stevenson,	Salem, N. J.,	" "
879. Elizabeth Middleton,	Philadelphia, Pa.,	" "
880. Martha Coffin,	"	6th mo., "

GENERAL CATALOGUE.

SECOND THOUSAND.

NAME.	RESIDENCE.	DATE OF ENTRY.
881. Elizabeth Truman,	Sadsbury, Pa.,	12th mo., 1821
882. Phebe S. Townsend,	Baltimore, Md.,	9th mo., "
883. H. P. Townsend,	"	" "
884. Sarah Darlington,	East Bradford, Pa.,	10th mo., "
885. Sarah Painter,	Middletown, Pa.,	" "
886. Jane Pennell,	"	9th mo., "
887. Hetty Ann Pierce,	Thornbury, Pa.,	10th mo., "
888. Sarah England,	Baltimore, Md.,	9th mo., "
889. Amy Darlington,	Middletown, Pa.,	10th mo., "
890. Sarah Gregg,	Kennet, Pa.,	" "
891. Ann G. Hill,	Darby, Pa.,	" "
892. Elizabeth Smith,	"	" "
893. Ann Pitfield,	Philadelphia, Pa.,	" "
894. Mary Gaskill,	Burlington, N. J.,	11th mo., "
895. Eliza A. Stratton,	Philadelphia, Pa.,	9th mo., "
896. Margaret G. Laing,	Rahway, N. J.,	10th mo., "
898. Elizabeth C. Garrett,	Philadelphia, Pa.,	" "
899. Margaret Garrett,	"	" "
900. C. B. Dilworth,	East Whiteland, Pa.,	" "
902. Hannah Yarnall,	Edgmont, Pa.,	" "
903. Susan Longstreth,	Horsham, Pa.,	11th mo., "
904. Mary Ann Kirk,	Uwchlan, Pa.,	1st mo., 1822.
905. Hannah A. Clement,	Woodbury, N. J.,	11th mo., 1821.
906. Letitia Brinton,	Thornbury, Pa.,	" "
907. Mary Grubb,	Willistown, Pa.,	" "
908. Lydia Grubb,	"	" "
909. Caroline Roberts,		
910. Susan Brinton,	Lampeter, Pa.,	1st mo., 1822.
911. Mary Cooper,	Woodbury, N. J.,	10th mo., 1821.
912. Maria Tatum,	Wilmington, Del.,	" "
913. Hannah Grubb,	"	" "
914. Mary Bassett,	Salem, N. J.,	11th mo., "
915. Abigail Borton,	Evesham, N. J.,	10th mo., "
916. Hannah Marshall,	Philadelphia, Pa.,	" "
917. Rebecca Smith,	Wrightstown, Pa.,	11th mo., "
918. Martha Woolman,	Rancocas, N. J.,	" "
919. Mary Conard,	Philadelphia, Pa.,	12th mo., "
920. Rebecca Taylor,	Kennet, Pa.,	11th mo., "
921. Mary M. Townsend,	Baltimore, Md.	" "
922. Rachel H. Garrett,	Willistown, Pa.,	12th mo., "
923. Rachel Miller,	Downingtown, Pa.,	" "
924. Elizabeth Passmore,	W. Marlborough, Pa.;	1st mo., 1822.
925. Maria Smith,	Sadsbury, Pa.,	4th mo., "
926. Mary Ann Kemp,	King's Creek, Md.,	" "
927. Henrietta Nixon,	Charlestown, Pa.,	" "
928. Ann Nixon,	"	" "
929. Frances Eastburn,	Buckingham, Pa.,	" "

STUDENTS.

SECOND THOUSAND.

NAME.	RESIDENCE.	DATE OF ENTRY.
930. Mary Lafetra,	Baltimore, Md.,	3d mo., 1822.
931. Rachel Johnson,	Philadelphia, Pa.,	11th mo., 1821.
932. Martha Stokes,	"	12th mo., "
933. Elizabeth M. Smith,	Fallsington, Pa.,	11th mo., "
934. Priscilla Parry,	Philadelphia, Pa.,	12th mo., "
935. Hannah Lippincott,	Westfield, N. J.,	" "
936. Rachel Burrough,	Evesham, N. J.,	11th mo., "
937. Sarah Evans,	"	" "
939. Sarah Corlies,	———, N. Y.,	4th mo., 1822.
940. Mary Nelson,	"	" "
941. Hannah M. Jefferson,	Philadelphia, Pa.,	3d mo., "
944. Hepzibah Norris,	"	" "
946. Ann Augusta Cocks,	———, N. Y.,	4th mo., "
947. Martha Jones,	Darby, Pa.,	2d mo., "
948. Em. Gillingham,	Frankford, Pa.,	3d mo., "
949. Eliz. Gillingham,	"	" "
950. Mary Sharpless,	Philadelphia, Pa.,	4th mo., "
951. Eliz. W. Haydock,	"	" "
952. Susanna Kite,	"	" "
953. Rebecca Levick,	Little Creek, Del.,	5th mo., "
954. Phebe Hustler,	Philadelphia, Pa.,	3d mo., "
956. Anna Gillingham,	Frankford, Pa.,	" "
957. Rebecca Abbott,	Philadelphia, Pa.,	4th mo., "
958. Elizabeth Woodnutt,	Salem, N. J.,	" "
959. Eliz. Ann White,	Rahway, N. J.,	" "
960. Elizabeth Mott,	Baltimore, Md.,	3d mo., "
961. Augusta Comegys,	"	" "
962. Ann Read,		4th mo., "
963. Mary Ann Mickle,	Sadsbury, Pa.,	" "
964. Eliza Mickle,	"	" "
965. Hannah Mechem,	East Bradford, Pa.,	9th mo., "
966. Mary Ann Chandler,	Centre, Del.,	5th mo., "
967. Mary Trimble,	Baltimore, Md.,	4th mo., "
968. Jane Trimble,	"	" "
969. Martha Garrett,	Newtown, Pa.,	10th mo., "
970. Patience Chambers,	London Grove, Pa.,	6th mo., "
971. Mary Ann Sinclair,	Baltimore, Md.,	5th mo., "
972. Mary Shotwell,	Rahway, N. J.,	6th mo., "
973. Rebecca Ann Hulme,	Mt. Holly, N. J.,	5th mo., "
974. Mary Butterworth,	"	" "
975. Abigail Butterworth,	"	" "
976. Susanna Matlack,	Baltimore, Md.,	" "
977. Elizabeth Hunt,	Darby, Pa.,	" "
978. Esther Price,	Merion, Pa.,	" "
979. Elizabeth Haines,	Rancocas, N. J.,	6th mo., "
980. Mary Laws,	Hillsborough, Md.,	4th mo, "
981. Margaret Robbins,	Mullica Hill, N. J.,	" "

SECOND THOUSAND.

NAME.	RESIDENCE.	DATE OF ENTRY.
982. Eliza Ann Buzby,	Burlington, N. J.,	7th mo., 1822.
983. Eliza Burdsall,	Rahway, N. J.,	6th mo., "
984. Mary Bringhurst,	Wilmington, Del.,	8th mo., "
985. Elizab'h Nicholson,	Philadelphia, Pa.,	6th mo., "
986. Deborah Willits,	Maiden Creek, Pa.,	9th mo., "
987. Mary A. Haydock,	Philadelphia, Pa.,	6th mo., "
988. Elizabeth Pancoast,	Springfield, N. J.,	" "
989. Hannah W. Jenks,	Philadelphia, Pa.,	" "
990. Sarah Haines,	East Bradford, Pa.,	8th mo., "
991. Hannah Simmons,	Penn, Pa.,	6th mo., "
992. Sarah Alricks,	Wilmington, Del.,	" "
993. Margaret C. Vail,	Plainfield, N. J.,	9th mo., "
994. Ann Sharpless,	Chester, Pa.,	10th mo., "
995. Hannah Morris,	Merion, Pa.,	9th mo., "
996. Martha Morris,	Philadelphia, Pa.,	11th mo., "
998. Ann Preston,	W. Nottingham, Md.,	5th mo., 1823.
999. Jane Gibbons,	Lampeter, Pa.,	9th mo., 1822.
1000. Eliza Burton,	Little Creek, Del.,	11th mo., "

THIRD THOUSAND.

NAME.	RESIDENCE.	DATE OF ENTRY.
1. Letitia E. Austin,	Buckingham, Pa.,	9th mo., 1822.
2. Rebecca J. Maule,	Philadelphia, Pa.,	8th mo., "
3. Rachel V. Massey,	W. Whiteland, Pa.,	10th mo., "
4. Rebecca Lower,	Philadelphia, Pa.,	8th mo., "
5. Rachel Passmore,	Darby, Pa.,	10th mo., "
6. Mary Hough,	New Mills, N. J.,	12th mo., "
7. Martha Thomas,	Germantown, Pa.,	9th mo., "
8. Mary Longstreth,	Horsham, Pa.,	" "
10. Susan Haines,	Rancocas, N. J.,	11th mo., "
11. Sarah Sharpless,	Chester, Pa.,	10th mo., "
13. Ruth Gilpin,	Birmingham, Pa.,	" "
14. Abigail Sharpless,	East Bradford, Pa.,	2d mo., 1823.
15. Mary Jefferis,	"	11th mo., 1822.
16. Hannah P. Baily,	"	10th mo., "
17. Sarah A. Pennock,	London Grove, Pa.,	" "
18. Sarah Hoopes,	Philadelphia, Pa.,	11th mo., "
19. Eliza A. Balderston,	Baltimore, Md.,	" "
20. Rachel Balderston,	"	" "
21. Phebe Lewis,	Newtown, Pa.,	10th mo., "
22. Hannah Pratt,	"	11th mo., "
23. Lydia S. Palmer,	Concord, Pa.,	1st mo., 1823.
24. Sarah Woodward,	Centre, Del.,	11th mo., 1822.
25. L. A. Buffington,	New Garden, Pa.,	4th mo., 1823.
26. Elizabeth Baily,	London Grove, Pa.,	10th mo., 1822.
27. Hannah Garrett,	Upper Darby, Pa.,	12th mo., "

STUDENTS.

THIRD THOUSAND.

NAME.	RESIDENCE.	DATE OF ENTRY.
28. Elizabeth Shoemaker,	Abington, Pa.,	11th mo., 1822
29. Esther Longstreth,	Horsham, Pa.,	" "
30. Eliza Taylor,	Pennsbury, Pa.,	10th mo., "
31. Abigail L. Middleton,	Philadelphia, Pa.,	" "
32. Rachel Evans,	"	" "
33. Rachel W. Stokes,	Rancocas, N. J.,	12th mo., "
34. Ann Hallowell,	Abington, Pa.,	5th mo., 1823.
35. Catharine Thompson,	"	" "
36. Hannah Newbold,	Springfield, N. J.,	4th mo., "
37. Rebecca Parry,	Horsham, Pa.,	5th mo., "
38. Hannah Singley,	Frankford, Pa.,	4th mo., "
39. Ann Tatum,	Wilmington, Del.,	5th mo., "
40. Mary Bennett,	Woodbury, N. J.,	4th mo., "
41. Eliza Pusey,	London Grove, Pa.,	11th mo., 1822.
42. Eliza Pennock,	"	" "
43. Mira Marshall,	E. Marlborough, Pa.,	" "
44. Sarah P. Hoopes,	West Chester, Pa.,	" "
45. Rebecca Thomas,	Charlestown, Pa.,	12th mo., "
46. Mary F. Walter,	Concord, Pa.,	1st mo., 1823.
47. Gulielma Hunn,	Camden, Del.,	12th mo., 1822.
48. Mary Griscom,	Salem, N. J.,	5th mo., 1823.
49. Elizabeth Price,	Baltimore, Md.,	6th mo., "
50. Elizabeth Marshall,	West Bradford, Pa.,	4th mo., "
52. Hannah Monaghan,	London Grove, Pa.,	" "
53. Martha Jefferis,	Sadsbury, Pa.,	" "
54. Frances Price,	Baltimore, Md.,	2d mo., "
55. Mary Phillips,	Hockessing, Del.,	7th mo., "
56. Mary J. Nixon,	Pikeland, Pa,	4th mo., "
57. Mary Wood,	Little Britain, Pa.,	9th mo., 1824.
58. Ruth Heald,	Hockessing, Del.,	7th mo., 1823.
59. Amy Green.	Chichester, Pa.,	4th mo., "
60. Asenath Cooper,	Columbia, Pa.,	" "
61. Mary Vickers,	Uwchlan, Pa.,	" "
62. Hannah Coleman,	Trenton, N. J.,	" "
63. Mary E. Mitchell,	Bristol, Pa.,	5th mo., "
64. Elizabeth Cooper,	Pleasant View, Pa.,	" "
65. Letitia Swain,	Bristol, Pa.,	" "
66. Mary Mendenhall,	Wilmington, Del.,	" "
67. Mary Fell,	Philadelphia, Pa.,	" "
68. Eliza Fell,	"	" "
69. Rebecca Dixon,		" "
70. Mary Ridgway,	Burlington, N. J.,	" "
71. Mary Hallowell,	Abington, Pa.,	" "
72. Sarah Whitelock,	Frankford, Pa.,	" "
73. Mary C. Evans,	Evesham, N. J.,	" "
74. Elizabeth Lippincott,	Mauch Chunk, Pa.,	" "
75. Sarah Kester,	Frankford, Pa.,	" "

GENERAL CATALOGUE.

THIRD THOUSAND.

NAME.	RESIDENCE.	DATE OF ENTRY.
76. Beulah Morris,	Philadelphia, Pa.,	5th mo., 1823.
77. Hannah Taylor,	Frankford, Pa.,	6th mo., "
78. Rebecca Mitchell,	Horsham, Pa.,	" "
79. Rachel Matlack,	Rancocas, N. J.,	7th mo., "
80. Ann Raleigh,	Philadelphia, Pa.,	6th mo., "
81. Eleanor Kenny,	Baltimore, Md.,	5th mo., "
82. Ann Chandlee,	"	9th mo., "
83. Ann Burrough,	Evesham, N. J.,	5th mo., "
84. Ann Sinclair,	Baltimore, Md.,	" "
85. Susanna Lamborn,	Wilmington, Del.,	8th mo., "
86. Rebecca Baker,	West Bradford, Pa.,	11th mo., "
87. Esther Meredith,	Uwchlan, Pa.,	4th mo., 1824.
89. Hannah Griffith,	New London, Pa.,	10th mo., 1823.
90. Henrietta Simmons,	Penn, Pa.,	" "
91. Mary Wilson,	Easton, Md.,	6th mo., "
92. Euphemia Wilson,	"	" "
93. Mary H. Wilson,	"	" "
94. Mary W. Haines,	Rancocas, N. J.,	10th mo., "
95. Ann T. Lippincott,	Westfield, N. J.,	" "
96. Kezia Warrington,	"	9th mo., "
97. Rebecca Warrington,	"	" "
98. Susanna Henderson,	Sadsbury, Pa.,	6th mo., "
99. Hannah Yerkes,	Jenkinton, Pa.,	5th mo., "
100. Sarah Hance,	Philadelphia, Pa.,	6th mo., "
101. Susan H. Trotter,	"	5th mo., "
102. Lydia Shoemaker,	Hatborough, Pa.,	6th mo., "
103. Rachel Shoemaker,	"	" "
104. Mary Sleeper,	Philadelphia, Pa.,	" "
105. Mary Haines,	Moorestown, N. J.,	8th mo., "
106. Ann Haines,	Philadelphia, Pa.,	" "
107. Ann Cooper,	Woodbury, N. J.,	11th mo., "
108. Mary Howell,	Philadelphia, Pa.,	7th mo., "
109. Elizabeth Howell,	"	" "
110. Mary C. Wood,	Woodbury, N. J.,	12th mo., "
111. Ruth Ann Lukens,	Philadelphia, Pa.,	11th mo., "
112. Sarah B. Reeves,	Camden, N. J.,	" "
113. Sarah Parry,	Philadelphia, Pa.,	" "
114. Sarah J. Leedom,	"	9th mo., "
115. Elizabeth H. Davis,	"	4th mo., 1825.
116. Elizabeth Stokes,	"	11th mo., 1823
117. Rachel Welding,	Frankford, Pa.,	" "
118. Hannah Kester,	"	10th mo., "
119. Susanna Brookes,	Wilmington, Del.,	" "
120. Mercy Field,	Makefield, Pa.,	4th mo., 1825.
122. Martha Poole,	Wilmington, Del.,	10th mo., 1823.
123. Eliz. D. England,	Baltimore, Md.,	9th mo , "
124. S. Y. Thomas,	Willistown, Pa.,	12th mo.. 1824

STUDENTS.

THIRD THOUSAND.

NAME.	RESIDENCE.	DATE OF ENTRY.
125. Beulah R. Wright,	Reading, Pa.,	11th mo., 1823.
126. Mary Kersey,	East Whiteland, Pa.,	" "
127. Han'h H. Sharpless,	Goshen, Pa.,	" "
129. Mary Wood,	Smithfield, Ohio,	10th mo., "
130. Susan Pierce,	Kennet, Pa.,	12th mo., "
131. Ann Comly,	Byberry, Pa.,	11th mo., "
132. Mary Knight,	"	" "
133. Esther Fennimore,	Springfield, N. J.,	" "
134. Lydia Sheppard,	Philadelphia, Pa.,	" "
135. Hannah Potts,	Abington, Pa.,	" "
136. Martha Potts,	Cheltenham, Pa.,	" "
137. Mary T. Newbold,	Springfield, N. J.,	" "
139. Sarah Ann Smith,	Salem, N. J.,	" "
140. Elizabeth T. Ogden,	Swedesboro, N. J.,	" "
141. Elizabeth Pennell,	Concord, Pa.,	12th mo., "
142. Martha Parker,	Mt. Pleasant, Ohio,	" "
143. Lydia Wood,	Smithfield, Ohio,	" "
144. Susanna Wood,	"	" "
145. Elizabeth Luff,	Camden, Del.,	3d mo., 1824.
146. Ruth Anna Moore,	W. Nottingham, Md.,	4th mo., "
147. Philena Woodrow,	Kennet Square, Pa.,	5th mo., "
148. Maria Haines,	West Chester, Pa.,	3d mo., "
149. Margaret Marshall,	Philadelphia, Pa.,	10th mo., "
150. Hannah Moore,	London Grove, Pa.,	3d mo., "
151. Hannah Powell,	Springfield, Pa.,	1st mo., "
152. Susan P. Bacon,	Philadelphia, Pa.,	5th mo., "
153. Hannah Pancoast,	Springfield, N. J.,	3d mo., "
154. Ann Zelley,	"	" "
155. Rachel Borton,	Evesham, N. J.,	12th mo., 1823.
156. Hannah Collins,	"	" "
157. Lydia Collins,	"	" "
158. Caroline Glover,	Woodbury, N. J.,	1st mo., 1824.
159. Susan D. Smith,	Burlington, N. J.,	" "
160. Hannah Thomas,	Providence, Pa.,	3d mo., "
161. Mary Stevenson,	Springfield, N. J.,	4th mo., 1825.
162. Lydia Cook,	Philadelphia, Pa.,	8th mo., 1824.
163. Mary Ann Haines,	Westfield, N. J.,	4th mo., 1825.
164. Sarah Matlack,	Moorestown, N. J.,	3d mo., 1824.
165. Ann R. Lippincott,	Westfield, N. J.,	4th mo., "
166. Anna Lippincott,	"	-
167. Letitia Parry,	Drumore, Pa.,	5th mo., "
168. Mary L. Nicholson,	Philadelphia, Pa.,	" "
170. Mary Updegraff,	Smithfield, Ohio,	" '
171. Mary Bell,	New York, N. Y.,	" "
172. Elizabeth A. Worth,	East Bradford, Pa.,	6th mo., "
173. Mary Ann Marshall,	London Grove, Pa.,	" "
174. Deborah Harry,	East Caln, Pa.,	5th mo., "

THIRD THOUSAND.

NAME.	RESIDENCE.	DATE OF ENTRY.
175. Mary Thompson,	New Garden, Pa.,	10th mo., 1824.
176. Adriana Moore,	W. Nottingham, Pa.,	4th mo., "
177. Emily Fell,	Philadelphia, Pa.,	7th mo., "
178. Rachel Garretson,	Smithfield, Ohio,	5th mo., "
179. Mary Ann Carmalt,	Philadelphia, Pa.,	10th mo., "
180. Ann L. Cowgill,	Little Creek, Del.,	5th mo., "
182. Ann W. Jenks,	Philadelphia, Pa.,	4th mo., "
184. Margaret L. Atlee,	"	6th mo., "
185. Catharine Smith,	"	4th mo., "
186. Julia Gaskill,	Springfield, N. J.,	3d mo., "
187. Beulah Mason,	"	" "
188. Ann Eliza Emerson,	Little Creek, Del.,	6th mo., "
189. Elizabeth Trump,	Newport, Pa.,	" "
190. Martha Newbold,	Frankford, Pa.,	" "
193. Elizabeth Hopper,	Philadelphia, Pa.,	" "
194. Catharine Peters,	"	" "
196. Jane Quinby,	Stanton, Del.,	7th mo., "
197. Rachel Alsop,	Kennet, Pa.,	6th mo., "
198. Eliza Dolby,	Camden, Del.,	" "
199. Sarah W. Potts,	Great Valley, Pa.,	" "
200. Deborah Kirk,	Little Britain, Pa.,	9th mo., "
201. Susanna Evans,	Evesham, N. J.,	11th mo., "
202. Edith Burr,	Philadelphia, Pa.,	6th mo., "
203. Esther M. Hancock,	"	8th mo., "
204. Sarah Ann Vandever,	"	11th mo., "
205. Catharine S. Paxson,	Fallsington, Pa.,	" "
206. Susan L. Thomas,	Whitpaine, Pa.,	8th mo., "
207. Elizabeth H. Knight,	Byberry, Pa.,	11th mo., "
208. Sarah Ferris,	Sadsbury, Pa.,	" "
209. Lydia McIlvain,	W. Philadelphia, Pa.,	3d mo., 1825.
210. Elizabeth Sharpless,	Chester, Pa.,	11th mo., 1824.
211. Elizabeth Powell,	"	" "
212. Priscilla S. Reeve,	Evesham, N. J.,	" "
213. Mary Shreeve,	Trenton, N. J.,	" "
214. Sarah E. Conrow,	Moorestown, N. J.,	" "
215. Rebecca Conard,	Tredyffrin, Pa.,	" "
216. Ann Mercer,	Westtown, Pa.,	" "
217. Alice Ann Wilson,	Baltimore, Md.,	10th mo., "
218. Anna Mott,	Rensselaerville, N. Y.,	11th mo., "
219. Ruth Conard,	New London, Pa.,	" "
220. Hannah S. Palmer,	Concord, Pa.,	" "
221. Sarah Thompson,	Abington, Pa.,	" "
222. Hannah Hallowell,	"	" "
223. Martha Hallowell,	"	" "
224. Ann Bishop,	Springfield, N. J.,	" "
225. Ann McIlvain,	Chester, Pa.,	" "
226. M. D. Lippincott,	Woodbury, N. J.,	10th mo., "

STUDENTS.

THIRD THOUSAND.

NAME.	RESIDENCE.	DATE OF ENTRY.
227. Eliz. Scattergood,	Philadelphia, Pa.,	11th mo., 1824.
229. Sarah Kay,	Woodbury, N. J.,	" "
230. Beulah Bacon,	Greenwich, N. J.,	" "
231. Sarah Hodgson,	Philadelphia, Pa.,	10th mo., "
232. Keturah Chapman,	Roxborough, Pa.,	" "
233. Sarah Waters,	Philadelphia, Pa.,	" "
234. Ann M. Oliver,	Milford, Del.,	11th mo., "
235. Tacy Williams,	Abington, Pa.,	" "
236. Sarah Mather,	"	" "
237. Sarah Ann Thomas,	Providence, Pa.,	3d mo., 1825.
238. Tacy Thomas,	"	" "
239. Lydia Laws,	Hillsborough, Md.,	" "
240. Hannah Darlington,	East Bradford, Pa.,	11th mo., 1824.
241. Mercy Moore,	W. Nottingham, Pa.,	12th mo., "
242. Beulah Haines,	Westfield, N. J.,	4th mo., 1825.
243. Rachel Miller,	Short Creek, Ohio,	12th mo., 1824.
244. Lydia Taylor,	London Grove, Pa.,	1st mo., 1825.
245. Sarah D. Sharpless,	Downingtown, Pa.,	4th mo., "
246. Elizabeth Owen,	Lampeter, Pa.,	" "
247. Elizabeth Kemp,	King's Creek, Md.,	" "
248. Mary A. Atkinson,	Easton, Md.,	" "
249. Edna Webb,	Middletown, Pa.,	5th mo., "
250. Mary Ann Abbott,	Salem, N. J.,	12th mo., 1824.
251. Kezia Burrough,	Chester, Pa.,	5th mo., 1825.
252. Mary A. Paschall,	Darby, Pa.,	4th mo., "
253. Ann Eliza Shinn,	Mt. Holly, N. J.,	" "
254. Henrietta Ridgway,	Philadelphia, Pa.,	" "
256. Elizabeth White,	"	5th mo., "
257. Sarah Ann Maule,	"	4th mo., "
258. Elizabeth Davis,	"	5th mo., "
259. Mary Lippincott,	Westfield, N. J.,	" "
260. Ann Howell,	Philadelphia, Pa.,	" "
261. Rachel Grellet,	Burlington, N. J.,	" "
262. Mary L. Somers,	Salem, N. J.,	4th mo., "
263. Abbe Ann Pancoast,	Springfield, N. J.,	5th mo., "
264. Rebecca B. Sterling,	Trenton, N. J.,	" "
265. Sarah Paxson,	Bristol, Pa.,	6th mo., "
266. Lydia S. Jones,	Philadelphia, Pa.,	5th mo., "
267. Mary Ann Evans,	"	" "
268. Hannah White,	Mauch Chunk, Pa.,	" "
269. Angelica Cowgill,	Smyrna, Del.,	7th mo., "
270. Mary Morton,	Wilmington, Del.,	6th mo., "
271. Rebecca Thomas,	Chichester, Pa.,	5th mo., "
272. Mary Ann Heald,	Hockessing, Del.,	" "
273. Mary Dutton,	Chichester, Pa.,	" "
274. Rachel Lukens,	E. Fallowfield, Pa.,	" "
275. Hannah Jones,	East Bradford, Del.,	" "

GENERAL CATALOGUE.

THIRD THOUSAND.

NAME.	RESIDENCE.	DATE OF ENTRY.	
276. Elizabeth Reed,	Westtown, Pa.,	5th mo.,	1825.
277. Susan C. Corse,	Smyrna, Del.,	7th mo.,	"
278. Margaret S. White,	Pasquotank, N. C.,	"	"
279. Elizabeth Stokes,	Rancocas, N. J.,	4th mo.,	"
280. Isabella Parker,	Pasquotank, N. C.,	7th mo.,	"
281. R. I. Richardson,	Middletown, Pa.,	2d mo.,	1827.
282. Charlotte Newbold,	Springfield, N. J.,	4th mo.,	"
283. Hannah E. McCollin,	Philadelphia, Pa.,	3d mo.,	"
284. Elizabeth Justice,	Fallsington, Pa.,	11th mo.,	1825.
285. Elizabeth Knight,	Washington Co., Pa.,	4th mo.,	"
286. Mary Palmer,	Little Creek, Del.,	6th mo.,	"
287. Rebecca D. Smith,	Philadelphia, Pa.,	5th mo.,	"
288. Martha Lukens,	East Fallowfield, Pa.,	"	"
289. Susan Ann Bruff,	Philadelphia, Pa.,	"	"
290. Ann Lawrence,	Suffolk, Va.,	7th mo.,	"
291. Hannah Painter,	Middletown, Pa.,	10th mo.,	"
292. Sidney Painter,	"	"	"
293. Lydia Ann Smith,	Sadsbury, Pa.,	"	"
294. Mary E. Meredith,	E. Nantmeal, Pa.,	1st mo.,	1826.
295. Sarah B. Chambers,	New Garden, Pa.,	11th mo.,	1825.
296. Anne Gibbons,	Lampeter, Pa.,	9th mo.,	"
297. Anna Poole,	Wilmington, Del.,	2d mo.,	1826.
298. Sarah Phillips,	Hockessing, Del.,	9th mo.,	1825.
299. Hannah Chandlee,	Baltimore, Md.,	10th mo.,	"
300. Susanna A. Jarrett,	Horsham, Pa.,	7th mo.,	"
301. Elizabeth Rhoads,	Blockley, Pa.,	6th mo.,	"
302. Mary Whitelock,	Frankford, Pa.,	7th mo.,	"
303. Sarah F. Smith,	Philadelphia, Pa.,	9th mo.,	"
304. Martha Longstreth,	Horsham, Pa.,	"	"
305. Sarah Stevens,	Burlington, N. J.,	"	"
306. Elizabeth Lloyd,	Philadelphia, Pa.,	"	"
307. Matilda Hodgson,	"	"	"
308. Margaret Paschall,	Darby, Pa.,	10th mo.,	"
309. Ann Conard,	Horsham, Pa.,	12th mo.,	"
310. Sarah A. Evans,	Baltimore, Md.,	10th mo.,	"
311. Mary M. Evans,	"	"	"
312. Lydia Hoopes,	West Chester, Pa.,	12th mo.,	"
313. A. B. Carpenter,	West Bradford, Pa.,	10th mo.,	"
314. Susanna Medcalf,	Baltimore, Md.,	"	"
315. Edith Jefferis,	East Bradford, Pa.,	12th mo.,	1826.
316. Eliza Thatcher,	Aston, Pa.,	3d mo.,	"
317. Eliz. Richardson,	Wilmington, Del.,	4th mo.,	"
318. Elizabeth Walker,	Hockessing, Del.,	5th mo.,	"
319. Dinah Hannum,	Kennet, Pa.,	4th mo.,	"
320. Rachel Garretson,	Little York, Pa.,	5th mo.,	"
321. Rebecca Daniel,	Lampeter, Pa.,	9th mo.,	1825
322. Deborah Conard,	Horsham, Pa.,	12th mo.,	"

STUDENTS.

THIRD THOUSAND.

NAME.	RESIDENCE.	DATE OF ENTRY.
323. Lydia Walton,	Byberry, Pa.,	12th mo., 1825.
324. Rebecca Clement,	Haddonfield, N. J.,	1st mo., 1826.
325. Mary Wood,	Philadelphia, Pa.,	11th mo., 1825.
326. Mary Foulke,	Richland, Pa.,	12th mo., "
327. Louisa Gatchel,	Philadelphia, Pa.,	11th mo., "
328. Eleanor Shotwell,	Rahway, N. J.,	" "
329. Sarah Comly,	Byberry, Pa.,	12th mo., "
330. Sarah S. Knight,	"	" "
331. Rebecca Biddle,	Philadelphia, Pa.,	" "
332. Martha H. Garrett,	"	" "
333. Mary L. Bonner,	Byberry, Pa.,	1st mo., 1826.
334. Lydia A. Walton,	"	" "
335. Anna M. Matlack,	Baltimore, Md.,	12th mo., 1825.
336. Phebe Ann Starr,	"	" "
337. Cath. Butterworth,	Mt. Holly, N. J.,	5th mo., 1826.
338. Eliz. H. Jackson,	Darby, Pa.,	" "
339. Sarah White,	Philadelphia, Pa.,	3d mo., "
340. Mary Ann Edwards,	"	5th mo., "
341. Margaret H. Eastlack,	Haddonfield, N. J.,	4th mo., "
342. Hannah Townsend,	Philadelphia, Pa.,	" "
343. Ann J. Foulke,	Gwynedd, Pa.,	5th mo., "
344. Sarah Gest,	Philadelphia, Pa.,	3d mo., "
345. Ellen Oliver,	Milford, Del.,	4th mo., "
346. Mary E. Oliphant,	Tuckerton, N. J.,	" "
347. Martha Comstock,	New York, N. Y.,	" "
348. Eliz. A. Comstock,	"	" "
349. Anna Mott,	Philadelphia, Pa.,	5th mo., "
350. Phebe Darlington,	East Bradford, Pa.,	" "
351. Margaret Husband,	Deer Creek, Md.,	3d mo., "
352. Ann Owen,	Lampeter, Pa.,	4th mo., "
353. Sarah Comly,	....	5th mo., "
354. Susan Worthington,	Deer Creek, Md.,	6th mo., "
355. Ann Phillips,	Wilmington, Del.,	9th mo., "
356. Eliz. K. Meredith,	East Nantmeal, Pa.,	10th mo., "
357. Mary Marshall,	E. Marlborough, Pa.,	5th mo., "
358. Elizabeth Jones,	Philadelphia, Pa.,	" "
359. Deborah Ferris,	Wilmington, Del.,	" "
361. Ann Walmsley,	Byberry, Pa.,	" "
362. Elizabeth Thornton,	"	" "
363. Martha Foulke,	Richland, Pa.,	" "
364. Mary H. Shoemaker,	Philadelphia, Pa.,	4th mo., "
365. Charlotte Pharo,	Barnegat, N. J.,	" 1827
366. Martha Biddle,	Philadelphia, Pa.,	5th mo., 1826
367. Rebecca Lippincott,	Westfield, N. J.,	" "
368. Elizabeth T. Green,	Richland, Pa.,	" "
369. Mary L. Davies,	Reading, Pa.,	" "
370. Eliz. Cunningham,	West Bradford, Pa.,	" "

21*

THIRD THOUSAND.

NAME.	RESIDENCE.	DATE OF ENTRY.	
371. Lydia D. Crawford,	Newtown, Pa.,	11th mo.,	1826
372. Rachel Jones,	East Bradford, Pa.,	2d mo.,	1827.
373. Ann Sykes,	Springfield, N. J.,	11th mo.,	1826.
374. Anna Marsh,	Concord, Pa.,	"	"
375. Margaret Evans,	Lampeter, Pa.,	10th mo.,	"
376. Hannah Warner,	Harford, Md.,	11th mo.,	"
377. Eliza Townsend,	New Garden, Pa.,	"	"
378. Elizabeth M. Hewes,	Baltimore, Md.,	10th mo.,	"
379. Anna Evans,	"	"	"
380. Hannah Lamborn,	New Garden, Pa.,	"	"
381. Mary Yarnall,	Frankford, Pa.,	5th mo.,	"
382. Susan Hunt,	Bordentown, N. J.,	"	"
383. Maria H. Harrison,	Upper Freehold, N. J.,	"	"
384. Hannah H. Mason,	Salem, N. J.,	"	1827.
385. Elizabeth Comfort,	Solesbury, Pa.,	6th mo.,	1826.
386. Maria Woodward,	Upper Freehold, N. J.,	"	"
387. Ann Penrose,	Horsham, Pa.,	8th mo.,	"
388. Deborah Craft,	Burlington, N. J.,	"	"
389. Martha S. Ecroyd,	Muncy, Pa.,	"	"
390. Phebe Ann Paxson,	Newtown, Pa.,	10th mo.,	"
391. Ann Pancoast,	Springfield, N. J.,	9th mo.,	"
392. Susan Shaw,	Philadelphia, Pa.,	"	"
393. Mary Kirkbride,	Fallsington, Pa.,	11th mo.,	"
394. Dinah Kinsey,	Frankford, Pa.,	10th mo.,	"
395. Mary Ann Mather,	Abington, Pa.,	"	"
396. Rachel Williams,	"	"	"
398. Miriam Lippincott,	Westfield, N. J.,	11th mo.,	"
399. Mary Ann Tyson,	Abington, Pa.,	"	"
400. Marg't M. Chambers,	New Garden, Pa.,	"	"
401. Elizabeth Sharpless,	Goshen, Pa.,	11th mo.,	"
402. Mary Messick,	Smyrna, Del.,	4th mo.,	1827.
403. Jane B. Bradshaw,	Baltimore, Md.,	12th mo.,	1826.
404. Sarah Smith,	Washington Co., Pa.,	"	"
405. Ann Matthews,	Baltimore, Md.,	"	"
406. Jane Comfort,	Byberry, Pa.,	5th mo.,	1828.
407. Susanna C. Marshall,	Concord, Pa.,	"	1827.
408. Ann Pusey,	London Grove, Pa.,	4th mo.,	"
409. Lydia A. Grave,	Centre, Del.,	3d mo.,	"
410. Melinda Woodward,	West Bradford, Pa.,	4th mo.,	"
411. Elizabeth Hallowell,	Abington, Pa.,	11th mo.,	1826.
412. Sarah Garrigues,	Merion, Pa.,	"	"
413. Martha Williams,	Plymouth, Pa.,	12th mo.,	"
414. Mary Logan,	Philadelphia, Pa.,	"	"
415. Margaret Jarrett,	Horsham, Pa.,	1st mo.,	1827.
417. Margaret M. Corlies,	———, N. Y.,	4th mo.,	"
418. Mary Hodgson,	Philadelphia, Pa.,	3d mo.,	"
419. Ann Cooper,	Salem, N. J.,	4th mo.,	"

STUDENTS. 273

THIRD THOUSAND.

NAME.	RESIDENCE.	DATE OF ENTRY.
420. Sarah Valentine,	East Caln, Pa.,	4th mo., 1827.
421. Hannah H. Webb,	Pennsbury, Pa.,	12th mo., "
422. Lydia Pierce,	East Caln, Pa.,	4th mo., "
423. Mary C. Wilson,	Cantwell's Bridge, Del.,	" "
424. Ann Parke,	Downingtown, Pa.,	3d mo., "
425. Elizabeth Edge,	"	" "
426. Susanna Evans,	Baltimore, Md.,	4th mo., "
427. Eliza Jane Register,	"	" "
428. Rachel Brookes,	"	" "
429. Sarah Ann Hewes,	Concord, Pa.,	5th mo., "
430. Eliza Lewis,	Newtown, Pa.,	6th mo., "
431. Elizabeth Spencer,	Horsham, Pa.,	4th mo., "
432. Ruth Pyle,	London Grove, Pa.,	" "
433. Hannah Wilkinson,	"	" "
434. P. Worthington,	Deer Creek, Md.,	" "
435. Hannah Pyle,	W. Marlborough, Pa.,	9th mo., "
436. Alice John,	West Whiteland, Pa.,	7th mo., "
437. Martha Furness,	Little Britain, Pa.,	4th mo., "
438. Lydia Lafetra,	Baltimore, Md.,	" "
439. Sarah Ann Pyle,	Kennet Square, Pa.,	8th mo., 1829.
440. Rebecca Snowdon,	Indian Spring, Va.,	4th mo., 1827.
441. Ann Magill,	London Grove, Pa.,	3d mo., "
442. Mary E. Smith,	Salem, N. J.,	6th mo., "
443. H. A. Woodnutt,	"	5th mo., "
444. Mary Trump,	Bristol, Pa.,	" "
445. Mira Righter,	Plymouth, Pa.,	4th mo., "
446. Rebecca Lancaster,	Philadelphia, Pa.,	5th mo., "
447. Ann L. Stokes,	Rancocas, N. J.,	" "
448. Jane Morris,	Merion, Pa.,	4th mo., "
449. Hannah Pharo,	Barnegat, N. J.,	" "
450. Priscilla Ballenger,	Woodbury, N. J.,	" "
451. Maria Cock,	Brownsville, Pa.,	" "
452. Margaret Hibberd,	Pipe Creek, Md.,	5th mo., "
453. Susanna Haines,	"	" "
454. Hannah Morrison,	Richmond, Ind.,	4th mo., "
455. Lydia T. King,	Springfield, Pa.,	8th mo., "
456. Mary Leeds,	G't Egg Harbor, N. J.,	9th mo., "
457. Edith Sharpless,	Birmingham, Pa.,	6th mo., "
458. Susanna Morthland,	Gunpowder, Md.,	" "
459. Dinah Pierce,	East Caln, Pa.,	" "
460. Ann Sheward,	W. Marlborough, Pa.,	12th mo., "
461. Ruth Eastburn,	Fallsington, Pa.,	5th mo., "
462. Mary Ann Wistar,	Philadelphia, Pa.,	" "
463. Amy Jones,	Newtown, N. J.,	6th mo., "
464. Beulah A. Griscom,	Salem, N. J.,	9th mo., "
465. Rachel Blakey,	Middletown, Pa.,	" "
466. Mary Lippincott,	Mauch Chunk, Pa.,	" "

GENERAL CATALOGUE.

THIRD THOUSAND.

NAME.	RESIDENCE.	DATE OF ENTRY.
467. Sarah Sharp,	Philadelphia, Pa.,	9th mo., 1827.
468. Esther Hunt,	Moorestown, N. J.,	10th mo., "
469. Rebecca Fisher,	Woodbury, N. J.,	2d mo., 1828.
470. Mary Hood,	Londonderry, Pa.,	10th mo., 1827.
471. Elizabeth Baker,	West Bradford, Pa.,	12th mo., "
472. Priscilla E. Yarnall,	Edgmont, Pa.,	10th mo., "
473. Hadassah Townsend,	Baltimore, Md.,	9th mo., "
474. Lydia S. Marsh,	Concord, Pa.,	10th mo., "
475. Margaret Marshall,	"	" "
476. Mary Carpenter,	Westtown, Pa.,	" "
477. Susan Harlan,	Little Falls, Md.,	2d mo., 1828.
478. Abigail Parker,	Mt. Pleasant, Ohio,	10th mo., 1827.
479. Hannah Steer,	"	" "
480. Sarah Ann Fell,	Ellicott's Mills, Md.,	11th mo., "
481. Elizabeth B. Cock,	Brownsville, Pa.,	12th mo., "
482. Caroline Phillips,	Hockessing, Del.,	1st mo., 1828.
483. Jane Kinsey,	"	" "
484. Ann M. Reynolds,	W. Nottingham, Md.,	12th mo., 1827.
485. Mary Hoopes,	West Chester, Pa.,	" "
486. Emma Seal,	E. Marlborough, Pa.,	" "
487. Ann G. Pennell,	Concord, Pa.,	" "
488. Rebecca Harlan,	Doe Run, Pa.,	1st mo., 1828.
489. Ruth Brinton,	West Chester, Pa.,	12th mo., 1827.
490. Hannah P. Allen,	Mannington, N. J.,	10th mo., "
491. Sarah H. Wood,	Philadelphia, Pa.,	11th mo., "
492. Elizabeth Shreeve,	Springfield, N. J.,	12th mo., "
493. Rebecca A. White,	Philadelphia, Pa.,	11th mo., "
494. Gulielma Garrett,	Upper Darby, Pa.,	12th mo., "
495. Lydia P. Garrett,	"	" "
496. H. M. Lightfoot,	Nantmeal, Pa.,	
497. Rebecca Haines,	....	11th mo., 1830.
499. Beulah Newbold,	Frankford, Pa.,	5th mo., 1828.
500. Hannah Woolman,	Darby, Pa.,	12th mo., 1827.
501. Maria Conard,	Egg Harbor, N. J.,	2d mo., 1828.
502. Mary Ann Walker,	Mt. Pleasant, Ohio,	5th mo., "
503. Mary Darlington,	East Bradford, Pa.,	" "
504. Deborah Cope,	"	" "
505. Susan Coale,	Deer Creek, Md.,	" "
506. Elizabeth A. Newlin,	Providence, Pa.,	6th mo., "
507. Hannah Corson,	Plymouth, Pa.,	5th mo., "
508. Ann Jefferis,	East Bradford, Pa.,	" "
509. Hannah Sharpless,	Birmingham, Pa.,	8th mo., "
510. Mary Eldridge,	East Goshen, Pa.,	" "
511. Abigail Evans,	Philadelphia, Pa.,	3d mo., "
512. Sarah Jones,	Cheltenham, Pa.,	5th mo., "
513. Jane Jones,	"	" "
514. Anna Shoemaker,	"	" "

STUDENTS.

THIRD THOUSAND.

NAME.	RESIDENCE.	DATE OF ENTRY.
515. Amy Haines,	Evesham, N. J.,	5th mo., 1828.
516. Martha Warrington,	Moorestown, N. J.,	" "
517. Rebecca Kite,	Philadelphia, Pa.,	" "
518. Ruth Ann Spencer,	Horsham, Pa.,	" "
519. Hannah Acton,	Salem, N. J.,	4th mo., "
520. M. Cowperthwaite,	Upper Evesham, N. J.,	5th mo., "
521. Martha Smith,	Chester, Pa.,	" "
522. Sarah Rhoads,	Blockley, Pa.,	" "
523. Rachel P. Townsend,	West Chester, Pa.,	9th mo., "
524. Sarah Hoopes,	"	5th mo., 1829.
525. Philena Griest,	Little Britain, Pa.,	9th mo., 1828.
526. Lydia Chambers,	New Garden, Pa.,	10th mo., "
527. Sarah S. Garrett,	Wilmington, Del.,	" "
528. Joanna R. Taylor,	New Garden, Pa.,	12th mo., "
529. Esther Bancroft,	Providence, Pa.,	" "
530. Martha Bancroft,	"	" "
531. Sarah Williams,	Plymouth, Pa.,	" "
532. Philena P. Swayne,	East Bradford, Pa.,	4th mo., 1829.
533. Anna Garrett,	Philadelphia, Pa.,	6th mo., 1828.
534. Hannah W. Buzby,	Burlington, N. J.,	" "
536. Elizabeth Stokes,	Evesham, N. J.,	9th mo., "
537. Grace A. Lippincott,	Greenwich, N. J.,	10th mo., "
538. Susan Folwell,	Allentown, Pa.,	11th mo., "
539. Hannah Neeld,	Middletown, Pa.,	" "
540. Tabitha Jenkins,	Darby, Pa.,	1st mo., 1829.
541. Eliza Jones,	Newtown, N. J.,	10th mo., 1828.
542. Elizabeth Eastlack,	Haddonfield, N. J.,	" "
543. Rebecca Evans,	Evesham, N. J.,	" "
544. Mary Atkinson,	"	" "
545. Rebecca Burton,	Little Creek, Del.,	11th mo., "
546. Elizabeth Cowgill,	Chester, Pa.,	" "
547. Mary M. Howell,	Middletown, Pa.,	12th mo., "
548. Lucy Page,	Moorestown, N. J.,	11th mo., "
549. Charlotte Brown,	Fallsington, Pa.,	" "
550. Lydia Sharpless,	Chester, Pa.,	" "
551. Sarah Powell,	"	" "
552. Mary Buffington,	Middletown, Pa.,	4th mo., 1829.
553. Ruth Anna Needles,	Baltimore, Md.,	11th mo., 1828.
554. Mary Richardson,	Wilmington, Del.,	1st mo., 1829.
555. Sarah T. Richardson,	"	" "
556. Hannah Forsythe,	Goshen, Pa.,	5th mo., "
557. Susanna Forsythe,	East Bradford, Pa.,	" "
558. Margaret Daniel,	Lampeter, Pa.,	4th mo., "
559. Ann Evans,	"	11th mo., "
560. Mary Ann Fulton,	Philadelphia, Pa.,	" 1828.
561. Charlotte W. Atlee,	"	12th mo., "
562. Emily Balderston,	Baltimore, Md.,	11th mo., "

THIRD THOUSAND.

NAME.	RESIDENCE.	DATE OF ENTRY.
563. Mary D. Cox,	Philadelphia, Pa.,	1st mo., 1829.
564. Han. F. Randolph,	"	3d mo., "
565. Marg. Shoemaker,	Cheltenham, Pa.,	" "
566. Lydia Stokes,	Evesham, N. J.,	5th mo., "
567. Agnes Page,	"	" "
568. Sarah Sheppard,	Greenwich, N. J.,	4th mo., "
569. Margaret Lowry,	Philadelphia, Pa.,	" "
570. Martha N. Jenkins,	Darby, Pa.,	5th mo., "
571. Martha Evans,	Evesham, N. J.,	" "
573. Mercy W. Ridgway,	Tuckerton, N. J.,	7th mo., "
574. Sarah Wistar,	Salem, N. J.,	4th mo., "
575. Mary N. Borton,	Evesham, N. J.,	" "
576. Rebecca Hughes,	London Grove, Pa.,	6th mo., "
577. Margaret Hughes,	"	" "
578. Sarah H. Brian,	Wilmington, Del.,	" "
579. Margaret Mercer,	Sadsbury, Pa.,	10th mo., "
580. Deborah Daniel,	Lampeter, Pa.,	12th mo., "
581. Eliza Thomas,	Willistown, Pa.,	" "
582. Lydia Ann Needles,	Easton, Md.,	4th mo., "
583. Ruth Ann Dawson,	"	" "
584. Martha E. Atkinson,	"	" "
585. Mary Hance,	Chichester, Pa.,	12th mo., "
586. Mary Neal,	Easton, Md.,	8th mo., "
587. Lucy Smith,	Philadelphia, Pa.,	5th mo., "
588. Mary S. Boone,	Georgetown, D. C.,	" "
589. Lydia Lippincott,	Westfield, N. J.,	6th mo., "
590. Lydia Warrington,	"	" "
591. Anna Sharpless,	Philadelphia, Pa.,	5th mo., "
592. Lydia J. Sharpless,	"	" "
593. Elizabeth Dolby,	"	7th mo., "
594. Margaret W. Miller,	"	6th mo., "
595. Mary Craft,	Upper Freehold, N. J.,	10th mo., "
596. Julia Welding,	Frankford, Pa.,	" "
598. S. M. Shoemaker,	Abington, Pa.,	11th mo., "
599. R. Deprefontaine,	Germantown, Pa.,	9th mo., "
600. Elizabeth Couplin,	Darby, Pa.,	10th mo., "
601. Hannah Ecroyd,	Muncy, Pa.,	9th mo., 1830.
602. Martha Ecroyd,	"	" "
603. Jane Boustead,	Philadelphia, Pa.,	10th mo., 1829.
604. Amy Eastlack,	Woodbury, N. J.,	12th mo., 1830.
605. Hannah Allen,	Philadelphia, Pa.,	10th mo., 1829.
606. Rebecca Price,	"	12th mo., 1830.
607. Priscilla A. Lukens,	Burlington, N. J.,	" "
608. Hannah E. Moore,	Evesham, N. J.,	" "
609. Cath. S. Shotwell,	Philadelphia, Pa.,	11th mo., "
610. Jane Lafetra,	Baltimore, Md.,	" "
611. Catharine Sharpless,	Downingtown, Pa.,	5th mo., "

STUDENTS.

THIRD THOUSAND.

NAME.	RESIDENCE.	DATE OF ENTRY.
612. Sarah Corson,	Plymouth, Pa.,	4th mo., 1830.
613. Lydia Evans,	Waynesville, Ohio,	" "
614. Fanny Edge,	Downingtown, Pa.,	5th mo., "
615. Ruth Anna Edge,	"	" "
616. Lydia Gibbons,	Lampeter, Pa.,	" "
617. Hannah Palmer,	Concord, Pa.,	" "
618. Elizabeth E. Horne,	Goshen, Pa.,	" "
619. Catharine Morris,	Salem, Ind.,	" "
620. Sarah Larkin,	Chichester, Pa.	6th mo., "
621. Ann Evans,	Springfield, Pa.,	11th mo., 1829.
622. Hannah Cooper,	Woodbury, N. J.,	12th mo., "
623. Sarah Wilkins,	Evesham, N. J.,	— "
624. Sarah Ann Engle,	"	" "
625. Esther T. Engle,	"	" "
626. Sarah C. Engle,	"	" "
627. Lydia Williams,	Plymouth, Pa.,	3d mo., 1830.
628. Sarah C. Paul,	Woodbury, N. J.,	4th mo., "
629. Hannah Saunders,	"	" "
630. Margaret Williams,	Philadelphia, Pa.,	" "
631. Sarah Allen,	"	" "
632. Sarah Balderston,	Solesbury, Pa.,	" "
633. Sarah Ann Fell,	Buckingham, Pa.,	" "
634. Hannah Edge,	Downingtown, Pa.,	5th mo., "
635. Mary Parke,	"	" "
636. Ellen Spencer,	Horsham, Pa.,	" "
637. Martha Comfort,	Byberry, Pa.,	7th mo., "
639. Beulah Lippincott,	Greenwich, N. J.,	5th mo., "
640. Hannah Smart,	Salem, N. J.,	" "
641. Sarah Scattergood,	Philadelphia, Pa.,	" "
642. Lydia Ann Welding,	Stroudsburg, Pa.,	" "
643. Susan Welding,	"	" "
644. Lavinia Maule,	Philadelphia, Pa.,	" "
645. Lydia N. Price,	"	" "
646. Ann Thompson,	Salem, N. J.,	6th mo., "
647. Sarah Waln,	Springfield, N. J.,	" "
648. Anna Walmsley,	Byberry, Pa.,	7th mo., "
649. Sarah R. Coates,	Philadelphia, Pa.,	5th mo., "
650. Lucy Conard,	"	6th mo., "
651. Mary H. Matlack,	"	" "
652. Elizabeth Smith,	"	5th mo., "
653. Rebecca Sheppard,	"	6th mo., "
654. S. A. Cowperthwaite,	Moorestown, N. J.,	" "
655. Ann Jess,	Philadelphia, Pa.,	" "
656. Eliz. M. Heacock,	Abington, Pa.,	" "
658. Cath. F. Gatchel,	Philadelphia, Pa.,	" "
659. Phebe Kimber,	"	" "
660. Sarah Thomas,	Chichester, Pa.,	11th mo., "

GENERAL CATALOGUE.

THIRD THOUSAND.

NAME.	RESIDENCE.	DATE OF ENTRY.
661. Mary Ann Hoopes,	Birmingham, Pa.,	8th mo., 1830.
662. Rebecca H. Hubbs,	Pilesgrove, N. J.,	7th mo., "
663. Mary Kirkwood,	Columbia, Pa.,	10th mo., "
664. Mary Dent,	Westtown, Pa.,	9th mo., "
665. Esther P. Jones,	East Bradford, Pa.,	10th mo., "
666. Hannah M. Lindley,	Perry Co., Pa.,	" "
667. Mary James,	East Bradford, Pa.,	" "
668. Eliz. D. Lindley,	Perry Co., Pa.,	" "
669. Hannah Maris,	Chester, Pa.,	" "
670. Mary Sharpless,	"	" "
671. Mary Coates,	Philadelphia, Pa.,	7th mo., "
672. Beulah Reeve,	Woodbury, N. J.,	" "
673. Elizabeth B. Jones,	Upper Merion, Pa.,	" "
674. Mary Ann Watson,	Upper Dublin, Pa.,	" "
675. Catharine M. Lea,	Philadelphia, Pa.,	" "
676. Mary Evans,	Evesham, N. J.,	9th mo., "
677. Rebecca Glover,	"	10th mo., "
678. Mary W. Dixon,	Philadelphia, Pa.,	" "
679. Mary W. Cresson,	"	" "
680. Alice Comfort,	Plymouth, Pa.,	" "
681. Susanna H. Garrett,	Philadelphia, Pa.,	9th mo., "
682. Ann Eliza Sloan,	Tuckerton, N. J.,	" "
683. Lydia Smith,	Chester, Pa.,	10th mo., "
684. Sidney Sharpless,	"	" "
685. Sarah Paxson,	"	" "
686. Martha Roberts,	Moorestown, N. J.,	" "
687. Elizabeth Garrett,	Darby, Pa.,	" "
688. Amy Ann Thomas,	"	" "
689. Deborah Hunt,	Evesham, N. J.,	4th mo., 1832.
690. Sarah Davis,	West Bradford, Pa.,	10th mo., 1830.
691. Jane Garrett,	Willistown, Pa.,	9th mo., "
692. Thomazin Valentine,	Uwchlan, Pa.,	" "
693. Lydia A. Baily,	W. Marlborough, Pa.,	" "
694. Sarah Pennell,	Concord, Pa.,	" "
695. Rachel Garrett,	Willistown, Pa.,	" "
696. Deborah Davis,	West Bradford, Pa.,	10th mo., "
697. Frances C. Morton,	Wilmington, Del.,	" "
698. Mary F. Clement,	"	" "
700. Malvina Register,	Smyrna, Del.,	11th mo., "
701. Mercy Buckman,	Newtown, Pa.,	" "
702. Susanna Buckman,	"	" "
703. Esther Evans,	Muncy, Pa.,	" "
704. Ruth Anna Paxson,	Frankford, Pa.,	10th mo., "
705. Sarah Healy,	Fallsington, Pa.,	11th mo., "
706. Anna Nicholson,	Philadelphia, Pa.,	12th mo., "
707. Hannah Spencer,	Horsham, Pa.,	10th mo., "
708. Hannah Richie,	Philadelphia, Pa.,	" "

STUDENTS. 279

THIRD THOUSAND.

NAME.	RESIDENCE.	DATE OF ENTRY.
709. Sarah Scull,	Woodstown, N. J.,	10th mo., 1830.
710. Mary Emlen,	Middletown, Pa.,	" "
711. Mary Ann Pratt,	Newtown, Pa.,	" "
712. Amy S. Pierce,	Providence, Pa.,	" "
713. Susanna Sharpless,	Goshen, Pa.,	" "
714. Elizabeth Pusey,	Sadsbury, Pa.,	3d mo., 1831.
715. Mary Woolman,	Darby, Pa.,	10th mo., 1830.
716. Mary Sharpless,	New Garden, Pa.,	12th mo., "
717. Priscilla White,	Perquimans Co., N. C.,	9th mo., "
718. Rebecca Taylor,	Pennsbury, Pa.,	" "
719. Gulielma M. Thomas,	East Goshen, Pa.,	- 10th mo., "
720. Henrietta G. Levis,	Darby, Pa.,	" "
721. Rachel Eastburn,	Solesbury, Pa.,	11th mo., "
722. Eliz. W. Lukens,	Coatesville, Pa.,	" "
723. Mary Snowdon,	Philadelphia, Pa.,	" "
724. Mary Yerkes,	Plymouth, Pa.,	" "
725. Mary Troth,	Haddonfield, N. J.,	" "
726. Phebe Ann Heston,	Fallsington, Pa.,	" "
727. Hannah Lloyd,	Philadelphia, Pa.,	" "
728. Margaret Jones,	"	5th mo., 1831.
729. Eliza C. Atkinson,	Trenton, N. J.,	10th mo., 1830.
730. Mary Ann Comfort,	Middletown, Pa.,	11th mo., "
731. Phebe Sharpless,	Goshen, Pa.,	10th mo., "
732. Sibilla P. Entriken,	Chester Co., Pa.,	12th mo., "
733. Ann J. Lamborn,	West Bradford, Pa.,	5th mo., 1831.
734. Lydia Woodward,	"	" "
735. Anne Hill,	Trenton, N. J.,	3d mo., "
736. Elizabeth Hunt,	Downingtown, Pa.,	" "
737. Eliza Wilson,	Spring Mill, Md.,	4th mo., "
738. Jane Craft,	Crosswicks, N. J.,	9th mo., "
739. Sarah M. Taylor,	"	" "
740. Alice Welding,	Stroudsburg, Pa.,	4th mo., "
741. Deborah Cox,	Philadelphia, Pa.,	12th mo., 1830.
742. Lydia Conard,	Horsham, Pa.,	3d mo., 1831.
743. Rebecca Y. Conard,	"	" "
744. Elizabeth Price,	Philadelphia, Pa.,	5th mo., 1832.
745. Lydia Abbott,	Salem, N. J.,	3d mo., 1831.
746. Deborah Clark,	Woodbury, N. J.,	4th mo., "
747. Sarah E. Morris,	Wellsborough, Pa.,	" "
748. Sarah H. Deacon,	Mt. Holly, N. J.,	" "
749. Eliz. R. Lippincott,	Westfield, N. J.,	6th mo., "
750. Margaret Wendell,	Frankford, Pa.,	5th mo., "
751. Elizabeth Dillon,	Plymouth, Pa.,	4th mo., "
752. Eliza Jane Cotant,	Stroudsburg, Pa.,	5th mo., "
753. Sarah Lippincott,	Haddonfield, N. J.,	3d mo., "
754. Mary Scull,	Woodstown, N. J.,	5th mo., "
755. Martha W. Haydock,	Philadelphia, Pa.,	4th mo., "

22

280　　　GENERAL CATALOGUE.

THIRD THOUSAND.

NAME.	RESIDENCE.	DATE OF ENTRY.
756. Sarah Mickle,	Woodbury, N. J.,	4th mo., 1831.
757. Mary E. Thomas,	Philadelphia, Pa.,	5th mo., "
758. Margaret Taylor,	Mt. Holly, N. J.,	3d mo., "
759. Hannah Taylor,	"	" "
760. Caroline T. Vail,	Plainfield, N. J.,	4th mo., "
761. Ruth Anna Taylor,	New Garden, Pa.,	" "
762. Martha E. Wilson,	Spring Mill, Md.,	" "
763. Sarah Ann Starr,	Bradford, Pa.,	5th mo., "
764. Ann Painter,	Middletown, Pa.,	3d mo., "
765. Juliana Saul,	Appoquinnimink, Del.,	7th mo., "
766. Susanna P. Baily,	Pennsbury, Pa.,	6th mo., "
767. Lydia Yearsley,	*Wagontown, Pa.,	8th mo., "
768. Mary Walker,	Mill Creek, Del.,	" "
769. Ruth W. Pennock,	Marlborough, Pa.,	11th mo., "
770. Phebe Emlen,	Middletown, Pa.,	7th mo., "
771. Hannah Alsop,	Philadelphia, Pa.,	5th mo., "
772. Rebecca S. Leeds,	G't Egg Harbor, N. J.,	3d mo., "
773. Catharine Vail,	Plainfield, N. J.,	4th mo., "
774. Beulah Townsend,	Philadelphia, Pa.,	5th mo., "
775. Mary Ann Bellangee,	"	" "
776. Ann Kirkbride,	Fallsington, Pa.,	" "
777. Elizabeth Kirkbride,	"	" "
778. Jane W. Edwards,	Muncy, Pa.,	4th mo., "
779. Jane B. Temple,	Philadelphia, Pa.,	5th mo., "
780. Massey Lownes,	Springfield, Pa.,	11th mo., "
781. Frances Gibbons,	Lampeter, Pa.,	4th mo., 1832.
782. Hannah Yarnall,	Edgmont, Pa.,	6th mo., "
783. Mary Ann Phillips,	Hockessing, Del.,	11th mo., 1831.
784. Mary Hunt,	Downingtown, Pa.,	12th mo., "
785. Mary Cox,	Kennet, Pa.,	" "
786. Sarah B. Pierce,	Concord, Pa.,	2d mo., 1832.
787. Susanna Mickle,	Sadsbury, Pa.,	5th mo., "
788. Elizabeth Hoopes,	New Garden, Pa.,	7th mo., "
789. Jane Harper,	Philadelphia, Pa.,	9th mo., 1831.
790. Susanna Pennell,	Concord, Pa.,	4th mo., 1832.
791. Mary S. Lippincott,	Philadelphia, Pa.,	5th mo., 1831.
792. Mary Newlin,	"	10th mo., "
793. Mary Maris,	New Hope, Pa.,	6th mo., "
794. Deborah C. Evans,	Evesham, N. J.,	9th mo., "
795. Sarah E. Roberts,	"	" "
796. Susanna Evans,	"	" "
797. Naomi Borton,	"	" "
798. Mary Bishop,	Burlington, N. J.,	" "
799. Sidney Stevenson,	Kingwood, N. J.,	4th mo., 1832.
800. Rebecca Rhoads,	Pottsville, Pa.,	10th mo., 1831.
801. Mary Ann Engle,	Evesham, N. J.,	9th mo., "
802. Lydia Saunders,	"	" "

STUDENTS.

THIRD THOUSAND.

NAME.	RESIDENCE.	DATE OF ENTRY.
803. Eliza P. Worrall,	Providence, Pa.,	10th mo., 1831.
804. Sarah Cresson,	Philadelphia, Pa.,	4th mo., 1832.
805. Phebe W. Heacock,	Plymouth, Pa.,	10th mo., 1831.
806. Ann Middleton,	Philadelphia, Pa.,	11th mo., "
807. Margaret A. Haney,	"	" "
808. Mary Fitzwater,	Plymouth, Pa.,	4th mo., "
809. Hannah S. Atherton,	Bethlehem, Pa.,	7th mo., "
810. Mary C. Matlack,	Moorestown, N. J.,	6th mo., "
811. Rachel S. Vail,	Plainfield, N. J.,	4th mo., 1832.
812. Mary E. Suiggett,	Cantwell's Bridge, Del.,	" 1831.
813. Phebe Way,	Kennet, Pa.,	10th mo., "
814. Mary Ann Ogden,	Woodbury, N. J.,	12th mo., "
815. Amy Chambers,	New Garden, Pa.,	10th mo., "
816. Mary Evans,	Lampeter, Pa.,	11th mo., "
817. Lydia A. Pratt,	Newtown, Pa.,	" "
818. Elizabeth Tatum,	Woodbury, N. J.,	9th mo., "
819. Rebecca Pierce,	Kennet, Pa.,	11th mo., "
820. R. A. Pennington,	Sadsbury, Pa.,	" "
821. Sarah Ann Sleeper,	Philadelphia, Pa.,	10th mo., "
823. Elizabeth H. Sloan,	Burlington, N. J.,	" "
824. Catharine Thorn,	Philadelphia, Pa.,	" "
825. Ellen J. Parker,	"	7th mo., 1832.
826. Mary Shaw,	Buckingham, Pa.,	11th mo., 1831.
827. Jane Bell,	Philadelphia, Pa.,	10th mo., "
828. Mary H. Chrisman,	Exeter, Pa.,	" "
829. Mary Ballangee,	Bordentown, N. J.,	" "
830. Eliza Ann Emlen,	Philadelphia, Pa.,	" "
831. Elizabeth Bell,	Plymouth, Pa.,	" "
832. Hannah Livezey,	Whitemarsh, Pa.,	
833. Elizabeth Watson,	Abington, Pa.,	5th mo., 1832.
835. Phebe S. Sinton,	Easton, Pa.,	10th mo., 1831.
836. Mary Sinton,	"	" "
837. Sally A. B. Sinton,	"	" "
838. Ann S. Woolston,	Fallsington, Pa.,	11th mo., "
839. Rebecca Moon,	Philadelphia, Pa.,	12th mo., "
840. Sarah Baily,	Pennsbury, Pa.,	9th mo., 1832.
841. Frances L. Clement,	Wilmington, Del.,	7th mo., 1831.
842. Isabella Ladd,	Jefferson Co., Ohio,	" "
843. Deborah Bates,	"	" "
844. Rebecca Allen,	Salem, N. J.,	4th mo., 1832.
845. Sarah Richardson,	Wilmington, Del.,	" "
846. Deborah D. Suiggett,	Dover, Del.,	5th mo., "
847. Esther James,	East Bradford, Pa.,	" "
848. Mary Ann Chambers,	New Garden, Pa.,	" 1833.
849. Lydia Phillips,	"	" "
850. Sarah Forsythe,	West Goshen, Pa.,	11th mo., 1832.
851. Rebecca Ogden,	Port Elizabeth, N. J.,	5th mo., "

THIRD THOUSAND.

NAME.	RESIDENCE.	DATE OF ENTRY.
852. Mary Yarnall,	Philadelphia, Pa.,	5th mo., 1832.
853. Sarah Jennings,	Haddonfield, N. J.,	" "
854. Martha P. Williams,	Blockley, Pa.,	" "
855. Jane Livezey,	Whitemarsh, Pa.,	" "
856. Elizabeth Marshall,	Philadelphia, Pa.,	" "
857. Phebe Marshall,	"	" "
858. Mary Gummere,	Haverford, Pa.,	4th mo., 1834.
859. Sarah Harman,	Smyrna, Del.,	5th mo., 1832.
860. Ann M. Lowry,	Philadelphia, Pa.,	" "
861. Rebecca Cope,	"	" "
862. Edith Craft,	Crosswicks, N. J.,	9th mo., 1833.
863. Elizabeth Willits,	Philadelphia, Pa.,	3d mo., 1832.
864. Mercy Ann Ellis,	Muncy, Pa.,	11th mo., "
865. Francinia Ely,	Buckingham, Pa.,	5th mo., "
866. Mary Humphreys,	Philadelphia, Pa.,	" "
867. Louisa P. Michener,	Penn, Pa.,	10th mo., "
868. Elizabeth Hunn,	Camden, Del.,	5th mo., "
869. Louisa Willits,	Philadelphia, Pa.,	" "
870. Anna Smedley,	Little Britain, Pa.,	11th mo., 1833.
871. Hannah Sharpless,	Concord, Pa.,	" 1832.
872. Elizabeth Sharpless,	"	" "
873. Mary Hicks,	London Grove, Pa.,	10th mo., "
874. Elizabeth Lamborn,	New Garden, Pa.,	9th mo., "
875. Mary Warrington,	Westfield, N. J.,	10th mo., "
876. Margaret Alexander,	Fallsington, Pa.,	4th mo., "
877. Rebecca L. Hayes,	Fallowfield, Pa.,	1st mo., 1833.
878. Sarah R. Hallowell,	Wilmington, Del.,	10th mo., 1832.
879. Rebecca P. Hallowell,	"	" "
880. Eliza Painter,	Concord, Pa.,	9th mo., "
881. Rebecca T. West,	Philadelphia, Pa.,	" "
882. Elizabeth C. West,	"	" "
883. Mary T. Smith,	"	11th mo., "
884. Elizabeth Gummere,	Haverford, Pa.,	4th mo., 1834.
885. Teresa J. Kimber,	Philadelphia, Pa.,	10th mo., 1832.
886. Ann Kinsey,	Frankford, Pa.,	11th mo., "
887. Rachel Johnson,	Solesbury, Pa.,	9th mo., "
888. Phebe Roberts,	Moorestown, N. J.,	11th mo., "
889. Martha Nicholson,	Philadelphia, Pa.,	5th mo., "
890. Hannah G. Marsh,	Concord, Pa.,	10th mo., "
891. Susan M. Morris,	Wellsborough, Pa.,	11th mo., "
892. Susan Fulton,	East Fallowfield, Pa.,	" "
893. Esther Roberts,	Moorestown, N. J.,	" "
894. Rachel S. Matlack,	"	" "
895. Jane P. Thompson,	West Chester, Pa.,	4th mo., "
896. Eliza Atkinson,	Easton, Md.,	" 1833.
897. Susanna Kemp,	"	" "
898. Rachel Griscom,	E. Nottingham, Pa.	" 1832.

STUDENTS.

THIRD THOUSAND.

NAME.	RESIDENCE.	DATE OF ENTRY.
899. Hannah Richardson,	Wilmington, Del.,	11th mo., 1832.
900. Mary Edwards,	Westtown, Pa.,	10th mo., "
901. Hannah Spencer,	Horsham, Pa.,	" "
902. Sibilla Spencer,	"	" "
903. Susanna Williams,	Whitpaine, Pa.	" "
904. Ruth Ann Townsend,	Plainfield, N. J.,	11th mo., "
905. Phebe Pharo,	Tuckerton, N. J.,	9th mo., "
906. Eliza Pharo,	"	" "
907. Elizabeth C. Stokes,	Evesham, N. J.,	10th mo., "
908. Susan Edge,	Downingtown, Pa.,	" "
909. Emma Dixon,	Wilmington, Del.,	" "
910. Sarah Pyle,	Hockessing, Del.,	7th mo., "
911. Elizabeth F. Coale,	Sadsbury, Pa.,	4th mo., 1833.
912. Louisa Spencer,	London Grove, Pa.,	11th mo., 1832.
913. Lydia S. Painter,	West Chester, Pa.,	" "
914. Mary D. Thorn,	Fallowfield, Pa,	" "
915. Ann Evans,	Springfield, Pa.,	" "
916. Jane Simmons,	Sadsbury, Pa.,	9th mo., "
917. Albina Bradley,	East Bradford, Pa.,	1st mo., 1834.
918. Ann Harper,	Philadelphia, Pa.,	7th mo., 1832.
919. Eliz. M. Hannum,	Aston, Pa.,	12th mo , "
920. Hannah Wetherill,	Springfield, Pa.,	" "
921. Elizabeth M. Corse,	Wilmington, Del.,	11th mo., "
922. Sarah T. Eachus,	Haverford, Pa.,	" "
923. Mary W. Paxson,	Horsham, Pa.,	" "
924. Deborah Scull,	Woodstown, N. J.,	12th mo., "
925. Beulah Jones,	Camden, N. J.,	11th mo., "
926. Sarah M. Thomas,	Philadelphia, Pa.,	5th mo., 1833.
927. Elizabeth Comfort,	Middletown, Pa.,	11th mo., "
928. Mary L. Newbold,	Springfield, N. J.,	" 1832.
929. Margaret Taylor,	Makefield, Pa.,	" "
930. Margaret Trimble,	Concord, Pa.,	" "
931. Ann B. Lamborn,	Kennet, Pa.,	10th mo., 1833.
932. Sarah Ann Cooper,	Sadsbury, Pa.,	12th mo., 1832.
933. Lydia Edwards,	Westtown, Pa.,	3d mo., 1833.
934. Elizabeth Forsythe,	Birmingham, Pa.,	2d mo., "
935. Susanna Foulke,	Gwynedd, Pa.,	5th mo., "
936. Sarah Moore,	Sadsbury, Pa.,	12th mo., 1832.
937. Susanna M. Thomas,	Abington, Pa.,	" "
938. Juliana Powell,	Easton, Md.,	4th mo., 1833.
939. Mary Willits,	Philadelphia, Pa.,	11th mo., 1832.
940. Grace Worthington,	Cheltenham, Pa.,	10th mo., "
941. Eliz. Y. Stackhouse,	Bristol, Pa.,	5th mo., 1834.
942. Mary W. Bacon,	Greenwich, N. J.,	3d mo., 1833.
943. Mary Allen,	Philadelphia, Pa.,	4th mo., "
944. Rebecca Gaskill,	Burlington, N. J.,	3d mo., "
945. Elizabeth Troth,	Waterford, N. J.,	" "

22*

R

THIRD THOUSAND.

NAME.	RESIDENCE.	DATE OF ENTRY.
946. R. W. Hinchman,	Philadelphia, Pa.,	4th mo., 1833
947. Marg. E. Thatcher,	Springfield, Pa.,	" "
948. Lydia Betts,	Wilmington, Del.,	" "
949. Lydia Gaskill,	Burlington, N. J.,	3d mo., "
950. Priscilla Jones,	New London, Pa.,	12th mo., 1832.
951. Elizabeth S. Ferris,	Wilmington, Del.,	4th mo., 1833.
952. Mary P. Newlin,	Providence, Pa ,	5th mo., "
953. Mary C. Wilson,	Coatesville, Pa.,	6th mo., "
954. Phebe G. Thatcher,	Aston, Pa.,	4th mo., "
955. Sarah Mendenhall,	Kennet, Pa.,	6th mo., "
956. Martha Mendenhall,	"	" "
957. Hannah Matson,	Concord, Pa.,	" "
958. Sarah H. Letchworth,	Philadelphia, Pa.,	9th mo., "
959. Lydia Palmer,	Concord, Pa.,	4th mo., "
960. Beulah Palmer,	"	" "
961. Mary Williams,	Whitpaine, Pa.,	" "
962. Sarah Snowdon,	Philadelphia, Pa.,	12th mo., 1832.
963. Sarah B. Shreeve,	Springfield, N. J.,	4th mo., 1833.
964. Elizabeth Reeve,	Greenwich, N. J.,	3d mo., 1834.
965. Sarah Taylor,	Philadelphia, Pa.,	11th mo., 1832.
966. Ann M. Foulke,	Richland, Pa.,	3d mo., 1833.
967. Letitia Foulke,	"	" "
968. Elizabeth Roberts,	Cropwell, N. J.,	4th mo., "
969. R. C. Gillingham,	Fallsington, Pa.,	12th mo., 1832.
970. Lydia H. Palmer,	Concord, Pa.,	5th mo., 1833.
971. Deborah Wetherill,	Springfield, N. J.,	6th mo., "
972. Caroline Chambers,	White Clay Creek, Del.,	11th mo., "
973. Deborah Cope,	East Bradford, Pa.,	5th mo., "
974. Lydia Taylor,	Lower Makefield, Pa.,	12th mo., "
975. Ann Tatum,	Woodbury, N. J.,	4th mo., "
976. Phebe A. Whitson,	Sadsbury, Pa.,	" "
977. Mary Whitson,	"	1st mo., 1834.
978. Rebecca W. Taylor,	West Chester, Pa.,	10th mo., 1833.
979. Anna Phillips,	Sadsbury, Pa.,	4th mo., 1834.
980. Deborah P. Yarnall,	Edgmont, Pa.,	6th mo., 1833.
981. Sarah Mather,	Gwynedd, Pa.,	10th mo., "
982. Jane Mather,	"	" "
983. Eliz. P. Williams,	Germantown, Pa.,	6th mo., "
984. Chlotilda Cook,	Isle of Wight Co., Va.,	4th mo., 1835.
985. Sarah S. Newlin,	Philadelphia, Pa.,	6th mo., 1833.
986. Rebecca Walton,	"	5th mo., 1834.
987. Rachel M. North,	"	" 1833.
988. Mary H. Bacon,	Greenwich, N. J.,	9th mo., "
989. Hannah Hogeland,	Muncy, Pa.,	8th mo., 1834.
990. Susanna Lightfoot,	Uwchlan, Pa.,	4th mo., 1833.
991. Ruth Anna Gause,	Concord, Pa.,	10th mo., "
992. Eliz. E. Redman,	Haddonfield, N. J.,	11th mo., "

STUDENTS.

THIRD THOUSAND.

NAME.	RESIDENCE.	DATE OF ENTRY.
993. Lydia Eldridge,	Goshen, Pa.,	9th mo., 1833.
994. Emily Evans,	Lampeter, Pa.,	11th mo., "
995. Anna Garrett,	Wilmington, Del.,	4th mo., "
996. Elizabeth Hoopes,	Westtown, Pa.,	3d mo., 1835.
997. Ann Jones,	Valley Forge, Pa.,	12th mo., 1833.
998. Jane Ann Passmore,	London Grove, Pa.,	11th mo., "
999. Naomi Gibbons,	Lampeter, Pa.,	" "
1000. Susanna Magarge,	Germantown, Pa.,	6th mo., 1834.

FOURTH THOUSAND.

NAME.	RESIDENCE.	DATE OF ENTRY.
1. Priscilla Lippincott,	Salem, N. J.,	12th mo., 1833.
2. Amy C. Wills,	Evesham, N. J.,	9th mo., "
3. Ann Williams,	White Marsh, Pa.,	10th mo., "
4. Mary H. Holgate,	Philadelphia, Pa.,	9th mo., "
5. Hannah Battin,	Elkland, Pa.,	8th mo., 1834.
6. Martha Levis,	Springfield, Pa.,	10th mo., 1833.
7. Mary Kirkbride,	Morrisville, Pa.,	" "
8. Gulielma Hilles,	Wilmington, Del.,	4th mo., 1834.
9. Eliz. Kenderdine,	Horsham, Pa.,	12th mo., 1833.
10. Prudence Ferguson,	Philadelphia, Pa.,	3d mo., 1835.
11. Lydia Ann Wood,	London Grove, Pa.	5th mo., 1833.
12. P. Worthington,	Deer Creek, Md.,	11th mo., 1834.
13. Henrietta M. Horne,	Philadelphia, Pa.,	12th mo., 1833.
14. Eliz. Richardson,	Wilmington, Del.,	1st mo., 1834.
15. Emeline Darlington,	Birmingham, Pa.,	6th mo., 1833.
16. Sally Thomas,	Goshen, Pa.,	9th mo., 1834.
17. Elizabeth Baily,	Parkersville, Pa.,	2d mo., "
18. Ann Eliza Powell,	West Chester, Pa.,	12th mo., 1833.
19. Sarah Matson,	Concord, Pa.,	4th mo., 1834.
20. Mary C. Price,	Philadelphia, Pa.,	7th mo., "
21. Rebecca Spencer,	Horsham, Pa.,	11th mo., 1833.
22. Eliza Moon,	Fallsington, Pa.,	10th mo., "
23. Ann Brown,	"	" "
24. Maria Balderston,	"	" "
25. Rachel S. Yarnall,	Edgmont, Pa.,	3d mo., 1834.
26. Mary Merrefield,	Philadelphia, Pa.,	6th mo., 1833.
27. Sarah E. Updegraff,	Mt. Pleasant, Ohio,	7th mo., "
28. Mary Ann Ladd,	"	" "
29. Cath. Van Hoesen,	———, N. Y.,	10th mo., "
30. Caroline R. Maule,	Richmond, Va.,	8th mo., "
31. Margaret J. Maule,	"	" "
32. Elizabeth L. Maule,	"	" "
33. Jane Edge,	Downingtown, Pa.,	12th mo., "
34. Sarah Ann Bates,	Smithfield, Ohio,	7th mo., "
35. Marg. B. Fletcher,	Philadelphia, Pa.,	3d mo., 1834.

FOURTH THOUSAND.

NAME.	RESIDENCE.	DATE OF ENTRY.
36. Agnes Spencer,	Gwynedd, Pa.,	12th mo., 1833.
37. Rachel Wilson,	Ayrestown, N. J.,	5th mo., 1834.
38. Anne Porter,	———, Va.	" "
39. Anna C. Temple,	Philadelphia, Pa.,	4th mo., "
40. Dinah Taylor,	Westtown, Pa.,	3d mo., "
41. Sarah C. Palmer,	Dover, Del.,	5th mo., 1835.
42. Mary E. Haines,	Muncy, Pa.,	1st mo., 1834.
43. Emily Dutton,	Chichester, Pa.,	10th mo., "
44. Eliza W. Bassett,	Moorestown, N. J.,	5th mo., "
45. Sarah Ann Sharpless,	Concord, Pa.,	" "
46. Hannah Eastlack,	Camden, N. J.,	6th mo., "
47. Mary Hill,	....	4th mo., "
48. Mary Ann Spencer,	New London, Pa.,	10th mo., 1835.
49. Deborah Phillips,	Sadsbury, Pa.,	5th mo., 1836.
50. Elizabeth Knight,	Philadelphia, Pa.,	3d mo., 1834.
51. Ruth Anna Moore,	Penningtonville, Pa.,	4th mo., "
52. Mary E. Decou,	Crosswicks, N. J.,	5th mo., "
53. Mary E. Woodward,	"	" "
54. Mary C. Newlin,	Philadelphia, Pa.,	" 1835.
55. Martha N. Reeve,	Medford, N. J.,	" 1834.
56. Mary S. Reeve,	"	" "
57. Charlotte Acton,	Salem, N. J.,	" "
58. Mary Anna West,	Philadelphia, Pa.,	4th mo., "
59. Elizabeth Stackhouse,	"	12th mo., 1833.
60. Rachel Kirkbride,	Morrisville, Pa.,	11th mo., 1834.
61. Mary Rhoads,	Springfield, Pa.,	5th mo., "
62. Elizabeth Webb,	Philadelphia, Pa.,	7th mo., "
63. Elizabeth Shinn,	"	5th mo., "
64. Martha S. Haines,	Evesham, N. J.,	" "
65. Mary Jones,	Newtown, N. J.,	11th mo., "
66. Martha E. Hillman,	Haddonfield, N. J.,	" "
67. Esther S. Hacker,	Philadelphia, Pa.,	5th mo., 1835.
68. Sarah M. Kaighn,	Kaighn's Point, N. J.,	9th mo., 1834.
69. Sarah Ann Haydock,	Philadelphia, Pa.,	5th mo., "
70. Sarah Starr,	Cecil Co., Md.,	10th mo., "
71. Deborah Davis,	Caln, Pa.,	11th mo., "
72. Eliza Ann Hayes,	Philadelphia, Pa.,	8th mo., "
73. Mary R. Richardson,	Wilmington, Del.,	" "
74. Elizabeth Smith,	....	6th mo., "
75. Mary Ann Parsons,	Easton, Md.,	3d mo., "
76. Susan Woolman,	....	5th mo., "
77. Sarah Ann Edge,	Downingtown, Pa.,	11th mo., "
78. Mary Nicholson,	Haddonfield, N. J.,	6th mo., "
79. Sarah P. Wilson,	Philadelphia, Pa.,	3d mo., "
80. Hetty Ann Atkinson,	Easton, Md.,	4th mo., "
81. Martha White,	———, N. C.,	" 1835
82. Hannah L. Brown,	Fallsington, Pa.,	10th mo., 1834.

STUDENTS.

FOURTH THOUSAND.

NAME.	RESIDENCE.	DATE OF ENTRY.
83. Anna W. Hinchman,	Philadelphia, Pa.,	5th mo., 1834.
84. Hannah T. Cook,	London Grove, Pa.,	4th mo., 1844.
85. Frances C. Stokes,	Stroudsburg, Pa.,	6th mo., 1834.
86. Angeline Lee,	Exeter, Pa.,	4th mo., 1835.
87. Elizabeth D. Stroud,	Stroudsburg, Pa.,	6th mo., 1834.
88. Lydia B. Stroud,	"	" "
89. Sarah Page,	Philadelphia, Pa.,	5th mo., 1835.
90. Rebecca B. Matlack,	"	8th mo., 1834.
91. Sarah Hood,	Doe Run, Pa.,	10th mo., "
92. Hannah Newlin,	Middletown, Pa.,	" "
93. Hannah Wiley,	Sadsbury, Pa.,	5th mo., "
94. Sarah A. Longstreth,	Goshen, Pa.,	11th mo., "
95. Mary Smith,	Philadelphia, Pa.,	6th mo., 1835.
96. Susanna Buzby,	Moorestown, N. J.,	12th mo., 1834.
97. Elizabeth Steer,	Cincinnati, Ohio,	7th mo., 1835.
98. Alice Lewis,	New Garden, Pa.,	5th mo., 1834.
99. Sarah K. Baily,	Wilmington, Del.,	6th mo., "
100. Joanna Haight,	Washington, N. J.,	" "
101. Mary T. Black,	Bordentown, N. J.,	9th mo., "
102. Avolina Haines,	Medford, N. J.,	5th mo., 1835.
103. Elizabeth Davidson,	Cropwell, N. J.,	6th mo., 1834.
104. Julia White,	———, N. C.,	11th mo., "
105. Anna B. Hubbs,	Philadelphia, Pa.,	10th mo., "
106. Sarah Richie,	"	8th mo., "
107. Adeline Glover,	West Chester, Pa.,	" 1835.
108. Sarah Janney,	Loudon Co., Va.,	4th mo., 1834.
109. Sarah E. Janney,	"	" "
110. Ann Eliza Pyle,	Kennet Square, Pa.,	11th mo., "
111. Rebecca Matson,	Concord, Pa.,	10th mo., "
112. Sarah Cook,	Deer Creek, Md.,	7th mo., "
113. Rebecca Worthington,	"	" "
114. Frances Gummere,	Haverford, Pa.,	" "
115. Sarah Ann Andrews,	Somer's Point, N. J.,	6th mo., "
116. Hannah A. Harlan,	Kennet, Pa.,	11th mo., "
117. Sarah Babb,	Isle of Wight Co., Va.,	" "
118. Mary Burgess,	Attleboro', Pa.,	9th mo., "
119. Sarah Walter,	Hockessing, Del.,	8th mo., "
120. Sarah E. Ellis,	Muncy, Pa.,	10th mo., 1837.
121. Martha Abbott,	Salem, N. J.,	11th mo., 1834.
122. Ann T. Updegraff,	Mt. Pleasant, Ohio,	7th mo., "
123. Ann W. Janney,	Philadelphia, Pa.,	4th mo., 1835.
124. Elizabeth P. Smith,	"	8th mo., 1834.
125. Anne Boone,	Georgetown, D. C.,	9th mo., "
126. Sarah Proctor,	Baltimore, Md.,	11th mo., "
127. Elizabeth Proctor,	"	" "
128. Eliza Hunt,	Moorestown, N. J.,	" "
129. Matilda Pharo,	Barnegat, N. J.,	5th mo., 1835.

GENERAL CATALOGUE.

FOURTH THOUSAND.

NAME.	RESIDENCE.	DATE OF ENTRY.
130. Mary Humphreys,	Woodbury, N. J.,	9th mo., 1834.
131. Catharine S. Palmer,	Concord, Pa.,	2d mo., 1835.
132. Edith Sharpless,	Goshen, Pa.,	10th mo., 1834.
133. Lavinia Hawley,	Edgmont, Pa.,	11th mo., "
134. Ann Hoopes,	New Garden, Pa.,	" "
135. R. A. Kirkwood,	Columbia, Pa.,	12th mo., "
136. Hannah Williams,	Baltimore, Md.,	11th mo., "
137. Phebe Ann Pharo,	Tuckerton, N. J.,	3d mo., 1836.
138. Elizabeth Phillips,	Christiana, Pa.,	9th mo., 1835.
139. Alvina Carpenter,	Marshallton, Pa.,	6th mo., "
140. Elizabeth Davis,	Birmingham, Pa.,	3d mo., "
141. Mary Ann Walton,	Byberry, Pa.,	5th mo., "
142. Deborah Bunting,	Crosswicks, N. J.,	4th mo., "
143. Mary Tomlinson,	Springfield, Pa.,	" 1844.
144. Margaretta Elkinton,	Philadelphia, Pa.,	5th mo., 1835.
145. Elizabeth Allen,	"	4th mo., "
146. Elizabeth C. Thomas,	"	" "
147. Ellen Boone,	Georgetown, D. C.,	6th mo., "
148. Susan Boone,	"	8th mo., "
149. Lydia C. Fisher,	Woodbury, N. J.,	4th mo., 1844.
150. Martha H. Webb,	....	" 1835.
151. Ann Michener,	Philadelphia, Pa.,	6th mo., "
152. Susan T. West,	"	8th mo., "
153. Edith Whitall,	Woodbury, N. J.,	10th mo., "
154. Miriam Lee,	Exeter, Pa.,	5th mo., "
155. Mary Bell,	Germantown, Pa.,	4th mo., "
156. Sarah A. Merrefield,	Philadelphia, Pa.,	5th mo., "
157. Hannah Brown,	Fallsington, Pa.,	9th mo., "
158. Hannah C. Williams,	Newtown, Pa.,	" "
159. Mary Fox,	Philadelphia, Pa.,	5th mo., "
160. Rachel Hoopes,	Birmingham, Pa.,	3d mo.,
161. Margaretta Griffith,	Richland, Pa.,	4th mo., "
162. Eliza Bullock,	Arneystown, N. J.,	7th mo., "
163. Mary L. Thomas,	Goshen, Pa.,	10th mo., "
164. Mary Thomas,	"	" "
165. Elizabeth Hooton,	Moorestown, N. J.,	4th mo., "
166. Sarah Emlen,	Middletown, Pa.,	" "
167. Anne Emlen,	"	" "
168. Susan Emlen,	"	" "
169. Emily Wilson,	Chester Town, Md.,	9th mo., "
170. Hannah Lamborn,	New Garden, Pa.,	2d mo., 1836.
171. Eliza M. Janney,	Philadelphia, Pa.,	10th mo., 1835.
172. Amelia Spencer,	Gwynedd, Pa.,	" "
173. Elizabeth Heston,	Fallsington, Pa.,	" "
174. Rebecca R. Stroud,	Philadelphia, Pa.,	3d mo., 1836.
175. Lydia Roberts,	Moorestown, N. J.,	10th mo., 1835.
176. Tacy Roberts,	Newportville, Pa.,	4th mo., 1836.

STUDENTS.

FOURTH THOUSAND.

NAME.	RESIDENCE.	DATE OF ENTRY.
177. Rebecca Warrington,	Moorestown, N. J.,	10th mo., 1835.
178. Mary Comfort,	Fallsington, Pa.,	9th mo., "
179. Sarah Pike,	Burlington, N. J.,	6th mo., "
180. Charlotte Beesley,	Philadelphia, Pa.,	4th mo., "
181. Rebecca Williams,	Baltimore, Md.,	" "
182. Sophia Morris,	———, Ind.,	11th mo., "
183. Joanna Morris,	"	" "
184. Emily Lewis,	Springfield, Pa.,	5th mo., "
185. Sarah M. Medcalf,	Baltimore, Md.,	" "
186. Sarah Ann Norris,	"	" "
187. Lydia Allen,	Salem, N. J.,	" "
188. Rebecca Morgan,	Aston, Pa.,	4th mo., 1837.
189. Marg. Worthington,	Deer Creek, Md.,	6th mo., 1835.
190. Lydia Williams,	Baltimore, Md.,	8th mo., "
191. Sarah Mickle,	Woodbury, N. J.,	10th mo., "
192. Martha Mickle,	"	" "
193. Anna Miller,	Philadelphia, Pa.,	5th mo., "
194. Elizabeth Borton,	Haddonfield, N. J.,	10th mo., "
195. Rebecca Troth,	Camden, N. J.,	" "
196. Mary Ann Taylor,	Springfield, N. J.,	9th mo., "
197. Deborah Taylor,	Mt. Holly, N. J.,	" "
198. Dinah Hilles,	Frankford, Pa.,	10th mo., "
199. Anna Warrington,	Westfield, N. J.,	12th mo., "
200. Ellen M. Bolton,	Woodstown, N. J.,	7th mo., "
201. Claranda White,	Perquimans Co., N. C.,	6th mo., "
202. Rachel Robinson,	"	" "
203. Penina White,	"	" "
204. Lydia J. Sharpless,	Goshen, Pa.,	10th mo., "
205. Edith Hickman,	"	4th mo., "
206. Mary Cooper,	Sadsbury, Pa.,	9th mo., "
207. Hannah P. Peters,	Concord, Pa.,	10th mo., "
208. Rebecca Cassin,	Providence, Pa.,	" "
209. Jane D. Haines,	West Chester, Pa.,	3d mo., 1836.
210. Sarah Bunting,	Darby, Pa.,	12th mo., 1835.
211. Mary Pancoast,	Mullica Hill, N. J.,	9th mo., "
212. A. E. Deprefontaine,	Philadelphia, Pa.,	6th mo., "
213. Mary P. Hull,	Dutchess Co., N. Y.,	10th mo., "
214. Martha Brown,	Fallsington, Pa.,	2d mo., 1836.
215. Rebecca E. Jenks,	Newtown, Pa.,	10th mo., 1835.
216. Hannah Jenks,	"	" "
217. Sarah R. Jones,	Blockley, Pa.,	5th mo., 1836.
218. H. Gillingham,	Frankford, Pa.,	10th mo., 1835.
219. Rebecca Jones,	———, N. J.,	5th mo., 1837.
220. Ellen Reeve,	Greenwich, N. J.,	3d mo., 1836.
221. Ann H. Sutton,	Dutchess Co., N. Y.,	10th mo., 1835.
222. Abigail Matlack,	Moorestown, N. J.,	5th mo., 1836
223. Mary Parker,	Shrewsbury, N. J.,	1st mo., "

GENERAL CATALOGUE.

FOURTH THOUSAND.

NAME.	RESIDENCE.	DATE OF ENTRY.
224. Susanna Parker,	Shrewsbury, N. J.,	1st mo., 1836
225. Rachel Moon,	Fallsington, Pa.,	4th mo., "
226. Mary Ann Janney,	Kennet, Pa.,	" "
227. Mary D. B. Levis,	Philadelphia, Pa.,	3d mo., "
228. Hannah L. Silver,	Medford, N. J.,	4th mo., "
229. Elizabeth Kaighn,	Kaighn's Point, N. J.,	5th mo., 1837.
230. Mary Ann Webb,	Pennsbury, Pa.,	11th mo., 1836.
231. Hannah E. Decou,	Trenton, N. J.,	5th mo., 1837.
232. Hannah A. Livezey,	Medford, N. J.,	4th mo., 1836.
233. Sarah W. Stockton,	Burlington, N. J.,	5th mo., "
234. Susan K. Stockton,	"	" "
235. A. A. J. Woolman,	....	4th mo., "
236. Sarah Ann Harrison,	Burlington, N. J.,	" "
237. Emily Harrison,	"	" "
238. Mary Pike,	"	" "
239. Jane White,	Milton, Ind.,	" 1837.
240. Lucy A. Pancoast,	Springfield, N. J.,	5th mo., 1836.
241. Beulah Tatum,	Woodbury, N. J.,	11th mo., "
242. Susan Haines,	Christiana, Del.,	4th mo., "
243. Hannah Thompson,	Salem, N. J.,	5th mo., "
244. Lydia Healy,	Fallsington, Pa.,	11th mo., "
245. Eliz. A. Boustead,	Philadelphia, Pa.,	5th mo., "
246. Mary T. Wilson,	....	" "
247. Beulah R. Lippincott,	Chester, N. J.,	" "
248. Elizabeth Cumming,	Philadelphia, Pa.,	10th mo., 1838.
249. Rebecca Allen,	Salem, N. J.,	5th mo., 1836.
250. Anna M. Worrall,	Fallsington, Pa.,	4th mo., "
251. Margaret Pyle,	....	" 1838.
252. Elizabeth Pierson,	Concord, Pa.,	9th mo., 1836.
253. Mary E. Carey,	Bucks Co., Pa.,	5th mo., "
254. Edith Fox,	Philadelphia, Pa.,	4th mo., "
255. Abi Walton,	"	" "
256. Ann E. Wetherill,	Burlington, N. J.,	" "
257. Louisa A. Bartlett,	Egg Harbor, N. J.,	3d mo., "
258. Marcia White,	Robinson, Ind.,	4th mo., "
259. Esther Smith,	"	" "
260. Elizabeth Webb,	Kennet, Pa.,	11th mo., "
261. Sarah Thompson,	West Chester, Pa.,	4th mo., "
262. Abigail Eldridge,	Evesham, N. J.,	" 1837.
263. Elizabeth Lightfoot,	West Whiteland, Pa.,	9th mo., 1836.
264. Rebecca Mendenhall,	Edgmont, Pa.,	10th mo., "
265. Jane C. Hoag,	———, Vt.,	7th mo., 1837.
266. Hannah Townsend,	New Garden, Pa.,	5th mo., 1836.
267. Sarah Satterthwaite,	———, Mich.,	10th mo., 1837.
268. Ruth H. Carter,	Kennet, Pa.,	5th mo., 1836
269. Rachel S. House,	"	11th mo., "
270. Sarah E. Edwards,	Muncy, Pa.,	4th mo., "

STUDENTS.

FOURTH THOUSAND.

NAME.	RESIDENCE.	DATE OF ENTRY.
271. Rebecca Levis,	Philadelphia, Pa.,	4th mo., 1836.
272. Mercia White,	Milton, Ind.,	" "
273. Juliann Webster,	Blockley, Pa.,	5th mo., "
274. Ruth A. Hunt,	Burlington, N. J.,	" "
275. Jane Ellicott,	Baltimore, Md.,	11th mo., 1843.
276. Sarah Farrington,	....	5th mo., 1836.
277. Rachel T. Jones,	Perry Co., Pa.,	4th mo., 1844.
278. Mary Hunt,	Burlington Co., N. J.,	5th mo., 1836.
279. Isabella Pancoast,	Mullica Hill, N. J.,	8th mo., "
280. Jane W. Green,	Muncy, Pa.,	4th mo., "
281. Susan D. Parker,	Philadelphia, Pa.,	5th mo., "
282. Rebecca W. Symons,	——, Ind.,	4th mo., 1837.
283. Elizabeth Stroud,	Wilmington, Del.,	5th mo., 1836.
284. Martha M. Haines,	Lockport, N. Y.,	" 1837.
285. Mary Maddock,	Springfield, N. J.,	9th mo., 1836.
286. Martha Butcher,	Burlington, N. J.,	4th mo., "
287. Elizabeth Dent,	Providence, Pa.,	5th mo., "
288. Margaret Walmsley,	Byberry, Pa.,	" "
289. Rachel White,	Shrewsbury, N. J.,	6th mo., "
290. Mira Townsend,	Beaver Co., Pa.,	4th mo., "
291. Mary N. Thompson,	Salem, N. J.,	9th mo., "
292. Mary Wistar,	"	" "
293. Anna Jenks,	Newtown, Pa.,	5th mo., "
294. Elizabeth Clement,	Woodbury, N. J.,	4th mo., 1837.
295. Ann Deacon,	Mt. Holly, N. J.,	8th mo., 1836.
296. Mary Bell,	Germantown, Pa.,	4th mo., 1837.
297. Mary L. Thomas,	Burlington, N. J.,	11th mo., 1836.
298. Rebecca M. Thomas,	Philadelphia, Pa.,	" "
299. Sarah Pancoast,	Springfield, Pa.,	" "
300. Rachel Wilson,	Centre, Del.,	5th mo., "
301. Mary R. Evans,	Springfield, Pa.,	" "
302. Mary H. Rhoads,	"	" "
303. Jael Cooper,	Sadsbury, Pa.,	6th mo., "
304. Cassandra Brinton,	"	" "
305. Deborah Rhoads,	Springfield, Pa.,	" "
306. Mary E. Wilson,	Caroline Co., Md.,	4th mo., "
307. Ann Evans,	Willistown, Pa.,	6th mo., "
308. Mary Pugh,	Unionville, Pa.,	4th mo., 1837.
309. Ann Woolman,	Goshen, Pa.,	11th mo., "
310. Martha Harry,	New Garden, Pa.,	" "
311. Mary Fletcher,	Philadelphia, Pa.,	9th mo., 1836.
312. Rebecca Haines,	"	10th mo., "
313. Sarah Eastlack,	Newtown, Pa.,	12th mo., "
314. Margaret A. Cotant,	Stroudsburg, Pa.,	4th mo., 1838.
315. Susan Hibberd,	East Whiteland, Pa.,	1st mo., 1837.
316. Mary P. Malin,	"	" "
317. Sidney A. Welding,*	Philadelphia, Pa.,	10th mo., 1836.

* Deceased at the school, 5th of Twelfth month, 1836.

FOURTH THOUSAND.

NAME.	RESIDENCE.	DATE OF ENTRY.
318. Hannah Allen,	Salem, N. J.,	9th mo., 1838.
319. Martha Burdsall,	New York, N. Y.,	10th mo., "
320. Ruth Ann Jones,	Plymouth, Pa.,	4th mo., 1844.
321. Edith S. Lippincott,	Moorestown, N. J.,	9th mo., 1836.
322. Rachel Garetson,	....	3d mo., 1837.
323. Beulah Leeds,	G't Egg Harbor, N. J.,	10th mo., 1836.
324. Ann Walton,	Byberry, Pa.,	4th mo., 1837.
325. Achsah E. Ward,	Woodbury, N. J.,	5th mo., "
326. Beulah Middleton,	....	" "
327. Anna Ogden,	Swedesborough, N. J.,	" "
328. Jane Scott,	Gwynedd, Pa.,	" "
329. Esther Griffin,	New York, N. Y.,	4th mo., 1837.
330. Mary Ann Phipps,	Uwchlan, Pa.,	10th mo., 1836.
331. Sarah Vail,	Plainfield, N. J.,	" 1837.
332. Martha P. Vail,	"	4th mo., "
333. Lydia S. Brinton,	Lancaster, Pa.,	10th mo., 1836.
334. Anna Smedley,	Little Britain, Pa.,	" "
335. Harriet Eldridge,	Whiteland, Pa.,	" "
336. Eleanor Baily,	Parkersville, Pa.,	11th mo., "
337. Rachel Eastlack,	Newtown, Pa.,	12th mo., "
338. Isabella S. Peters,	Concord, Pa.,	1st mo., 1837.
340. Mary Hall,	——, Ohio,	4th mo., 1838.
341. Sarah W. Rulon,	Philadelphia, Pa.,	" "
342. Elizabeth A. Rulon,	"	" "
343. M. R. Cadwallader,	Plumstead, Pa.,	10th mo., 1844.
344. Tacy T. Haycock,	Abington, Pa.,	5th mo., 1837.
345. Rachel S. Lewis,	Philadelphia, Pa.,	" "
346. Elizabeth Lewis,	"	" "
347. Sarah W. Merritt,	Salem, N. J.,	4th mo., 1844.
348. Mary N. Jenkins,	——, N. Y.,	" 1837.
349. Ann Magarge,	Germantown, Pa.,	10th mo., "
350. Susanna M. Jarrett,	Horsham, Pa.,	5th mo., "
351. Sarah Holmes,	Pedricton, N. J.,	6th mo., "
352. Ann Eliza Holmes,	"	" "
353. Han. A. Hutchinson,	Philadelphia, Pa.,	5th mo., "
354. Priscilla Foulke,	Gwynedd, Pa.,	" "
355. Mary H. Shreeve,	Wrightstown, N. J.,	" "
356. Hannah L. Folwell,	Philadelphia, Pa.,	" "
357. Mary Hughes,	London Grove, Pa.,	10th mo., "
358. Hannah A. Green,	Edgmont, Pa.,	" "
359. Lucy A. Leeds,	Egg Harbor, N. J.,	" "
360. Phebe Quinby,	Brandywine, Pa.,	4th mo., "
361. Rebecca Shoemaker,	Shoemakertown, Pa.,	" 1839.
362. Mary Atkinson,	Philadelphia, Pa.,	5th mo., 1837
363. Mary C. Wilkins,	"	" "
364. Mariba Hampton,	"	" "
365. Sarah Jones,	Norristown, Pa.,	4th mo., "

STUDENTS.

FOURTH THOUSAND.

NAME.	RESIDENCE.	DATE OF ENTRY.
366. Elizabeth Dawson,	Chestertown, Md.,	4th mo., 1837.
367. Mary Roberts,	Moorestown, N. J.,	5th mo., "
368. Rebecca Roberts,	"	" "
369. Rebecca R. Simmons,	Philadelphia, Pa.,	11th mo., 1840.
370. Lydia Cox,	"	5th mo., 1837.
371. Abigail W. Brown,	Darby, Pa.,	" "
372. Mary Ann Eldridge,	Woodbury, N. J.,	" "
373. Mary H. Buzby,	Moorestown, N. J.,	" "
374. Margaret Masters,	Muncy, Pa.,	10th mo., "
375. Eliz. C. Worthington,	Deer Creek, Md.,	5th mo., "
376. Mary Evans,	Springfield, Pa.,	" "
377. Jane Brinton,	Lancaster Co., Pa.,	" "
378. Mary Ann Trimble,	West Whiteland, Pa.,	" "
379. Philena Swain,	West Chester, Pa.,	" "
380. Rebecca Reeve,	....	" "
381. Mary Brown,	Fallsington, Pa.,	10th mo., "
382. Frances Gillingham,	Philadelphia, Pa.,	" "
383. Caroline Gillingham,	"	" "
384. Hephziba Matlack,	"	" "
385. Cath. Gillingham,	"	" "
386. Margaret Thompson,	Penn's Manor, Pa.,	" "
387. Rosanna Thompson,	"	" "
388. Beulah Ogden,	Swedesborough, N. J.,	4th mo., 1838.
389. Lydia Ann Parker,	Long Branch, N. J.,	10th mo., 1837.
390. Hannah Ellis,	Plymouth, Pa.,	" "
391. Susan J. Wilson,	"	" "
392. Elizabeth Wilson,	"	" "
393. Eliz. Cadwallader,	Philadelphia, Pa.,	" "
394. Mary Cadwallader,	"	" "
395. Elizabeth Pratt,	Upper Darby, Pa.,	" "
396. Anne Brown,	Fallsington, Pa.,	" "
397. Lydia Price,	"	" "
398. Sarah A. Lippincott,	Haddonfield, N. J.,	4th mo., 1838.
399. Hannah Wetherill,	Manayunk, Pa.,	10th mo., 1837.
400. Ann Matlack,	Philadelphia, Pa.,	4th mo., 1838.
401.*Mary L. Smith,	"	" "
402. Sarah F. Phillips,	Parkesburg, Pa.,	10th mo., "
403. Mary Binns,	Brownsville, Pa.,	5th mo., 1847.
404. Mary Cleaver,	Valley, Pa.,	10th mo., 1838.
405. R. E. Caulk,	Philadelphia, Pa.,	4th mo., "
406. Mary B. Caulk,	"	" "
407. H. P. Kirkbride,	"	" "
408. Abigail A. Haines,	Medford, N. J.,	" "
409. Tacy S. Penrose,	Horsham, Pa.,	10th mo., 1837.
410. Elizabeth S. Fell,	West Grove, Pa.,	" "
411. Phebe Hoopes,	New Garden, Pa.,	" "
412. Lydia Wetherill,	Stroudsburg, Pa.,	" 1839

* This number duplicated. Read also:
Mary Woodward, Philadelphia, Pa., 11th mo., 1840.

FOURTH THOUSAND.

NAME.	RESIDENCE.	DATE OF ENTRY.
413. Mary L. Packer,	Woodbury, N. J.,	11th mo., 1840
414. Jane Griffith,	Hockessing, Del.,	10th mo., 1837.
415. Priscilla Walter,	"	" "
416. Jane Webb,	Kennet, Pa.,	" "
417. Mary V. Trimble,	Whiteland, Pa.,	" "
418. Matilda Pyle,	W. Marlborough, Pa.,	" "
419. Sarah Newlin,	Middletown, Pa.,	" "
420. Anna C. Smith,	Philadelphia, Pa.,	" "
421. Ellen L. Smith,	"	" "
422. Sidney M. England,	Chester Co., Pa.,	4th mo., 1839.
423. Mary H. Painter,	West Chester, Pa.,	10th mo., 1837.
424. Hannah Garretson,	———, N. Y.,	5th mo., 1841.
425. Abigail S. Reed,	West Chester, Pa.,	10th mo., 1837.
426. Mary A. Lippincott,	Moorestown, N. J.,	" "
427. Lydia Simmons,	Philadelphia, Pa.,	" "
428. Deborah S. Smith,	"	" "
429. Sarah Trimble,	Whiteland, Pa.,	" "
430. Lydia Morgan,	Philadelphia, Pa.,	" "
431. Mary A. Green,	Salem, N. J.,	4th mo., 1839.
432. Ann Lippincott,	Philadelphia, Pa.,	" 1838.
433. Mary W. Paxson,	Bucks Co., Pa.,	" "
434. Elizabeth B. Garrett,	Philadelphia, Pa.,	4th mo., "
435. Eliz. P. Simmons,	Bristol, Pa.,	10th mo., "
436. Ann R. Butcher,	Philadelphia, Pa.,	" "
437. Martha C. Barton,	Camden, N. J.,	4th mo., "
438. Anna Spencer,	Moreland, Pa.,	" "
439. Lydia S. Garrigues,	Philadelphia, Pa.,	" "
440. Hannah G. Reeve,	Allowaystown, N. J.,	" 1839.
441. Elizabeth Eastburn,	Makefield, Pa.,	" 1839.
442. Patience Lowber,	Camden, Del.,	10th mo., 1838.
443. Mary Ann Jones,	Plumstead, Pa.,	4th mo., 1839.
444. Sarah Townsend,	Plainfield, N. J.,	10th mo., 1838.
445. Hannah A. Bell,	Philadelphia, Pa.,	4th mo., "
446. Hannah Ecroyd,	Muncy, Pa.,	" 1839.
447. Phebe Burgess,	Bucks Co., Pa.,	11th mo., 1838.
448. Elizabeth Cumming,	Philadelphia, Pa.,	10th mo., "
449. Mary Randolph,	"	5th mo., "
450. Hannah N. Pyle,	E. Marlborough, Pa.,	4th mo., "
451. Elizabeth M. Pyle,	"	" "
452. Mary Martin,	Moorestown, N. J.,	" "
453. Mary Ball,	Bucks Co., Pa.,	" "
454. Mary Burgess,	"	" 1839.
455. Eliz. Cadwallader,	Fallsington, Pa.,	10th mo., 1838
456. Eliz. Shoemaker,	Shoemakertown, Pa.,	4th mo., "
457. Ruth Michener,	Plumstead, Pa.,	" "
458. Georgiana Janney,	Kennet, Pa.,	" "
459. Chloe M. Comstock,	Lockport, N. Y.,	10th mo., "

STUDENTS.

FOURTH THOUSAND.

NAME.	RESIDENCE.	DATE OF ENTRY.
460. Sarah Ann Wilkins,	Philadelphia, Pa.,	4th mo., 1838.
461. Margaret Comfort,	Whitemarsh, Pa.,	" 1839.
462. Margaret Lightfoot,	Goshen, Pa.,	10th mo., "
463. Rebecca W. Brinton,	Lancaster Co., Pa.,	4th mo., "
464. Sarah D. Powell,	Burlington, N. J.,	" 1838.
465. Mary Ann Lewis,	Springfield, N. J.,	" 1839.
466. Hannah Pusey,	Wilmington, Del.,	" 1838.
467. Mary Pusey,	New Castle Co., Del.,	" "
468. Sarah Hoopes,	London Grove, Pa.,	" "
469. Elizabeth Clemson,	"	" "
470. Mary Rudolph,	Springfield, N. J.,	" "
471. Lavinia R. Hoopes,	Goshen, Pa.,	5th mo., "
472. Caroline E. Hoopes,	"	" "
473. Elizabeth Yarnall,	Concord, Pa.,	" "
474. Sarah Atkinson,	Talbot Co., Md.,	10th mo., "
475. Sarah K. Powell,	Easton, Md.,	" "
476. Sarah Baily,	Coatesville, Pa.,	" "
477. Anna M. Ellis,	Muncy, Pa.,	" "
478. Mary H. Rea.	Hunterdon, N. J.,	" "
479. Elizabeth J. Cox,	Springfield Co., N. J.,	" 1839.
480. Martha Knight,	Philadelphia, Pa.,	" 1838.
481. Rachel Jarrett,	Horsham, Pa.,	" "
482. Elizabeth Comfort,	Fallsington, Pa.,	" "
483. Emily Jones,	Philadelphia, Pa.,	5th mo., "
484. Elizabeth Ann Jones,	"	" "
485. Helen D. Thompson,		4th mo., 1839.
486. Hope Lippincott,	Haddonfield, N. J.,	10th mo., 1838.
487. Lydia Medcalf,	Baltimore, Md.,	4th mo., 1839.
488. Sarah Ann Bacon,	Bacon's Neck, N. J.,	10th mo., 1838.
489. Mary Ellis,	Muncy, Pa.,	" "
490. Eliz. Hollingsworth,	———, Va.,	" "
491. Rebecca Fox,	Philadelphia, Pa.,	" "
492. Letitia Sheppard,	Greenwich, N. J.,	" "
493. Elizabeth F. Page,	Medford, N. J.,	" "
494. Sarah Ann Starr,	Newlin, Pa.,	" "
495. Elizabeth Smith,	Philadelphia, Pa.,	" "
496. Rebecca Pitman,	Mansfield, Pa.,	" "
497. Mary Stokes,	Philadelphia, Pa.,	" "
498. Ruth R. Townsend,	Palmyra, Pa.,	" "
499. Elizabeth Wilson,	Philadelphia, Pa.,	" 1844.
500. Susan P. Smith.	Chester Co., Pa.,	" 1838.
501. Fan. E. Gillingham,	Kensington, Pa.,	" "
502. Anna Mary Kirk,	Goshen, Pa.,	" "
503. Hannah P. Morgan,	Aston, Pa.,	" "
504. Eliza Pennell,	Chichester, Pa.,	" "
505. Mary Larkin,	Bethel, Pa.,	" "
506. Rachel Warrington,	Westfield, N. J.,	" "

GENERAL CATALOGUE.

FOURTH THOUSAND.

NAME.	RESIDENCE.	DATE OF ENTRY.
507. Ann Kersey,	East Bradford, Pa.,	10th mo., 1838.
508. Rebecca G. Cope,	"	" "
509. Jane Gordon,	Uwchlan, Pa.,	" "
510. Mary M. Allen,	New York, N. Y.,	" "
511. Rebecca Hawley,	Edgmont, Pa.,	4th mo., 1839.
512. Mary Hutchinson,	——, N. Y.,	10th mo. 1838.
513. Philena Sharpless,	Goshen, Pa.,	" "
514. Sarah Pratt,	Newtown, Pa.,	" "
515. Elizabeth Woolman,	Goshen, Pa.,	" "
516. Mary Ann Pyle,	London Grove, Pa.,	5th mo., 1840.
517. Miriam Allen,	New York, N. Y.,	10th mo., 1838.
518. Ann Cope,	East Bradford, Pa.,	" "
519. Elizabeth Paxson,	Bucks Co., Pa.,	" "
520. Margaret Lightfoot,	Goshen, Pa.,	" "
521. Maria Harvey,	East Caln, Pa.,	10th mo., "
522. Louisa S. Wilson,	Salem Co., N. J.,	" "
523. Elizabeth Chambers,	Newark, Del.,	" "
524. Rachel Eldridge,	Moorestown, N. J.,	4th mo., 1839.
525. Deborah Roberts,	"	" "
526. Han. B. Lishman,	Evesham, N. J.,	" "
527. Margaret Wiley,	Sadsbury, Pa.,	" "
528. Hannah Fulton,	"	" "
529. Ruth Anna Hoopes,	East Bradford, Pa.,	" "
530. Emma Richards,	Wilmington, Del.,	" "
531. Eleanor Tyson,	....	" "
532. Mary A. Bostwick,	Rancocas, N. J.,	10th mo., 1844.
533. Lydia Ann Hawley,	Goshen, Pa.,	" "
534. Marg. F. Haines,	Medford, N. J.,	4th mo., 1839.
535. R. S. Kirkbride,	Fallsington, Pa.,	" "
536. Sarah W. Stevens,	Tredyffrin, Pa.,	" "
537. Sarah Lippincott,	Moorestown, N. J.,	" "
538. Margaret Chandler,	Penn, Pa.,	10th mo., 1844.
539. Eliza J. Stroud,	Stroudsburg, Pa.,	" 1839.
540. Anna Stackhouse,	Philadelphia, Pa.,	4th mo., "
541. Mary Harper,	Bristol, Pa.,	" "
542. Hannah Evans,	Philadelphia, Pa.,	" "
543. Ann N. Lukens,	....	" "
544. Juliana R. Parry,	Philadelphia, Pa.,	" "
545. Jane P. Parry,	"	" "
546. Juliana R. Maule,		" "
547. Sarah H. Redman,	Haddonfield, N. J.,	" "
548. Margaret Williams,	Philadelphia, Pa.,	" "
549. Ruth B. Sheppard,	Greenwich, N. J.,	" "
550. Mary M. Morthland,	Gunpowder, Md.,	" "
551. Rebecca A. Abbott,	Philadelphia, Pa.,	" "
552. Ann E. Grubb,	"	" "
553. Rachel Roberts,	Evesham, N. J.,	5th mo., 1840

STUDENTS. 297

FOURTH THOUSAND.

NAME.	RESIDENCE.	DATE OF ENTRY.
554. Lydia A. Eldridge,	Whiteland, Pa.,	10th mo., 1844.
555. Rebecca C. Garrett,	Philadelphia, Pa.,	" 1839.
556. Matilda Norris,	Baltimore, Md.,	" "
557. Susan Ecroyd,	Muncy, Pa.,	" "
558. Elizabeth S. Lloyd,	Philadelphia, Pa.,	" "
559. Narcissa Mendenhall,	Muncy, Pa.,	5th mo., 1840.
560. Mary Cooper,	Sadsbury, Pa.,	4th mo., 1839.
561. Lucy Richardson,	Wilmington, Del.,	" "
562. Elizabeth Hickman,	Goshen, Pa.,	" "
563. Elizabeth Jones,	New London, Pa.,	" "
564. Ann Benington,	Concord, Pa.,	" "
565. Lydia Wood,	....	" "
566. Ann Trimble,	Concord, Pa.,	" "
567. Sarah J. Coates,	Coatesville, Pa.,	" "
568. Sarah Ann Pierce,	Kennet, Pa.,	" "
569. Mary C. Emlen,	Philadelphia, Pa.,	" "
570. Huldah H. Bonwell,	Frederica, Del.,	" "
571. Mary A. Bonwell,	"	" "
572. Gulielma M. Wilson,	Easton, Md.,	" "
573. Elizabeth Tucker,	Philadelphia, Pa.,	" "
574. Elizabeth Evans,	Willistown, Pa.,	" "
575. Mary Ann Morgan,	Aston, Pa.,	" "
576. Mary Pratt,	Goshen, Pa.,	" "
577. Isabella Kemp,	Smyrna, Del.,	10th mo., "
578. Mary Moore,	Sadsbury, Pa.,	" "
579. Rachel Cox,	Springfield, Pa.,	" "
580. Sarah Eaves,	Muncy, Pa.,	" "
581. Ann Lightfoot,	Maiden Creek, Pa.,	5th mo., 1840.
582. Eleanor Lightfoot,	"	" "
583. Ann Quinby,	———, N. Y.,	10th mo., 1839.
584. Sarah Wetherill,	Manayunk, Pa.,	" "
585. Anna M. Reeves,	Philadelphia, Pa.,	" "
586. Mary Levis,	Springfield, Pa.,	" "
587. Sarah G. Carmalt,	Montrose, Pa.,	" "
588. Anna A. Stevenson,	Philadelphia, Pa.,	11th mo., 1840.
589. Lydia Post,	———, N. Y.,	10th mo., 1839.
590. Esther Rushmore,	"	" "
591. Rachel E. Sharpless,	Downingtown, Pa.,	11th mo., 1840.
592. Ann Prickitt,	Medford, N. J.,	5th mo., "
593. Abigail Page,	"	" "
594. Lydia C. Shinn,	Philadelphia, Pa.,	" "
595. Regina S. Kimber,	"	" "
596. Joanna S. Kimber,	"	" "
597. Lydia Smedley,	Middletown, Pa.,	10th mo., 1844.
598. Phebe J. Hutchinson,	Philadelphia, Pa.,	5th mo., 1840.
599. Mary L. Betts,	Bucks Co., Pa.,	" "
600. Mary Albertson,	Plymouth, Pa.,	10th mo., 1839.

FOURTH THOUSAND.

NAME.	RESIDENCE.	DATE OF ENTRY.
601. Sarah E. Cooper,	Sadsbury, Pa.,	5th mo., 1840.
602. Sarah Pusey,	E. Marlborough, Pa.,	6th mo., "
603. Elizabeth Larkin,	Concord, Pa.,	10th mo., 1839.
604. Susan Williams,	Sadsbury, Pa.,	" "
605. Hannah Pratt,	Newtown, Pa.,	" "
607. Mary House,	Pennsbury, Pa.,	" "
608. Marg. A. Hallowell,	Bucks Co., Pa.,	" "
609. Sarah Warner,	Bristol, Pa.,	" "
610. Lydia Thompson,	New Garden, Pa.,	" "
611. Ann Buzby,	Moorestown, N. J.,	11th mo., 1840.
612. Elizabeth Walter,	Kennet, Pa.,	10th mo., 1839.
613. Rachel S. Saunders,	....	" "
614. Rebecca Reeve,	Philadelphia, Pa.,	" "
615. Sarah Lukens,	Bucks Co., Pa.,	" "
616. Sarah P. Moore,	Sadsbury Pa.,	" "
617. Margaret S. Dawson,	Wilmington, Del.,	" "
618. Mary Gause,	Concord, Pa.,	11th mo., 1840.
619. Albina Garrett,	Willistown, Pa.,	" 1839.
620. Susanna F. Ogborn,	Millville, Pa.,	" 1840.
621. Martha W. Moore,	Strickersville, Pa.,	5th mo., "
622. Anna Mary Hoopes,	Goshen, Pa.,	" "
623. Huldah Walker,	New Garden, Pa.,	" "
624. Henrietta Woodward,	Moorestown, N. J.,	" "
625. Eliza W. Pusey,	E. Marlborough, Pa.,	" "
626. Sarah Lewis,	Philadelphia, Pa.,	11th mo., "
627. Maria Hall,	Harrisville, Ohio,	4th mo., 1844.
628. Esther Massey,	....	5th mo., 1840.
629. Hannah Scattergood,	Millville, N. J.,	" "
630. Ann Scattergood,	"	" "
631. Eliza Martin,	Allentown, Pa.,	" 1841.
632. Catharine H. Smith,	Buckingham, Pa.,	11th mo., 1840.
633. Frances J. Simpson,	Solesbury, Pa.,	" "
634. Mary S. Merritt,	Salem, N. J.,	5th mo., "
635. Jane Johnson,	Bucks Co., Pa.,	" "
636. Anna Potts,	Philadelphia, Pa.,	" "
637. Martha Hampton,	Wrightstown, Pa.,	11th mo., "
638. Mary W. Wistar,	Philadelphia, Pa.,	5th mo., "
639. Sarah J. Dutton,	Burlington, N. J.,	" "
640. Ann Eyre,	Chichester, Pa.,	" "
641. Susanna Palmer,	Concord, Pa.,	" "
642. Letitia Harmer,	Bacon's Neck, N. J.,	" "
643. Hannah H. Yarnall,	Concord, Pa.,	10th mo., 1842.
644. Rebecca A. Wilson,	Denton, Md.,	5th mo., 1840.
645. Rebecca Buzby,	Bordentown, N. J.,	11th mo., "
646. Rebecca Pierce,	Kennet, Pa.,	5th mo., "
647. Martha M. Pratt,	Goshen, Pa.,	" 1843.
648. Caroline Churchman,	Wilmington, Del.,	" 1840.

STUDENTS. 299

FOURTH THOUSAND.

NAME.	RESIDENCE.	DATE OF ENTRY.
649. Margaret M. Garrett,	East Whiteland, Pa.,	5th mo., 1840.
650. Albina Phillips,	Mill Village, Del.,	" "
651. Rachel Comfort,	Penn's Manor, Pa,	" "
652. Lydia Heald,	Hockessing, Del.,	" "
653. Ann Eliza Rankin,	Coatesville, Pa.,	" 1841.
654. Emma Conklin,	———, N. Y.,	" 1840.
655. Deborah Lightfoot,	Whiteland, Pa.,	" "
656. Ann S. Hutton,	Wilmington, Del.,	" "
657. Margaret J. Pyle,	London Grove, Pa.,	" "
658. Catharine Evans,	Willistown, Pa.,	" "
659. Mary Morris,	———, Ind.,	" "
660. Ann Eliza Phipps,	Uwchlan, Pa.,	11th mo., "
661. Anna Pharo,	Barnegat, N. J.,	" "
662. Caroline Parker,	Philadelphia, Pa.,	5th mo., "
663. Martha T. Cox,	Merion, Pa.,	11th mo., "
664. Frances Edge,	London Grove, Pa.,	" "
665. Anna Williamson,	Philadelphia, Pa.,	" "
666. Pamelia Tomlinson,	Bucks Co., Pa.,	" "
667. Sarah Harvey,	Columbus, N. J.,	" "
668. Sarah P. Lee,	Exeter, Pa.,	5th mo., 1841.
669. Mary F. Newbold,	Springfield, N. J.,	11th mo., 1840.
670. Hannah Pierson,	Concord, Pa.,	4th mo., 1844.
671. Susan Whitall,	Woodbury, N. J.,	11th mo., 1840.
673. Mary Parke,	Philadelphia, Pa.,	" "
674. Martha Ogborn,	Germantown, Pa.,	" "
675. Hannah Chrisman,	Reading, Pa.,	" "
676. Rebecca W. Brown,	Bucks Co., Pa.,	5th mo., 1841.
677. Mary Ann Wetherill,	Manayunk, Pa.,	11th mo., 1840.
678. Isabella L. Pennock,	Darby, Pa.,	5th mo., 1841.
679. Jane Bettle,	Philadelphia, Pa.,	" "
680. Elizabeth Rhoads,	Springfield, Pa.,	11th mo., 1840.
681. Ann Yarnall,	Edgmont, Pa.,	" "
682. Sarah Pyle,	East Fallowfield, Pa.,	" "
683. Sarah Thompson,	New Garden, Pa.,	" "
684. Anna Mary Starr,	"	" "
685. Sarah Starr,	Chester Co., Pa.,	" "
686. Hannah Thomas,	Goshen, Pa.,	" "
687. Rebecca Paxson,	New London, Pa.,	" "
688. Eliza Larkin,	Concord, Pa.,	4th mo., 1843.
689. Mary Cranstone,	London Grove, Pa.,	10th mo., "
690. Anna B. Passmore,	Edgmont, Pa.,	" 1844.
691. Mary K. Passmore,	"	" "
692. Mary Ann Hoopes,	East Caln, Pa.,	11th mo, 1840.
693. Susan H. Pratt,	East Whiteland, Pa.,	" "
694. Susan Pierson,	Concord, Pa.,	" "
695. Sally Howell,	Edgmont, Pa.,	" "
696. Elizabeth Willits,	White Plain, N. Y.,	" "

S

GENERAL CATALOGUE.

FOURTH THOUSAND.

NAME.	RESIDENCE.	DATE OF ENTRY.
697. Phebe Wilson,	Hockessing, Del.,	11th mo., 1840.
698. Sarah E. Haines,	Muncy, Pa.,	" "
699. Louisa Woodward,	New Garden, Pa.,	" "
700. Phebe Seal,	London Grove, Pa.,	" "
701. Hannah Whitson,	Sadsbury, Pa.,	" "
702. Leah Whitson,	"	" "
703. Hannah Thompson,	New Garden, Pa.,	" "
704. Susan M. Fallis,	——, Ohio,	8th mo., 1841.
705. Martha L. Pennell,	Chichester, Pa.,	11th mo., 1840.
706. Susanna Rhoads,	Springfield, Pa.,	" "
707. Hannah Rudolph,	Springfield, N. J.,	" "
708. Amanda Garretson,	York, Pa.,	4th mo., 1842.
709. Maria Harry,	East Caln, Pa.,	11th mo., 1840.
710. Caroline Haworth,	——, Ohio,	8th mo., 1844.
711. Lydia M. Eachus,	Edgmont, Pa.,	11th mo., 1840.
712. Rachel Eldridge,	Willistown, Pa.,	" "
714. Abigail W. Heacock,	Jenkintown, Pa.,	" "
715. Elizabeth Lamborn,	Lancaster Co., Pa.,	" "
716. Anne Sharpless,	Chester, Pa.,	10th mo., "
717. Ann Eliza Palmer,	Dover, Del.,	5th mo., 1841.
718. Beulah T. Grubb,	Chichester, Pa.,	" "
719. Mary Yearsley,	Coatesville, Pa.,	" "
720. Rachel Michener,	Bradford, Pa.,	10th mo., 1843.
721. Eliz. Humphreys,	Philadelphia, Pa.,	5th mo., 1841.
722. Sarah Branson,	Bristol, Pa..	11th mo., "
723. Lydia Tucker,	Philadelphia, Pa.,	" "
724. Phebe Rhoads,	Newtown, Pa.,	4th mo., 1844.
725. Jane Walton,	Philadelphia, Pa.,	5th mo., 1841.
726. Elizabeth Thompson,	Salem, N. J.,	" "
727. M. P. Sharpless,	Philadelphia, Pa.,	" "
728. Susanna Lukens,	Horsham, Pa.,	" "
729. Mary Scattergood,	Philadelphia, Pa.,	" "
730. Ann Eliza Haines,	Evesham, N. J.,	" "
731. Ann Trimble,	West Whiteland, Pa.,	" "
732. Rachel Price,	West Chester, Pa.,	" "
733. Mary Nicholson,	Haddonfield, N. J.,	" "
734. Kezia Flanner,	Zanesville, Ohio,	" "
735. Jane Yarnall,	Edgmont, Pa.,	11th mo., "
736. Letitia Acton,	Salem, N. J.,	5th mo., "
737. Catharine Acton,	"	" "
738. Sarah Stroud,	Wilmington, Del.,	4th mo., 1844.
739. Deborah Smedley,	Middletown, Pa.,	11th mo., 1841.
740. Sarah Cole,	Sadsbury, Pa.,	" "
741. Anna Fulton,	East Fallowfield, Pa.,	4th mo., 1842.
742. Mary B. Hayes,	"	11th mo., 1841.
743. Lucy Burton,	Fallsington, Pa.,	" "
744. Sarah Gibbons,	Lancaster, Pa.,	. " "

STUDENTS.

FOURTH THOUSAND.

NAME.	RESIDENCE.	DATE OF ENTRY.
745. Susan Valentine,	Downingtown, Pa.,	4th mo., 1842.
746. Sarah Ann Harry,	Sadsbury, Pa.,	11th mo., 1841.
747. Sophia Harry,	"	" "
748. Elizabeth Pennock,	Marlborough, Pa.,	" "
749. Mary W. Thompson,	New Garden, Pa.,	" "
750. Mary Smedley,	Middletown, Pa.,	10th mo., 1841.
751. Jane B. Twining,	Northampton, Pa.,	11th mo., 1841.
752. Elizabeth Jones,	Moorestown, N. J.,	5th mo., "
753. Eliz. H. Twining,	Wrightstown, Pa.,	11th mo., "
754. Rachel Whitson,	Sadsbury, Pa.,	5th mo., "
755. M. J. Cowperthwaite,	Philadelphia, Pa.,	" "
756. Gulielma Jenkins,	Camden, Del.,	11th mo., "
757. Eliz. D. Meredith,	Pughtown, Pa.,	" "
758. Lydia S. Foulke,	Gwynedd, Pa.,	" "
759. Mary Balderston,	Fallsington, Pa.,	" "
760. Anna Brotherton,	Dover, N. J.,	10th mo., 1844.
761. Ann M. Lamborn,	Chatham, Pa.,	5th mo., 1846.
762. Elizabeth Wilson,	Philadelphia, Pa.,	11th mo., 1841.
763. Elizabeth Wright,	"	" "
764. Frances Potts,	"	" "
765. Rachel T. Dickinson,	Reading, Pa.,	" "
766. Lydia Wistar,	Philadelphia, Pa.,	" "
767. Lydia Ann Willits,	"	" "
768. Hannah Kirby,	Salem, N. J.,	" "
769. Mary H. Moore,	Rochester, N. Y.,	" "
770. Orpha Pratt,	Newtown, Pa.,	" "
771. Anna Harlan,	Little Britain, Pa.,	10th mo., 1842.
772. Rachel B. Evans,	Wilmington, Del.,	11th mo., 1841.
773. Deb. A. Passmore,	Edgmont, Pa.,	10th mo., 1842.
774. Abigail Lippincott,	Woodstown, N. J.,	" 1843.
775. Sarah Chambers,	New Garden, Pa.,	" 1842.
776. Frances Garrett,	Philadelphia, Pa.,	12th mo., 1841.
777. Martha Thomas,	Newtown, Pa.,	11th mo., "
778. Sarah Ann Eldridge,	Evesham, N. J.,	" "
779. Eliz. A. Hancock,	Mansfield, N. J.,	" "
780. Rebecca Sharpless,	Waterville, Pa.,	4th mo., 1842.
781. Rebecca L. Chrisman,	Reading, Pa.,	" "
782. Jane Sharpless,	Chester, Pa.,	" . "
783. Amanda Townsend,	Penn, Pa.,	" "
784. Edith Barnard,	London Grove, Pa.,	" "
785. Sidney J. Walter,	New Garden, Pa.,	" "
786. Mary Ann Passmore,	London Britain, Pa.,	10th mo., "
787. Elizabeth Bradley,	East Bradford, Pa.,	4th mo., "
788. Sarah Wiley,	Sadsbury, Pa.,	" "
789. Catharine Dell,	Bridgeville, N. J.,	" "
790. Marg. D. Michener,	Bradford, Pa.,	" "
791. Jane M. Cope,	Whiteland, Pa.,	10th mo., 1844.

GENERAL CATALOGUE.

FOURTH THOUSAND.

NAME.	RESIDENCE.	DATE OF ENTRY.
792. Margaret Kirk,	Whiteland, Pa.,	10th mo., 1844.
793. Elizabeth Poole,	Mill Creek, Del.,	" 1842.
794. Phebe W. Pyle,	Kennet, Pa.,	" "
795. Edith Webb,	Pennsbury, Pa.,	" "
796. Martha D. House,	"	" "
797. Rachel Garrett,	Birmingham, Pa.,	" "
798. Mercy Healy,	Fallsington, Pa.,	" 1843.
799. Hannah S. Pyle,	E. Marlborough, Pa.,	" 1842.
800. Lydia E. Cox,	"	" "
801. Cynthia E. Jones,	Gulf Mills, Pa.,	11th mo., 1841.
802. Cath. B. Trimble,	Whiteland, Pa.,	10th mo., 1844.
803. Lydia Haines,	Medford. N. J.,	4th mo., 1842.
804. S. A. Hendrickson,	Crosswicks, N. J.,	11th mo., 1841.
805. Rebecca Smart,	Salem, N. J.,	" "
806. Lydia Ann Eldridge,	Goshen, Pa.,	10th mo., 1844.
807. Sarah Ann Ogborn,	Germantown, Pa.,	11th mo., 1841.
808. Mary S. Mott,	Rochester, N. Y.,	12th mo., "
809. Rebecca Elkinton,	Philadelphia, Pa.,	4th mo., 1842.
810. Edith Elkinton,	"	" "
811. Sarah Downing,	Downingtown, Pa.,	10th mo., 1844.
812. Henrietta Haines,	Moorestown, N. J.,	4th mo., 1842.
813. Sally Ann Tyson,	——, Ohio,	1st mo., "
814. Elizabeth R. Reeve,	Medford, N. J.,	4th mo., "
815. Priscilla W. Reeve,	"	" "
816. Rachel Knight,	Frankford, Pa.,	" "
817. Eleanor Hunt,	Philadelphia, Pa.,	" "
818. Anna Hunt,	"	" "
819. Marianna Haines,	Trenton, N. J.,	" "
820. Sarah North,	Philadelphia, Pa.,	" "
821. Martha Hancock,	Burlington Co., N. J.,	" "
822. Elizabeth T. Troth,	Philadelphia, Pa.,	" "
823. Sarah Hayes,	"	" "
824. Mary A. Wetherill,	Manayunk, Pa.,	" "
825. Susanna Townsend,	New Market, N. J.,	" "
826. Han. S. Remington,	Philadelphia, Pa.,	" "
827. Sarah J. Remington,	"	" "
828. Meribah Warner,	Princeton, N. J.,	" "
829. Mary Ecroyd,	Muncy, Pa.,	" "
830. Mary Middleton,	Crosswicks, N. J.,	" "
831. Ann E. Clark,	Trenton, N. J.,	" "
832. Hannah Tatum,	Wilmington, Del.,	" "
833. Catharine Stabler,	Sandy Springs, Md.,	
834. Rebecca E. Haines,	Muncy, Pa.,	5th mo., 1845.
835. Deborah J. Baldwin,	Downingtown, Pa.,	4th mo., 1842.
836. Susan Jones,	Philadelphia, Pa.,	10th mo., 1844.
837. Susan Thomas,	Burlington, N. J.,	" 1842.
838. Sarah Morris,	Philadelphia, Pa.,	7th mo., "

STUDENTS.

FOURTH THOUSAND.

NAME.	RESIDENCE.	DATE OF ENTRY.
839. Mary T. Comfort,	Fallsington, Pa.,	10th mo., 1842.
840. Elizabeth R. Evans,	Philadelphia, Pa.,	" "
841. Ann Wills,	Rancocas, N. J.,	" "
842. Mary Borton,	"	" "
843. Mary Masters,	Greenwood, Pa.,	" "
844. Martha Eves,	Fishing Creek, N. J.,	" "
845. Beulah S. Morris,	Germantown, Pa.,	" "
846. Sarah Elkinton,	Philadelphia, Pa.,	" "
847. Sarah Comfort,	Solesbury, Pa.,	" "
848. Rachel Reeves,	Philadelphia, Pa.,	" "
849. Mary Ann Rulon,	"	12th mo., "
850. Mary Ann Jones,	Germantown, Pa.,	10th mo., "
851. Sarah Lee,	Oley, Pa.,	" "
852. Mary Downing,	Downingtown, Pa.,	" "
853. Lydia Spencer,	Horsham, Pa.,	" "
854. Mary Reeve,	Philadelphia, Pa.,	4th mo., 1843.
855. Priscilla Kirby,	Salem, N. J.,	10th mo., 1842.
856. Lydia S. Russell,	Syracuse, N. Y.,	" "
857. Hannah Albertson,	Plymouth, Pa.,	" "
858. Ruth E. Parry,	Philadelphia, Pa.,	4th mo., 1843.
859. Sarah Scattergood,	"	" "
860. Sarah W. Acton,	Salem, N. J.,	10th mo., 1842.
861. Elizabeth Howell,	Edgmont, Pa.,	" "
862. Margaret Tucker,	Philadelphia, Pa.,	" 1843.
863. Anna W. Smith,	———, N. Y.,	1st mo., "
864. Martha A. Burrough,	Waterford, N. J.,	4th mo., "
865. Mary Jane Pound,	Plainfield, N. J.,	" "
866. Tacy Trump,	Philadelphia, Pa.,	" "
867. Susan W. Harlan,	Doe Run, Pa.,	" "
868. Mary Barnard,	London Grove, Pa.,	" "
869. Martha S. Matlack,	Moorestown, N. J.,	" "
870. Deborah Harry,	Uwchlan, Pa.,	10th mo., 1844.
871. Sarah Shoemaker,	Downingtown, Pa.,	4th mo., 1843.
872. Elizabeth Leaver,	Burlington, N. J.,	10th mo., "
873. Martha W. Bostwick,	Moorestown, N. J.,	4th mo., "
874. Jemima A. Gifford,	Rancocas, N. J.,	" "
875. Marg. J. Walter,	Kennet, Pa.,	12th mo., "
876. Mary A. Wetherill,	Chester, Pa.,	10th mo., 1844.
877. Sarah Lightfoot,	Philadelphia, Pa.,	5th mo., 1843.
878. Sarah Yearsley,	Coatesville, Pa.,	" "
879. Frances Bullock,*	Bordentown, N. J.,	10th mo., "
880. Sarah Ann Maris,	Chester, Pa.,	" "
881. Mary J. Townsend,	New Market, N. J.,	" "
882. Elizabeth Ogborn,	Frankford, Pa.,	" 1844.
883. Hannah P. Webb,	E. Marlborough, Pa.,	" 1843.

* Deceased at the school, 18th of Eleventh month, 1843.

FOURTH THOUSAND.

NAME.	RESIDENCE.	DATE OF ENTRY.
884. Deborah Huey,	Hamorton, Pa.,	10th mo., 1843.
885. Elizabeth Pratt,	Goshen, Pa.,	" "
886. Sarah Bradley,	East Bradford, Pa.,	" "
887. Mary M. Jenkinson,	Kennet, Pa.,	" "
888. Esther P. Taylor,	West Chester, Pa.,	" "
889. Edith White,	Guthrieville, Pa.,	" "
890. Sarah Ann Fogg,	Philadelphia, Pa.,	" "
891. Anna Mekeel,	Hector, N. Y.,	" 1842.
892. Eliz. Letchworth,	Philadelphia, Pa.,	" "
893. Elizabeth Mekeel,	Hector, N. Y.,	" "
894. Elizabeth H. Dudley,	Evesham, N. J.,	" "
895. Deborah Smith,	———, N. Y.,	" "
896. Martha R. Bacon,	Bacon's Neck, N. J.,	" "
897. Margaret B. Levis,	Springfield, Pa.,	4th mo., 1843.
898. Mary E. Harvey,	Columbus, N. J.,	" "
899. Mary Parry,	Moorestown, N. J.,	" "
900. Hannah E. Shipley,	Philadelphia, Pa.,	" "
901. Elizabeth S. Jones,	"	" "
902. Sarah S. Bassett,	"	" "
903. Mary Abbott,	Salem, N. J.,	" "
904. Agnes Neville,	———, N. Y.,	" "
905. Mary C. Swayne,	Centerville, Del.,	" "
906. Lydia Lippincott,	Philadelphia, Pa.,	" "
907. Sarah E. Lloyd,	Wilmington, Del.,	10th mo., 1844.
908. Mary Hayes,	Fallowfield, Pa.,	" "
909. Phebe P. Cooper,	Sadsbury, Pa.,	5th mo., 1845.
910. Marg. C. Stephens,	King of Prussia, Pa.,	10th mo., 1843.
911. Hannah Evans,	Springfield, Pa.,	5th mo., 1845.
912. Alice E. Moore,	Sadsbury, Pa.,	10th mo., "
913. Diana Richards,	Nottingham, Md.,	" "
914. Sarah Starr Pearson,	Philadelphia, Pa.,	" 1843.
915. Sarah R. Sheppard,	Greenwich, N. J.,	" "
916. Mary Burton,	Fallsington, Pa.,	" "
917. Rebecca Harned,	Rahway, N. J.,	" 1845.
918. Asenath Heacock,	Muncy, Pa.,	" 1844.
919. Agnes Ann Martin,	Philadelphia, Pa.,	4th mo., "
920. Susan W. Rich,	Moreland, Pa.,	" "
921. Eliz. A. Crenshaw,	———, Va.,	" "
922. Eliz. B. Griffith,	Hopewell, Va.,	" "
923. Hannah G. Allen,	Salem, N. J.,	" "
924. Ann E. Pleasants,	Philadelphia, Pa.,	" "
925. Mary Valentine,	Bellefonte, Pa.,	" "
926. Caroline Valentine,	"	" "
927. Catharine Shipley,	Philadelphia, Pa.,	" "
928. Hannah Fox,	"	" "
929. Rebecca Fox,	"	" "
930. Phebe Davis,	Coatesville, Pa.,	10th mo., 1845.

STUDENTS.

FOURTH THOUSAND.

NAME.	RESIDENCE.	DATE OF ENTRY.
931. Martha Larkin,	Concord, Pa.,	10th mo., 1845.
932. Elmira S. Baily,	Cincinnati, Ohio,	" "
933. Hannah Baily,	Douglass, Pa.,	" "
934. Hannah Foulke,	Gwynedd, Pa.,	" "
935. Hannah Woodward,	Marshallton, Pa.,	5th mo., 1844.
936. Susan Hancock,	Burlington, N. J.,	10th mo., 1845.
937. Phebe Moore,	Bart, Pa.,	" "
938. Phebe Ann Moore,	Sadsbury, Pa.,	" "
939. Alice Hallowell,	Middletown, Pa.,	" "
940. Rachel Benington,	Concord, Pa.,	" "
941. Anne Cooper,	Sadsbury, Pa.,	5th mo., 1846.
942. Sarah Ann Thorn,	Philadelphia, Pa.,	" "
943. Beulah Harvey,	Radnor, Pa.,	" "
944. Mary D. Harvey,	"	" "
946. E. J. Cowperthwaite,	Philadelphia, Pa.,	" "
947. Sarah C. Gillespie,	Lampeter, Pa.,	" "
948. Margaret Passmore,	London Britain, Pa.,	10th mo., "
949. Jane Wright,	Leesburg, Ohio,	9th mo., "
950. Mary Ann Cope,	East Bradford, Pa.,	10th mo., "
951. Deborah Garrett,	Birmingham, Pa.,	" "
952. Albina Lamborn,	Chatham, Pa.,	" "
953. Jane S. Eachus,	Edgmont, Pa.,	" "
954. Sarah Morris,	Bradford, Pa.,	" "
955. Phebe B. Price,	Fallsington, Pa.,	" "
956. Mary E. Coleman,	Trenton, N. J.,	" "
957. Eliza W. House,	Pennsbury, Pa.,	" "
958. Jane C. Moon,	Fallsington, Pa.,	" "
959. Mary P. Cope,	Whiteland, Pa.,	" "
960. Susanna Roberts,	Moorestown, N. J.,	" "
961. Martha Corson,	Plymouth, Pa.,	4th mo., "
962. Elizabeth Decou,	Trenton, N. J.,	" "
963. Judith Ann Willits,	Philadelphia, Pa.,	" "
964. Abby Ann Taylor,	Mt. Holly, N. J.,	" "
965. Deborah Lee,	Maiden Creek, Pa.,	" "
966. Rebecca S. Matlack,	Moorestown, N. J.,	" "
967. R. Satterthwaite,	Crosswicks, N. J.,	" "
968. Ann Brown,	Plumstead, Pa.,	" "
969. Margaret O. Wilson,	Buckingham, Pa.,	10th mo., 1844.
970. Elizabeth Hall,	Mt. Pleasant, Ohio,	4th mo., "
971. Kezia S. Jones,	——, Ohio,	5th mo., "
972. Frances A. Jenkins,	Hudson, N. Y.,	6th mo., "
973. Hannah L. Robinson,	Rochester, N. Y.,	" "
974. Anna Stokes,	Westfield, N. J.,	10th mo., 1846.
975. P. A. Mendenhall,	Greenwood, Pa.,	" 1844.
976. Rebecca W. Haines,	Medford, N. J.,	" 1846.
977. Susan Winner,	Williamsport, Pa.,	5th mo., 1845.
978. Mary Warner,	Muncy, Pa.,	10th mo., 1844.

FOURTH THOUSAND.

NAME.	RESIDENCE.	DATE OF ENTRY.
979. Deborah Ecroyd,	Muncy, Pa.,	10th mo., 1844.
980. Martha D. Ball,	Richmond, Pa.,	" "
981. Mercy Wilson,	Rahway, N. J.,	" "
982. Catharine Wistar,	Salem, N. J.,	" "
983. Anna B. Roberts,	Moorestown, N. J.,	5th mo., 1845.
984. Elizabeth Bacon,	Philadelphia, Pa.,	10th mo., 1844.
985. Deborah Whitall,	Woodbury, N. J.,	" "
986. Mary E. Woolman,	Rancocas, N. J.,	" "
987. Sarah Ann Price,	Fallsington, Pa.,	" "
988. Elizabeth Knight,	Haddonfield, N. J.,	" "
989. Rebecca J. Foulke,	Gwynedd, Pa.,	" "
990. Catharine Evans,	Willistown, Pa.,	" "
991. Mary Evans,	"	" "
992. Sarah Ann Rudolph,	Springfield, N. J.,	5th mo., 1845
993. Mary A. Eastburn,	Attleboro', Pa.,	" "
994. Elizabeth Buckman,	Makefield, Pa.,	" "
995. Susanna Bates,	Montpelier, Va.,	" "
996. Sarah Bates,	"	" "
997. Mary B. Gardiner,	Mt. Holly, N. J.,	" "
998. Abby Ann Trump,	Salem, N. J.,	" "
999. Hannah Cooper,	Sadsbury, Pa.,	" "
1000. Rebecca Cooper,	"	" "

FIFTH THOUSAND.

NAME.	RESIDENCE.	DATE OF ENTRY.
1. Margaret Wilson,	Perquimans Co., N. C.,	5th mo., 1845.
2. Isabella Wilson,	"	" "
3. Margaret Newby,	"	" "
4. Sarah Glover,	Burlington, N. J.,	" "
5. Eliz. W. Wistar,	Abington, Pa.,	" "
6. Anna Pharo,	Philadelphia, Pa.,	" "
7. Mary S. West,	Nottingham, Md.,	" "
8. Catharine Lee,	Exeter, Pa.,	10th mo., "
9. Amy G. Abbott,	Salem, N. J.,	" "
10. Sarah C. Tatum,	Woodbury, N. J.,	" "
11. Mary Wood,	Rahway, N. J.,	" "
12. Miriam Lippincott,	Moorestown, N. J.,	" "
13. Frances A. Adams,	Philadelphia, Pa.,	" "
14. Sarah Jane Willits,	——, N. Y.,	" "
15. Sarah C. Wilbur,	Fall River, Mass.,	" "
16. Rachel Buffington,	"	" "
17. Susan J. Kinney,	Camden, Del.,	" "
18. Beulah Cattell,	Brownsville, Pa.,	5th mo., 1847.
19. Susan E. Dickinson,	Philadelphia, Pa.,	10th mo., 1845.
20. Mary Warner,	Muncy, Pa.,	5th mo., 1847.
21. Lucinda Lake,	Philadelphia, Pa.,	10th mo., 1845.

STUDENTS.

FIFTH THOUSAND.

NAME.	RESIDENCE.	DATE OF ENTRY.
22. Sarah Whitall,	Philadelphia, Pa.,	10th mo., 1845.
23. Amelia A. Pennell,	Chichester, Pa.,	" "
24. Marg. M. Webster,	Plainfield, N. J.,	" "
25. Lucy E. Healy,	Milestown, Pa.,	" "
26. Sarah Ann Hayward,	Baltimore, Md.,	" "
27. Josephine Carroll,	Port Carbon, Pa.,	5th mo., 1846.
28. Jane H. Fisher,	Cayuga Co., N. Y.,	" "
29. Sarah N. Fletcher,	Richmond, Ind.,	" "
30. Semira Hiatt,	Milton, Ohio,	" "
31. Rachel Scattergood,	Philadelphia, Pa.,	" "
32. Hannah Dilworth,	Solesbury, Pa.,	" "
33. Eliza P. Wilson,	Rahway, N. J.,	" "
34. Martha Ecroyd,	Muncy, Pa.,	" "
35. Laura Pleasants,	Philadelphia, Pa.,	" "
36. Miriam L. Vail,	Woodbridge, N. J.,	" "
37. Emma Williams,	Philadelphia, Pa.,	" "
38. Caroline Martin,	"	" "
39. Susan B. Trump,	"	" "
40. Anna Spencer,	Gwynedd, Pa.,	" "
41. Mary A. Rhoads,	Marple, Pa.,	" "
42. Anna C. Valentine,	Philadelphia, Pa.,	" "
43. Ellen Remington,	"	" "
44. Caroline Remington,	"	" "
45. Henrietta Haines,	Evesham, N. J.,	" "
46. Caroline B. Wood,	Philadelphia, Pa.,	" "
47. Elizabeth B. Wood,	"	" "
48. Mary J. Crenshaw,	———, Va.,	" "
49. Martha Ann Bates,	Richmond, Va.,	" "
50. Catharine Bates,	"	" "
51. Anna Lee,	Exeter, Pa.,	10th mo., "
52. Henrietta Warrington,	Westfield, N. J.,	" "
53. Tacy Bates,	Smithfield, Ohio,	" "
54. Josephine Clark,	Princeton, N. J.,	" "
55. Rebecca R. Haines,	Marlton, N. J.,	" "
56. Hannah B. Child,	Jefferson Co., N. Y.,	" "
57. Marianna Haines,	Trenton, N. J.,	" "
58. Elizabeth Balderston,	Fallsington, Pa.,	" "
59. Ann E. McGrew,	Smithfield, Ohio,	" "
60. Hannah J. Parker,	Parkersville, Pa.,	" "
61. Maria Eldridge,	Willistown, Pa.,	" "
62. Lucy Ann Burr,	Mt. Holly, N. J.,	" "
63. Rachel Griffith,	Middletown, Pa.,	" "
64. Hannah Gibbons,	West Chester, Pa.,	" "
65. Elizabeth L. Hayes,	East Fallowfield, Pa.,	" "
66. Hannah S. Pennell,	Middletown, Pa.,	" "
67. Mary Brinton,	Lampeter, Pa.,	" "
68. Elizabeth A. Dingee,	West Bradford, Pa.,	5th mo., 1847.

24*

FIFTH THOUSAND.

NAME.	RESIDENCE.	DATE OF ENTRY.
69. Elizabeth A. Brinton,	Lancaster Co., Pa.,	5th mo., 1847
70. Mary G. Hoopes,	Westtown, Pa.,	10th mo., 1846.
71. Anna Baily,	Pine Iron Works, Pa.,	5th mo., 1847.
72. Wilhelm'a Townsend,	Plainfield, N. J.,	" "
73. Keturah L. Roberts,	Haddonfield, N. J.,	" "
74. Deborah C. Parker,	Woodbury, N. J.,	" "
75. Hannah Heacock,	Muncy, Pa.,	" "
76. Sarah R. Conard,	Philadelphia, Pa.,	" "
77. Lydia Ann Hoopes,	West Bradford, Pa.,	" "
78. Hannah Underhill,	Sing Sing, N. Y.,	" "
79. Caroline Hallowell,	Alexandria, Va.,	10th mo., "
80. Mary Harlan,	Little Britain, Pa.,	" "
81. Edith T. Phillips,	Hockessin, Del.,	" "
82. Anna Mary Harvey,	Birmingham, Pa.,	" "
83. Mary Webb,	"	" "
84. Anna Knight,	Philadelphia, Pa.,	" "
85. Rachel Sheppard,	Greenwich, N. J.,	" "
86. Malvina Stokes,	Philadelphia, Pa.,	" "
87. Elmira Stevenson,	Bloomsbury, N. J.,	4th mo., 1848.
88. Hannah Hannum,	Kennet Square, Pa.,	5th mo., 1859.
89. Sarah T. House,	Pennsbury, Pa.,	10th mo., 1847.
90. Rachel Hoopes,	Goshen, Pa.,	" "
91. Philena Webb,	E. Marlborough, Pa.,	" "
92. Rebecca Judkins,	Cincinnati, Ohio,	4th mo., 1848.
93. Rebecca S. Williams,	Germantown, Pa.,	10th mo., 1847.
94. Sarah Williams,	"	" "
95. Sarah Ann Griffith,	East Whiteland, Pa.,	" "
96. Martha J. Reynolds,	Harrisville, Md.,	4th mo., 1848.
97. Hannah Llewellyn,	London Grove, Pa.,	" "
98. Phebe D. Phillips,	Kennet Square, Pa.,	" "
99. Emily B. Phillips,	"	" "
100. Sarah A. P. Brown,	New London, Pa.,	" "
101. Mary G. Hazard,	Dutchess Co., N. Y.,	10th mo., 1846.
102. Rachel L. Albertson,	Plymouth, Pa.,	" "
103. Clarissa Fussell,	Baltimore, Md.,	" "
104. Lydia C. Hazard,	Dutchess Co., N. Y.,	" "
105. Hannah W. Burton,	Fallsington, Pa.,	" "
106. Rebecca Haines,	Marlton, N. J.,	4th mo., 1848.
107. Emma Reeve,	Allowaystown, N. J.,	10th mo., 1846.
108. Edith Dawson,	Easton, Md.,	5th mo., 1847.
109. Elizabeth Smith,	Sadsbury, Pa.,	" "
110. Mary B. Spencer,	Moreland, Pa.,	" "
111. Rebecca B. Price,	Smithfield, Ohio,	" "
112. Elizabeth P. Wood,	Chesterfield, Ohio,	" "
113. Esther T. Haines,	Medford, N. J.,	" "
114. Susan S. Reeve,	"	" "
115. Ann H. Nicholson,	Haddonfield, N. J.,	" "

STUDENTS.

FIFTH THOUSAND.

NAME.	RESIDENCE.	DATE OF ENTRY.
116. Anna Collins,	Philadelphia, Pa.,	5th mo., 1847.
117. Hannah Wills,	Rancocas, N. J.,	" "
118. Sarah M. Brown,	Plymouth, Pa.,	" "
119. Hannah Pancoast,	Springfield, Pa.,	" "
120. Rebecca H. Merritt,	Salem, N. J.,	" "
121. Susan Pound,	Plainfield, N. J.,	" "
122. Catharine Griffin,	Clinton, N. Y.,	10th mo., "
123. Lydia Griffin,	"	" "
124. Sarah L. West,	Rowlandsville, Md.,	5th mo., 1859.
125. Tacy E. Carey,	Trenton, N. J.,	10th mo., 1847.
126. Mary C. Eastburn,	Newtown, Pa.,	" "
127. Mary Knight,	Philadelphia, Pa.,	" "
128. Miriam Decou,	Trenton, N. J.,	" "
129. Eliz. M. Lippincott,	Haddonfield, N. J.,	" "
130. Sarah M. Taylor,	Mt. Holly, N. J.,	" "
131. Thom. M. Borton,	Evesham, N. J.,	" "
132. Sidney Ann Bonsall,	Salem, Ohio,	5th mo., 1859.
133. Temperance Foster,	Hopkinton, R. I.,	10th mo., 1847.
134. Lydia B. Evans,	Cropwell, N. J.,	" "
135. Rachel Borton,	Rancocas, N. J.,	" "
136. Sarah H. Albertson,	Philadelphia, Pa.,	" "
137. Rachel Pennell,	Darby, Pa.,	" "
138. Elizabeth Tatnall,	Wilmington, Del.,	5th mo., 1859.
139. Mary H. Roberts,	Evesham, N. J.,	10th mo., 1847.
140. Mary W. Haines,	Milford, N. J.,	4th mo., 1848.
141. Caroline Williams,	Philadelphia, Pa.,	" "
142. Mary Parke,	"	" "
143. Rebecca G. Wood,	Rahway, N. J.,	" "
144. Anna Scattergood,	Philadelphia, Pa.,	" "
145. Mary Dutton,	Burlington, N. J.,	" "
146. Anna Maria Vail,	Rahway, N. J.,	" "
147. Rachel Haines,	Moorestown, N. J.,	" "
148. Mary C. Haines,	"	" "
149. Sarah M. Richards,	Nottingham, Md.,	" "
150. Susan Brinton,	Leacock, Pa.,	" "
151. Catharine Cooper,	Lampeter, Pa.,	" "
152. Sarah H. Matson,	Chadd's Ford, Pa.,	" "
153. Philena Yarnall,	Middletown, Pa.,	" "
154. Lydia H. Yarnall,	"	" "
155. Deborah Brookes,	Burlington, N. J.,	" "
156. Elizabeth Kirk,	Goshen, Pa.,	" "
157. Rebecca Healy,	Fallsington, Pa.,	" "
158. Elizabeth Snowdon,	Philadelphia, Pa.,	" "
159. Rebecca D. Maris,	West Pikeland, Pa.,	5th mo., 1853.
160. Mary Ann Haydock,	Wilmington, Del.,	6th mo., 1848.
161. Mary A. Pennell,	Upper Chichester, Pa.,	10th mo., "
162. Sarah Linton,	Newtown, Pa.,	" "

FIFTH THOUSAND.

NAME.	RESIDENCE.	DATE OF ENTRY.
163. Mary Pyle,	East Fallowfield, Pa.,	10th mo., 1848.
164. Emily Roberts,	Lower Merion, Pa.,	" "
165. Mary Pennell,	Middletown, Pa.,	" "
166. Mary Dingee,	West Bradford, Pa.,	" "
167. Minerva Webb,	Pennsbury, Pa.,	" "
168. Han. H. Thompson,	Newark, Del.,	" "
169. Elizabeth Cope,	East Bradford, Pa.,	" "
170. Ellen Cope,	"	" "
171. Zilla Monks,	Chester Co., Pa.,	" "
172. Margaret Fothergill,	Philadelphia, Pa.,	" "
173. Emily R. Temple,	Middletown, Pa.,	" "
174. Rebecca Webster,	Philadelphia, Pa.,	4th mo., 1849.
175. Elizabeth P. Ogborn,	Germantown, Pa.,	10th mo., 1848.
176. Eliz. A. Thompson,	W. Marlborough, Pa.,	" "
177. Esther Roberts,	Haddonfield, N. J.,	" "
178. Susanna Evans,	Springfield, Pa.,	" "
179. Emily Baily,	Westtown, Pa.,	" "
180. Susan Gibbons,	Salem, N. J.,	5th mo., 1853.
181. Marg. M. Webster,	Plainfield, N. J.,	4th mo., 1849.
182. Sarah A. Webster,	"	" "
183. Hannah A. Scott,	Downingtown, Pa.,	" "
184. Emily Pusey,	London Grove, Pa.,	" "
185. Abigail P. Townsend,	Plainfield, N. J.,	" "
186. Sarah L. Passmore,	London Britain, Pa.,	" "
187. Loretta Thomas,	Goshen, Pa.,	" "
188. Cornelia Janney,	Loudon Co., Va.,	" "
189. Hannah B. Gifford,	Tuckerton, N. J.,	" "
190. Mary W. Cox,	"	" "
191. Mary Ann Brookes,	Woodstown, N. J.,	" "
192. Sally A. Westbrook,	———, N. J.,	" "
193. Hannah M. Wilson,	Philadelphia, Pa.,	" "
194. Eleanor Haydock,	Wilmington, Del.,	" "
195. Rachel Poole,	Hockessing, Del.,	" "
196. Catharine Levis,	Springfield, Pa.,	10th mo., "
197. Hannah W. Bassett,	Philadelphia, Pa.,	" "
198. Eliz. M. Hoagland,	Rahway, N. J.,	" "
199. Elizabeth Garrett,	Willistown, Pa.,	" "
200. Sarah Brown,	New Garden, Pa.,	" "
201. Phebe Embree,	Marshallton, Pa.,	4th mo., 1848.
202. Elizabeth R. Wills,	Rancocas, N. J.,	" "
203. Sarah E. Healy,	Abington, Pa.,	" "
204. Elizabeth Swift,	Philadelphia, Pa.,	5th mo., "
205. Mary J. Lewis,	New Garden, Pa.,	10th mo., "
206. Hannah Roberts,	Moorestown, N. J.	" "
207. Anna M. Hilyard,	Rancocas, N. J.,	" "
208. Rachel Ballinger,	Haddonfield, N. J.,	" -"
209. Rachel Roberts,	Moorestown, N. J.,	" "

STUDENTS.

FIFTH THOUSAND.

NAME.	RESIDENCE.	DATE OF ENTRY
210. Rebecca Nicholson,	Haddonfield, N. J.,	10th mo., 1848.
211. Ann Foulke,	Somerton, Va.,	" "
212. Phebe Jane Wood,	Rahway, N. J.,	" "
213. Lydia L. Ashead,*	Cropwell, N. J.,	" "
214. Hannah A. Haines,	Marlton, N. J.,	" "
215. Ruth A. Albertson,	Plymouth, Pa.,	4th mo., 1849.
216. Mary A. Sheppard,	Greenwich, N. J.,	10th mo., 1848.
217. Ellen Moore,	Merion, Pa.,	" "
218. Mary E. Tyson,	Fairfax Co., Va.,	" "
219. Mary Lippincott,	Moorestown, N. J.,	" "
220. Keziah Webster,	Philadelphia, Pa.,	" "
221. Lydia S. Gifford,	Westport, Mass.,	" "
222. Louisa Buffington,	Fall River, Mass.,	" "
223. Emeline Ogborn,	Philadelphia, Pa.,	" "
224. Mary Bacon,	Salem, N. J.,	4th mo., 1849.
225. Hannah B. Roberts,	Rancocas, N. J.,	5th mo., 1859.
226. Mary A. Harris,	Bellefonte, Pa.,	4th mo., 1849.
227. Eliza Miller,	"	" "
228. Anna Whitall,	Philadelphia, Pa.,	" "
229. Harriet Brown,	———, N. Y.,	" "
230. Rebecca Magarge,	Germantown, Pa.,	" "
231. Anna Thomas,	Burlington, N. J.,	" "
232. Jane E. Masters,	Millville, Pa.,	5th mo., 1859.
233. Sarah A. Levick,	Philadelphia, Pa.,	4th mo., 1849.
234. Caroline M. Rulon,	"	" "
235. Rebecca Shinn,	"	" "
236. Elizabeth Matlack,	"	" "
237. Hannah E. Collins,	Salem, Iowa,	" "
238. Rebecca Wistar,	Salem, N. J.,	" "
239. Ann E. Butler,	Petersburg, Va.,	" "
240. Matilda Willits,	Danville, Pa.,	" "
241. Elizabeth Pyle,	East Fallowfield, Pa.,	10th mo., "
242. Amy J. Roberts,	Evesham, N. J.,	5th mo., 1859.
243. Elizabeth H. Rhoads,	Springfield, Pa.,	10th mo., 1849.
244. Phebe M. Larkin,	Concord, Pa.,	" "
245. Anna Eliza Gough,	———, N. Y.,	" "
246. Cath. W. Bostwick,	Rancocas, N. J.,	4th mo., 1850.
247. Mary G. Fogg,	Philadelphia, Pa.,	10th mo., 1849.
250. Lydia S. Pennell,	Middletown, Pa.,	4th mo., 1850.
251. Hannah Pennell,	"	" "
252. Mary S. Parker,	West Chester, Pa.,	" "
253. Sarah Pennock,	Sadsbury, Pa.,	" "
254. Lydia G. Thomas,	Goshen, Pa.,	" "
255. Phebe T. Cook,	Harford Co., Md.,	" "
256. Elizabeth Linton,	Marshallton, Pa.,	" "

* Deceased at the school, 8th of First month, 1849.

GENERAL CATALOGUE.

FIFTH THOUSAND.

NAME.	RESIDENCE.	DATE OF ENTRY.
257. Martha Cowgill,	Kent Co., Del.,	4th mo., 1850.
258. Martha Griffith,	Winchester, Va.,	" "
259. Sarah Saunders,	Salem, N. J.,	" "
260. Rosina A. Aronson,	Mansfield, N. J.,	" "
261. Sarah E. Knight,	Fallsington, Pa.,	10th mo., "
262. Sarah H. Price,	West Chester, Pa.,	5th mo., 1859.
263. Hannah P. Smedley,	Middletown, Pa.,	10th mo., 1850.
264. Martha Pierson,	Concord, Pa.,	" "
265. Esther Roberts,	Evesham, N. J.,	5th mo., 1859.
266. Esther Good,	West Grove, Pa.,	10th mo., 1850.
267. Emily Kinsey,	"	" "
268. Anna P. Sharpless,	Strickersville, Pa.,	11th mo., 1859.
269. Edith Sharpless,	Birmingham, Pa.,	10th mo., 1850.
270. Rebecca R. Preston,	Nottingham, Md.,	" "
271. Mary Louisa Walter,	Parkersville, Pa.,	11th mo., 1859.
272. Philena P. Jackson,	Rising Sun, Md.,	10th mo., 1850.
273. Mary J. Hopkins,	Baltimore, Md.,	" "
274. Anne Ecroyd,	Muncy, Pa.,	" "
275. Indiana Underhill,	———, Ind.,	" "
276. Hannah A. Griffith,	Middletown, Pa.,	" "
277. Amy Griffith,	"	" "
278. Sarah E. Swain,	York Co., Pa.,	" "
279. Mary W. Moore,	Sadsbury, Pa.,	" "
280. Edith Cooper,	Bart, Pa.,	" "
281. Phebe Lukens,	Horsham, Pa.,	" "
282. Emma Bassett,	Wilmington, Del.,	5th mo., 1852.
283. Abigail C. Woolman,	Frankford, Pa.,	10th mo., 1850.
284. Priscilla Hutton,	Lancaster Co., Pa.,	" "
285. Philena Pyle,	East Fallowfield, Pa.,	6th mo., 1851.
286. Portia Haines,	Pipe Creek, Md.,	" "
287. Louisa A. Corbit,	Cantwell's Bridge, Del.,	11th mo., "
288. Phebe J. Underhill,*	Poughkeepsie, N. Y.,	6th mo., "
289. Edith D. Scott,	Gunpowder, Md.,	" "
291. Mary E. Simmons,	Bart, Pa.,	11th mo., 1859.
292. Sarah J. Cooper,	Sadsbury, Pa.,	6th mo., 1851.
293. Charity Baldwin,	Downingtown, Pa.,	" "
294. Elizabeth C. Smith,	Darlington, Md.,	11th mo., 1859.
295. Anna M. Smedley,	West Chester, Pa.,	6th mo., 1851.
296. Hannah J. James,	"	11th mo., 1859.
297. Ruth Anna Brown,	Burlington, N. J.,	" 1851.
298. Susanna House,	Pennsbury, Pa.,	" "
299. Abigail Eldridge,	Goshen, Pa.,	" "
300. Phebe Lamborn,	New Garden, Pa.,	" "
301. M. E. Satterthwaite,	Tecumseh, Mich.,	10th mo., 1849.
302. Mary A. Haines,	Medford, N. J.,	" "
303. Agnes H. Haines,	"	" "
304. Mary R. Dilks,	Philadelphia, Pa.,	" "

* Deceased at the school, 10th of Fourth mo., 1852.

STUDENTS.

FIFTH THOUSAND.

NAME.	RESIDENCE.	DATE OF ENTRY.
305. Elizabeth S. Richie,	Philadelphia, Pa.,	10th mo., 1849.
306. Sarah Darnell,	Cropwell, N. J.,	" "
307. Mary W. Hilyard,	Rancocas, N. J.,	" "
308. Eleanor K. Wood,	New York, N. Y.,	" "
309. Debby E. Cope,	Whiteland, Pa.,	" "
310. Harriet H. Thorn,	Crosswicks, N. J.,	" "
311. Hannah Haines,	Medford, N. J.,	" "
312. Rebecca M. Hopkins,	....	" "
313. Deborah Jones,	McCartyville, N. J.,	" "
314. C. A. Hendrickson,	Crosswicks, N. J.,	" "
315. Mary N. Ogborn,	Philadelphia, Pa.,	" "
316. Jane Croasdale,	Stroudsburg, Pa.,	" "
317. Anna Hazard,	Poplar Ridge, N. Y.,	11th mo., 1859
318. Anna Reeve,	Medford, N. J.,	4th mo., 1850.
319. Hannah Magarge,	Germantown, Pa.,	" "
320. Elizabeth Jones,	"	" "
321. Frances Pleasants,	"	" "
322. Elizabeth Woolman,	Frankford, Pa.,	" "
323. Anna M. Bolton,	Philadelphia, Pa.,	" "
324. Martha Parker,	Tuckerton, N. J.,	" "
325. Jane E. Haines,	Cropwell, N. J.,	" "
326. Sarah P. Buzby,	Evesham, N. J.,	" "
327. Mary Whitson,	Sadsbury, Pa.,	" "
328. Elizabeth Pettit,	Philadelphia, Pa.,	" "
329. Deborah S. Evans,	Cropwell, N. J.,	10th mo., "
330. Sarah E. Atwater,	Lockport, N. Y.,	" "
331. Emily Hilyard,	Rancocas, N. J.,	" "
332. Susan Wills,	"	" "
333. Mary W. Maris,	Chester, Pa.,	" "
334. Rebecca C. Darnell,	Evesham, N. J.,	" "
335. Ann Eliz. Comfort,	Penn's Manor, Pa.,	" "
336. Anna C. Underhill,	Poughkeepsie, N. Y.,	" "
337. Mary W. Underhill,	"	" "
338. Rachel J. Dilks,	Philadelphia, Pa.,	" "
339. Martha H. Garrett,	"	" "
340. Elizabeth Burton,	Fallsington, Pa.,	" "
341. Emily Temple,	Philadelphia, Pa.,	" "
342. Sarah E. Wilson,	"	" "
343. Rachel A. Wright,	Winchester, Va.,	11th mo., 1859.
344. Hannah Levick,	Philadelphia, Pa.,	10th mo., 1850.
345. Elizabeth Hazard,	Wash'n Hollow, N. Y.,	11th mo., 1851.
346. Eliz. W. Blakey,	Byberry, Pa.,	10th mo., 1850.
347. Hannah C. Saunders,	Woodbury, N. J.,	" "
348. Sarah G. Smith,	Harford Co., Md.,	" "
349. Sarah Nicholson,	Haddonfield, N. J.,	6th mo., 1851
350. Virginia Russell,	Baltimore, Md.,	" "
351. Mary Sharpless,	Philadelphia, Pa.,	" "

FIFTH THOUSAND.

NAME.	RESIDENCE.	DATE OF ENTRY.
352. Anna Deacon,	Burlington, N. J.,	6th mo., 1851.
353. Margaretta Thomas,	"	" "
354. Mary L. Hibberd,	East Bradford, Pa.,	" "
355. Hannah H. Stokes,	Westfield, N. J.,	" "
356. Amanda Russell,	Baltimore, Md.,	" "
357. R. C. Lippincott,	Haddonfield, N. J.,	" "
358. Ann Bishop,	Mt. Holly, N. J.,	" "
359. Lydia Bishop,	"	" "
360. Anna Hopkins,	Annapolis, Md.,	" "
361. Ellen Deacon,	Burlington, N. J.,	11th mo., "
362. Isabella S. Phipps,	Lionville, Pa.,	" "
363. Elizabeth Haviland,	South Dover, N. Y.,	" "
364. Rebecca J. Allen,	Springfield, Pa.,	" "
365. Amanda M. Ash,	West Caln, Pa.,	" "
366. Mary Yearsley,	"	" "
367. Ann E. Maule,	Radnor, Pa.,	5th mo., 1852.
368. Ruth Ann Riker,	Medford, N. J.,	" "
369. Mary Lownes,	Buckingham, Pa.,	" "
370. Mary J. Walton,	E. Marlborough, Pa.,	" "
371. Elizabeth Harry,	Uwchlan, Pa.,	" "
372. Jane Flagler,	Dutchess Co., N. Y.,	" "
374. Agnes Alderson,	Cincinnati, Ohio,	" "
375. Anna M. Alderson,	"	" "
376. Lydia Wilson,	Perquimans Co., N. C.,	" "
377. Ann Hayes,	E. Marlborough, Pa.,	" "
378. Lydia J. Brown,	Pughtown, Pa.,	" "
379. Hannah Ann Cox,	Philadelphia, Pa.,	" "
380. Jane G. Hoopes,	New Garden, Pa.,	" "
381. Rebecca H. Harlan,	Doe Run, Pa.,	" "
383. Sidney Temple,	Parkersville, Pa.,	" "
384. Mary Tomlinson,	Edgmont, Pa.,	11th mo., "
385. Phebe Ogborn,	Germantown, Pa.,	" "
386. Lydia Ann Kinsey,*	Centreville, Del.,	" "
387. Hannah Kester,	Bloomsburg, Pa.,	" "
388. Martha Sankey,	Westtown, Pa.,	" "
389. Jane H. Garrett,	Birmingham, Pa.,	" "
390. Jane Garrett,	Willistown, Pa.,	" "
391. Rebecca Smedley,	Middletown, Pa.,	" "
392. Edith E. Haworth,	Wilmington, Ohio,	5th mo., 1853.
393. Marianna Hunt,	Mahoning Co., Ohio,	11th mo., 1852.
394. Fanny Hayes,	Westtown, Pa.,	" "
395. Anne Pennell,	Middletown, Pa.,	" "
396. Rachel M. Ellis,	Kirkwood, Ohio,	" "
397. Anna Townsend,	Palmyra, N. Y.,	" "
398. Margaret Townsend,	"	" "

*Hannah Elma Kinsey was admitted on same number, Eleventh month, 1857.

STUDENTS.

FIFTH THOUSAND.

NAME.	RESIDENCE.	DATE OF ENTRY.
399. Sarah Ann Pusey,	London Grove, Pa.,	5th mo., 1853.
400. Anne Snowdon,	Westtown, Pa.,	11th mo., 1852.
401. Marian B. Lloyd,	Wilmington, Del.,	" 1851.
402. Esther C. Miller,	Salem, N. J.,	" "
403. Anna M. Taylor,	Burlington, N. J.,	" "
404. Sarah S. Wills,	Rancocas, N. J.,	" "
405. Sarah S. Reeve,	Medford, N. J.,	" "
406. Caroline Whitall,	Philadelphia, Pa.,	" "
407. Rebecca W. Zelley,	Moorestown, N. J.,	" "
408. Henrietta Vail,	Plainfield, N. J.,	" "
410. Susanna D. Buzby,	Burlington, N. J.,	" "
411. Jane Eachus,	Edgmont, Pa.,	" "
412. Mary Walmsley,	Philadelphia, Pa.,	" "
413. Sarah Jane Grubb,	"	" "
414. Mary R. Masters,	Muncy, Pa.,	" "
415. Mary W. Lee,	Stonersville, Pa.,	5th mo., 1852.
416. Sarah L. Allen,	Philadelphia, Pa.,	" "
417. Helen R. Bacon,	"	" "
418. Sally Wistar,	"	" "
419. Mary E. Harry,	E. Marlborough, Pa.,	" "
420. Hannah Evans,	Philadelphia, Pa.,	" "
421. Catharine Evans,	"	" "
422. Eliz. C. Ballenger,	Evesham, N. J.,	" "
423. Rachel S. Fogg,	Philadelphia, Pa.,	" "
424. Elizabeth B. Collins,	Burlington, N. J.,	" "
425. Abigail E. Haines,	Medford, N. J.,	" "
426. Sarah Savery,	Philadelphia, Pa.,	" "
427. Deborah F. Haines,	Medford, N. J.,	" "
428. Anna M. Bartlett,	Huron Co., Ohio,	11th mo., "
429. Martha W. Bartlett,	"	" "
430. Elizabeth G. Evans,	Philadelphia, Pa.,	" "
431. Lydia Evans,	Marlton, N. J.,	" "
432. Em. J. Gillingham,	Philadelphia, Pa.,	" "
433. Mary Thompson,	Newport, Del.,	5th mo., 1854.
434. Elizabeth G. King,	Burlington, N. J.,	11th mo., 1852.
435. Elizabeth Reeves,	Woodbury, N. J.,	" "
436. Jane Darnell,	Mt. Laurel, N. J.,	" "
437. Agnes M. Darnell,	"	" "
438. Elizabeth Pennock,	Holmesburg, Pa.,	" "
439. Deborah Warner,	Muncy, Pa.,	" "
440. Harriet Griffith,	Winchester, Va.,	" "
441. Mary Anna Roberts,	Moorestown, N. J.,	" "
442. Priscilla W. Haines,	Medford, N. J.,	" "
443. Amy Haines,	"	" "
444. Sallie W. Carpenter,	Salem, N. J.,	" "
445. Anna S. Haines,	Medford, N. J.,	" "
446. Deborah O. Ricks,	Prospect Hill, Va.,	" 1859.

25 T

GENERAL CATALOGUE.

FIFTH THOUSAND.

NAME.	RESIDENCE.	DATE OF ENTRY.
447. Alice Hallowell,	Upper Merion, Pa.,	11th mo., 1852.
448. Phebe Lukens,	Horsham, Pa.,	" "
449. Elizabeth Potts,	Springfield, Pa.,	" "
450. Hannah Vivian,	Burlington, N. J.,	" "
451. Hannah D. Mitchell,	Philadelphia, Pa.,	12th mo., "
452. Asenath Hill,	Hill's Store, N. C.,	11th mo., "
453. Sarah Henly,	Caraway, N. C.,	" "
454. Jane M. Eldridge,	Willistown, Pa.,	" "
455. Eliz. E. Lippincott,	Moorestown, N. J.,	5th mo., 1853.
456. Sally E. Pim,	Downingtown, Pa.,	" "
457. Sarah D. Hoopes,	"	" "
458. Alice P. Gruwell,	Damascus, Ohio,	" "
459. Sarah Ellen Thomas,	Midway, Pa.,	" "
460. Margaret Eldridge,	Warren Tavern, Pa.,	" "
461. Sarah A. Michener,	Rising Sun, Md.,	" "
462. Elizabeth Cope,	Whiteland, Pa.,	" "
463. Susanna R. Cooper,	Parkesburg, Pa.,	" "
464. Deborah P. Smedley,	Willistown, Pa.,	" "
465. Mary E. Cooper,	Christiana, Pa.,	10th mo., 1853.
466. Rachel A. Fawkes,	Giger's Mill, Pa.,	" "
467. Phebe Jane Walter,	Parkersville, Pa.,	11th mo., 1859.
468. Ann E. Jones,	Philadelphia, Pa.,	5th mo., 1853.
469. Sarah M. Thompson,	Newport, Del.,	10th mo., "
470. Mary Gubbings,	New Garden, Pa.,	" "
471. Esther Kite,	Birmingham, Pa.,	" "
472. Hannah Boone,	Pickering, Can. West,	" "
473. Rachel A. Holloway,	Flushing, Ohio,	" "
474. Rebecca J. Townsend,	Plainfield, N. J.,	" "
475. Lydia Ann Scarlet,	Birdsboro', Pa.,	" "
476. Anna M. J. Brown,	Avondale, Pa.,	" "
477. Annie E. Windle,	Guthrieville, Pa.,	" "
478. Thomazine T. Miller,	Bellefonte, Pa.,	" "
479. Josephine M. Hoge,	Pleasant Valley, Va.,	" "
480. Hannah Baily,	Parkersville, Pa.,	" "
( ) Rachel G. Preston,	Westtown, Pa.,	" "
481. Annie Cheyney,	London Grove, Pa.,	" "
482. Elmira Wickersham,	West Grove, Pa.,	" "
483. Anna G. Edge,	Wilmington, Del.,	5th mo., 1854.
484. Mary Jane Peckham,	Somerset, N. Y.,	10th mo., 1853.
485. Phebe C. Brown,	Jennerville, Pa.,	5th mo., 1854.
486. Elizabeth D. Edge,	Downingtown, Pa.,	" "
487. Amy R. Sheffield,	Hopkinton, R. I.,	" "
488. Deborah J. Windle,	Guthrieville, Pa.,	" "
489. Phebe Ann Moore,	Christiana, Pa.,	" "
490. Mary E. Reed,	Darlington, Md.,	" "
491. Elizabeth J. Brown,	New Garden, Pa.,	" "
492. Susan Underhill,	Brooklyn, N. Y.,	11th mo., "

STUDENTS. 317

FIFTH THOUSAND.

NAME.	RESIDENCE.	DATE OF ENTRY.
493. Mary Ann Temple,	Parkersville, Pa.,	11th mo., 1854.
494. Philena Smedley,	West Chester, Pa.,	5th mo., "
495. Martha Larkin,	Guthrieville, Pa.,	" "
496. Sarah E. Harlan,	Doe Run, Pa.,	" "
497. Susanna M. Sutton,	Norwich, Can. West,	" "
498. Eliza T. Harris,	Downingtown, Pa.,	" "
499. Sarah F. Cloud,	Woodbury, N. J.,	11th mo., "
500. Mary B. Thompson,	New London, Pa.,	5th mo., 1853.
501. Caroline E. Cope,	Woodbourne, Pa.,	" "
502. Annette Cope,	"	" "
503. Sarah Dilworth,	New Hope, Pa.,	" "
504. Edith L. Chase,	Burlington, N. J.,	" "
505. Mary W. Pharo,	Philadelphia, Pa.,	" "
506. Eliz. W. Hilyard,	Rancocas, N. J.,	" "
507. Mercy W. Brown,	Fallsington, Pa.,	" "
508. Elizabeth B. Kaighn,	Philadelphia, Pa.,	" "
509. Sarah M. Richie,	"	" "
510. Mary T. Hilyard,	Rancocas, N. J.,	" "
511. Martha W. Hilyard,	New York, N. Y.,	" "
512. Elizabeth Deacon,	Mt. Holly, N. J.,	" "
513. Eliz. P. Albertson,	Plymouth, Pa.,	" "
514. Hannah Whitall,	Philadelphia, Pa.,	" "
515. Sarah Maule,	Port Royal, Pa.,	" "
516. Ann E. Jones,	Conshohocken, Pa.,	" "
517. Mary Lawrence,	Philadelphia, Pa.,	" "
518. Anna Lawrence,	"	" "
519. Caroline Hoagland,	Muncy, Pa.,	" "
520. Elizabeth B. Allen,	Bristol, Pa.,	" "
521. Mary E. Allinson,	Crosswicks, N. J.,	" "
522. Anna Eliz. Dickinson,	Philadelphia, Pa.,	" "
523. Elizabeth S. Hoge,	Pleasant Valley, Va.,	" "
524. Phebe Ann Pyle,	Strickersville, Pa.,	" "
525. Martha Heacock,	Greenwood, Pa.,	" "
526. Anna W. King,	Burlington, N. J.,	" "
527. Emma Larkin,	Concordville, Pa.,	" "
528. Mary P. Lee,	Stonersville, Pa.,	" "
529. Anna Lippincott,	Woodstown, N. J.,	" "
530. Elizabeth Lownes,	Springfield, Pa.,	" "
531. Annabella C. Ogborn,	Germantown, Pa.,	" "
532. Mary H. Ash,	Philadelphia, Pa.,	10th mo., "
533. Sarah Garrett,	Upper Darby, Pa.,	" "
534. Mary Maule,	Radnor, Pa.,	" "
535. Ruth Kite,	Philadelphia, Pa.,	" "
536. Mercy E. Brown,	Centre Bridge, Pa.,	" "
537. Martha E. Stokes,	Stroudsburg, Pa.,	" "
538. Mary Kite,	Philadelphia, Pa.,	" "
539. Mercy Eastburn,	Newtown, Pa.,	" "

GENERAL CATALOGUE.

FIFTH THOUSAND.

NAME.	RESIDENCE.	DATE OF ENTRY.
540. Martha Bettle,	Philadelphia, Pa.,	10th mo., 1853
541. Deborah G. Passmore,	Edgmont, Pa.,	" "
542. S. N. Warrington,	Philadelphia, Pa.,	" "
543. M. E. Warrington,	"	" "
544. Maline Tostenson,	Stawage, Norway, Ee.,	" "
545. Anna Hazard,	Wash'n Hollow, N. Y.,	" "
546. Rachel E. Balderston,	Philadelphia, Pa.,	" "
547. Sarah Ann Seal,	Avondale, Pa.,	" "
548. Mary Jane Seal,	"	" "
549. Elizabeth P. Lee,	Stonersville, Pa.,	" "
550. Lydia P. Haviland,	Clinton Corners, N. Y.,	5th mo., 1860.
551. Lydia C. Hughes,	Jennerville, Pa.,	" 1856.
552. Mary R. Parry,	Philadelphia, Pa.,	" 1854.
553. Emma Parry,	"	" "
554. Eleanor S. Baker,	"	" "
555. Rebecca Pennell,	Middletown, Pa.,	" "
556. Sarah Richie,	Philadelphia, Pa.,	" "
557. Elizabeth W. Cope,	"	" "
558. Mary Anna Cope,	"	" "
559. Catharine Morris,	Marlton, N. J.,	" "
560. Margaret W. Richie,	Philadelphia, Pa.,	" "
561. Mary Sheppard,	Greenwich, N. J.,	" "
562. Elizabeth E. Haines,	Marlton, N. J.,	" "
563. Sarah Scull,	Philadelphia, Pa.,	" "
564. Elizabeth Carlile,	"	" "
565. Ann J. Kirkbride,	"	" "
566. Elizabeth L. Evans,	Marlton, N. J.,	" "
567. Hannah Ballenger,	Haddonfield, N. J.,	" "
568. Mary P. Lee,	Stonersville, Pa.,	" "
569. Mary C. Wildman,	Morrisville, Pa.,	" "
570. Mary G. Wood,	Clinton Corners, N. Y.,	" 1860.
571. Hannah Gubbings,	Germantown, Pa.,	" 1854.
572. Phebe C. Brown,	Jennerville, Pa.,	" "
573. Sidney Dilks,	Germantown, Pa.,	" "
574. E. L. Mendenhall,	Muncy, Pa.,	" "
575. Phebe W. Wilson,	Philadelphia, Pa.,	" "
576. Abigail Haviland,	Wing's Station, N. Y.,	" "
577. Abby Newhall,	Philadelphia, Pa.,	" "
578. Leontine R. Corse,	Wilmington, Del.,	" "
579. Rebecca J. Roberts,	Moorestown, N. J.,	11th mo., "
580. Mary Ann Cope,	Marshallton, Pa.,	" "
581. Ruth Anna Hallock,	Stanfordville, N. Y.,	5th mo., 1860.
582. Elizabeth C. Maule,	Philadelphia, Pa.,	11th mo., 1854.
583. Asenath Haines,	Medford, N. J.,	" "
584. Annie W. Hutton,	Chester, Pa.,	" "
585. Mary Hewes,	"	" "
586. Sarah Pennock,	Holmesburg, Pa.,	" "

STUDENTS.

FIFTH THOUSAND.

NAME	RESIDENCE	DATE OF ENTRY
587. Mary Anna Tilton,	Barnegat, N. J.,	11th mo., 1854.
588. Lydia T. Cumming,	Philadelphia, Pa.,	" "
589. Sarah E. Hacker,	"	" "
590. Susan Scattergood,	"	" "
591. Sarah Scattergood,	"	" "
592. Ruth Anna Richie,	"	" "
593. Rachel M. Johnson,	Parkesburg, Pa.,	" "
594. Rebecca Trimble,	Chester, Pa.,	5th mo., 1855.
595. Mary L. Buzby,	Mt. Laurel, N. J.,	" "
596. Rachel R. Haines,	Vincenttown, N. J.,	" "
597. Marg. M. Smith,	Philadelphia, Pa.,	" "
598. A. W. Albertson,	Plymouth, Pa.,	" "
599. Mary E. Ellison,	Kensington, Pa.,	" "
600. Ann E. Moore,	Richmond, Ind.,	11th mo., "
601. Mary J. Windle,	Guthrieville, Pa.,	" 1854.
602. Hannah T. Cope,	Kimbleville, Pa.,	" "
603. Elizabeth A. Joliffe,	Stephenson's Dep., Va.,	" "
604. Hannah W. Roberts,	Paoli, Pa.,	" "
605. Deborah L. Smedley,	Lima, Pa.,	" "
606. Elizabeth Evans,	Darlington, Md.,	" "
607. Rachel Dingee,	Uwchlan, Pa.,	" "
608. Sarah Embree,	Marshallton, Pa.,	" "
609. Hannah Ann Hoge,	Hamilton Store, Va.,	" "
610. Anna N. Watson,	Philadelphia, Pa.,	" "
611. Hannah Larkin,	Concordville, Pa.,	" "
612. Lydia Harvey,	Jennerville, Pa.,	" "
613. Rachel W. Cope,	West Chester, Pa.,	" "
614. Eliz. A. Sheffield,	Hopkinton, R. I.,	" "
615. Hannah M. Smedley,	Lima, Pa.,	" "
616. Ellen Knight,	Philadelphia, Pa.,	" "
617. Elizabeth Sankey,	Westtown, Pa.,	" "
618. Mary Anna Moore,	Bart, Pa.,	" "
619. Maria F. Cooper,	Camden, N. J.,	5th mo., 1855.
620. Hannah A. Cooper,	Gap, Pa.,	" "
621. Elizabeth Masters,	Millville, Pa.,	" "
622. Mary Jones,	Frankford, Pa.,	" "
623. Hannah J. Troth,	Columbus, N. J.,	" "
624. Hannah W. Roberts,	Willistown, Pa.,	11th mo., 1854.
625. Emily Kinsey,	Chatham, Pa.,	5th mo., 1855.
626. Ellen Parker,	West Chester, Pa.,	11th mo., "
627. Elizabeth Hoopes,	Downingtown, Pa.,	5th mo., "
628. Sidney Pennell,	Lima, Pa.,	" "
629. Wilhelmina Bell,	Richmond, Ind.,	" "
630. Phebe Davis,	Coatesville, Pa.,	" "
631. Sarah Wilson,	Newby's Bridge, N. C.,	" "
632. Anna Mckeel,	Tompkins Co., N. Y.,	" "
633. Martha J. Lightfoot,	Malaga, Ohio,	11th mo., 1856.

25*

FIFTH THOUSAND.

NAME.	RESIDENCE.	DATE OF ENTRY.	
634. Caroline Cope,	Warren Tavern, Pa.,	5th mo.,	1855.
635. Sarah E. Hallock,	Searsburg, N. Y.,	7th mo.,	1858.
636. Ph. P. Mendenhall,	Westminster, N. C.,	5th mo.,	1855.
637. Elizabeth Mckeel,	Tompkins Co., N. Y.,	"	"
638. Susan S. Way,	West Chester, Pa.,	"	"
639. Mary Barker,	Richmond, Ind.,	"	"
640. Mary E. Whitacre,	Muncy, Pa.,	"	"
( ) Margaret Benington,	Westtown, Pa.,	"	"
641. Elizabeth F. Perry,	Westerly, R. I.,	"	1860.
642. L. H. Tomlinson,	Ivy Mills, Pa.,	"	1855.
643. Mary Emma Stokes,	Cinnaminson, N. J.,	11th mo.,	"
644. Mary E. Harris,	Westminster, N. C.,	"	"
646. Rebecca Lippincott,	Woodstown, N. J.,	"	"
647. Mary M. Rote,	Millville, Pa.,	"	"
648. Mary J. Maris,	Kimberton, Pa.,	"	"
649. Sarah Jane Scott,	Marshallton, Pa.,	"	"
650. Annie E. Sheppard,	Greenwich, N. J.,	"	"
651. Phebe Ann Griffith,	Warren Tavern, Pa.,	"	"
652. Abigail N. Hill,	Hill's Store, N. C.,	"	"
653. Mary E. Scott,	Butler's P. O., Md.,	5th mo.,	1860.
654. Anna W. Tatnall,	Wilmington, Del.,	"	1856.
655. Margaret Tatnall,	"	"	"
656. Mary W. Savery,	Parkersville, Pa.,	"	"
657. Rebecca C. Smedley,	Paoli, Pa.,	"	"
658. Mary H. Huey,	Smyrna, Del.,	"	"
659. Sarah W. Huey,	"	"	"
660. Martha J. White,	Newby's Bridge, N. C.,	"	"
661. Anna Pim,	Thorndale, Pa.,	"	"
662. Mary Pim,	"	"	"
663. Deborah Cope,	West Chester, Pa.,	"	"
664. Edith H. Pusey,	London Grove, Pa.,	"	"
665. Phebe Ann Pharo,	Philadelphia, Pa.,	"	"
666. Margaret H. Janney,	Baltimore, Md.,	"	"
667. Lydia W. Taylor,	Chatham, Pa.,	"	"
669. Mary A. M. Irwin,	Guthrieville, Pa.,	11th mo.,	"
670.		"	"
671. Hannah Way,	Centerville, Del.,	"	"
672. Abby Gould,	Newport, R. I.,	"	"
673. Mercy S. Townsend,	Plainfield, N. J.,	"	"
674. Sarah Mendenhall,	Parkersville, Pa.,	"	"
675. Susanna T. Ballinger,	Leed's Point, N. J.,	"	"
676. Anna French,	Salem, Ohio,	"	"
677. Susan Jolliffe,	Stephenson's Dep., Va.,	"	"
678. Beulah Palmer,	Media, Pa.,	"	1858.
679. Mary E. Webb,	Parkersville, Pa.,	"	1856.
680. Rachel Hall,	Mt. Pleasant, Ohio,	"	"
681. Elvira Hall,	Barnesville, Ohio,	"	"

STUDENTS.

FIFTH THOUSAND.

NAME.	RESIDENCE.	DATE OF ENTRY.
682. Emily Thomas,	Booth's Corner, Pa.	11th mo., 1856.
683. Achsah A. Blakey,	Fallston, Md.,	5th mo., 1857.
684. Lydia C. Johnson,	Parkesburg, Pa.,	" "
685. Phebe W. Hoge,	Flushing, Ohio,	" "
686. Amy S. Barton,	Fellowship, N. J.,	" "
687. Rachel Moore,	Nine Points, Pa.,	" "
688. Jemima D. Johnson,	Danboro', Pa.,	" "
689. Matilda P. Ellison,	Philadelphia, Pa.,	" "
690. Mary R. Tatnall,	Wilmington, Del.,	" "
691. Rachel E. Allinson,	Yardville, N. J.,	" 1858.
692. Elizabeth Eldridge,	Johnstown, Pa.,	" 1857.
693. Virginia Griffith,	White Hall, Va.,	" "
694. Clara Moyse,	Cincinnati, Ohio,	" "
695. Emma Cope,	West Chester, Pa.,	" "
696. Mary S. Gilkeson,	Winchester, Va.,	" "
697. Sarah Worth,	Marshallton, Pa.,	" "
698. Elizabeth Sharpless,	Birmingham, Pa.,	11th mo., "
699. Susanna S. Kite,	"	" "
700. Susan Decou,	Trenton, N. J.,	5th mo., 1855.
701. Elizabeth Gubbings,	Germantown, Pa.,	" "
702. Jane Gubbings,	"	" "
703. Mary T. Evans,	Willistown, Pa.,	" "
704. Eunice Fawcett,	Salem, Ohio,	" "
705. Ann Street,	"	" "
706. Mary S. White,	Newby's Bridge, N. C.,	" "
707. Martha T. Lukens,	Horsham, Pa.,	" "
708. Mary L. Michener,	Chester Hill, Ohio,	" "
709. Ellen Matlack,	Germantown, Pa.,	" "
710. Rebecca Ballenger,	Marlton, N. J.,	11th mo., "
711. Mary Taylor,	West Grove, Pa.,	" "
712. Hannah Webster,	Middletown, Pa.,	" "
713. Sarah Webster,	"	" "
714. Mary R. Matlack,	Moorestown, N. J.,	" "
715. Marian A. Bartlett,	Bethlehem, Pa.,	" "
716. Esther G. Evans,	Haddonfield, N. J.,	" "
717. Abigail B. Evans,	"	" "
718. Annie B. Shoemaker,	Jenkintown, Pa.,	" "
719. Han. B. Shoemaker,	"	" "
720. Anna Smith,	Darlington, Md.,	" "
721. Sidney H. Brown,	Philadelphia, Pa.,	" "
722. Eliza L. Brown,	Fallsington, Pa.,	" "
723. Marg. E. McCollin,	Philadelphia, Pa.,	" "
724. Hannah E. Moore,	Bart, Pa.,	" "
725. Rachel Alexander,	Landisburg, Pa.,	" "
726. Rachel Barton,	Fellowship, N. J.,	" "
727. Anna M. Thorp,	Frankford, Pa.,	5th mo., 1856.
728. Mary Anna Kaighn,	Philadelphia, Pa.,	" "

FIFTH THOUSAND.

NAME.	RESIDENCE.	DATE OF ENTRY.
729. Mary E. Smith,	Philadelphia, Pa.,	5th mo., 1856
730. Elizabeth Wiggins,	Wrightstown, Pa.,	" "
731. Rachel Wiggins,	"	" "
732. Eliz. Mendenhall,	Parkersville, Pa.,	" 1860.
733. Anna D. Bacon,	Philadelphia, Pa.,	" 1856.
734. Rebecca Kite,	"	" "
735. Martha A. Haines,	Marlton, N. J.,	" "
736. Hettie W. Gardiner,	Mt. Holly, N. J.,	" "
737. Emily B. Gardiner,	"	" "
738. Rachel R. Yarnall,	Lima, Pa.,	" "
739. Emily A. Taylor,	Columbus, N. J.,	" "
740. Anna Eliza Gruwell,	Damascoville, Ohio,	" "
741. Mary Anna Bassett,	Stanton, Del.,	" "
742. Mary Susan Wright,	White Hall, Va.,	" 1860.
743. Alice R. Stokes,	Philadelphia, Pa.,	" 1856.
744. Sarah J. Cooper,	Gap, Pa.,	" "
745. Phebe Ann Parker,	Tuckerton, N. J.,	11th mo., "
746. Hannah Ann Cox,	West Creek, N. J.,	" "
747. Louisa P. Pharo,	Tuckerton, N. J.,	" "
748. Margaret T. Decou,	Georgetown, Pa.,	" "
749. Rachel Griffith,	Eagle, Pa.,	5th mo., 1860.
750. Mary S. Reeves,	Woodbury, N. J.,	11th mo., 1856.
751. Mary Griffith,	Eagle, Pa.,	5th mo., 1860.
752. Lydia Eldridge,	Goshenville, Pa.,	11th mo., 1856.
753. Margaret N. Thorp,	Frankford, Pa.,	" "
754. Hannah Matlack,	Germantown, Pa.,	" "
755. Rebecca C. Reeve,	Allowaystown, N. J.,	" "
756. Mary E. Rudolph,	Woodbury, N. J.,	" "
757. Rebecca Lee,	Stonersville, Pa.,	" "
758. Sarah Emma Masters,	Millville, Pa.,	" 1860.
759. Eliza J. Barton,	Fellowship, N. J.,	" 1856.
760. Anna R. Cooper,	Gap, Pa.,	" "
761. Mary J. Lee,	Stonersville, Pa.,	" "
762. Hannah S. Leeds,	Moorestown, N. J.,	" "
763. Anna Livezey,	Centre Bridge, Pa.,	" "
764. Rach. W. Middleton,	Crosswicks, N. J.,	5th mo., 1857.
765. Sarah L. Rudolph,	Woodbury, N. J.,	" "
766. Ruth Anna Thomas,	Philadelphia, Pa.,	" "
767. Edith S. Middleton,	Crosswicks, N. J.,	11th mo., "
768. Eliz. L. Woolman,	Philadelphia, Pa.,	5th mo., "
769. Caroline Deacon,	Burlington, N. J.,	" "
770. Mary Ann Pierson,	Avondale, Pa.,	" "
771. Mary E. Jones,	Philadelphia, Pa.,	" "
772. Eliz. H. Tatnall,	Wilmington, Del.,	" "
773. Ann Sharpless,	Chester, Pa.,	" "
774. Hannah Kite,	Philadelphia, Pa.,	" "
775. Phebe H. Chambers,	New Garden, Pa.,	" "

STUDENTS.

FIFTH THOUSAND.

NAME.	RESIDENCE.	DATE OF ENTRY.
776. Mary E. Dickinson,	Parkesburg, Pa.,	5th mo., 1857.
777. Rebecca A. Leeds,	Barnegat, N. J.,	" "
778. Esther R. Reid,	Brandywine Manor, Pa.,	" "
779. Sarah L. Woolman,	Mantuaville, Pa.,	" "
780. Harriet J. McCluen,	Marple, Pa.,	" 1863.
781. Achsah R. Taylor,	Columbus, N. J.,	11th mo., 1857.
782. Lucretia Way,	Centreville, Del.,	" "
783. Mary S. Haines,	Pleasant Grove, Pa.,	" "
784. Anna Cope,	Milltown, Pa.,	" "
785. Hannah Mitchell,	Flushing, Ohio,	" "
786. E. Jane Pennell,	Lima, Pa.,	" "
787. Sibilla S. Parvin,	Leesport, Pa.,	" 1860.
788. Anna M. Marshall,	Loveville, Del.,	" 1857.
789. Sarah T. Wilson,	"	" "
790. Anna E. Thompson,	New London, Pa.,	" "
791. Lydia A. Hoge,	Hughesville, Va.,	" 1860.
792. Jane B. Temple,	Parkersville, Pa.,	5th mo., 1858.
793. Lydia W. Mussey,	Mt. Pleasant, Ohio,	" "
794. Lydia Embree,	Marshallton, Pa.,	" "
795. Rachel W. Yearsley,	West Caln, Pa.,	" "
796. Susan W. Janney,	Hillsborough, Va.,	" "
797. Anna Eugenia Hoge,	Union Bridge, Md.,	11th mo., 1860.
798. Catharine S. Grubb,	Philadelphia, Pa.,	7th mo., 1858.
799. Mannah E. Maule,	Port Royal, Pa.,	11th mo., "
800. Deborah Y. Rich,	Plumstead, Pa.,	" "
( ) L. H. Tomlinson,	Westtown, Pa.,	" "
( ) Mary Thompson,	Darlington, Md.,	" "
801. Elizabeth P. Cook,	Rolandsville, Md.,	" "
802. Hannah E. Kirk,	Hickory Hill, Pa.,	" "
803. Mary A. Forsythe,	West Chester, Pa.,	" "
804. Deborah S. Yarnall,	Middletown, Pa.,	" "
805. Martha L. Sharpless,	Chester, Pa.,	" "
806. Cath. M. Stackhouse,	Howellville, Pa.,	" "
807. Rebecca L. Windle,	Milltown, Pa.,	" "
808. Anna W. Roberts,	Moorestown, N. J.,	" "
809. Elizabeth H. Roberts,	"	5th mo., 1860.
810. Elizabeth Smith,	Parkesburg, Pa.,	11th mo., 1858.
811. Amy Q. Mekeel,	Searsburg, N. Y.,	" "
812. Catharine Mekeel,	"	" "
813. Elizabeth Lippincott,	Woodstown, N. J.,	" "
814. Emily H. Pim,	Thorndale, Pa.,	" 1860.
815. Rebecca Moore,	Christiana, Pa.,	" "
816. Rachel Alsop,	Chatham, Pa.,	" "
817. Mary S. Jackson,	Wilmington, Del.,	" 1862.
818. Hannah R. Haines,	Marple, Pa.,	" 1860.
819. Mary Louisa Brown,	Jennerville, Pa.,	" "
820. Sarah Speakman,	Coatesville, Pa.,	" 1862.

GENERAL CATALOGUE.

FIFTH THOUSAND.

NAME.	RESIDENCE.	DATE OF ENTRY.
821. Phebe Taylor,	West Chester, Pa.,	11th mo., 1857.
822. Susanna G. Lear,	Warren Tavern, Pa.	" 1860.
823. Hannah Ladd,	Smithfield, Ohio,	" 1857.
824. Martha J. Wood,	"	" "
825. Rebecca B. Moore,	West Grove, Pa.,	" "
827. Hannah P. Husband,	Dublin, Md.,	" 1860.
828. Edna Stanton,	Richmond, Ind.,	12th mo., 1857.
829. Rebecca S. Walton,	Jenkintown, Pa.,	5th mo., 1858.
830. Hannah P. Rudolph,	Woodbury, N. J.,	" "
831. Susan Farnum,	Philadelphia, Pa.,	" "
832. Mary Anna Brown,	"	" "
833. Anna B. Warrington,	Cinnaminson, N. J.,	" "
834. Mary Scull,	Philadelphia, Pa.,	" "
835. Eliz. S. Garrett,	Upper Darby, Pa.,	" "
836. Sarah H. Roberts,	Moorestown, N. J.,	" "
837. Helen R. Parry,	Philadelphia, Pa.,	" "
838. Rachel Ann Cooper,	Chatham, Pa.,	" "
839. Angeline Rundell,	Eldredville, Pa.,	" "
840. Ellen McCarty,	"	" "
841. Ruthanna Potter,	Westtown, Pa.,	" "
842. Sarah Lukens,	Morrisville, Pa.,	" "
843. Hester Ann Green,	West Chester, Pa.,	11th mo., 1860.
844. Rebecca F. Brown,	Fallsington, Pa.,	" 1858.
845. Sarah Wiggins,	Wrightstown, Pa.,	" "
846. Lydia E. Wills,	Rancocas, N. J.,	" "
847. Sarah J. Borton,	"	" "
848. Mary Allen,	Woodstown, N. J.,	" "
849. Hannah K. Evens,	Marlton, N. J.,	" "
850. Elizabeth F. Haines,	Medford, N. J.,	" "
851. Sarah C. Haines,	Rancocas, N. J.,	" "
852. Rebecca H. Wilkins,	"	" "
853. Hannah Linton,	Cochranville, Pa.,	" "
854. Sarah E. Warner,	Muncy, Pa.,	" "
855. Sylvania Cooper,	Christiana, Pa.,	5th mo., 1860.
856. Hannah Dutton,	Philadelphia, Pa.,	11th mo., 1858.
857. Anna B. Allinson,	Burlington, N. J.,	" "
858. Anna Scattergood,*	Philadelphia, Pa.,	" "
859. Rachel E. Collins,	Mt. Laurel, N. J.,	" "
860. Emily N. Balderston,	Port Deposit, Md.,	" "
861. Sarah L. Evens,	Marlton, N. J.,	" "
862. Sarah W. Stokes,	Woodbury, N. J.,	5th mo., 1859.
863. Elizabeth Branson,	Philadelphia, Pa.,	" "
864. Elizabeth Dunn,	Trenton, N. J.,	" "
865. Anne T. Baily,	Germantown, Pa.,	" "
866. Susan R. Lippincott,	Westfield, N. J.,	" "
867. Lydia S. Lowry,	Philadelphia, Pa.,	" "
868. Elizabeth Kaighn,	Chew's Landing, N. J.,	" "

* Deceased at the school, 3d of Fourth month, 1859.

STUDENTS.

FIFTH THOUSAND.

NAME.	RESIDENCE.	DATE OF ENTRY.
869. Hannah C. Wills,	Rancocas, N. J.,	5th mo., 1859.
870. Hannah M. Haines,	"	" "
871. Sarah Ann Whitall,	Philadelphia, Pa.,	" "
872. Mary L. Haines,	Haverford, Pa.,	" "
873. Anna H. Haines,	"	" "
874. Prudence E. Haines,	Medford, N. J.,	" "
875. Eliz. R. Moore,	Gap, Pa.,	" "
876. Rachel Ogborn,	Germantown, Pa.,	" "
877. Hannah Evans,	Haddonfield, N. J.,	" "
878. Lydia Kite, Jr.,	Philadelphia, Pa.,	" "
879. Fanny Lloyd,	Camden, N. J.,	11th mo., "
880. Sarah H. Reeves,	Woodbury, N. J.,	" "
881. Mercy Buckman,	Newtown, Pa.,	" "
882. Marianna Darnell,	Mt. Laurel, N. J.,	" "
883. Susan Cope,	Kimbleville, Pa.,	" "
884. Cornelia B. Maule,	Philadelphia, Pa.,	" "
885. Sarah McCarty,	Eldredville, Pa.,	" "
886. Sarah Barton,	Fellowship, N. J.,	" "
887. Anna Mary Moore,	Christiana, Pa.,	" 1860.
888. H. V. Whitlock,	Richmond, Va.,	" 1859.
889. Anna E. Comfort,	Attleboro', Pa.,	12th mo., "
890. Mary J. Haines,	Marlton, N. J.,	5th mo., 1860.
891. Elizabeth B. Evens,	"	" "
892. Alice Roberts,	Paoli, Pa.,	" "
893. Sarah W. Roberts,	"	" "
894. Eliza Ann Bell,	Plymouth, Pa.,	" "
895. Rebecca W. Borton,	Rancocas, N. J.,	" "
896. Elizabeth M. Cooper,	Erceildoun, Pa.,	" "
897. Anna C. Wright,	Columbus, N. J.,	" "
898. Julia Wood,	Philadelphia, Pa.,	" "
899. Deb. A. Crenshaw,	Richmond, Va.,	" "
900. Marg. E Crenshaw,	"	" "
901. Deb. E. Wetherill,	Medford, N. J.,	" "
902. Eliza M. Thomas,	Bellefonte, Pa.,	11th mo., "
903. Deborah D. Thomas,	"	" "
904. Martha C. Roberts,	West Chester, Pa.,	" "
905. Lydia H. Remington,	Philadelphia, Pa.,	" "
906. Marianna Maris,	Darlington, Md.,	" "
907. Margaret H. Jones,	Milestown, Pa.,	" "
908. Mary Anna Griffith,	Winchester, Va.,	5th mo., 1863.
909. Hannah Ann Lovett,	Fallsington, Pa.,	11th mo., 1860.
910. Esther A. Kashner,	Columbus, N. J.,	" "
911. Rachel L. Hilyard,	Rancocas, N. J.,	" "
912. Mary Ellen Stone,	Sandy Spring, Md.,	" 1863.
913. Mary N. Smith,	Darlington, Md.,	" 1860.
914. Emily S. Haines,	Marlton, N. J.,	" "
915. Anna L. Ellison,	Philadelphia, Pa.,	" "

GENERAL CATALOGUE.

FIFTH THOUSAND.

NAME.	RESIDENCE.	DATE OF ENTRY.
916. Hannah H. Dilks,	Germantown, Pa.,	11th mo., 1860.
917. Mary Mickle,	Marple, Pa.,	5th mo., 1861.
918. Annie Mickle,	"	" "
919. Elizabeth G. Fogg,	Philadelphia, Pa.,	" "
920. Ruth Anna Brown,	New Garden, Pa.,	" "
921. Rebecca A. Frame,	Lloydsville, Ohio,	" "
922. Caroline Cadbury,	Philadelphia, Pa.,	" "
923. Rachel M. Roberts,	Moorestown, N. J.,	" "
924. Anna B. Temple,	Hamorton, Pa.,	" "
926. Jane A. Kester,	Millville, Pa.,	" "
927. Abigail Kite,	Philadelphia, Pa.,	" "
928. Elizabeth Balderston,	Lahaska, Pa.,	11th mo., "
929. Deb. Satterthwaite,	Attleboro', Pa.,	" "
930. Elizabeth H. Kester,	Millville, Pa.,	" "
931. Sarah B. Bishop,	Columbus, N. J.,	" "
932. Ruth Anna Clement,	Leed's Point, N. J.,	" "
933. Rachel A. Wills,	Rancocas, N. J.,	" "
934. R. W. Thompson,	Salem, N. J.,	" "
935. Sarah H. Alexander,	Philadelphia, Pa.,	" "
936. Rebecca M. Cooper,	Londonderry, Pa.,	" 1863.
937. Mary H. Canby,	Hulmeville, Pa.,	12th mo., 1861.
938. Anna B. Decou,	Trenton, N. J.,	5th mo., 1862.
939. Sarah Dunn,	"	" "
940. Mary L. Evans,	Middletown, Pa.,	" "
941. Mary Branson,	Philadelphia, Pa.,	" "
942. Ann Lippincott,	Moorestown, N. J.,	" "
943. Elizabeth Lukens,	Horsham, Pa.,	" "
944. Susanna Kite,	Philadelphia, Pa.,	" "
945. Martha A. Shreeve,	Long-a-coming, N. J.,	' "
946. Mary E. Maris,	Lionville, Pa.,	" "
947. Anna Mary Fawkes,	Beckersville, Pa.,	" . "
948. Lydia Sharpless,	McClellandsville, Del.,	" "
949. Mary Sharpless,	"	11th mo., "
950. Anna J. Bell,	Philadelphia, Pa.,	5th mo., "
951. Catharine Masters,	Millville, Pa.,	" "
952. Marianna Hobbs,	Bloomingdale, Ind.,	" "
953. Martha C. Smith,	Darlington, Md.,	" "
954. Catharine L. Smith,	Smyrna, Ohio,	" "
955. Mary Ann Abbott,	Salem, N. J.,	" "
956. Mary Redman,	Haddonfield, N. J.,	" "
957. Sarah M. Wildman,	Morrisville, Pa.,	" "
958. Emma England,	Thornbury, Pa.,	" "
959. Emma H. Walter,	Parkersville, Pa.,	" "
960. Anna C. Collins,	Morrisville, Pa.,	11th mo., "
961. Anna P. Canby,	Hulmeville, Pa.,	" "
962. Martha J. Murray,	Bart, Pa.,	" "
963. Hettie T. Borton,	Mt. Laurel, N. J.,	" "

STUDENTS. 327

FIFTH THOUSAND.

NAME.	RESIDENCE.	DATE OF ENTRY.
964. Elma Heacock,	Greenwood, Pa.,	11th mo., 1862.
965. Rachel F. Warner,	Muncy, Pa.,	" "
966. Nancy M. Stanley,	Haddonfield, N. J.,	5th mo., 1863.
967. Anna B. Harlan,	Salem, N. J.,	" "
968. Sarah Harlan,	Philadelphia, Pa.,	" "
969. Abby S. Reeves,	Woodbury, N. J.,	" "
970. Martha Lee,	Stonersville, Pa.,	11th mo., 1861.
971. Rachel C. Kinsey,	Centreville, Del.,	5th mo., "
972. Ann Gubbings,	Germantown, Pa.,	" "
973. Sarah Allen,	Moorestown, N. J.,	" "
974. Sarah E. Bell,	Bloomington, Ill.,	11th mo., "
975. Minerva Parker,	Greenwood, Pa.,	5th mo., "
976. Mary Pusey,	Thorndale, Pa.,	" "
977. R. Scattergood,	Philadelphia, Pa.,	" 1862.
979. Mary Embree,	Marshallton, Pa.,	" 1861.
980. Emily E. Bundy,	Pugh, Ohio,	11th mo., 1862.
981. Phebe E. Hoopes,	Avondale, Pa.,	5th mo., 1861.
982. Jane S. Davis,	Barnesville, Ohio,	11th mo., 1862.
983. Eliz. Hollingsworth,	Fallston, Md.,	" 1861.
984. Alice E. Cope,	Milltown, Pa.,	" "
985. R. Em. Kinsey,	Chatham, Pa.,	" "
986. J. Anna Embree,	West Chester, Pa.,	" "
987. Elizabeth T. Kemp,	Jerusalem Mills, Md.,	" "
988. Anne Warner,	Westtown, Pa.,	12th mo., "
989. Rebecca Warner,	"	" "
990. Sibilla Smith,	Maiden Creek, Pa.,	5th mo., 1862.
991. Jane E. Way,	Port Deposit, Md.,	" "
992. Mary E. Levering,	Ashley, Ohio,	" "
993. Susan Hathaway,	"	" "
994. Mary E. Clinger,	Philadelphia, Pa.,	" "
995. Phebe E. Baker,	Avondale, Pa.,	" "
996. Sarah S. Jolliffe,	Winchester, Va.,	" "
997. Lydia S. Willits,	Smithfield, Ohio,	11th mo., "
998. Alice E. Evans,	Elizabethtown, N. J.,	" "
999. Mary K. Evans,	"	" "
1000. Emily E. Maris,	Darlington, Md.,	" "

SIXTH THOUSAND.

NAME.	RESIDENCE.	DATE OF ENTRY.
1. Jane Miller,	Bellefonte, Pa.,	5th mo., 1863
2. Rebecca Matlack,	Moorestown, N. J.,	" "
3. Sarah C. Comfort,	Conshohocken, Pa.,	11th mo., "
4. Jane Johnson,	Parkesburg, Pa.,	5th mo., "
5. Margaret Maule, Jr.,	London Grove, Pa.,	" "
6. Jane Bishop,	Columbus, N. J.,	11th mo., "
7. Eliz. K. Hulme,	Bristol, Pa.,	5th mo., "

SIXTH THOUSAND

NAME.	RESIDENCE.	DATE OF ENTRY.	
8. Rachel Maule,	Port Royal, Pa.,	5th mo.,	1863
9. Ellen Walton,	Fallston, Md.,	11th mo.,	"
10. Mary S. Hackney,	Winchester, Va.,	5th mo.,	"
11. Marg. M. Gummere,	Germantown, Pa.,	"	"
12. Sarah Jane Kinsey,	Centreville, Del.,	11th mo.,	"
13. Frances Gummere,	Germantown, Pa.,	5th mo.,	"
14. Esther A. Linton,	West Grove, Pa.,	"	"
15. Emma Speakman,	Coatesville, Pa.,	11th mo.,	"
16. Anna R. Edwards,	Huntington, Ind.,	5th mo.,	"
17. Emma L. Cooper,	Christiana, Pa.,	"	"
18. Elizabeth Parvin,	Leesport, Pa.,	11th mo.,	"
19. Anna Hilyard,	New York, N. Y.,	5th mo.,	"
20. Susanna Price,	Media, Pa.,	"	"
21. Anna Miller,	Sandy Spring, Md.,	11th mo.,	"
22. Ann Thomas,	Harrisville, Ohio,	5th mo.,	"
23. Elizabeth L. Baily,	Yardville, N. J.,	"	"
24. Mary W. Newlin,	Concordville, Pa.,	11th mo.,	"
25. Josephine Cooper,	Gap, Pa.,	5th mo.,	"
26. Elizabeth A. Leeds,	Cinnaminson, N. J.,	11th mo.,	"
27. Susanna J. Thatcher,	Paoli, Pa.,	"	"
28. Rebecca Haverstick,	Moorestown, N. J.,	"	"
29. Anna Warrington,	Cinnaminson, N. J.,	"	"
30. Emily Gilpin,	Baltimore, Md.,	"	"
31. Mary B. Evens,	Marlton, N. J.,	"	"
32. Elizabeth Wright,	Columbus, N. J.,	"	"
33. Lucy Sutton,	Baltimore, Md.,	"	"
34. Sarah B. Garrigues,	West Haverford, Pa.,	"	"
35. Elizabeth Garrigues,	"	"	"
36. Annie M. Bartlett,	Bethlehem, Pa.,	"	"
37. Rebecca Wilkins,	Rancocas, N. J.,	"	"
38. Ruth Anna Sharpless,	Chester, Pa.,	"	"
39. Lydia Pim,	Thorndale, Pa.,	"	"
40. M. A. Satterthwaite,	Oxford Valley, Pa.,	"	"
41. Margaret Sheppard,	Greenwich, N. J.,	"	"
42. Fannie W. Pim,	Thorndale, Pa.,	"	"
43. S. A. Satterthwaite,	Attleboro', Pa.,	"	"
44. Lydia C. Whitall,	Philadelphia, Pa.,	"	"
45. Lydia D. Woodward,	Marshallton, Pa.,	"	"
46. Hannah Lee,	Stonersville, Pa.,	"	"
47. Mary Frances Leeds,	Barnegat, N. J.,	"	"
48. Mary Janney,	Hillsboro', Va.,	"	"
50. Elizabeth S. Woolman,	Fallsington, Pa.,	"	"
51. Mercy A. Roberts,	West Chester, Pa.,	"	"
52. Sarah Worthington,	Philadelphia, Pa.,	"	"
53. Martha E. Wright,	Winchester, Va.,	"	"
54. Priscilla Hoopes,	Avondale, Pa.,	"	"
55. Mary M. Warren,	Burlington, N. J.,	"	"

STUDENTS.

SIXTH THOUSAND.

NAME.	RESIDENCE.	DATE OF ENTRY.
56. Hannah Street,	Salem, Ohio,	11th mo., 1863
57. Anne Garrett,	West Chester, Pa.,	" "
58. Elizabeth K. Roberts,	Medford, N. J.,	5th mo., 1864.
59. Eliz. C. Nicholson,	Mt. Ephraim, N. J.,	" "
60. Elizabeth M. Jenness,	Burlington, N. J.,	11th mo., 1863.
61. Eliza C. Nicholson,	Haddonfield, N. J.,	5th mo., 1864.
62. Sarah R. Haines,	Marlton, N. J.,	" "
63. Julia Harvey,	Chadd's Ford, Pa.,	11th mo., 1863.
64. Rebecca A. Haines,	Philadelphia, Pa.,	5th mo., 1864.
65. Sarah N. Lippincott,	Haddonfield, N. J.,	" "
66. Edith Shoemaker,	Point of Rocks, Md.,	11th mo., 1863.
67. Mary L. Collins,	Burlington, N. J.,	5th mo., 1864.
68. Anna Brown,	Fallsington, Pa.,	" "
69. Helen Cromwell,	New York, N. Y.,	11th mo., 1863.
70. Hannah W. Lukens,	Horsham, Pa.,	5th mo., 1864.
71. Rachel C. Wildman,	Morrisville, Pa.,	" "
72. Rebecca S. Edge,	Downingtown, Pa.,	" "
73. Anna Bishop,	Columbus, N. J.,	" "
74. Anna S. Collins,	Barnegat, N. J.,	" "
75. Emma Bell,	Experiment Mills, Pa.,	" "
76. Margaret A. Masters,	Millville, Pa.,	" "
77. Sarah A. Taylor,	Eldredville, Pa.,	" "
78. Ellen Speakman,	Marshallton, Pa.,	" "
79. Emily Maule,	London Grove, Pa.,	" "
80. A. L. Mendenhall,	Muncy, Pa.,	" "
81. Angelina Gray,	Elkton, Md.,	" "
82. Sarah H. Kaighn,	Haddonfield, N. J.,	" 1865.
83. Phebe R. Lear,	Warren Tavern, Pa.,	11th mo., 1864.
84. Mary E. Thomas,	Kennet Square, Pa.,	5th mo., "
85. Sidney P. Walter,	Parkersville, Pa.,	11th mo., "
86. Sophia R. Pusey,	Thorndale, Pa.,	" "
87. Helen E. Bartlett,	Bethlehem, Pa.,	5th mo., "
88. Margaret Rote,	Sereno, Pa.,	12th mo., "
89. Acintha Heacock,	Greenwood, Pa.,	11th mo., "
90. Mary E. Bartlett,	Bethlehem, Pa.,	5th mo., "
91. Susan Masters,	Millville, Pa.,	11th mo., "
92. Sophia K. Taylor,	Oxford Valley, Pa.,	" "
93. Gertrude Cromwell,	New York, N. Y.,	5th mo., "
94. R. Anna Price,	Fallsington, Pa.,	11th mo., "
95. Sarah F. Wills,	Rancocas, N. J.,	" 1865
96. Abby W. Brown,	New York, N. Y.,	5th mo., 1864
97. Eliz. C. French,	Philadelphia, Pa.,	11th mo., "
98. Marg. B. Haines,	Medford, N. J.,	" "
99. Mary C. Corbit,	Odessa, Del.,	5th mo., "
100. Anna C. Eastburn,	Attleboro', Pa.,	11th mo., "
101. Margaret T. Cook,	Glenville, Md.,	5th mo., "
102. Sarah T. Hilyard,	New York, N. Y.,	" "

SIXTH THOUSAND.

NAME.	RESIDENCE.	DATE OF ENTRY.
103. Anna Wills,	Rancocas, N. J.,	5th mo., 1864.
104. Mary K. Wood,	Trenton, N. J.,	" "
105. Anna R. Hopkins,	Baltimore, Md.,	" "
106. Bessie J. Hopkins,	"	" "
107. Mary P. Thomas,	Sandy Spring, Md.,	" "
108. Anna M. Masters,	Millville, Pa.,	" "
109. Pen. F. Michener,	Springdale, Iowa,	11th mo., "
110. Hannah P. Smith,	Village Green, Pa.,	5th mo., 1865.
111. Lizzie A. Moore,	Rancocas, N. J.,	" "
112. Bernice Allinson,	Yardville, N. J.,	" "
113. Mary J. Warrington,	Cinnaminson, N. J.,	" "
114. L. W. Satterthwaite,	Fallsington, Pa.,	" "
115. Rebecca B. Bacon,	Greenwich, N. J.,	" "
116. Elizabeth Price,	Fallsington, Pa.,	" "
117. Sarah B. Twining,	Richboro', Pa.,	" "
118. Ann Trimble,	Chester, Pa.,	11th mo., "
119. Julia C. Kirkbride,	Burlington, N. J.,	5th mo., 1866.
120. Anna S. House,	Goshenville, Pa.,	11th mo., 1865.
121. Eliza C. Crenshaw,	Richmond, Va.,	" "
122. Sarah T. Sharpless,	Chester, Pa.,	" "
123. E. F. Worthington,	Philadelphia, Pa.,	" "
124. Rachel A. Williams,	Rancocas, N. J.,	" "
125. Susan P. Leeds,	Cinnaminson, N. J.,	" "
126. Mary V. Cooper,	Glendale, N. J.,	" "
127. Mary T. Brown,	Danboro', Pa.,	" "
128. Asenath Hunt,	Salem, Ohio,	" "
129. Sarah J. Perkins,	Goldsboro', N. C.,	" "
130. Rachel M. Perkins,	"	" "
131. Martha C. Smith,	Village Green, Pa.,	" "
132. Sarah S. Cadbury,	Philadelphia, Pa.,	5th mo., 1866.
133. Ellen M. Taylor,	"	" "
134. Hetty E. Haines,	Medford, N. J.,	" "
135. Sarah N. Hunt,	Rome, N. Y.,	" "
136. Caroline S. Knowles,	Smyrna, N. Y.,	" "
137. Sarah C. Reeve,	Salem, N. J.,	" 1867.
138. Sarah B. Boswell,	Springdale, Iowa,	" 1866.
139. Anna Mary Richie,	New Paris, Ohio,	" "
140. Martha J. Tylor,	Richmond, Ind.,	" "
141. Samuella T. Ricks,	Ruther Glen, Va.,	" "
142. Rachel P. Stewart,	Salem, Ohio,	" "
143. Lydia Millhouse,	Pennsville, Ohio,	" "
144. Marg. E. Thatcher,	West Chester, Pa.,	" "
145. Jos. M. Tomlinson,	Bush Hill, N. C.,	" "
146. Sarah M. Taylor,	Burlington, N. J.,	" "
147. Mary E. Taylor,	"	" "
148. Emma A. Taylor,	"	" "
149. Ann Sharpless,	Birmingham, Pa.,	" "

STUDENTS.

SIXTH THOUSAND.

NAME.	RESIDENCE.	DATE OF ENTRY.
150. Rebecca B. Embree,	Marshallton, Pa.,	5th mo., 1866
151. Elizabeth Wistar,	Salem, N. J.,	11th mo., 1864
152. Anna T. Matthews,	Monkton, Md.,	" "
153. Jane Maule,	London Grove, Pa.,	" "
154. Sarah M. Evans,	"	" "
155. Mary E. Harvey,	West Grove, Pa.,	" "
156. Isabella E. Stabler,	Sandy Spring, Md.,	" "
157. Thomazin T. Zook,	Downingtown, Pa.,	" "
158. Mary Anna Haines,	Uniontown, Md.,	" "
159. Mary J. Haines,	"	" "
160. Mary R. Carpenter,	Salem, N. J.,	" "
161. Hannah R. Hopkins,	Darlington, Md.,	" "
162. Mary R. Walker,	West Chester, Pa.,	" "
163. Margaret J. Scott,	Concordville, Pa.,	" "
164. Anna E. Gove,	Hamilton, Min.,	" "
165. Hannah G. Jessop,	York, Pa.,	" "
166. Mary B. Valentine,	Bellefonte, Pa.,	" "
167. Elizabeth H. Jolliffe,	Baltimore, Md.,	" "
168. Fannie M. Jolliffe,	"	" "
169. Sarah Ann Brown,	Circleville, Va.,	" "
170. Hannah Brown,	"	" "
171. Sarah B. Bentley,	Sandy Spring, Md.,	" "
172. Anna L. Stone,	"	" "
173. Mary R. Lytle,	Philadelphia, Pa.,	" "
174. Ruth Anna Lytle,	"	" "
175. Hannah Elma Hoge,	Flushing, Ohio,	" "
176. Edith Sharpless,	McClellandsville, Del.,	" "
177. Eliz. E. Lippincott,	Salem, N. J.,	5th mo., 1867
178. Deborah H. Roberts,	Medford, N. J.,	" 1865.
179. Mary E. Hilyard,	Rancocas, N. J.,	" "
180. Ann J. Faron,	Wilmington, Del.,	" "
181. Elizabeth Cope,	Jennerville, Pa.,	" "
182. Sarah E. Whitacre,	Muncy, Pa.,	" "
183. Annie Zook,	Downingtown, Pa.,	" "
184. Elizabeth Savery,	Parkersville, Pa.,	" "
185. Hannah Bacon,	Greenwich, N. J.,	" "
186. Sarah G. Embree,	Marshallton, Pa.,	" "
187. Sarah E. Windle,	Guthrieville, Pa.,	" "
188. Elizabeth C. Dilks,	New Paris, Ohio,	" "
189. Amy E. Michener,	Springdale, Iowa,	" "
190. Marg. W. White,	Belvidere, N. C.,	" 1866.
191. Ellen Painter,	Springdale, Iowa,	" 1865.
192. Esther Painter,	"	" "
193. Eliza A. Willits,	Smithfield, Ohio,	" "
194. Laura A. White,	Belvidere, N. C.,	" 1866.
195. Cidney E. Williams,	Flushing, Ohio,	" 1865
196. Guli A. Purviance,	"	" "

GENERAL CATALOGUE.

SIXTH THOUSAND.

NAME.	RESIDENCE.	DATE OF ENTRY.
197. Corinne Cattell,	Muscatine, Iowa,	5th mo., 1865
198. Mary A. McConnell,	East Fairfield, Ohio,	" "
199. Anna H. Taylor,	Cinnaminson, N. J.,	11th mo., "
200. Elizabeth Bonsall,	Philadelphia, Pa.,	" "
201. Anna Simmons,	Bart, Pa.,	" "
202. Elizabeth Smith,	Leesport, Pa.,	" "
203. Susanna Forsythe,	West Chester, Pa.,	" "
204. Hannah Maule,	London Grove, Pa.,	" "
205. Emma H. Edge,	Downingtown, Pa.,	" "
206. Anna P. Harvey,	West Grove, Pa.,	" "
207. Elizabeth E. Masters,	Millville, Pa.,	" "
208. Anna G. Shreeve,	Long-a-Coming, N. J.,	" "
209. Elizabeth E. Borton,	Mt. Laural, N. J.,	" "
210. Sarah L. Brown,	"	" "
211. Mary Penrose,	Pennsville, Ohio,	5th mo., 1866.
212. Mary S. Willis,	Glenville, Md.,	" 1865.
213. Elizabeth Butler,	Damascoville, Ohio,	" "
214. Lydia Butler,	"	" "
215. Hannah Butler,	"	" "
216. Eliz. A. McGrew,	Smithfield, Ohio,	" "
217. Anna E. Kite,	Cincinnati, Ohio,	" 1866.
218. Martha Bonsall,	Salem, Ohio,	" 1865.
219. Mary Ann Elliott,	Rich Square, N. C.,	" 1866.
220. Elizabeth A. White,	Belvidere, N. C.,	" "
221. Matilda Masters,	Benton, Pa.,	" "
222. Cordelia B. Johnson,	West Chester, Pa.,	11th mo., 1865.
223. M. E. Mendenhall,	Deep River, N. C.,	5th mo., 1866.
224. Anna M. Wrigley,	Philadelphia, Pa.,	" "
225. Anna L. Edgerton,	Barnesville, Ohio,	" "
226. Susanna Lear,	Warren Tavern, Pa.,	" "
227. Ruth B. Leeds,	Cinnaminson, N. J.,	" "
228. Anna M. Cook,	Philadelphia, Pa.,	" "
229. Rebecca Hutton,	"	" "
230. Anna Moore,	Nine Points, Pa.,	" "
231. Sarah M. Calley,	Camden, Del.,	" "
232. Anna E. Scott,	Concordville, Pa.,	" "
233. Ann Eliza Wilson,	Barnesville, Ohio,	" "
234. Anna J. Cooper,	Woodbury, N. J.,	11th mo., "
235. Lydia Balderston,	Philadelphia, Pa.,	" "
236. Caroline E. Smith,	Parkesburg, Pa.,	" "
237. Rebecca S. Smith,	Darlington, Md.,	" "
238. Sarah P. Thomas,	Philadelphia, Pa.,	" "
239. Alice D. Lamborn,	West Chester, Pa.,	" 1871.
240. Hannah P. Morris,	Olney, Pa.,	5th mo., 1867.
( ) Melissa Cope,	Redstone, Pa.,	" "
241. Rachel E. Plummer,	Barnesville, Ohio,	" 1866.
242. Ruanna E. Frame,	"	" "

STUDENTS.

SIXTH THOUSAND.

NAME.	RESIDENCE.	DATE OF ENTRY.
243. Rebecca W. Hopkins,	Havre-de-Grace, Md.,	5th mo., 1866.
244. Sarah C. Harris,	Franklin Depot, Va.,	" "
245. Elizabeth H. Wills,	Princeton, N. J.,	11th mo., "
246. Josephine G. Harlan,	New York, N. Y.,	" "
247. Anna R. Whitson,	New London, Pa.,	" "
248. A. H. Warrington,	Cinnaminson, N. J.,	" "
249. Laura Jones,	Haddonfield, N. J.,	" "
250. M. Jane Lovett,	Bristol, Pa.,	" "
251. Hannah F. Gardiner,	Glendale, N. J.,	" "
252. Susan Hutton,	Philadelphia, Pa.,	" "
253. Mary W. Yarnall,	Howellville, Pa.,	" "
254. Sidney S. Garrett,	West Chester, Pa.,	" "
255. Eliz. J. Bonsall,	Salem, Ohio,	" "
256. Lydia B. McGrew,	Smithfield, Ohio,	" "
257. Charlotte White,	Belvidere, N. C.,	" "
258. Anna E. Prickitt,	Medford, N. J.,	" "
259. Eliz. H. Atwater,	Somerset, N. Y.,	" "
260. Hannah G. Atwater,*	"	" "
261. Naomi C. Fulghum,	Richmond, Ind.,	" "
262. Anna E. Marshall,	Hamorton, Pa.,	" "
263. Mary E. Cannon,	Belvidere, N. C.,	" "
264. Anna H. Welding,	Brooklyn, N. Y.,	" "
265. Harriet Wrigley,	Jackson, N. J.,	" "
266. Mary Ellen Ash,	Wagontown, Pa.,	5th mo., 1867.
267. S. Rebecca Larkin,	Chelsea, Pa.,	" "
268. Rebecca W. Abbott,	Salem, N. J.,	" "
269. Kath. W. Abbott,	"	" "
270. Deb. Cadwallader,	East Fairfield, Ohio,	" "
271. Jane Penrose,	Pennsville, Ohio.	" "
272. M. Elizabeth Hill,	Hill's Store, N. C.,	" "
273. Beulah E. Haines,	Mt. Laurel, N. J.,	11th mo., "
274. Rebecca W. Hoge,	Flushing, Ohio,	" "
275. Lucilla R. Hedley,	Medina, N. Y.,	" "
276. Jane C. Balderston,	West Nottingham, Md.,	" "
277. Almedia Dewees,	Pennsville, Ohio,	" "
278. Emily T. Hilyard,	New York, N. Y.,	" "
279. Eliza Gardiner,	Mt. Laurel, N. J.,	" 1868.
280. Sarah L. Brown,	Fallsington, Pa.,	" 1867.
( ) Lucinda Cope,	Redstone, Pa.,	5th mo., 1868
281. Marg. M. McCollin,	West Chester, Pa.,	" 1867
282. Anna G. McCollin,	"	" "
283. Elizabeth C. Wills,	Medford, N. J.,	" "
284. Frances Baily,	Yardville, N. J.,	" "
285. Harriet Randolph,	Chester, Pa.,	" "
286. Ella T. Gause,	Philadelphia, Pa.,	" "
287. Caroline B. Canby,	"	" "

*Deceased at the school, 12th of Ninth month, 1867.

GENERAL CATALOGUE

SIXTH THOUSAND.

NAME.	RESIDENCE.	DATE OF ENTRY.
288. Sarah M. Gould,	Moorestown, N. J.,	5th mo., 1867.
289. Esther A. Engle,	Mt. Laurel, N. J.,	11th mo., "
290. Emma A. Roberts,	Bristol, Pa.,	5th mo., "
291. Anna G. Willits,*	Haddonfield, N. J.,	" "
292. Clara England,	Quakertown, Pa.,	" "
293. Elizabeth E. Roberts,	Rancocas, N. J.,	11th mo., "
294. Deborah B. Prickitt,	Vincentown, N. J.,	" "
295. Rachel H. Brown,	Mt. Laurel, N. J.,	" "
296. Mary C. Moon,	Morrisville, Pa.,	" "
297. Sarah R. Harmer,	Greenwich, N. J.,	5th mo., 1869.
298. Martha Leeds,	Barnegat, N. J.,	11th mo., 1867.
299. Elizabeth S. Warren,	Burlington, N. J.,	" "
300. Helen F. Price,	Media, Pa.,	5th mo., "
301. Sallie Maris,	Darlington, Md.,	11th mo., "
302. Susan Parvin,	Leesport, Pa.,	" "
303. Helen A. Smith,	"	" "
304. Anna M. Haines,	Muncy, Pa.,	" "
305. Anna T. Wills,	Princeton, N. J.,	" "
306. Lydia Ann Haines,	Medford, N. J.,	" "
307. Philena Harvey,	Chadd's Ford, Pa.,	" "
308. Hannah G. Pusey,	Thorndale, Pa.,	" 1868.
309. Anna Hedley,	Medina, N. Y.,	" 1867.
310. Eliz. J. McFadgen,	Ercildoun, Pa.,	" 1868.
311. Eva Henley,	Richmond, Ind.,	5th mo., "
312. Emma Hedley,	Medina, N. Y.,	" "
313. Frederica P. Hoge,	Lincoln, Va.,	" "
314. M. Ella Hoge,	Hughesville, Va.,	" "
315. Margaret Henrie,	Greenwood, Pa.,	" "
316. Mary Anna Brown,	Mt. Laurel, N. J.,	11th mo., "
317. Julia T. Walter,	Parkersville, Pa.,	" "
318. Mary B. Phipps,	Lionville, Pa.,	" "
319. Jane H. Harvey,	Chadd's Ford, Pa.,	" "
320. S. E. Satterthwaite,	Oxford Valley, Pa.,	" "
( ) Mary D. Forsythe,	Westtown, Pa.,	5th mo., "
( ) Alice Hoopes,	"	" "
( ) Phebe Hoopes,	"	11th mo., "
321. Mary Chambers,	Strickersville, Pa.,	" "
322. M. W. Satterthwaite,	Fallsington, Pa.,	" "
323. Phebe L. Collins,	Barnegat, N. J.,	" "
324. Sallie T. Cope,	Kimbleville, Pa.,	" "
325. S. Roselma Paist,	Danboro', Pa.,	" "
326. Mary Y. Hutton,	Chester, Pa.,	" 1867.
327. Anna K. Thorp,	West Chester, Pa.,	" "
328. Anna M. Heacock,	Greenwood, Pa.,	" "
329. Eliza Collins,	Barnegat, N. J.,	" "
330. Lydia Cooper,	Chatham, Pa.,	5th mo., 1868

* Deceased at the school, 22d of Third month, 1869.

STUDENTS. 335

SIXTH THOUSAND.

NAME.	RESIDENCE.	DATE OF ENTRY.
331. Margaretta Gray,	Elkton, Md.,	11th mo., 1867.
332. Sarah Fawkes,	Bakersville, Pa.,	" "
333. Mary D. Fawkes,	"	" "
334. Sarah H. Jones,	Moorestown, N. J.,	5th mo., 1868.
335. Mary C. Kester,	Greenwood, Pa.,	" "
336. Mary W. Woolman,	Philadelphia, Pa.,	" "
337. Elizabeth Balderston,	West Chester, Pa.,	11th mo., "
338. Mary B. Willits,	Philadelphia, Pa.,	5th mo., "
339. Anna Mary Kaighn,	Moorestown, N. J.,	" "
340. Mary C. Stokes,	Philadelphia, Pa.,	" "
341. Anna M. Stokes,	Berlin, N. J.,	" "
342. Rebecca O. Tilton,	Manahawkin, N. J.,	" "
343. Phebe E. Middleton,	Crosswicks, N. J.,	" "
344. Susan M. Brown,	Germantown, Pa.,	" 1869.
345. Regina S. Heacock,	Benton, Pa.,	" 1868.
346. Frances B. McCollin,	Philadelphia, Pa.,	" 1869.
347. Hannah E. Pharo,	Tuckerton, N. J.,	11th mo., 1868.
348. Anna Garrigues,	West Haverford, Pa.,	" "
349. Elizabeth Shoemaker,	Jarrettown, Pa.,	" "
350. Mary H. Dutton,	Frankford, Pa.,	" "
351. Caroline B. Collins,	Burlington, N. J.,	5th mo., 1869.
352. Sarah E. Decou,	Trenton, N. J.,	" "
353. Lucy Branson,	Philadelphia, Pa.,	" "
354. Rachel Rich,	Danboro', Pa.,	" "
355. Hannah M. Jones,	Germantown, Pa.,	" "
356. Anna M. Taylor,	Avondale, Pa.,	" "
357. Lydia R. Parker,	West Chester, Pa.,	" 1871.
358. Elizabeth W. Reeves,	Philadelphia, Pa.,	" 1869.
359. Hannah W. Ogden,	Kingsessing, Pa.,	" 1871.
360. M. Ella Ogden,	"	11th mo., 1869.
( ) Frances E. Forsythe,	Westtown, Pa.,	5th mo., "
( ) Susanna Sharpless,	"	" "
361. Elizabeth R. Ogden,	Kingsessing, Pa.,	11th mo., "
362. Anna E. Kirkbride,	Burlington, N. J.,	" "
363. Harriet F. Kirkbride,	"	" "
364. Elizabeth H. Sexton,	Crosswicks, Pa.,	" "
365. Isabella L. Pennock,	Philadelphia, Pa.,	" "
366. R. S. Satterthwaite,	Attleboro', Pa.,	" "
367. Annabella Sellers,	Upper Darby, Pa.,	" "
368. Sarah G. Reed,	Chester, Pa.,	5th mo., 1870
369. Catharine E. Stanley,	Oskaloosa, Iowa,	" "
370. Sarah F. Jones,	Germantown, Pa.,	" "
371. Miriam E. Buzby,	Rancocas, N. J.,	" "
372. Hannah H. Ivins,	Trenton, N. J.,	" "
373. Mary Saunders,	Woodbury, N. J.,	" "
374. Lydia J. Evans,	Burlington, N. J.,	" "
375. Josephine D. Moore,	Rancocas, N. J.,	" "

GENERAL CATALOGUE.

SIXTH THOUSAND.

NAME.	RESIDENCE.	DATE OF ENTRY.
376. Lydia S. Wood,	Chester Hill, Ohio,	11th mo., 1868.
377. Annie Thomas,	Street Road, Pa.,	5th mo., 1869.
378. Eliza A. Cheyney,	West Nottingham, Md.,	" "
379. Mary E. Woodward,	Marshallton, Pa.,	" "
380. Anna Foulke,	Pennsville, Ohio,	" "
381. Hettie B. Deacon,	Princeton, N. J.,	" "
382. Anna M. Janney,	Hillsboro', Va.,	" "
383. Elma Windle,	Guthrieville, Pa.,	" "
384. Elizabeth Hunt,	Salem, Ohio,	" "
385. Lucy Sharpless,	Strickersville, Pa.,	11th mo., "
386. Emma S. Chambers,	Philadelphia, Pa.,	" "
387. Sarah E. Heacock,	Greenwood, Pa.,	" 1870.
388. Regina S. Rote,	Millville, Pa.,	" 1869.
389. Rachel F. Warner,	Benton, Pa.,	" "
390. Sarah C. Leeds,	Barnegat, N. J.,	" "
391. Narcissa Rote,	Millville, Pa.,	" 1870.
392. Anna Forsythe,	Chadd's Ford, Pa.,	" 1869.
393. Sarah W. Passmore,	Concordville, Pa.,	" "
394. Anna Yarnall,	Howellville, Pa.,	" "
395. Susan T. Hoopes,	Downingtown, Pa.,	" "
396. Deb. P. Chambers,	Toughkenamon, Pa.,	" "
397. Damaris Bradshaw,	Somerton, Va.,	" "
398. Emily P. Maxwell,	Richmond, Ind.,	5th mo., 1870.
399. Ruth Bundy,	Barnesville, Ohio,	11th mo., 1869.
400. Sarah Baily.	"	" "
401. Sarah M. Sharpless,	Strickersville, Pa.,	" "
402. Geneva M. Babb,	Franklin Depot, Va.,	" "
403. Fanny Maris,	Darlington, Md.,	5th mo., 1871.
404. H. Jane Walter,	Norway, Pa.,	" 1870.
405. Emma G. Heacock,	Benton, Pa.,	11th mo., 1869.
406. Anna H. Darnell,	Medford, N. J.,	5th mo., 1870.
407. Mary Jones,	Camden, N. J.,	11th mo., 1869.
408. Mary C. England,	Quakertown, Pa.,	" "
409. Anna Pandrich,	Warren Tavern, Pa.,	5th mo., 1870.
410. Caroline Allinson,	Yardville, N. J.,	" "
411. Elizabeth H. Decou,	Trenton, N. J.,	" "
412. Mary C. Lippincott,	Haddonfield, N. J.,	" "
413. Henrietta Hoge,	Hughesville, Va.,	" "
414. Ruth A. Forsythe,	Oak Hill, Pa.,	" "
415. Emily Forsythe,	"	" "
416. Annie Thompson,	Newark, Del.,	" "
417. Anna Morgan,	Village Green, Pa.,	11th mo., "
418. Mary Thomas,	Chelsea, Pa.,	" "
419. Ellen P. Cope,	Kimbleville, Pa.,	" "
420. Fannie E. Zook,	Downingtown, Pa.	" "
421. Elizabeth Zook,	Exton, Pa.,	" "
422. Jane D. Zook,	"	" "

STUDENTS. 337

SIXTH THOUSAND.

NAME.	RESIDENCE.	DATE OF ENTRY.
423. Ruth Anna Trimble,	Chester, Pa.,	11th mo., 1870.
424. M. C. Shoemaker,	Jarrettown, Pa.	" "
425. Rebecca T. Janney,	Hillsboro', Va.,	" "
426. Edith B. Walker,	Waterford, Va.,	" "
427. Mary Wood,	Springdale, Iowa,	" "
428. Sallie F. Downing,	Downingtown, Pa.,	" "
429. Louisa Kimber,	Brooklyn, N. Y.,	" "
430. Mary Tatum,	Wilmington, Del.,	" "
431. Martha Albertson,	Norristown, Pa.,	5th mo., 1871.
432. Sarah Wilcox,	Shunk P. O., Pa.,	11th mo., 1870.
433. Mary E. Roberts,	Moorestown, N. J.,	" "
434. Anna B. Taylor,	Fallsington, Pa.,	" "
435. Sarah R. McFadgen,	West Chester, Pa.,	" 1871.
436. Edith Decou,	Trenton, N. J.,	5th mo., "
437. Phebe Nicholson,	Haddonfield, N. J.,	" "
438. Mary Nicholson,	"	" "
439. Anne Evans,	Glen Mills, Pa.,	" "
440. Lydia Evans,	"	" "
441. Cynthia Battin,	Shunk, Pa.,	" "
442. Hannah E. Forsythe,	Lenape, Pa.,	11th mo., "
443. Deb'h C. Passmore,	Concordville, Pa.,	" "
444. Mary O. Reeve,	Medford, N. J.	5th mo., 1872.
445. Debby C. Pusey,	Thorndale, Pa.	11th mo., 1871.
446. Ellen S. Parvin,	Leesport, Pa.,	" "
447. Lydia K. Edge,	Downingtown, Pa.,	" "
448. Sidney S. Larkin,	Chelsea, Pa.,	" "
449. Anna Harvey Chace,	Valley Falls, R. I.,	" "
450. Emma C. Isaac,	Lahaska, Pa.,	5th mo., 1870.
451. Lucetta McCarty,	Eldredville, Pa.,	" "
452. Lucy R. Tatnall,	Wilmington, Del.,	11th mo., 1872.
453. Mary M. Lownes,	Oakdale, Pa.,	5th mo., 1870.
454. Catharine E. Rhoads,	Haddonfield, N. J.,	" "
455. Lydia S. Winn,	Muscatine, Iowa,	11th mo., "
456. Anna T. Bacon,	Greenwich, N. J.,	" "
457. Emily Hulme,	Bristol, Pa.,	" "
458. Mary H. Lippincott,	Haddonfield, N. J.,	" "
459. Anna H. Deacon,	Mt. Holly, N. J.,	" "
460. Alwilda Collins,	Barnegat, N. J.,	" "
461. C. Eleanor Battin,	Shunk, Pa.,	" "
462. Jane J. Wetherill,	Philadelphia, Pa.,	" "
463. Amelia S. Mott,	Burlington, N. J.,	5th mo., 1871
464. Hannah W. Haines,	Kirkwood, N. J.,	" "
465. Anna B. Kirkbride,	Morrisville, Pa.,	" "
466. Caro. W. Randolph,	Overbrook, Pa.,	" "
467. Laura H. Page,	Fellowship, N. J.,	" "
468. Virginia Nicholson,	Camden, N. J.,	11th mo., "
469. Ruth Ann Leeds,	Cinnaminson, N. J.,	" "

GENERAL CATALOGUE.

SIXTH THOUSAND.

NAME.	RESIDENCE.	DATE OF ENTRY.
470. Rebecca Kite,	Philadelphia, Pa.,	5th mo., 1873.
471. Lizzie T. Canby,	Hulmeville, Pa.,	11th mo., 1871
472. Penelope Kashner,	Columbus, N. J.,	" "
473. Rebecca F. Bishop,	"	" "
474. Lucy Taylor,	Fallsington, Pa.,	" "
475. Lydia T. Cope,	New Garden, Pa.,	" "
476. Eliza C. Pidgeon,	Wadesville, Va.,	" "
477. Cordelia A. Davis,	Westminster, N. C.,	" "
478. Emma J. Fawkes,	Beckersville, Pa.,	" "
479. Lydia D. Jones,	Germantown, Pa.,	5th mo., 1872.
480. Elizabeth H. Brown,	Mt. Laurel, N. J.,	11th mo., 1871.
481. Lydia A. Cooper,	Toughkenamon, Pa.,	" "
482. Mary E. Cooper,	"	" "
483. Edith S. Reeve,	Medford, N. J.,	" "
484. Anna G. Brinton,	Chadd's Ford, Pa.,	5th mo., 1872.
485. Rebecca R.J.Pidgeon,	Wadesville, Va.,	11th mo., 1872.
486. Rebecca Fell,	Marshalton, Pa.,	" "
487. M. Ella Mendenhall,	Howellville, Pa.,	" "
488. Emily Thomas,	Chelsea, Pa.,	" "
489. Margaretta Cheyney,	Doe Run, Pa.,	" "
490. Edith Fawcett,	Salem, Ohio,	" "
491. Carrie W. Hayes,	Thorndale, Pa.,	" "
492. Hannah Thomas,	Avondale, Pa.,	5th mo., 1873.
493. Cordelia Hilyard,	Rancocas, N. J.,	11th mo., 1872.
494. Rebecca S. Ashead,	Marlton, N. J.,	" "
495. Elizabeth Webster,	Glen Riddle, Pa.,	" "
496. Lydia H. Smedley,	Lima, Pa.,	" "
497. Harriet J. Smedley,	" "	" "
498. Elmira C. Humes,	Chesterville, Pa.,	" "
499. Mehetable F. Cox,	Goldsboro, N. C.,	" "
500. Phebe A. Roberts,	Norristown, Pa.,	" "
501. Mary P. Elkinton,	Philadelphia, Pa.,	" 1871.
502. Hannah C. Williams,	Rancocas, N. J.,	5th mo., 1872
503. Martha T. Buzby,	" "	" "
504. R. M. Ballinger,	Haddonfield, N. J.,	" "
505. Mary Anna Lukens,	Horsham, Pa.,	" "
506. Anna Woolman,	Philadelphia, Pa.,	" "
507. Eliz. C. Stokes,	" "	" "
508. Sarah B. Chambers,	Toughkenamon, Pa.,	" "
509. E. Jennette Miner,	Bloomington, Ill.,	11th mo., "
510. Rachel S. Warren,	Columbus, N. J.,	" "
511. Helen M. Allinson,	Pemberton, N. J.,	" "
512. Eliz. N. Powell,	Trappe, Md.,	" "
513. Caroline H. Maule,	Village Green, Pa.,	" "
514. Mary W. Leeds,	Moorestown, N. J.,	" "
515. Mary D. Bell,	Mt. Ephraim, N. J.,	" "
516. Ada M. Leeds,	Moorestown, N. J.,	" "
517. Rachel H. Taber,	Mt. Pleasant, Ohio,	" "

STUDENTS.

SIXTH THOUSAND.

NAME.	RESIDENCE.	DATE OF ENTRY.
518. Georgianna Buzby,	Masonville, N. J.,	5th mo., 1873.
519. Josephine H. Borton,	Atlantic City, N. J.,	" "
520. Elizabeth A. Shreve,	Mount Laurel, N. J.,	" "
521. Gulielma Harvey,	West Grove, Pa.,	" "
522. Margaret C. Bell,	Mount Ephraim, N. J.,	" "
523. Mary Alice Heulings,	Trenton, N. J.,	" "
524. Elizabeth L. Sholl,	Burlington, N. J.,	" "
525. Maria E. Pennock,	Philadelphia, Pa.,	" "
526. Mary S. Thorp,	Lionville, Pa,	11th mo., 1872.
527. Caroline H. Cooper,	Westtown, Pa.,	5th mo., 1873.
528. Sarah Whitson,	Gum Tree P. O., Pa.,	" "
529. Josephine Winner,	Wolf Run, Pa.,	" "
530. Mary W. Cook,	Glenville, Md.,	" "
531. Sarah H. Bailey,	Thorndale, Pa.,	" "
532. Alice S. Townsend,	Rahway, N. J.,	" "
533. Rebecca Parker,	Parkersville, Pa.,	" "
534. Susan B. Satterthwaite,	Fallsington, Pa.,	" "
535. Mary L. Cooper,	Christiana, Pa.,	11th.mo., "
536. Margaret Pandrich,	Warren Tavern, Pa.,	5th mo., "
537. Mary F. Heacock,	Benton, Pa.,	" "
538. Priscilla Hunt,	Moorestown, N. J.,	" "
539. Sallie E. Cheyney,	Colora, Md.,	" "
540. Louisa Masters,	Wolf Run, Pa.,	" "
541. Laura Walter,	Parkersville. Pa.,	11th mo., "
542. Harriet E. Masters,	Wolf Run, Pa.,	5th mo., 1874.
543. Ella Wills,	Princeton, N. J.,	11th mo., 1873.
544. Emma Wills,	" "	" "
545. Elizabeth P. Webb,	Parkersville, Pa.,	" "
546. Sarah P. Ballinger,	West Chester, Pa.,	" "
547. Abbie T. Walter,	Parkersville, Pa.,	" "
548. Mary B. Taylor,	Greensburg, Pa.,	" "
549. Susan L. Haines,	Muncy, Pa.,	" "
550. Abbie L. Evens,	Marlton, N. J.,	" "
551. Ida R. Buzby,	Rancocas, N. J.,	" "
552. Martha M. Sholl,	Burlington, N. J.,	" "
553. Anna M. Comfort,	Moorestown, N. J.,	" "
554. Elizabeth E. Prickett,	Vincenttown, N. J.,	" "
555. Anna H. Kite,	Chester Hill, Ohio,	5th mo., 1874.
556. Caroline W. Bacon,	Greenwich, N. J.,	" "
557. Annie H. Barton,	Mt. Ephraim. N. J.,	" "
558. Esther Williams,	Fellowship, N. J.,	" "
559. Keziah Elma Cox,	Ashboro, N. C.,	" "
560. Artilla Ann Cox,	Franklinville, N. C.,	" "
561. Lydia C. Mendenhall,	Wolf Run, Pa.,	" "
562. Laura Heacock,	Benton, Pa.,	" "
563. Mary Dingee.	Quincy, Illinois,	" "
564. Margaretta P. Dingee,	" "	" "

27

SIXTH THOUSAND.

NAME.	RESIDENCE.	DATE OF ENTRY.
565. Anna T. Griffith,	Carthage, Mo.,	11th mo., 1874.
566. Lydia H. Lippincott,	Moorestown, N. J.,	" "
567. Mary C. Price,	Fallsington, Pa.,	" "
568. Hannah Garrigues,	Bryn Mawr, Pa.,	" "
569. Mary Garrigues,	" "	" "
570. L. Gertrude Haviland,	Bryantown, Md.,	" "
571. Jessie Nicholson,	Camden, N. J.,	" "
572. R. Louisa Troth,	Philadelphia, Pa.,	5th mo., 1875.
573. Huldah M. Atwater,	Somerset, N. Y.,	11th mo., 1874.
574. Myra A. Atwater,	" "	" "
575. M. Ella Kirkbride,	Columbus, N. J.,	5th mo., 1875.
576. Mary Evans,	Strickersville, Pa.,	11th mo., 1873.
577. Beulah T. Evans,	" "	" "
578. Elizabeth A. Lippincott,	Moorestown, N. J.,	" "
579. Adelaide Buzby,	Rancocas, N. J.,	" "
580. Rebecca J. Pusey,	Lionville, Pa.,	5th mo., 1874.
581. E. Elizabeth Kille,	Medford, N. J.,	11th mo., 1873.
582. Mary R. Lamborn,	West Chester, Pa.,	" "
583. Eliz. F. Neely,	" "	" "
584. Anna Bell Preston,	Darlington, Md.,	" "
585. H. Anna Powell,	Easton, Md.,	5th mo., 1874.
586. Lydia E. Hayes,	Salem, Ohio,	" "
587. Mary Hayes,	" "	" "
588. Marietta DeCou,	Trenton, N. J.,	" "
589. Eleanor Rhoads,	Haddonfield, N. J.,	" "
590. Sarah R. Evens,	Marlton, N. J.,	" "
591. Rachel S. Evens,	" "	" "
592. Beulah Thompson,	Strickersville, Pa.,	" "
593. Lydia T. James,	West Chester, Pa.,	11th mo., "
594. Rachel W. Jolliffe,	Stephenson's Depot, Va.,	" "
595. Mary E. Pennell,	Linwood, Pa.,	" "
596. Susanna H. Walter,	Parkersville, Pa.,	" "
597. Amanda Michener,	Colora, Md.,	" "
598. Harriet M. Headley,	Rising Sun, Md.,	" "
599. Ella Hill,	West Chester, Pa.,	" "
600. Anna S. Taylor,	Greensburg, Pa.,	" "
601. Anna Livezey,	Barnesville, Ohio,	" "
602. Annie S. Good,	London Grove, Pa.,	" "
603. Frances C. Tatum,	Wilmington, Del.,	" "
604. Leonora Neely,	West Chester, Pa.,	" "
605. Sarah E. Whiteley,	Philadelphia, Pa.,	" "
606. Mary J. Whiteley,	" "	" "
607. Emma A. Wistar,	" "	" 1876.
608. Julianna R. Manle,	Village Green, Pa.,	5th mo., 1875.
609. Ellen L. Bartlett,	Tuckerton, N. J.,	" "
610. Frances J. Neely,	Frankford, Pa.,	" "
611. Hannah T. Lytle,	Germantown, Pa.,	" "

STUDENTS.

SIXTH THOUSAND.

NAME.	RESIDENCE.	DATE OF ENTRY.
612. Anna N. Reeves,	Philadelphia, Pa.,	5th mo., 1875.
( ) Abbie H. Davis,	Westtown Farm, Pa.,	" "
( ) Mary S. Davis	" " "	" "
613. Corinne Ridgway,	Tuckerton, N. J.,	11th mo., "
614. Susan Heacock,	Greenwood, Pa.,	" "
615. Ezraetta Jones,	Germantown, Pa.,	" "
616. Anna Babb,	Franklin, Va.,	5th mo., 1876.
617. Zada V. Hare.	Suffolk, Va.,	" "
618. Eliz. H. Lippincott,	Philadelphia, Pa.,	" "
619. Mary L. Crew,	Chester Hill, Ohio,	" "
620. Marion Edith Russell,	Philadelphia, Pa.,	11th mo., "
621. Marg'n P. Wickersham,	Kennett Square, Pa.,	" "
622. Anna E. Wickersham,	" " "	" 1877.
623. Sarah E. Paxson,	New Hope, Pa.,	" 1876.
624. Cassandra Smith,	Parkesburg, Pa.,	" "
625. Anna C. Tatnall,	Wilmington, Del.,	" "
626. Anna S. Jones,	Philadelphia, Pa.,	" "
627. Edith H. Dutton,	Burlington, N. J.,	5th mo., 1877.
628. Mary S. Johnson,	West Chester, Pa.,	" "
629. Ida Wilkins,	Medford, N. J.,	11th mo., "
630. Sarah L. Collins,	Philadelphia, Pa.,	" "
631. Elizabeth W. Warner,	Wolf Run, Pa.,	5th mo., 1875.
632. Mary E. Harrison,	Richmond, Ind.,	" "
633. Sarah M. Baxter,	" "	" "
634. Mary E. Baxter,	" "	" "
635. Elizabeth S. Forsythe,	Chadd's Ford, Pa.,	" "
636. Lucy A. Winston,	Richmond, Va.,	" "
637. Eliza D. Hall,	Barnesville, Ohio,	" "
638. Alice Calley,	Wilmington, Del.,	" "
639. Mary E. Kennard,	Barnesville, Ohio,	" "
640. Emma P. Forsythe,	Lenape P. O., Pa.,	11th mo., "
641. Phebe Hatton,	East Whiteland, Pa.,	" "
642. Mary E. Smith,	Village Green, Pa.,	" "
643. Martha B. Hoag,	Lawrence, Kansas,	" "
644. Rachel E. Barton,	Mt. Ephraim, N. J.,	" "
645. Emma Bailey,	Pottstown, Pa.,	" "
646. Elizabeth Cowgill,	West Branch, Iowa,	" "
647. Sarah E. Copeland,	Rich Square, N. C.,	" "
648. Mary F. Copeland,	" " "	" "
649. Ellen G. Copeland,	" " "	5th mo., 1876.
650. Amy French,	Salem, Ohio,	11th mo., 1875.
651. Ann Elizabeth White,	Belvidere, N. C.,	" "
652. Mary H. Whitson,	Chatham, Pa.,	" 1876.
653. Elizabeth W. Thorp,	Howellville, Pa.,	" 1875.
654. Rebecca W. Roberts,	Haddonfield, N. J.,	" "
655. Clara E. Swayne,	New London, Pa.,	" "
656. Lydia Jane Sidwell,	Colerain, Ohio,	" "

SIXTH THOUSAND.

NAME.	RESIDENCE.	DATE OF ENTRY.	
657. Sina A. Hall,	Barnesville, Ohio,	11th mo.,	1875.
658. Anna Nicholson,	Haddonfield, N. J.,	5th mo.,	1876.
659. Sarah E. Nicholson,	" "	"	"
660. Anna S. Heacock,	Greenwood, Pa.,	"	"
661. Sophronia Rich,	West Branch, Iowa,	"	"
662. Susanna Sharpless,	Birmingham, Pa.,	"	"
663. Laura P. Minster,	West Chester, Pa.,	"	"
664. Frances E. Linton,	Cochranville, Pa.,	"	"
665. Elizabeth S. Kite,	Chester Hill, Ohio,	"	"
666. Mary C. Moore,	Camden, N. J.,	11th mo.,	"
667. Anna H. Cooper,	Toughkenamon, Pa.,	"	"
668. Annie Palmer,	Media, Pa.,	"	"
669. Mary D. Forsythe,	Westtown, Pa.,	"	"
670. Louisa L. Smedley,	West Chester, Pa.,	"	"
671. Sarah Palmer,	Media, Pa.,	"	"
672. Emily Cheyney,	Marshallton, Pa.,	"	"
673. Hannah Rhoads,	Marple, Pa.,	"	"
674. Jane S. Rhoads,*	" "	"	"
675. Charlotte Mendenhall,	Kennett Square, Pa.,	"	"
676. Mary E. Ballinger,	Haddonfield, N. J.,	"	"
677. Sarah Fitzwater,	Thompson P. O., Del.,	5th mo.,	1877.
678. Elizabeth C. Sharpless,	Strickersville, Pa.,	"	"
679. Lydia T. Yarnall,	West Chester, Pa.,	"	"
680. Mary E. Outland,	Woodland, N. C.,	"	"
681. Sarah J. Outland,	" "	"	"
682. Mary J. White,	Belvidere, "	"	"
683. A. Helena Goodwin,	Greenwich, N. J.,	"	"
684. Louisa C. Brackman,	Shunk P. O., Pa.,	"	"
685. Elsie R. Yarnall,	Newtown Square, Pa.,	11th mo.,	1878.
686. Mary D. Snowdon,	Woodbury, N. J.,	5th mo.,	1877.
687. Mary L. Wetherill,	Philadelphia, Pa.,	"	"
688. Elizabeth Thompson,	Darlington, Md.,	11th mo.,	"
689. Lydia E. Hayes,	Doe Run, Pa.,	"	"
690. Mary T. Wilson,	Newportville, Pa.,	"	"
691. Emma Collins,	Barnegat, N. J.,	"	"
692. Anna M. Cheyney,	Colora, Md.,	"	"
693. Louisa W. Heacock,	Benton, Pa.,	5th mo.,	1878.
694. Louisa E. Priest,	Wolf Run, Pa.,	"	"
695. Susan M. Mendenhall,	" "	"	"
696. Sarah B. Taylor,	Oxford Valley, Pa.,	"	"
697. Car. C. Scattergood,	West Chester, Pa.,	11th mo.,	"
698. Melissa C. Hallett,	Moorestown, N. J.,	5th mo.,	"
699. Mary Moore,	Nine Points, Pa.,	"	"
700. Hannah D. Moore,	West Creek, N. J.,	"	"
701. Louisa M. Dewees,	Pennsville, Ohio,	"	"

* Deceased at the school, 27th of third mo., 1879.

STUDENTS.

SIXTH THOUSAND.

NAME.	RESIDENCE.	DATE OF ENTRY.
702. Mary Anna Jones,	Germantown, Pa.,	5th mo., 1878.
703. Mary F. Alsop,	Haverford College, Pa.,	11th mo., "
704. Rachel G. Alsop,	" "	" "
705. Susan K. Alsop,	" "	" "
706. Martha Balderston,	Philadelphia, Pa.,	" "
707. Rebecca T. DeCou,	Columbus, N. J.,	" "
708. Priscilla R. Nicholson,	Haddonfield, N. J.,	" "
709. Elizabeth E. Gardiner,	Kirkwood, N. J.,	" "
710. Margaret E. Paxson,	New Hope, Pa.,	" "
711. Mary P. Smedley,	Paoli, Pa.,	" "
712. Elizabeth N. Woolman,	Philadelphia, Pa.,	" "
713. Emily Hoffecker,	West Whiteland, Pa.,	5th mo., 1879.
714. Sarah K. Powell,	Easton, Md.,	" "
715. Harriet J. Taylor,	Woodstown, N. J.,	" "
716. Hannah R. Roberts,	Philadelphia, Pa.,	" "
717. Margaretta W. Roberts,	" "	" "
718. Sibyl J. Lindley,	Monrovia, Ind..	" "
719. Adelaide E. White,	Belvidere, N. C.,	" "
720. Emily W. Borton,	Rancocas. N. J.,	" "
721. Sarah S. Kirk,	Montoursville, Pa.,	" "
722. Sarah White,	Belvidere, N. C.,	" "
723. Ella T. Good,	West Grove, Pa.,	5th mo., 1880.
724. Z. Amy Larkin,	Toughkenamon, Pa.,	" "
725. Anna V. Haines,	Medford, N. J.,	11th mo., 1877.
727. Emily S. Aaronson,	Columbus, N. J.,	" "
728. Louisa H. Bishop,	Burlington, N. J.,	" "
729. Elizabeth Deacon,	Pemberton. N. J.,	5th mo., 1878.
730. Maria E. Garner,	Maryville, Tenn.,	" "
731. Martha E. Garner,	" "	" "
732. Miriam Elfreth,	Millville, N. J.,	" "
733. Elizabeth R. Russell,	Philadelphia, Pa.,	" "
734. Mary B. C. Lippincott,	Atlantic City, N. J.,	11th mo., "
735. Margaretta Kashner,	Columbus, N. J.,	" "
736. Elizabeth Roberts,	Centre Square, Pa.,	" "
737. Clara P Gifford,	Media, Pa.,	5th mo., 1879.
738. Helen Bonsall,	Philadelphia, Pa.,	" "
739. Mary M. Hartz,	Reading, Pa.,	" "
740. Sarah W. Paxson,	Aquetong, Pa.,	" "
741. Charlotte W. Bishop,	Columbus, N. J.,	" "
742. Emily B. Haines,	Medford, N. J.,	11th mo., "
743. Mary W. Matlack,	Moorestown, N. J.,	" "
744. Emily A. Darnell,	Mount Holly, N. J.,	" "
745. Ella S. Wills,	Philadelphia, Pa.,	" "
746. Bertha E. Atwater,	Somerset. N. Y.,	" "
747. Mary E. Lippincott,	Moorestown, N. J.,	" "
748. Caroline E. Paxson,	New Hope, Pa.,	" "
749. Sidney W. Eastburn,	Trenton, N. J.,	5th mo., 1880.

27*

SIXTH THOUSAND.

NAME.	RESIDENCE.	DATE OF ENTRY.	
750. Beulah F. Pennell,	Fairville, Pa.,	11th mo.,	1879.
751. Anna Walton,	Barnesville, Ohio,	"	"
752. Mary C. Bundy,	" "	"	"
753. Emma Thompson,	New London, Pa.,	"	"
754. Mary T. Frame,	Barnesville, Ohio,	"	"
755. Anna L. Ogborn,	Philadelphia, Pa.,	"	"
756. Estella H. Aaronson,	Columbus, N. J.,	"	"
757. Anna L. Seal,	Londonderry, Pa.,	"	"
758. Mary E. Peelo,	Winfall, N. C.,	"	"
759. Edith A. Edge,	London Grove, Pa.,	"	"
760. Sarah M. Edge,	" " "	"	"
761. Lydia C. Wilkins,	Medford, N. J.,	5th mo.,	1880.
762. Mary E. Wilkins,	" "	"	"
763. Rebecca Bailey,	Pine Iron Works, Pa.,	"	"
764. Margaret A. Futrell,	Rich Square, N. C.,	"	"
765. Ellen M. Griffin,	Woodland, N. C.,	"	"
766. Hannah Paxson,	Aquetong, Pa.,	"	"
767. Hannah J. Littler,	Kemp's Mills, N. C.,	"	"
768. Anna N. Rhoads,	Haddonfield, N. J.,	11th mo.,	"
769. Hannah C. Reeve,	Camden, N. J.,	"	"
770. Mary C. L. Bishop,	Columbus, N. J.,	"	"
771. Caroline R. Bell,	Mount Ephraim, N. J.,	"	"
772. Rachel R. Williams,	Fellowship, N. J.,	5th mo.,	1881.
774. Anna Heston,	Frankford, Pa.,	"	"
775. Susanna G. Fisher,	Dymond City, N. C.,	"	"
776. Mary E. Shreve,	Mount Laurel, N. J.,	"	1882.
777. Ollie S. Hall,	Mount Vernon, N. C.,	"	"
778. Eunice C. Winslow,	Jackson's Creek, N. C.,	"	"
779. Anna A. Mickle,	Millville, N. J.,	"	"
780. Edith F. Smedley,	Philadelphia, Pa.,	"	"
781. Emily F. Winslow,	Jackson's Creek, N. C.,	"	"
782. Sarah M. Tatum,	Woodbury, N. J.,	"	"
783. Anna G. Fell,	Suffolk, Va.,	11th mo.,	"
784. Lucy B. Child,	Wilmington, Del.,	"	"
785. Cornelia M. Atwater,	Somerset, N. Y.,	"	"
786. Elizabeth H. Smedley,	Howellville, Pa.,	"	"
787. Hannah Smedley,	Media, Pa.,	"	"
788. Emily Haines,	Rancocas, N. J.,	5th mo.,	1883.
789. Edith Dalziel,	Germantown, Pa.,	"	"
790. Ella Hatton,	West Chester, Pa.,	"	1880.
791. Caroline B. Hoopes,	" "	"	"
793. Eleanor H. Cooper,	Buffalo, N. Y.,	"	"
794. Elizabeth D. Fisher,	Dymond City, N. C.,	"	"
795. Hannah M. Worth,	Marshallton, Pa.,	"	"
796. Agnes V. McGrew,	Chester Hill, Ohio,	"	"
797. Abbie W. Parker,	West Chester, Pa.,	"	"
798. Caroline R. Parker,	" "	"	"

STUDENTS. 345

SIXTH THOUSAND.

NAME.	RESIDENCE.	DATE OF ENTRY.
799. Eliza L. Thomas,	Toughkenamon, Pa.,	5th mo., 1880.
800. Cynthia N. Cox,	Kemp's Mills, N. C.,	" "
801. Lydia E. Cope,	Philadelphia, Pa.,	" "
802. Abigail H. Heacock,	Greenwood, Pa.,	" "
804. Mary H. Bailey,	Thorndale, Pa.,	11th mo., "
805. Margaret Bentley,	Horsham, Pa.,	" "
806. Frances E. Forsythe,	West Grove, Pa.,	" "
807. Mary P. Good,	London Grove, Pa.,	" "
808. Emily E. Rockwell,	Rome, N. Y.,	" "
809. Martha Scarlett,	Reading, Pa.,	" "
810. Emily L. Allinson,	Camden, N. J.,	" "
811. Lillian H. Eastburn,	Edgewood, Pa.,	" "
812. Amy Heacock,	Greenwood, Pa.,	" "
813. Edda M. Satterthwaite,	Crosswicks, N. J.,	" "
814. Mary R. Wood,	Viola, Iowa,	" "
815. Anna L. Prindle,	Buffalo, N. Y.,	" "
816. Martha M. Holloway,	Flushing, Ohio,	" "
817. Mary Y. Coale,	Baltimore, Md.,	" "
818. Anna Jones,	Chestnut Hill, Pa.,	5th mo., 1881.
819. J. Della Hall,	Mount Vernon, N. C.,	" "
( ) Anna T. Hutton,	Westtown Mills, Pa.,	" "
( ) Susan E. Williams,	Westtown, Pa.,	11th mo., "
821. Elizabeth F. Babb,	Franklin, Va.,	5th mo., "
822. Caroline Myers,	Nicholson's Mills, N. C.,	" "
823. Hannah Thompson,	Thompson P. O., Del.,	" "
824. Fanny Cooper,	Chatham, Pa.,	" "
825. Margaretta A. Mercer,	Kennett Square, Pa.,	" "
826. Mary H. Wickersham,	" " "	" "
827. Gertrude Seal,	Londonderry, Pa.,	" "
828. Johnetta S. Griscom,	Philadelphia, Pa.,	" "
829. Mary E Hopkins,	Thompson P. O., Del.,	" "
830. Carrie E. Haviland,	Bryantown, Md.,	" "
831. Sarah E. Brackman,	Shunk P. O., Pa.,	" "
832. Mary A. Brackman,	" "	" "
833. M. Ella Penrose,	West Branch, Iowa,	" "
834. Elizabeth S. Ecroyd,	Wolf Run, Pa.,	11th mo, "
835. Laura F. Masters,	Millville, Pa.,	" "
836. Mary A Pearson,	Maiden Creek, Pa.,	" "
837. Ellen P. Foster,	Westerly, R. I.,	" "
838. Elizabeth R. Allen,	Cinnaminson, N. J.,	" "
839. Anna R. Mendenhall,	Howellville, Pa.,	" "
840. Susan S. Forsythe,	West Grove, Pa.,	" "
841. Rebecca Smedley,	Media, Pa.,	" "
842. Emma Smedley,	" "	" "
843. Elizabeth S. Thorp,	Wilmington, Del.,	" "
844. Sallie C. Garrett,	West Chester, Pa.,	" "
845. Mabel P. Sharpless,	Chester, Pa.,	" "

SIXTH THOUSAND.

NAME.	RESIDENCE.	DATE OF ENTRY.
846. Abby Walton,	Barnesville, Ohio,	11th mo., 1881.
847. Marian W. Haviland,	Hughesville, Md.,	" "
848. Julia S. White,	Belvidere, N. C.,	" "
849. Josephine L. Kester,	Bloomsburg, Pa.,	" "
850. Caroline Edgerton,	Barnesville, Ohio,	" "
851. S. Virginia Pearson,	Barclay, Kansas,	" "
852. Bethia B. Elder,	Angora, Pa.,	" "
853. Ella Leeds,	Spread Eagle, Pa.,	5th mo., 1882.
854. Eliza Hall,	Harrisville, Ohio,	" "
( ) Mary R. Williams,	Fellowship, N. J.,	" "
855. Emma Lamborn,	Russellville, Pa.,	" "
856. Melvina Dawson,	Barnesville, Ohio,	" "
857. Elma A. Cooper,	Philadelphia, Pa.,	" "
858. Elizabeth Garrett,	West Chester, Pa.,	" "
859. Alice M. Garrett,	" " "	11th mo., "
860. Susan A. Roberts,	Centre Square, Pa.,	" "
861. Anna Scarlett,	Reading, Pa.,	" "
862. Helen G. Birdsall,	East Coldenham, N. Y.,	" "
863. Eva Hoopes,	Downingtown, Pa.,	" "
864. Sibyl T. Howey,	Woodstown, N. J.,	" "
865. A. Clara Hatton,	Malvern, Pa.,	" "
866. Martha L. Pratt,	Toughkenamon, Pa.,	" "
867. Anna E. Garrett,	Lansdowne, Pa.,	" "
868. Pearl L. Mendenhall,	Greensboro, N. C.,	" "
869. S. Jane Ballinger,	Marlton, N. J.,	" "
870. Elizabeth M. Ballinger,	" "	" "
871. Ella M. Ballinger,	" "	" "
872. Caroline Whiteley,	Philadelphia, Pa.,	" "
873. Elizabeth H Tatum,	Wilmington, Del.,	" "
874. Emma C. Stanton,	Barnesville, Ohio,	" "
875. Hannah R. Lippincott,	Moorestown, N. J.,	" "
876. Elizabeth Harmer,	" "	" "
877. Jane Thorp,	Howellville, Pa.,	" "
878. Sarah J. Kennard,	Barnesville, Ohio,	" "
879. Christianna Schill,	Lake Run, Pa.,	" "
880. Katharine E. Kirk,	Muncy, Pa.,	" "
881. Annie L. Branson,	Flushing, Ohio,	5th mo., 1883.
882. Anna Holloway,	" "	11th mo., 1882.
883. Mary C. Scott,	West Chester, Pa.,	" "
884. Susan E. Williams,	Fellowship, N. J.,	" "
885. Luella E. Jones,	Hughesville, Md.,	5th mo., 1883.
886. Rettie W. Hoopes,	Downingtown, Pa.,	11th mo., "
887. Elizabeth R. Howell,	West Chester, Pa.,	5th mo., "
888. Frances A. Worth,	Marshallton, Pa.,	" "
889. Mary H. Smith,	Parkesburg, Pa.,	" "
890. Anna P. Smith,	" "	" "
891. Mary Scattergood,	West Chester, Pa.,	" "

STUDENTS.

SIXTH THOUSAND.

NAME.	RESIDENCE.	DATE OF ENTRY.
892. Anna R. Hoopes,	West Chester, Pa.,	5th mo., 1883.
893. Sarah J. Woody,	Saxapahaw, N. C.,	" "
894. Sarah F. Futrell,	Rich Square, N. C.,	" "
895. Elizabeth M. Whitacre,	Pine Iron Works, Pa.,	" "
896. Susan H. Winner,	Wolf Run, Pa.,	" "
897. Anna M. Winner,	" " "	" "
898. Louisa W. Parker,	" " "	" "
899. Elizabeth M. Bedford,	Shunk, P. O., Pa.,	" "
900. Frances Rhoads,	Wilmington, Del.,	" "
901. Elizabeth T. Haines,	Medford, N. J.,	" "
902. Elizabeth N. Henley,	Westminster, N. C.,	" "
903. Anna M. Llewelyn,	Pennsville, Ohio,	" "
904. Rachel B. Lamborn,	Setzler's Store, Pa.,	" "
905. Sarah R. Matlack,	Moorestown, N. J.,	11th mo., "
906. Jane S. Jones,	Germantown, Pa.,	" "
907. J. Gen've Mendenhall,	Westminster, N. C.,	" "
908. Mary Ward,	Coal Creek, Iowa,	" "
909. Ozella C. Outland,	Woodland, N. C.,	" "
910. Mary G. Haines,	Medford, N. J.,	5th mo., 1884.
911. Lydia M. Roberts,	Moorestown, N. J.,	" "
951. Elizabeth H. Goodwin,	Greenwich, N. J.,	" 1883.
952. Ida M. Votaw,	Richmond, Ind.,	" "
953. Edith Smedley,	Lima P. O, Pa.,	" "
954. Phebe A. Cope,	Kimbleville, Pa.,	11th mo., "
955. Miriam R. Copeland,	Woodland, N. C.,	5th mo., "
956. Margaret H. Scott,	Darlington, Md.,	" "
957. Mary H. C. Wright,	Conshohocken, Pa.,	11th mo., "
958. Esther H. Eldridge,	Goshenville, Pa.,	5th mo., "
959. Annie Way,	Fishertown, Pa.,	11th mo., "
960. Ellen Edgerton,	Barnesville, Ohio,	5th mo., "
961. R. Anna Coates,	Baltimore, Md.,	" "
962. Mary F. Chilton,	Westfield, N. C.,	11th mo., "
963. Hettie W. Gardiner,	Mount Holly, N. J.,	" "
964. Ada Blair,	High Point, N. C.,	" "
965. Emma H. Blair,	" " "	" "
966. Elizabeth W. Haines,	Mount Laurel, N. J.,	" "
967. J. Isabella Crenshaw,	Richmond, Va.,	" "
968. Sarah A. Wood,	Greenwich, N. J.,	" "
969. Annie Ecroyd,	Muncy, Pa.,	" "
970. Mary H. Cope,	London Grove, Pa.,	" "
971. Martha S Reynolds,	Bush Hill, N. C.,	" "
972. Naomi B. Dewees,	Pennsville, Ohio,	" "
973. Elizabeth B. Boone,	Pickering, Canada,	" "
974. Ella P. Lippincott,	Moorestown, N. J.,	" "
975. Felicia H. Thomas,	Elam P. O., Pa.,	" "
976. Clara Bedford,	Lake Run, Pa.,	5th mo., 1884.
977. Elizabeth Moore,	Ercildoun, Pa.,	11th mo., 1883.

v

SIXTH THOUSAND.

NAME.	RESIDENCE.	DATE OF ENTRY.
978. Sarah Hartz,	Reading, Pa.,	5th mo., 1884.
979. Sallie M. Test,	Springville, Iowa,	" "
980. Lydia M. Young,	" "	" "
981. Jane Dalziel,	Germantown, Pa.,	" "
982. Bertha A. Brown,	Lincoln Falls, Pa.,	" "
983. Jane L. Roberts,	Centre Square, Pa.,	" "
984. Beulah Palmer,	Media, Pa.,	" "
986. Elizabeth Mellor,	West Chester, Pa.,	" "
987. Sarah B. Stanton,	Barnesville, Ohio,	" "
988. Annie B. Griscom,	Philadelphia, Pa.,	" "
989. Mary K. Jackson,	" "	" "
990. Elspeth J. Trotter,	Bryantown, Md.,	" "
991. Rebecca W. Elder,	Germantown, Pa.,	" "

SUMMARY.

NOTE.—Those who were students at the school, but did not board in the Institution, or receive register numbers, are not included in the following.

	Boys.	Girls.
Highest Register number issued	4,874	5,991
Deducting for vacant numbers and those known to be re-admissions	159	125
Actual number of students (boarders)	4,715	5,866

Distributed as follows;

	Boys	Girls
Philadelphia, city and county	1,020	1,018
Pennsylvania (exclusive of above)	1,766	2,524
New Jersey	1,009	1,256
Maryland	256	275
Delaware	195	249
New York	143	114
Ohio	110	132
Virginia	90	90
North Carolina	24	73
Indiana	10	27
Illinois	8	3
Iowa	9	10
Massachusetts	10	4
Kansas	7	2
Canada	5	3
Rhode Island	4	7
Long Island	5	2
District of Columbia	6	4
Michigan	6	2
Colorado	3	
Tennessee		2
Minnesota	1	1
Vermont		1
Connecticut	1	
Missouri		1
Norway, Europe		1
Unknown	27	65
Total	4,715	5,866

TABULAR STATEMENT OF THE AVERAGE NUMBER OF STUDENTS AT WESTTOWN BOARDING SCHOOL, AS SHOWN BY THE ANNUAL REPORTS.

Date of Report.	Boys.	Girls.	Total.	Date of Report.	Boys.	Girls.	Total.
1800				1843	109	97	206
1801	100	100	200	1844	95	88	183
1802	90	90	180	1845	86	76	162
1803			130	1846	95	84	179
1804	80	80	160	1847	86	80	166
1805	70	100	170	1848			200
1806			170	1849	110	83	193
1807	79	97	176	1850	100	91	191
1808	45	85	130	1851	104	88	192
1809	65	90	155	1852	87	80	167
1810	82	93	175	1853	103	77	180
1811	93	95	188	1854	108	105	213
1812			193	1855	115	112	227
1813	74	92	166	1856	110	116	226
1814	71	98	169	1857	115	111	226
1815	75	100	175	1858	106	90	196
1816	62	103	165	1859	91	84	175
1817	73	104	177	1860	82	86	168
1818	68	93	161	1861	84	73	157
1819			140	1862	74	75	149
1820	73	83	156	1863	95	73	168
1821	58	87	145	1864	77	79	154
1822				1865	102	108	210
1823	63	113	176	1866	112	120	232
1824	59	102	161	1867	121+	121+	243
1825	58	93	151	1868	121	110	231
1826	57	82	139	1869	112+	87+	200
1827	51	81	132	1870	108	81	189
1828	35	75	110	1871	103+	96+	200
1829	45	64	109	1872	106	91	197
1830	45	58	103	1873	109+	75+	185
1831	70	83	153	1874	104	84	188
1832	100	107	207	1875	106	84	190
1833	101	105	206	1876	113	83	196
1834	122	115	237	1877	113	72	185
1835			238	1878	112+	69+	182
1836	114	116	230	1879	117	68	185
1837	102	129	231	1880	101	66	167
1838	102	120	222	1881	94	74	168
1839			243	1882	97+	70+	168
1840			244	1883	99	79	178
1841	123	120	243	1884	108	101	209
1842			212				

ALPHABETICAL INDEX.

NOTE.—Names of Officers at the Institution and Members of the Committee in *italics.*

Name	PAGE
Aaronson, Emily S.,	343
Aaronson, Estella H.,	344
Aaronson, Hor. L. F.,	199
Abbott, Amy G.,	306
Abbott, Charles T.,	179
Abbott, Eleanor S.,	250
Abbott, George.	117
Abbott, George,	140
" " (Com.,)	103
Abbott, George, Jr.,	183
Abbott, George B.,	139
Abbott, Hannah,	244
Abbott, Hannah,	246
Abbott, Helena,	226
Abbott, Henry,	123
Abbott, Henry B.,	181
Abbott, Howard,	120
Abbott, Kath'ine W.,	353
Abbott, Lucy,	229
Abbott, Lydia,	279
Abbott, Martha,	287
Abbott, Mary,	304
Abbott, Mary Ann,	269
Abbott, Mary Ann,	326
Abbott, Rebecca,	242
Abbott, Rebecca,	263
Abbott, Rebecca A.,	296
Abbott, Rebecca W.,	333
Abbott, Ruth S.,	103
Abbott, Samuel,	140
Abbott, Samuel,	188
Abbott, Sarah,	226
Abbott, Thomas,	124
Abbott, William,	121
Abbott, William,	202
Acton, Benjamin,	133
Acton, Caspar W.,	144
Acton, Catharine,	300
Acton, Charlotte,	286
Acton, Hannah,	275
Acton, Letitia,	300
Acton, Richard M.,	130
Acton, Sarah W.,	303
Adams, Eliza,	246
Adams, Frances A.,	306
Adams, Frank,	187
Adams, George,	165
Adams, John Q.,	156
Adams, Robert H.,	187
Adams, William,	113
Adams, Wm.,(Teacher,)	83
Adamson, Rebecca,	258
Albertson, Abigail W.,	319
Albertson, Amos L.,	190
Albertson, Benjamin,	113
Albertson, Benjamin,	175
Albertson, Charles,	163
Albertson, Eliz. P.,	317
Albertson, Hannah,	223
Albertson, Hannah,	229
" (Teacher,)	83
(Williams,) (Com.,)	100
Albertson, Hannah,	303
Albertson, Henry,	165
Albertson, Henry,	175
Albertson, J. Morton,	153
Albertson, Jacob,	113
Albertson, Joseph,	163
Albertson, Josiah,	110
Albertson, Lewis J.,	165
Albertson, Martha,	337
Albertson, Mary,	297
Albertson, Rachel L.,	308
Albertson, Rebecca,	235
Albertson, Ruth A.,	311
Albertson, Samuel L.,	157
Albertson, Samuel L.,	162
Albertson, Sam'l M.,	157
Albertson, Sarah H.,	309
Albertson, William,	162
Albertson, Wm. E.,	190
Alderson, Agnes,	314
Alderson, Anna M.,	314
Alderson, William C.,	166
Alexander, Chris. H.,	176
Alexander, Margaret,	282
Alexander, Rachel,	321
Alexander, Sarah H.,	326
Alexander, William,	140
Allen, Benjamin,	136
Allen, Charles,	98
Allen, Charles B.,	125
Allen, Charles J.,	149
" " (Com.,)	101
" " (Sup't,)	80
Allen, Edward, Jr.,	189
Allen, Elizabeth,	288
" " (Com.,)	102
Allen, Elizabeth B.,	317
Allen, Elizabeth R.,	345
Allen, George B.,	123
Allen, George B.,	171
Allen, Hannah,	276
" " (Teacher,)	85
(Warner,) " (Gov'ss,)	81
" " (Com.,)	102
Allen, Hannah,	292
Allen, Hannah G.,	304
Allen, Hannah P.,	274
Allen, Henry D.,	205
Allen, John C.,	127
Allen, Joseph E.,	145
Allen, Joshua G.,	160
Allen, Joshua M.,	134
Allen, Lydia,	289
Allen, MarmadukeW.,	139
Allen, Martha D.,	102
" " (Matron,)	80
(See House.)	
Allen, Mary,	283
Allen, Mary,	324
Allen, Mary M.,	296
Allen, Miriam,	296
Allen, Rebecca, (Com.,)	99
Allen, Rebecca,	281
Allen, Rebecca,	290
Allen, Rebecca J.,	314
" " (Teacher,)	91
Allen, Rebecca S.,	102
(See Leeds.)	
Allen, Richard J.,	157
" " (Teacher,)	86
Allen, Robert G.,	166
Allen, Rowland D.,	189
Allen, Samuel,	172
Allen, Samuel L.,	170
Allen, Sarah,	277
" " (Com.,)	101
(See Richie.)	
Allen, Sarah,	327
Allen, Sarah L.,	315
Allen, Thomas,	112
Allen, William C.,	194
Allen, William E.,	177
Allinson, Anna B.,	324
Allinson, Bernice,	330
Allinson, Caroline,	336
Allinson, Charles,	198
Allinson, Edward P.,	185
Allinson, Emily L.,	345
Allinson, Helen M.,	338
Allinson, James,	175
Allinson, John C.,	105

377

378 INDEX.

Name	Page
Allinson, Josiah T.,	193
Allinson, Mary. (Com.,)	97
" " (Teacher,)	83
Allinson, Mary E.,	317
Allinson, Rachel E.,	321
Allinson, Rebecca,	260
Allinson, Samuel,	127
" " (Com.,)	102
Allinson, William,	98
Allinson, William W.,	195
Alricks, Sarah,	264
Alsop, Edmund,	203
Alsop, Edward B.,	167
Alsop, George M.,	130
Alsop, Hannah,	280
Alsop, Mary F.,	343
Alsop, Rachel,	268
Alsop, Rachel,	323
Alsop, Rachel G.,	343
Alsop, Rebecca,	259
Alsop, Reece,	167
Alsop, Robert,	128
Alsop, Samuel,	87
Alsop, Samuel, Jr.,	170
" " (B'k-keeper,)	93
" " (Teacher,)	87, 88
Alsop, Susan K.,	343
Alsop, William K.,	205
Altemus, Francis L.,	137
Alston, Hannah J.,	232
" " (Com.,)	99
Alston, Susanna,	237
Ambler, Mary,	249
Andrews, Hannah,	239
Andrews, Hannah,	246
Andrews, Sarah,	258
Andrews, Sarah Ann,	287
Antrim, Benajah,	139
Archer, Rebecca,	96
Arnold, C. William,	192
Aronson, Rosina A.,	312
Ash, Amanda M.,	314
Ash, Charles W.,	176
Ash, Elizabeth,	236
Ash, Hannah,	227
Ash, Isaac Y.,	171
Ash, Lewis P.,	185
Ash, Mary Ellen,	333
Ash, Mary H.,	317
Ash, Phineas,	92
Ash, Samuel,	192
Ash, Walter P.,	200
Ash, William G.,	174
Ash, William R.,	169
Ashbridge, Ab'm S.,	145
Ashbridge, George,	137
Ashbridge, George G.,	99
Ashead, Amos, Jr.,	202
Ashead, Benjamin S.,	194
Ashead, Joseph H.,	198
Ashead, Lydia L.,	311
Ashead, Morris,	204
Ashead, Rebecca S.,	338
Aston, Ann,	223
Aston, George,	105
Atherton, Charles,	125
Atherton, Hannah S.,	281
Atherton, Lydia,	260
Atkinson, Ann,	251
Atkinson, Benjamin,	141
Atkinson, Eliza,	282
Atkinson, Eliza C.,	279
Atkinson, Elizabeth,	228
Atkinson, Ellen,	225
Atkinson, Ellen,	242
Atkinson, Hetty Ann,	286
Atkinson, James E.,	131
Atkinson, Joseph H.,	138
Atkinson, Martha E.,	276
Atkinson, Mary,	275
Atkinson, Mary,	292
Atkinson, Mary A.,	269
Atkinson, Rachel,	261
Atkinson, Sarah,	295
Atkinson, Stephen,	145
Atlee, Charlotte W.,	275
Atlee, Edwin P.,	120
Atlee, Esther B.,	254
Atlee, Margaret L.,	268
Atlee, Samuel Y.,	128
Atwater, Bertha E,	343
Atwater, Cornelia M.,	344
Atwater, Eliz. H.,	333
Atwater, Hannah G.,	333
Atwater, Huldah M.,	340
Atwater, Myra A.,	340
Atwater, Sarah E.,	313
Atwater, Stephen,	197
Atwater, William L.,	186
Austin, Joseph,	166
Austin, Letitia E.,	264
Austin, Lydia,	236
Austin, Martha N.,	252
Austin, Sarah,	227
Ayres, Mary Ann,	250
Babb, Anna,	341
Babb, Elizabeth F.,	345
Babb, Geneva M.,	336
Babb, Sarah,	287
Bacon, Ann,	225
" " (Teacher,)	83
Bacon, Anna D.,	322
Bacon, Anna T.,	337
Bacon, Beulah,	269
Bacon, Caroline W.,	339
Bacon, Charles W.,	128
Bacon, Charles W.,	135
Bacon, David,	105
Bacon, Elizabeth,	306
Bacon, George S.,	201
Bacon, George W.,	177
Bacon, George W.,	205
Bacon, Hannah,	331
Bacon, Helen R.,	315
Bacon, Henry,	182
Bacon, Herbert M.,	204
Bacon, Horatio W.,	200
Bacon, Job,	165
Bacon, John,	200
Bacon, John M.,	128
Bacon, John M.,	152
Bacon, J. Murray,	192
Bacon, Jonah M.,	172
Bacon, Josiah,	134
Bacon, Josiah,	165
Bacon, Joseph E.,	172
Bacon, Joseph K.,	148
Bacon, Martha R.,	304
Bacon, Mary,	242
Bacon, Mary,	259
Bacon, Mary,	311
Bacon, Mary H.,	284
Bacon, Mary W.,	283
Bacon, Maurice W.,	205
Bacon, Morris,	172
Bacon, Rebecca B.,	330
Bacon, Samuel,	111
Bacon, Samuel A.,	184
Bacon, Samuel W.,	141
Bacon, Sarah,	239
Bacon, Sarah Ann,	295
Bacon, Susan P.,	267
Bacon, Thomas,	108
Bacon, Thomas,	126
" " (Com.,)	100
Bacon, William S.,	189
Bailey, Emma,	341
Bailey, George,	200
Bailey, Joseph, Jr.,	201
Bailey, Joseph,	118
" " (Farmer,)	92
Bailey, Joseph L.,	160
Bailey, Mary H.,	345
Bailey, Rebecca,	344
Bailey, Richard W.,	201
Bailey, Sarah H.,	339
Bailey, William L.,	155
" " (Com.,)	103
Baily, Abiah,	110
Baily, Alfred W.,	195
Baily, Ann,	244
Baily, Anna,	308
Baily, Anne T.,	324
Baily, Charles L.,	141
Baily, Dempsey,	192
Baily, Edward,	151
Baily, Eleanor,	292
Baily, Elizabeth,	241
Baily, Elizabeth,	264
Baily, Elizabeth,	285
" " (Teacher,)	85
Baily, Elizabeth L.,	328
Baily, Elmira S.,	305
Baily, Emily,	310
Baily, Frances,	333
Baily, George,	151
" " (Teacher,)	86
Baily, Hannah,	237
Baily, Hannah,	305
Baily, Hannah,	316
Baily, Hannah P.,	264
Baily, James,	109
Baily, Jesse J.,	143
Baily, Joseph,	139
Baily, Joshua,	109
Baily, Joshua L.,	150
Baily, Josiah T.,	188
Baily, Lloyd,	182
Baily, Lydia,	228
Baily, Lydia A.,	278
Baily, Mary,	240
Baily, Mary,	256
Baily, Olive,	239

INDEX.

Name	PAGE
Baily, Richard B.,	132
" " (Com.,)	102
Baily, Samuel L.,	141
Baily, Samuel P.,	144
Baily, Sarah,	249
Baily, Sarah,	281
" " (Teacher,)	85
Baily, Sarah,	295
Baily, Sarah,	336
Baily, Sarah K.,	287
Baily, Susanna P.,	280
Baily, Thomas,	144
Baily, Thomas L.,	145
Baily, William E.,	126
Baily, William L.,	153
Baker, Ann,	255
Baker, Eleanor S.,	318
Baker, Elizabeth,	274
Baker, George R.,	136
Baker, Hannah,	247
Baker, Lydia,	238
Baker, Phebe E.,	327
Baker, Rachel,	251
Baker, Rebecca,	266
Baker, William,	116
Balderston, Anne,	90
Balderston, C. Canby,	180
" (*Teacher,*) 88, 89, 90	
Balderston, Cath. C.,	103
Balderston, Charles,	190
Balderston, Cl'yton N.,	188
Balderston, Edward,	167
Balderston, Eliza A.,	264
Balderston, Eliz.,(Com.,)	98
Balderston, Eliz.,	307
Balderston, Eliz.,	326
Balderston, Eliz.,	335
Balderston, Elwood,	197
Balderston, Emily,	275
Balderston, Emily N.,	324
Balderston, George,	179
Balderston, George W.,	203
Balderston, Henry G.,	199
Balderston, Isaiah,	123
Balderston, Isaiah,	171
Balderston, Jane C.,	333
Balderston, John E.,	170
Balderston, John L.,	187
Balderston, John P.,	182
Balderston, Joseph H.,	180
Balderston, Lloyd, Jr.,	198
Balderston, Lydia,	332
Balderston, Marcellus,	124
Balderston, Marcellus,	177
Balderston, Maria,	285
Balderston, Martha,	343
Balderston, Mary,	301
Balderston Mary A.,	91
(See Brown.)	
Balderston, Rachel,	264
Balderston, Rachel E.,	318
Balderston, Sam'l F.,	130
Balderston, Sarah,	277
Balderston, William,	177
Balderston, William,	193
Balderston, William,	102
Balderston, Wm. H.,	158
Balderston, Wilson,	123

Name	PAGE
Baldwin, Caleb,	147
Baldwin, Cath'ine W.,	256
Baldwin, Charity,	312
Baldwin, Deborah J.,	302
Baldwin, Hannah,	232
Baldwin, J. Hanover,	160
Baldwin, John,	83
Baldwin, John E.,	149
Baldwin, Jonathan C.,	176
Baldwin, Joseph,	123
Baldwin, Thomas,	131
Baldwin, William,	115
Ball, Aaron,	160
Ball, Ellwood,	179
Ball, Martha D.,	306
Ball, Mary,	294
Ball, Thomas,	195
Ballance, James M.,	176
Ballance, John,	176
Ballance, Joseph L.,	153
Ballance, Merrick,	164
Ballangee, Mary,	281
Ballenger, Charles,	171
Ballenger, Eliz. C.,	315
Ballenger, Hannah,	318
Ballenger, J. T.,	156
Ballenger, John,	156
Ballenger, John H.,	156
Ballenger, Joseph E.,	165
Ballenger, Joshua C.,	175
Ballenger, Priscilla,	273
Ballenger, Rebecca,	321
Ballenger, Thomas,	123
Ballenger, Thomas,	143
Ballinger, Charles D.,	205
Ballinger, Eliz M.,	346
Ballinger, Ella M.,	346
Ballinger, Mary E.,	342
Ballinger, Rachel,	310
Ballinger, Rebecca N.,	338
Ballinger, S. Jane,	346
Ballinger, Sarah P.,	339
Ballinger, Susan T.,	320
Bancroft, Esther,	275
Bancroft, Harvey,	136
Bancroft, Martha,	275
Bancroft, William,	136
Bane, Mary,	258
Bangs, James E.,	179
Bangs, William,	184
Barker, Abigail,	99
Barker, Elizabeth,	84
Barker, Elizabeth,	244
Barker, Elizabeth D.,	236
Barker, John R.,	135
Barker, Martha,	83
(*Hilles.*) " (*Com.,*)	99
Barker, Mary,	320
Barker, Peter,	96
Barker, Solomon E.,	203
Barnard, Ann,	247
Barnard, Anne,	261
Barnard, Dinah,	240
Barnard, Edith,	301
Barnard, Eliza,	256
Barnard, Elizabeth,	225
Barnard, Ephraim,	140
Barnard, Eusebius,	125

Name	PAGE
Barnard, Grace,	251
Barnard, Lettice,	248
Barnard, Margaret,	238
Barnard, Mary,	239
Barnard, Mary	303
Barnard, Mary P.,	240
Barnard, Moses,	116
Barnard, Reuben,	158
Barnard, Richard,	99
Barnard, William,	124
Barnard, Wilson,	141
Barnes, Sarah L.,	239
Barnett, Thomas F.,	145
Barney, Mabel,	240
Barrington, John A.,	109
Bartlett, Alfred R.,	189
Bartlett, Amos R.,	174
Bartlett, Anna M.,	315
Bartlett, Annie M.,	328
Bartlett, Charles A.,	202
Bartlett, Duncan O.,	183
Bartlett, Fayre P.,	169
Bartlett, Ellen L.,	340
Bartlett, George G.,	171
Bartlett, Helen E.,	329
Bartlett, J. Henry,	196
" " (B'k-kpr.,)	93
Bartlett, John,	114
Bartlett, John K.,	162
Bartlett, John W.,	182
Bartlett, Joseph,	132
Bartlett, Louisa A.,	290
Bartlett, Marian A.,	321
Bartlett, Martha W.,	315
Bartlett, Mary E.,	329
Bartlett, Samuel P.,	181
Bartlett, Thomas R.,	172
Bartlett, William O.,	176
Barton, Amy S.,	321
Barton, Annie H.,	339
Barton, Bathsheba,	256
Barton, Eliza J.,	322
Barton, Martha C.,	294
" " (*Teacher,*)	86
Barton, John,	157
Barton, Joseph E.,	168
Barton, Joshua,	185
Barton, Nathaniel,	165
Barton, Rachel,	321
Barton, Rachel E.,	341
Barton, Sarah,	325
Burtram, Elizabeth,	254
Bartram, George,	105
Bartram, Isaac,	119
Bartram, Mary,	223
Bartram, Rachel C.,	99
Bartram, Sarah,	227
Bartram, Thomas,	128
Bartram, Thomas,	157
Bartram, William S.,	116
Bassett, Elisha,	113
Bassett, Eliza W.,	286
Bassett, Emma,	312
Bassett, Franklin,	183
Bassett, Granville,	100
Bassett, Hannah W.,	310
Bassett, Irena,	169
Bassett, Joseph,	98

28*

380 INDEX.

Name	Page
Bassett, Mary,	251
Bassett, Mary,	262
Bassett, Mary Anna,	322
Bassett, Samuel,	122
Bassett, Sarah S.,	304
Bassett, William,	130
Bates, Catharine,	307
Bates, Deborah,	281
Bates, Martha Ann,	307
Bates, Sarah,	306
Bates, Sarah Ann,	285
Bates, Susanna,	306
Bates, Tacy,	307
Battey, Thomas C.,	161
Battin, Andrew J.,	203
Battin, C. Eleanor,	337
Battin, Cynthia,	337
Battin, Hannah,	285
Battin, Henry,	196
Battin, Reuben,	161
Battin, Susanna,	254
Baxter, Mary E.,	341
Baxter, Sarah M.,	341
Beans, William, Jr.,	191
Bedell, Charles C.,	174
Bedell, Charles C.,	176
Bedell, Thomas H.,	168
Bedford, Clara,	347
Bedford, Eliz. M.,	347
Bedford, Thomas,	118
Beesley, Charlotte,	289
Bell, Abraham,	122
Bell, Albert T.,	206
Bell, Anna J.,	326
Bell, Arthur H.,	190
Bell, Caroline R.,	344
Bell, Chalkley,	142
Bell, Charles,	145
Bell, Charles,	181
Bell, Charles,	193
Bell, Edward,	141
Bell, Edwin A.,	172
Bell, Edwin R.,	194
Bell, Eliza Ann,	325
Bell, Elizabeth,	281
Bell, Emma,	329
Bell, Ezra,	154
Bell, Francis J.,	172
Bell, Franklin,	158
Bell, Frederic D.,	206
Bell, Hannah A.,	294
Bell, Henry A.,	190
Bell, Howard H.,	196
Bell, Hughes,	122
" " (Farmer,)	92
Bell, James,	133
Bell, James,	164
Bell, James E.,	175
Bell, Jane,	281
Bell, John H.,	194
Bell, Jonathan,	117
Bell, Jonathan, Jr.,	182
Bell, Levi,	128
Bell, Margaret C.,	339
Bell, Mary,	267
Bell, Mary,	288
Bell, Mary,	291
Bell, Mary D.,	388
Bell, Mifflin,	179
Bell, Robert B.,	157
Bell, Samuel,	132
Bell, Samuel E.,	185
Bell, Sarah E.,	327
Bell, Thomas A.,	175
" " (Teacher,)	88
Bell, Thomas J.,	151
Bell, Walter,	175
Bell, Wilhelmina,	319
Bell, William,	128
Bell, William B.,	179
Bell, William E.,	173
Bellach, James,	121
Bellangee, Aaron,	107
Bellangee, Benj. S.,	141
Bellangee, James B.,	158
Bellangee, Mary Ann,	280
Bellerby, Elizabeth,	83
Benington, Ann,	297
Benington, Henry,	160
Benington, John,	101
" " (Farmer,)	92
Benington, John, Jr.,	173
Benington, Margaret,	320
Benington, Rachel,	305
Benington, Robert H.,	156
Benington, Samuel,	153
Bennett, Daniel R.,	127
Bennett, Edith,	236
Bennett, Gilpin,	118
Bennett, James,	121
Bennett, Mary,	265
Bentley, David F.,	203
Bentley, Margaret,	345
Bentley, Richard L.,	198
Bentley, Sarah B.,	331
Berry, Thomas,	97
Bettle, Charles,	172
Bettle, Edward,	122
Bettle, Jane,	99
Bettle, Jane,	299
Bettle, Martha,	318
Bettle, Samuel,	97
Bettle, Samuel, Jr.,	101
Bettle, William,	112
Betts, Benjamin,	145
Betts, Henry E.,	191
Betts, Lydia,	281
Betts, Martha,	233
Betts, Mary L,	297
Betts, William,	156
Biddle, Anna,	241
Biddle, Anna,	249
Biddle, Anne,	98
(*Tatum*,) "	100
Biddle, Edward,	129
Biddle, James C.,	123
Biddle, James G.,	205
Biddle, John,	117
Biddle, John W.,	103
Biddle, Martha,	271
Biddle, Owen,	128
Riddle, Owen,	95
Biddle, Philip G.,	172
Biddle, Rebecca,	271
" " (*Teacher*,)	86
" " (*Com.*,)	101
(*Cope*)Biddle,R.(*Com.*,)	101
Biddle, Samuel,	117
Biddle, Samuel,	155
Biddle, William,	124
" " (*Com..*)	102
Biddle, William, Jr.,	202
Biddle, William W.,	178
Biles, Rachel,	234
Bines, David A.,	196
Bines, Samuel M.,	149
Bines, S. Mason,	188
Bines, William H.,	149
Bines, William T.,	188
Binns, Mary,	293
Birdsall, Charles C.,	204
Birdsall, Helen G.,	346
Bishop, Ann,	268
Bishop, Ann,	314
Bishop, Anna,	329
Bishop, Biddle,	189
Bishop, Charlotte W.,	343
Bishop, Edward N.,	159
Bishop, Jane,	327
Bishop, John,	142
" " (*Com.*,)	102
Bishop, John I.,	182
Bishop, Louisa H.,	343
Bishop, Lucy,	253
Bishop, Lydia,	314
Bishop, Mary,	280
Bishop, Mary C. L.,	344
Bishop, Rebecca F.,	338
Bishop, Sarah B.,	326
Bishop, Thomas S.,	181
Bishop, William,	192
Bishop, William R.,	163
Black, Joseph,	83
Black, Mary T.,	287
Black, Rebecca,	239
Black, Samuel W.,	85
Black, Thomas N.,	142
Black, William,	117
Black, William H.,	156
Blackburn, Wm. J.,	203
Blackledge, Mary,	84
Blackwood, Abigail,	243
Blackwood, Ann,	253
Blackwood, Benj.,	122
Blackwood, Eliz.,	241
Blackwood, John,	120
Blackwood, John,	178
Blackwood, Samuel,	106
Blackwood, Sarah,	246
Blackwood, Wm. H.,	182
Blair, Ada,	347
Blair, Emma H.,	347
Blakey, Achsah A.,	321
Blakey, Elizabeth W.,	318
Blakey, John,	169
Blakey, Rachel,	273
Blakey, Thomas,	132
Blakey, William,	95
Bolton, Alfred,	175
Bolton, Anna M.,	313
Bolton, Ellen M.,	289
Bolton, Gideon S.,	167
Bolton, Hannah S.,	256
Bolton, James,	125

INDEX.

Name	PAGE	Name	PAGE	Name	PAGE
Bolton, Samuel,	128	Borton, John W.,	184	Briggs, Lætitia,	238
Bolton, Sarah,	232	Borton, Joseph H.,	159	Briggs, Mary,	236
Bolton, Thomas S.,	167	Borton, Josephine H.,	339	Bringhurst, James,	114
Bond, Jesse,	111	Borton, Mary,	240	Bringhurst, Mary,	264
Bonner, Benjamin,	131	Borton, Mary,	303	Bringhurst, Sarah A.,	234
Bonner, Mary L.,	271	Borton, Mary N.,	276	Bringhurst, Sarah A.,	244
Bonsall, Anna,	232	Borton, Naomi,	280	Brinton, Anna G.,	338
Bonsall, Anna,	244	Borton, Rachel,	267	Brinton, Cassandra,	291
Bonsall, Charles,	121	Borton, Rachel,	309	Brinton, Edward,	189
Bonsall, Charles S.,	201	Borton, Rebecca W.,	325	Brinton, Elizabeth,	226
Bonsall, Charles T.,	164	Borton, Sarah,	234	(*Smith*,) " (*Com*.,)	100
Bonsall, Daniel,	124	Borton, Sarah J.,	324	Brinton, Elizabeth A.,	308
Bonsall, Edmund H.,	141	Borton, Thomazin M.,	309	Brinton, Emmor,	151
Bonsall, Edward,	181	Borton, Uriah,	167	Brinton, Ferree.	118
Bonsall, Edward H.,	114	Borton, William T.,	171	Brinton, Hannah,	227
Bonsall, Edwin,	121	Bostwick, Mary Anna,	296	Brinton, Howard,	192
Bonsall, Elizabeth,	332	Bostwick, Cath'ne W.,	311	Brinton, James,	111
Bonsall, Elizabeth J.,	333	Bostwick, Martha W.,	303	Brinton, Jane,	293
Bonsall, Ellwood,	165	Boswell, Sarah B.,	340	Brinton, John F.,	148
Bonsall, Helen,	343	" (*Teacher*,)	88	Brinton, Joseph,	149
Bonsall, Henry L.,	121	Boustead, Eliz. A.,	290	Brinton, Joseph,	167
Bonsall, Isaac,	96	Boustead, James,	140	Brinton, Letitia,	262
Bonsall, James,	122	Boustead, Jane,	276	Brinton, Lydia,	231
Bonsall, James H.,	163	Boustead, William,	143	Brinton, Lydia S.,	292
Bonsall, Jeremiah,	146	Bowerman, Elijah,	172	Brinton, Maria,	245
Bonsall, Joseph,	116	Bowers, Thomas,	167	Brinton, Mary,	228
Bonsall, Joseph,	120	Bowman, Esther,	237	Brinton, Mary,	307
Bonsall, Joseph E.,	190	Bowne, Hugh H.,	136	Brinton, Nathan S.,	151
Bonsall, Lewis E.,	183	Bowne, John,	139	Brinton, Ralph Lee,	198
Bonsall, Martha,	332	Bowne, Richard H.,	130	Brinton, Rebecca W.,	295
Bonsall, Martha G.,	241	Bowne, William,	136	Brinton, Robert M.,	174
Bonsall, Mary,	98	Bowne, William,	139	Brinton, Ruth,	274
Bonsall, Rebecca,	237	Brackin, Lemuel,	180	Brinton, Samuel,	111
Bonsall, Ruth,	255	Brackman, Adolph,	200	Brinton, Sarah,	241
Bonsall, Samuel,	126	Brackman, Louisa C.,	342	Brinton, Susan,	262
Bonsall, Sidney,	243	Brackman, Mary A.,	345	Brinton, Susan,	309
Bonsall, Sidney Ann,	309	Brackman, Sarah E.,	345	Brinton, Walter,	196
Bonsall, Spencer,	138	Bradley, Albina,	283	Britt, George,	116
Bonsall, Thomas,	106	Bradley, Elizabeth,	301	Britt, Mary,	229
Bonsall, Thomas S.,	165	Bradley, Sarah,	304	Britt, Mary,	241
Bonwell, Huldah H.,	297	Bradshaw, Damaris,	336	Brooke, John T.,	109
Bonwell, Mary A.,	297	Bradshaw, James M.,	192	Brooke, Richard,	109
Book, Henry,	151	Bradshaw, Jane B.,	272	Brookes, Deborah,	309
Book, Mary,	260	Bradshaw, Robert B.,	199	Brookes, Mary,	247
Boone, Ambrose,	171	Bramner, George,	121	Brookes, Mary Ann,	310
Boone, Anne,	287	Branson, Annie L.,	346	Brookes, Rachel,	273
Boone, Elizabeth B.,	347	Branson, Asa,	160	Brookes, Susanna,	266
Boone, Ellen,	288	*Branson, David*,	92	Brotherton, Anna,	301
Boone, Hannah,	316	Branson, David,	172	Brown, Abby W.,	329
Boone, Mary,	232	Branson, Elizabeth,	324	Brown, Abiah,	116
Boone, Mary S.,	276	Branson, Ellis,	159	Brown, Abigail W.,	293
Boone, Samuel S.,	146	Branson, John D.,	187	Brown, Abram,	137
Boone, Susan,	288	Branson, Joseph,	173	Brown, Allen N.,	206
Booth, George S.,	161	Branson, Joseph H.,	145	Brown, Ann,	285
Booth, Thomas,	131	Branson, Joseph H.,	187	Brown, Ann,	305
Borton, Aaron E.,	180	Branson, Lucy,	335	Brown, Anna,	329
Borton, Abigail,	262	Branson, Mary,	229	Brown, Anna M. J.,	316
Borton, C. Walter,	202	Branson, Mary,	326	Brown, Anne,	293
Borton, Elizabeth,	289	Branson, Sarah,	300	Brown, Barclay,	126
Borton, Elizabeth E.,	332	Branson, Thomas F.,	206	Brown, Bertha A.,	348
Borton, Emily W.,	343	Brandingham, Sarah,	244	Brown, Charles H.,	190
Borton, Frank L.,	196	Breaor, Abel,	140	Brown, Charlotte,	275
Borton, George B.,	162	Brian, Ann,	226	Brown, Crosby M.,	195
Borton, George W.,	205	Brian, Sarah H.,	276	Brown, David,	169
Borton, Hettie T.,	326	Brick, Ann,	252	Brown, David J.,	180
Borton, J. Harvey,	205	Brick, Deborah,	237	Brown, Delbert L.,	204
Borton, J. Howard,	194	Brick, Rebecca,	246	Brown, Edward,	128
Borton, James C.,	187	Briggs, Anna,	236	Brown, Eleanor,	228

INDEX.

Name	PAGE
Brown, Eliza L.,	321
Brown, Elizabeth H.,	338
Brown, Elizabeth J.,	316
Brown, Ezra H.,	186
Brown, George,	140
Brown, Hannah,	246
Brown, Hannah,	258
Brown, Hannah,	288
Brown, Hannah,	331
Brown, Hannah L.,	286
Brown, Harriet,	311
Brown, Henry H.,	195
Brown, Howell,	163
Brown, Isaac,	198
Brown, Isaac B.,	138
Brown, Jane H.,	251
Brown, J. Morton,	193
Brown, John,	117
Brown, John,	128
Brown, John,	148
Brown, John,	175
Brown, John,	96
Brown, Joseph,	149
Brown, Joshua,	180
Brown, Lydia J.,	314
Brown, Martha,	289
Brown, Mary,	258
Brown, Mary,	293
Brown, Mary Anna,	324
" " (*Teacher*,)	89
(*Balderston*),"(*Teacher*,)	91
Brown, Mary Anna,	334
Brown, Mary J.,	254
Brown, Mary Louisa,	323
Brown, Mary T.,	330
Brown, Matthias,	124
Brown, Mercy E.,	317
Brown, Mercy W.,	317
Brown, N. Howland,	195
Brown, Nathaniel B.,	150
Brown, Phebe C.,	316
Brown, Phebe C.,	318
Brown, Rachel,	247
Brown, Rachel H.,	334
Brown, Rebecca,	240
Brown, Rebecca F.,	324
Brown, Rebecca W.,	299
Brown, Richard C.,	206
Brown, Richard J.,	182
Brown, Robert P.,	182
Brown, Ruth Anna,	312
Brown, Ruth Anna,	89
" " (*Governess*,)	81
Brown, Ruth Anna,	326
Brown, Sarah,	258
Brown, Sarah,	310
Brown, Sarah Ann,	331
Brown, Sarah A. P.,	308
Brown, Sarah L.,	332
Brown, Sarah L.,	333
Brown, Sarah M.,	309
Brown, Sidney H.,	321
Brown, Susan M.,	335
Brown, Thomas,	140
Brown, Thomas K.,	183
" " (*Teacher*,)	90
Brown, Thornton,	163
Brown, Thornton E.,	192

Name	PAGE
Brown, Wm. Lewis,	195
Brown, Wistar P.,	188
Brown, Yardley,	168
Bruce, Ann,	234
Bruce, Elizabeth,	235
Bruff, Ebenezer L.,	147
Bruff, Hannah,	234
Bruff, Lydia,	234
Bruff, Richard,	150
Bruff, Susan Ann,	270
Bryant, Hewlings,	132
Buckbee, Sarah,	225
Buckley, Ann,	241
" " (*Com*.,)	100
Buckley, Sarah,	99
(*Cope*,) " (*Com*.,)	100
Buckman, Elizabeth,	306
Buckman, John B.,	181
Buckman, Mercy,	278
Buckman, Mercy,	325
Buckman, Susanna,	278
Budd, Mary,	224
Budd, Mary,	256
Budd, Paul C.,	126
Budd, Rebecca,	223
Budd, Rebecca,	223
Budd, Rebecca,	83
(*Comly*,) " (*Com*.,)	99
Buffington, Lee H.,	180
Buffington, Lee W.,	136
Buffington, Louisa,	311
Buffington, Lydia A.,	264
" " (*Teacher*.)	84
" " "(*G'ss*,)	80
Buffington, Mary,	275
Buffington, Rachel,	306
Buffum, Arthur H.,	194
Buffum, Frederic C.,	193
Bullock, Amos,	84
Bullock, Edith,	234
Bullock, Edith,	246
Bullock, Eliza,	240
Bullock, Eliza,	288
Bullock, Frances,	303
Bullock, George,	122
Bullock, John,	111
Bullock, John,	84
Bullock, Lydia,	229
Bullock, Margaret,	250
Bullock, Mary,	242
Bullock, Susanna,	229
Bundy, Caleb,	176
Bundy, Emily E.,	327
Bundy, Jefferson,	194
Bundy, Jesse E.,	193
Bundy, Mary C.,	344
Bundy, Nathan,	173
Bundy, Ruth,	336
Bundy, T. Clarkson,	193
Bundy, Thomas W.,	179
Bundy, William E.,	179
Bunting, Deborah,	288
Bunting, Edward M.,	202
Bunting, Edwin M.,	159
Bunting, Elizabeth,	233
Bunting, Esther S.,	226
Bunting, Jacob,	111
Bunting, Jacob T.,	115

Name	PAGE
Bunting, John H.,	98
Bunting, Josiah,	95
Bunting, Margery,	234
Bunting, Samuel,	138
Bunting, Sarah,	289
Bunting, Walter F.,	202
Burdsall, Burnett,	110
Burdsall, Daniel T.,	165
Burdsall, Eliza,	264
Burdsall, Joseph C.,	133
Burdsall, Martha,	292
Burdsall, Thomas,	163
Burgess, Jane,	237
Burgess, Mary,	287
Burgess, Mary,	294
Burgess, Phebe,	294
Burgess, William,	146
Burling, Thomas C.,	115
Burr, Charles W.,	125
Burr, Edith,	268
Burr, Elizabeth,	232
Burr, Elizabeth,	239
Burr, Elizabeth,	255
Burr, George,	110
Burr, George W.,	117
Burr, Lucy Ann,	307
Burr, Lydia,	233
Burr, Miriam,	240
Burr, Rebecca,	233
Burr, Sarah,	226
Burr, Sarah Ann,	249
Burr, Tylee W.,	125
Burr, William W.,	122
Burrough, Ann,	266
Burrough, Kezia,	239
Burrough, Kezia,	269
Burrough, Lydia,	253
Burrough, Martha A.,	303
Burrough, Mary,	231
Burrough, Rachel,	239
Burrough, Rachel,	263
Burrough, Samuel L.,	158
Burson, Ann,	235
Burson, David S.,	138
" " (*Teacher*,)	85
Burson, John,	142
Burton, Charles, Jr.,	180
Burton, Eliza,	264
Burton, Elizabeth,	313
Burton, Hannah W.,	308
Burton, Lucy,	300
Burton, Mary,	304
Burton, Rebecca,	275
Burton, Robert,	176
Bushman, John,	144
Butcher, Ann R.,	294
Butcher, Elizabeth,	223
Butcher, Elizabeth,	229
Butcher, Elizabeth,	250
Butcher, Hannah W.,	84
Butcher, Martha,	291
Butcher, Mary,	229
Butcher, Rebecca,	223
Butcher, Sarah,	223
Butcher, Thomas,	106
Butler, Ann E.,	311
Butler, Elizabeth,	332
Butler, Hannah,	332

INDEX. 383

Name	PAGE	Name	PAGE	Name	PAGE
Butler, James,	155	Canby, John P.,	182	Carver, Elizabeth,	238
Butler, Lydia,	332	Canby, Joseph,	134	Carver, Henry,	119
Butterworth, Abigail,	263	Canby, Lizzie T.,	338	Carver, Mary,	256
Butterworth, Cath'ne,	271	*Canby, Margaret,*	97	Carver, Samuel H.,	112
Butterworth, Mary,	263	Canby, Mary,	246	Cary, Egbert S.,	205
Buzby, Adelaide,	340	Canby, Mary H.,	326	Cassin, Isaac S.,	156
Buzby, Ann,	298	Canby, Merrit,	108	Cassin, John,	137
Buzby, Augustus C.,	191	*Canby, Samuel,*	95	Cassin, Rebecca,	289
Buzby, David,	151	Canby, Samuel, Jr.,	107	Cattell, Beulah,	306
Buzby, Eliza Ann,	264	Canby, Samuel R.,	128	Cattell, Corinne,	332
Buzby, Elizabeth,	228	Canby, Sarah,	225	Caulk, Elizabeth,	235
Buzby, Georgiana,	339	Canby, William,	143	Caulk, Mary B.,	293
Buzby, Hannah W.,	275	Canby, William J.,	149	Caulk, R. E.,	293
Buzby, Ida R.,	339	Canby, William M.,	156	Cawley, Lydia,	238
Buzby, Isaac,	190	Cannon, Mary E.,	333	Chace, Anna Harvey,	337
Buzby, John W.,	148	Carey, George,	117	Chambers, Amy,	281
Buzby, Joseph,	110	Carey, James,	111	Chambers, Caroline,	284
Buzby, Martha,	231	Carey, Mary E.,	290	Chambers, Charles,	194
Buzby, Martha T.,	338	Carey, Samuel,	111	Chambers, Charles P.,	197
Buzby, Mary,	230	Carey, Tacy E.,	309	Chambers, David,	122
Buzby, Mary H.,	293	Carey, Thomas C.,	149	Chambers, David,	151
Buzby, Mary L.,	319	Carey, Thomas K.,	183	Chambers, Deborah P.,	336
Buzby, Miriam E.,	335	Carlile, Elizabeth,	318	Chambers, Edm'd M.,	195
Buzby, Rebecca,	298	Carlile, Henry C.,	176	Chambers, Elizabeth,	296
Buzby, Sarah P.,	313	Carlile, Joseph E.,	177	" (*Teacher*,)	87
Buzby, Stacy,	158	Carlile, Thomas J.,	113	(Dunn,) " (Com.,)	102
Buzby, Susanna,	287	Carlile, William K.,	169	Chambers, Emma S.,	336
Buzby, Susanna D.,	315	Carlisle, Ann,	227	Chambers, George R.,	188
Buzby, Thomas T.,	199	*Carmalt, Caleb,*	95	Chambers, James,	189
Buzby, Walter J.,	202	Carmalt, Mary Ann,	268	Chambers, John J.,	185
Buzby, William,	125	Carmalt, Sarah G.,	297	Chambers, John W.,	141
Buzby, William P.,	170	Carmalt, Susanna,	249	Chambers, Joseph,	144
Byrd, Josephus,	205	Carnahan, Abigail,	245	Chambers, Joseph C.,	198
Byrnes, Hannah P.,	244	Carpenter, Albina B.,	270	Chambers, Lydia,	275
Byrnes, Jonathan,	125	Carpenter, Alvina,	288	Chambers, Mahlon,	144
		Carpenter, Charles,	193	Chambers, Marg't M.,	272
Cadbury, Caroline,	326	Carpenter, Charles G.,	168	Chambers, Mark P.,	194
Cadbury, John W.,	168	Carpenter, John R.,	127	Chambers, Mary,	334
Cadbury, Richard T.,	186	Carpenter, John R.,	170	Chambers, Mary Ann,	281
Cadbury, Sarah S.,	330	Carpenter, Joseph,	127	Chambers, Patience,	263
Cadwallader, Allen J.,	205	Carpenter, Mary,	274	Chambers, Phebe H.,	322
Cadwallader, Cyrus,	158	Carpenter, Mary R.,	331	Chambers, Phillips,	178
Cadwallader, Deb'ah,	333	Carpenter, Phebe,	258	Chambers, Richard,	160
Cadwallader, Edw'd,	190	Carpenter, Rachel,	259	Chambers, Rich'd M.,	168
Cadwallader, Eliz.,	237	Carpenter, Richard,	170	Chambers, Sam'l K.,	176
Cadwallader, Eliz.,	293	Carpenter, S. Preston,	180	Chambers, Sarah,	301
Cadwallader, Eliz.,	294	Carpenter, Sallie W.,	315	Chambers, Sarah B.,	270
Cadwallader, Elma,	248	Carpenter, William,	183	Chambers, Sarah B.,	338
Cadwallader, Frank,	192	Carr, Caleb,	106	Chambers, Thos. L.,	170
Cadwallader, M'tha R.,	292	Carr, Mary,	229	Chambers, William,	155
Cadwallader, Mary,	293	Carr, Samuel,	110	Chance, Armily,	243
Cadwallader, Mifflin,	126	Carroll, Josephine,	307	Chance, Elizabeth,	243
Cadwallader, Moses,	161	Carslake, Wm. J.,	203	Chandlee, Ann,	266
Cadwallader, Rees,	105	Carter, Ann,	250	Chandlee, Edward,	120
Cadwallader, Thos. S.,	190	Carter, Aurelius N.,	206	Chandlee, Hannah,	227
Calley, Alice,	341	Carter, Caleb,	107	Chandlee, Hannah,	235
Calley, Joseph K.,	178	*Carter, Charles S.,*	103	Chandlee, Hannah,	270
Calley, Sarah M.,	332	Carter, Daniel,	124	Chandlee, Mahlon,	112
Canby, Anna P.,	326	Carter, Henry,	122	Chandler, Ann,	254
Canby, Caleb,	149	Carter, Jacob,	134	Chandler, Daniel W.,	158
Canby, Caroline B.,	333	Carter, James,	118	Chandler, Jacob,	154
Canby, Charles,	143	Carter, John,	122	Chandler, Margaret,	296
Canby, Charles,	199	*Carter, John E.,*	103	Chandler, Mary Ann,	263
Canby, Esther,	232	Carter, Joseph,	138	Chandler, Thomas,	123
Canby, Frances,	243	Carter, Lydia,	239	Chandler, William G.,	123
Canby, George,	154	Carter, Rebecca,	259	Chapman, Elizabeth,	252
Canby, James, Jr.,	128	Carter, Ruth H.,	290	Chapman, John,	121
Canby, John,	143	Carter, William,	206	Chapman, Joseph,	120

INDEX.

Name	PAGE
Chapman, Josiah,	126
Chapman, Keturah,	269
Chapman, Mary R.,	253
Chapman, Mercy A.,	253
Chapman, Sarah,	244
Chapman, William,	126
Chase, Edith L.,	317
Chase, Richard W.,	169
Chase, William B.,	172
Chase, William C.,	195
Cheyney, Anna M.,	342
Cheyney, Annie,	316
Cheyney, Charles,	194
Cheyney, Eliza A.,	336
" " (*Teacher*,)	91
Cheyney, Emily,	342
Cheyney, J. Passmore,	195
Cheyney, Jesse S.,	169
" " (*Teacher*,)	87
Cheyney, John P.,	156
Cheyney, Margaretta,	338
Cheyney, Sallie E.,	339
Cheyney, Wilmer,	184
Child, Hannah B.,	307
Child, John T.,	132
Child, Lucy B.,	344
Child, Willard,	201
Child, William L.,	194
Chilton, Mary F.,	347
Chrisman, Hannah,	299
Chrisman, Isaac,	165
Chrisman, Mary H.,	281
Chrisman, Rebec. L.,	301
Church, Antrim,	131
Church, Matlack,	121
Church, Rebecca,	256
Church, Sarah,	256
Churchman, Caroline,	298
Churchman, Edward,	92
Churchman, George,	95
Churchman, Hannah,	236
Churchman, Marg.,	243
" "(*Com.,*)	101
Churchman, Owen,	108
Churchman, Rebecca,	97
Clark, Achsah,	245
Clark, Ann,	254
Clark, Ann E.,	302
Clark, Benjamin,	95
Clark, Beulah,	239
Clark, Charles G.,	184
Clark, Deborah,	279
Clark, Edith H.,	252
Clark, Elisha,	147
Clark, Elisha L.,	124
Clark, Eliza,	245
Clark, Elizabeth G.,	254
Clark, Jane,	100
Clark, Joseph G.,	129
Clark, Josephine,	307
Clark, Mary,	234
Clark, Rachel,	250
Clark, Susan,	261
Clark, Thomas,	112
Clarke, Joseph O.,	117
Clarke, Mary,	100
Cleaver, Charlotte,	254
Cleaver, Emily,	259

Name	PAGE
Cleaver, Isaac,	106
Cleaver, Jonathan,	152
Cleaver, Mary,	293
Clement, Allan B.,	204
Clement, Ann,	248
Clement, Charles A.,	175
Clement, Edgar,	199
Clement, Elizabeth,	244
Clement, Elizabeth,	291
Clement, Evan,	109
Clement, Frances L.,	281
Clement, Hannah A.,	262
Clement, Joseph,	134
Clement, Joseph C.,	127
Clement, Josiah,	106
Clement, Lydia,	244
Clement, Mary F.,	278
Clement, Mickle,	129
Clement, Rebecca,	271
Clement, Ruth Anna,	326
Clement, Samuel C.,	151
Clement, Samuel E.,	117
Clement, William W.,	129
Clemson, Elizabeth,	295
Clemson, Hannah,	231
Clemson, James L.,	151
Clemson, Mary,	235
Clemson, Sarah,	235
Clendenon, Ann,	241
Clendenon, Eliz.,	239
Clendenon, Hannah,	241
Clifton, Henry,	95
Clinger, Mary E.,	327
Cloud, Benjamin F.,	179
Cloud, Charles R.,	174
Cloud, Edward H.,	183
Cloud, George W.,	174
Cloud, J. Harper,	191
Cloud, Josiah, Jr.,	195
Cloud, Henry J.,	192
Cloud, John W.,	188
" " (*Teacher*,)	89
Cloud, Samuel H.,	177
Cloud, Sarah Ann,	242
Cloud, Sarah F.,	317
Coale, Elizabeth F.,	283
Coale, George M.,	131
Coale, Margaret,	261
Coale, Mary Y.,	345
Coale, Samuel,	134
Coale, Sarah,	261
Coale, Sarah W.,	233
Coale, Skipwith H.,	179
Coale, Susan,	274
Coale, Thomas E.,	161
Coale, Thomas E.,	202
Coale, William B.,	145
Coale, William E.,	161
Coates, Amy,	97
Coates, Ann G.,	260
Coates, R. Anna,	317
Coates, Charles,	152
Coates, Charles E.,	204
Coates, Deborah,	99
Coates, George,	151
Coates, George T.,	159
Coates, George W. P.,	194
Coates, Jesse,	204

Name	PAGE
Coates, Josiah,	108
Coates, L. Roberts,	194
Coates, Lydia,	226
Coates, Mary,	278
Coates, Moses,	112
Coates, Reynall,	122
Coates, Samuel,	159
Coates, Sarah,	233
Coates, Sarah J.,	297
Coates, Sarah R.,	277
Coates, Sidney,	100
Coates, Zillah,	235
Cock, Elizabeth B.,	274
Cock, Maria,	273
Cocks, Ann Augusta,	263
Cocks, Eliza F.,	255
Coe, Esther,	240
Coe, Robert,	122
Coe, Samuel E.,	117
Coe, William,	119
Coffin, Edward H.,	182
Coffin, Elizabeth,	241
Coffin, James A.,	172
Coffin, Martha,	261
Coffin, Mary,	240
Coffin, Oliver G.,	172
Coffin, Stephen,	139
Coffin, Thomas M.,	115
Cohn, Joseph S.,	142
Cole, Alvin,	191
Cole, Lydia,	100
Cole, Sarah,	300
Cole, William B.,	148
Coleman, Elizabeth,	98
Coleman, Hannah,	236
Coleman, Hannah,	265
Coleman, James,	136
Coleman, Mary E.,	305
Collins, Alwilda,	337
Collins, Amos S.,	155
Collins, Anna,	309
Collins, Anna C.,	326
Collins, Anna S.,	329
Collins, Arthur,	107
Collins, Caroline B.,	335
Collins, Charles,	182
Collins, Eliza,	334
Collins, Elizabeth B.,	315
Collins, Emma,	342
Collins, George,	146
Collins, Hannah,	267
Collins, Hannah E.,	311
Collins, John,	95
Collins, Josiah,	191
Collins, Lydia,	267
Collins, Mary L.,	329
Collins, Percival,	162
Collins, Phebe L.,	334
Collins, Rachel E.,	324
Collins, Samuel C.,	181
Collins, Sarah A.,	81
Collins, Sarah L.,	341
Collins, Stephen G.,	162
Collins, Stokes,	196
Collins, William L.,	196
Comegys, Augusta,	263
Comfort, Aaron R.,	167
Comfort, Albert,	161

INDEX. 385

Name	Page
Comfort, Alice,	98
Comfort, Alice,	84
Comfort, Alice,	278
Comfort, Ann Eliz.,	313
" " " (Com.),	102
Comfort, Anna E.,	325
Comfort, Anna M.,	339
Comfort, Benjamin C.,	189
Comfort, Charles W.,	189
Comfort, Cyrus C.,	167
Comfort, David,	144
Comfort, Edward,	140
Comfort, Edward W.,	204
Comfort, Eliza,	252
Comfort, Elizabeth,	272
(Scattergood,) " (Com.),	102
Comfort, Elizabeth,	283
Comfort, Elizabeth,	295
Comfort, Ellis,	114
Comfort, Ellwood,	119
Comfort, Ezra,	182
Comfort, George M.,	167
" " (Com.),	103
Comfort, Harvey S.,	190
Comfort, Henry W.,	199
Comfort, Howard,	188
Comfort, I. Roberts,	197
Comfort, James C.,	135
Comfort, James C.,	192
Comfort, Jane,	272
Comfort, Jeremiah,	138
Comfort, Jesse,	139
Comfort, John B.,	183
Comfort, John S.,	102
Comfort, Jonathan J.,	163
Comfort, Margaret,	295
Comfort, Martha,	277
Comfort, Mary,	230
Comfort, Mary,	289
Comfort, Mary Ann,	279
Comfort, Mary T.,	303
Comfort, Maurice,	190
Comfort, Mercy,	102
Comfort. Moses,	101
Comfort, Rachel,	299
Comfort, Samuel,	83
Comfort, Samuel,	141
Comfort, Sarah,	303
Comfort, Sarah C.,	327
Comfort, Stephen,	97
Comfort, Susan E.,	102
(See Edge.)	
Comfort, Thomas,	131
Comfort, William,	188
Comfort, William S.,	199
Comly, Ann,	267
Comly, Charles,	133
Comly, Ethan,	109
Comly, Franklin,	114
Comly, John,	83
Comly, Rebecca B.,	99
(See Budd.)	
Comly, Samuel,	108
Comly, Sarah,	271
Comly, Sarah,	271
Comstock, Chloe M.,	294
Comstock, Eliz. A.,	271
Comstock, Isaac T.,	149
Comstock, Martha,	271
Comstock, Nathan D.,	149
Conard, Alfred S.,	167
Conard, Ann,	270
Conard, Deborah,	270
Conard, Elizabeth,	251
Conard, Lucy,	277
Conard, Lydia,	279
Conard, Maria,	274
Conard, Mary,	262
Conard, Milton,	137
Conard, Nathan,	135
Conard, Rachel,	260
Conard, Rebecca,	268
" " (Teacher,)	86
Conard, Rebecca S.,	102
Conard, Rebecca Y.,	279
Conard, Ruth,	268
Conard, Sarah,	81
Conard, Sarah R.,	308
Conard, Susanna,	259
Conard, Thomas,	133
" " (Com.),	102
Conard, Thomas P.,	172
Congdon, Edward,	168
Congdon, Robert D.,	154
Conklin Emma,	299
Conrad, James S.,	175
Conrad, Sarah,	258
Conrad, Solomon,	140
Conrad, Timothy A.,	121
Conrad, William B.,	181
Conrow, Elizabeth,	237
Conrow, Joseph,	179
Conrow, Sarah,	255
Conrow, Sarah E.,	268
Cook, Amos M.,	206
Cook, Anna M.,	352
Cook, Barton,	127
Cook, C. Carroll,	184
Cook, Charles G.,	205
Cook, Chlotilda,	284
Cook, Edwin,	190
Cook, Elisha,	188
Cook, Elisha,	125
Cook, Elizabeth P.,	323
Cook, George,	193
Cook, Hannah T.,	287
Cook, J. Howard,	202
Cook, Jesse,	124
Cook, J. Horace,	194
Cook, Joel,	125
Cook, John,	98
Cook, John,	126
Cook, John T.,	174
Cook, John William,	184
Cook, Jonas P.,	185
Cook, Josiah T.,	142
Cook, Lydia,	267
Cook, Margaret T.,	329
Cook, Mary,	260
Cook, Mary W.,	339
Cook, Nathan,	135
Cook, Phebe T.,	311
Cook, Richard,	118
Cook, Ruth,	231
Cook, Sarah,	287
Cook, Stacy,	141
Cook, Thomas,	119
Cook, William H.,	174
Cook, William P.,	161
Cooke, John,	99
Cookson, Mary,	229
Cooper, Alexander,	129
Cooper, Ann,	228
Cooper, Ann,	259
Cooper, Ann,	266
Cooper, Ann,	272
Cooper, Anna H.,	342
Cooper, Anna J.,	332
" " (Teacher,)	89
Cooper, Anna R.,	322
Cooper, Anne,	305
Cooper, Asahel,	176
Cooper, Asahel W.,	177
Cooper, Asenath,	265
Cooper, Benjamin,	97
Cooper, Benjamin,	126
Cooper, Benjamin,	162
Cooper, Benjamin C.,	113
Cooper, Benjamin W.,	204
Cooper, Brinton P.,	196
Cooper, Caleb M.,	106
Cooper, Caleb P.,	178
Cooper, Catharine,	309
Cooper, Caroline H.,	339
Cooper, Charles,	149
Cooper, Charles,	152
Cooper, Charles M.,	137
Cooper, Clayton,	163
Cooper, Cyrus,	198
Cooper, David E.,	200
Cooper, Edith,	312
Cooper, Edwin,	193
Cooper, Edwin H.,	198
Cooper, Eleanor H.,	344
Cooper, Elizabeth,	226
Cooper, Elizabeth,	265
Cooper, Elizabeth M.,	325
Cooper, Ellwood,	177
Cooper, Elma A.,	346
Cooper, Emma L.,	328
Cooper, Fanny,	345
Cooper, George,	179
Cooper, Hannah,	277
Cooper, Hannah,	306
Cooper, Hannah A.,	319
Cooper, Harry E.,	204
Cooper, Howard,	194
Cooper, Isaac,	107
Cooper, J. Morris,	193
Cooper, Jael,	291
Cooper, James,	96
Cooper, James,	86
Cooper, James,	147
Cooper, James P.,	182
Cooper, Joseph,	114
Cooper, Joseph,	84
Cooper, Joseph B.,	154
Cooper, Joseph B.,	156
Cooper, Josephine,	328
Cooper, Lydia,	226
Cooper, Lydia,	334
Cooper, Lydia A.,	338
Cooper, Maria F.,	319
Cooper, Mary,	228

INDEX.

Name	PAGE	Name	PAGE	Name	PAGE
Cooper, Mary,	262	Cope, Edward Y.,	163	Cope, William,	173
Cooper, Mary,	289	Cope, Eleanor,	258	Cope, Wilmer,	200
Cooper, Mary,	297	Cope, Elizabeth,	310	Copeland, Ellen G.,	341
Cooper, Mary E.,	319	Cope, Elizabeth,	316	Copeland, Mary F.,	341
Cooper, Mary E.,	328	Cope, Elizabeth,	331	Copeland, Miriam R.,	347
Cooper, Mary L.,	339	Cope, Elizabeth C.,	255	Copeland, Sarah E.,	311
Cooper, Mary V.,	330	Cope, Elizabeth W.,	318	Coppock, Joseph J.,	198
Cooper, Pennock,	196	Cope, Ellen,	310	Corbit, Ann,	252
Cooper, Phebe P.,	304	Cope, Ellen P.,	336	Corbit, Daniel W.,	173
Cooper, Prudence,	254	Cope, Emeline,	256	Corbit, Elizabeth,	257
Cooper, Rachel Ann,	324	Cope, Emma,	258	Corbit, John C.,	162
" " (Teacher,)	88	Cope, Emma,	321	Corbit, Louisa A.,	312
Cooper, Rebecca,	246	Cope, Francis,	112	Corbit, Mary C.,	329
Cooper, Rebecca,	249	Cope, Franklin,	191	Corbit, Thomas,	120
Cooper, Rebecca,	306	Cope, Frederick H.,	204	Corbit, William C.,	170
Cooper, Rebecca M.,	326	Cope, Gilbert,	173	Corbit, William F.,	106
Cooper, Richard M.,	195	Cope, Hannah,	237	Corbitt, Jemima,	228
Cooper, Samuel,	119	Cope, Hannah T.,	316	Corlies, Benjamin,	118
Cooper, Samuel,	160	Cope, Henry,	112	Corlies, Britton,	111
Cooper, Samuel,	162	" " (Com.,)	99	Corlies, Britton,	140
Cooper, Samuel C.,	119	Cope, Henry,	172	Corlies, Charles,	135
Cooper, Sarah,	98	Cope, Henry, Jr.,	181	Corlies, Edward G.,	108
Cooper, Sarah Ann,	283	Cope, James,	183	Corlies, George W.,	130
Cooper, Sarah E.,	298	Cope, James B.,	189	Corlies, Henry,	126
Cooper, Sarah J.,	312	Cope, Jane M.,	301	Corlies, Henry,	147
Cooper, Sarah J.,	322	" " (Com.,)	103	Corlies, Joseph,	136
Cooper, Susanna R.,	316	Cope, Jasper,	132	Corlies, Joseph W.,	110
Cooper, Sylvania,	324	Cope, John,	107	Corlies, Margaret M.,	272
" " (Teacher,)	89	Cope, Jonathan,	196	*Corlies, Mary,*	99
" " (Gov'ness,)	81	Cope, Joseph E.,	174	*Corlies, Patience,*	98
Cooper, Warner,	193	Cope, Lucinda,	333	Corlies, Sarah,	263
Cooper, William,	99	Cope, Lydia E.,	345	Corlies, Thomas,	138
Cooper, William A.,	202	Cope, Lydia T.,	338	Corlies, William W.,	136
Cooper, William B.,	137	Cope, Marmaduke,	121	Cornthwaite, Ann P.,	257
Cooper, William B.,	202	Cope, Mary,	245	Corse, Elizabeth M.,	283
Cooper, William B.,	203	*Cope, Mary,*	99	Corse, Frank,	186
Cooper, William T.,	188	Cope, Mary Ann,	246	Corse, James M.,	130
Cooper, William T.,	198	Cope, Mary Ann,	305	Corse, John R.,	135
Cope, Abiah,	179	Cope, Mary Ann,	318	Corse, Leontine R.,	318
Cope, Albert,	194	Cope, Mary Anna,	318	Corse, Susan C.,	270
Cope, Albert B.,	91	Cope, Mary H.,	347	Corse, William H.,	143
Cope, Alexis T.,	179	Cope, Mary P.,	305	Corse, William J.,	186
Cope, Alfred,	101	Cope, Melissa,	332	Corson, Hannah,	274
Cope, Alice E.,	327	Cope, Morris S.,	179	Corson, Martha,	305
Cope, Ann,	296	Cope, Nathan,	176	Corson, Sarah,	277
Cope, Anna,	323	Cope, Oliver,	130	Cotant, Charles,	155
Cope, Annette,	317	Cope, Paschall,	158	Cotant, Daniel B.,	166
Cope, Barclay,	176	Cope, Phebe A.,	347	Cotant, Eliza Jane,	279
Cope, Benjamin,	98	*Cope, Rachel,*	97	Cotant, Gideon,	147
Cope, Benjamin,	174	Cope, Rachel W.,	252	Cotant, Joseph H.,	157
Cope, Benjamin H.,	200	Cope, Rachel W.,	319	Cotant, Margaret A.,	291
Cope, Caleb D.,	204	Cope, Rebecca,	282	Couch, Deborah,	234
Cope, Caleb S.,	136	*Cope, Rebecca B.,*	101	Couch, Rebecca,	235
Cope, Caroline,	320	(See Biddle.)		Coulson, Thomas M.,	173
Cope, Caroline E.,	317	Cope, Rebecca G.,	296	Couplin, Elizabeth,	276
Cope, Caroline R.,	245	(Passmore,) " (Matron,)	80	Cowgill, Angelica,	269
Cope, Charity,	224	" " (Com.,)	103	Cowgill, Ann L.,	268
Cope, Charity,	83	*Cope, Rest,*	99	Cowgill, Charles,	121
Cope, Charles S.,	120	(See Swayne.)		Cowgill, Charles,	156
Cope, Daniel,	175	Cope, Sallie T.,	334	*Cowgill, Clayton,*	98
Cope, David,	176	Cope, Samuel,	169	*Cowgill, Daniel,*	96
Cope, Debbie E.,	313	Cope, Samuel S.,	168	Cowgill, Daniel S.,	121
Cope, Deborah,	274	*Cope, Sarah B.,*	100	Cowgill, Edward D.,	173
" " (Teacher,)	85	(See Buckley.)		Cowgill, Elizabeth,	275
Cope, Deborah,	284	Cope, Susan,	325	" " (Teacher,)	85
Cope, Deborah,	320	*Cope, Thos. P.,*	102	Cowgill, Elizabeth,	341
Cope, Edgar,	168	Cope, William,	117	Cowgill, James,	122
Cope, Edward D.,	172	Cope, William,	160	Cowgill, John Henry,	166

INDEX.

Name	Page
Cowgill, Martha,	312
Cowgill, Mary,	261
Cowgill, Nathaniel,	133
Cowgill, Sarah,	97
Cowgill, Warner,	119
Cowgill, William,	131
Cowperthwait, Eliz.,	227
Cowperthwait, Eliz.,	228
Cowperthwait Eliz.,	234
Cowperthwait, Eliz. J.,	305
Cowperthwait, Esther,	226
Cowperthwait, Han'h,	228
Cowperthwait, Jos. C.,	144
Cowperthwait, Levi,	170
Cowperthwait. Ma'ha,	275
Cowperthwait, M. J.,	301
Cowperthwait, Mary	256
Cowperthwait. Sar.A.,	277
Cox, Aaron,	135
Cox, Amy,	232
Cox, Ann,	97
Cox, Artilla Ann,	339
Cox, Clarkson J.,	201
Cox, Cynthia N.,	315
Cox, Deborah,	279
Cox, Elizabeth J.,	295
Cox, Hannah Ann,	314
Cox, Hannah Ann,	322
Cox, Howard,	204
Cox, Isaac J.,	134
Cox, Isaac P.,	117
Cox, John,	95
Cox, John, Jr.,	96
Cox, John E.,	195
Cox, Joseph,	137
Cox, Keziah Elma,	339
Cox, Lydia,	293
Cox, Lydia E.,	302
Cox, Margaret,	250
Cox, Martha T.,	299
Cox, Mary,	260
Cox, Mary D.,	276
Cox, Mary L.,	232
Cox, Mary W.,	310
Cox, Mehetabel F.,	338
Cox, Phebe,	83
Cox, Rachel,	234
Cox, Rachel,	297
Cox, Samuel,	115
Cox, Sarah,	234
Cox, Silas W.,	195
Cox, Susan H.,	236
Cox, Susanna,	227
Craft, Agnes,	240
Craft, Deborah,	272
Craft, Edith,	282
Craft, Elizabeth,	240
Craft, Elizabeth,	250
Craft, Isaac,	139
Craft, Jane,	279
Craft, Mary,	276
Craig, Ann,	236
Craig, Sarah,	224
Cranstone, Alfred H.,	186
Cranstone, Charles,	186
Cranstone, Mary,	299
Crawford, Ann,	259
Crawford, Hannah,	257

Name	Page
Crawford, Lydia D.,	272
Crawford, Margaret,	257
Crenshaw, Deb. A.,	325
Crenshaw, Edm'd A.,	148
Crenshaw, Edm'd A.,	155
Crenshaw, Eliza C.,	330
Crenshaw, Eliz'h A.,	304
Crenshaw, J. Isabella,	347
Crenshaw, James H.,	186
Crenshaw, Marg't E.,	325
Crenshaw, Mary J.,	307
Crenshaw, Nath'l B.,	177
Cresson, Elizabeth,	225
" " (Com.,)	99
(Mason,) " "	100
Cresson, Emlen,	130
Cresson, James,	126
Cresson, James,	128
Cresson, John,	139
Cresson, John B.,	138
Cresson, Jonathan L.,	177
Cresson, Joshua,	146
Cresson, Mary W.,	278
Cresson, Rebecca W.,	255
Cresson, Sarah,	96
Cresson, Sarah,	225
Cresson, Sarah,	99
Cresson, Sarah,	281
Cresson, Warder,	119
Crew, Jacob L.,	160
Crew, James H.,	149
Crew, Mary L.,	341
Crew, Thomas M.,	149
Crew, William B.,	189
Crim, James S.,	129
Croasdale, Jane,	313
Cromwell, Daniel,	187
Cromwell, Edward,	190
Cromwell, Everett,	193
Cromwell, Gertrude,	329
Cromwell, H. Maur'c,	185
Cromwell, Helen,	329
Cromwell, Morton,	201
Crownover, Sabina,	239
Croxson, Hannah,	230
Crukshank, Rachel,	97
Cumming, Asher,	105
Cumming, Charles,	159
Cumming, David,	95
Cumming, David B.,	106
Cumming, Deborah,	233
Cumming, Edward,	159
Cumming, Elizabeth,	290
Cumming, Elizabeth,	294
Cumming, John,	164
Cumming, Lydia T.,	319
Cumming, Rachel,	227
Cumming, Rebecca,	223
Cumming, Thomas,	113
Cunningham, Eliz'h,	271
Curtis, Charles,	129
Curtis, James T.,	196
Curtis, William E.,	190
Dallam, Thomas B.,	146
Dallam, William,	146
Dalziel, Edith,	314
Dalziel, Jane,	343

Name	Page
Daniel, Deborah,	276
Daniel, Margaret,	275
Daniel, Rebecca,	270
Daniel, William,	140
Darlington, Amos,	136
Darlington, Amy,	262
Darlington, Em'line,	285
Darlington, Hannah,	247
Darlington, Hannah,	269
Darlington, Isaac,	131
Darlington, Mary,	229
Darlington, Mary,	274
Darlington, Phebe,	271
Darlington, Rhoda,	238
Darlington, Samuel,	118
Darlington, Sarah,	262
Darnell, Agnes M.,	315
Darnell, Anna H.,	336
Darnell, Charles,	155
Darnell, David E.,	182
Darnell, Edward,	161
Darnell, Edward,	163
Darnell, Emily A.,	343
Darnell, Ezra E.,	182
Darnell, Howard,	175
Darnell, Jane,	315
Darnell, Job,	124
Darnell, John E,	177
Darnell, Joseph H.,	192
Darnell, Mariana,	325
Darnell, Rachel,	241
Darnell, Rebecca C.,	313
Darnell, Samuel B.,	178
Darnell, Sarah,	313
Davids, Benjamin,	114
Davidson, Benjamin,	142
Davidson, Elizabeth,	287
Davidson, William,	136
Davidson, William H.,	166
Davies, Mary L.,	271
Davis, Aaron,	157
Davis, Abbie H.,	341
Davis, Benjamin,	151
Davis, Caleb W.,	199
Davis, Charles,	128
Davis, Cordelia A.,	338
Davis, Deborah,	259
Davis, Deborah,	278
Davis, Deborah,	286
Davis, Edward M.,	135
Davis, Elizabeth,	269
Davis, Elizabeth,	288
Davis, Elizabeth H.,	266
Davis, Franklin,	194
Davis, Hannah,	231
Davis, Hannah G.,	245
Davis, Hannah P.,	101
(See Price.)	
Davis, Isaac R.,	132
Davis, James,	121
Davis, James,	152
" " (Farmer,)	92
Davis, Jane S.,	327
Davis, John F.,	179
Davis, Joseph,	122
Davis, Joshua H.,	198
Davis, Lydia,	233
Davis, Martha,	234

INDEX.

Name	PAGE	Name	PAGE	Name	PAGE
Davis, Martha,	255	Deacon, Sarah H.,	279	Dickinson, Rachel,	247
Davis, Mary,	236	Deacon, Thomas E.,	110	Dickinson, Rachel T.,	301
Davis, Mary,	246	Deacon, William R.,	163	Dickinson, Samuel E.,	168
Davis, Mary C.,	259	Decou, Amelia,	247	*Dickinson, Sally N.,*	98
Davis, Mary C.,	260	Decou, Anna B.,	326	Dickinson, Susan E.,	306
Davis, Mary S.,	341	Decou, Barclay,	188	*Dicks, Roger,*	95
Davis, Mary W.,	99	Decou, Charles,	163	Dilks, Elizabeth C.,	331
Davis, Phebe,	304	Decou, Clayton,	106	Dilks, George R.,	191
Davis, Phebe,	319	Decou, Daniel,	177	Dilks, Hannah H.,	326
Davis, Richard W.,	137	Decou, Edith,	337	Dilks, Mary R.,	312
Davis, Ruthana,	249	Decou, Elizabeth,	305	Dilks, Rachel J.,	313
Davis, Samuel,	118	Decou, Elizabeth H.,	336	Dilks, Sidney,	318
Davis, Sarah,	278	Decou, Francis,	172	Dilks, William W.,	177
Davis, Tacy,	245	Decou, Hannah E.,	290	*Dillin, Sarah Ann,*	85
Davis, William,	118	Decou, Margaret T.,	322	Dillon, Elizabeth,	279
Davis, Wm. Morris,	137	Decou, Mary E.,	286	Dillon, Hannah,	241
Dawes, Edward,	105	Decou, Miriam,	309	Dillon, Isaac,	114
Dawes, Elizabeth,	226	Decou, Peter Ellis,	175	Dillon, Martha,	237
Dawes, Jonathan,	105	Decou, Sarah E.,	335	*Dillwyn, George,*	97
Dawes, Samuel F.,	105	Decou, Susan,	321	Dilworth, Brinton,	132
Dawson, Anne,	243	Decou, Thomas B.,	186	Dilworth, Charlotte,	245
Dawson, Caleb,	206	De Cou, George,	201	Dilworth, Christi'a B.,	262
Dawson, Chalkley,	173	De Cou, Joseph E.,	203	Dilworth, Hannah,	259
Dawson, Edith,	308	De Cou, Marietta,	340	Dilworth, Hannah,	307
Dawson, Elizabeth,	293	De Cou, Rebecca T.,	343	Dilworth, Martha,	246
Dawson, Ellis,	154	De Cou, Thomas J.,	199	Dilworth, Mary T.,	254
Dawson, Margaret S.,	298	De Cou, Walter E.,	201	Dilworth, Mary T.,	261
Dawson, Melvina,	346	Dell, Catharine,	301	Dilworth, Sarah,	317
Dawson, Mordecai I.,	120	Dell, Joseph S.,	162	Dilworth, Thomas,	146
Dawson, Mordecai M.,	163	Dell, Thomas,	169	Dingee, Elizabeth,	235
Dawson, Ruth Ann,	276	Denn, Rachel,	259	Dingee, Elizabeth A.,	307
Dawson, Thomas S.,	133	Dennis, Edward G.,	166	Dingee, Jacob,	114
Dawson, Thomas M.,	199	Dennis, Sarah,	239	Dingee, Jacob,	161
Dawson, William,	117	Denny, Charles,	114	Dingee, Margaretta P.,	339
Dawson, William P.,	158	Denny, Charles,	124	Dingee, Mary,	251
Day, Samuel M.,	129	Denny, Daniel C.,	134	Dingee, Mary,	310
" " (Teacher,)	85	Denny, Elizabeth,	246	Dingee, Mary,	339
Deacon, Ann,	228	Denny, Evelina,	256	Dingee, Obadiah,	115
Deacon, Ann,	291	Denny, Mary,	226	Dingee, Rachel,	319
Deacon, Anna,	314	Denny, Samuel,	134	Dingee, Rebecca,	254
Deacon, Anna H.,	337	Denny, Sarah,	254	Dingee, William E.,	173
Deacon, Caroline,	322	Denny, William,	131	Dixon, Emma,	288
Deacon, Charles R.,	178	Denny, William,	154	Dixon, Isaac,	124
Deacon, Charles T.,	130	Dent, Elizabeth,	291	Dixon, James,	165
Deacon, Edmund,	132	Dent, Mary,	278	Dixon, John,	134
Deacon, Elizabeth,	343	" " (Teacher,)	85	Dixon, Joseph,	109
Deacon, Elizabeth,	317	Dent, Thomas,	135	Dixon, Joseph,	123
Deacon, Ellen,	314	Deprefontaine, Ann E.,	289	Dixon, Joseph E.,	141
Deacon, Frederic H.,	187	Deprefontaine, John	147	Dixon, Mary,	261
Deacon, George B.,	129	Deprefontaine, R.,	276	Dixon, Mary W.,	278
Deacon, George E.,	187	Dewees, Almedia,	333	Dixon, Rebecca,	265
Deacon, Hannah,	252	Dewees, Lonisa M.,	342	Dixon, Robert,	164
Deacon, J. Herbert,	204	Dewees, Naomi B.,	347	Dixon, Samuel,	132
Deacon, Hettie B.,	336	Dewees, Richard S.,	197	Dixon, William B.,	156
Deacon, Howard,	175	Dewees, Watson W.,	185	Dolby, Eliza,	268
Deacon, James,	163	" "(Ast. Gov.,)	88	Dolby, Elizabeth,	276
Deacon, Jervis B.,	198	" " (Gov.,)	80	Dolby, James B.,	144
Deacon, John,	165	" " (Teacher,)	90	Donaldson, Isaac M.,	139
Deacon, John C.,	126	Dewell, George S.,	168	*Dorsey, Elizabeth,*	97
Deacon, John C., Jr.,	181	Dickinson, Anna E.,	317	Dorsey, Stanton,	129
Deacon, John E.,	148	Dickinson, Benjamin,	171	Dorsey, William,	129
Deacon, John L.,	172	Dickinson, Benjamin,	174	Doudna, Josiah W.,	192
Deacon, Joseph H.,	139	Dickinson, Betty,	243	Douglass, William,	112
Deacon, Keturah,	233	Dickinson, Edwin L.,	166	Downing, Charles,	166
Deacon, Kezia,	248	Dickinson, Henry,	112	*Downing, Charles,*	100
Deacon, Mary,	255	Dickinson, John,	163	Downing, Edward,	174
Deacon, Rebecca,	248	Dickinson, Mary,	249	Downing, Elizabeth,	226
Deacon, Samuel B.,	191	Dickinson, Mary Elma,	323	Downing, Elizabeth,	246

INDEX.

Name	PAGE
Downing, Esther,	251
Downing, George,	117
Downing, George A.,	122
Downing, Henry D.,	193
Downing, Jane,	97, 98
Downing, Joseph R.,	170
Downing, Mary,	227
Downing, Mary,	303
Downing, Phebe,	226
Downing, Richard T.,	127
Downing, Sallie F.,	337
Downing, Samuel A.,	139
Downing, Samuel S.,	153
Downing, Sarah,	260
Downing, Sarah,	302
Downing, Thomas,	123
Downing, Thomazin,	250
Downing, William M.,	139
Downing, William W.,	113
Drinker, Elizabeth,	243
Drinker, Esther,	242
Drinker, Henry,	95
Drinker, Henry,	108
Drinker, Henry,	126
Drinker, John,	95
Drinker, Sandwith,	134
Drinker, Sarah,	246
Dudley, Elizabeth H.,	304
Duell, Joseph John,	173
Dugdale, Elizabeth,	239
Dugdale, Samuel,	145
Dunkin, Elizabeth,	238
Dunkin, Gulielma,	244
Dunn, Elizabeth,	324
Dunn, Elizabeth C.,	102
(See Chambers.)	
Dunn, Philip,	187
Dunn, Philip P.,	161
" " (Com.,)	102
Dunn, Sarah,	326
Dutton, Charles S.,	178
Dutton, Edith H.,	341
Dutton, Emily,	286
Dutton, Hannah,	324
Dutton, Jacob,	122
Dutton, John,	115
Dutton, Jonathan,	110
Dutton, Mary,	269
Dutton, Mary,	309
Dutton, Mary H.,	335
Dutton, Rebecca,	241
Dutton, Rowland,	115
Dutton, Rowland J.,	161
Dutton, Samuel,	138
Dutton, Sarah J.,	298
Dutton, Thomas,	180
Dutton, William R.,	161
Eachus, Jane,	315
Eachus, Jane S.,	305
Eachus, Lydia M.,	300
Eachus, Samuel S. G.,	142
Eachus, Sarah T.,	283
Earl, Caleb,	116
Earl, Charlotte,	253
Earl, Daniel S.,	129
Earl, Elizabeth,	233
Earl, Leah,	235

Name	PAGE
Earl, Martha,	250
Earl, Mary,	237
Earl, Mary,	242
Earl, Mary,	251
Earl, Rebecca,	247
Earl, Rebecca,	252
Earl, Sarah B.,	261
Earl, Thomas,	116
Earl, William,	106
Earl, William,	121
Eastburn, Amos,	155
Eastburn, Anna C.,	329
Eastburn, Cyrus,	165
Eastburn, Eliza,	247
Eastburn, Elizabeth,	238
Eastburn, Elizabeth,	294
Eastburn, Frances,	262
Eastburn, Franklin,	178
Eastburn, Isaac S.,	159
Eastburn, Joseph W.,	161
Eastburn, Lillian H.,	345
Eastburn, Martha,	254
Eastburn, Mary,	250
Eastburn, Mary Anna,	306
Eastburn, Mary C.,	309
Eastburn, Mercy,	317
Eastburn, Rachel,	279
Eastburn, Ruth,	273
Eastburn, Samuel C.,	183
Eastburn, Sarah,	250
Eastburn, Sidney W.,	343
Eastburn, Thomas,	191
Eastlack, Amy,	276
" " (*Teacher,*)	85
Eastlack, Elizabeth,	275
Eastlack, Hannah,	286
Eastlack, M. H.,	271
Eastlack, Rachel,	292
Eastlack, Sarah,	291
Eaves, Sarah,	297
Fayre, Kezia,	233
Ecroyd, Anne,	312
Ecroyd, Annie,	347
Ecroyd, Charles E.,	203
Ecroyd, Deborah,	306
Ecroyd, Elizabeth S.,	345
Ecroyd, Hannah,	276
(*Snowdon*,) " (*Com.*,)	102
" (*Matron*,)	79
Ecroyd, Hannah,	294
Ecroyd, Henry,	195
Ecroyd, James,	163
Ecroyd, Martha,	276
Ecroyd, Martha,	307
Ecroyd, Martha S.,	272
Ecroyd, Mary,	302
Ecroyd, Richard,	175
Ecroyd, Susan,	297
(*Lippincott,*) " (*Com.*,)	102
Eddy, Charles,	116
Eddy, George,	111
Eddy, James,	119
Eddy, Lewis,	106
Edge, Alfred P.,	183
Edge, Anna G.,	316
Edge, Anna V.,	102
Edge, Benjamin,	189
Edge, Edith,	101

Name	PAGE
Edge, Edith A.,	344
Edge, Edward S.,	194
Edge, Elizabeth,	273
Edge, Elizabeth D.,	316
Edge, Emma H.,	332
Edge, Fanny,	277
Edge, Frances,	299
Edge, Hannah,	277
Edge, Jacob,	101
Edge, Jacob V.,	173
Edge, Jane,	285
Edge, John,	146
Edge, Jonas,	147
Edge, Joshua P.,	93
Edge, Lydia K.,	337
Edge, Mary,	226
Edge, Mary,	259
Edge, Rebecca S.,	329
Edge, Ruth Anna,	277
Edge, Samuel H.,	176
Edge, Sarah Ann,	286
Edge, Sarah M.,	344
Edge, Susan,	283
(*Comfort,*) " (*Com.*,)	102
Edge, Thomas,	142
Edge, Thomas J.,	165
Edge, Vincent,	188
Edge, William,	140
Edgerton, Anna L.,	332
Edgerton, Caroline,	346
Edgerton, Ellen,	347
Edgerton, James, Jr.,	191
Edgerton, Jesse,	156
" " (*Teacher,*)	86
Edgerton, Nathan H.,	180
" " (*Teacher,*)	87
Edgerton, Thomas D.,	205
Edget, Webster,	167
Edkin, Aaron S.,	205
Edkin, Robert B.,	205
Edmondson, Eliza,	236
Edmondson, John F.,	150
Edmondson, Martha,	251
Edmondson, Mary,	256
Edmondson, Rebecca,	245
Edwards, Anna R.,	328
Edwards, Benj. J.,	146
Edwards, Edward,	117
Edwards, Howard,	162
Edwards, Jane W.,	280
" " (*Teacher,*)	87
(*Knight,*) " (*Matron,*)	80
Edwards, Joseph J.,	147
Edwards, Lydia,	283
Edwards, Mary,	283
Edwards, Mary Ann,	271
Edwards, Rebecca,	241
Edwards, S. Hildeburn,	183
Edwards, Sarah,	230
Edwards, Sarah E.,	290
Edwards, William,	159
Elder, Bethia B.,	346
Elder, Rebecca W.,	348
Elder, Theodore E.,	204
Eldridge, Abigail,	290
Eldridge, Abigail,	312
Eldridge, Abra'm S.,	192
Eldridge, Charles,	150

INDEX.

Name	PAGE
Eldridge, David,	150
Eldridge, Deborah M.,	251
Eldridge, Edward T.,	194
Eldridge, Elizabeth,	321
Eldridge, Elmer E.,	199
Eldridge, Enos P.,	181
Eldridge, Esther H.,	347
Eldridge, Hannah P.,	251
Eldridge, Harriet,	292
Eldridge, Isaac,	130
Eldridge, Issachar,	164
Eldridge, James,	174
Eldridge, Jane M.,	316
Eldridge, John,	178
Eldridge, Jonathan,	158
Eldridge, Jonathan,	193
" " (B'k-kpr.,)	98
Eldridge, Joseph,	187
Eldridge, Joseph P.,	171
Eldridge, Joseph P.,	173
Eldridge, Lydia,	285
Eldridge, Lydia,	322
Eldridge, Lydia Ann,	297
Eldridge, Lydia Ann,	302
Eldridge, Margaret,	316
Eldridge, Maria,	307
Eldridge, Maris H.,	190
Eldridge, Mary,	274
Eldridge, Mary Ann,	293
Eldridge, Rachel,	296
Eldridge, Rachel,	300
Eldridge, Reuben,	181
Eldridge, Sarah Ann,	301
Eldridge, Thomas C.,	164
Eldridge, William,	156
Eldridge, William,	168
Eldridge, William P.,	152
Elfreth, Jacob,	105
" " (B'k-kpr.,)	92
Elfreth, J. Benington,	194
Elfreth, Joseph,	147
Elfreth, Miriam,	343
" " (Teacher,)	92
Elkinton, Alfred C.,	201
Elkinton, Asa,	158
Elkinton, Charles,	163
Elkinton, Edith,	302
Elkinton, George E.,	157
Elkinton, Henry H.,	183
Elkinton, Joseph,	112
Elkinton, Joseph S.,	149
Elkinton, Lindley M.,	153
Elkinton, Margaretta,	288
Elkinton, Mary P.,	338
Elkinton, Rebecca,	233
Elkinton, Rebecca,	302
Elkinton, Sarah,	254
Elkinton, Sarah,	303
Elkinton, William T.,	197
Ellet, Hannah C.,	232
Ellicott, Andrew,	124
Ellicott, Elizabeth,	232
Ellicott, Evan T.,	113
Ellicott, Hannah,	229
Ellicott, James,	112
Ellicott, Jane,	291
Ellicott, John,	110
Ellicott, Rachel,	232

Name	PAGE
Ellicott, William,	113
Elliott, Daniel,	98
Elliott, George S.,	147
Elliott, John,	118
Elliott, Hannah,	98
Elliott, Mary Ann,	332
Ellis, Abigail,	243
Ellis, Anna,	232
Ellis, Anna M.,	295
Ellis, Benj. W. M.,	149
Ellis, David,	108
Ellis, Elizabeth,	234
Ellis, Hannah,	231
Ellis, Hannah,	243
Ellis, Hannah,	293
Ellis, Henry D.,	124
Ellis, Mary,	223
Ellis, Mary,	248
Ellis, Mary,	295
Ellis, Mercy,	253
Ellis, Mercy Ann,	282
Ellis, Peter,	95
Ellis, Phebe,	252
Ellis, Rachel,	223
Ellis, Rachel M.,	314
Ellis, Reuben,	150
Ellis, Sarah E.,	287
Ellis, Susanna,	248
Ellis, William C.,	105
Ellison, Anna L.,	325
Ellison, John B.,	114
Ellison, Mary E.,	319
Ellison, Matilda P.,	321
Elston, Agnes,	97
Elston, Sarah,	224
Ely, Charles,	116
Ely, Charles B.,	147
Ely, Elias,	118
Ely, Elizabeth,	242
Ely, Francinia,	282
Ely, Hannah,	260
Ely, Henry,	133
Ely, Hugh,	97
Ely, Joseph,	116
Ely, Joseph O.,	143
Ely, Letitia,	257
Ely, Ruth,	97
Ely, Seneca,	133
Ely, William P.,	148
Embree, Alfred,	190
Embree, Anne,	254
Embree, Edwin E.,	176
Embree, George E.,	189
Embree, J. Anna,	327
Embree, Joshua G.,	173
Embree, Lydia,	323
" "(Teacher,)	89
Embree, Martha,	260
Embree, Mary,	327
Embree, Phebe,	228
Embree, Phebe,	310
Embree, Rebecca,	247
Embree, Rebecca B.,	331
Embree, Sarah,	319
Embree, Sarah G.,	331
Embree, Sibilla,	248
" " (Teacher,)	84
Embree, T. Walter,	195

Name	PAGE
Embree, William G.,	174
" " (Teacher,)	88
Embree, Zillah,	257
" " (Teacher,)	85
Emerson, Ann Eliza,	268
Emerson, Gouverneur,	115
Emerson, Mary,	250
Emerson, Ruth,	228
Emerson, Sarah,	250
Emerson, Susan,	260
Emlen, Ann,	224
Emlen, Anne,	288
Emlen, Caleb,	144
Emlen, Deborah,	227
Emlen, Eliza Ann,	281
Emlen, James,	96
Emlen, James,	109
" " (Teacher,)	85
" " (Com.,)	99
Emlen James V.,	139
Emlen, Jeremiah,	108
Emlen, Joshua,	107
Emlen, Mary,	224
Emlen, Mary,	279
" " (Teacher,)	86
Emlen, Mary C.,	297
Emlen, Phebe,	224
Emlen, Phebe,	229
Emlen, Phebe,	280
Emlen, Samuel,	107
" " (Com.,)	102
Emlen, Samuel,	98
Emlen, Sarah,	288
Emlen, Susan,	288
Emlen, Susanna,	98
England, Alfred,	184
England, Clara,	334
England, Elizabeth D.,	266
England, Emma,	326
England, Hannah,	230
England, Hastings,	187
England, Howell S.,	202
England, Joseph K.,	197
England, Mary C.,	336
England, Sarah,	262
England, Sidney M.,	294
Engle, Deborah,	235
Engle, David D.,	196
Engle, Elizabeth,	260
Engle, Esther A.,	334
Engle, Esther T.,	277
Engle, Ezra C.,	194
Engle, Josiah P.,	187
Engle, Mary Ann,	280
Engle, Maurice D.,	202
Engle, Rebecca,	259
Engle, Robert B.,	171
Engle, Robert F.,	201
Engle, Sarah Ann,	277
Engle, Sarah C.,	277
Entriken, Mary,	237
Entriken, Sibilla P.,	279
Evans, Abigail,	274
(*Wood*,) " (*Com*.,)	101
Evans, Abigail B.,	321
Evans, Alice E.,	327
Evans, Amelia,	224
Evans, Amos,	144

INDEX. 391

Name	PAGE	Name	PAGE	Name	PAGE
Evans, Ann,	260	Evans, *Joseph*,	99	*Evans*, *William*,	102
Evans, Ann,	275	Evans, Joseph,	119	Evans, William,	197
Evans, Ann,	277	Evans, Joseph,	170	Evans, William,	204
Evans, Ann,	283	Evans, Joseph,	185	Evans, William J.,	181
Evans, Ann,	291	Evans, Joseph,	185	Evans, William P.,	184
Evaus, Anna,	272	Evans, Joseph B.,	165	*Eraul, Henry,*	89
Evans, Anne,	337	Evans, Joseph G.,	178	Evens, Abbie L.,	339
Evans, Beulah T.,	340	Evans, Josiah,	135	Evens, Clayton L.,	201
Evans, Caleb G.,	174	Evans, Josiah B.,	133	Evens, Elizabeth B.,	325
Evans, Catharine,	254	Evans, Joshua D.,	182	Evens, Hannah K.,	324
Evans, Catharine,	299	Evans, Lewis,	132	Evens, Henry,	192
Evans, Catharine,	306	Evans, Lydia,	260	Evens, Isaac S.,	199
Evans, Catharine,	315	Evans, Lydia,	277	Evens, Joseph J.,	192
Evans, Catharine,	102	Evans, Lydia,	315	Evens, Joseph K.,	182
(See Wistar.)		Evans, Lydia,	337	Evens, Joshua R.,	197
Evans, Charles,	170	Evans, Lydia B.,	309	Evens, Mary,	255
Evans, Charles,	102	Evans, Lydia J.,	335	*Evens, Mary,*	101
Evans, Charles,	206	Evans, Margaret,	272	Evens, Mary B.,	328
Evans, Charles B.,	129	(*Maule,*) " (*Com.,*)	102	Evens, Rachel S.,	340
Evans, Clayton H.,	200	Evans, Martha,	276	Evens, Sarah L.,	324
Evans, David,	96	Evans, Martha A.,	252	Evens, Sarah R.,	340
Evans, David,	133	Evans, Mary,	225	Evens, Thomas J.,	197
Evans, David,	153	Evans, Mary,	233	Eves, Martha,	303
Evans, David R.,	116	Evans, Mary,	278	Eves, Priscilla,	256
Evans, Deborah C.,	280	Evans, Mary,	281	Eves, Samuel,	162
Evans, Deborah S.,	313	Evans, Mary,	293	Eyre, Ann,	298
Evans, Edwin,	200	Evans, Mary,	306	Eyre, Jesse B.,	115
Evans, Elizabeth,	297	Evans, Mary,	340	Eyre, Joshua,	154
Evans, Elizabeth,	100	Evans, Mary Ann,	269		
Evans, Elizabeth,	319	Evans, Mary C.,	265	Fairlamb, Francis,	109
" " (*Teacher,*)	89	Evans, Mary K.,	327	Fairlamb, Harriet,	240
Evans, Elizabeth G.,	315	Evans, Mary L.,	326	Fairlamb, Lydia,	250
Evans, Elizabeth L.,	318	Evans, Mary M.,	270	Fairlamb, Susanna,	277
Evans, Elizabeth R.,	308	Evans, Mary R.,	291	Fallas, Isaac C.,	160
" " (*Com.,*)	102	Evans, Mary T.,	321	Fallis, Susan M.,	300
Evans, Ellwood,	175	Evans, Owen,	156	Farnum, Susan,	324
Evans, Emily,	285	Evans, Rachel,	242	Faron, Ann J.,	331
Evans, Esther,	278	Evans, Rachel,	265	Farquhar, Charles,	121
Evans, Esther G.,	321	Evans, Rachel B.,	301	*Farquhar, Charles,*	84
Evans, Ezra,	123	Evans, Rebecca,	275	*Farquhar, Sarah,*	84
Evans, Francis W.,	136	Evans, Robert,	116	(See Foulke.)	
Evans, Grace,	100	Evans, Rowland,	197	Farrington, Sarah,	291
(See Trimble.)		Evans, Samuel,	120	Farson, Ann,	254
Evans, Hannah,	97	Evans, Samuel,	129	Farson, Mary,	245
Evans, Hannah,	296	Evans, Samuel,	171	Fawcett, Edith,	338
" " (*Com.,*)	102	Evans, Samuel B.,	141	Fawcett, Eunice,	321
Evans, Hannah,	249	Evans, Samuel J.,	169	Fawcett, Joseph,	185
Evans, Hannah,	304	Evans, Samuel R.,	172	Fawkes, Anna Mary,	326
Evans, Hannah,	315	Evans, Sarah,	229	Fawkes, Emma J.,	338
Evans, Hannah,	325	Evans, Sarah,	263	Fawkes, Mary D.,	335
Evans, Hannah, Jr.,	99	Evans, Sarah A.,	270	Fawkes, Rachel A.,	316
Evans, Hannah,	236	Evans, Sarah M.,	331	Fawkes, Sarah,	335
(*Rhoads,*) " (*Com.,*)	100	Evans, Susanna,	268	Fell, Ann,	218
Evans, Isaac,	143	Evans, Susanna,	273	Fell, Anna G.,	344
Evans, Isaac,	191	Evans, Susanna,	280	Fell, David,	122
Evans, Jane,	235	Evans, Susanna,	310	Fell, Eliza,	265
Evans, Jane,	237	Evans, Thomas,	110	Fell, Elizabeth S.,	293
Evans, Jesse,	110	Evans, Thomas,	129	Fell, Emily,	268
Evans, Jesse,	138	*Evans, Thomas,*	100	Fell, Jane,	245
Evans, Joel,	101	Evans, Thomas,	141	Fell, Jonathan,	138
Evans, Joel,	176	Evans, Thomas,	158	Fell, Joseph,	114
Evans, John,	121	Evans, William,	105	Fell, Joseph,	156
Evans, John,	166	" " (*Com.,*)	98	Fell, Lydia,	248
Evans, John B.,	200	Evans, William,	125	Fell, Maria,	230
Evans, John T.,	164	Evans, William,	129	Fell, Marshall, Jr.,	186
Evans, John W.,	169	Evans, William,	127	Fell, Mary,	265
Evans, Jonathan, Jr.,	95	Evans, William,	151	Fell, Rebecca,	338
Evans, Joseph,	105	Evans, William,	163	Fell, Samuel S.,	206

29*

INDEX.

Name	Page
Fell, Sarah Ann,	274
Fell, Sarah Ann,	277
Fell, Thomas J.,	126
Fenimore, Edward L.,	175
Fennimore, Esther,	267
Fennimore, Jason L.,	118
Fentham, Priscilla,	242
Ferris, Benjamin,	99
Ferris, Charleton,	130
Ferris, Deborah,	271
Ferris, Elizabeth S.,	284
Ferris, Sarah,	268
Ferris, Ziba,	107
Ferris, Ziba,	156
Field, Deborah,	96
Field, John,	95
Field, Mary Ann,	255
Field, Mercy,	266
Fincher, Jeremiah,	126
Fisher, Elizabeth,	237
Fisher, Elizabeth,	240
Fisher, Elizabeth D.,	344
Fisher, Esther,	224
Fisher, Hannah, Sr.,	98
Fisher, Henry W.,	201
Fisher, Jane H.,	307
Fisher, Joseph R.,	146
Fisher, Lydia,	223
Fisher, Lydia C.,	288
Fisher, Mary,	99
Fisher, Rebecca,	240
Fisher, Rebecca,	274
Fisher, Samuel R.,	105
Fisher, Susanna G.,	344
Fisher, Thomas,	95
Fisher, William,	147
Fisher, William J.,	201
Fitzwater, George,	141
Fitzwater, George, Jr.,	185
Fitzwater, Jacob,	110
Fitzwater, Mary,	281
Fitzwater, Matthew,	110
Fitzwater, Sarah,	342
Flagler, Jane,	314
Flanner, Abigail,	248
Flanner, Kezia,	300
Fletcher, Ann,	256
Fletcher, Daniel,	153
Fletcher, Hannah,	242
Fletcher, Margaret B.,	285
Fletcher, Mary,	291
Fletcher, Priscilla,	227
Fletcher, Sarah,	226
Fletcher, Sarah N.,	307
Fletcher, Tacy,	233
Fogg, Elisha,	160
Fogg, Elizabeth G.,	326
Fogg, Joseph G.,	182
Fogg, Lindley,	198
Fogg, Mary G.,	311
Fogg, Rachel S.,	315
Fogg, Sarah Ann,	304
Folger, Francis J.,	118
Folger, William,	124
Folwell, Ann,	260
Folwell, Charles,	116
Folwell, Charles,	158
Folwell, Edward,	129
Folwell, Elizabeth,	226
Folwell, Hannah L.,	292
Folwell, James,	118
Folwell, John	125
Folwell, Mary,	243
Folwell, Nathan,	155
Folwell, Richard S.,	141
Folwell, Sarah,	100
Folwell, Susan,	275
Folwell, William,	108
Forsythe, Amos,	155
Forsythe, Amos,	156
Forsythe, Ann,	235
Forsythe, Anna,	336
Forsythe, Charles,	193
Forsythe, Davis H.,	190
Forsythe, Edward,	192
Forsythe, Edwin C.,	174
Forsythe, Elizabeth.	283
Forsythe, Elizabeth S.,	341
Forsythe, Emily,	336
Forsythe, Emma P.,	341
Forsythe, Frances E.,	335
Forsythe, Frances E.,	345
Forsythe, George,	202
Forsythe, Hannah,	223
Forsythe, Hannah,	253
Forsythe, Hannah,	275
" "(*Teacher,*)	86
" "(*Gov's,*)	81
(*Wood*), "(*Com.,*)	102
Forsythe, Hannah E.,	337
Forsythe, H. Lea,	190
Forsythe, Henry,	195
Forsythe, Henry W.,	204
Forsythe, Isaac,	193
Forsythe, James,	107
" " (*Com.,*)	99
Forsythe, James,	141
Forsythe, James L.,	176
Forsythe, John,	136
Forsythe, John,	83
" " (*Com.,*)	97
Forsythe, John, Jr.,	100
Forsythe, John E.,	187
" (*Teacher,*)	90, 91
Forsythe, Joseph P.,	171
Forsythe, Lewis,	151
"(*B'k-kpr.,*)	93
Forsythe, Mary Anna,	323
" (*Teacher,*)	88, 90, 91
Forsythe, Mary D.,	334
Forsythe, Mary D.,	342
Forsythe, Michael,	125
Forsythe, Ruth Anna,	336
Forsythe, Samuel,	195
Forsythe, Sarah,	281
" (*Com.,*)	102
Forsythe, Susan S.,	345
Forsythe, Susanna,	275
(*Sharpless,*) " (*Com.,*)	102
" (*Mat.,*)	80
Forsythe, Susanna,	332
Forsythe, Truman,	143
" " (*Com.,*)	103
Forsythe, William,	135
" " (*Teacher,*)	85
Forsythe, William T.,	180
Foster, Ellen P.,	345
Foster, George W.,	125
Foster, Temperance,	309
Fothergill, Henry,	168
Fothergill, Margaret,	310
Fothergill, William,	166
Foulke, Anna,	248
Foulke, Anna,	336
Foulke, Ann,	311
Foulke, Ann J.,	271
Foulke, Ann M.,	284
Foulke, Charles,	139
Foulke, Hannah,	231
" " (*Teacher,*)	83
Foulke, Hannah,	257
Foulke, Hannah,	305
Foulke, Jesse,	95
Foulke, John M.,	116
Foulke, Letitia,	284
Foulke, Levi,	119
Foulke, Lydia S.,	301
Foulke, Martha,	271
Foulke, Mary,	271
Foulke, Phebe,	249
Foulke, Priscilla,	292
Foulke, Rebecca J.,	306
Foulke, Sarah,	234
(*Farquhar,*) " (*Teacher,*)	84
Foulke, Sidney,	239
Foulke, Susanna,	283
Fox, Charles H.,	158
Fox, Edith,	290
Fox, Edward B.,	200
Fox, George,	116
Fox, Hannah,	304
Fox, Joseph,	159
Fox, Joseph J.,	200
Fox, Mary,	268
Fox, Rebecca,	295
Fox, Rebecca,	304
Fox, Robert E.,	204
Fox, Samuel L.,	163
Frame, Ira S.,	198
Frame, Joseph,	182
Frame, Mary T.,	344
Frame, Rebecca Ann,	326
Frame, Ruanna E.,	332
Frame, Thompson,	80
Frame, William A.,	198
Frampton, Deborah,	256
Freeman, Joseph,	118
French, Amy,	341
French, Anna,	320
French, Clarkson S.,	203
French, Elizabeth C.,	329
French, George J.,	177
French, Mary,	225
French, Rachel,	235
French, Rachel,	243
French, Robert R.,	194
Fulghum, Naomi C.,	333
Fulton, Anna,	300
Fulton, Hannah,	296
Fulton, Joshua,	145
Fulton, Mary Ann,	275
Fulton, Susan,	282
Furguson, Prudence,	285
Furness, Martha,	273

INDEX.   393

Name	PAGE	Name	PAGE	Name	PAGE
Furness, Phebe,	253	Garrett, Martha,	263	Gaskill, Mary,	262
Fussell, Clarissa,	308	Garrett, Martha H.,	271	Gaskill, Rachel,	233
Fussell, Sarah,	238	Garrett, Martha H.,	313	Gaskill, Rebecca,	245
Futrell, Margaret A.,	344	Garrett, Mary,	250	Gaskill, Rebecca,	283
Futrell, Sarah F.,	347	Garrett, Mary,	259	Gatchell, Cath. F.,	277
		Garrett, Nathan,	146	Gatchell, Louisa,	271
Gamble, Elisha,	198	*Garrett, Philip,*	98	Gauntt, Benjamin U.,	177
Gardiner, Albert,	185	Garrett, Philip C.,	165	Gauntt, Nathan C.,	182
Gardiner, Eliza,	333	Garrett, Rachel,	253	Gause, Charles E.,	159
Gardiner, Eliza'th E.,	343	Garrett, Rachel,	278	Gause, Charles E., Jr.,	195
Gardiner, Emily B.,	322	Garrett, Rachel,	302	Gause, Eber N.,	202
Gardiner, Hannah F.,	333	Garrett, Rachel H.,	262	Gause, Ella T.,	333
Gardiner, Hettie W.,	322	Garrett, Rebecca C.,	297	Gause, Lea,	134
Gardiner, Hettie W.,	347	Garrett, Robert,	136	Gause, Lewis,	146
Gardiner, Henry T.,	183	Garrett, Robert,	171	Gause, Mary,	298
Gardiner, James,	189	Garrett, Sallie C.,	345	Gause, Ruth Anna,	284
Gardiner, John,	188	Garrett, Samuel L.,	138	Gawthrop, Sarah,	252
Gardiner, Joseph,	139	Garrett, Sarah,	255	George, Amos,	109
Gardiner, Mary,	260	Garrett, Sarah,	317	George, Lewis B.,	177
Gardiner, Mary B.,	306	Garrett, Sarah S.,	275	George, William,	109
Gardiner, Micajah,	147	Garrett, Sidney S.,	333	Gest, John,	111
Gardiner, S. Harrison,	201	Garrett, Susanna H.,	278	Gest, Sarah,	271
Gardiner, Thomas W.,	143	Garrett, Thomas,	128	Gibbons, Abraham,	111
Gardiner, William,	201	Garrett, William,	132	*Gibbons, Abraham,*	101
Garner, Maria E.,	343	Garrett, William S.,	203	Gibbons, Anne,	270
Garner, Martha E.,	343	Garretson, Amanda,	300	Gibbons, Dillon,	187
Garrett, Albin,	176	Garretson, George F.,	121	Gibbons, Frances,	280
Garrett, Albina,	298	Garretson, Hannah,	294	*Gibbons, Hannah,*	98
Garrett, Alice M.,	346	Garretson, Rachel,	268	Gibbons, Hannah,	251
Garrett, Ann,	248	Garretson, Rachel,	270	Gibbons, Hannah,	307
Garrett, Anna,	275	Garretson, Rachel,	292	Gibbons, Hannah B.,	254
Garrett, Anna,	285	Garrigues, Anna,	335	Gibbons, Henry,	169
Garrett, Anna E.,	346	Garrigues, Benjamin,	116	Gibbons, Jane,	264
Garrett, Anne,	329	Garrigues, Benj. D.,	135	*Gibbons, Jane,*	101
Garrett, Charles,	108	Garrigues, Beulah,	256	Gibbons, Joseph,	119
Garrett, David,	173	Garrigues, Caspar,	118	Gibbons, Joseph H.,	175
Garrett, Davis,	136	Garrigues, David W.,	186	Gibbons, Lydia,	228
Garrett, Deborah,	305	Garrigues, Deborah,	256	Gibbons, Lydia,	277
Garrett, Edward,	123	*Garrigues, Edward,*	98	Gibbons, Martha,	248
Garrett, Elizabeth,	259	Garrigues, Edward,	118	" "(*Teacher,*)	85
Garrett, Elizabeth,	278	Garrigues, Edward,	184	Gibbons, Mary,	246
Garrett, Elizabeth,	310	Garrigues, Edward H.,	144	Gibbons, Mary P.,	254
Garrett, Elizabeth,	346	Garrigues, Elizabeth,	328	Gibbons, Massey,	226
Garrett, Elizabeth R.,	294	Garrigues, Hannah,	244	Gibbons, Naomi,	285
Garrett, Elizabeth C.,	262	Garrigues, Hannah,	340	Gibbons, Richard,	140
Garrett, Elizabeth S.,	324	Garrigues, Isaac,	108	Gibbons, Sarah,	300
Garrett, Ellwood,	156	Garrigues, James R.,	118	Gibbons, Susan,	310
Garrett, Frances,	301	Garrigues, John S.,	186	Gibbons, Thomas,	145
Garrett, George S.,	172	Garrigues, Lydia S.,	294	Gibbons, William,	160
Garrett, Gulielma,	274	Garrigues, Mary,	226	Gibbons, William A.,	132
Garrett, Hannah,	264	Garrigues, Mary,	225	Gibbons, William M.,	106
Garrett, Henry S.,	164	Garrigues, Mary,	340	Gibbs, Lydia,	237
Garrett, Isaac P.,	178	Garrigues, Mary M.,	250	Gibson, Ann,	234
Garrett, Jane,	278	Garrigues, Robert,	112	Gibson, Webster,	185
Garrett, Jane,	314	Garrigues, Sarah,	272	Gifford, Charles,	166
Garrett, Jane H.,	314	Garrigues, Sarah B.,	328	Gifford, Clara P.,	343
Garrett, James,	176	Garrigues, Sarah M.,	243	Gifford, Elton B.,	152
Garrett, Jesse,	166	Garrigues, Susan H.,	244	Gifford, Hannah B.,	310
Garrett, Jesse H.,	170	*Garrigues, William,*	96	Gifford, Jemima A.,	303
Garrett, John B.,	165	Garrigues, William,	108	Gifford, Lydia S.,	311
Garrett, John K.,	116	Garrigues, William H.,	144	Gifford, Thomas,	166
Garrett, Lydia P.,	274	Garwood, Daniel,	173	Gifford, William B.,	169
Garrett, Margaret,	224	Gaskill, Ann,	225	Gilbert, Ann,	83
(*Malin,*) " (*Com.*)	100	Gaskill, Beulah,	233	Gilbert, Joshua,	106
Garrett, Margaret,	279	Gaskill, Jane,	242	Gilkeson, Hunter B.,	178
Garrett, Margaret,	262	Gaskill, Josiah,	107	Gilkeson, Mary S.,	321
(*Sheppard,*) " (*Com.*)	192	Gaskill, Julia,	268	Gill, Ephraim T.,	197
Garrett, Margaret M.,	299	Gaskill, Lydia,	284	Gill, John,	157

INDEX.

Name	PAGE	Name	PAGE	Name	PAGE
Gill, John, Jr.,	192	Grave, Lydia A.,	272	*Griffiths, Samuel P.,*	95
Gill, Mary,	226	Gray, Angelina,	329	*Grigg, Ann,*	99
Gill, William H.,	161	Gray, Margaretta,	335	Griscom, Andrew,	122
Gillam, Isaac,	112	Gray, Martha,	238	Griscom, Annie B.,	348
Gillam, Simon,	98	Gray, Martha,	230	Griscom, Beulah A.,	273
Gillespie, Sarah C.,	305	Gray, William,	119	Griscom, David B.,	150
Gillingham, Anna,	263	Greaves, Alfred,	131	Griscom, Johnetta S.,	345
Gillingham, Caroline,	293	Greaves, Charles,	138	Griscom, Mary,	254
Gillingham, Cathar'e,	293	Greaves, James,	111	Griscom, Mary,	265
Gillingham, Edw. C.,	128	Green, Abel,	105	Griscom, Rachel,	282
Gillingham, Elizab'h,	263	Green, Amy,	265	Griscom, Sarah,	248
Gillingham, Emeline,	263	Green, Elizabeth T.,	271	Griscom, William,	125
Gillingham, Emma J.,	315	Green, Hannah A.,	292	Grubb, Ann E.,	296
Gillingham, Fannie E.,	295	Green, Hester Ann,	324	Grubb, Beulah T.,	300
Gillingham, Frances,	293	Green, Jane,	223	Grubb, Catharine S.,	323
Gillingham, Hannah,	85	Green, Jane W.,	291	Grubb, Edward,	122
Gillingham, Henrie'a,	289	Green, Joseph,	107	Grubb, Franklin M.,	176
Gillingham, James,	122	Green, Mary,	260	Grubb, Hannah,	262
Gillingham, Mahlon,	107	Green, Mary A.,	294	Grubb, Joseph,	132
Gillingham, M. H.,	148	Green, Mary Ann,	253	Grubb, Lydia,	262
Gillingham, Nath. H.,	117	Green, Nathan G.,	187	Grubb, Mary,	262
Gillingham, Rachel C.,	284	*Green, Robert,*	90	Grubb, Samuel S.,	122
Gillingham, Sam'l H.,	122	Green, William,	170	Grubb, Sarah Jane,	315
Gillingham, Theo. T.,	165	Green, William L.,	143	Grubb, William R.,	156
Gillingham, Thomas,	121	Greenfield, Betsey,	256	Gruwell, Alice P.,	316
Gillingham, Wm. H.,	118	Gregg, Ann E.,	235	Gruwell, Anna Eliza,	322
Gillingham, Yeamans,	125	Gregg, Ann Eliza,	240	Gruwell, Charles,	177
Gilpin, Abigail,	247	Gregg, Deborah,	240	Gubbings, Ann,	327
Gilpin, Ann,	223	Gregg, Elizabeth,	257	Gubbings, Elizabeth,	321
Gilpin, Elizabeth,	242	Gregg, Sarah,	262	Gubbings, Hannah,	318
Gilpin, Emily,	328	Gregory, Azor,	111	Gubbings, James,	174
Gilpin, Richard B.,	121	Grellet, Rachel,	269	Gubbings, Jane,	321
Gilpin, Ruth,	264	Griest, Philena,	275	Gubbings, Mary,	316
Gilpin, Sidney A.,	240	Griffin, Ann,	245	Guell, George,	140
Glover, Adeline,	287	Griffin, Catharine,	309	Gummere, Elizabeth,	282
Glover, Beulah,	251	Griffin, Daniel,	204	Gummere, Frances,	287
Glover, Caroline,	267	Griffin, Elisha,	153	Gummere Frances,	328
Glover, James,	107	Griffin, Ellen M.,	344	Gummere, John,	111
Glover, Rebecca,	278	Griffin, Esther,	292	" "(B'k-k'r,)	92
Glover, Sarah,	306	Griffin, Jacob,	155	" "(Teacher,)	84
Good, Annie S.,	340	Griffin, John D.,	165	Gummere, Marg't M.,	328
Good, Ella T.,	343	Griffin, Lydia,	309	Gummere, Mary,	282
Good, Esther,	312	Griffin, William D.,	155	Gummere, Rachel J.,	247
Good, Francis,	157	Griffith, Aaron H.,	173	*Gummere, Samuel R.,*	84
Good, Isaac,	157	Griffith, Amy,	312		
Good, Joel P.,	203	Griffith, Anna T.,	340	*Hacker, Beulah M.,*	101
Good, Joseph,	156	Griffith, David L.,	176	Hacker, Edward,	199
Good, Louis P.,	190	Griffith, Elizabeth B.,	304	Hacker, Esther S.,	286
Good, Mary P.,	345	Griffith, Hannah,	257	*Hacker, Jeremiah,*	101
Good, Thomas,	170	Griffith, Hannah,	266	Hacker, Morris,	165
Goodwin, A. Helena,	342	Griffith, Hannah A.,	312	Hacker, Sarah E.,	319
Goodwin, Elizabeth,	232	Griffith, Harriet,	315	Hackney, Mary S.,	328
Goodwin, Eliz. H.,	347	Griffith, Isaac H.,	171	Haight, Joanna,	287
Goodwin, Frank'n H.,	204	Griffith, Jane,	294	Haines, Aaron Engle,	203
Goodwin, Warren C.,	202	Griffith, John,	189	Haines, Aaron N.,	146
Gordon, Jane,	296	Griffith, John C.,	165	Haines, Abigail A.,	293
Gordon, Mordecai L.,	108	Griffith, John M.,	182	Haines, Abigail E.,	315
Gough, Anna Eliza,	311	Griffith, Margaretta,	288	Haines, Agnes H.,	312
Gould, Abby,	320	Griffith, Martha,	312	Haines, Albert,	202
Gould, Henry E.,	177	Griffith, Mary,	322	Haines, Alfred,	178
Gould, Sarah M.,	334	Griffith, Mary Anna,	325	Haines, Alfred C.,	203
Gould, Thomas B.,	188	Griffith, Phebe Ann,	320	Haines, Amy,	275
Gould, William,	167	Griffith, Rachel,	307	Haines, Amy,	315
Gove, Anna E.,	331	Griffith, Rachel,	322	Haines, Ann,	229
Gove, Frederic D.,	186	Griffith, Richard E.,	176	Haines, Ann,	266
Gover, Jesse,	111	Griffith, S. Smith,	181	Haines, Ann Eliza,	300
Govett, Ellen,	250	Griffith, Sarah Ann,	308	Haines, Anna H.,	325
Grant, Lukens,	126	Griffith, Virginia,	321	Haines, Anna M.,	334

INDEX. 395

Name	PAGE
Haines, Anna S.,	315
Haines, Anna V.,	343
Haines, Asenath,	318
Haines, Avolina,	287
Haines, Benjamin H.,	154
Haines, Benjamin M.,	205
Haines, Bethuel,	159
Haines, Beulah,	269
Haines, Beulah E.,	333
Haines, Caspar W.,	168
Haines, Caspar W.,	189
Haines, Charles C.,	200
Haines, Clayton,	172
Haines, David,	155
Haines, David S.,	203
Haines, Deborah,	249
Haines, Deborah F.,	315
Haines, Edwin M.,	153
Haines, Elizabeth,	245
Haines, Elizabeth,	252
Haines, Elizabeth,	263
Haines, Elizabeth E.,	318
Haines, Elizabeth F.,	324
Haines, Elizabeth T.,	347
Haines, Elizabeth W.,	347
Haines, Ellis,	189
Haines, Emily,	344
Haines, Emily B.,	343
Haines, Emily S.,	325
Haines, Emmor,	148
Haines, Ephraim,	168
Haines, Erasmus W.,	154
Haines, Esther,	257
Haines, Esther T.,	308
Haines, George,	153
Haines, George,	166
Haines, George R.,	170
Haines, George R.,	205
Haines, Hamilton,	183
Haines, Hannah,	313
Haines, Hannah A.,	311
Haines, Hannah M.,	325
Haines, Hannah R.,	323
Haines, Hannah W.,	337
Haines, Harrison W.,	196
Haines, Henrietta,	302
Haines, Henrietta,	307
Haines, Henry,	143
Haines, Henry E.,	193
Haines, Hetty E.,	330
Haines, J. Clifford,	203
Haines, J. Leander,	186
Haines, Jacob,	81
Haines, J. Gardiner,	175
Haines, James G.,	191
Haines, James W.,	181
Haines, Jane,	240
Haines, Jane D.,	289
Haines, Jane E.,	313
Haines, Jesse,	153
Haines, Job,	152
Haines, John,	135
Haines, John,	180
Haines, John D.,	158
Haines, John G.,	184
Haines, John N.,	184
Haines, John W.,	134
Haines, Joseph A.,	181
Haines, Joseph E.,	145
Haines, Joseph H.,	180
Haines, Joseph S.,	180
Haines, Josiah,	135
Haines, Joshua,	143
Haines, Levi,	176
Haines, Lindley,	137
Haines, Lindley, Jr.,	180
Haines, Lydia,	302
Haines, Lydia Ann,	334
Haines, Margaret B.,	329
Haines, Margaretta F.,	296
Haines, Maria,	267
Haines, Martha A.,	322
Haines, Martha M.,	291
Haines, Martha S.,	286
Haines, Mary,	252
Haines, Mary,	266
Haines, Mary A.,	312
Haines, Mary Ann,	254
Haines, Mary Ann,	267
Haines, Mary Anna,	331
Haines, Marianna,	302
Haines, Marianna,	307
Haines, Mary C.,	309
Haines, Mary E.,	286
Haines, Mary G.,	347
Haines, Mary J.,	325
Haines, Mary J.,	331
Haines, Mary L.,	325
Haines, Mary S.,	323
Haines, Mary W.,	266
Haines, Mary W.,	309
Haines, Mulford,	188
Haines, Nathan,	124
Haines, Nathan,	135
Haines, Newbold R.,	183
Haines, Newlin,	202
Haines, Portia,	312
Haines, Priscilla W.,	315
Haines, Prudence E.,	325
Haines, Rachel,	309
Haines, Rachel R.,	319
Haines, Rebecca,	251
Haines, Rebecca,	274
Haines, Rebecca,	291
Haines, Rebecca,	308
Haines, Rebecca A.,	329
Haines, Rebecca E.,	302
" " (Teacher,)	86
Haines, Rebecca R.,	307
Haines, Rebecca W.,	305
Haines, Reuben,	105
Haines, Richard,	172
Haines, Samuel,	138
Haines, Samuel S.,	168
Haines, S. Howard,	201
Haines, Sarah,	264
Haines, Sarah C.,	324
Haines, Sarah E.,	300
Haines, Sarah R.,	329
Haines, Sophia,	259
Haines, Stacy B.,	162
Haines, Susan,	264
Haines, Susan,	290
Haines, Susanna,	273
Haines, Susan L.,	319
Haines, Thomas Lee,	202
Haines, William B.,	159
Haines, William C.,	181
Haines, William E.,	139
Haines, Wm. Henry,	185
Haines, Zebedee,	182
" " (Teacher,)	88
" " (Com.,)	103
Hall, Abigail W.	102
(See Williams.)	
Hall, Albert,	152
Hall, Ann,	248
Hall, Deborah K.,	241
Hall, Edward H.,	154
Hall, Eliza,	346
Hall, Eliza D.,	341
Hall, Elizabeth,	238
Hall, Elizabeth,	305
Hall, Elvira,	320
Hall, Francis D.,	203
Hall, George E.,	152
Hall, Hannah,	256
Hall, Henry,	197
Hall, Isaac,	165
" " (Teacher,)	86
" " (Com.,)	102
Hall, J. Della,	345
Hall, James M.,	141
Hall, John C.,	180
Hall, Joseph,	187
Hall, Josiah,	181
Hall, Ollie S.,	344
Hall, Maria,	298
Hall, Mary,	292
Hall, Morris,	113
Hall, Prudence,	249
Hall, Rachel,	320
Hall, Rebecca,	245
Hall, Ruth,	239
Hall, Sarah,	243
Hall, Sarah,	249
Hall, Sina A.,	342
Hall, Susanna,	258
Hall, Thomas,	181
Hall, Thomas H.,	150
Hall, Wilson,	169
Hallett, Melissa C.,	342
Hallock, Allen,	133
Hallock, Daniel H.,	195
Hallock, James C.,	132
Hallock, Ruth Anna,	318
Hallock, Sarah E.,	320
Hallowell, Alice,	305
Hallowell, Alice,	316
Hallowell, Ann,	265
Hallowell, Benjamin,	81
Hallowell, Benjamin,	168
Hallowell, Caleb,	129
Hallowell, Caroline,	308
Hallowell, Edwin,	125
Hallowell, Elizabeth,	272
Hallowell, Hannah,	268
Hallowell, John,	131
Hallowell, Jonah,	131
Hallowell, M. A.,	298
Hallowell, Martha,	268
Hallowell, Mary,	250
Hallowell, Mary,	258
" " (Teacher,)	84

INDEX.

Name	Page
Hallowell, Mary,	205
Hallowell, Morris L.,	129
Hallowell, R. P.,	282
Hallowell, Sarah A.,	256
Hallowell, Sarah R.,	282
Hallowell, Susan,	243
Hallowell, William,	123
Hambleton, Stephen,	113
Hamblin, C. Allen,	192
Hamblin, Howard,	189
Hamblin, Wm. J. A.,	196
Hamilton, Osborn,	142
Hampton, Charles,	110
Hampton, Mariba,	292
Hampton, Martha,	298
Hampton, Mary,	229
Hampton, Mercy,	229
Hampton, William,	134
Hance, Mary,	276
Hance, Sarah,	266
Hancock, Asa,	145
Hancock, Eliz. A.,	301
Hancock, Ellis,	148
Hancock, Esther M.,	268
Hancock, George C.,	161
Hancock, Martha,	302
Hancock, Reading K.,	164
Hancock, Susan,	305
Handy, Charles,	153
Handy, Henry,	146
Handy, William,	153
Haney, Margaret A.,	281
Hannum, Dinah,	270
Hannum, Eliz. M.,	283
Hannum, Hannah,	308
Hannum, Sarah,	254
Hanson, Samuel,	106
Hanson, Thomas,	107
Hare, John L.,	205
Hare, Jonathan C.,	200
Hare, William T.,	202
Hare, Zada V.,	341
Harlan, Anna,	301
Harlan, Anna B.,	327
Harlan, Charles N.,	160
Harlan, Edith,	248
Harlan, Elizabeth,	246
Harlan, Enoch,	169
Harlan, George P.,	122
Harlan, George W.,	176
Harlan, Hannah A.,	287
Harlan, John M.,	164
Harlan, Joseph,	109
Harlan, Joseph G.,	156
" " (Teacher,)	86
Harlan, Josephine G.,	333
Harlan, Lydia,	237
Harlan, Martha,	236
Harlan, Mary,	261
Harlan, Mary,	308
Harlan, Rebecca,	274
Harlan, Rebecca H.,	314
Harlan, Samuel,	97
Harlan, Sarah,	259
Harlan, Sarah,	327
Harlan, Sarah E.,	317
Harlan, Susan,	274
Harlan, Susan W.,	303
Harlan, Thomas W.,	157
Harlan, William B.,	183
Harman, Andrew,	133
Harman, John A.,	133
Harman, Sarah,	282
Harmer, Edward S.,	265
Harmer, Elizabeth,	346
Harmer, Hannah,	249
Harmer, Joshua L.,	103
Harmer, Letitia,	298
Harmer, Sarah R.,	334
" "(Teacher.)	80
Harned, Rebecca,	304
Harper, Ann,	283
Harper, Benjamin,	153
Harper, Daniel R.,	141
Harper, James,	108
Harper, Jane,	280
Harper, Mary,	296
Harper, Nathan,	98
Harris, Deborah,	234
Harris, Eliza T.,	317
Harris, Hilt H.,	204
Harris, John S.,	174
Harris, Lucy,	234
Harris, Mary A.,	311
Harris, Mary E.,	320
Harris, Sarah C.,	333
Harrison, Charlotte,	253
Harrison, Eliz. B.,	239
Harrison, Emily,	290
Harrison, Maria H.,	272
Harrison, Mary E.,	341
Harrison, Sarah Ann,	290
Harry, Deborah,	267
Harry, Deborah,	303
Harry, Edward,	164
Harry, Elizabeth,	314
Harry, Maria,	300
Harry, Martha,	291
Harry, Mary E.,	315
Harry, Sarah Ann,	301
Harry, Sophia,	301
Harry, William,	178
Hart, Margaret,	96
Hartley, Thomas B.,	130
Hartshorne, Catharine,	97
" "(Mat'n,)	79
Hartshorne, Hannah,	99
Hartshorne, R., (Supt.)	79
" " (Com.)	96
Hartshorne, Sam'l H.,	130
Hartshorne, Sarah,	224
Hartshorne, Sarah,	97
Hartshorne, William,	95
Hartshorne, Wm. D.,	187
Hartz, John S.,	204
Hartz, Lee D.,	203
Hartz, Mary M.,	343
Hartz, Sarah,	348
Hartz, Wilbern,	202
Harvey, Alban,	179
Harvey, Amos,	97
Harvey, Anna Mary,	308
Harvey, Anna P.,	332
Harvey, Beulah,	305
Harvey, Edwin,	158
Harvey, Gulielma,	339
Harvey, Hannah,	238
Harvey, Hannah,	250
Harvey, Jane H.,	334
Harvey, Joseph,	123
Harvey, Joseph C.,	194
Harvey, Julia,	329
Harvey, Lydia,	238
Harvey, Lydia,	244
Harvey, Lydia,	319
Harvey, Maria,	296
Harvey, Mary D.,	305
Harvey, Mary E.,	304
Harvey, Mary E.,	331
Harvey, Phebe,	230
Harvey, Philena,	334
Harvey, Sarah,	299
Harvey, Thomas M.,	151
" " (Com.,)	103
Harvey William B.,	198
Hathaway, Caleb,	117
Hathaway, Susan,	327
Hathaway, Thos. W.,	117
Hatton, A. Clara,	346
Hatton, Ella,	344
Hatton, Jonathan,	189
Hatton, Phebe,	341
Hatton, Samuel C.,	179
Hauxhurst, Ann,	235
Hauxhurst, Mary B.,	241
Hauxhurst, Sarah,	235
Havard, Jane,	228
Haverstick, Rebecca,	328
Haviland, Abigail,	318
Haviland, Alfred,	185
Haviland, Carrie E.,	345
Haviland, Daniel P.,	205
Haviland, David S.,	178
Haviland, Edward,	187
Haviland, Elizabeth,	314
Haviland, Francis,	184
Haviland, Isaac,	169
Haviland, L. Gertrude,	340
Haviland, Lydia P.,	318
Haviland, Marian W.,	346
Haviland, Philip H.,	171
Haviland, Walter,	178
Hawley, Abner G.,	138
Hawley, Lavinia,	288
Hawley, Lydia Ann,	296
Hawley, Mary,	254
Hawley, Rachel,	260
Hawley, Rebecca,	296
Haworth, Caroline,	300
Haworth, Edith E.,	314
Haworth, Mary,	225
Haworth, Mary,	227
Haycock, Tacy T.,	292
Haydock, Ann J.,	225
Haydock, Benjamin,	119
Haydock, Eleanor,	310
Haydock, Eliz. W.,	263
Haydock, Hannah,	236
Haydock, Hannah,	241
Haydock, John,	118
Haydock, Martha W.,	279
Haydock, Mary Ann,	264
Haydock, Mary Ann,	309
Haydock, Robert,	119

INDEX.

Name	Page
Haydock, Sarah Ann,	286
Haydock, Susanna,	98
Haydock, William,	106
Haydock, William,	115
Hayes, Albert L.,	205
Hayes, Ann,	314
Hayes, Benjamin,	158
Hayes, Carrie W.,	338
Hayes, Charles,	157
Hayes, Edward,	164
Hayes, Eliza Ann,	286
Hayes, Elizabeth L.,	307
Hayes, Fanny,	314
Hayes, Isaac,	92
Hayes, Isaac I.,	160
Hayes, J. Borton,	160
Hayes, Jacob,	121
Hayes, Lydia E.,	340
Hayes, Lydia E.,	342
Hayes, Mary,	304
Hayes, Mary,	340
Hayes, Mary B.,	300
Hayes, Rebecca L.,	252
Hayes, Robert,	168
Hayes, Sarah,	302
Hayes, William B.,	196
Hayward, Sarah Ann,	307
Hazard, Anna,	313
Hazard, Anna,	318
Hazard, Elizabeth,	238
Hazard, Elizabeth,	313
Hazard, Isaac P.,	116
Hazard, Isaac P.,	179
Hazard, John W.,	156
Hazard, Joseph,	124
Hazard, Lydia C.,	308
Hazard, Mary G.,	308
Hazard, Rowland G.,	121
Hazard, Rowland H.,	170
Hazard, Thomas R.,	116
Hazard, William,	123
Hazard, William W.,	177
Heacock, Abigail H.,	315
Heacock, Abigail W.,	300
Heacock, Acintha,	329
Heacock, Amy,	345
Heacock, Anna M.,	334
Heacock, Anna S.,	342
Heacock, Asenath,	304
Heacock, Charles C.,	194
Heacock, Eli,	197
Heacock, Eliz. M.,	277
Heacock, Elma,	327
Heacock, Emma G.,	326
Heacock, Hannah,	308
Heacock, Harvey E.,	191
Heacock, Jesse W.,	153
Heacock, Joseph,	179
Heacock, Joseph,	188
Heacock, Laura,	339
Heacock, Louisa W.,	342
Heacock, Martha,	317
" (*Teacher*,)	88, 89
Heacock, Mary F.,	339
Heacock, Phebe W.,	281
Heacock, Regina S.,	335
Heacock, Sarah E.,	336
Heacock, Stacy L.,	195
Heacock, Susan,	341
Heacock, William W.,	197
Headley, Aaron M.,	197
Headley, Harriet M.,	340
Headley, Oliver H.,	198
Heald, Jacob,	129
" " (*Teacher*,)	84
Heald, Lydia,	259
Heald, Mary Ann,	269
Heald, Ruth,	265
Healy, Jeremiah,	147
Healy, John,	140
Healy, Joseph,	175
Healy, Lucy E.,	307
Healy, Lydia,	290
Healy, Mark,	154
Healy, Mercy,	302
Healy, Rebecca,	309
Healy, Sarah,	278
Healy, Sarah E.,	310
Hedley, Alfred,	190
Hedley, Anna,	334
Hedley, David B.,	186
Hedley, Emma,	334
Hedley, James L.,	190
Hedley, Lucilla R.,	353
Hedley, William J.,	172
Henderson, Susanna,	266
Henderson, Thos. A.,	205
Hendrickson, Albert,	157
Hendrickson, Ben. E.,	167
Hendrickson, Cath. A.,	318
Hendrickson, Edwin,	168
Hendrickson, Nathan,	133
Hendrickson, Sar. A.,	342
Hendrickson, Wm.,	166
Hendrickson, Wm. L.,	191
Henley, Elizabeth N.,	347
Henley, Eva,	334
Henley, John G.,	173
Henley, Wm. Edgar,	190
Henly, Sarah,	316
" " (*Teacher*,)	87
Henrie, Clemuel R.,	193
Henrie, George W.,	196
Henrie, Josiah T.,	188
Henrie, Margaret,	334
Henzey, Joshua,	107
Hercndeen, George,	171
Heston, Anna,	341
Heston, Charles B.,	186
Heston, David,	155
Heston, Eber,	153
Heston, Elizabeth,	220
Heston, Elizabeth,	288
Heston, Enoch W.,	167
Heston, George D.,	156
Heston, Jane,	270
Heston, John B.,	195
Heston, Mary,	232
Heston, Phebe Ann,	279
Heulings, Howard M.,	196
Heulings, Mary Alice,	339
Hewes, Caleb,	155
Hewes, Charles P.,	152
Hewes, Elizabeth M.,	272
Hewes, Isaac,	111
Hewes, Jacob,	116
Hewes, Jacob,	151
Hewes, James A.,	123
Hewes, Jane,	230
Hewes, Jesse,	143
Hewes, John,	111
Hewes, John G.,	132
Hewes, Mary,	318
Hewes, Rebecca,	227
Hewes, Samuel,	154
Hewes, Sarah Ann,	273
Hewlings, Esther,	225
Hiatt, Semira,	307
Hibberd, Ann,	247
Hibberd, Ann,	254
Hibberd, Edward,	132
Hibberd, Eli M.,	185
Hibberd, Hannah,	238
Hibberd, Hannah,	251
Hibberd, Josiah,	148
Hibberd, Margaret,	273
Hibberd, Mary,	234
Hibberd, Mary,	234
Hibberd, Mary L.,	314
Hibberd, Norris,	106
Hibberd, Rebecca,	249
Hibberd, Rebecca,	257
Hibberd, Susan,	291
Hibberd, William,	128
Hickman, Edith,	289
Hickman, Elizabeth,	297
Hickman, Eninor,	147
Hicks, Edward,	123
Hicks, John,	136
Hicks, Mary,	282
Hildeburn, Samuel,	105
Hill, Abigail N.,	320
Hill, Ann G.,	262
Hill, Anne,	279
Hill, Asenath,	316
" " (*Teacher*,)	87
Hill, Elizabeth M.,	258
Hill, Ella,	310
Hill, Hannah W.,	258
Hill, John H.,	110
Hill. M. Elizabeth,	333
Hill, Mary,	224
Hill, Mary,	219
Hill, Mary,	286
Hill, Rachel,	258
Hill, Sidney,	224
(*Temple,*) " (*Com.*,)	99
Hilles, Albert L.,	186
Hilles, Dinah,	299
Hilles, Edward B.,	189
Hilles, Eli,	114
" " (*Teacher,*)	83
Hilles, Gulielma,	285
Hilles, Joseph T.,	201
Hilles, Margaret H.,	99
(See Smith.)	
Hilles, Martha,	99
(See Barker.)	
Hilles, Nathan,	138
Hilles, Samuel,	83
" " (*Com.*,)	100
Hilles, Samuel,	139
Hilles, William P.,	186
Hillman, Albert H.,	165

INDEX.

Name	PAGE
Hillman, John B.,	151
Hillman, Martha E.,	286
Hillman, Nathaniel B.,	142
Hillman, Richard J.,	148
Hillman, Sarah,	241
Hilyard, Anna,	328
Hilyard, Anna M.,	310
Hilyard, Cordelia,	338
Hilyard, Elizabeth W.,	317
Hilyard, Emily,	313
Hilyard, Emily T.,	333
Hilyard, Franklin W.,	187
Hilyard, George D.,	161
Hilyard, J. Barclay,	184
Hilyard, J. Franklin,	183
Hilyard, James, Jr.,	181
Hilyard, John W.,	169
Hilyard, Jonathan H.,	174
Hilyard, Junia,	234
Hilyard, Lavinia,	234
Hilyard, Martha W.,	317
Hilyard, Mary E.,	331
Hilyard, Mary T.,	317
Hilyard, Mary W.,	313
Hilyard, Rachel L.,	325
Hilyard, Sarah T.,	329
Hilyard, Thomas,	114
Hinchman, Allen,	142
Hinchman, Anna W.,	287
Hinchman, Barclay,	136
Hinchman, Eliza,	243
Hinchman, Griffith,	122
Hinchman, Mary,	247
Hinchman, Morgan,	136
Hinchman, Reb'ca W.,	284
Hinshaw, John E.,	202
Hinshaw, Stephen C.,	200
Hirons, John,	106
Hoag, Jane C.,	290
Hoag, Martha B.,	341
Hoag, Nicholas W.,	164
Hoagland, Caroline,	317
Hoagland, Eliz. M.,	310
Hobbs, Marianna,	326
Hobson, Dorothy,	88
Hobson, Martha,	253
Hodgin, Asenath,	245
Hodgson, Matilda,	270
Hodgson, Mary,	272
Hodgson, Sarah,	269
Hoffecker, Emily,	343
Hoge, Anna Eugenia,	323
Hoge, Edward B.,	197
Hoge, Elizabeth S.,	317
Hoge, Frederica P.,	334
Hoge, Hannah Ann,	319
Hoge, Hannah Elma,	331
Hoge, Henrietta,	336
Hoge, Isaac C.,	179
Hoge, J. Barclay,	190
Hoge, James,	171
Hoge, James L.,	205
Hoge, Josephine M.,	316
Hoge, Lewis N.,	176
Hoge, Lindley M.,	185
Hoge, Lydia A.,	323
Hoge, M. Ella,	334
Hoge, Phebe W.,	321
Hoge, Rebecca W.,	333
Hoge, Thomas C.,	187
" " (*Teacher*,)	88
Hogeland, Hannah,	284
Holgate, Mary H.,	285
Hollingshead, Hud'n,	125
Hollingsworth, Eliz.,	295
Hollingsworth, Eliz.,	327
Hollinshead, Benj. H.,	117
Hollinshead, Rachel,	233
Holloway, Anna,	346
Holloway, Chalk'y C.,	200
Holloway, Edwin F.,	197
Holloway, Eph'm W.,	187
Holloway, Martha M.,	345
Holloway, Murray S.,	205
Holloway, Rachel A.,	316
Holloway, Walter S.,	206
Holloway, William C.,	183
Holmes, Ann Eliza,	292
Holmes, Elizabeth,	231
Holmes, Sarah,	292
Hood, Mary,	274
Hood, Sarah,	287
Hoopes, Alice,	334
Hoopes, Amy,	249
Hoopes, Amy C.,	251
Hoopes, Ann,	288
Hoopes, Anna Mary,	298
Hoopes, Anna R.,	317
Hoopes, Barton,	157
Hoopes, Benjamin,	148
Hoopes, Benjamin,	93
" (*Teacher*,)	86, 87
Hoopes, Benjamin P.,	185
Hoopes, Caleb,	92
" " (*Com.*,)	108
Hoopes, Caroline B.,	344
Hoopes, Caroline E.,	295
Hoopes, Charles,	189
Hoopes, Cyrus,	140
Hoopes, David,	99
Hoopes, David,	107
Hoopes, David R.,	169
Hoopes, Davis,	117
Hoopes, Edward,	141
Hoopes, Edward J.,	206
Hoopes, Edwin A.,	189
Hoopes, Elizabeth,	280
Hoopes, Elizabeth,	285
Hoopes, Elizabeth,	319
Hoopes, Elizabeth W.,	81
(See Walters.)	
Hoopes, Enoch P.,	126
Hoopes, Esther,	227
Hoopes, Eva,	346
Hoopes, Franklin T.,	197
Hoopes, Hannah,	242
Hoopes, Hannah,	248
Hoopes, Henry,	149
Hoopes, Jane,	230
Hoopes, Jane G.,	314
Hoopes, Jasper,	137
Hoopes, John,	155
Hoopes, Joseph D.,	202
Hoopes, Joshua,	109
Hoopes, Joshua,	164
Hoopes, Lavinia R.,	295
Hoopes, Levi,	176
Hoopes, Lydia,	260
Hoopes, Lydia,	270
Hoopes, Lydia Ann,	308
Hoopes, Margaret,	256
Hoopes, Mary,	274
Hoopes, Mary Ann,	278
Hoopes, Mary Ann,	299
Hoopes, Mary G.,	308
Hoopes, Morris,	192
Hoopes, Passmore,	115
Hoopes, Peirce,	124
Hoopes, Phebe,	100
(See Pennock.)	
Hoopes, Phebe,	293
Hoopes, Phebe,	334
Hoopes, Phebe Emma,	327
Hoopes, Priscilla,	328
Hoopes, Rachel,	288
Hoopes, Rachel,	308
Hoopes, Ralston R.,	173
Hoopes, Rettie W.,	346
Hoopes, Ruth Anna,	296
Hoopes, Samuel,	111
Hoopes, Sarah,	264
Hoopes, Sarah,	275
Hoopes, Sarah,	295
Hoopes, Sarah D.,	316
Hoopes, Sarah P.,	295
Hoopes, Susan T.,	336
Hoopes, Susanna,	235
Hoopes, Thomas,	115
Hoopes, Thomas,	163
Hoopes, Thomas D.,	164
Hoopes, Townsend,	149
Hoopes, Towns'd W.,	191
Hoopes, W. Walter,	186
Hoopes, William,	164
Hooton, Anna W.,	102
(See Warrington.)	
Hooton, Charles,	121
Hooton, Elizabeth,	268
Hooton, Hannah,	232
Hooton, Joseph,	143
Hooton, Mary,	250
Hooton, Priscilla A.,	255
Hopkins, Anna,	314
Hopkins, Anna R.,	330
Hopkins, Beulah,	100
(*Nicholson*,) "	100
Hopkins, Bessie J.,	330
Hopkins, C. Canby,	200
Hopkins, Daniel W.,	190
Hopkins, Deborah,	242
Hopkins, Edward C.,	179
Hopkins, Elizabeth,	235
Hopkins, Frank N.,	179
Hopkins, Gerard,	160
Hopkins, Hannah,	97
Hopkins, Hannah R.,	331
Hopkins, Hannah W.,	241
Hopkins, John,	182
Hopkins, John A.,	198
Hopkins, Johns,	193
Hopkins, Law'nce H.,	168
Hopkins, Lewis N.,	162
Hopkins, Mary E.,	345
Hopkins, Mary J.,	312

INDEX. 399

Name	Page	Name	Page	Name	Page
Hopkins, Nicholas,	109	Howell, Patience,	261	Hunn, Gulielma,	265
Hopkins, Priscilla,	256	Howell, Sally,	299	Hunn, John,	140
Hopkins, Rebecca,	224	*Howell, Samuel,*	95	Hunn, Jonathan,	98
Hopkins, Rebecca,	226	Howell, Samuel,	108	*Hunn, Patience,*	98
Hopkins, Rebecca,	227	Howell, Samuel D.,	125	Hunn, Patience,	261
Hopkins, Rebecca M.,	313	Howell, Sarah,	248	Hunt, Ann,	261
Hopkins, Rebecca W.,	333	Howell, Susanna,	227	Hunt, Anna,	302
Hopkins, Robert G.,	139	Howey, Martha,	260	Hunt, Asenath,	330
Hopkins, Samuel,	165	Howey, Rebecca,	256	Hunt, Benjamin,	133
Hopkins, Sarah,	229	Howey, Sibyl T.,	346	Hunt, Caleb S.,	139
Hopkins, Sarah, Jr.,	98	Howland, Mary R.,	259	Hunt, Charles,	157
Hopkins, William T.,	155	*Hozie, Henry N.,*	88	Hunt, Daria W.,	161
Hopper, Elizabeth,	268	Hoyle, William G.,	186	Hunt, David,	127
Hopper, Sarah,	243	Hubbs, Anna B.,	287	Hunt, Deborah,	278
Horne, Elizabeth E.,	277	Hubbs, Beulah,	256	Hunt, Edmund,	150
Horne, Henrietta M.,	285	Hubbs, Rebecca H.,	278	Hunt, Eleanor,	302
Horney, Charles,	177	Huey, Deborah,	304	Hunt, Elisha H.,	152
Hoskins, Abigail,	83	Huey, Joseph D.,	159	Hunt, Eliza,	287
Hoskins, Anna M.,	241	Huey, Mary H.,	320	Hunt, Eliza W.,	256
Hoskins, Anna Maria,	235	Huey, Pennock,	153	Hunt, Elizabeth,	225
Hoskins, Dorothea,	244	Huey, Sarah W.,	320	Hunt, Elizabeth,	263
Hoskins, Henry G.,	121	Hughes, Alfred,	167	Hunt, Elizabeth,	279
Hoskins, John,	95	Hughes, Ann,	230	Hunt, Elizabeth,	336
Hoskins, Mary,	254	Hughes, George P.,	161	Hunt, Ellwood,	162
Hough, Mary,	95	Hughes, Hannah,	253	Hunt, Emmor,	126
Hough, Mary,	241	Hughes, James T.,	164	Hunt, Esther,	274
Hough, Mary,	264	Hughes, Joseph,	157	Hunt, Ezra,	148
Hough, Oliver,	127	Hughes, Lydia C.,	318	Hunt, George A.,	184
Hough, Rebecca,	237	*Hughes, Lydia, Jr.,*	100	Hunt, Gibbons,	107
House, Amos W.,	143	Hughes, Margaret,	232	Hunt, Hannah,	223
House, Anna S.,	330	Hughes, Margaret,	276	Hunt, Howard A.,	160
House, Benjamin S.,	174	Hughes, Mark,	167	Hunt, John,	113
House, Eliza W.,	305	Hughes, Mary,	292	*Hunt, John,*	96
House, Jehu,	114	Hughes, Rebecca,	276	Hunt, Joshua,	142
House, Martha D.,	302	Hughes, Richard,	165	Hunt, Marianna,	314
" " (Teacher,)	86	Hughes, Samuel,	155	Hunt, Marshall J.,	133
(Allen,) " (Com.,)	102	Hughes, William,	144	Hunt, Mary,	280
" " (Matron,)	80	Hull, Mary P.,	289	Hunt, Mary,	291
House, Mary,	298	Hulme, Edward S.,	194	Hunt, Naomi,	227
House, Rachel S.,	230	Hulme, Elizabeth K.,	327	Hunt, Nathan C.,	167
House, Sarah T.,	308	Hulme, Emily,	337	Hunt, Priscilla,	339
House, Susanna,	312	Hulme, James,	125	*Hunt, Rachel,*	96
House, William E.,	159	Hulme, John,	128	Hunt, Rachel,	235
House, William H.,	183	Hulme, John K.,	180	Hunt, Rachel,	237
Howard, Charles D.,	123	Hulme, Joseph R.,	116	(Roberts,) " (Com.,)	99
Howard, Henry,	112	Hulme, Joshua S.,	127	" " (Matron,)	79
Howell, Ann,	269	Hulme, Rebecca,	253	Hunt, Ruth A.,	291
Howell, Anna E.,	103	Hulme, Rebecca Ann,	263	Hunt, Sarah M.,	330
(See Emlen.)		Hulme, Robert R.,	186	Hunt, Susan,	272
Howell, Arthur,	136	Hulme, Samuel,	139	Hunt, William,	169
Howell, Catharine,	95	Hulme, Samuel, Jr.,	197	Huntington, Chas. E.,	189
Howell, Deborah,	99	Hulme, Sarah,	259	Hurford, Hannah,	232
Howell, Elizabeth,	97	Hulme, Susan,	253	Husband, Ann,	251
Howell, Elizabeth,	266	Hulme, T. Kirkbride,	197	Husband, Hannah P.,	324
Howell, Elizabeth,	303	Hulme, Thomas C.,	127	Husband, Harman,	122
Howell, Elizabeth R.,	316	Humes, Elmira C.,	338	Husband, John,	123
Howell, Hannah,	227	Humes, J. Edwin,	194	Husband, Joshua,	129
Howell, Hannah,	230	Humphreys, Eliz.,	224	Husband, Joshua, Jr.,	186
Howell, Hannah,	252	Humphreys, Eliz.,	300	Husband, Joseph,	114
Howell, Jacob,	152	Humphreys, John,	155	Husband, Margaret,	271
Howell, John R.,	140	Humphreys, Mary,	282	Husband, Mary,	234
Howell, Joseph,	97	Humphreys, Mary,	288	Husband, Thomas J.,	136
Howell, Joshua,	149	Humphreys, Richard,	129	Husband, William P.,	179
Howell, Margaret A.,	248	Humphreys, Wm. L.,	138	Hussey, Mary,	228
Howell, Mary,	228	Humphreys, Wm. W.,	137	Hussey, William F.,	118
Howell, Mary,	252	Hunn, Ann,	228	Hustler, Isabel,	259
Howell, Mary,	266	Hunn, Elizabeth,	282	Hustler, Mary,	259
Howell, Mary M.,	275	Hunn, Ezekiel,	130	Hustler, Phebe,	263

30

INDEX.

Name	Page
Hutchinson, Abigail,	244
" "(Com.,)	102
Hutchinson, David,	111
Hutchinson, Eliza'h,	234
Hutchinson, Han. A.,	292
Hutchinson, John,	106
Hutchinson, John F.,	151
Hutchinson, John P.,	148
Hutchinson, Joseph,	117
Hutchinson, Jos. P.,	151
Hutchinson, Mary,	296
Hutchinson, Phebe J.,	297
Hutchinson, Samuel,	128
Hutchinson, Thos. T.,	112
Hutton, Ann S.,	299
Hutton, Anna T.,	345
Hutton, Annie W.,	318
Hutton, George S.,	184
Hutton, Hannah,	229
Hutton, Harmon L.,	190
Hutton, J. Wetherill,	199
Hutton, James,	116
Hutton, John,	107
Hutton, Mabel,	248
Hutton, Mary Ann,	254
Hutton, Mary Y.,	334
Hutton, Priscilla,	312
Hutton, Rebecca,	332
Hutton, Richard W.,	172
Hutton, Samuel T.,	206
Hutton, Susan,	333
Hutton, William,	178
Iden, Elizabeth,	238
Iden, Jane,	235
Iden, Sarah,	238
Iden, Susanna,	245
Ingham, Isaiah,	109
Ingham, Lydia,	254
Ingham, Mary,	227
Ingram, Abigail,	235
Iredell, Charles,	125
Irish, Franklin,	135
Irish, Washington,	135
Irwin, Hannah,	228
Irwin, Mary A. M.,	320
Irwin, Thomas,	114
Isaac, Emma C.,	337
Isaac, Stephen B.,	192
Ivins, Ann,	239
Ivins, George W.,	160
Ivins, George W.,	178
Ivins, Hannah H.,	335
Ivins, Lambert,	154
Ivins, Peter Ellis,	203
Ivins, Robert B.,	177
Ivins, Wardell,	148
Ivins, William C.,	144
Jackson, Abigail,	251
Jackson, Elizabeth H.,	271
Jackson, Ephraim J.,	160
Jackson, Hannah B.,	234
Jackson, Holiday,	97
Jackson, Isaac,	92
Jackson, Isaac P.,	166
Jackson, Jacob,	123
Jackson, James C.,	137
" (Teacher,)	85, 86
Jackson, Jane,	100
Jackson, John,	132
Jackson, G. John,	141
" "(Teacher,)	85
Jackson, John H.,	160
Jackson, Lydia,	230
Jackson, Lydia,	255
Jackson, Martha,	233
Jackson, Mary H.,	256
Jackson, Mary K.,	318
Jackson, Mary S.,	257
Jackson, M'ry S.,	323
Jackson, Philena P.,	312
Jackson, Samuel S.,	121
Jackson, Thomas,	128
Jackson, Thomas,	174
Jackson, William,	95
Jackson, William,	113
Jackson, William B.,	174
Jacob, Charles P.,	206
Jacob, Frederick,	206
Jacob, Joseph P.,	206
Jacob, Walter W.,	206
Jacobs, Camilla,	260
Jacobs, Isaac,	109
Jacobs, John,	98
Jacobs, Margaret,	245
Jacobs, Margaretta T.,	84
Jacobs, Richard,	132
Jacobs, Samuel,	129
Jacobs, Sarah,	228
Jacobs, Sarah,	83
Jacobs, Sidney,	257
Jacobs, Thomas,	108
Jacobs, William,	110
James, Cheyney,	157
James, Edwin,	136
James, Edwin S.,	195
James, Esther,	281
James, Hannah J.,	312
James, J. Edwin,	204
James, Jesse,	160
James, John,	118
James, John,	99
James, John,	145
James, John M.,	176
James, Joseph,	115
James, Lydia T.,	340
James, Mary,	278
James, Phincas P.,	176
James, Ruth,	223
Janney, Ann W.,	287
Janney, Anna M.,	336
Janney, Bernard T.,	174
Janney, Charles,	136
Janney, Charles,	146
Janney, Charles P.,	173
Janney, Cornelia,	310
Janney, Daniel,	110
Janney, Eliza M.,	288
Janney, Francis,	146
Janney, Georgiana,	294
Janney, Hannah,	229
Janney, Israel,	111
Janney, James W.,	183
Janney, John,	186
Janney, John W.,	162
Janney, Johns H.,	162
Janney, Jonas,	164
Janney, Margaret H.,	320
Janney, Martha,	255
Janney, Mary,	328
Janney, Mary Ann,	290
Janney, Nathaniel E.,	173
Janney, Pemberton,	163
Janney, Rebecca T.,	337
Janney, Robert M.,	186
Janney, Samuel A.,	162
Janney, Sarah,	225
Janney, Sarah,	287
Janney, Sarah E.,	287
Janney, Susan W.,	323
Janney, Thomas M.,	184
Janney, William,	157
Janney, William W.,	162
Jarrett, Alice,	240
Jarrett, Ann,	237
Jarrett, Chalkley,	120
Jarrett, Elizabeth,	243
Jarrett, Hannah,	231
Jarrett, Jonathan,	109
Jarrett, Margaret,	272
Jarrett, Martha,	244
Jarrett, Mary,	231
Jarrett, Mary,	233
Jarrett, Rachel,	295
Jarrett, Susan,	245
Jarrett, Susanna A.,	270
Jarrett, Susanna M.,	292
Jarrett, Tacy,	234
Jeanes, Jacob,	119
Jeanes, Leah,	238
Jeanes, Rachel,	233
Jefferis, Ann,	274
" "(Teacher,)	85
Jefferis, Cheyney,	96
Jefferis, Cheyney,	124
Jefferis, Edith,	270
Jefferis, Hannah,	235
Jefferis, Jacob,	131
Jefferis, James,	113
Jefferis, Joshua,	143
Jefferis, Lydia,	244
Jefferis, Malinda,	238
Jefferis, Martha,	99
" "(Matron,)	79
(See Sharpless.)	
Jefferis, Martha,	265
Jefferis, Mary,	264
Jefferis, William L.,	179
Jefferson, Hannah M.,	263
Jenkins, Ann,	240
Jenkins, Elizabeth,	242
Jenkins, Ezekiel,	122
Jenkins, Frances A.,	305
Jenkins, Gulielma,	301
Jenkins, Halliday,	130
Jenkins, Jabez,	136
Jenkins, Jabez H.,	163
Jenkins, John H.,	168
Jenkins, Martha N.,	276
Jenkins, Mary,	241
Jenkins, Mary N.,	292
Jenkins, Samuel H.,	166
Jenkins, Tabitha,	275
Jenkins, William L.,	128

INDEX. 401

Name	PAGE
Jenkinson, Eliza,	243
Jenkinson, Mary M.,	304
Jenks, Alexander R.,	197
Jenks, Ann W.,	268
Jenks, Anna,	291
Jenks, Eliza,	232
Jenks, Hannah,	289
Jenks, Hannah W.,	264
Jenks, M H.,	189
Jenks, Rebecca E.,	289
Jenks, Richard L.,	196
Jenks, Watson,	111
Jenks, William E.,	196
Jenks, William H.,	177
Jenness, Elizabeth M.,	329
Jenness, William S.,	182
Jennings, George L.,	185
Jennings, Sarah,	282
Jess, Ann,	240
Jess, Ann,	277
Jess, Rachel,	245
Jessop, Alfred,	187
Jessop, Hannah G.,	331
Jobson, Joseph,	130
Jobson, Joseph,	134
John, Alice,	273
John, Sarah,	238
Johnson, Benjamin,	128
Johnson, Caleb,	120
Johnson, Cordelia B.,	332
Johnson, Edward,	109
Johnson, Edward,	134
Johnson, Ellwood,	151
Johnson, Frederick B.,	190
Johnson, George B.,	191
Johnson, George K.,	142
Johnson, Hannah,	248
Johnson, Hannah H.,	247
Johnson, J. Anderson,	202
Johnson, Jane,	99
Johnson, Jane,	298
Johnson, Jane,	327
Johnson, Jemima D.,	321
Johnson, John,	97
Johnson, Joseph,	115
Johnson, Joseph,	186
Johnson, Lindley F.,	199
Johnson, Lydia,	218
Johnson, Lydia C.,	321
Johnson, Mary,	257
Johnson, Mary S.,	341
Johnson, Nathan H.,	156
Johnson, Rachel,	236
Johnson, Rachel,	244
Johnson, Rachel,	263
Johnson, Rachel,	282
Johnson, Rachel M.,	319
Johnson, Richards,	119
Johnson, Richards H.,	178
Johnson, Rowland,	139
Johnson, Ruth,	252
Johnson, Samuel,	120
Johnson, Samuel,	179
Johnson, William,	186
Johnson, William C.,	171
Johnson, William S.,	126
Jolliffe, Elizabeth A.,	319
Jolliffe, Elizabeth H.,	331
Jolliffe, Fannie M.,	331
Jolliffe, George J.,	194
Jolliffe, Joseph J.,	185
Jolliffe, Rachel W.,	340
Jolliffe, Sarah S.,	327
Jolliffe, Susan,	320
Jolliffe, Thomas H.,	176
Jolliffe, Townsend S.,	203
Jolliffe, William,	178
Jolliffe, William H.,	176
Jones, Abraham,	174
Jones, Alfred,	159
Jones, Alfred B.,	202
Jones, Amy,	273
Jones, Ann,	227
Jones, Ann,	247
Jones, Ann,	285
Jones, Ann E.,	316
Jones, Ann E.,	317
Jones, Anna,	216
Jones, Anna,	345
Jones, Anna S.,	341
Jones, Arthur H.,	206
Jones, Beulah,	283
Jones, Caleb,	141
Jones, Charles,	138
Jones, Christopher H.,	182
Jones, Cynthia E.,	302
Jones, Cyrus,	118
Jones, Deborah,	313
Jones, Edward B.,	200
Jones, Edward C.,	175
Jones, Edward H.,	190
Jones, Edward M.,	196
Jones, Eliza,	275
Jones, Elizabeth,	271
Jones, Elizabeth,	297
Jones, Elizabeth,	301
Jones, Elizabeth,	313
Jones, Elizabeth Ann,	295
Jones, Elizabeth B.,	278
Jones, Elizabeth S.,	304
Jones, Emily,	295
Jones, Enos S.,	195
Jones, Esther P.,	278
Jones, Ezra,	121
Jones, Ezraetta,	341
Jones, George,	153
Jones, Hannah,	223
Jones, Hannah,	228
Jones, Hannah,	231
Jones, Hannah,	234
Jones, Hannah,	250
Jones, Hannah,	269
Jones, Hannah M.,	335
Jones, Harriet,	240
Jones, Henry E.,	194
Jones, Henry M.,	188
Jones, Howard F.,	200
Jones, Isaac,	153
Jones, Isaac,	180
Jones, Israel,	116
Jones, J. Albertson,	195
Jones, James H.,	171
Jones, James S.,	152
Jones, Jane,	232
Jones, Jane,	274
Jones, Jane S.,	317
Jones, Jeremiah,	164
Jones, Jesse,	98
Jones, Jesse,	132
Jones, John,	95
Jones, John,	109
Jones, John B.,	181
Jones, John Barclay,	192
Jones, John P.,	135
Jones, John T.,	177
Jones, Jonathan,	119
Jones, Jonathan, Jr.,	181
Jones, Jonathan C.,	131
Jones, Jonathan T.,	144
Jones, Joseph,	107
Jones, Joseph,	136
Jones, Joseph,	146
Jones, Joseph,	174
Jones, Joseph W.,	172
Jones, Josiah,	139
Jones, Josiah F.,	152
Jones, Kezia S.,	305
Jones, Lambert J.,	201
Jones, Laura,	333
Jones, Letitia,	244
Jones, Luella E.,	346
Jones, Lydia,	245
Jones, Lydia A.,	236
Jones, Lydia D.,	338
Jones, Lydia S.,	269
Jones, Margaret,	279
Jones, Margaret H.,	325
Jones, Maria,	251
Jones, Maria A.,	240
Jones, Martha,	263
Jones, Mary,	224
Jones, Mary,	231
Jones, Mary,	240
Jones, Mary,	286
Jones, Mary,	319
Jones, Mary,	336
Jones, Mary Ann,	258
Jones, Mary Ann,	294
Jones, Mary Ann,	343
Jones, Mary Anna,	313
Jones, Mary C.,	258
Jones, Mary E.,	322
Jones, Nathan,	133
Jones, Nathaniel,	186
Jones, Priscilla,	238
Jones, Priscilla,	244
Jones, Priscilla,	246
Jones, Rachel,	272
Jones, Rachel T.,	291
Jones, Rebecca,	95
Jones, Rebecca,	224
Jones, Rebecca,	289
Jones, Ruth Ann,	292
Jones, S. Morris,	193
Jones, Samuel,	165
Jones, Samuel T.,	120
Jones, Sarah,	237
Jones, Sarah,	253
Jones, Sarah,	274
Jones, Sarah,	292
Jones, Sarah F.,	335
" (Teacher,)	90, 91
Jones, Sarah H.,	335
Jones, Sarah R.,	289

	PAGE		PAGE		PAGE
Jones, Solomon,	105	Kersey, Joseph,	116	Kinsey, Lydia Ann,	314
Jones. Solomon,	152	Kersey, Mary,	248	Kinsey, Pearson,	136
Jones, Stacy,	163	Kersey, Mary,	267	Kinsey, R. Emmarine,	327
Jones, Susan,	302	Kester, Benjamin,	108	Kinsey, Rachel,	247
Jones, Susanna,	228	Kester, Elizabeth H.,	326	Kinsey, Rachel C.,	327
Jones, Thomas B.,	180	Kester, Hannah,	266	Kinsey, Sarah Jane,	274
Jones, Walter,	193	Kester, Hannah,	314	Kinsey, Sarah Jane,	328
Jones, Walter M.,	200	Kester, Jane A.,	326	Kinsey, Thomas,	176
Jones, John,	118	Kester, John,	133	Kinsey, William,	141
Jones, William,	181	Kester, Joseph,	184	Kinsey, William,	145
Jones, William H.,	126	Kester, Josephine L.,	346	Kirby, Hannah,	301
Jones, William P.,	166	Kester, Mary C.,	335	Kirby, Priscilla,	303
Jones, William P.,	177	Kester, Samuel B.,	188	Kirby, Robert,	118
Jordan, Ann,	240	Kester, Sarah,	265	Kirk, Abner G.,	132
Jordan, David,	121	Kille, Horace L.,	198	Kirk, Alphonso,	171
Jordan, Robert W.,	115	Kille, Elizabeth E.,	340	Kirk, Anna Mary,	295
Judkins, Rebecca,	308	Kimber, Anna,	249	(*Townsend*,) " (*Com*.,)	103
Justice, Edward R.,	124	*Kimber, Emmor*,	83	Kirk, Caleb,	111
Justice, Elizabeth,	270	" " (*Com*.,)	98	Kirk, Deborah,	268
Justice, George R.,	124	Kimber, George D.,	151	Kirk, Elizabeth,	248
		Kimber, Isaac,	119	*Kirk, Elizabeth*,	99
Kaighn, Amos E.,	171	Kimber, Joanna S.,	297	Kirk, Elizabeth,	309
Kaighn, Anna Mary,	335	Kimber, Joshua,	168	Kirk, Hannah E.,	323
Kaighn, Bartram,	85	Kimber, Louisa,	337	Kirk, Isaiah,	164
Kaighn, Charles,	126	Kimber, Marm'ke C.,	184	Kirk, John S.,	166
Kaighn, Edward B.,	172	Kimber, Phebe,	277	Kirk, Katherine E.,	346
Kaighn, Elizabeth,	290	Kimber, Regina S.,	297	Kirk, Mahlon,	110
Kaighn, Elizabeth,	324	Kimber, Samuel,	120	Kirk, Margaret,	302
Kaighn, Elizabeth B.,	317	Kimber, Samuel S.,	165	Kirk, Mary,	229
Kaighn, John,	118	Kimber, Susan,	252	Kirk, Mary,	240
Kaighn, John,	175	Kimber, Teresa J.,	282	Kirk, Mary Ann,	262
Kaighn, John M.,	100	Kimber, Thomas,	111	Kirk, Priscilla,	224
Kaighn, John M.,	189	" " (*B'k-kpr*.,)	92	Kirk, Samuel,	110
Kaighn, Joseph,	98	" " (*Com*.,)	100	Kirk, Sarah S.,	343
Kaighn, Joseph M.,	151	Kimber, Thomas,	150	Kirk, William,	154
Kaighn, Mary Anna,	321	Kimber, William,	119	Kirkbride, Ann,	280
Kaighn, Richard,	192	Kimber, William B.,	165	Kirkbride, Ann J.,	318
Kaighn, Sarah H.,	329	Kimber, William G.,	193	Kirkbride, Anna B.,	337
Kaighn, Sarah M.,	286	Kimberly, Samuel,	146	Kirkbride, Anna E.,	335
Kaighn, William B.,	89	King, Abigail,	246	Kirkbride, Elizabeth,	245
Kaighn, William B.,	129	King, Anna W.,	317	Kirkbride, Elizabeth,	260
Kashner, Daniel S.,	201	King, Annabella,	249	Kirkbride, Frances,	230
Kashner, Edward A.,	186	King, Eleanor,	242	Kirkbride, George B.,	186
Kashner, Esther Ann,	325	King, Eleanor,	216	*Kirkbride, Hannah*,	97
Kashner, Margaretta,	313	King, Elizabeth G.,	315	Kirkbride, Harriet,	238
Kashner, Penelope,	338	King, George C.,	178	Kirkbride, Harriet F.,	335
Kashner, William H.,	187	King, Lydia T.,	273	Kirkbride, Harriet P.,	293
Kay, Clement H.,	124	King, Martha,	231	Kirkbride, J. Paul,	186
Kay, Deborah E.,	236	King, Mary,	256	*Kirkbride, John*,	100
Kay, Ellwood,	147	King, Vincent,	108	Kirkbride, John P.,	111
Kay, James W.,	151	King, William G.,	178	Kirkbride, Julia A.,	238
Kay, Sarah,	269	King, William W.,	116	Kirkbride, Julia C.,	330
Kemp, Eleanor,	254	Kinney, Susan J.,	306	Kirkbride, M. Ella,	340
Kemp, Elizabeth,	269	Kinsey, Ann,	282	Kirkbride, Mahlon,	144
Kemp, Elizabeth T.,	327	Kinsey, Cyrus G.,	141	Kirkbride, Mahlon,	191
Kemp, Isabella,	297	Kinsey, Dinah,	272	Kirkbride, Mahlon S.,	135
Kemp, Mary Ann,	262	Kinsey, Edward,	205	Kirkbride, Mary,	238
Kemp, Susanna,	282	Kinsey, Emily,	312	Kirkbride, Mary,	272
Kemp, William,	137	Kinsey, Emily,	319	Kirkbride, Mary,	285
Kenderdine, Eliza'h,	285	Kinsey, Ezra,	150	Kirkbride, Rachel,	246
Kennard, Mary E.,	341	Kinsey, George,	136	Kirkbride, Rebecca S.,	296
Kennard, Sarah J.,	346	Kinsey, George C.,	182	Kirkbride, Rich'd M.,	139
Kenny, Eleanor,	266	Kinsey, Hannah Elma,	314	*Kirkbride, Robert*,	95
Kenny, Jane,	246	Kinsey, Isaac L.,	205	Kirkbride, Sarah A.,	249
Kersey, Ann,	296	*Kinsey, John*,	98	Kirkbride, Wm. B.,	194
Kersey, Gerard C.,	152	Kinsey, John F.,	179	Kirkwood, John,	133
Kersey, Hannah,	245	Kinsey, John W.,	186	Kirkwood, Mary,	278
Kersey, Jesse,	98	Kinsey, Lewis C.,	184	Kirkwood, Reb'ca A.,	288

INDEX. 403

Name	PAGE	Name	PAGE	Name	PAGE
Kirkwood, Wm. F.,	160	Ladd, Anna Maria,	257	Larkin, Mary,	295
Kitchen, Samuel,	166	Ladd, Hannah,	324	Larkin, Milton W.,	197
Kite, Abigail,	326	Ladd, Isabella,	234	Larkin, Mordecai,	168
Kite, Anna E.,	332	Ladd, Isabella,	281	Larkin, Pennell,	147
Kite, Anna H.,	339	Ladd, James,	144	Larkin, Pennell,	193
Kite, Benjamin,	120	Ladd, Oliver,	116	Larkin, Phebe M.,	311
Kite, Elizabeth S.,	342	Ladd, Mary Ann,	285	Larkin, Reece,	170
Kite, Esther,	316	Ladd, Sarah,	235	Larkin, S. Rebecca,	343
" " (Teacher,)	87	Lafetra, Jane,	276	Larkin, Sarah,	277
Kite, Hannah,	322	Lafetra, Lydia,	273	Larkin, Shelly,	201
Kite, J. Albin,	197	Lafetra, Mary,	263	Larkin, Sidney S.,	337
Kite, James,	127	Laing, Annabella,	233	Larkin, William S.,	205
Kite, James,	159	Laing, Joel,	113	Larkin, Z. Amy,	343
Kite, James R.,	176	Laing, John F.,	129	Latimer, John R.,	115
Kite, Jehu L.,	139	Laing, Margaret G.,	262	Latimer, Mary R.,	210
Kite, John L.,	117	Lake, Lucinda,	306	*Latimer, Sarah*,	99
Kite, Lydia, Jr.,	325	" " (Teacher,)	92	Lawrence, Ann,	270
Kite, Mary,	317	Lamb, George M.,	184	Lawrence, Anna,	317
Kite, Nathan,	195	Lamb, John E.,	124	Lawrence, Elizabeth,	257
Kite, Rebecca,	275	Lamb, Philena,	252	Lawrence, Henry,	163
" " (Teacher,)	85, 86	Lamborn, Albina,	305	Lawrence, Isaac,	112
Kite, Rebecca,	322	Lamborn, Alice D.,	332	Lawrence, Marsha,	240
Kite, Ruth,	317	Lamborn, Ann B.,	283	Lawrence, Mary,	317
Kite, Susanna,	263	Lamborn, Ann J.,	279	Lawrence, Mordecai,	123
Kite, Susanna,	326	Lamborn, Ann M.,	301	Lawrence, Samuel,	108
Kite, Susanna S.,	321	Lamborn, Arthur,	206	Lawrence, Sarah,	245
Kite, Thomas,	138	Lamborn, Benjamin,	164	Lawrie, Abigail,	256
Kite, Thomas,	100	Lamborn, Charles,	197	Lawrie, Ann,	250
Kite, William,	88	Lamborn, Eli W.,	131	Lawrie, James,	127
Kite, William, Jr.,	185	Lamborn, Elizabeth,	282	Lawrie, Lucy Ann,	216
Kite, William Henry,	190	Lamborn, Elizabeth,	300	Lawrie, Susanna,	211
Klein, John E.,	146	Lamborn, Emma,	346	*Lawrie, Thomas*,	98
Knight, Anna,	308	Lamborn, Ezra,	198	Lawrie, William,	117
Knight, Dubre,	93	Lamborn, Hannah,	272	Lawrie, William,	159
" " (Supt.,)	80	Lamborn, Hannah,	288	Laws, Ann,	217
Knight, Eliza,	247	Lamborn, John,	131	Laws, Daniel,	122
Knight, Elizabeth,	258	Lamborn, Louis,	195	Laws, Elijah,	117
Knight, Elizabeth,	270	Lamborn, Mary,	238	Laws, Elizabeth,	259
Knight, Elizabeth,	286	Lamborn, Mary R.,	340	Laws, George W.,	120
Knight, Elizabeth,	306	Lamborn, Phebe,	312	Laws, John M.,	123
Knight, Elizabeth H.,	268	Lamborn, Rachel B.,	347	Laws, Lydia,	209
" " (Teacher,)	81	Lamborn, Samuel,	198	Laws, Mary,	263
(Passmore,)" (Com.,)	100	Lamborn, Susanna,	266	Laws, Nelson,	126
Knight, Ellen,	319	Lamborn, Thomas,	144	Laws, Thomas,	120
Knight, Esther,	225	Lamborn, Thomas,	149	Laws, William,	121
Knight, Israel,	133	Lamborn, William,	168	Lea, Catharine M.,	278
Knight, Jane W.,	80	Lamborn, Ziba,	166	Lea, Elizabeth,	242
(See Edwards.)		Lancaster, Elizabeth,	275	Lea, George,	108
Knight, Joseph,	119	Lancaster, Harriet,	251	Lea, Joseph,	137
Knight, Martha,	295	Lancaster, John,	123	Lea, Margaret,	223
Knight, Mary,	267	Lancaster, Letitia,	253	Lea, Mary,	226
Knight, Mary,	309	Lancaster, Mary,	250	Lea, Ruth,	233
Knight, Nathan T.,	119	Lancaster, Rebecca,	273	Lea, Thomas,	106
Knight, Oliver,	151	Lancaster, Sarah,	247	Lea, Thomas,	108
Knight, Rachel,	302	Landis, Henry,	108	Lea, Thomas T.,	128
Knight, Samuel,	106	Lane, Henry D.,	194	Lea, Susan,	244
Knight, Samuel,	151	Large, Isaiah,	119	Lear, Barclay,	188
Knight, Sarah E.,	312	Large, Joseph,	120	Lear, Isaac H.,	184
Knight, Sarah S.,	271	Larkin, Edgar D.,	205	Lear, Malin,	193
Knight, Thomas,	135	Larkin, Eliza,	299	Lear, Phebe R.,	329
Knight, Walter,	137	Larkin, Elizabeth,	298	Lear, Robert G.,	178
Knight, William K.,	166	Larkin, Emma,	317	Lear, Susanna,	332
Knight, William R.,	174	Larkin, Enos,	158	Lear, Susanna G.,	334
Knowles, Anna,	257	Larkin, Hannah,	319	Leaver, Elizabeth,	303
Knowles, Caroline S.,	330	Larkin, Isaac,	173	Leaver, George D.,	155
Knowles, Hannah,	235	Larkin, Joseph,	165	Lee, Angeline,	287
Knowles, Mary,	245	Larkin, Martha,	305	Lee, Anna,	307
Knowles, Rebecca,	242	Larkin, Martha,	317	Lee, Armat W.,	161

30 *   X

INDEX.

Name	PAGE
Lee, Catharine,	306
Lee, Charles,	156
Lee, Charles,	188
Lee, Deborah,	305
Lee, Elizabeth P.,	318
Lee, Ellis P.,	177
Lee, Francis W.,	152
Lee, Hannah,	328
Lee, John,	171
Lee, Joshua B.,	148
Lee, Lewis P.,	135
Lee, Margaret,	235
Lee, Martha,	327
Lee, Mary J.,	322
Lee, Mary P.,	317
Lee, Mary P.,	318
Lee, Mary W.,	315
Lee, Miriam,	288
Lee, Rachel,	231
Lee, Rebecca,	322
Lee, Samuel,	112
Lee, Sarah,	303
Lee, Sarah P.,	299
Lee, Thomas,	111
Leedom, Benjamin,	126
Leedom, Edward,	111
Leedom, Erwin J.,	120
Leedom, Jonathan,	134
Leedom, Lydia,	249
Leedom, Mary,	250
Leedom, Sarah J.,	266
Leeds, Ada M.,	338
Leeds, Alfred W.,	199
Leeds, Arthur N.,	206
Leeds, B. Rush,	193
Leeds, Barzillai,	148
Leeds, Beulah,	292
Leeds, Catharine,	244
Leeds, Charles,	148
Leeds, Chas. Henry,	181
Leeds, Charles W.,	202
Leeds, Daniel L., Jr.,	205
Leeds, Elizabeth A.,	328
Leeds, Ella,	346
Leeds, Ezra,	149
Leeds, Hannah S.,	322
Leeds, Henry B.,	201
Leeds, Henry W.,	203
Leeds, Herman H.,	204
Leeds, J. Howell,	184
Leeds, J. Powell,	186
Leeds, Joseph S.,	198
Leeds, Lewis W.,	158
Leeds, Lucy A.,	292
Leeds, Martha,	334
Leeds, Mary,	273
Leeds, Mary Frances,	328
Leeds, Mary W.,	338
Leeds, Morris E.,	205
Leeds, Nathan B.,	191
Leeds, Rebecca A.,	323
Leeds, Rebecca S.,	280
" " (*Teacher,*)	85
(*Allen,*) " (*Com.,*)	102
Leeds, Ruth Ann,	337
Leeds, Ruth B.,	332
Leeds, S. Bolton,	204
Leeds, Samuel,	139

Name	PAGE
Leeds, Samuel,	85
Leeds, Samuel,	167
Leeds, Samuel S.,	188
Leeds, Sarah C.,	336
Leeds, Susan P.,	330
Leeds, Walton B.,	198
Leeds, William W.,	189
Leeds, Wilmer P.,	196
" " (*Teacher,*)	91
Leggett, William F.,	128
Letchworth, Alb't L.,	141
Letchworth, Eliz.,	223
Letchworth, Eliz.,	304
Letchworth, John,	98
Letchworth, Sar. H.,	284
Levering, Mary E.,	327
Levick, Hannah,	313
Levick, James J.,	151
Levick, Peter L.,	139
Levick, Peter S.,	143
Levick, Rebecca,	263
Levick, Robert,	174
Levick, Samuel J.,	141
Levick, Sarah A.,	311
Levick, Susanna,	252
Levick, Thomas J.,	159
Levis, Alice,	230
Levis, Ann,	228
Levis, Anna P.,	252
Levis, Catharine,	310
Levis, Elmer,	171
Levis, Evan,	151
Levis, Franklin,	102
Levis, George,	160
Levis, Henrietta G.,	279
Levis, Isaac,	109
Levis, Margaret B.,	304
Levis, Martha,	285
Levis, Mary,	297
Levis, Mary D. B.,	290
Levis, Morris,	159
Levis, Oborn,	142
Levis, Pancoast,	124
Levis, Rebecca,	291
Levis, Samuel,	152
Levis, William,	108
Levis, William,	142
Lewis, Alice,	98
Lewis, Alice,	287
Lewis, Charles,	150
Lewis, Charles W.,	185
Lewis, Davis,	141
Lewis, Elijah,	120
Lewis, Eliza,	278
Lewis, Elizabeth,	292
Lewis, Emily,	289
Lewis, Enoch,	83, 85
" " (*Com.,*)	98
Lewis, Enoch,	141
Lewis, Esther,	258
Lewis, Evan,	109
Lewis, Evan,	120
Lewis, Hannah, Jr.,	98
Lewis, Hannah J.,	246
Lewis, Jane,	227
Lewis, Job M.,	152
Lewis, John G.,	120
Lewis, John P.,	144

Name	PAGE
Lewis, Joseph S.,	155
Lewis, Mary,	239
Lewis, Mary Ann,	295
Lewis, Mary J.,	310
Lewis, Mordecai,	143
Lewis, Pamela,	232
Lewis, Phebe,	264
Lewis, Phebe Ann,	257
Lewis, Rachel S.,	292
Lewis, Samuel S.,	145
Lewis, Sarah,	298
Lewis, Thomas M.,	122
Lightfoot, Ann,	297
Lightfoot, Benjamin,	108
Lightfoot, Benj. H.,	155
Lightfoot, Benj. H.,	157
Lightfoot, Deborah,	299
Lightfoot, Eleanor,	297
Lightfoot, Elizabeth,	290
Lightfoot, Francis,	147
Lightfoot, Hannah M.,	274
Lightfoot, John,	138
Lightfoot, Margaret,	295
Lightfoot, Margaret,	296
" " (*Teacher,*)	86
Lightfoot, Martha J.,	319
Lightfoot, Sarah,	303
Lightfoot, Susanna,	226
Lightfoot, Susanna,	231
Lightfoot, Susanna,	231
Lightfoot, Susanna,	284
" " (*Teacher,*)	85
(*Wood,*) " (*Com.,*)	101
Lightfoot, William,	109
Lindley, Elizabeth D.,	278
Lindley, Hannah M.,	278
Lindley, Jacob,	96
Lindley, Jacob,	108
Lindley, John M.,	156
Lindley, Sarah,	98
Lindley, Sibyl J.,	343
Lindley, T. Ellicott,	183
Lindley, Thomas D.,	133
Lindley, Thomas R.,	123
Lindley, William,	123
Line, Joseph,	126
Linton, Cyrus,	150
Linton, Elizabeth,	311
Linton, Esther A.,	328
Linton, Frances E.,	342
Linton, Hannah,	324
Linton, Harvey,	167
Linton, Morris,	195
Linton, Sarah,	309
Lippincott, Abigail,	301
Lippincott, Allen,	169
Lippincott, Ann,	294
Lippincott, Ann,	326
Lippincott, Ann R.,	267
Lippincott, Ann T.,	266
Lippincott, Anna,	249
Lippincott, Anna,	267
Lippincott, Anna,	317
Lippincott, Asa,	130
Lippincott, Benjamin,	130
Lippincott, Benj. A.,	191
Lippincott, Benj. H.,	122
Lippincott, Beulah,	228

INDEX.
405

Name	PAGE	Name	PAGE	Name	PAGE
Lippincott, Beulah,	228	Lippincott, Miriam,	306	Lloyd, Susanna,	245
Lippincott, Beulah,	277	Lippincott, Nathaniel,	150	Lloyd, William,	144
Lippincott, Beulah R.,	290	Lippincott, Paul S.,	182	*Lockwood, Moses B.*,	85
Lippincott, Charles,	148	Lippincott, Priscilla,	285	Lodge, Mary,	249
Lippincott, Charles,	191	Lippincott, Rebecca,	271	Logan, Harriet,	225
Lippincott, CharlesA.,	205	Lippincott, Rebecca,	320	Logan, Mary,	272
Lippincott, Daniel,	170	Lippincott, Reb'ca C.,	314	Longshore, Mary,	241
Lippincott, Darling,	128	Lippincott, Sam'l H.,	184	Longstreth, Ann,	224
Lippincott, Dinah H.,	102	Lippincott, Sarah,	279	Longstreth, Anna,	255
(See Hilles.)		Lippincott, Sarah,	296	Longstreth, Charles,	106
Lippincott, Edith S.,	292	Lippincott, Sarah A.,	253	Longstreth, Charl'te,	234
Lippincott, Edmund,	131	Lippincott, Sarah A.,	293	Longstreth, Elwood,	203
Lippincott, Edward,	186	Lippincott, Sarah N.,	329	Longstreth, Esther,	265
Lippincott, Elizabeth,	256	Lippincott, Seth,	111	Longstreth, Hannah,	241
Lippincott, Elizabeth,	265	Lippincott, Stacy,	119	Longstreth, Howell,	123
Lippincott, Elizabeth,	323	*Lippincott, Susan E.*,	102	Longstreth, Jane,	225
Lippincott, Eliz'h A.,	310	(See Ecroyd.)		Longstreth, John,	134
Lippincott, Eliz h E.,	316	Lippincott, Susan R.,	324	Longstreth, Lydia,	246
Lippincott, Eliz'h E.,	331	Lippincott, Thos. E.,	162	Longstreth, Martha,	270
Lippincott, Eliz'h H.,	341	Lippincott, Wallace,	123	Longstreth, Mary,	264
Lippincott, Eliz'h N.,	309	Lippincott, Wm. F.,	145	Longstreth, Morris,	120
Lippincott, Eliz'h R.,	279	Lishman, Hannah B.,	296	Longstreth, Morris,	201
Lippincott, Ella P.,	317	Litler, Hannah J.,	344	Longstreth, Samuel,	109
Lippincott, George,	133	Litler, John Oxley,	201	Longstreth, Sarah A.,	287
Lippincott, GraceAnn,	275	Litler, Rachel,	213	Longstreth, Susan,	262
Lippincott, Hannah,	255	Litler, Sarah Ann,	214	Longstreth, Susanna,	246
Lippincott, Hannah,	263	Little, Charles,	115	Longstreth, Thomas,	112
Lippincott, Han'h R.,	346	Little, John,	115	Longstreth, Thomas,	120
Lippincott, Henry,	180	Livezey, Anna,	322	Longstreth, Wm. W.,	121
Lippincott, Henry A.,	198	Livezey, Anna,	340	Lord, Benjamin,	139
Lippincott, HenryW.,	137	" " (*Teacher*,)	90	Lord, James,	126
Lippincott, Hilles,	188	Livezey, Asenath,	238	Lord, James,	143
Lippincott, Hope,	295	Livezey, Charles,	204	Lord, Joshua,	124
Lippincott, Isaac,	173	Livezey, David H.,	148	*Lord, Phineas*,	98
Lippincott, Isaac,	198	Livezey, Hannah,	281	Love, Eleanor,	243
Lippincott, James,	110	Livezey, Han'h Ann,	290	Lovett, George,	171
Lippincott, James S.,	141	Livezey, Jane,	282	Lovett, Hannah Ann,	325
Lippincott, Jesse,	145	Livezey, John, Jr.,	117	Lovett, M. Jane,	333
Lippincott, John,	132	Livezey, Martha,	248	Lovett, Robert P.,	167
Lippincott, John H.,	194	Livezey, Moses,	131	Lowber, Patience,	294
Lippincott, Joseph,	128	Livezey, Oliver,	139	Lower, Amos,	124
Lippincott, Joseph K.,	158	Livezey, Rachel,	251	Lower, Rebecca,	264
Lippincott, JosephK.,	180	Livezey, Thomas,	120	Lowler, Jonathan H.,	139
Lippincott, Jos. K., Jr.,	195	Livezey, William,	182	Lownes, Edward,	199
Lippincott, Joseph T.,	199	Llewellyn, Auron,	128	Lownes, Elias P.,	176
Lippincott, JosephW.,	157	Llewelyn, Anna M.,	347	Lownes, Elizabeth,	317
Lippincott, Lydia,	231	Llewellyn, Baily,	163	Lownes, George,	111
Lippincott, Lydia,	239	Llewellyn, Hannah,	308	Lownes, George B.,	153
Lippincott, Lydia,	252	Llewellyn, John,	174	Lownes, Henry E.,	160
Lippincott, Lydia,	276	*Lloyd, Ann*,	96	Lownes, Hugh M.,	136
(*Walton*,) "(*Com.*,)	102	Lloyd, Bolton,	153	Lownes, Joseph,	110
Lippincott, Lydia,	304	Lloyd, Clement E.,	170	Lownes, Joseph,	157
Lippincott, Lydia H.,	340	Lloyd, Elizabeth,	243	Lownes, Joseph,	183
Lippincott, MarthaD.,	268	Lloyd, Elizabeth,	270	Lownes, Martha,	243
Lippincott, Mary,	228	Lloyd, Elizabeth S.,	297	Lownes, Mary,	314
Lippincott, Mary,	234	Lloyd, Fanny,	325	Lownes, Mary M.,	337
Lippincott, Mary,	244	Lloyd, Franklin,	156	Lownes, Massey,	280
Lippincott, Mary,	269	Lloyd, Hannah,	260	Lownes, Phineas,	142
Lippincott, Mary,	273	Lloyd, Hannah,	279	Lownes, Sidney,	257
Lippincott, Mary,	311	Lloyd, Horace,	169	Lownes, William,	158
Lippincott, Mary A.,	291	Lloyd, Isaac B.,	169	Lowrie, Lydia,	231
Lippincott, MaryB.C.,	343	Lloyd, James,	105	Lowry, Alfred,	192
Lippincott, Mary C.,	336	Lloyd, Joseph,	169	Lowry, Ann M.,	282
Lippincott, Mary E.,	343	Lloyd, Marian B.,	315	Lowry, Benjamin H.,	191
Lippincott, Mary H.,	337	Lloyd, Mary,	254	Lowry, Charles,	170
Lippincott, Mary S.,	280	Lloyd, Richard,	131	Lowry, Edward S.,	170
Lippincott, Miriam,	100	Lloyd, Samuel E.,	154	Lowry, Isaac M.,	150
Lippincott, Miriam,	272	Lloyd, Sarah E.,	304	Lowry, Isaac S.,	182

INDEX.

Name	PAGE
Lowry, John S.,	182
Lowry, Lydia S.,	324
Lowry, Margaret,	276
Lowry, William C.,	192
Luff, Elizabeth,	267
Luff, Susanna,	226
Luff, Thomas,	107
Lukens, Alice,	238
Lukens, Ann N.,	296
Lukens, Casper P.,	155
Lukens, Charlotte,	246
Lukens, Elizabeth,	326
Lukens, Elizabeth W.,	279
Lukens, Hannah W.,	329
Lukens, Harriet,	260
Lukens, John,	112
Lukens, Martha,	245
Lukens, Martha,	270
Lukens, Martha T.,	321
Lukens, Mary Anna,	338
Lukens, Phebe,	312
Lukens, Phebe,	316
Lukens, Priscilla A.,	276
Lukens, Rachel,	269
Lukens, Rebecca,	246
Lukens, Reuben,	151
Lukens, Ruth Ann,	266
Lukens, Sarah,	238
Lukens, Sarah,	298
Lukens, Sarah,	324
Lukens, Solomon,	101
Lukens, Susanna,	300
Lukens, Tacy,	255
Lukens, Thomas E.,	151
Lukens, Violetta,	256
Lukens, Willet,	171
Lukens, William,	125
Lukens, William F.,	147
Lundy, Abigail,	253
Lunny, Lydia,	257
Lupton, Sarah Ann,	257
Lynn, Mary,	229
Lytle, Cidney,	164
Lytle, Hannah T.,	340
Lytle, Mary R.,	331
Lytle, Richard H.,	202
Lytle, Ruth Anna,	331
McCarty, Ellen,	324
McCarty, Francis,	193
McCarty, Frederic,	192
McCarty, Job,	180
McCarty, Lydia,	246
McCarty, Lucetta,	337
McCarty, Sarah,	325
McCay, Richard B.,	147
McCluen, Harriet J.,	323
McCluen, William,	184
McCollin, Anna G.,	333
McCollin, Frances B.,	355
McCollin, Hann'h E.,	270
McCollin, Marg't M.,	353
" " (*Teacher,*)	91
McCollin, M'rg'tta E.,	321
McCollin, Rebecca,	85
" " (*Gov'ness.*)	80
McCollin, Samuel M.,	175
McCollin, William T.,	184
McConnell, Mary A.,	332

Name	PAGE
McCoy, John C.,	124
McCoy, William,	124
McCnrach, James G.,	122
McFadgen, Cyrus W.,	204
McFadgen, Eliz. J.,	334
McFadgen, Sarah R.,	337
McFadgen, Wilmer L.,	262
McGrew, Agnes V.,	314
" " (*Teacher,*)	91
McGrew, Ann E.,	307
McGrew, Eliz. A.,	332
McGrew, Eulysses A.,	192
McGrew, Gilbert,	192
McGrew, Jasper C.,	195
McGrew, Lydia B.,	333
McGuire, George W.,	195
McIlvain, Abr'am G.,	146
McIlvain, Ann,	268
McIlvain, Eliza,	248
McIlvain, J. H'ph'ys,	132
McIlvain, John H.,	132
McIlvain, Lydia,	268
McIlvain, Rachel,	261
McKand, Martha,	241
McMillan, Maria,	248
McPherson, Eliz.,	225
McPherson, Esther,	241
McPherson, Jane,	225
McPherson, Mary,	241
Macy, Jonathan G.,	116
Macy, William H.,	165
Maddock, Mary,	291
Magarge, Ann,	292
Magarge, Ezra,	156
Magarge, Hannah,	313
Magarge, Rebecca,	311
Magarge, Susanna,	285
Magill, Ann,	273
Magill, Edward H.,	154
Magill, Jacob W.,	157
Magill, Mary,	245
Malin, George,	100
Malin, Jane,	225
" " (*Com.,*)	100
Malin, John,	111
Malin, Joseph,	97
Malin, Joseph A.,	146
Malin, Margaret,	100
Malin, Mary P.,	291
Malin, Rachel,	96
Malin, Randall,	113
Malin, Randall,	157
Malone, Charles T.,	185
Malone, William C.,	185
Manchester, Jerem'h,	127
Mann, Lydia,	232
Maris, Alfred E.,	199
Maris, Beaumont,	140
Maris, Edward,	159
Maris, Emily E.,	327
Maris, Fanny,	336
Maris, Hannah,	278
Maris, Jesse E.,	152
Maris, John M.,	138
Maris, Margaret,	255
Maris, Marianna,	325
Maris, Mary,	280
Maris, Mary,	101

Name	PAGE
Maris, Mary E,	326
Maris, Mary J.,	320
Maris, Mary W.,	313
Maris, Rachel S.,	102, 103
(See Scattergood.)	
Maris, Rebecca D.,	309
Maris, Richard,	177
Maris, Richard W.,	197
Maris, Robert W.,	199
Maris, Sallie,	334
Maris, Samuel W.,	147
Maris, Sarah,	255
Maris, Sarah Ann,	303
Maris, William,	140
Maris, William,	147
Marsh, Agnes E.,	255
Marsh, Anna,	272
Marsh, Benjamin,	139
Marsh, Catharine,	232
Marsh, Elias,	112
Marsh, Elizabeth,	241
Marsh, Gibbons,	127
Marsh, Hannah,	234
Marsh, Hannah G.,	282
Marsh, John H.,	137
Marsh, Joseph R.,	152
Marsh, Lydia S.,	274
Marsh, Phineas,	114
Marsh, Rebecca,	228
Marsh, William,	142
Marshall, Anna E.,	333
Marshall, Anna M.,	323
Marshall, Elizabeth,	265
Marshall, Elizabeth,	282
Marshall, Hannah,	262
Marshall, Henry,	186
Marshall, Humphrey,	95
Marshall, James,	96
Marshall, Margaret,	96
Marshall, Margaret,	247
Marshall, Margaret,	267
Marshall, Margaret,	274
Marshall, Mary,	271
Marshall, Mary Ann,	267
Marshall, Myra,	265
Marshall, Phebe,	282
Marshall, Philena,	99
Marshall, Rebecca,	227
Marshall, Samuel,	109
Marshall, Samuel,	143
Marshall, Sarah,	260
Marshall, Susanna C.,	272
Marshall, Thomas,	140
Marshall, William,	152
Marshall, William L.,	152
Marshall, Wilmer W.,	179
Martin, Agnes Ann,	304
Martin, Caroline,	307
Martin, Eliza,	298
Martin, George,	141
Martin, George,	151
Martin, Henry,	141
Martin, Isaac,	134
Martin, James,	110
Martin, Mary,	294
Martin, Nathan S.,	151
Martin, Oliver,	119
Martin, Oliver D.,	166

INDEX. 407

Name	PAGE	Name	PAGE	Name	PAGE
Martin, Robert T.,	176	Matlack, Ann,	261	Maule, Edward,	168
Martin, Sanderson R.,	160	Matlack, Ann,	293	Maule, Edward R.,	155
Martin, Sarah,	229	Matlack, Anna M.,	271	Maule, Elisha P.,	138
Martin, Sarah,	83	Matlack, Atlantic,	242	Maule, Elizabeth C.,	318
Mason, Beulah,	268	Matlack, Eliza,	244	Maule, Elizabeth L.,	285
Mason, Elizabeth C.,	100	Matlack, Elizabeth,	311	Maule, Emily,	329
(See Cresson.)		Matlack, Ellen,	321	Maule, Evert P.,	182
Mason, Hannah H.,	272	Matlack, George,	171	Maule, Hannah,	229
Mason, Jane,	242	Matlack, Hannah,	236	Maule, Hannah,	260
Mason, John,	84	Matlack, Hannah,	322	Maule, Hannah,	332
Mason, Lewis G.,	136	Matlack, Hephziba,	293	Maule, Hannah E.,	323
Mason, Rachel,	235	Matlack, Jane,	259	Maule, Henry,	151
Mason, Samuel,	119	Matlack, Joseph H.,	199	Maule, Isaac,	172
Mason, Vincent,	142	Matlack, Martha S.,	303	Maule, Israel,	137
Massey, Anne,	260	Matlack, Mary,	237	Maule, Jacob,	124
Massey, Aquila B.,	130	Matlack, Mary C.,	281	Maule, Jacob,	173
Massey, Enmor K.,	150	Matlack, Mary H.,	277	Maule, James,	171
Massey, Enos,	125	Matlack, Mary R.,	321	Maule, Jane,	331
Massey, Esther,	298	Matlack, Mary W.,	343	Maule, John,	171
Massey, George,	96	Matlack, Rachel,	266	Maule, John C.,	178
Massey, George,	156	Matlack, Rachel S.,	282	Maule, Joseph E.,	138
Massey, George V.,	123	Matlack, Rebecca,	290	Maule, Joseph L.,	138
Massey, Hannah,	254	Matlack, Rebecca,	327	Maule, Juliana R.,	296
Massey, Isaac,	122	Matlack, Rebecca B.,	287	Maule, Juliana R.,	340
Massey, Isaac,	131	Matlack, Rebecca S.,	305	Maule, Lavinia,	277
Massey, Lydia,	256	Matlack, Samuel R.,	182	*Maule, Margaret*,	102
Massey, Rachel V.,	264	Matlack, Samuel R.,	180	(See Evans.)	
Massey, Robert V.,	116	Matlack, Sarah,	267	Maule, Margaret, Jr.,	327
Masters, Anna M.,	330	Matlack, Sarah R.,	347	Maule, Margaret J.,	285
Masters, Arthur H.,	296	Matlack, Susanna,	263	Maule, Mary,	317
Masters, Catharine,	326	Matlack, Sidney,	244	" " (*Teacher,*)	88
Masters, David W.,	196	Matlack, Tacy,	258	Maule, Mercy,	225
Masters, Dubre K.,	200	Matlack, William,	181	Maule, Mordecai L.,	151
Masters, Elizabeth,	319	Matlack, William C.,	161	Maule, Penrose,	177
Masters, Elizabeth E.,	332	Matson, Hannah,	284	Maule, Rachel,	328
Masters, Ellis H.,	184	Matson, Rebecca,	287	Maule, Rebecca J.,	264
Masters, Francis,	173	Matson, Sarah,	243	Maule, Samuel,	173
Masters, Harriet E.,	339	Matson, Sarah,	285	*Maule, Sarah*,	97
Masters, J. Howard,	183	Matson, Sarah H.,	309	Maule, Sarah,	317
Masters, J. Parvin,	184	Matthews, Ann,	272	Maule, Sarah Ann,	269
Masters, Jane E.,	311	Matthews, Anna T.,	331	Maule, William D.,	183
Masters, Jas. Wilson,	178	Matthews, David L.,	187	Maule, Zillah,	224
Masters, Laura F.,	345	Matthews, Edith,	234	Maule, Zillah,	227
Masters, Louisa,	339	Matthews, Edward,	127	Maulsby, Alice,	258
Masters, Margaret,	293	Matthews, Edward,	184	Maulsby, George,	134
Masters, Margaret A.,	329	Matthews, Edw'd H.,	178	Maulsby, Hannah,	251
Masters, Mary,	303	Matthews, Eliza,	239	Maxfield, William R.,	119
Masters, Mary R.,	315	Matthews, Elizabeth,	237	Maxwell, Emily P.,	336
Masters, Matilda,	332	Matthews, George,	127	May, Joseph,	139
Masters, Morris E.,	175	Matthews, Henry C.,	168	Mayberry, Jer. W.,	106
Masters, Parvin,	151	Matthews, Joseph,	127	Mears, Charles,	118
Masters, Sarah Emma,	322	Matthews, Joshua,	186	Mears, Edward B.,	134
Masters, Susan,	329	Matthews, Matilda,	236	Mears, Susanna,	242
Masters, William G.,	201	Matthews, Rachel,	232	Mechem, Hannah,	263
Mather, Barthol'ew,	106	Matthews, Rhoda,	228	Mechem, John,	132
Mather, Benjamin,	108	Matthews, Richard,	157	Medcalf, Lydia,	295
Mather, Charles,	150	Matthews, Rich'd J.,	204	Medcalf, Sarah M.,	289
Mather, Charles,	150	Matthews, Samuel,	115	Medcalf, Susanna,	270
Mather, Jane,	284	Matthews, Thos. F.,	178	Meeteer, George,	127
Mather, Joseph,	114	Matthews, Thos. R.,	158	Megear, Thomas J.,	131
Mather, Joseph,	143	Maule, Ann,	249	Megear, William,	128
Mather, Mary Ann,	272	Maule, Ann E.,	314	Mekeel, Amy Q.,	323
Mather, Sarah,	269	Maule, Benjamin,	117	Mekeel, Anna,	301
Mather, Sarah,	281	Maule, Caleb,	113	Mekeel, Anna,	319
Mathis, Joseph,	181	Maule, Caroline H.,	338	Mekeel, Catharine,	323
Mathis, William,	187	Maule, Caroline R.,	285	Mekeel, Elizabeth,	301
Matlack, Abigail,	289	Maule, Cornelia B.,	325	Mekeel, Elizabeth,	320
Matlack, Ann,	233	Maule, Edward,	142	Mekeel, James,	168

408 INDEX.

Name	Page	Name	Page	Name	Page
Mekeel, Jesse,	174	Messick, Mary,	272	*Mifflin*, Ann, Jr.,	97
Mellor, Elizabeth,	348	Michener, Amanda,	340	*Mifflin, Anna,*	97
Meloney, George R.,	199	Michener, Amos J.,	168	Mifflin, Deborah,	223
Meloney, William L.,	204	Michener, Amy E.,	331	Mifflin, Deborah A.,	259
Mendenhall, Anna L.,	329	Michener, Ann,	288	Mifflin, James,	131
Mendenhall, Anna R.,	345	Michener, Aaron J.,	150	Mifflin, John H.,	127
Mendenhall, Anne,	239	Michener, John D.	201	Mifflin, Jonathan W.,	108
Mendenhall, Chas. E.,	189	Michener, Lonisa P.,	282	Mifflin, Joseph,	131
Mendenhall, Ch'lotte,	342	Michener, Marg't D.,	301	Mifflin, Lemuel,	109
Mendenhall, Cyrus,	108	Michener, Mary L.,	321	Mifflin, Lloyd,	105
" " (*Book-keeper,*)	93	" " (*Teacher,*)	88	Mifflin, Mary,	232
Mendenhall, Edward,	178	Michener, Penina F.,	330	Mifflin, Samuel E.,	107
Mendenhall, Eliz.,	322	Michener, Rachel,	300	Mifflin, Thomas,	116
Mendenhall, Esth. L.,	318	Michener, Ruth,	294	*Mifflin, Warner,*	95
Mendenhall, Geo. A.,	201	Michener, Sarah A.,	316	Miller, Anna,	289
Mendenhall, Hannah,	243	Mickle, Anna A.,	344	Miller, Anna,	328
Mendenhall, Henry,	151	Mickle, Annie,	326	Miller, Arthur,	170
Mendenhall, J.Gen'e,	347	Mickle, Eliza,	263	Miller, Benjamin H.,	169
Mendenhall, J.How'd,	200	Mickle, Isaac,	157	Miller, Caleb S.,	198
Mendenhall, Jacob H.	135	Mickle, J. Howard,	202	Miller, Eliza,	311
Mendenhall, Jas. M.,	181	Mickle, John B.,	157	Miller, Elizabeth,	225
Mendenhall, John,	136	Mickle, Joseph,	106	Miller, Esther C.,	315
Mendenhall, JohnW.,	191	Mickle, Joseph E.,	187	Miller, Franklin,	132
Mendenhall, Joseph,	109	Mickle, Keziah,	224	Miller, Guion,	200
Mendenhall, Joseph,	157	*Mickle, Margary,*	97	Miller, Hannah,	237
Mendenhall, Lydia C.,	339	Mickle, Martha,	289	Miller, Isaac,	119
Mendenhall, M. Ella,	338	Mickle, Mary,	326	Miller, James,	108
Mendenhall, Marga't,	252	Mickle, Mary Ann,	263	Miller, Jane,	327
Mendenhall, Martha,	224	Mickle, Priscilla,	225	Miller, John S.,	123
Mendenhall, Martha,	281	Mickle, Robert T.,	201	Miller, Joseph A.,	142
Mendenhall, Mary,	265	Mickle, Samuel,	135	Miller, Joseph H.,	171
Mendenhall, Mary E.,	332	Mickle, Sarah,	280	Miller, Letitia,	225
Mendenhall, Narcissa,	297	Mickle, Sarah,	289	Miller, Levis,	130
Mendenhall, Newlin,	200	(*Tatum,*) " (*Com.,*)	102	Miller, Llewellyn,	171
Mendenhall, Pearl C.,	346	Mickle, Susanna,	280	*Miller, Lydia L.,*	99
Mendenhall, Ph'e A.,	305	Mickle, William,	192	Miller, Margaret,	253
Mendenhall, Ph'e P.,	320	Middleton, Abigail L.,	265	Miller, Margaret W.,	276
Mendenhall, Rachel,	239	Middleton, Amos,	140	Miller, Mary,	243
Mendenhall, Reb'ca,	290	Middleton, Ann,	281	Miller, Mary,	253
Mendenhall, Sarah,	281	Middleton, Benj. H.,	181	Miller, Mary Ann,	259
Mendenhall, Sarah,	320	Middleton, Beulah,	292	*Miller, Phebe,*	97
Mendenhall, Sus. M.,	342	Middleton, Charles,	143	Miller, Phebe,	226
Mendenhall, Wm. P.,	203	Middleton, Edith S.,	322	Miller, Phebe,	243
Mendenhall, Wm.,	180	Middleton, Edward,	1"8	Miller, Rachel,	262
Mendenhall, Wm. L.,	148	Middleton,EdwardT.,	203	Miller, Rachel,	269
Mercer, Ann,	268	Middleton, Elizabeth,	261	Miller, Robert,	121
Mercer, C. Sharpless,	200	Middleton, Ellis,	130	Miller, Robert H.,	185
Mercer, Charles J.,	200	Middleton, Ellis,	182	Miller, Robert V.,	185
Mercer, Margaret,	276	Middleton, Howard,	186	Miller, S. Grant,	206
Mercer, M'garetta A.,	345	Middleton, Jacob R.,	127	Miller, Samuel,	176
Meredith, Eliz'h D.,	301	Middleton, John,	134	Miller, Sarah,	225
" " (*Com.,*)	103	Middleton, Joseph,	134	Miller, Sarah,	231
Meredith, Eliza'h K.,	271	Middleton, Joseph H.,	158	Miller, Sarah,	257
Meredith, Esther,	264	Middleton, Joseph S.,	170	Miller, Thomas P.,	173
Meredith, Isaac,	122	Middleton, Joshua B.,	169	Miller, Thomazine T.,	316
Meredith, Jesse,	92	Middleton, Josiah,	126	Miller, Warwick,	115
Meredith, Mary E.,	270	Middleton, Lydia A.,	247	Miller,WarwickP.,Jr.,	198
Merrefield, Amelia G.,	246	Middleton, Mary,	302	Miller, William,	166
Merrefield, John G.,	119	Middleton, Nathan,	138	*Miller, William P,*	99
Merrefield, Joseph,	141	Middleton,NathanH.,	182	Miller, William H.,	144
Merrefield, Mary,	285	*Middleton, Phebe,*	100	Millhouse, Jane,	231
Merrefield, Sarah A.,	288	(See Sharpless.)		Millhouse, Lydia,	330
Merritt, Alfred C.,	164	Middleton, Phebe E.,	335	Millhouse, Phebe,	228
Merritt, Mary,	230	Middleton, Rachel W.,	322	Milnor, Daniel,	113
Merritt, Mary S.,	298	Middleton, Samuel,	131	Milnor, Mary,	239
Merritt, Rebecca H.,	309	Middleton, Samuel B.,	154	Miner, E. Jannette,	338
Merritt, Sarah,	230	Middleton, Spencer,	149	Minster, Laura P.,	342
Merritt, Sarah W.,	292	Middleton, Thomas,	155	Minster, William W.,	189

INDEX. 409

Name	PAGE	Name	PAGE	Name	PAGE
Mitchell, Hannah,	323	Moore, Isaac,	112	Morgan, Thomas,	108
Mitchell, Hannah D.,	316	Moore, J. Willits,	298	*Morgan, William B.,*	87
Mitchell, Jonathan,	109	Moore, Jane,	245	Morgan, William P.,	199
Mitchell, Joshua,	117	Moore, John,	174	Morris, Alfred,	170
Mitchell, Mary E.,	295	Moore, John M.,	196	Morris, Anthony P.,	117
Mitchell, Rebecca,	266	Moore, John W.,	187	Morris, Benjamin W.,	144
Mitchell, Robert,	172	Moore, Joseph S.,	182	Morris, Beulah,	266
Mitchell, Samuel,	150	Moore, Joseph T.,	165	(*Hacker,*) " (*Com.,*)	101
Mitchell, William,	108	Moore, Josephine D.,	335	Morris, Beulah S.,	303
Mode, James B.,	145	Moore, Joshua,	168	" " (*Com.,*)	102
Mode, William,	96	Moore, Kirkwood,	168	(*Rhoads,*) " (*Com.,*)	103
Monaghan, Hannah,	265	Moore, Leah W.,	230	Morris, Caspar,	129
Monks, Zillah,	310	Moore, Levi,	176	Morris, Catharine,	249
Moon, Alfred H.,	200	Moore, Lizzie A.,	330	Morris, Catharine,	277
Moon, Charles,	143	Moore, Lydia,	245	Morris, Catharine,	318
Moon, Charles H.,	201	Moore, Lydia,	218	*Morris, Catharine,*	97
Moon, Eliza,	285	Moore, Martha W.,	298	Morris, Elliston P.,	163
Moon, Everett,	197	Moore, Mary,	342	Morris, Francis,	181
Moon, James,	107	*Moore, Mary,*	98	Morris, Geo. Spencer,	205
Moon, James,	195	Moore, Mary,	236	Morris, Hannah,	261
Moon, James H.,	162	Moore, Mary,	239	Morris, Hannah P.,	332
Moon, Jane,	100	Moore, Mary,	297	Morris, Isaac P.,	122
Moon, Jane C.,	305	Moore, Mary Anna,	319	*Morris, Isaac W.,*	97
Moon, John B.,	193	Moore, Mary C.,	342	Morris, Israel,	129
Moon, Mahlon,	137	Moore, Mary H.,	301	Morris, James W.,	189
Moon, Mary C.,	334	Moore, Mary W.,	312	Morris, Jane,	273
Moon, Rachel,	290	Moore, Marcy,	269	Morris, Joanna,	289
Moon, Rebecca,	281	Moore, Paschall,	195	Morris, Joseph P.,	127
Moon, Samuel C.,	189	Moore, Pemberton,	176	Morris, Levi,	128
Moon, William B.,	203	Moore, Peter R.,	126	Morris, Luke W.,	192
Moon, William H.,	184	Moore, Phebe,	305	Morris, Margaret,	231
Moore, Adrian,	175	Moore, Phebe Ann,	305	Morris, Margaret,	236
Moore, Adriana,	268	Moore, Phebe Ann,	316	Morris, Martha,	236
Moore, Alice E.,	304	Moore, Rachel,	321	Morris, Martha,	264
Moore, Allen,	108	Moore, Rebecca,	323	Morris, Mary,	299
Moore, Ann E.,	319	Moore, Rebecca B.,	324	*Morris, Mary H.,*	99
Moore, Anna,	243	Moore, Ridgway,	145	Morris, Mifflin,	145
Moore, Anna,	332	*Moore, Robert,*	95	Morris, Morton,	166
Moore, Anna Mary,	325	Moore, Robert R.,	132	Morris, Paschall,	173
Moore, Asa,	115	Moore, Robert S,	157	Morris, Powell,	128
Moore, Ashel W.,	192	Moore, Ruth Anna,	267	Morris, Priscilla,	250
Moore, Benjamin,	108	Moore, Ruth Anna,	286	Morris, Robert,	147
Moore, Burrwood,	191	Moore, Samuel L.,	170	*Morris, Samuel,*	102
Moore, Caleb,	195	Moore, Samuel W.,	179	*Morris, Samuel B.,*	101
Moore, Calvin C.,	160	Moore, Sarah,	228	Morris, Sarah,	302
Moore, Casandra,	232	Moore, Sarah,	283	Morris, Sarah,	305
Moore, Catharine,	243	Moore, Sarah P.,	298	Morris, Sarah E.,	279
Moore, Charles,	160	*Moore, Sarah W.,*	88	Morris, Sophia,	289
Moore, Charles T.,	205	" (*Goddess,*)	81	Morris, Susan M.,	282
Moore, Christiana,	251	(See Walter.)		Morris, Susanna,	261
Moore, Clarkson,	168	Moore, Sidney,	248	*Morris, Thomas,*	95
Moore, Edward A.,	204	Moore, Susanna,	244	Morris, William,	107
Moore, Edward D.,	173	Moore, Walter C.,	173	Morris, William,	107
Moore, Edwin P.,	205	Moore, Walter L.,	196	Morrison, Evan,	108
Moore, Eliza,	239	Moore, Walter T.,	188	Morrison, Hannah,	273
Moore, Elizabeth,	228	Moore, William B.,	173	Morthland, Mary M.,	296
Moore, Elizabeth,	230	Moore, William W.,	105	Morthland, Susanna,	273
Moore, Elizabeth,	317	Moore, Wilmer J.,	202	Morton, Esther,	243
Moore, Elizabeth R.,	325	Morgan, Abraham P.,	138	Morton, Frances C.,	278
Moore, Ellen,	311	Morgan, Anna,	336	*Morton, John,*	95
Moore, Hannah,	267	Morgan, Hannah P.,	295	*Mort n, John, Jr.,*	97
Moore, Hannah D.,	342	Morgan, Isaac,	141	*Morton, Margaret,*	99
Moore, Hannah E.,	276	Morgan, Isaac,	150	*Morton, Mary,*	97
Moore, Hannah E.,	321	*Morgan, Isaac,*	102	Morton, Mary,	269
Moore, Hartshorne,	111	Morgan, Lydia,	294	Morton, Robert,	121
Moore, Harry E.,	203	Morgan, Mary Ann,	297	Morton, Samuel,	127
Moore, Hibbard D.,	197	Morgan, Mordecai,	110	Morton, Samuel G.,	121
Moore, Horace C.,	201	Morgan, Rebecca,	289	Mott, Amelia S.,	337

INDEX.

Name	PAGE
Mott, Anna,	268
Mott, Anna,	271
Mott, Edward,	114
Mott, Elizabeth,	263
Mott, James,	130
Mott, John W.,	197
Mott, Mary,	97
Mott, Mary S.,	302
Mott, Richard,	130
Mott, Sarah,	235
Mott, Thomas E.,	197
Mott, William E.,	203
Moyse, Clara,	321
Murphy, Letitia,	98
Murray, Edward L.,	178
Murray, John J.,	154
Murray, Joseph R.,	163
Murray, Martha J.,	326
Murray, William R.,	163
Musgrave, Abigail,	254
Musgrave, Esther,	253
Mussey, Lydia W.,	323
Myers, Caroline,	345
Myers, Joseph E.,	196
Neal, Lydia,	251
Neal, Mary,	276
Neal, William,	81
Neave, Alexander,	114
Needles, John,	95
Needles, John,	160
Needles, Lydia,	242
Needles, Lydia Ann,	276
Needles, Ruth Anna,	275
Needles, Sarah,	241
Neeld, Hannah,	275
Neely, Elizabeth F.,	340
Neely, Frances J.,	340
Neely, Leonora,	340
Nelson, Mary,	263
Nesbit, John,	113
Neville, Agnes,	304
Neville, Benjamin G.,	159
Neville, James,	159
Neville, Joseph W.,	159
Newbold, Albert G.,	201
Newbold, Ann,	224
Newbold, Ann T.,	245
Newbold, Beulah,	274
Newbold, Charlotte,	270
Newbold, Clayton,	118
Newbold, Edith,	223
Newbold, Edith,	235
Newbold, Edward,	117
Newbold, Elizabeth,	247
Newbold, Hannah,	244
Newbold, Hannah,	265
Newbold, Henry,	118
Newbold, James S.,	119
Newbold, James S.,	169
Newbold, John,	122
Newbold, Joseph,	113
Newbold, Joshua,	143
Newbold, Martha,	231
Newbold, Martha,	239
Newbold, Martha,	268
Newbold, Mary, Jr.,	97
Newbold, Mary A.,	244
Newbold, Mary F.,	299
Newbold, Mary L.,	283
Newbold, Mary T.,	267
Newbold, Rebecca,	256
Newbold, Susan H.,	256
Newbold, Susanna,	99
Newbold, Thomas H.,	139
Newbold, Thomas H.,	201
Newbold, Watson,	124
Newbold, William,	96
Newbold William L.,	118
Newbold, William R.,	163
Newbold, Wm. R., Jr.,	202
Newbold, Wistar,	182
Newby, John L.,	120
Newby, Margaret,	306
Newby, Robert B.,	120
Newhall, Abby,	318
Newkirk, I. Roberts,	200
Newkirk, John B.,	195
Newlin, Ann,	230
Newlin, Cyrus,	96
Newlin, Eliza,	235
Newlin, Elizabeth A.,	274
Newlin, Hannah,	287
Newlin, Hetty Ann,	259
Newlin, John,	143
Newlin, John,	86
Newlin, John S.,	114
Newlin, Levis,	143
Newlin, Levis,	85
Newlin, Levis P.,	190
Newlin, Martha,	223
Newlin, Mary,	97
Newlin, Mary,	280
Newlin, Mary C.,	286
Newlin, Mary P.,	284
Newlin, Mary S.,	243
Newlin, Mary W.,	328
Newlin, Nathaniel,	113
Newlin, Nicholas,	149
Newlin, Sarah,	96
Newlin, Sarah,	226
Newlin, Sarah,	294
Newlin, Sarah S.,	284
Newlin, Thomas,	120
Newlin, Thomas S.,	120
Newlin, William P.,	137
Nichols, Amor,	179
Nichols, Hannah,	226
Nichols, Lydia,	228
Nichols, Rebecca,	223
Nicholson, Ann H.,	308
Nicholson, Anna,	278
Nicholson, Anna,	312
Nicholson, Beulah H.,	100
(See Hopkins.)	
Nicholson,Col'man L.,	161
Nicholson, Elisha,	122
Nicholson, Eliza C.,	329
Nicholson, Elizabeth,	264
Nicholson, Eliz. C.,	329
Nicholson, Esther,	237
Nicholson, Hannah,	239
Nicholson,Herbert M.,	191
Nicholson, Isaac,	162
Nicholson, Isaac,	185
Nicholson, James,	115
Nicholson, Jessie,	340
Nicholson, Joseph L.,	191
Nicholson, J.Whitall,	191
Nicholson, Martha,	282
Nicholson, Mary,	286
Nicholson, Mary,	300
Nicholson, Mary,	337
Nicholson, Mary L.,	267
Nicholson, Phebe,	337
" (Teacher,)	90, 91
Nicholson,Priscilla R.,	343
Nicholson, Rachel,	259
Nicholson, Rebecca,	237
Nicholson, Rebecca,	311
Nicholson, Rich'd L.,	158
Nicholson, Robert P.,	196
Nicholson, Samuel,	101
Nicholson, Sam'l P.,	153
Nicholson, Sarah,	313
Nicholson, Sarah E.,	342
Nicholson, William C.,	187
Nicholson, William H.,	155
Nicholson, Virginia,	337
Nicholson, Zebedee,	145
Nields, David,	150
Nisbett, Mary,	244
Nixon, Abigail,	236
Nixon, Ann,	262
Nixon, Beulah,	237
Nixon, Hannah,	252
Nixon, Henrietta,	262
Nixon, Mary J.,	265
Nock, David,	115
Nock, Sarah W.,	249
Norris, Deborah L.,	245
Norris, Hepzibah,	263
Norris, Mary E.,	245
Norris, Matilda,	297
Norris, Oliver,	155
Norris, Oliver,	161
Norris, Sarah Ann,	289
Norris, William T.,	159
North, Abel,	136
North, Jesse,	126
North, Rachel M.,	284
North, Sarah,	302
Norton, Thomas,	96
Oakford, Ann,	238
Oakford, Charles,	119
Oakford, Deborah,	251
Oakford, Elizabeth,	242
Oakford, Hannah A.,	257
Oakford, Lloyd,	132
Oakford, Mary,	248
Oakford, William L.,	133
Offley, John N.,	106
Offley, Mary,	238
Offley, Rachel,	236
Ogborn, Anna L.,	344
Ogborn, Annabella C.,	317
Ogborn, Elizabeth,	303
Ogborn, Elizabeth P.,	310
Ogborn, Emeline,	311
Ogborn, Henry F.,	203
Ogborn, James,	170
Ogborn, Martha,	299
Ogborn, Mary N.,	313

INDEX. 411

Name	PAGE	Name	PAGE	Name	PAGE
Ogborn, Phebe,	314	Painter, Ann,	280	Palmer, Sarah C.,	286
Ogborn, Rachel,	325	Painter, Charles,	136	Palmer, Susanna,	242
Ogborn, Sarah Ann,	302	Painter, Darwin,	140	Palmer, Susanna,	298
Ogborn, Susanna F.,	298	Painter, Edward,	134	Palmer, T. Chalkley,	197
Ogden, Anna,	292	Painter, Eliza,	282	Palmer, William C.,	190
Ogden, Beulah,	293	Painter, Elizabeth,	236	Palmer, William G.,	148
Ogden, Charles S.,	148	Painter, Ellen,	331	Palmer, William P.,	112
Ogden, Charles G.,	100	Painter, Esther,	331	Palmer, William S.,	203
Ogden, Clarkson,	150	Painter, George B.,	169	Palmer, William W.,	130
Ogden, Clement,	165	Painter, Hannah,	270	Pancoast, Abbe Ann,	269
Ogden, David,	121	Painter, Howard T.,	201	Pancoast, Abigail,	226
Ogden, Elizabeth R.,	335	Painter, Jacob,	137	Pancoast, Albert,	175
Ogden, Elizabeth T.,	267	Painter, John,	142	Pancoast, Ann,	272
Ogden, Hannah W.,	335	Painter, Joseph G.,	183	Pancoast, Anna,	233
Ogden, James H.,	145	Painter, Lydia S.,	283	Pancoast, Charles,	172
Ogden, John,	143	Painter, Mary,	259	Pancoast, Charles H.,	153
Ogden, M. Ella,	335	Painter, Mary H.,	294	Pancoast, David,	113
Ogden, Martha,	229	Painter, Milton,	108	Pancoast, Elizabeth,	253
Ogden, Mary Ann,	281	Painter, Milton,	135	Pancoast, Elizabeth,	264
Ogden, Orpha,	248	Painter, Rachel,	246	Pancoast, Esther,	236
Ogden, Rebecca,	281	Painter, Samuel,	131	Pancoast, Hannah,	253
Ogden, Samuel,	142	Painter, Samuel,	134	Pancoast, Hannah,	267
Ogden, Samuel,	151	Painter, Samuel G.,	179	Pancoast, Hannah,	309
Ogden, Sarah,	257	Painter, Sarah,	262	Pancoast, Hannah C.,	289
Ogden, William,	141	Painter, Sidney,	232	Pancoast, Isabella,	291
Oldden, Anna,	225	Painter, Sidney,	270	Pancoast, Jane,	252
Oldden, Catharine,	236	Painter, William,	107	Pancoast, Lucy A.,	248
Oldden, Elizabeth,	240	Paist, Charles,	111	Pancoast, Lucy A.,	290
Oldden, Emley,	117	Paist, James,	124	Pancoast, Martha,	261
Oldden, Giles,	123	Paist, Mary,	237	Pancoast, Mary,	289
Oldden, James,	132	Paist, S. Roselma,	334	Pancoast, Rebecca,	233
Oldden, John W.,	132	Palen, Arthur,	133	Pancoast, Samuel,	171
Oldden, Mary H.,	223	Palen, Ezekiel,	133	Pancoast, Samuel A.,	130
Oldden, Rebecca B.,	221	Palmer, Abiah J.,	190	Pancoast, Sarah,	291
Oldden, Samuel,	134	Palmer, Ann Eliza,	300	Pancoast, Sarah Ann,	261
Oldden, Thomas H.,	107	Palmer, Annie,	342	Pancoast, Stephen,	116
Oliphant, Duncan S.,	135	Palmer, Arthur W.,	181	Pancoast, Thomas,	157
Oliphant, Eayre,	151	Palmer, Beulah,	284	Pancoast, William A.,	137
Oliphant, Mary E.,	271	Palmer, Beulah,	320	Pandrich, Anna,	336
Oliver, Ann M.,	269	Palmer, Beulah,	348	Pandrich, Margaret,	339
Oliver, Ellen,	271	Palmer, Catharine S.,	288	Pardoe, Albert,	174
Oliver, Joshua C.,	116	Palmer, Charles M.,	171	Parke, Ann,	273
Osborne, Sophronia,	260	Palmer, Daniel,	146	Parke, Jonathan E.,	142
Otis, Jesse M.,	201	Palmer, Edward E.,	137	Parke, Mary,	277
Outland, Jeptha E.,	200	Palmer, Eliza,	214	Parke, Mary,	299
Outland, Mary E.,	342	Palmer, Gideon G.,	127	Parke, Mary,	309
Outland, Ozella C.,	347	Palmer, Hannah,	277	Parker, Abbie W.,	344
Outland, Sarah J.,	342	Palmer, Hannah S.,	268	Parker, Abigail,	274
Outland, William F.,	206	Palmer, Henry,	169	Parker, Benjamin C.,	150
Owen, Ann,	271	Palmer, John,	129	Parker, Beulah T.,	261
Owen, Charles,	128	Palmer, John M.,	180	Parker, Caroline,	299
Owen, Elizabeth,	269	Palmer, John S.,	161	Parker, Caroline R.,	344
Owen, Rachel,	229	Palmer, John W.,	204	Parker, Charles,	133
Owen, Parker,	127	Palmer, J. Howard,	179	Parker, Charles,	171
Owen, Thomas,	147	Palmer, Joseph H.,	172	Parker, Charles H.,	145
Owen, William W.,	124	Palmer, Levick,	146	Parker, Deborah C.,	308
		Palmer, Lewis,	127	Parker, Dillwyn,	171
Packer, Coleman,	168	Palmer, Lewis,	155	Parker, Edward A.,	138
Packer, Mary L.,	294	" " (Teacher,)	86	Parker, Edward T.,	147
Page, Abigail,	297	Palmer, Lydia,	281	Parker, Elias,	138
Page, Agnes,	276	Palmer, Lydia H.,	284	Parker, Ellen,	319
Page, Elizabeth F.,	295	Palmer, Lydia S.,	261	Parker, Ellen J.,	281
Page, Laura H.,	337	Palmer, Mary,	270	Parker, Ezra,	191
Page, Lucy,	275	*Palmer, Moses,*	98	Parker, Hannah J.,	307
Page, Sally,	84	Palmer, Moses,	136	Parker, Henry,	150
Page, Sarah,	287	Palmer, Moses G.,	118	Parker, Henry,	165
Page, William,	132	Palmer, Sallie Ann,	240	Parker, Ira J.,	180
Page, William A.,	144	Palmer, Sarah,	342	Parker, Isabella,	270

31

INDEX.

Name	PAGE
Parker, Jacob,	170
Parker, Jesse,	135
Parker, John,	98
Parker, John J.,	159
Parker, John W.,	150
Parker, Joseph,	133
Parker, J. Walter,	193
Parker, J. Warner,	191
Parker, Louisa W.,	317
Parker, Lydia Ann,	293
Parker, Lydia R.,	335
Parker, Margaret,	100
Parker, Martha,	267
Parker, Martha,	313
Parker, Mary,	289
Parker, Mary S.,	311
Parker, Minerva,	327
Parker, Phebe Ann,	322
Parker, Rebecca,	339
Parker, Samuel J.,	160
Parker, Susan D.,	291
Parker, Susanna,	236
Parker, Susanna,	290
Parker, T. Elwood,	193
Parker, Thomas S.,	133
Parker, William,	137
Parker, William J.,	150
Parker, William M.,	184
Parker, William W.,	138
Parker, William W.,	157
Parker, Willits,	175
Parkins, Maria,	241
Parkins, Sarah H.,	240
Parrish, Dillwyn,	128
Parrott, Benjamin,	121
Parrott, John B.,	149
Parry, Anna,	249
Parry, Benjamin,	140
Parry, Caleb,	144
Parry, Charles,	152
Parry, Edward R.,	157
Parry, Emma,	318
Parry, George R.,	166
Parry, Helen R.,	324
Parry, Isaac,	133
Parry, Jane,	255
Parry, Jane P.,	296
Parry, Julianna R.,	296
Parry, Letitia,	267
Parry, Margaret,	255
Parry, Martha,	241
Parry, Martha,	249
Parry, Mary,	304
Parry, Mary R.,	318
Parry, Oliver,	116
Parry, Priscilla,	263
Parry, Rachel,	241
Parry, Rachel,	84
Parry, Rebecca,	265
Parry, Richard,	161
Parry, Robert,	84
Parry, Ruth,	245
Parry, Ruth E.,	303
Parry, Samuel,	131
Parry, Sarah,	266
Parry, Thomas,	162
Parsons, Mary Ann,	286
Parsons, Nathaniel,	113

Name	PAGE
Parvin, Elizabeth,	242
Parvin, Elizabeth,	328
Parvin, Ellen S.,	337
Parvin, Mordecai S.,	195
Parvin, Sibilla S.,	323
Parvin, Susan,	334
Paschall, Beulah,	239
Paschall, Margaret,	270
Paschall, Mary A.,	269
Paschall, Stephen,	130
Passmore, Abiah,	160
Passmore, Abigail,	248
" " (*Teacher,*)	84
Passmore, Anna B.,	299
Passmore, Benj. W.,	150
" " (*Com.,*)	102
" " (*Supt.,*)	80
Passmore, Beulah,	246
Passmore, Carleton,	110
Passmore, Deborah,	253
Passmore, Deb. A.,	253
Passmore, Deb. C.,	337
Passmore, Deb. G.,	318
Passmore, Elizabeth,	230
Passmore, Elizabeth,	262
Passmore, Elizab. K.,	100
(See Knight.)	
Passmore, Esther,	258
Passmore, Everett G.,	158
Passmore, Jane Ann,	285
Passmore, John L.,	133
Passmore, Joseph,	149
" " (*Teacher,*)	87
" " (*Com.,*)	101
Passmore, Lewis,	155
Passmore, Margaret,	305
Passmore, Mary,	242
Passmore, Mary,	84, 85
" " (*Com.,*)	101
Passmore, Mary Ann,	301
Passmore, Mary K.,	299
Passmore, Pennock.	92, 93
" " (*Teacher,*)	84
" " (*Supt.,*)	79
" " (*Com.,*)	100
Passmore, Phebe,	289
Passmore, Rachel,	257
Passmore, Rachel,	264
Passmore, Rebecca G.,	80
" " (*Com.,*)	103
(See Cope.)	
Passmore, Ruth,	239
Passmore, Sarah,	79
(See West.)	
Passmore, Sarah L.,	310
Passmore, Sarah W.,	336
" (*Teacher,*)	90, 91
Passmore, Thomas H.,	168
Passmore, Thomas L.,	203
Passmore, William C.,	199
Patterson, John W.,	199
Patton, Francis J.,	202
Patton, Hannah,	239
Patton, James M.,	202
Paul, Ann,	228
Paul, Ann,	235
Paul, Ann,	98
Paul, Elizabeth,	253

Name	PAGE
Paul, Elizabeth F.,	99
Paul, Hannah,	230
Paul, Hannah,	99
Paul, Jacob W.,	6
Paul, John,	98
Paul, Joseph,	110
Paul, Joseph M.,	99
Paul, Sarah C.,	277
" " (*Com.,*)	101
Paul, Yeamans,	111
Paxson, Ann,	225
Paxson, Anna,	255
Paxson, Anna Maria,	251
Paxson, Benjamin W.,	134
Paxson, Caroline E.,	343
Paxson, Catharine S.,	268
Paxson, Charles,	144
Paxson, David,	142
Paxson, Edward,	127
Paxson, Elizabeth,	296
Paxson, Hannah,	344
Paxson, John,	116
Paxson, John W.,	139
Paxson, Jonathan,	112
Paxson, Louis,	139
Paxson, Margaret E.,	343
Paxson, Mary,	257
Paxson, Mary W.,	283
Paxson, Mary W.,	294
Paxson, Oliver,	98
Paxson, Oliver,	84
Paxson, Oliver,	142
" " (*Com.,*)	102
Paxson, Oliver Wilson,	201
Paxson, Phebe Ann,	272
Paxson, Rebecca,	299
Paxson, Richard,	108
Paxson, Richard,	159
Paxson, Ruth Anna,	278
Paxson, Samuel,	159
Paxson, Samuel W.,	201
Paxson, Sarah,	269
Paxson, Sarah,	278
Paxson, Sarah E.,	341
Paxson, Sarah W.,	343
Paxson, Susanna,	244
Payne, Susanna M.,	256
Peach, Samuel,	113
Pearl, Rachel,	263
Pearsall, Charles,	129
Pearsall, Robert,	117
Pearsall, Robert,	129
Pearson, Mary,	231
Pearson, Mary A.,	345
Pearson, S. Virginia,	316
Pearson, Sarah Starr,	304
Peckham, Henry K.,	184
Peckham, Mary J.,	316
Pedrich, Isaac,	146
Peele, James L.,	204
Peele, Mary E.,	344
Pell, Gilbert T.,	116
Pemberton, Phebe,	96
Pennell, Abraham,	96
Pennell, Abraham,	127
Pennell, Amelia Ann,	307
Pennell, Ann G.,	274
Pennell, Anne,	314

INDEX.

Name	PAGE	Name	PAGE	Name	PAGE
Pennell, Beulah F.,	344	Pennock, Hannah,	231	Pharo, Harvey E.,	203
Pennell, Dell,	145	Pennock, Hannah J.,	284	Pharo, Horatio W.,	163
Pennell, E. Jane,	323	Pennock, Herbert A.,	186	Pharo, Joseph W.,	135
Pennell, Eliza,	295	Pennock, Isaac W.,	119	Pharo, Joseph W.,	202
Pennell, Elizabeth,	259	Pennock, Isabella,	235	Pharo, Louisa P.,	322
Pennell, Elizabeth,	267	Pennock, Isabella L.,	299	Pharo, Mary W.,	317
Pennell, Hannah,	238	Pennock, Isabella L.,	335	Pharo, Merritt W.,	204
Pennell, Hannah,	258	Pennock, Joseph,	137	Pharo, Matilda,	287
Pennell, Hannah,	311	Pennock, Joseph E.,	191	Pharo, Orrin,	146
Pennell, Hannah S.,	307	Pennock, Levis,	128	Pharo, Phebe,	283
Pennell, Hill,	115	Pennock, Maria E.,	339	Pharo, Phebe Ann,	288
Pennell, Hill,	199	Pennock, Mary,	225	Pharo, Phebe Ann,	320
Pennell, James,	128	Pennock, Mary,	235	Pharo, Robert,	135
Pennell, Jane,	262	Pennock, Mary,	257	Pharo, S. Clarence,	192
Pennell, John L.,	142	Pennock, Phebe,	241	Pharo, T. Franklin,	190
Pennell, John S.,	185	(*Hoopes*,) " (*Com*.,)	100	Pharo, Timothy A.,	177
Pennell, Joseph,	139	Pennock, Philena,	261	Philips, Benjamin,	149
Pennell, Joseph,	181	Pennock, Rachel B.,	254	Philips, Charles H.,	194
Pennell, Larkin,	145	Pennock, Reb'ca W.,	235	Philips, Edward,	189
Pennell, Lydia S.,	311	Pennock, Ruth W.,	280	*Philips, John*,	97
Pennell, Maria,	251	Pennock, Sarah,	231	*Philips, Lydia*,	97
Pennell, Martha L.,	300	Pennock, Sarah,	232	*Philips, Lydia*,	86
Pennell, Mary,	228	Pennock, Sarah,	239	Philips, Moses,	114
Pennell, Mary,	239	Pennock, Sarah,	311	Philips, William M.,	194
Pennell, Mary,	245	Pennock, Sarah,	318	Phillips, Aaron,	110
Pennell, Mary,	310	Pennock, Sarah Ann,	264	Phillips, Albina,	299
Pennell, Mary A.,	309	Pennock, Susanna,	237	Phillips, Ann,	271
Pennell, Mary E.,	340	Pennock, William,	126	Phillips, Anna,	284
Pennell, Meredith,	109	Penrose, Abigail,	256	Phillips, Caroline,	274
Pennell, Nathan,	109	Penrose, Ann,	272	Phillips, Deborah,	227
Pennell, Nathan,	143	Penrose, Ann P.,	256	Phillips, Deborah,	230
Pennell, Priscilla W.,	261	Penrose, Charles,	187	Phillips, Deborah,	286
Pennell, Rachel,	231	Penrose, Jane,	333	Phillips, Edith T.,	308
Pennell, Rachel,	309	Penrose, M. Ella,	345	Phillips, Edward C.,	152
Pennell, Rebecca,	318	Penrose, Margaret,	252	Phillips, Elizabeth,	229
Pennell, Robert,	161	Penrose, Mary,	332	Phillips, Elizabeth,	288
Pennell, Samuel F.,	199	Penrose, Tacy S.,	293	Phillips, Emily B.,	308
Pennell, Sarah,	278	Penrose, Thomas,	116	Phillips, Hannah,	234
Pennell, Sarah A.,	250	Perkins, Benj. D.,	159	Phillips, Harvey,	133
Pennell, Sarah G.,	251	Perkins, Lindley M.,	153	Phillips, Isaac D.,	142
Pennell, Sidney,	226	Perkins, Rachel M.,	330	Phillips, James,	135
Pennell, Sidney,	239	Perkins, Sarah J.,	330	Phillips, Josiah,	132
Pennell, Sidney,	319	Perry, Elizabeth F.,	320	Phillips, Lydia,	281
Pennell, Susanna,	280	Perry, George F.,	149	Phillips, Mary,	265
Pennell, Thomaz. R.,	261	Peters, Catharine,	268	Phillips, Mary Ann,	280
Pennell, William,	139	Peters, Charles V.,	148	Phillips, Mercy,	256
Pennell, William,	148	Peters, Dell P.,	144	Phillips, Phebe D.,	308
Pennell, William H.,	191	Peters, Hannah P.,	289	Phillips, Rachel,	257
Pennington, Cyrus,	174	Peters, Isabella,	246	Phillips, Richard S.,	193
Pennington, Dan'l L.,	187	Peters, Isabella S.,	292	Phillips, Sarah,	261
Pennington, Ellis,	173	Peters, Joseph H.,	154	Phillips, Sarah,	270
Pennington, Lewis,	180	Peters, Samuel J.,	147	Phillips, Sarah F.,	293
Pennington, Milton C.,	191	Peters, William R.,	154	Phillips, Sidney,	251
Pennington, Morris,	174	Pettit, Elizabeth,	313	Phillips, Thomas, Jr.,	184
Pennington, Rach.A.,	281	Pettit, Nathaniel,	113	Phillips, William,	109
Pennington, Tow'd T.,	193	Pettit, Martha,	232	Phillips, William G.,	144
Pennington, Wilson,	187	Pharo, Albert,	151	Phillips, William H.,	176
Pennock, Abra'm L.,	155	Pharo, Albert E.,	190	Phipps, Amy R.,	241
Pennock, Abram L.,	192	Pharo, Allen R.,	206	Phipps, Ann Eliza,	299
Pennock, Benjamin,	118	Pharo, Anna,	299	Phipps, Charles,	126
Pennock, Caspar,	191	Pharo, Anna,	306	Phipps, Isabella S.,	314
Pennock, Charles E.,	191	Pharo, Archelaus R.,	135	Phipps, James,	152
Pennock, E. Eldridge,	191	Pharo, Archie,	195	Phipps, Jonathan T.,	292
Pennock, Eliza,	265	Pharo, Charlotte,	271	Phipps, Mary,	258
Pennock, Elizabeth,	97	Pharo, Eliza,	283	Phipps, Mary Ann,	292
Pennock, Elizabeth,	301	Pharo, George B.,	133	Phipps, Mary B.,	334
Pennock, Elizabeth,	315	Pharo, Hannah,	273	Phipps, Rachel,	257
Pennock, George L.,	199	Pharo, Hannah E.,	335	Phipps, Sarah,	223

INDEX.

Name	PAGE	Name	PAGE	Name	PAGE
Phipps, Sarah,	245	Pitman, Rebecca,	295	Pound, Daniel,	114
Phipps, Stephen,	119	Pitman, Robert,	113	Pound, Hugh,	146
Phipps, Susanna,	232	Pleasants, Ann,	259	Pound, John T.,	168
Phipps, Thomas,	126	Pleasants, Ann E.,	304	Pound, Joseph J.,	168
Phipps, Wm. P., Jr.,	200	Pleasants, Caleb,	125	Pound, Margaret,	231
Pickering, Elihu.	83	Pleasants, Charles P.,	162	Pound, Mary Jane,	303
Pickering, Jonathan,	96	Pleasants, Elizabeth,	226	Pound, Richard,	156
Pidgeon, Eliza C.,	338	Pleasants, Frances,	242	Pound, Samuel,	146
Pidgeon, Mary,	258	Pleasants, Frances,	313	Pound, Silas D.,	149
Pidgeon, Reb'ca R. J.,	338	Pleasants, George,	121	Pound, Susan,	309
Pierce, Abigail,	247	Pleasants, John,	161	Powell, Albina,	247
Pierce, Albin,	145	Pleasants, Joseph,	117	Powell, Ann B.,	261
Pierce, Amy S.,	279	Pleasants, Laura,	307	Powell, Ann Eliza,	285
Pierce, Ann,	96	*Pleasants, Mary,*	96	Powell, Benjamin,	122
Pierce, Anna,	258	Pleasants, Mary,	226	Powell, Edward A.,	187
Pierce, Cyrus,	109	Pleasants, Mary,	242	Powell, Elizabeth,	268
Pierce, David,	108	Pleasants, Robert,	121	Powell, Elizabeth N.,	338
Pierce, Dinah,	273	Pleasants, Thomas S.,	116	Powell, H. Anna,	340
Pierce, Hannah,	232	Plummer, Rachel E.,	332	Powell, Hannah,	267
Pierce, Hannah,	245	Poits, Joseph E.,	131	Powell, Isaac,	113
Pierce, Hetty Ann,	262	Poits, William,	124	Powell, John,	122
Pierce, Isaac,	110	Pole, Edward,	107	Powell, Juliana,	283
Pierce, Jane,	233	Pole, Joseph W.,	107	Powell, Margaret,	235
Pierce, John,	95	Pole, Rachel,	225	Powell, Sarah,	275
Pierce, John D.,	139	Poole, Anna,	270	Powell, Sarah D.,	295
Pierce, Lydia,	273	Poole, Elizabeth,	238	Powell, Sarah K.,	295
Pierce, Phebe,	249	Poole, Elizabeth,	302	Powell, Sarah K.,	343
Pierce, Rachel,	246	Poole, Hannah,	247	Powell, Shotwell,	126
Pierce, Rebecca,	259	Poole, J. Morton,	131	Powell, William,	145
Pierce, Rebecca,	281	Poole, Joseph,	152	Pownall, Levi,	156
Pierce, Rebecca,	298	Poole, Martha,	266	Pratt, Christiana,	246
Pierce, Sarah,	229	Poole, Mary,	242	Pratt, David G.,	137
Pierce, Sarah,	250	Poole, Rachel,	310	Pratt, Elizabeth,	293
Pierce, Sarah Ann,	297	Poole, Samuel,	118	Pratt, Elizabeth,	304
Pierce, Sarah B.,	280	*Poole, Sarah,*	99	Pratt, George,	143
Pierce, Sidney,	242	Poole, Sarah,	258	Pratt, Hannah,	264
Pierce, Susan,	267	Poole, Thomas H.,	164	Pratt, Hannah,	298
Pierson, Edward W.,	177	*Poole, William,*	98	Pratt, Jane,	229
Pierson, Elizabeth,	100	Poole, William,	166	Pratt, Lydia A.,	281
Pierson, Elizabeth,	290	Porter, Anne,	286	Pratt, Martha L.,	346
Pierson, Hannah,	299	Post, Edmund,	191	Pratt, Martha M.,	298
Pierson, John,	160	Post, Lydia,	297	Pratt, Mary,	297
Pierson, Martha,	312	Post, Stephen W.,	179	Pratt, Mary Ann,	279
Pierson, Mary Ann,	322	Post, William,	195	Pratt, Massey,	259
Pierson, Susan,	299	Potter, Ruthanna,	324	Pratt, Orpha,	249
Pierson, Thomas,	153	Potts, Anna,	298	Pratt, Orpha,	301
Pierson, William,	158	*Potts, Anne,*	99	Pratt, Priscilla,	259
Pike, Mary,	290	Potts, Charles,	148	Pratt, Sarah,	296
Pike, Sarah,	289	" " (*Teacher,*)	86, 88	Pratt, Susan H.,	299
" " (*Com.,*)	103	Potts, David D.,	128	Pratt, Thomas,	139
Pike, Thomas S.,	147	Potts, Deborah,	227	Preston, Albert W.,	178
Pim, Ann,	229	Potts, Deborah,	231	Preston, Ann,	264
Pim, Anna,	320	Potts, Edward,	155	Preston, Anna Bell,	340
Pim, Emily H.,	323	" " (*Teacher,*)	86	Preston, Edward S.,	166
Pim, Fannie W.,	328	Potts, Elizabeth,	316	Preston, Joseph,	118
Pim, George E.,	168	Potts, Frances,	241	Preston, Rachel G.,	316
Pim, Hannah,	230	Potts, Frances,	301	Preston, Rebecca,	252
Pim, Jonathan,	130	Potts, Franklin M.,	192	Preston, Rebecca R.,	312
Pim, Lydia,	328	Potts, Hannah,	267	Preston, Thomas R.,	174
Pim, Mary,	320	Potts, Isaac W.,	127	Price, Ann M.,	237
Pim, Richard P.,	187	*Potts, Joseph,*	95	Price, Benjamin,	115
Pim, Sallie E.,	316	Potts, Joseph,	162	Price, Benjamin,	184
Pim, Thomas,	164	Potts, Martha,	267	Price, Callender,	129
Pitfield, Ann,	262	Potts, Rebecca,	227	Price, Daniel B.,	150
Pitfield, Benjamin H.,	145	Potts, Rebecca,	230	Price, David,	127
Pitfield, Elizabeth,	99	Potts, Sarah W.,	268	Price, Edith,	257
Pitfield, Robert L.,	98	Potts, William,	167	Price, Eli K.,	120
Pitfield, William,	129	Poultney, Lydia,	224	Price, Elizabeth,	248

	PAGE		PAGE		PAGE
Price, Elizabeth,	265	Pryor, Edmund,	111	Pyle, Elizabeth M.,	294
Price, Elizabeth,	279	Pryor, Hannah,	232	Pyle, Hannah,	240
Price, Elizabeth,	330	Pryor, Rebecca,	234	Pyle, Hannah,	273
Price, Esther,	263	Pryor, Sarah Ann,	251	Pyle, Hannah N.,	294
Price, Ezra,	130	Puckett, Henry W.,	155	Pyle, Hannah S.,	302
Price, Frances,	265	Pugh, Howard,	148	Pyle, Isaac,	150
Price, Francis L.,	186	Pugh, Isaac,	116	Pyle, Margaret,	250
Price, Hannah,	225	Pugh, Mary,	291	Pyle, Margaret J.,	299
Price, Hannah,	230	Pugh, Sarah,	246	Pyle, Mary,	310
(*Davis,*) " (*Com.*,)	101	Purviance, Guli A.,	331	Pyle, Mary Ann,	296
Price, Helen F.,	334	Pusey, Ann,	229	Pyle, Matilda,	294
Price, Isaac,	122	Pusey, Ann,	250	Pyle, Phebe Ann,	317
Price, Isaac C.,	138	Pusey, Ann,	258	Pyle, Phebe W.,	302
Price, Jacob L.,	184	Pusey, Ann,	272	Pyle, Philena,	312
Price, James B.,	118	Pusey, Benjamin,	110	Pyle, Ruth,	273
Price, James M.,	146	Pusey, Caleb,	109	Pyle, Sarah,	283
" " (*Teacher,*)	86	Pusey, Caleb W.,	135	Pyle, Sarah,	299
Price, Joseph,	128	Pusey, Charles,	120	Pyle, Sarah Ann,	273
Price, Lydia,	293	Pusey, Debby C.,	337	Pyle, William,	146
Price, Lydia N.,	277	Pusey, Edith,	226	Pyle, Ziba,	110
Price, Margaret,	235	Pusey, Edith H.,	320		
Price, Martha,	223	Pusey, Eliza,	265	Quinby, Ann,	297
Price, Mary,	234	Pusey, Eliza W.,	298	Quinby, Isaac C.,	149
Price, Mary C.,	285	Pusey, Elizabeth,	279	Quinby, Jane,	268
Price, Mary C.,	310	Pusey, Ellis,	152	Quinby, Phebe,	234
Price, Phebe B.,	305	Pusey, Emily,	310	Quinby, Phebe,	292
Price, Philip, Jr.,	96	*Pusey, Hannah*,	98	Quinby, Rachel,	253
" " (*Supt.*,)	79	*Pusey, Hannah, Jr.*,	97	Quinby, Watson F.,	149
Price, Philip,	106	Pusey, Hannah,	295		
Price, Philip,	124	Pusey, Hannah G.,	334	Raisin, Warner M.,	148
Price, R. Anna,	329	Pusey, Hibberd,	144	Raleigh, Ann,	266
Price, Rachel,	97	Pusey, Isaac,	100	Raley, Robert F.,	167
" " (*Matron,*)	79	Pusey, Isaac,	154	Randolph, Car'ne W.,	337
Price, Rachel,	300	Pusey, Isaac,	171	Randolph, Charles,	122
Price, Rebecca,	251	Pusey, Israel,	154	Randolph, Edward,	106
Price, Rebecca,	276	Pusey, Jacob,	114	Randolph, Edward,	195
Price, Rebecca B.,	308	Pusey, James,	147	Randolph, George,	140
Price, Richard,	135	Pusey, Joel B.,	155	Randolph, Han'h F.,	276
Price, Sarah,	247	Pusey, John G.,	150	Randolph, Harriet,	333
Price, Sarah Ann,	306	Pusey, Joseph,	140	Randolph, John F.,	112
Price, Sarah H.,	312	*Pusey, Joshua B.*,	101	Randolph, Juliana,	261
Price, Sibilla,	231	*Pusey, Joshua E.*,	95	Randolph, Mary,	249
Price, Susanna,	328	Pusey, Lea,	109	Randolph, Mary,	291
Price, Walter,	189	Pusey, Lea,	142	Randolph, Nathaniel,	138
Price, William,	106	Pusey, Lewis,	154	Randolph, Rachel,	249
Price, William B.,	123	Pusey, Mary,	295	Randolph, Richard,	107
Price, William G.,	185	Pusey, Mary,	327	Randolph, Richard,	141
Price, William L.,	198	Pusey, Mary Ann,	240	Randolph, Rich'd W.,	178
Prickett, Elizabeth E.,	339	Pusey, Massey,	230	Randolph, William,	106
Prickett, Elmer D.,	198	Pusey, Pennock,	152	Randolph, Wm. H.,	181
Prickett, Frank W.,	199	Pusey, Phebe,	226	Rankin, Ann Eliza,	299
Prickett, William S.,	198	Pusey, Philena J.,	242	Rawlings, Jane,	242
Prickitt, Ann,	297	Pusey, Rebecca,	340	Rawlings, Margaret,	242
Prickitt, Anna F.,	333	Pusey, Samuel N.,	133	Ray, William,	115
Prickitt, Deborah B.,	331	Pusey, Samuel R.,	157	Rea, Mary H.,	295
Prickitt, Ezra E.,	188	Pusey, Sarah,	298	Read, Ann,	263
Prickitt, Josiah,	195	Pusey, Sarah Ann,	315	Reckerfuse, Samuel,	123
Priest, Louisa E.,	312	Pusey, Sophia R.,	329	Redman, Charles F.,	153
Priest, William E.,	203	Pusey, William,	113	Redman, Eliz. E.,	284
Prior, Hannah,	210	Pusey, William,	145	Redman, Joseph S.,	142
Prindle, Anna L.,	345	Pusey, William J.,	185	Redman, Mary,	326
Proctor, Elizabeth,	287	Pyle, Abigail,	261	Redman, Samuel G.,	186
Proctor, Mary,	247	Pyle, Ann Eliza,	287	Redman, Sarah H.,	296
Proctor, Samuel T.,	162	Pyle, Cloud,	155	*Reece, Davis*,	84
Proctor, Sarah,	287	Pyle, Edward,	168	" " (*Governor,*)	80
Proctor, Stephen,	131	Pyle, Elizabeth,	237	Reece, Eli Y.,	135
Prosser, Elizabeth,	248	" " (*Teacher,*)	84	Reece, Thomas,	110
Prosser, Mary,	247	Pyle, Elizabeth,	311	Reed, Abigail S.,	291

31 *

INDEX.

Name	PAGE
Reed, David,	123
Reed, Elizabeth,	270
Reed, James,	160
Reed, J. Harris,	195
Reed, Mary E.,	316
Reed, Ruth,	260
Reed, Sarah G.,	335
Reed, Thomas M.,	198
Reed, William,	140
Reed, William,	92
Reed, William T.,	172
Reed, William T.,	199
Reese, Maria,	233
Reese, Walter,	185
Reeve, Ann,	231
Reeve, Anna,	313
Reeve, Benjamin C.,	178
Reeve, Beulah,	278
Reeve, Charles,	140
Reeve, Clayton,	123
Reeve, Dallas,	168
Reeve, Edith S.,	338
Reeve, Edward, .	152
Reeve, Edward B.,	201
Reeve, Elizabeth,	226
Reeve, Elizabeth,	243
Reeve, Elizabeth,	99
Reeve, Elizabeth,	284
Reeve, Elizabeth R.,	302
Reeve, Ellen,	289
Reeve, Emma,	308
Reeve, Emmor,	134
Reeve, Hannah A.,	259
Reeve, Hannah C.,	344
Reeve, Hannah G.,	294
Reeve, Job W.,	119
Reeve, John,	95
Reeve, John,	124
Reeve, John N.,	106
Reeve, John N.,	150
Reeve, John N.,	198
Reeve, Joseph,	151
Reeve, Josiah,	96
Reeve, Josiah,	174
Reeve, Josiah M.,	112
Reeve, Josiah R.,	127
Reeve, Letitia,	250
Reeve, Mark M.,	175
Reeve, Mark S.,	163
Reeve, Martha,	224
Reeve, Martha,	228
" " (Com.,)	99
(*Wislar,*) "	100
Reeve, Martha,	260
Reeve, Martha N.,	286
Reeve, Mary,	258
Reeve, Mary,	303
Reeve, Mary O.,	337
Reeve, Mary S.,	286
Reeve, Priscilla S.,	268
Reeve, Priscilla W.,	302
Reeve, Rachel,	238
Reeve, Rebecca,	293
Reeve, Rebecca,	298
Reeve, Rebecca C.,	322
Reeve, Richard H.,	175
Reeve, Richard M.,	130
Reeve, Richardson S.,	174
Reeve, Ruth,	260
Reeve, Samuel,	126
Reeve, Sarah C.,	330
Reeve, Sarah S.,	315
Reeve, Sarah W.,	259
Reeve, Susan S.,	308
Reeve, Walter S.,	192
Reeves, Abby S.,	327
Reeves, Ann,	256
Reeves, Anna M.,	297
Reeves, Anna N.,	341
Reeves, Biddle,	138
Reeves, Biddle,	184
Reeves, Elizabeth,	315
Reeves, Elizabeth W.,	345
Reeves, Joseph,	125
Reeves, Mary,	226
Reeves, Mary S.,	322
Reeves, Mary W.,	255
Reeves, Paul S.,	165
Reeves, Rachel,	303
Reeves, Sarah,	224
Reeves, Sarah B.,	266
Reeves, Sarah H.,	320
Register, Eliza Jane,	273
Register, Malvina,	278
Register, Robert,	134
Register, Samuel,	142
Reid, Esther R.,	323
Remington, Caroline,	307
Remington, Charles,	119
Remington, Clement,	130
Remington, Edward,	131
Remington, Edward,	135
Remington, Ellen,	307
Remington, Han'h S.,	302
Remington, Isaac,	183
Remington, James.	1. 5
Remington, James A.,	161
Remington, John C.,	157
Remington, Lydia H.,	325
Remington, Sarah J.,	302
Remington, Thomas,	128
Remington, William,	131
Remington, William,	135
Resin, Abraham,	122
Resin, Margaret,	98
Reynolds, Ann M.,	274
Reynolds, Charles,	123
Reynolds, David,	164
Reynolds, Ebenezer,	111
Reynolds, Haines,	124
Reynolds, Jacob,	164
Reynolds, Jeremiah,	112
Reynolds, Martha J.,	308
Reynolds, Martha S.,	347
Reynolds, Stephen,	164
Reynolds, Theodore,	165
Rhoads, Anna N.,	344
Rhoads, Beulah M.,	102
(See Morris.)	
Rhoads, Catharine E.,	337
Rhoads, Charles,	158
" " (Com.,)	102
Rhoads, Daniel J.,	110
Rhoads, Deborah,	291
" " (Com.,)	101
Rhoads, Edward G.,	200
Rhoads, Eleanor,	340
Rhoads, Elizabeth,	230
Rhoads, Elizabeth,	230
Rhoads, Elizabeth,	270
Rhoads, Elizabeth,	299
" (*Teacher.*)	87, 89
" (Com.,)	102
Rhoads, Elizabeth H.,	311
Rhoads, Francis,	347
Rhoads, George,	152
Rhoads, George A.,	197
Rhoads, Hannah,	230
Rhoads, Hannah,	254
Rhoads, Hannah,	100
(See Evans.)	
Rhoads, Hannah.	342
Rhoads, J. Snowdon,	203
Rhoads, James,	134
Rhoads, James E.,	158
Rhoads, Jane S.,	342
Rhoads, John,	157
Rhoads, John B.,	202
Rhoads, John O.,	110
Rhoads, John P.,	154
Rhoads, Jonathan E.,	160
" (Com.,)	102
Rhoads, Joseph,	107
Rhoads, Joseph,	146
Rhoads, Joseph, Jr.,	191
" " (*Teacher,*)	91
Rhoads, Joshua,	129
Rhoads, Levi P.,	141
Rhoads, Mary,	286
Rhoads, Mary A.,	307
Rhoads, Mary H.,	291
Rhoads, Owen,	127
Rhoads, Owen,	139
Rhoads, Phebe,	241
Rhoads, Phebe,	300
Rhoads, Rebecca,	233
Rhoads, Rebecca,	280
Rhoads, Rebecca G.,	103
(See Garrett.)	
Rhoads, Samuel,	129
Rhoads, Samuel N.,	199
Rhoads, Sarah,	275
Rhoads, Susanna,	233
Rhoads, Susanna,	300
Rhoads, Thomas G.,	194
Rhoads, William,	120
" " (Com.,)	100
Rhoads, William,	152
Rhoads, William E.,	206
Rich, Atkinson H.,	177
Rich, Deborah Y.,	323
Rich, Howard,	184
Rich, Rachel,	335
Rich, Sophronia,	342
Rich, Susan W.,	301
Richards, Abigail,	238
Richards, Ann,	260
Richards, Diana,	304
Richards, Emma,	296
Richards, Frederic,	149
Richards, Hannah T.,	244
Richards, Isaac,	125
Richards, Isaac H.,	170
Richards, Jacob,	125

INDEX. 417

Name	PAGE
Richards, Jonathan,	137
Richards, Joshua,	109
Richards, Lydia,	223
Richards, Mary,	226
Richards, Mary,	252
Richards, Rachel,	97
Richards, Rachel,	223
Richards, Rachel,	258
Richards, Rachel,	251
Richards, Samuel,	125
Richards, Samuel,	131
Richards, Sarah H.,	237
Richards, Sarah M.,	309
Richards, William,	118
Richardson, Ann,	230
Richardson, Anne,	99
Richardson, Ashton,	158
Richardson, Charles,	175
Richardson, Clayton,	129
Richardson, Eliz.,	226
" " (Com.,)	100
Richardson, Eliz.,	255
Richardson, Eliz.,	270
Richardson, Eliz.,	285
Richardson, Francis.	163
Richardson, Hannah,	235
Richardson, Hannah,	100
Richardson, Han. W.,	283
" " (Com.,)	102
Richardson, John,	153
Richardson, Jos. G.,	163
Richardson, Jos. P.,	153
Richardson, Lucy,	297
Richardson, Mary,	247
Richardson, Mary,	275
(*Wistar,*) " (Com.,)	102
Richardson, Mary R.,	286
Richardson, Reb'ca J.,	270
Richardson, Ruth,	98
Richardson, Sarah,	226
Richardson, Sarah,	245
Richardson, Sarah,	281
Richardson, Sarah T.,	275
Richardson, Susan,	255
Richardson, Thomas,	108
Richie, Anna Mary,	310
Richie, Edward,	133
" " (*Teacher,*)	85
" " (*Com.,*)	102
Richie, Edward B.,	181
Richie, Elizabeth S.,	313
Richie, Gideon L.,	169
Richie, Hannah,	278
Richie, John,	170
Richie, Margaret W.,	318
Richie, Ruth Anna,	319
Richie, Samuel,	133
Richie, Sarah,	287
Richie, Sarah,	318
Richie, Sarah A.,	103
(See Allen.)	
Richie, Sarah M.,	317
Ricks, Deborah O.,	315
Ricks, Samuella T.,	330
Ricks, Walter A.,	178
Ridgway, Amos A.,	172
Ridgway, Andrew C.,	114
Ridgway, Catharine,	224

Name	PAGE
Ridgway, Corinne,	341
Ridgway, David W.,	114
Ridgway, Henrietta,	269
Ridgway, Henry W.,	125
Ridgway, Jacob,	110
Ridgway, Jacob,	123
Ridgway, Job,	121
Ridgway, Job,	174
Ridgway, John,	149
Ridgway, Mary,	251
Ridgway, Mary,	265
Ridgway, Mercy W.,	276
Ridgway, Sarah,	223
Ridgway, Sarah,	250
Ridgway, Thomas,	118
Ridgway, Thomas,	165
Ridgway, William,	114
Righter, Elizabeth,	252
Righter, Hannah,	219
Righter, Mira,	273
Riker, Ruth Ann,	311
Riley, Ann,	228
Ring, Charles A.,	193
Ring, Welding,	181
Risley, Joseph P.,	147
Rively, Sarah C.,	252
Robbins, Margaret,	263
Roberts, Abigail B.,	261
Roberts, Albina N.,	260
Roberts, Alice,	325
Roberts, Allen H.,	197
Roberts, Amy J.,	311
Roberts, Ann,	237
Roberts, Ann,	247
Roberts, Anna B.,	306
Roberts, Anna W.,	323
Roberts, Arthur E.,	196
Roberts, Beulah,	237
Roberts, C. William,	200
Roberts, Caroline,	262
Roberts, Charles,	109
Roberts, Charles H.,	189
Roberts, David,	99
" " (Supt.,)	79
Roberts, David, Jr.,	191
Roberts, Deborah,	296
Roberts, Deborah D.,	259
Roberts, Deborah H.,	331
Roberts, Ebenezer,	166
Roberts, Edward,	132
Roberts, Edwin,	144
Roberts, Edwin,	166
Roberts, Elihu,	133
Roberts, Elisha,	141
" " (*Farmer,*)	92
Roberts, Elizabeth,	97
Roberts, Elizabeth,	281
Roberts, Elizabeth,	343
Roberts, Elizabeth E.,	331
Roberts, Elizabeth H.,	323
Roberts, Elizabeth K.,	329
Roberts, Ellen,	244
Roberts, Emily,	310
Roberts, Emma A.,	334
Roberts, Esther,	282
Roberts, Esther,	310
Roberts, Esther,	312
" " (*Com.,*)	103

Name	PAGE
Roberts, Everett P.,	188
Roberts, Franklin,	192
Roberts, George,	116
Roberts, George,	121
Roberts, George A.,	160
Roberts, Hannah,	237
Roberts, Hannah,	310
Roberts, Hannah B.,	311
Roberts, Hannah R.,	343
Roberts, Hannah W.,	319
Roberts, Hannah W.,	319
Roberts, Henry W.,	163
Roberts, Hepzibah,	223
Roberts, Hiram,	146
Roberts, Howard E.,	192
Roberts, I. Henry,	189
Roberts, Isaac L.,	292
Roberts, Jacob,	102
Roberts, James C.,	183
Roberts, Jane L.,	318
Roberts, Jehu,	96
Roberts, Jehu,	160
Roberts, John,	115
Roberts, John,	98
Roberts, John,	131
Roberts, John,	154
Roberts, John,	156
Roberts, John M.,	163
Roberts, Joseph,	171
Roberts, Joseph H.,	191
Roberts, Josiah,	98
Roberts, Josiah A.,	170
Roberts, Keturah L.,	308
Roberts, Lydia,	288
Roberts, Lydia M.,	317
Roberts, Marga'ta W.,	343
Roberts, Martha,	225
Roberts, Martha,	278
Roberts, Martha C.,	325
Roberts, Mary,	293
Roberts, Mary Ann,	256
Roberts, Mary Ann,	261
Roberts, Mary Anna,	315
Roberts, Mary E.,	337
Roberts, Mary H.,	309
(*Woolman,*) (*Gov'ness,*)	81
Roberts, Matthew,	132
Roberts, Mercy,	241
Roberts, Mercy A.,	328
Roberts, Nathan,	147
Roberts, Nathan H.,	205
Roberts, Nathan S.,	188
Roberts, Phebe,	282
Roberts, Phebe A.,	338
Roberts, Phebe W.,	102
Roberts, Rachel,	296
Roberts, Rachel,	310
Roberts, Rachel H.,	99
" " (*Matron,*)	79
(See Hunt.)	
Roberts, Rachel M.,	326
Roberts, Rebecca,	237
Roberts, Rebecca,	259
Roberts, Rebecca,	293
Roberts, Rebecca J.,	318
Roberts, Rebecca W.,	341
Roberts, Samuel,	143
Roberts, Samuel,	164

418 INDEX.

Name	PAGE
Roberts, Samuel M.,	205
Roberts, Sarah,	252
Roberts, Sarah E.,	280
Roberts, Sarah H.,	324
Roberts, Sarah S.,	253
Roberts, Sarah W.,	325
Roberts, Septimus,	110
Roberts, Septimus,	84
Roberts, Septimus,	155
Roberts, Susan,	261
Roberts, Susan A.,	346
Roberts, Susanna,	305
(*Williams,*) " (*Com.,*)	103
" " (*Matron,*)	80
Roberts, Tacy,	288
Roberts, Thomas S.,	111
Roberts, William,	98
Roberts, William,	180
Roberts, William H.,	190
Roberts, William J.,	168
Robeson, Andrew,	105
Robeson, Elizabeth,	99
Robeson, Sarah Ann,	225
Robeson, Sarah Ann,	231
Robinson, Abigail,	227
Robinson, Abigail,	249
Robinson, Amy,	247
Robinson, Ann,	227
Robinson, Betty,	243
Robinson, Edward,	120
Robinson, Elizabeth,	227
Robinson, Hannah L.,	305
Robinson, Jacob,	106
Robinson, Mary,	252
Robinson, Nathaniel,	167
Robinson, Rachel,	289
Robinson, William A.,	120
Rockhill, Hannah C.,	224
Rockwell, Emily E.,	345
Rodman, Henry,	86
Rogers, Ann,	255
Rogers, Elizabeth,	249
Rogers, Grace,	235
Rogers, Jane M.,	99
Rogers, Mary D.,	250
Rogers, Minerva,	249
Rogers, Rachel,	231
Rogers, Samuel,	117
Rogers, Timothy,	111
Roman, Asenath,	230
Roman, Hannah,	233
Rose, John,	116
Ross, Sarah,	233
Ross, Thomas,	109
Rote, James M.,	183
Rote, Margaret,	329
Rote, Mary M.,	320
Rote, Milton,	189
Rote, Narcissa,	336
Rote, Regina S.,	336
Rowand, Robert B.,	157
Rowland, Ann,	224
Rowland, Catharine,	223
Rowland, Elizabeth,	224
Rowland, Elizabeth,	228
Rowland, Elizabeth,	237
Rowland, Elizabeth,	250
Rowland, Hannah,	244

Name	PAGE
Rowland, Janet,	224
Rowland, Joseph,	115
Rowland, Joseph G.,	164
Rowland, Joshua G.,	98
Rowland, Mary,	237
Rowland, Mifflin,	123
Rowland, Samuel,	106
Rowland, Samuel,	123
Rowland, Tabitha,	224
Rowland, Tabitha,	229
Rowland, Thomas,	109
Rudolph, Abra'm P.,	143
Rudolph, Hannah,	300
Rudolph, Hannah P.,	324
Rudolph, Mary,	295
Rudolph, Mary E.,	322
Rudolph, Samuel F.,	180
Rudolph, Sarah Ann,	306
Rudolph, Sarah L.,	322
Rudolph, Thomas,	153
Rulon, Caroline M.,	311
Rulon, Elizabeth A.,	292
Rulon, John W.,	160
Rulon, Mary Ann,	303
Rulon, Sarah W.,	292
Rundle, Angelina,	324
Rushmore, Esther,	297
Russell, Amanda,	314
Russell, Elizabeth R.,	343
Russell, Lydia S.,	303
Russell, Marion Edith,	341
Russell, Robert H.,	196
Russell, Thomas,	134
Russell, Thomas W.,	201
Russell, Virginia,	313
Rutter, Thomas,	109
Salter, Sarah,	226
Sanderson, Ann W.,	247
Sankey, Elizabeth,	319
Sankey, Martha,	314
" (*Teacher.*) 87, 88, 89	
" (*Governess,*)	81
Sansom, Beulah,	98
Sansom, Joseph,	95
Satterthwait, George,	199
Satterthwaite, Alfred,	161
Satterthwaite, Al. H.,	202
Satterthwaite, Benj. C.,	182
Satterthwaite, Daniel,	167
Satterthwaite, Dan. C.,	177
Satterthwaite, Deb'h,	326
Satterthwaite, E. H.,	198
Satterthwaite, E. M.,	345
Satterthwaite, Edw'd,	203
Satterthwaite, Ellw'd,	188
Satterthwaite, Emlen,	157
Satterthwaite, H. E.,	197
Satterthwaite, H. W.,	191
Satterthwaite, Hut'n,	141
Satterthwaite, Is'c H.,	110
Satterthwaite, Jon'n,	141
Satterthwaite, Jos. C.,	150
Satterthwaite, Jos. H.,	145
Satterthwaite, Jos. H.,	194
Satterthwaite, Liz.W.,	330
Satterthwaite, Lydia,	254
Satterthwaite, M. C.,	188

Name	PAGE
Satterthwaite, Mar. W.,	334
Satterthwaite, Mary,	244
Satterthwaite, Mary A.,	328
Satterthwaite, Mary E.,	312
Satterthwaite, Reb'ca,	305
Satterthwaite, Reu'n,	175
Satterthwaite, Rho. S.,	335
Satterthwaite, Rich'd,	133
Satterthwaite, R. T.,	203
Satterthwaite, Sam'l,	113
Satterthwaite, Sarah,	250
Satterthwaite, Sn'h A.,	328
Satterthwaite, Sa'h E.,	334
Satterthwaite, Su'n B.,	339
Satterthwaite, Thos. C.,	206
Satterthwaite, Wm.,	125
Saul, Juliana,	280
Saunders, David,	110
Saunders, Hannah,	277
Saunders, Hannah C.,	313
Saunders, James,	137
Saunders, James,	175
Saunders, James M.,	140
Saunders, Lydia,	280
Saunders, Mary,	253
Saunders, Mary,	335
Saunders, Rachel S.,	298
Saunders, Sarah,	99
Saunders, Sarah,	312
Savery, Addison H.,	235
Savery, Albert H.,	205
Savery, Edward,	172
Savery, Elizabeth,	331
Savery, Mary W.,	320
Savery, Sarah,	96
Savery, Sarah,	315
Savery, Stephen W.,	162
Savery, Thomas,	101
Savery, Thomas H.,	162
Savery, William,	96
Savery, William,	163
Savery, William H.,	202
Say, Benjamin,	107
Say, Thomas,	105
Scarlett, Anna,	346
Scarlett, J. Miller,	186
Scarlett, John J.,	204
Scarlett, Lydia Ann,	306
Scarlett, Martha,	345
Scattergood, Ann,	98
Scattergood, Ann,	248
Scattergood, Anna,	324
Scattergood, Anna,	309
Scattergood, Caro. C.,	312
Scattergood, Chas. C.,	206
Scattergood, David,	128
Scattergood, David,	182
Scattergood, Eliz.,	269
Scattergood, Eliz. C.,	102
(See Comfort.)	
Scattergood, Geo. J.,	162
" " (*Com.,*)	102
Scattergood, Hannah,	298
Scattergood, Joseph,	130
" " (*Com.,*)	101
Scattergood, Joseph,	169
" " (*Com.,*)	103
Scattergood, Jos., Jr.,	206

INDEX. 419

Name	PAGE
Scattergood, Jos. B.,	177
Scattergood, Mary,	300
Scattergood, Mary,	346
Scattergood, Rachel,	307
" " (Com.,)	102
(Maris.) "	103
Scattergood, Rebecca,	226
Scattergood, Rebecca,	232
Scattergood, Rebecca,	327
Scattergood, Samuel,	132
Scattergood, Sam'l H.,	187
Scattergood, Sarah,	277
Scattergood, Sarah,	303
Scattergood, Sarah,	319
Scattergood, Susan,	319
Scattergood, Thomas,	97
Scattergood, Thomas,	121
Scattergood, Thomas,	169
Scattergood, Thos..Jr.,	178
Scattergood, William,	125
Scattergood, William,	177
Schill, Christiana,	346
Schofield, Edith,	248
Schofield, Esther,	253
Schofield, Joseph,	115
Schofield, Rachel,	227
Schooley, Samuel,	141
Schureman, John D.,	174
Scofield, Lewis N.,	204
Scott, Anna E.,	332
Scott, Charles,	165
Scott, David J.,	162
" " (Teacher,)	87, 89
" " (Governor,)	80
Scott, Edith D.,	312
Scott, Edmund W.,	181
Scott, Edward E.,	200
Scott, Edwin,	150
Scott, Ellwood W.,	162
Scott, Esther,	235
Scott, George W.,	205
Scott, Hannah,	244
Scott, Hannah A.,	310
Scott, Irving M.,	200
Scott, Israel R.,	181
Scott, Jane,	292
Scott, Job,	155
Scott, John,	162
Scott, John,	198
Scott, Jonathan,	157
Scott, Margaret H.,	347
Scott, Margaret J.,	331
Scott, Mary C.,	346
Scott, Mary E.,	320
Scott, Nelson W.,	176
Scott, Norris J.,	177
Scott, Oliver,	149
Scott, Rachel,	257
Scott, Rossiter,	130
Scott, Samuel J.,	178
Scott, Sarah,	247
Scott, Sarah Jane,	320
Scott, Townsend,	128
Scott, Wakeman H.,	199
Scott, Walter A.,	201
Scull, Abigail,	225
Scull, David,	163
Scull, Deborah,	283
Scull, Gideon,	107
Scull, Gideon D.,	148
Scull, Henry C.,	178
Scull, Isaac,	142
Scull, James,	107
Scull, Mary,	279
Scull, Mary,	324
Scull, Paul,	113
Scull, Sarah,	240
" " (Com.,)	100
Scull, Sarah,	279
Scull, Sarah,	318
Seal, Anna L.,	344
Seal, Charles,	135
Seal, Elizabeth P.,	260
Seal, Emma,	274
Seal, Francis J.,	204
Seal, Gertrude,	345
Seal, Isaac,	108
Seal, Joel A.,	173
Seal, Joseph G.,	177
Seal, Joshua T.,	121
Seal, Lydia,	249
Seal, Mary Jane,	318
Seal, Phebe,	300
Seal, Sarah Ann,	318
Seal, Thomas,	148
Seal, William,	174
Seaman, Anna,	261
Seaman, Marianna,	260
Seaman, Percival,	128
Seaman, Willet,	128
Sellers, Annabella,	335
Sellers, Charles C.,	161
Sellers, Edward,	162
Sellers, George,	158
Sellers, George H.,	158
Sellers, Samuel,	158
Serrill, Thomas,	161
Sexton, Elizabeth H.,	385
Sexton, Townsend,	199
Shallcross, Esther,	238
Sharp, Joseph,	97
Sharp, Sarah,	274
Sharpless, Aaron,	131
" " (Com.,)	101
" " (Supt.,)	80
Sharpless, Abigail,	264
Sharpless, Abraham,	129
Sharpless, Abraham,	96
Sharpless, Alfred,	186
Sharpless, Ann,	79
Sharpless, Ann,	242
Sharpless, Ann,	264
Sharpless, Ann,	322
Sharpless, Ann,	330
" " (Teacher,)	89
Sharpless, Anna,	276
Sharpless, Anna P.,	312
Sharpless, Anne,	239
Sharpless, Anne,	243
Sharpless, Anne,	300
Sharpless, Benjamin,	98
Sharpless, Benjamin,	140
Sharpless, Benjamin,	164
Sharpless, Blakey,	111
" (B'k-kpr.,)	92
" (Teacher,)	84
Sharpless, Beulah,	234
Sharpless, Caspar T.,	178
Sharpless, Caspar W.,	128
Sharpless, Catharine,	97
Sharpless, Catharine,	276
Sharpless, Charles,	143
Sharpless, Charles,	161
Sharpless, Charles L.,	138
Sharpless, Charles L.,	181
Sharpless, Edith,	227
Sharpless, Edith,	245
Sharpless, Edith,	273
Sharpless, Edith,	288
Sharpless, Edith,	312
Sharpless, Edith,	331
Sharpless, Edward,	135
Sharpless, Edward,	159
" " (Com.,)	102
Sharpless, Edward,	202
Sharpless, Eli,	178
Sharpless, Elizabeth,	253
Sharpless, Elizabeth,	268
Sharpless, Elizabeth,	272
Sharpless, Elizabeth,	282
Sharpless, Elizabeth,	321
Sharpless, Eliza'h C.,	342
Sharpless, George,	132
Sharpless, George, Jr.,	201
Sharpless, Hannah,	261
Sharpless, Hannah,	274
Sharpless, Hannah,	282
Sharpless, Han'h H.,	267
Sharpless, Harvey,	144
Sharpless, Harvey,	189
Sharpless, Henry,	113
Sharpless, Henry,	150
Sharpless, Henry P.,	135
Sharpless, Henry W.,	180
Sharpless, Isaac,	110
Sharpless, Isaac,	98
Sharpless, Isaac,	115
Sharpless, Isaac,	180
" " (Teacher,)	89
Sharpless, J. Clemson,	149
Sharpless, James F.,	190
Sharpless, Jane,	301
Sharpless, John M.,	133
" " (Com.,)	101
Sharpless, John P.,	189
Sharpless, Joseph,	106
Sharpless, Joseph,	117
Sharpless, Joseph,	153
Sharpless, Joseph C.,	183
Sharpless, Joshua,	79
Sharpless, Joshua,	113
Sharpless, Joshua,	182
Sharpless, Joshua B.,	113
" " (Com.,)	99
Sharpless, Lewis,	113
Sharpless, Lewis,	170
Sharpless, Lewis P.,	183
Sharpless, Lucy,	336
Sharpless, Lydia,	233
Sharpless, Lydia,	275
Sharpless, Lydia,	326
Sharpless, Lydia J.,	276
Sharpless, Lydia J.,	289
Sharpless, Mabel P.,	345

Y

INDEX.

Name	Page
Sharpless, Martha,	83
(Jefferis,) " (Com.,)	99
" (Matron,)	80
Sharpless, Martha L.,	323
Sharpless, Martha P.,	300
Sharpless, Mary,	238
Sharpless, Mary,	263
Sharpless, Mary,	278
Sharpless, Mary,	279
Sharpless, Mary,	313
Sharpless, Mary,	326
Sharpless, Mary A.,	255
Sharpless, Mercy,	247
Sharpless, Nathan,	96, 98
Sharpless, Nathan,	98
Sharpless, Nathan,	99
" (Supt.,)	79
Sharpless, Nathan,	173
Sharpless, Nathan,	179
Sharpless, Nathan H.,	98
Sharpless, Nathan J.,	146
Sharpless, Oliver,	153
Sharpless, Phebe,	99
(Middleton,) " (Com.,)	100
Sharpless, Phebe,	279
Sharpless, Philena,	296
Sharpless, Philip,	134
Sharpless, Rachel,	99
Sharpless, Rachel,	253
Sharpless, Rachel E.,	297
Sharpless, Rachel V.,	224
Sharpless, Rebecca,	238
Sharpless, Rebecca,	301
Sharpless, Robert,	106
Sharpless, Robert M.,	164
Sharpless, Ruth Anna,	328
Sharpless, Sarah,	223
Sharpless, Sarah,	264
Sharpless, Sarah Ann,	286
Sharpless, Sarah D.,	269
Sharpless, Sarah M.,	336
Sharpless, Sarah T.,	330
Sharpless, Sidney,	278
Sharpless, Susanna,	279
Sharpless, Susanna,	335
Sharpless, Susanna,	342
Sharpless, Susanna F.,	102
" (Mat'n,)	80
(See Forsythe.)	
Sharpless, Thomas,	165
Sharpless, Thomas,	167
Sharpless, Townsend,	196
Sharpless, Town'd T.,	167
Sharpless, William,	131
Sharpless, William,	138
Sharpless, William,	181
Sharpless, William P.,	154
Sharpless, William T.,	192
Shaw, Alexander,	142
Shaw, Deborah,	258
Shaw, Janet,	229
Shaw, Joshua H.,	179
Shaw, Maria,	247
Shaw, Mary,	260
Shaw, Mary,	281
Shaw, Rebecca,	260
Shaw, Sarah,	229
Shaw, Susan,	272
Sheffield, Amy R.,	316
Sheffield, Eliza'h A.,	319
Shelley, Joshua M.,	185
Sheppard, Annie E.,	320
Sheppard, Charles B.,	174
Sheppard, Clarkson,	132
" (Com.,)	101
Sheppard, Edward,	172
Sheppard, George W.,	153
Sheppard, Hannah,	230
Sheppard, Henry,	175
Sheppard, John E.,	100
Sheppard, John E., Jr.,	194
Sheppard, John M.,	169
Sheppard, John M.,	173
Sheppard, Letitia,	295
Sheppard, Lydia,	267
Sheppard, Lydia W.,	102
(See Warrington.)	
Sheppard, Margaret,	240
" (Com.,)	101
Sheppard, Margaret,	328
Sheppard, Margaret G.,	102
(See Garrett.)	
Sheppard, Mary,	318
Sheppard, Mary Ann,	311
Sheppard, Philip G.,	175
Sheppard, Rachel,	308
Sheppard, Rebecca,	239
(Warder,) " (Com.,)	100
Sheppard, Rebecca,	277
Sheppard, Rebeca C.,	103
Sheppard, Ruth B.,	296
Sheppard, Samuel M.,	152
Sheppard, Sarah,	276
Sheppard, Sarah R.,	304
Sheppard, William C.,	155
Sheward, Ann,	273
Sheward, Isaac G.,	135
Sheward, William,	135
Shinn, Ann Eliza,	269
Shinn, Earl, Jr.,	172
Shinn, Elizabeth,	286
Shinn, James T.,	165
Shinn, Joseph B.,	117
Shinn, Lydia C.,	297
Shinn, Rebecca,	241
Shinn, Rebecca,	311
Shinn, Sarah,	243
Shipley, Anna,	227
Shipley, Catharine,	304
Shipley, Charles I.,	169
Shipley, Hannah,	251
Shipley, Hannah E.,	304
Shipley, Jacob W.,	159
Shipley, Joseph,	117
Shipley, Joseph M.,	132
Shipley, Samuel R.,	150
Shipley, Thomas,	106
Shipley, Thomas,	129
Shipley, William L.,	130
Shober, H. Regina,	100
Shoemaker, Ann,	231
Shoemaker, Ann,	246
Shoemaker, Anna,	236
Shoemaker, Anna,	274
Shoemaker, Annie B.,	321
Shoemaker, Canby B.,	170
Shoemaker, Charles,	98
Shoemaker, Charles,	133
Shoemaker, Edith,	329
Shoemaker, Elisha,	116
Shoemaker, Eliza,	242
Shoemaker, Eliz.,	236
Shoemaker, Eliz.,	265
Shoemaker, Eliz.,	294
Shoemaker, Eliz.,	335
Shoemaker, Ezek'l C.,	184
Shoemaker, Hannah,	254
Shoemaker, Han'h B.,	321
Shoemaker, Isaac,	127
Shoemaker, Isaac L.,	117
Shoemaker, Jane,	97
Shoemaker, John,	95
Shoemaker, John, Jr.,	96
Shoemaker, John J.,	107
Shoemaker, Lydia,	266
Shoemaker, Marg'ta,	276
Shoemaker, M'tha C.,	337
Shoemaker, Mary,	239
Shoemaker, Mary,	240
Shoemaker, Mary H.,	271
Shoemaker, Rachel,	238
Shoemaker, Rachel,	266
Shoemaker, Rebecca,	292
Shoemaker, Samuel,	111
Shoemaker, Sarah,	303
Shoemaker, Sarah M.,	276
Shoemaker, Thos. S.,	184
Shoemaker, Wm. C.,	161
Sholl, A. Lincoln,	203
Sholl, Elizabeth L.,	339
Sholl, Henry Lloyd,	204
Sholl, Martha M.,	339
Shotwell, Abraham,	133
Shotwell, August F.,	159
Shotwell, Cath'ne S.,	276
Shotwell, Eden,	184
Shotwell, Edward,	130
Shotwell, Eleanor,	271
Shotwell, Elizabeth R.,	100
Shotwell, Harriet,	258
Shotwell, Henry L.,	143
Shotwell, Jacob R.,	134
Shotwell, Jacob V.,	134
Shotwell, Joseph,	95
Shotwell, Joseph F.,	159
Shotwell, Mary,	263
Shotwell, Mercy,	100
Shotwell, Nathan,	111
Shotwell, Nathan,	153
Shotwell, Sarah,	98
Shotwell, Thomas D.,	113
Shotwell, Wm. P. G.,	180
Shourds, Charlotte,	237
Shourds, Elizabeth,	228
Shreeve, Alexander,	128
Shreeve, Anna G.,	332
Shreeve, Arthur D.,	119
Shreeve, Caleb,	119
Shreeve, Elizabeth,	210
Shreeve, Elizabeth,	274
Shreeve, John,	109
Shreeve, Joseph N.,	193
Shreeve, Martha A.,	326
Shreeve, Mary,	232

INDEX. 421

Name	PAGE	Name	PAGE	Name	PAGE
Shreeve, Mary,	268	Smedley, Benj. D.,	158	Smith, Anna P.,	346
Shreeve, Mary H.,	292	Smedley, Bennett L.,	170	Smith, Anna W.,	303
Shreeve, Richard S.,	128	Smedley, Charles,	173	Smith, B. Gilpin,	188
Shreeve, Sarah B.,	284	Smedley, Deborah,	300	Smith, Barclay,	159
Shreeve, Stacy B.,	133	Smedley, Deborah L.,	319	Smith, Barzillai,	118
Shreeve, Thomas,	182	Smedley, Deborah P.,	316	Smith, Beulah,	232
Shreeve, Walter O.,	180	Smedley, Edith,	270	Smith, Caroline E.,	332
Shreve, Elizabeth A.,	339	Smedley, Edith,	347	*Smith, Caroline M.,*	101
Shreve, Ephraim G.,	197	Smedley, Edith F.,	344	Smith, Cassandra,	341
Shreve, John G.,	197	Smedley, Edward G.,	164	Smith, Catharine,	224
Shreve, Mary E.,	344	Smedley, Eliza H.,	314	Smith, Catharine,	248
Shreve, Samuel N.,	199	Smedley, Ellis,	149	Smith, Catharine H.,	298
Sidwell, Lydia Jane,	341	Smedley, Emma,	345	Smith, Catharine L.,	326
Sidwell, Wilson T.,	198	Smedley, George L.,	164	Smith, Charles,	107
Silver, Hannah L.,	290	Smedley, Hannah,	344	Smith, Charles,	107
Simmons, Anna,	332	Smedley, Hannah M.,	319	Smith, Charles,	136
Simmons, Deborah,	252	Smedley, Hannah P.,	312	Smith, Charles,	169
Simmons, Edward,	109	Smedley, Harriet J.,	338	Smith, Charles E.,	142
Simmons, Edward R.,	134	Smedley, Horace W.,	204	Smith, Clement W.,	144
Simmons, Eliz. P.,	294	Smedley, Isaac Y.,	156	Smith, Cyrus,	115
Simmons, Hannah,	274	Smedley, J. Larkin,	186	Smith, Daniel,	129
Simmons, Henrietta,	266	Smedley, Jacob,	130	Smith, Deborah,	224
Simmons, James D.,	161	Smedley, Jacob,	166	Smith, Deborah,	304
Simmons, Jane,	283	Smedley, James,	158	Smith, Deborah B.,	255
Simmons, Joseph S.,	196	" " (Teacher,)	86	" " (Gov'ness,)	81
Simmons, Lydia,	294	" " (Com.,)	103	Smith, Deborah S.,	204
Simmons, Mary Elma,	312	*Smedley, Jeffrey,*	97	Smith, Dilwyn,	137
Simmons, Rebecca R.,	293	Smedley, Jonathan,	174	*Smith, Edmund,*	97
Simmons, Samuel R.,	118	Smedley, Joseph F.,	199	Smith, Edward B.,	194
Simmons, Sarah,	255	Smedley, Joseph P.,	155	Smith, Edward H.,	167
Simpson, Frances J.,	298	Smedley, Louisa L.,	342	Smith, Edward M.,	147
Sinclair, Ann,	242	Smedley, Lydia,	297	Smith, Edward T.,	127
Sinclair, Ann,	247	Smedley, Lydia H.,	338	Smith, Eliza Ann,	261
Sinclair, Ann,	266	Smedley, Mary,	301	Smith, Eliza H.,	257
Sinclair, Eliza,	247	Smedley, Mary P.,	343	Smith, Elizabeth,	231
Sinclair, Elizabeth G.,	257	Smedley, Otto,	158	Smith, Elizabeth,	250
Sinclair, Mary Ann,	263	Smedley, Philena,	317	Smith, Elizabeth,	262
Sinclair, Rebecca,	240	Smedley, Rebecca,	314	Smith, Elizabeth,	277
Sinclair, Samuel,	116	" " (Teacher,)	87	Smith, Elizabeth,	286
Sinclair, Sarah,	240	Smedley, Rebecca,	345	*Smith, Elizabeth,*	100
Sinclair, William,	122	Smedley, Rebecca C.,	320	Smith, Elizabeth,	295
Singley, Hannah,	265	Smedley, Rowland,	202	Smith, Elizabeth,	318
Sinnickson, Sinnick,	109	Smedley, Samuel L.,	160	Smith, Elizabeth,	323
Sinton, John,	111	Smedley, Sam'l L., Jr.,	197	Smith, Elizabeth,	332
Sinton, Mary,	281	Smedley, Samuel W.,	159	Smith, Elizabeth C.,	312
Sinton, Phebe,	246	Smedley, Thomas,	164	Smith, Elizabeth M.,	263
Sinton, Phebe S.,	281	Smedley, Thomas,	167	Smith, Elizabeth P.,	287
Sinton, Sallie A. B.,	281	Smedley, Walter,	199	Smith, Ellen L.,	204
Sipple, Eliza T.,	233	Smedley, William,	157	Smith, Ephraim,	173
Sisom, Jane,	240	Smedley, William,	169	" " (Teacher,)	87
Skelton, Eli,	127	Smedley, William,	206	" " (Com.,)	103
Skyrin, Mary,	246	Smedley, Wm. Alfred,	204	Smith, Esther,	228
Sleeper, Benjamin,	151	Smedley, William H.,	187	Smith, Esther,	231
Sleeper, Mary,	256	Smedley, William J.,	153	*Smith, Esther,*	99
Sleeper, Sarah Ann,	281	Smedley, William W.,	116	Smith, Esther,	290
Sloan, Ann Eliza,	278	Smith, Abigail B.,	224	Smith, Franklin,	127
Sloan, Charles,	154	Smith, Abram H.,	183	Smith, Franklin W.,	192
Sloan, Elizabeth H.,	251	Smith, Alban,	117	Smith, George D.,	129
Sloan, John,	154	Smith, Albanus,	143	Smith, Grace,	249
Sloan, Richard,	152	Smith, Albert H.,	161	Smith, Hannah,	237
Slocum, Marshall,	126	Smith, Alfred,	133	Smith, Hannah P.,	330
Smart, Hannah,	277	Smith, Alfred K.,	180	Smith, Helen A.,	334
Smart, Rebecca,	302	Smith, Ambrose,	137	Smith, Henry,	125
Smedley, Abra'm P.,	156	*Smith, Amelia,*	100	Smith, Henry,	130
Smedley, Alfred,	202	Smith, Ann,	210	Smith, Henry H.,	162
Smedley, Anna,	282	Smith, Anna,	252	Smith, Hugh,	119
Smedley, Anna,	292	Smith, Anna,	321	Smith, Hugh O.,	131
Smedley, Anna M.,	312	Smith, Anna C.,	294	Smith, Isaac J.,	130

INDEX.

Name	PAGE	Name	PAGE	Name	PAGE
Smith, J. Walters,	201	Smith, Rebecca,	227	Speakman, Stephen,	126
Smith, Jacob,	106	Smith, Rebecca,	262	Speakman, Townsend,	112
Smith, James,	112	Smith, Rebecca D.,	270	Spencer, Agnes,	286
Smith, James,	113	Smith, Rebecca S.,	332	Spencer, Amelia,	288
Smith, James,	147	Smith, Richard,	106	Spencer, Ann,	233
Smith, James,	200	Smith, Richard,	125	Spencer, Anna,	294
Smith, James B.,	117	Smith, Robert,	112	Spencer, Anna,	307
Smith, James W.,	130	Smith, Rowen,	129	*Spencer, Anne,*	100
Smith, Jesse,	153	*Smith, Samuel,*	95	Spencer, Elizabeth,	273
Smith, John,	115	*Smith, Samuel*	95	Spencer, Ellen,	277
Smith, John J.,	119	Smith, Samuel,	148	Spencer, George,	148
Smith, John L.,	135	Smith, Samuel N.,	138	Spencer, George,	150
Smith, Jonathan D.,	131	Smith, Samuel S.,	108	Spencer, Hannah,	230
Smith, Joseph,	114	Smith, Sarah,	229	Spencer, Hannah,	278
Smith, Joseph,	121	Smith, Sarah,	247	Spencer, Hannah,	283
Smith, Joseph,	126	Smith, Sarah,	272	*Spencer, Jesse,*	100
Smith, Joseph R.,	112	Smith, Sarah Ann,	246	Spencer, John,	146
Smith, Joshua C.,	195	Smith, Sarah Ann,	267	Spencer, Louisa,	283
Smith, Judith,	257	*Smith, Sarah E.,*	103	Spencer, Lydia,	251
Smith, Letitia,	233	(See Elkinton.)		Spencer. Lydia,	303
Smith, Lucy,	276	Smith, Sarah F.,	270	Spencer, Maria,	252
Smith, Lydia,	278	Smith, Sarah G.,	313	Spencer, Mary Ann,	286
Smith, Lydia Ann,	270	Smith, Sarah R.,	251	Spencer, Mary B.,	308
Smith, Margaret,	225	Smith, Septimus,	125	Spencer, Rachel,	251
(*Hilles,*) " (Com.,)	99	*Smith, Seth,*	84	Spencer, Rebecca,	245
Smith, Margaret,	236	Smith, Sibilla,	327	Spencer, Rebecca,	285
Smith, Margaret,	236	Smith, Susan D.,	267	Spencer, Ruth Ann,	275
Smith, Margaret,	245	Smith, Susan P.,	295	Spencer, Samuel,	110
Smith, Margaret,	246	Smith, Susanna,	249	Spencer, Sarah,	223
Smith, Margaret,	99	Smith, Susanna,	260	Spencer, Sibilla,	283
Smith, Margaret M.,	230	Smith, Tabitha R.,	239	Spencer, Susanna,	231
" " (Com.,)	101	Smith, Thornton,	149	Spencer, William F.,	162
Smith, Margaret M.,	319	Smith, Walter B.,	183	Squibb, Jacob H.,	120
Smith, Margery,	225	Smith, William A.,	127	Squibb, James,	119
Smith, Maria,	262	Smith, William B.,	129	Squibb, James R.,	150
Smith, Marshall,	111	Smith, William B.,	138	Squibb, Thomas,	124
Smith, Marshall B.,	161	Smith, William B.,	210	Stabler, Caleb,	114
Smith, Martha,	275	Smith, William F.,	196	Stabler, Catharine,	302
Smith, Martha C.,	326	Smith, William K.,	183	Stabler, Charles M.,	185
Smith, Martha C.,	330	Smith, Willianna,	232	Stabler, Edward,	114
Smith, Mary,	97	Snowdon, Anne,	315	Stabler, Isabella E.,	331
Smith, Mary,	231	Snowdon, Edward,	137	Stabler, John,	114
Smith, Mary,	236	Snowdon, Elizabeth,	309	Stabler, Robinson,	123
Smith, Mary,	250	*Snowdon, Hannah E.,*	102	Stabler, Russell,	204
Smith, Mary,	287	" " (*Mat'n,*)	79	Stabler, Thomas P.,	114
Smith, Mary B.,	248	(See Ecroyd.)		Stabler, Walter,	185
Smith, Mary E.,	273	Snowdon, John C.,	155	Stabler, William,	114
Smith, Mary E.,	322	Snowdon, Joseph,	135	Stabler, William H.,	125
Smith, Mary E.,	341	*Snowdon, Joseph,*	100	Stackhouse, Anna,	296
Smith, Mary H.,	346	" " (*Supt.,*)	79	Stackhouse, Cath. M.,	323
Smith, Mary L.,	85	Snowdon, Joseph D.,	195	Stackhouse, Chas. D.,	133
Smith, Mary L.,	293	Snowdon, Leonard,	172	Stackhouse, Chas. D.,	186
Smith, Mary N.,	325	Snowdon, Mary,	279	Stackhouse, Eliz.,	286
Smith, Mary T.,	282	Snowdon, Mary D.,	342	Stackhouse, Eliz. Y.,	283
Smith, Mary W.,	239	Snowdon, Rebecca,	273	Stackhouse, Grace,	238
Smith, Mary W.,	248	Snowdon, Sarah,	284	Stackhouse, Mercy,	238
Smith, Milnor D.,	189	Somers, Ann,	250	Stackhouse, Howell,	153
Smith, Milton,	124	Somers, Mary L.,	269	Stackhouse, Robert,	124
Smith, Milton,	147	South, Edward L.,	196	Stalker, Grace,	231
Smith, Morris,	119	South, Walter,	199	Stalker, Hannah B.,	256
Smith, N. Newlin,	180	Spackman, Ann,	261	Stanley, Catharine E.,	335
Smith, Nathan B.,	156	Speakman, Ellen,	329	Stanley, Nancy M.,	327
Smith, Parvin,	146	Speakman, Emma,	328	Stanley, T. Wistar,	203
Smith, Priscilla,	232	Speakman, Esther,	282	Stanton, Edna,	324
Smith, Rachel,	230	Speakman, Esther,	232	Stanton, Emma C.,	346
Smith, Rachel,	236	Speakman, P'be Ann,	256	Stanton, Sarah B.,	348
Smith, Raper,	119	Speakman, Samuel,	184	Stapler, Achsah,	236
Smith, Rebecca,	225	Speakman, Sarah,	323	Stapler, Charles,	116

INDEX. 423

Name	PAGE
Stapler, Esther,	226
Stapler, John,	95
Stapler, John,	108
Stapler, John,	115
Stapler, Joseph,	116
Stapler, Stephen,	107
Stapler, Thomas,	105
Stapler, William W.,	177
Starbuck, Milton,	180
Starr, Anna Mary,	299
Starr, Charles,	111
Starr, Elizabeth T.,	233
Starr, Isaac,	115
Starr, James,	111
Starr, John,	122
Starr, Joseph,	117
Starr, Lydia,	250
" " (Com.,)	101
Starr, Mary Anne,	259
Starr, Phebe Ann,	271
Starr, Samuel,	118
Starr, Sarah,	239
Starr, Sarah,	286
Starr, Sarah,	299
Starr, Sarah Ann,	280
Starr, Sarah Ann,	295
Starr, William,	127
Steel, Andrew,	92
Steel, Sidney,	245
Steer, Elizabeth,	287
Steer, Hannah,	274
Steer, Joseph E.,	198
Steer, Lindley B.,	185
Steer, Mary,	257
Steer, Samuel L.,	134
Steer, William G.,	197
Steer, William M.,	194
Stephens, Marg'ret C.,	304
Stephens, Richard,	155
Stephens, William,	153
Sterling, James S.,	131
Sterling, Rebecca B.,	269
Stevens, Ann,	249
Stevens, Sarah,	270
Stevens, Sarah W.,	296
Stevenson, Anna A.,	297
Stevenson, Daniel W.,	170
Stevenson, Edw'd B.,	168
Stevenson, Edw'd B.,	170
Stevenson, Elizabeth,	230
Stevenson, Elmira,	309
Stevenson, Emily,	261
Stevenson, James W.,	151
Stevenson, Joseph,	151
Stevenson, Mary,	224
Stevenson, Mary,	267
Stevenson, Samuel,	152
Stevenson, Sidney,	280
" (Teacher,)	85
Stevenson, Walter R.,	175
Stevenson, William L.,	107
Stevenson, William,	167
Stewardson, Anna,	97
Stewardson, Eliza'th,	241
Stewardson, John H.,	124
Stewardson, Thomas,	95
Stewart, Hannah,	253
Stewart, Mary,	255

Name	PAGE
Stewart, Rachel P.,	330
Stockton, Ann,	217
" " (Teacher,)	84
Stockton, Edith B.,	257
Stockton, Edith D.,	256
Stockton, Jane,	259
Stockton, Sarah W.,	290
Stockton, Susan K.,	290
Stokely, Harriet,	255
Stokes, Alice R.,	322
Stokes, Ann L.,	273
Stokes, Anna,	305
Stokes, Anna M.,	335
Stokes, Barzillia B.,	164
Stokes, Chalkley,	144
Stokes, Charles,	144
Stokes, Edwin,	153
Stokes, Elizabeth,	266
Stokes, Elizabeth,	270
Stokes, Elizabeth,	275
Stokes, Elizabeth C.,	283
Stokes, Elizabeth C.,	338
Stokes, Ezra,	153
Stokes, Frances C.,	287
Stokes, Francis,	159
Stokes, George C.,	168
Stokes, George P.,	175
Stokes, Hannah H.,	314
Stokes, Henry W.,	159
Stokes, Horace,	196
Stokes, Isaac,	178
Stokes, J. Stogdell,	205
Stokes, John,	121
Stokes, John C.,	188
Stokes, John H.,	156
Stokes, John W.,	183
Stokes, Joseph,	154
Stokes, Joseph,	197
Stokes, Joseph W.,	129
Stokes, Joseph W.,	165
Stokes, Joshua,	133
Stokes, Lydia,	276
(Wills,) " (Com.,)	101
Stokes, Malvina,	308
Stokes, Martha,	263
Stokes, Martha E.,	317
Stokes, Mary,	247
Stokes, Mary,	252
Stokes, Mary,	295
Stokes, Mary C.,	335
Stokes, Mary Emma,	320
Stokes, Nathaniel B.,	165
Stokes, Nathaniel N.,	123
" " (Com.,)	100
Stokes, Nathaniel N.,	160
Stokes, N. Newlin,	194
Stokes, Rachel W.,	265
Stokes, Samuel,	112
Stokes, Samuel,	136
Stokes, Samuel S. H.,	201
Stokes, Samuel W.,	172
Stokes, Sarah,	237
Stokes, Sarah W.,	324
Stokes, Stogdell,	113
Stokes, Susanna,	231
Stokes, Susanna,	255
Stokes, Thomas C.,	175
Stokes, Walter P.,	192

Name	PAGE
Stokes, William C.,	175
Stokes, Wistar,	163
Stone, Anna L.,	331
Stone, Mary Ellen,	325
Storer, John W.,	170
Story, Hannah,	243
Story, Rebecca,	237
Stowe, Isaac,	117
Stratton, Benjamin,	134
Stratton, Charles,	198
Stratton, Clayton,	128
Stratton, Dillwyn,	204
Stratton, Eliza Ann,	262
Stratton, Jacob,	133
Stratton, Joseph C.,	198
Stratton, Joseph D.,	128
Stratton, Lydia,	232
Strawbridge, Ed. R.,	291
Strawn, Johnson P.,	185
Street, Ann,	321
Street, Hannah,	329
Street, John,	144
Street, Samuel W.,	193
Street, Webster,	185
Street, William J.,	184
Strode, Richard,	96
Stroud, Ann,	227
Stroud, Charles,	115
Stroud, Eliza J.,	296
Stroud, Elizabeth,	291
Stroud, Elizabeth D.,	287
Stroud, George M.,	115
Stroud, Jacob,	119
Stroud, James,	119
Stroud, Jemima,	239
Stroud, Joseph R.,	163
Stroud, Lydia B.,	287
Stroud, Morris R.,	145
Stroud, Rebecca R.,	288
Stroud, Sarah,	300
Stroud, William,	116
Stroud, William D.,	145
Stubbs, John W.,	115
Styer, Albanus,	155
Styer, Samuel,	145
Sniggett, Deborah D.,	281
Sniggett, Mary E.,	281
Sutton, Adna H.,	187
Sutton, Ann H.,	289
Sutton, Lucy,	328
Sutton, Susanna M.,	317
Swain, Andrew,	118
Swain, Letitia,	265
Swain, Mary,	97
Swain, Philena,	293
Swain, Sarah E.,	312
Swayne, Benj. W.,	154
Swayne, Clara E.,	311
Swayne, Caleb,	118
Swayne, Caleb,	98
Swayne, Hannah,	240
Swayne, Howard R.,	202
Swayne, Joel,	127
Swayne, Joseph,	146
Swayne, Mary C.,	304
Swayne, Philena P.,	275
Swayne, Rest,	227
" " (Com.,)	99

32

424 INDEX.

Name	PAGE
Swayme, Rest, (Cope,)	99
Swayme, Samuel,	98
Swayne, Susanna,	257
Swayne, Walter S.,	197
Swayne, Wm. M'shall,	154
Swett, Benjamin,	95
Swett, Mary.	97
Swift, Elizabeth,	310
Sykes, Ann,	272
Symons, Rebecca W.,	291
Taber, J. John H.,	190
Taber, Rachel H.,	338
Talbot, John,	96
Tatnall, Anna C.,	341
Tatnall, Anna W.,	320
Tatnall, Ashton R.,	189
Tatnall, Charles M.,	177
Tatnall, Edward,	100
Tatnall, Edward,	174
Tatnall, Elizabeth,	309
Tatnall, Elizabeth H.,	322
Tatnall, Henry,	154
Tatnall, Henry,	190
Tatnall, James W.,	176
Tatnall, Lucy R.,	337
Tatnall, Margaret,	320
Tatnall, Mary R.,	321
Tatnall, Richard R.,	190
Tatnall, Robert R.,	205
Tatnall, Samuel W.,	194
Tatnall, Sarah,	98
Tatnall, Thomas,	190
Tatnall, William,	143
Tatnall, William, Jr.,	199
Tatum, Amy Y.,	100
(See Yarnall.)	
Tatum, Ann,	265
Tatum, Ann,	284
Tatum, Anne,	100
(See Biddle.)	
Tatum, Ashton R.,	189
Tatum, Beulah,	290
Tatum, Charles,	195
Tatum, Daniel O.,	136
Tatum, David,	128
Tatum, Edward,	144
Tatum, Edward P.,	193
Tatum, Elizabeth,	281
Tatum, Elizabeth H.,	346
Tatum, Frances C.,	340
Tatum, George W.,	170
Tatum, Hannah,	99
Tatum, Hannah,	302
Tatum, Henry,	192
Tatum, John,	121
Tatum, John,	149
Tatum, John, Jr.,	97
Tatum, John C.,	162
Tatum, John W.,	99
Tatum, John W.,	193
Tatum, Joseph,	125
Tatum, Josiah,	113
" " (Com.,)	99
Tatum, Josiah,	140
Tatum, Lawrence,	189
Tatum, Maria,	259
Tatum, Maria,	262

Name	PAGE
Tatum, Mary,	253
Tatum, Mary,	337
Tatum, Oliver P.,	199
Tatum, Richard P.,	193
Tatum, Sarah C.,	306
Tatum, Sarah M.,	102
(See Mickle.)	
Tatum, Sarah M.,	344
Tatum, William E.,	182
Tatum, William R.,	203
Taylor, Abby Ann,	305
Taylor, Achsah R.,	323
Taylor, Alfred B.,	179
Taylor, Amos,	146
Taylor, Anna B.,	337
Taylor, Anna H.,	322
Taylor, Anna M.,	315
Taylor, Anna M.,	335
Taylor, Anna S.,	340
Taylor, Benjamin,	122
Taylor, Benjamin,	147
Taylor, Benjamin B.,	163
Taylor, Benjamin F.,	154
Taylor, Benjamin H.,	199
Taylor, Bolton L.,	158
Taylor, Caleb,	111
Taylor, Caleb,	144
Taylor, Caleb C. W.,	148
Taylor, Charles,	149
Taylor, Charles J.,	181
Taylor, Charles P.,	175
Taylor, Charles S.,	187
Taylor, Charles W.,	136
Taylor, Deborah,	289
Taylor, Dinah,	286
Taylor, Edward,	158
Taylor, Edward B.,	183
Taylor, Edward H.,	143
Taylor, Eliza,	265
Taylor, Elizabeth,	237
Taylor, Elizabeth,	258
Taylor, Ellen M.,	330
Taylor, Emily A.,	322
Taylor, Emma A.,	330
Taylor, Esther P.,	304
Taylor, George B.,	177
Taylor, George K.,	167
Taylor, George P.,	136
Tayl r, George W.,	85
Taylor, George W.,	179
Taylor, Hannah,	252
Taylor, Hannah,	255
Taylor, Hannah,	266
Taylor, Hannah,	280
Taylor, Harriet J.,	343
Taylor, Henry,	143
Taylor, Henry,	185
Taylor, Henry W.,	157
Taylor, Hudson B.,	181
Taylor, J. Gardiner,	153
Taylor, Jacob,	115
Taylor, James,	170
Taylor, Jesse W.,	139
Taylor, Joanna R.,	275
Taylor, John H.,	175
Taylor, John W.,	148
Taylor, Joseph,	115
Taylor, Joseph,	161

Name	PAGE
Taylor, Joseph B.,	146
Taylor, Joseph G.,	157
Taylor, Joshua,	188
Taylor, Levis W.,	196
Taylor, Lewis,	193
Taylor, Lownes,	114
Taylor, Lucy,	338
Taylor, Lydia,	209
Taylor, Lydia,	284
Taylor, Lydia W.,	320
Taylor, Mahlon,	112
Taylor, Margaret,	280
Taylor, Margaret,	283
Taylor, Maris,	112
Taylor, Mark B.,	186
Taylor, Marshall,	152
Taylor, Mary,	97
Taylor, Mary,	238
Taylor, Mary,	321
Taylor, Mary Ann,	289
Taylor, Mary B.,	339
Taylor, Mary E.,	330
Taylor, Morris H.,	198
Taylor, Nicholas,	116
Taylor, Nicholas,	154
Taylor, Oliver A.,	141
Taylor, Phebe,	324
Taylor, Rebecca,	235
Taylor, Rebecca,	250
Taylor, Rebecca,	262
Taylor, Rebecca,	279
Taylor, Rebecca W.,	284
Taylor, Richard,	140
Taylor, Robert,	177
Taylor, Ruth Anna,	280
Taylor, Samuel C.,	130
Taylor, Samuel W.,	145
Taylor, Sarah,	227
Taylor, Sarah,	230
Taylor, Sarah,	236
Taylor, Sarah,	246
Taylor, Sarah,	284
Taylor, Sarah A.,	329
Taylor, Sarah B.,	342
Taylor, Sarah H.,	261
Taylor, Sarah M.,	279
Taylor, Sarah M.,	309
Taylor, Sarah M.,	330
Taylor, Sophia K.,	329
Taylor, Thomas B.,	188
Taylor, Thomas K.,	147
Taylor, Walter S.,	206
Taylor, William,	110
Taylor, William,	178
Taylor, William H.,	181
Taylor, Wm. Henry,	182
Teas, Rebecca,	240
Temple, Anna B.,	326
Temple, Anna C.,	286
Temple, Charles,	167
Temple, Edward,	164
Temple, Edward B.,	179
Temple, Emily,	313
Temple, Emily R.,	310
Temple, George,	173
Temple, Hannah S.,	261
Temple, James B.,	169
Temple, Jane,	259

INDEX. 425

Name	PAGE	Name	PAGE	Name	PAGE
Temple, Jane B.,	258	Thomas, George,	130	Thomas, Sarah,	277
Temple, Jane B.,	280	Thomas, George, Jr.,	179	Thomas, Sarah Ann,	269
Temple, Jane B.,	323	Thomas, Gulielma M.,	279	Thomas, Sarah Ellen,	316
Temple, Joseph E.,	131	Thomas, Hannah,	283	Thomas, Sarah M.,	283
Temple, Mary Ann,	317	Thomas, Hannah,	267	Thomas, Sarah P.,	332
Temple, Mira E.,	258	Thomas, Hannah,	299	Thomas, Susan,	302
Temple, Norris,	127	*Thomas, Harvey,*	85	Thomas, Susanna J.,	248
Temple, Norris G.,	202	Thomas, Harvey M.,	205	Thomas, Susan L.,	268
Temple, Sarah,	252	Thomas, Henry M.,	196	Thomas, Susanna M.,	283
Temple, Sidney,	99	Thomas, Howard,	170	Thomas, Susanna Y.,	266
(See Hill.)		Thomas, Howard,	191	Thomas, Tacy,	260
Temple, Sidney,	314	Thomas, Isaac,	166	Thomas, Tacy,	269
Test, Sallie M.,	348	Thomas, Jacob V.,	142	Thomas, Thomazine,	226
Thatcher, Benjamin,	147	Thomas, James M.,	137	Thomas, William,	143
Thatcher, Charity,	253	Thomas, Jane,	252	Thomas, William,	161
Thatcher, Eliza,	270	Thomas, Jane L.,	253	Thomas, Wm. Penn,	122
Thatcher, Enos E.,	173	Thomas, Jane W.,	256	Thompson, Ann,	216
Thatcher, Garrett,	134	Thomas, John,	108	Thompson, Ann,	277
Thatcher, Jesse P.,	176	Thomas, John,	114	Thompson, Anna,	254
Thatcher, Marg'etta F.,	284	Thomas, John,	136	Thompson, Anna E.,	323
Thatcher, Marg'etta E.,	330	Thomas, John H.,	189	Thompson, Annie,	336
Thatcher, Phebe G.,	284	Thomas, Jonathan,	147	Thompson, Beulah,	340
Thatcher, Richard,	140	Thomas, Joseph,	114	Thompson, C. Wistar,	201
Thatcher, Richard,	141	Thomas, Joseph,	125	Thompson, Caspar W.,	148
Thatcher, Sarah,	259	Thomas, Joseph W.,	113	Thompson, Catharine,	265
Thatcher, Sidney,	242	Thomas, Joshua,	196	Thompson, Daniel,	204
Thatcher, Susanna J.,	328	Thomas, Levi S.,	180	Thompson, David,	130
Thatcher, William P.,	141	Thomas, Loretta,	310	Thompson, Deborah,	242
Thomas, Alfred,	140	Thomas, Louisa A.,	248	Thompson, Eli,	154
Thomas, Amy,	248	Thomas, Lydia A.,	255	Thompson, Elizabeth,	300
Thomas, Amy Ann,	278	Thomas, Lydia G.,	311	Thompson, Elizabeth,	342
Thomas, Ann,	83	Thomas, Margaretta,	314	Thompson, Eliz'h A.,	310
Thomas, Ann,	249	Thomas, Martha,	241	Thompson, Eliz'h M.,	259
Thomas, Ann,	258	Thomas, Martha,	255	Thompson, Emma,	344
Thomas, Ann,	328	Thomas, Martha,	264	Thompson, Francis,	173
Thomas, Anna,	227	Thomas, Martha,	301	Thompson, Geo. H.,	190
Thomas, Anna,	311	Thomas, Mary,	234	Thompson, Hannah,	228
Thomas, Annie,	336	Thomas, Mary,	288	Thompson, Hannah,	258
Thomas, Anthony,	116	Thomas, Mary,	336	Thompson, Hannah,	260
Thomas, Barclay,	187	Thomas, Mary E.,	280	Thompson, Hannah,	290
Thomas, Benjamin F.,	166	Thomas, Mary E.,	329	Thompson, Hannah,	300
Thomas, Bond V.,	196	Thomas, Mary L.,	288	Thompson, Hannah,	345
Thomas, Charles,	195	Thomas, Mary L.,	291	Thompson, Han'h H.,	310
Thomas, Charles T.,	179	Thomas, Mary P.,	330	Thompson, Helen D.,	205
Thomas, Charles W.,	164	Thomas, Orpha,	253	Thompson, Henry D.,	167
Thomas, Daniel,	96	Thomas, Peter,	132	Thompson, Horace D.,	152
Thomas, Daniel,	114	Thomas, Priscilla,	213	Thompson, Isaac H.,	164
Thomas, Deborah D.,	325	Thomas, Rebecca,	232	Thompson, Israel,	105
Thomas, Edward,	147	Thomas, Rebecca,	265	Thompson, James,	152
Thomas, Edward A.,	172	Thomas, Rebecca,	269	Thompson, Jane P.,	282
Thomas, Eliza,	276	Thomas, Rebecca M.,	291	Thompson, Joel,	152
Thomas, Eliza L.,	345	Thomas, Reece,	169	Thompson, Joseph,	141
Thomas, Eliza M.,	325	Thomas, Reece L.,	190	Thompson, Joseph,	169
Thomas, Elizabeth,	225	Thomas, Richard,	123	Thompson, Joseph,	173
Thomas, Elizabeth,	252	Thomas, Richard,	186	Thompson, Lydia,	298
Thomas, Elizabeth C.,	288	Thomas, Ridgway,	114	Thompson, Margaret,	293
Thomas, Ellwood,	154	Thomas, Robert,	130	Thompson, Mary,	268
Thomas, Elton,	154	*Thomas, Robert,*	101	Thompson, Mary,	315
Thomas, Emilla,	231	Thomas, Robert H.,	144	Thompson, Mary,	323
Thomas, Emily,	321	Thomas, Robert P.,	146	Thompson, Mary B.,	317
Thomas, Emily,	338	Thomas, Robert P.,	192	Thompson, Mary N.,	291
Thomas, Enos,	153	Thomas, Ruth Anna,	322	Thompson, Mary W.,	301
Thomas, Enos,	180	Thomas, Sally,	285	Thompson, Pleasant,	228
Thomas, Esther L.,	253	Thomas, Samuel C.,	187	Thompson, Reb'a W.,	326
Thomas, Esther M.,	229	Thomas, Samuel D.,	114	Thompson, Rosanna,	293
Thomas, Evan,	114	Thomas, Sarah,	226	Thompson, Sam'l S.,	166
Thomas, Evan,	138	Thomas, Sarah,	227	Thompson, Sarah,	228
Thomas, Felicia,	347	Thomas, Sarah,	228	Thompson, Sarah,	268

INDEX.

Name	PAGE
Thompson, Sarah,	290
Thompson, Sarah,	299
Thompson, Sarah B.,	241
Thompson, Sarah E.,	257
Thompson, Sarah M.,	316
Thompson, Spencer,	165
Thompson, Thos. H.,	199
Thompson, William,	147
Thompson, Wm. H.,	204
Thompson, Wm. S.,	150
Thompson, Wilson,	170
Thompson, Wilson,	171
Thorne, Barton T.,	167
Thorne, Catharine,	
Thorne, Chalkley N.,	138
Thorne, Edgar,	145
Thorne, Harriet H.,	313
Thorne, Joseph W.,	142
Thorne, Mary D.,	283
Thorne, Sarah,	238
Thorne, Sarah Ann,	305
Thorne, William,	137
Thornton, Elizabeth,	271
Thornton, James,	107
Thorp, Anna K.,	334
Thorp, Anna M.,	321
Thorp, Benjamin, Jr.,	186
Thorp, Benjamin S.,	200
Thorp, Charles N.,	184
Thorp, Edward A.,	194
Thorp, Edwin,	189
" " (*Teacher*,)	90
Thorp, Elizabeth S.,	345
Thorp, Elizabeth W.,	341
Thorp, George S.,	193
Thorp, Henry A.,	201
Thorp, Howard J.,	203
Thorp, James Albin,	190
Thorp, Jane,	346
Thorp, John M.,	205
Thorp, John P.,	195
Thorp, Joseph,	200
Thorp, Lewis W.,	204
Thorp, Leonard T.,	206
Thorp, Margaret N.,	322
Thorp, Mary S.,	339
Thorp, Mary S.,	338
Thorp, Robert M.,	203
Thorp, Samuel R.,	198
Thorp, Thomas W.,	196
Thorp, William H.,	195
Thorp, William K.,	189
Tilton, Allen P.,	161
Tilton, Henry R.,	165
Tilton, John Henry,	194
Tilton, Mary Anna,	319
Tilton, Rebecca O.,	335
Titus, Daniel,	153
Titus, Robert W.,	153
Tomkins, Joseph,	109
Tomkins, Joseph Y.,	112
Tomlinson, Benj. H.,	164
Tomlinson, David,	177
Tomlinson, Ellwood,	179
Tomlinson, Joseph,	125
Tomlinson, Joseph,	178
Tomlinson, Jos'ine,	330
Tomlinson, Lav'la H.,	320

Name	PAGE
Tomlinson, Lav'ia H.,	323
Tomlinson, Mary,	288
Tomlinson, Mary,	314
Tomlinson, Pamella,	299
Tomlinson, Robert K.,	164
Tomlinson, Sarah,	224
Tomlinson, Wm. H.,	179
Tostenson, Maline,	318
Townsend, Abel,	111
Townsend, Abigail P.,	310
Townsend, Alice S.,	339
Townsend, Amanda,	301
Townsend, Anna,	314
Townsend, Anna Mary,	103
(See Kirk.)	
Townsend, Beulah,	208
Townsend, Charles,	98
Townsend, Edward,	125
Townsend, Elisha,	122
Townsend, Eliza,	272
Townsend, Elizabeth,	252
Townsend, Elizabeth,	252
Townsend, Eusebius,	110
Townsend, George C.,	142
Townsend, Grace,	240
Townsend, Hadassah,	274
Townsend, Hannah,	249
Townsend, Hannah,	271
Townsend, Hannah,	290
Townsend, Han'h P.,	262
Townsend, Henry C.,	142
Townsend, Hugh,	174
Townsend, Israel H.,	192
Townsend, James,	113
Townsend, John,	109
Townsend, John K.,	127
Townsend, Joseph,	141
Townsend, Joseph S.,	159
Townsend, Jotham,	120
Townsend, Margaret,	314
Townsend, Mary,	230
Townsend, Mary,	242
Townsend, Mary J.,	303
Townsend, Mary M.,	262
Townsend, Mercy S.,	320
Townsend, Mira,	291
Townsend, Phebe S.,	262
Townsend, Philip P.,	154
Townsend, Rachel,	234
Townsend, Rachel P.,	275
Townsend, Rebecca J.,	316
Townsend, Richard,	125
Townsend, Ruth Ann,	283
Townsend, Ruth R.,	295
Townsend, Sabina,	241
Townsend, Samuel,	127
Townsend, Sarah,	231
Townsend, Sarah,	294
Townsend, Susanna,	210
Townsend, Susanna,	302
Townsend, Tacy,	257
Townsend, Wil'mina,	308
Townsend, Wm. P.,	102
Townsend, Wilson,	193
Trasel, Edward G.,	156
Trasel, John L.,	156
Trimble, Abraham,	154
Trimble, Ann,	242

Name	PAGE
Trimble, Ann,	297
Trimble, Ann,	300
Trimble, Ann,	330
Trimble, Catharine B.,	302
Trimble, David,	132
Trimble, David B.,	160
Trimble, Elizabeth,	261
Trimble, George,	181
Trimble, George T.,	111
Trimble, George W.,	143
Trimble, Grace,	236
(*Evans,*) " (*Com.*,)	100
Trimble, Henry,	187
Trimble, Isaac,	122
Trimble, Jane,	263
Trimble, John,	131
Trimble, John,	172
" " (*Com.*,)	108
Trimble, John R.,	113
Trimble, Joseph,	132
Trimble, Joseph,	193
Trimble, Lydia,	230
Trimble, Lydia,	245
Trimble, Lydia,	256
Trimble, Margaret,	283
Trimble, Mary,	263
Trimble, Mary Ann,	293
Trimble, Mary V.,	294
Trimble, Phebe,	228
Trimble, Phebe,	230
Trimble, Rebecca,	319
Trimble, Ruth Anna,	337
Trimble, Samuel,	150
Trimble, Samuel,	175
Trimble, Sarah,	101
Trimble, Sarah,	294
Trimble, Stephen,	134
Trimble, Thomas,	141
Trimble, Thomazine,	241
Trimble, William,	112
Trimble, William,	149
Trimble, William,	183
" " (*Teacher*,)	90
Troth, Alfred,	186
Troth, Daniel,	120
Troth, Elizabeth,	244
Troth, Elizabeth,	283
Troth, Elizabeth T.,	302
Troth, Esther,	260
Troth, Hannah J.,	319
Troth, Isaac L.,	179
Troth, Jacob M.,	156
Troth, Lucy Ann,	260
Troth, Mary,	244
Troth, Mary,	279
Troth, Morgan,	184
Troth, Paul H.,	144
Troth, R. Louisa,	340
Troth, Rebecca,	289
Troth, Samuel,	154
Trotter, Edward H.,	132
Trotter, Elspeth J.,	348
Trotter, Mary,	237
Trotter, Nathan,	108
Trotter, Rebecca,	234
Trotter, Samuel,	131
Trotter, Susan H.,	266
Trotter, Thomas,	108

INDEX. 427

Name	PAGE
Trotter, William H.,	143
Trueman, Thomas S.,	118
Truman, Ann,	232
Truman, Elizabeth,	262
Truman, Rebecca,	229
Truman, Rebecca,	258
Truman, Ruth,	245
Trump, Abby Ann,	306
Trump, Charles,	130
Trump, David,	140
Trump, Elizabeth,	268
Trump, Grace,	242
Trump, Mary,	273
Trump, Michael,	141
Trump, Susan B.,	307
Trump, Tacy,	303
Trump, Thomas,	112
Trump, William B.,	158
Tucker, Benjamin C.,	126
Tucker, Elizabeth,	297
Tucker, Howard,	159
Tucker, Lydia,	310
Tucker, Margaret,	303
Tucker, Martha,	254
Tucker, Mary,	253
Tudor, Isaac,	151
Tudor, John,	136
Tudor, William,	154
Tunis, Hannah,	227
Turner, John,	98
Turner, Joseph,	97
Turner, Joseph,	113
Turner, Samuel R.,	115
Turner, Sarah,	243
Twining, Edward W.,	181
Twining, Eliz. H.,	301
Twining, Jacob,	192
Twining, Jane B.,	301
Twining, Rachel,	253
Twining, Sarah B.,	330
Twining, Susanna,	246
Tyler, Hannah G.,	215
Tyler, Mary,	260
Tyler, Martha J.,	330
Tyson, Ann,	214
Tyson, Daniel T.,	120
Tyson, Edwin A.,	143
Tyson, Eleanor,	296
Tyson, Elizabeth,	230
Tyson, Evan T.,	123
Tyson, Hannah,	244
Tyson, Hannah,	248
Tyson, Isaac,	110
Tyson, Isaac,	161
Tyson, John,	114
Tyson, Jonathan,	123
Tyson, Levi,	134
Tyson, Martha H.,	258
Tyson, Mary Ann,	272
Tyson, Mary E.,	311
Tyson, Nathan,	110
Tyson, Richard W.,	146
Tyson, Sally Ann,	302
Tyson, Sarah Ann,	255
Tyson, Thomas,	113
Tyson, William,	123
Underhill, Albert,	173

Name	PAGE
Underhill, Alex.,	187
Underhill, Alfred A.,	170
Underhill, Andrew,	117
Underhill, Anna C.,	313
Underhill, Clayton E.,	202
Underhill, Edm'd B.,	163
Underhill, Frederick,	160
Underhill, Hannah,	308
Underhill, Henry,	171
Underhill, Indiana,	312
Underhill, James E.,	155
Underhill, Mary W.,	313
Underhill, Phebe J.,	312
Underhill, Reuben H.,	161
Underhill, Robert,	153
Underhill, Robert B.,	170
Underhill, Silas A.,	168
Underhill, Stephen,	169
Underhill, Susan,	316
Underhill, Wm. H.,	171
Underhill, Wm. W.,	166
Updegraff, Ann T.,	297
Updegraff, Hannah,	230
Updegraff, Mary,	267
Updegraff, Sarah E.,	285
Vail, Abel C.,	127
Vail, Abraham M.,	149
Vail, Albert L.,	137
Vail, Anna Maria,	309
Vail, Benjamin,	90
Vail, Benjamin A.,	178
Vail, Bethiah,	233
Vail, Bethiah,	236
Vail, Caroline T.,	280
Vail, Catharine,	280
Vail, Christiana,	236
Vail, Clarkson,	113
Vail, Daniel,	126
Vail, David L.,	148
Vail, Henrietta,	315
Vail, Hugh D.,	142
" " (Teacher,)	86
Vail, Isaac N.,	178
" " (Teacher,)	89, 90
Vail, James,	131
Vail, John T.,	117
Vail, John W.,	137
Vail, Lindley,	130
Vail, Mahlon,	137
Vail, Margaret C.,	264
Vail, Martha P.,	292
Vail, Miriam L.,	307
Vail, Nathan R.,	147
Vail, Phebe,	251
Vail, Rachel,	258
Vail, Rachel S.,	281
Vail, Robert,	118
Vail, Samuel,	131
Vail, Sarah,	292
Vail, Sarah W.,	255
Vail, Wallace,	159
Vail, William,	117
Valentine, Anne C.,	307
Valentine, Caroline,	301
Valentine, Chas. M.,	131
Valentine, Eliza Ann,	258
Valentine, Eliza D.,	100

Name	PAGE
Valentine, George,	161
Valentine, Henry C.,	179
Valentine, Jacob,	150
Valentine, Jacob,	158
Valentine, Jacob D.,	142
Valentine, James C.,	150
Valentine, John B.,	179
Valentine, Mary,	304
Valentine, Mary B.,	331
Valentine, Samuel R.,	163
Valentine, Sarah,	273
Valentine, Susan,	301
Valentine, Thomazin,	278
Valentine, Wm. T.,	161
Vandeveer, Sarah A.,	268
Van Hoesen, Cath'ine,	285
Van Horn, Sarah,	232
Vanlaw, Ann,	224
Vansant, Mary,	243
Vernon, Charles D.,	194
Vezey, Elizabeth,	258
Vickirs, Isaac,	115
Vickirs, Mary,	265
Vickirs, Sarah,	230
Vivian, Hannah,	316
Vivian, William,	169
Votaw, Albert H.,	91
Votaw, Ida M.,	347
Walcott, Joseph,	98
Walker, Ann,	245
Walker, Catharine,	234
Walker, Edith B.,	337
Walker, Elizabeth,	270
Walker, Enoch,	126
Walker, George,	118
Walker, Huldah,	298
Walker, Isaac R.,	136
Walker, James,	107
Walker, James,	117
Walker, John,	152
Walker, Joshua,	115
Walker, Mary,	280
Walker, Mary Ann,	274
Walker, Mary R.,	331
Walker, Peter R.,	115
Walker, Phebe,	261
Walker, Phebe M.,	254
Walker, Priscilla,	243
Walker, Rebecca,	247
Walker, Richard,	166
Walker, Robert,	163
Walker, Samuel,	111
Walker, Sarah,	243
Walker, Sarah,	247
Walker, William,	107
Wall, Ann,	258
Walmsley, Ann,	271
Walmsley, Anna,	277
Walmsley, Charles,	125
Walmsley, Daniel W.,	159
Walmsley, Margaret,	291
Walmsley, Mary,	315
Walmsley, Morris,	161
Walmsley, Richard,	143
Walmsley, Thomas,	180
Walmsley, William,	158
Waln, Elizabeth,	241

32 *

INDEX.

Name	Page
Waln, Elizabeth,	99
Waln, Nicholas,	95
Waln, Richard,	125
Waln, Sarah,	96
Waln, Sarah,	277
Walter, Abbie T.,	339
Walter, Alban W.,	194
Walter, Carpenter,	173
Walter, Davis P.,	182
Walter, Elizabeth,	298
" " (Teacher,)	86
(Hoopes,) " (Gov's,)	81
Walter, Emma H.,	326
Walter, H. Jane,	336
Walter, Henry,	142
Walter, Joseph S.,	158
Walter, Julia T.,	334
" " (Teacher,)	90
Walter, Laura,	339
Walter, Louis H.,	193
Walter, Margaretta J.,	303
Walter, Marshall J.,	183
Walter, Mary F.,	265
Walter, Mary Louisa,	312
Walter, Phebe Jane,	316
Walter, Priscilla,	294
" " (Teacher,)	86
Walter, Robert H.,	195
Walter, Sarah,	287
(Moore,) " (Teacher,)	88
" " (Gov's,)	81
Walter, Sidney J.,	301
Walter, Sidney P.,	329
Walter, Susanna H.,	340
Walter, William H.,	154
Walter, William M.,	201
Walter, Ziba D.,	177
" " (Teacher,)	87
Walters, Edward,	115
Walton, Abby,	346
Walton, Abi,	290
Walton, Alfred,	146
Walton, Ann,	292
Walton, Anna,	344
" (Teacher,)	91, 92
Walton, Benj. L.,	119
Walton, Charles,	136
Walton, Charles J.,	127
Walton, Charles J.,	186
Walton, Elizabeth,	241
" " (Teacher,)	84
Walton, Elizabeth,	258
Walton, Ellen,	328
Walton, Gilpin F.,	152
Walton, James,	120
Walton, James,	197
Walton, Jane,	251
Walton, Jane,	300
Walton, Joseph,	137
" " (Teacher,)	85
" " (Com.,)	102
Walton, Lydia,	271
Walton, Lydia Ann,	271
Walton, Lydia L.,	102
(See Lippincott.)	
Walton, Martha,	253
Walton, Mary Ann,	254
Walton, Mary Ann,	288
Walton, Mary J.,	314
Walton, Nathan,	127
Walton, Rebecca,	284
Walton, Rebecca S.,	324
Walton, S. Francis,	205
Walton, Samuel,	152
Walton, Samuel B.,	146
Walton, Sarah,	254
Walton, Sarah,	260
Walton, William M.,	151
Ward, Aaron,	166
Ward, Achsah E.,	292
Ward, Allen,	167
Ward, Charles,	120
Ward, John B.,	124
Ward, Mary,	347
Ward Rachel,	231
Warder, Ann,	97
Warder, Caroline,	247
Warder, Charles,	108
Warder, Elizabeth,	229
Warder, John,	106
Warder, Rebecca,	100
(See Sheppard.)	
Ware, Charles,	162
Ware, Sarah,	229
Ware, Sarah,	238
Waring, Edward,	171
Waring, Joshua,	171
Waring, Thomas,	166
" " (Teacher,)	87
Warner, Anne,	327
" " (Teacher,)	89
Warner, Benjamin,	149
Warner, Benjamin,	171
Warner, Charles L.,	162
Warner, Deborah,	315
Warner, Edward A.,	130
Warner, Edward A.,	162
Warner, Elizabeth W.,	341
Warner, Esther,	226
Warner, Hannah,	272
Warner, Hannah A.,	81
" " (Com.,)	102
(See Allen.)	
Warner, John W.,	200
Warner, Joseph F.,	131
Warner, Mary,	305
Warner, Mary,	306
Warner, Meribah,	302
Warner, Rachel F.,	327
Warner, Rachel F.,	336
Warner, Rebecca,	327
Warner, Sarah,	298
Warner, Sarah E.,	324
Warner, Silas,	168
Warner, Thomas,	162
Warner, Yardley,	139
" (Teacher,)	86, 87
" (Com.,)	102
Warren, Elizabeth S.,	334
Warren, Henry E.,	203
Warren, Mary M.,	328
Warren, Rachel S.,	338
Warren, Thomas M.,	183
Warren, William C.,	201
Warrington, Abraham,	96
Warrington, Anna,	289
Warrington, Anna,	328
Warrington, Anna B.,	324
Warrington, Anna H.,	333
Warrington, Chas. W.,	189
Warrington, Curtis H.,	190
Warrington, Edward,	197
Warrington, Esther,	237
Warrington, Hannah,	100
Warrington, Hen'ta,	307
Warrington, Hen.,Jr.,	107
" " (Com.,)	99
Warrington, Henry,	145
Warrington, Henry,	193
Warrington, Joseph,	129
Warrington, Joseph,	160
Warrington, Josiah,	147
Warrington, Kezia,	266
Warrington, Lydia,	276
(Sheppard,) " (Com.,)	102
Warrington, Martha,	275
Warrington, Martha N.,	102
(See Jenkins.)	
Warrington, Mary,	282
Warrington, Mary J.,	330
Warrington, Rachel,	225
Warrington, Rachel,	295
Warrington, Rebecca,	266
Warrington, Rebecca,	289
Warrington, Seth,	140
Warrington, Susan N.,	318
Warrington, Susanna,	259
Warrington, T. Fran.,	193
Warrington, Thomas,	153
Warrington, William,	132
Warrington, Wm. H.,	181
Waterman, Mary,	234
Waters, Edward,	140
Waters, Elizabeth,	250
Waters, George,	133
Waters, Mary,	261
Waters, Sarah,	269
Watson, Anna,	238
Watson, Anna N.,	319
Watson, Betsy,	254
Watson, Elizabeth,	257
Watson, Elizabeth,	281
Watson, Jacob M.,	162
Watson, John,	162
Watson, Josiah J.,	157
Watson, Martha,	257
Watson, Mary,	246
Watson, Mary,	253
Watson, Mary Ann,	278
Watson, Rachel,	258
Watson, Sarah,	246
Watson, Susanna M.,	244
Watson, Thomas,	120
Way, Annie,	347
Way, Charles C.,	176
Way, Hannah,	320
Way, Jane E.,	327
Way, John,	206
Way, Lucretia,	323
Way, Mary,	229
Way, Melmoth H.,	176
Way, Phebe,	228
Way, Phebe,	281
Way, Rebecca,	232

INDEX. 429

Name	Page	Name	Page	Name	Page
Way, Sarah,	255	Welding, Alice,	279	Wheeler, Ann,	226
Way, Susan S.,	320	Welding, Anna H.,	333	Wheeler, Ann,	231
Way, William,	106	Welding, Charles,	137	*Wheeler, Mary*,	97
Weaver, Edwin A.,	135	Welding, Charles F.,	183	Whinery, Nathan,	175
Weaver, Elijah,	110	Welding, David,	137	Whitacre, Alfred,	179
Webb, Alban,	160	Welding, Elizabeth,	261	Whitacre, Edwin,	183
Webb, Ambrose,	125	Welding, Ellwood,	137	Whitacre, Eliz. M.,	347
Webb, Ann,	252	Welding, Emily,	246	Whitacre, Henry P.,	182
Webb, Edith,	302	Welding, Julia,	276	Whitacre, Henry W.,	200
Webb, Edna,	269	Welding, Lydia Ann,	277	Whitacre, John,	167
Webb, Elizabeth,	286	Welding, Rachel,	266	Whitacre, Mary,	252
Webb, Elizabeth,	290	Welding, Sidney Ann,	291	Whitacre, Mary E.,	320
Webb, Elizabeth P.,	339	Welding, Susan,	277	Whitacre, Nehemiah,	178
Webb, Ellis,	129	Welding, Watson J.,	131	Whitacre, R. Harlan,	188
Webb, Hannah,	252	Welding, William H.,	180	Whitacre, Sarah E.,	331
Webb, Hannah H.,	273	Welsh, Mary,	229	Whitacre, Wm. S.,	200
Webb, Hannah P.,	308	Wendell, Evert J.,	158	Whitall, Ann C.,	233
Webb, Isaac B.,	164	Wendell, Margaret,	279	Whitall, Anna,	311
Webb, James,	160	*West, Ann*,	99	Whitall, Benjamin,	119
Webb, James L.,	146	West, Ann,	258	Whitall, Caroline,	315
Webb, Jane,	294	*West, Catharine V.*,	85	*Whitall, David*,	84
Webb, John B.,	195	West, Clarkson,	137	Whitall, Deborah,	306
Webb, Martha H.,	288	West, Eli,	124	Whitall, Ebenezer,	120
Webb, Mary,	308	West, Elizabeth,	235	Whitall, Edith,	288
Webb, Mary Ann,	290	West, Elizabeth C.,	282	*Whitall, Hannah*,	98
Webb, Mary E.,	320	West, George,	106	" " (*Matron*,)	79
Webb, Minerva,	247	*West, Hannah*,	96	Whitall, Hannah,	243
Webb, Minerva,	310	West, James H.,	129	Whitall, Hannah,	317
Webb, Philena,	308	West, Lydia,	235	Whitall, Henry,	145
Webb, Samuel,	115	West, Martha,	224	*Whitall, Joseph*,	97
Webb, Samuel P.,	166	*West, Martha*,	83	" " (Supt.,)	79
Webb, Sally Ann,	244	West, Mary Anna,	286	Whitall, Joseph,	165
Webb, Stephen A.,	142	West, Mary S.,	306	Whitall, Joshua,	119
Webb, Thomas H.,	159	West, Rebecca T.,	282	Whitall, Lydia C.,	328
Webb, William,	96	West, Sarah,	226	Whitall, Mark,	105
Webb, William H.,	152	West, Sarah,	244	Whitall, Samuel,	172
Webster, Ann,	245	" " (*Teacher*,)	84	Whitall, Sarah,	307
Webster, Catharine,	232	(*Passmore*.) " (*Matron*,)	79	Whitall, Sarah Ann,	325
Webster, Crowell,	112	West, Sarah L.,	309	Whitall, Susan,	299
Webster, David,	133	West, Susan T.,	288	Whitall, William,	139
Webster, Edward,	112	Westbrook, Sally A.,	310	Whitall, William,	144
Webster, Edward,	185	Wetherald, Samuel J.,	187	Whitall, William H.,	168
Webster, Edmund G.,	158	Wetherill, Ann E.,	290	White, Adelaide E.,	343
Webster, Eliza,	243	Wetherill, Benj. K.,	165	White, Alfred R.,	198
Webster, Elizabeth,	338	Wetherill, Charles,	148	White, Ann Elizabeth,	341
Webster, George C.,	195	Wetherill, Deborah,	284	White, Barclay,	140
Webster, Hannah,	321	Wetherill, Deborah E.,	325	*White, Britton*,	95
Webster, Isaac M.,	191	Wetherill, George,	160	White, Charlotte,	333
Webster, Joseph,	185	Wetherill, George,	163	White, Claranda,	289
Webster, Juliann,	291	Wetherill, George S.,	192	White, Daniel,	129
Webster, Keziah,	311	Wetherill, Hannah,	283	White, Edith,	304
Webster, Louisa,	219	Wetherill, Hannah,	293	White, Elias A.,	143
Webster, Margaret M.,	307	Wetherill, Isaac,	140	White, Elizabeth,	233
Webster, Margaret M.,	310	Wetherill, James P.,	293	White, Elizabeth,	269
Webster, Mary J.,	224	Wetherill, Jane J.,	337	White, Elizabeth A.,	332
Webster, Pennell L.,	196	Wetherill, John,	167	White, Elizabeth Ann,	263
Webster, Phebe,	232	Wetherill, John,	198	White, Francis,	144
Webster, Prudence,	260	Wetherill, Joseph,	142	White, George,	143
Webster, Rebecca,	310	Wetherill, Lydia,	293	White, Hannah,	269
Webster, Richard G.,	290	Wetherill, Mary Ann,	299	White, Howard,	140
Webster, Samuel C.,	198	Wetherill, Mary Ann,	302	White, Jane,	290
Webster, Sarah,	321	Wetherill, Mary Ann,	303	White, John,	126
Webster, Sarah L.,	310	Wetherill, Mary L.,	312	White, Julia,	287
Webster, Susanna,	232	Wetherill, Richard,	156	White, Julia S.,	346
Webster, Thomas M.,	185	Wetherill, Robert,	138	White, Laura A.,	331
Webster, William,	142	Wetherill, Sarah,	297	White, Lydia,	253
Webster, William,	148	Wetherill, William,	136	White, Marcia,	290
Webster, William,	191	Wetherill, William,	146	White, Margaret S.,	270

430 INDEX.

Name	PAGE
White, Margaret W.,	331
White, Martha,	286
White, Martha J.,	320
White, Mary J.,	342
White, Mary S.,	321
White, Mercia,	291
White, Nixon,	138
White, Penina,	289
White, Priscilla,	279
White, Rachel,	229
White, Rachel,	291
White, Rebecca,	226
White, Rebecca,	233
White, Rebecca A.,	274
White, Robert C.,	148
White, Sarah,	271
White, Sarah,	343
Whiteley, Caroline,	346
Whiteley, George T.,	200
Whiteley, Mary J.,	340
Whiteley, Sarah E.,	340
Whitelock, Elizabeth,	261
Whitelock, Mary,	270
Whitelock, Sarah,	265
Whitlock, H. Virginia,	325
Whitson, Amos,	144
Whitson, Anna R.,	333
Whitson, Benj. F.,	204
Whitson, Hannah,	300
Whitson, Joseph T.,	199
Whitson, Leah,	300
Whitson, Mary,	284
Whitson, Mary,	313
Whitson, Mary H.,	341
Whitson, Phœbe A.,	284
Whitson, Rachel,	301
Whitson, Samuel L.,	197
Whitson, Sarah,	339
Wickersham, Anna E.,	341
Wickersham, B. F., Jr.,	196
Wickersham, Elmira,	316
Wickersham, John B.,	149
Wickersham, John M.,	205
Wickersham, Jos. A.,	172
Wickersham, Levi,	158
Wickersham, Mar. P.,	341
Wickersham, Mary H.,	345
Wickersham, Preston,	148
Wickersham, Wm. F.,	200
Widdefield, Eleanor,	260
Widdefield, Eliza'th,	256
Widdefield, Sarah,	238
Widdefield, Wm. A.,	125
Wiggins, Elizabeth,	322
Wiggins, Rachel,	322
Wiggins, Sarah,	324
Wilbur, Sarah C.,	306
Wilcox, C. Martin,	199
Wilcox, Eldaah,	197
Wilcox, M. Ellis,	200
Wilcox, Sarah,	337
Wildman, Elias,	177
Wildman, Mary C.,	318
Wildman, Rachel C.,	329
Wildman, Sarah M.,	326
Wildman, Thomas,	175
Wiley, Hannah,	287
Wiley, John,	107

Name	PAGE
Wiley, Margaret,	296
Wiley, Mary,	225
Wiley, Mary,	229
Wiley, Sarah,	301
Wilkins, Esther,	236
Wilkins, Henry H.,	183
Wilkins, Ida,	341
Wilkins, Jay,	205
Wilkins, Joshua P.,	138
Wilkins, Lydia C.,	344
Wilkins, Mary C.,	292
Wilkins, Mary E.,	344
Wilkins, Rebecca,	328
Wilkins, Rebecca H.,	324
Wilkins, Sarah,	277
Wilkins, Sarah A.,	295
Wilkins, William,	166
Wilkins, William H.,	185
Wilkinson, Hannah,	273
Wilkinson, Isaac,	109
Wilkinson, Isaac,	114
Wilkinson, Lewis P.,	140
Wilkinson, Mary,	257
Wilkinson, Nathan,	131
Wilkinson, William,	112
Williams, Abigail,	86
" " (Gov'ess,)	81
" " (Com.,)	101
(Hall,) " (Com.,)	102
Williams, Alice,	253
Williams, Ann,	285
Williams, Ann G.,	233
Williams, Anthony,	131
Williams, Benjamin,	164
Williams, Caroline,	309
Williams, Charles,	101
Williams, Charles B.,	145
Williams, Charles, Jr.,	195
Williams, Cidney E.,	331
" (Teacher.)	88, 89
Williams, D. Howard,	203
Williams, Deborah,	231
Williams, Edmund T.,	124
Williams, Edward B.,	192
Williams, Elizabeth,	223
Williams, Elizabeth,	230
Williams, Elizabeth,	231
Williams, Elizabeth,	232
Williams, Elizab'h P.,	284
Williams, Emma,	307
Williams, Esek H.,	124
Williams, Esther,	339
Williams, Francis C.,	169
Williams, George,	96
Williams, George,	97
Williams, George,	115
Williams, George,	139
Williams, George,	184
Williams, George G.,	113
Williams, George G.,	203
Williams, Hannah,	225
Williams, Hannah,	100
(See Albertson.)	
Williams, Hannah,	288
Williams, Hannah C.,	288
Williams, Hannah C.,	338
Williams, Henry,	154
Williams, Henry S.,	184

Name	PAGE
Williams, Henry W.,	191
Williams, Isaac,	109
Williams, Jesse,	113
Williams, Jesse,	92
Williams, Jesse,	197
Williams, John L.,	106
Williams, Jonathan G.,	102
" " (Supt.)	80
Williams, Joseph,	151
Williams, Joseph,	187
Williams, Joseph K.,	137
Williams, Lydia,	224
Williams, Lydia,	233
Williams, Lydia,	277
Williams, Lydia,	289
Williams, Margaret,	225
Williams, Margaret,	277
Williams, Margaret,	296
Williams, Martha,	272
Williams, Martha P.,	282
Williams, Mary,	248
Williams, Mary,	99
Williams, Mary,	284
Williams, Mary R.,	346
Williams, Phebe,	236
Williams, Phebe,	255
Williams, Rachel,	272
Williams, Rachel A.,	330
Williams, Rachel R.,	344
Williams, Rebecca,	289
Williams, Rebecca S.,	308
Williams, Reuben,	134
Williams, Richard J.,	157
Williams, Samuel,	106
Williams, Samuel,	140
Williams, Samuel R.,	143
Williams, Samuel S.,	183
Williams, Sarah,	225
Williams, Sarah,	248
Williams, Sarah,	275
Williams, Sarah,	308
Williams, Susan,	298
Williams, Susan E.,	345
Williams, Susan E.,	316
Williams, Susanna,	283
Williams, Susanna R.,	80
" " (Com.,)	103
(See Roberts.)	
Williams, Tacy,	269
Williams, Thomas,	121
Williams, William K.,	168
Williamson, Adam B.,	121
Williamson, Alfred,	157
Williamson, Anna,	299
Williamson, George,	146
Williamson, Hannah,	246
Williamson, Sarah,	257
Williamson, Thomas,	92
Willis, Achsah,	235
Willis, David,	107
Willis, Elizabeth,	249
Willis, Joel,	142
Willis, Mary,	225
Willis, Mary S.,	332
Willis, Thomas,	108
Willits, Alfred,	161
Willits, Anna G.,	334
Willits, Archie P.,	189

INDEX. 431

	PAGE		PAGE		PAGE
Willits, Charles,	189	Wills, Susan,	313	Wilson, Oliver,	96
Willits, Charles L.,	136	Wills, William R.,	162	Wilson, Oliver,	150
Willits, Deborah,	264	Wilson, Alexander,	96	Wilson, Peter,	114
Willits, Edmund,	191	Wilson, Alexander,	83	Wilson, Phebe,	300
Willits, Eliza A.,	331	Wilson, Alice Ann,	229	Wilson, Phebe W.,	318
Willits, Elizabeth,	282	Wilson, Alice Ann,	268	Wilson, Rachel,	227
Willits, Elizabeth,	290	Wilson, Allen J.,	206	Wilson, Rachel,	238
Willits, Henry,	148	Wilson, Andrew J.,	191	Wilson, Rachel,	245
Willits, James,	143	Wilson, Ann,	242	Wilson, Rachel,	286
Willits, James A.,	148	Wilson, Ann,	248	Wilson, Rachel,	291
Willits, Jeremiah,	151	Wilson, Ann,	254	Wilson, Rachel R.,	241
Willits, John,	112	Wilson, Ann Eliza,	332	Wilson, Rathmell,	128
Willits, John G.,	185	Wilson, Ann L.,	254	Wilson, Rebecca,	231
Willits, Joseph,	154	Wilson, Benjamin,	130	Wilson, Rebecca,	98
Willits, Joseph B.,	189	Wilson, Charles S.,	176	Wilson, Rebecca,	251
Willits, Joseph N.,	196	Wilson, Charles W.,	124	Wilson, Rebecca A.,	298
Willits, Judith,	228	Wilson, Charles W. L.,	198	Wilson, Richard H.,	151
Willits, Judith Ann,	305	Wilson, David,	105	Wilson, Samuel Alan,	200
Willits, Louisa,	282	Wilson, Edward,	126	Wilson, Sarah,	97
Willits, Lydia Ann,	301	Wilson, Edward E.,	205	Wilson, Sarah,	249
Willits, Lydia S.,	327	Wilson, Eliza,	279	Wilson, Sarah,	261
Willits, Matilda,	311	Wilson, Eliza B.,	226	Wilson, Sarah,	319
Willits, Mary,	283	Wilson, Eliza P.,	307	Wilson, Sarah E.,	313
Willits, Mary B.,	335	Wilson, Elizabeth,	244	Wilson, Sarah P.,	286
Willits, Nathan B.,	148	Wilson, Elizabeth,	257	Wilson, Sarah T.,	323
Willits, Samuel A.,	178	Wilson, Elizabeth,	293	Wilson, Susan J.,	293
Willits, Samuel C.,	142	Wilson, Elizabeth,	295	Wilson, Susanna,	247
Willits, Samuel S.,	140	Wilson, Elizabeth,	301	Wilson, Thomas,	142
Willits, Sarah Jane,	306	Wilson, Emily,	288	Wilson, William,	129
Wills, Alfred S.,	184	Wilson, Ephraim,	97	Wilson, William,	123
Wills, Amy,	244	Wilson, Euphemia,	266	Wilson, William,	158
Wills, Amy C.,	285	Wilson, George,	136	Wilson, William P.,	151
Wills, Ann,	251	Wilson, George,	154	Windle, Anne E.,	316
Wills, Ann,	303	Wilson, Grace,	257	Windle, Deborah J.,	316
Wills, Anna,	330	Wilson, Gulielma M.,	297	Windle, Elma,	336
Wills, Anna T.,	334	Wilson, Hannah,	249	Windle, Isaac E.,	171
Wills, Chalkley,	144	Wilson, Hannah M.,	310	Windle, Mary J.,	319
Wills, Charles,	150	Wilson, Isaac,	110	Windle, Rebecca L.,	323
Wills, Charles T.,	188	Wilson, Isabella,	306	Windle, Sarah E.,	331
Wills, Clayton N.,	172	Wilson, James,	126	Windle, Thomas J.,	177
Wills, Daniel,	126	Wilson, James,	137	Windle, William E.,	176
Wills, Daniel,	162	Wilson, James,	161	Winn, Elizabeth,	254
Wills, Edmund D.,	182	Wilson, James H.,	155	Winn, Elliott,	169
Wills, Elizabeth C.,	333	Wilson, Jefferis,	144	Winn, Lydia S.,	337
Wills, Elizabeth H.,	333	Wilson, John,	132	Winner, Anna M.,	347
Wills, Elizabeth R.,	310	Wilson, John J.,	150	Winner, Charles E.,	199
Wills, Ella,	339	Wilson, John W.,	146	Winner, Josephine,	339
Wills, Ella S.,	343	Wilson, Joseph,	112	Winner, Susan,	305
Wills, Emma,	339	Wilson, Joseph,	147	Winner, Susan H.,	347
Wills, George J.,	191	Wilson, Joseph J.,	175	Winner, William,	167
Wills, Hannah,	235	Wilson, Louisa S.,	296	Winslow, Emily F.,	344
Wills, Hannah,	309	Wilson, Lydia,	251	Winslow, Eunice C.,	344
Wills, Hannah C.,	325	Wilson, Lydia,	314	Winston, James,	111
Wills, Howard H.,	181	Wilson, Margaret,	224	Winston, Lindley M.,	198
Wills, John,	126	Wilson, Margaret,	257	Winston, Lucy A.,	341
Wills, Joseph,	121	Wilson, Margaret,	306	Wistar, Bartholomew,	112
Wills, Joseph,	167	Wilson, Margaret O.,	305	" " (Com.,)	99
Wills, Joseph H.,	160	Wilson, Martha E.,	280	Wistar, B. Wyatt,	137
Wills, Joshua S.,	181	Wilson, Mary,	242	Wistar, Caspar,	96
Wills, Lydia E.,	324	Wilson, Mary,	296	Wistar, Caspar,	120
Wills, Lydia S.,	101	Wilson, Mary,		Wistar, Caspar,	161
(See Stokes.)		Wilson, Mary C.,	273	Wistar, Caspar,	162
Wills, R. Albert,	183	Wilson, Mary C.,	284	Wistar, Catharine,	96
Wills, Rachel,	247	Wilson, Mary E.,	291	Wistar, Catharine,	253
Wills, Rachel A.,	326	Wilson, Mary H.,	266	(Evans,) " (Com.,)	102
Wills, Samuel J.,	144	Wilson, Mary T.,	290	Wistar, Catharine,	306
Wills, Sarah F.,	329	Wilson, Mary T.,	342	Wistar, Charlotte,	241
Wills, Sarah S.,	315	Wilson, Mercy,	306	Wistar, Charlotte,	98

432 INDEX.

Name	PAGE
Wistar, Charlotte,	252
Wistar, Clayton,	112
" " (Com.,)	100
Wistar, Clayton,	180
Wistar, Dillwyn,	174
Wistar, Edward M.,	183
Wistar, Elizabeth,	331
Wistar, Elizabeth W.,	306
Wistar, Emma A.,	340
Wistar, Francis,	156
Wistar, Francis,	157
Wistar, Isaac E.,	152
Wistar, John,	95
Wistar, John,	137
Wistar, John,	182
Wistar, Joseph,	170
Wistar, Josiah,	157
Wistar, Lydia,	301
Wistar, Margaret,	242
Wistar, Martha,	100
(See Reeve.)	
Wistar, Mary,	224
Wistar, Mary,	98
Wistar, Mary,	291
Wistar, Mary,	102
(See Richardson.)	
Wistar, Mary Ann,	273
Wistar, Mary W.,	298
Wistar, Rebecca,	311
Wistar, Richard,	145
Wistar, Richard, Jr.,	183
Wistar, Sally,	315
Wistar, Sarah,	276
Wistar, Thomas,	117
Wistar, Thomas,	149
Wistar, Thomas,	169
Wistar, William H.,	159
Wistar, William W.,	169
Wollaston, Abigail,	227
Wollaston, Hannah,	237
Wood, Abigail,	101
(See Evans.)	
Wood, Alfred,	172
Wood, Anna Maria,	251
Wood, Caroline B.,	307
Wood, Catharine,	253
Wood, Charles,	156
Wood, Day,	134
Wood, Edward L.,	132
Wood, Edward R.,	167
Wood, Edward S.,	206
Wood, Edmund,	179
Wood, Eleanor K.,	313
Wood, Elizabeth B.,	307
Wood, Elizabeth P.,	308
Wood, George,	156
Wood, George,	161
Wood, George,	170
Wood, George,	186
Wood, George B.,	159
Wood, George R.,	167
Wood, Hannah,	260
Wood, Hannah A.,	240
Wood, Hannah F.,	102
(See Forsythe.)	
Wood, Hannah S.,	84
" " (Gov'ness,)	80
Wood, Horatio C.,	101

Name	PAGE
Wood, Horatio C.,	170
Wood, James,	106
Wood, James,	168
Wood, James T.,	177
Wood, John B.,	174
Wood, John Henry,	172
Wood, Joseph,	106
Wood, Julia,	325
Wood, Lydia,	267
Wood, Lydia,	297
Wood, Lydia Ann,	285
Wood, Lydia S.,	336
Wood, Martha J.,	324
Wood, Mary,	265
Wood, Mary,	267
Wood, Mary,	271
Wood, Mary,	306
Wood, Mary,	337
Wood, Mary C.,	266
Wood, Mary G.,	318
Wood, Mary K.,	330
Wood, Mary R.,	345
Wood, Mary S.,	236
Wood, Phebe Jane,	311
Wood, Randolph,	175
Wood, Rebecca,	250
Wood, Rebecca G.,	309
Wood, Richard,	155
Wood, Richard,	158
Wood, Robert,	171
Wood, Samuel,	110
Wood, Sarah A.,	347
Wood, Sarah H.,	274
Wood, Stephen,	168
Wood, Stephen,	181
Wood, Stuart,	183
Wood, Susanna,	267
Wood, Susanna L.,	101
(See Lightfoot.)	
Wood, Tacy,	231
Wood, Tacy,	237
Wood, Thomas,	110
Wood, Wager H.,	172
Wood, Walter,	180
Wood, William J.,	191
Wood, William W.,	124
Woodnut, Edward,	135
Woodnut, Elizabeth,	227
Woodnut, Elizabeth,	263
Woodnut, Han'h A.,	273
Woodnut, James M.,	130
Woodnut, Martha,	247
Woodnut, Preston,	140
Woodrow, Philena,	267
Woodward, Ann,	229
Woodward, Ann,	83
Woodward, Chas. E.,	178
Woodward, David C.,	145
Woodward, Dillwyn,	145
Woodward, Eliza'th,	259
Woodward, Francis,	185
Woodward, Hannah,	235
Woodward, Hannah,	305
Woodward, Henri'ta,	298
Woodward, Henry R.,	161
Woodward, Israel,	158
Woodward, Louisa,	300
Woodward, Lydia,	279

Name	PAGE
Woodward, Lydia D.,	328
Woodward, Margaret,	255
Woodward, Maria,	272
Woodward, Mary,	261
Woodward, Mary,	293
Woodward, Mary E.,	286
Woodward, Mary E.,	336
Woodward, Melinda,	272
Woodward, Sarah,	229
Woodward, Sarah,	231
Woodward, Sarah,	83
Woodward, Sarah,	264
Woody, Sarah J.,	347
Wooley, Edmund T.,	155
Wooley, Jacob,	97
Woollen, Hannah,	236
Woollen, Rebecca,	236
Woolman, Abigail C.,	312
Woolman, Alice A. J.,	290
Woolman, Ann,	251
Woolman, Ann,	291
Woolman, Anna,	328
Woolman, Benj. H.,	147
Woolman, Charles,	171
Woolman, Edward W.,	170
Woolman, Eliza,	248
Woolman, Elizabeth,	251
Woolman, Elizabeth,	296
Woolman, Elizabeth,	313
Woolman, Eliz'h L.,	322
Woolman, Eliz'h N.,	343
Woolman, Eliz'h S.,	328
Woolman, Giles S.,	182
Woolman, Hannah,	274
Woolman, John,	160
Woolman, Jon. H.,	157
Woolman, Joseph G.,	187
Woolman, Josiah N.,	180
Woolman, Lewis,	175
Woolman, Martha,	262
Woolman, Mary,	279
Woolman, Mary E.,	306
Woolman, Mary H.,	81
(See Roberts.)	
Woolman, Mary W.,	335
Woolman, Michael N.,	164
Woolman, Samuel B.,	138
Woolman, Samuel C.,	172
Woolman, Sarah L.,	323
Woolman, Susan,	286
Woolman, Thomas,	156
Woolman, William S.,	181
Woolston, Ann S.,	281
Woolston, Joshua,	147
Woolston, Martha,	255
Woolston, Mary,	259
Woolston, Samuel,	147
Woolston, Sarah,	226
Worrall, Anna Maria,	290
Worrall, Eliza P.,	281
Worth, Ebenezer,	168
Worth, Elizabeth A.,	267
Worth, Frances A.,	346
Worth, Francis,	166
Worth, Hannah M.,	344
Worth, John, Jr.,	196
Worth, Moses,	174
Worth, Paschall,	174

INDEX.   433

Name	PAGE	Name	PAGE	Name	PAGE
Worth, Samuel,	166	Wrigley, Harriet,	333	Yarnall, Priscilla E.,	274
Worth, Samuel, Jr.,	197	Wynn, William,	106	Yarnall, Rachel,	227
Worth, Sarah.	321			Yarnall, Rachel,	239
Worthington, Eliz. C.,	293	Yardley, George E.,	165	*Yarnall, Rachel,*	99
Worthington, Eliz. F,	330	Yardley, Thomas,	158	Yarnall, Rachel R.,	322
Worthington, Grace,	283	Yardley, Thomas M.,	151	Yarnall, Rachel S.,	285
Worthington, Han'h,	261	Yarnall, Albert E.,	293	Yarnall, Rebecca,	224
Worthington, H. W.,	184	Yarnall, Amos H.,	141	Yarnall, Rebecca,	254
Worthington, J. Kent,	188	Yarnall, Amy,	242	Yarnall, Sarah,	224
Worthington,J.Will's,	177	(*Tatum*.) " (*Com*.,)	100	Yarnall, Sarah,	225
Worthington, James,	145	Yarnall, Ann,	299	Yarnall, Sidney,	239
Worthington, Marg.,	289	Yarnall, Anna,	336	Yarnall, Susan,	242
Worthington, Prisc.,	273	Yarnall, Benjamin,	116	Yarnall, Walker,	106
Worthington, Benj, Prisc.,	285	Yarnall, Benj. H.,	107	Yarnall, William S.,	199
Worthington, Rebec.,	287	*Yarnall, Charles,*	100	Yearsley, Davis,	185
Worthington, Sam'l,	171	Yarnall, Deborah P.,	284	Yearsley, Humphrey,	135
Worthington, Sarah,	328	Yarnall, Deborah S.,	323	Yearsley, Isaac,	140
Worthington, Susan,	271	Yarnall, Edward,	120	Yearsley, Isaac,	169
Worthington, Wm.,	147	Yarnall, Edward S.,	173	Yearsley, Lydia,	280
Wright, Andrew C.,	112	*Yarnall. Eli,*	96	Yearsley, Mary,	300
Wright, Ann,	231	Yarnall, Eli,	112	Yearsley, Mary,	314
Wright, Anna C.,	325	Yarnall, Elizabeth,	234	Yearsley, Rachel W.,	323
Wright, Benjamin,	96	Yarnall, Elizabeth,	295	Yearsley, Sarah,	303
Wright, Beulah, R.,	267	*Yarnall, Ellis,*	96	Yearsley, Thomas,	152
Wright, Charles,	118	Yarnall, Ellis,	109	Yentman, Lydia,	261
Wright, Charles, Jr.,	188	Yarnall, Elsie R.,	342	Yerkes, Hannah,	266
Wright, Edwin,	171	Yarnall, Francis,	196	Yerkes, Jones,	156
Wright, Elizabeth,	225	Yarnall, George S..	193	Yerkes, Mary,	279
Wright, Elizabeth,	229	*Yarnall, Hannah,*	97, 98	Young, Lydia M.,	348
Wright, Elizabeth,	230	Yarnall, Hannah,	243		
Wright, Elizabeth,	254	Yarnall, Hannah,	262	Zane, Nathan T.,	120
Wright, Elizabeth,	301	Yarnall, Hannah,	280	Zane, Timothy,	120
Wright, Elizabeth,	328	Yarnall, Hannah H.,	298	Zell, Emma,	258
Wright, George,	173	Yarnall, Hibberd,	152	Zell, Hannah,	237
Wright, James,	106	Yarnall, Howard,	136	Zelley, Amos A.,	302
Wright, Jane,	305	" " (*Teacher*,)	85	Zelley, Ann,	267
Wright, Letitia,	253	Yarnall, Isaac,	149	Zelley, Charles E.,	188
Wright, Lucy,	228	Yarnall, James,	155	Zelley, Eliza,	249
Wright, Martha E.,	328	Yarnall, J. Howard,	188	Zelley, J. Howard,	193
Wright, Mary Ann,	258	Yarnall, Jane,	259	Zelley, Rebecca W.,	315
Wright, Mary H. C.,	347	Yarnall, Jane,	300	Zelley, Sarah,	250
Wright, Mary Susan,	322	Yarnall, Lydia H.,	309	Zelley, William H.,	190
Wright, Nehemiah,	187	Yarnall, Lydia T.,	342	Zook, Annie,	331
Wright, Rachel A.,	313	Yarnall, Mary,	272	Zook, Elizabeth,	336
Wright, Robert,	111	Yarnall, Mary,	282	Zook, Fannie E.,	336
Wright, Robert,	118	Yarnall, Mary A.,	251	Zook, George D.,	303
Wright, Robert K.,	141	Yarnall, Mary W.,	333	Zook, Henry,	197
Wright, Ruth,	250	Yarnall, Mordecai,	107	Zook, J. Trimble,	192
Wright, William,	185	Yarnall, Nathan S.,	145	Zook, Jane D.,	336
Wright, Willis W.,	139	Yarnall, Peter,	112	Zook, Thomazin T.,	331
Wrigley, Anna M.,	332	Yarnall, Philena,	309	Zook, William T.,	190

THE END

www.ingramcontent.com/pod-product-compliance
Lightning Source LLC
Chambersburg PA
CBHW030348230426
43664CB00007BB/575